The Political Economy of Socialism

AF734704

BY THE SAME AUTHOR:

The Yugoslav Economic System
Ekonomska politika stabilizacije
Self-governing Socialism (with M. Marković and R. Supek)
Ekonomska analiza
Yugoslav Economic Policy in the Post-War Period
Integrirani sistem društvenog računovodstva (with Z. Popov, D. Dimitrijević, and I. Vinski)
Business Cycles in Yugoslavia
An Essay on Yugoslav Society
Ekonomska nauka i narodna privreda
Ekonomski modeli
Medjusektorska analiza
Towards a Theory of Planned Economy
Ekonomika naftne privrede
Industrija nafte u Jugoslaviji, 3 vols.

BRANKO HORVAT

The Political Economy of Socialism

A MARXIST SOCIAL THEORY

Routledge
Taylor & Francis Group
LONDON AND NEW YORK

First published 1982 by M.E. Sharpe.Inc

Published 2016 by Routledge
2 Park Square, Milton Park, Abingdon, Oxon OX14 4RN
711 Third Avenue, New York, NY 10017, USA

Routledge is an imprint of the Taylor & Francis Group, an informa business
Copyright © 1982 by Taylor & Francis. All rights reserved.

No part of this book may be reprinted or reproduced or utilised in any form or by any electronic, mechanical, or other means, now known or hereafter invented, including photocopying and recording, or in any information storage or retrieval system, without permission in writing from the publishers.

Notices
No responsibility is assumed by the publisher for any injury and/or damage to persons or property as a matter of products liability, negligence or otherwise, or from any use of operation of any methods, products, instructions or ideas contained in the material herein.

Practitioners and researchers must always rely on their own experience and knowledge in evaluating and using any information, methods, compounds, or experiments described herein. In using such information or methods they should be mindful of their own safety and the safety of others, including parties for whom they have a professional responsibility.

Product or corporate names may be trademarks or registered trademarks, and are used only for identification and explanation without intent to infringe.

Library of Congress Cataloging in Publication Data

Horvat, Branko.
The political economy of socialism.

Includes index.
1. Marxian economics. 2. Communism and society.
I. Title.
HB97.5.H653 335.4 81-9430
ISBN 0-87332-184-7 AACR2

ISBN 13: 978-0-87332-184-6 (hbk)

Contents

PART TWO

Searching for an Alternative

PART FOUR

The Period of Transition

A Postscript

Foreword

In a sense, this book represents a life's work. Not in terms of actual writing—I have worked on it for only the last six years. But I have been thinking about its content throughout my life. Ever since my class left the secondary school of a small provincial town in Croatia to join the partisans in the Yugoslav Revolution, socialism has been my predominant concern. My generation undertook to accomplish what Marx called for in his famous thesis on Feuerbach: to change the world, not just to explain it. I threw myself fully into that business of changing.

It turned out that changing the world was not at all a simple or easy affair. Contrary to our original views, socialism proved to be rather elusive and far from obvious. Although explaining the world was not enough, it was still an indispensable condition for changing it in the desired fashion. The neglect of serious theoretical research could not but have disastrous consequences. Many of our "scientific" explanations did not survive the test of societal praxis. They were exposed as naive and simpleminded, occasionally as obscurantist and just simply wrong. Very soon—hardly three years had passed since the end of the armed struggle—the need for a thorough rethinking of the received socialist theory became obvious. Since then, I have been thinking about this book.

When I completed secondary school, somewhat more than a year after the Revolution, it was not clear to me in what way I could make myself most useful in building socialism. I studied engineering and then switched to economics, philosophy, and sociology. Eventually, I decided that economics, dealing as it did with the "basis" of the society, offered a proper occupation. Thus, I became an economist.

My long-run program included gaining practical experience in development planning and writing a fundamental book on the theory of socialist economy. In the beginning the program was followed pretty closely. My second dissertation, later published in several languages, was the theoretical exploration, *Towards a Theory of Planned Economy*. The term *socialist* was omitted from the title in order to avoid frightening Western publishers. As for practical experience, I was invited to join the

Federal Planning Bureau, where I became responsible for the methodology of planning. A few years later my department was transformed into an independent Institute of Economic Sciences, and I served as its director for the next seven years. That was a period of intensive empirical research into the problems of economic and social development, and planning.

The work on socialist economic theory, however, had to be postponed and pushed ever further into the future. Eventually, it became absolutely clear that one cannot study economics without exploring social relations and politics. Unfortunately, studies on socialist political systems and societal development failed to appear, and so it became necessary to develop simultaneously economic and sociopolitical theory. This, then, was the genesis of the present *Political Economy of Socialism*.

It should be mentioned, perhaps, that in my usage political economy has a somewhat special meaning. The term *political economy* was invented three centuries ago to denote the management of state economy in contrast to that of family households. With time, this meaning underwent a change. Classical political economy denoted the economics of a specific society: it meant the theory of the capitalist mode of social production. It is this theory that became the target of Marx's *Critique of Political Economy*. With the advent of neoclassical economics, social and political dimensions were eliminated, and what remained was uncontaminated economics. Soon pure economic theory came to mean model building irrelevant to any real-world economic decision making or problem solving. Only recently has interest in the classical political-economic approach, supplemented by economic sociology, been revived in the West. In the East, political economy has been petrified at its nineteenth-century developmental stage as if nothing had happened in the world or in thinking since then. Thus little help could be expected from either of these two sources. On the other hand, the problem with which I was grappling required a very definite unorthodox approach. Since socialist society—despite many promising beginnings—does not exist as yet, the classical approach was inappropriate. Both economic and political institutions first had to be designed before one could study their interaction. Consequently, political economy required a fusion of economic and political theory into one single social theory. That implied numerous methodological problems.

First of all, the idea of designing a social system is likely to be met with great suspicion. Does it not smack of utopianism, of wishful thinking? Joseph Schumpeter is quite emphatic in calling the endeavor "extra-scientific."[1] Unlike the engineer, whose task is to design new machines, the social scientist is not expected to design new social systems; his job is to analyze them critically and to explain them. Yet, logically, there is no difference between the two tasks—except that the latter is much more difficult. The design of a new bridge, for instance, may be unique, may replicate nothing existing before; yet we may confidently expect that the bridge will not collapse if all the calculations are carried out correctly and appropriate construction materials are used. Or, to take another example, Einstein's theory may have appeared fantastic in 1905, and scarcely anyone was willing to accept it. But nobody called it utopian. And after it passed the tests of theoretical consistency and correspondence to reality, it was accepted.

Social design is different because it affects values for which people are ready to fight to the death. It is also different because social reality includes an additional and vitally important dimension—consciousness. Unlike in the design of bridges, "construction materials" themselves change. This makes social design immensely more complex and difficult. In addition, social theory is not only part of the design but also becomes part of reality itself. The present book is an exploration into this uncharted territory. It is intended to meet Robert Heilbroner's request to convert "economics into an instrument of social science whose purpose and justification was not so much the elucidation of the way society actually behaves, as the formulation of the ways in which it should behave . . . the specification of necessary behavioral patterns to enable society to reach a postulated goal."[2]

The whole problem is vastly more important than an academic discussion about methodology would indicate. The tradition of not caring about the design of the future society—in fact, of openly denouncing any attempt at such design as utopian and antiscientific—has been long and well established in the socialist movement. It started with Marx and Engels, who perhaps might be excused because the society in which they lived—contrary to their own beliefs—was very far away from socialism. But the tradition is still alive, and with disastrous consequences. When, in 1891, the German Social Democratic Party was preparing its Erfurt Program, some of the members asked that the program contain a political and institutional design for the transition period. Karl Kautsky, the chief party theoretician, rejected the requests as unjustified, since the time was not yet ripe. When, two and a half decades later in 1918, the time was ripe, the party had no action program whatever. It tottered through the postwar chaos, lost power, antagonized various segments of the working class, and plunged the country into galloping inflation; the ensuing social and economic instability, colossal unemployment, and bitter fights between communists and socialists, cleared the way for Hitler and the Nazis. The history of Austrian socialism was almost identical. Similarly, Russian socialists were surprised by 1917 with nothing to guide them. To be sure, they wanted power. But what was to be done after the power had been conquered—that was a mystery with which no one was concerned. Toward the end of 1916, Lenin—apparently the only one aware of the problem, and also stimulated by a polemic with Bukharin—undertook to reread Marx, Engels, and Kautsky in the Zurich library in order to find out what they would have suggested. On this foundation, back in Russia, Lenin feverishly compiled his *State and Revolution* between the February and October revolutions in 1917. His labor was of no great avail, however, for the ideas in the book were not and/or could not be applied to the Russian scene. Soon Lenin died. The haphazard and uncontrolled social and political processes which were unleashed ended in Stalinist counterrevolution.

In citing these three historical examples, I do not wish to imply that a scientifically worked out action program and institutional design for the morrow of the revolution would have prevented nazism and Stalinism. Unfortunately, the social world is not that simple. But I do maintain that the absence of any meaningful long-run program enormously aided the counterrevolutions in those cases.

The subtitle of the book indicates that it is a Marxist exploration. The term *Marxist* must also be interpreted in a special sense. It does not mean the repetition of Marx's conclusions, which were applicable to a historical situation of a hundred years ago. That would belong to Marxology, not to Marxism. It means an approach such as Marx might have taken if he had lived today. One can easily disagree by calling this a hypothetical use of the term that cannot be tested against facts; after all, Marx is dead and cannot be consulted. Since my theory diverges from Marx's in certain important respects, while in others it deals with problems that Marx never encountered, one might argue that I am solely responsible for it. I would agree. Since it is obviously influenced by Marx, however, one could use a hyphenated term, Marxism-Horvatism, which Ben Ward applied to my early work. I would not mind. But I still prefer my subtitle.

There are at least two reasons why this book ought to be called simply Marxist. One is to deprive the critics of the pleasure of discovering triumphantly that, after all, this is a Marxist treatise and as such may be conveniently dismissed. It is good to know in advance that it is Marxist so that one cannot reject its findings without producing a satisfactory counterargument. The other reason is more fundamental. A friend of mine, a well-known Marxist philosopher, used to say that Marx achieved what he did because he was able to mount the shoulders of an intellectual giant—Hegel. As for myself, I freely mounted the broad shoulders of Marx. No science starts from scratch, and it is no false modesty to acknowledge one's debt to great forerunners.

It happened that my first reading in social theory was *The Communist Manifesto*. It happened also that, after reading it, I participated in one of the few genuine social revolutions of our time. Marx and the Revolution agreed beautifully, and my innocent mind took the rest as self-evident. Thus Marx's reasoning came very naturally to me; it became part of my own reasoning and of my own approach to social phenomena. I was not "taught" Marxism, I lived it. And precisely because I appropriated Marxism spontaneously as my own way of thinking, I felt no inhibition in revising the received theory whenever it did not square with facts. Marx would have done the same.

The quotations from Marx are more numerous than I would prefer; to a certain degree, this applies to quotations from other authors as well. There are four reasons for this. Marx, like all great thinkers, is so widely misunderstood and misinterpreted that it might be useful for those who are not familiar with his teachings to discover the original thinker. To those who know Marx, the quotations ought to indicate that a particular statement is not fortuitous. A third reason for quotations in general is that it seems worthwhile to explore the intellectual origin of the concepts we are using. More than once I was surprised to find that my own discoveries had been made before by others. As for some other seemingly superfluous quotations, their purpose is to prevent any accusation of bias. In an area where passions run high, it is almost impossible to avoid misunderstandings. But it is worth trying. It was, I think, Kenneth Galbraith who once suggested that one should always cherish one's critics and protect them where possible from foolish error.

I adopted the principle of quoting "Western" writers when criticizing the social order in which they live and of invoking "Eastern" writers when dissecting their own societies. Those living in the particular societies ought to know these societies best and may be considered their best representatives—or judges. The principle could not be followed with complete consistency—taboos exist in our societies, not only in "primitive" ones, and so certain themes simply are not discussed—but I did my best, searching through the literature in a dozen or so languages.

In order to expose the ideas developed in the book to qualified criticism, I discussed them at numerous international scholarly gatherings. The experience was occasionally rather curious: great difficulties were encountered in establishing communication. I was reminded of an observation made by Karl Mannheim: "Every new vision of improving institutions has seemed utopian to those who took the established order for granted." Often, the participants in the discussions would avoid any analysis and simply insist that the particular design was unrealistic, if not outright impossible. A closer scrutiny of what they meant invariably showed that they *implied* that *everything else remained unchanged*. Clearly, no radical change or improvement of any important social institution—that is, of a *subsystem*—is possible if the social *system* remains unchanged. Thus I must call the attention of the reader to the fact that this is an exercise in system design. The established order not only is not taken for granted; it is questioned at every point. To follow the argument, the reader is invited to accompany the author in an exploration of the possibilities for the transformation and change of the existing social systems.

The present book has at least one great deficiency: its institutional design stops at the boundaries of the national state. Socialism, however, is a world phenomenon. The political economy of socialism cannot be complete if it does not include socialist relations on an international scale. This is particularly obvious in the contemporary divided world. There are two reasons that prompted my choice to examine socialism in a single country. One of them is methodological realism. If, as a Marxist, one is interested in changing the world, one cannot change it all at once. In a world of established national sovereignties, changes can be carried out only within national jurisdictions. It is therefore appropriate to start exploring all the possibilities for building socialism in a single country. The second reason is pragmatic. It took too long to write the book as it is. It would necessarily delay its publication if the difficult field of international economic and political relations also had to be explored. I admit that a more general, global approach might change some of the findings of the study. But so will scholarly critique, which I expect. Sometime in the future a new edition will incorporate improvements and extensions.

In an endeavor like the present one, the author faces a great danger of being parochial. We all are very much influenced by our own social and national environments, by our own experiences and preferences. The only way to avoid making oneself silly by proclaiming national peculiarities to be globally valid truths is to expose one's ideas to international criticism. I did so, as any scholar does, by publishing books and papers. But that is far from sufficient. One must also live in different societal and national environments to be able to see things from different angles. In this respect, I was fortunate to study and teach in a number of countries. I learned much from my teachers in Manchester, London, and Cambridge, Massachusetts. My students in Stockholm and Paris; in Washington, Ann Arbor, and Notre Dame; in Santiago de Chile and Dar es Salaam; and, of course, in my own country, which is a cultural macrocosmos in miniature, were my first and most informative critics. It is difficult to say whether I learned more when they agreed with me or when they disagreed. This experience was complemented by my work in advising foreign governments interested in self-management and socialism, and by addresses to professional audiences as an invited lecturer at some fifty-odd universities and research institutions throughout the world, across all its dividing lines. If, after all this filtering of ideas, some of them still bear traces of parochialism, that must be considered as the hard core of my own limitations.

I have also been privileged to belong to a group of social scientists who have been meeting for several years now in Zagreb under the guidance of Rudi Supek and Eugen Pusić. The unifying theme of all these meetings has been "Man and the System." Most of the ideas contained in this book were discussed at the group's meetings, and I benefited enormously from the friendly but ruthless criticism of my colleagues.

I received valuable comments from Vučina Vasović and Robert Lane, who read chapters 10 and 11, and from Jozo Županov, who read chapter 14. They are in no way responsible, however, for the present version of these chapters. I am also indebted to various publishers and editors who have granted the necessary permissions to use quotations and my own published material.

Even a full-blooded socialist needs leisure time to reflect and write about socialism. I am grateful to the Swedish Institute for International Economic Studies and its director, Assar Lindbeck, for the generous invitation to spend seven months at the institute without any obligations. The change of environment—Sweden is so different from Yugoslavia—the friendly and stimulating atmosphere at the institute, the lack of pressure of administrative and other duties, and a good library provided all that was necessary for the long-postponed beginning of the work. All of part I was written in Stockholm. Most of the rest of the book was written in Belgrade at the Institute of Economic Sciences. I should like to express my sincere thanks to the institute for the financial and other help extended to me.

I am particularly obliged to Mrs. Ljuba Martinović, librarian of the Institute of Economic Sciences. Without her help, this book would have taken much longer to write, or would have contained inadmissible lacunae. I used to drive Mrs. Martinović to despair with long lists of requested books, many of which were not available in Belgrade or even in the country. Month after month she patiently searched out my "required reading" and, in the end, the books would appear on my desk. It is my pleasant duty to acknowledge her unselfish concern.

Belgrade

Branko Horvat

PART ONE

A Critique of Contemporary Socioeconomic Systems

I am speaking of a *ruthless criticism of everything existing,* ruthless in two senses: The criticism must not be afraid of its own conclusions, nor of conflict with the powers that be.

MARX to Arnold Ruge (1843)

The possessing class and the proletarian class express the same human alienation. But the former is satisfied with its situation, feels itself well established in it, recognizes this self-alienation as its *own* power and thus has the *appearance* of a human existence. The latter feels itself crushed by this *self-alienation,* sees in it its own impotence and the reality of an inhuman situation.

MARX AND ENGELS, The Holy Family (1844)

I

IN THE SECOND HALF of the twentieth century, two gigantic blocs of countries are fighting for world supremacy. The two blocs are identified with two socioeconomic systems: capitalism and socialism (or communism). Capitalism is characterized by a free market and private productive property, socialism by central planning and state property. People debate whether it is possible—and necessary—for the two systems to coexist peacefully and whether the paths of development of the two systems tend to converge. The recently liberated, less developed countries can choose only between market-oriented capitalism and state-controlled socialism.

This is the popular view of the contemporary world scene—so popular, in fact, that even most social scientists adhere to it without questioning it in the least. They disagree only in their answers to the questions posed, particularly in their predictions as to the final winner in the battle.

Such a view is false, however. Even the terms used are confused. True, big powers are fighting for supremacy. Big powers have always been fighting for supremacy: now, during the two world wars, in the nineteenth century. . . . But this has had little to do with socialism. Neither is socialism at stake in the present battle. In fact, *the only important interest that the two blocs have in common is to prevent genuine socialist development anywhere.* The often mutually tolerated interventions and military aggressions in Greece, China, Vietnam, Latin America, Hungary, and Czechoslovakia, together with the total blockade of Yugoslavia by the Cominform countries and of Cuba by the United States, demonstrate this externally. Numerous trials and persecutions of progressive individuals demonstrate it internally.

To many simple-minded people, that looks puzzling. Wasn't the October Revolution in Russia a genuine socialist revolution? Of course it was! Since this revolution was victorious, and no counterrevolution occurred afterward, clearly the Soviet Union must be a socialist country. True, Stalin was responsible for many grave mistakes—millions of people perished in concentration camps—and for many deviations. These were the unfortunate results of the cult of personality. But mistakes can be corrected and deviations eliminated. Once this is done, we shall have a truly socialist society.

A moment of reflection shows that the same reasoning applies to capitalism. And, of course, it is being used all the time. Bourgeois revolutions were inspired by lofty ideals just as were socialist revolutions. Unfortunately, the implementation did not quite reach the desired standards. Yet, once the shortcomings of capitalism are eliminated, we shall achieve a decent society that, if one wishes, one may call "socialist" (or "free," or whatever one likes).

The difficulty with such reasoning is that it makes little sense in the real world. In order to eliminate the basic shortcomings of capitalism, it is necessary to eliminate—occasionally to destroy by force—capitalism itself. It took some time—and the life work of a Marx—before people began to understand this simple truth. No wonder that the same truth about Stalinist systems is still not well comprehended. In a way history repeats itself. In the last century bourgeois ideology mystified the capitalist society as the incarnation of freedom and equality of opportunity for all. In our century the ideology of the ruling bureaucracies mystifies their own societies as the best of all possible ones. Now—as then—demystification is vitally needed.

Let us therefore start our inquiry by a brief critical survey of the salient features of the two contending social systems.

1

Capitalism

Capitalism has been with us for a couple of centuries by now. Thus, we may assume that its manifestations are well known and adopt a shortcut by approaching our problem somewhat schematically.

As Marx made clear, the development of productive forces and antagonistic class relationships represented basic dynamic elements in social development. When the productive forces outgrow the old system of productive relationships—social relationships among people participating in production—the conflict must be resolved by transforming the latter into a new and compatible social system. In the pioneering countries, the conflict is usually resolved by revolutions that change the class structure of the society.

I. Bourgeois Revolutions and the Process of Political Liberalization

The best-known and most important bourgeois revolution is undoubtedly the French Revolution. This revolution was not intended to bring about small improvements in the society as compared with the feudal order. The revolution had to achieve nothing less than the emancipation of the human race. It was fought under the triple banner of *liberté, égalité,* and *fraternité.* Its advocates believed that all that had to be done to achieve these imposing goals was to smash feudal barriers in order to make possible the free initiative of individuals, who were equal before the law; this initiative was to be protected by a representative government.[1] As a result liberty, equality, and brotherhood would follow as a matter of course.

Based on eighteenth-century political theory, the celebrated *Declaration of the Rights of Man,* issued by the French revolutionary assembly in 1789 and incorporated into the revolutionary constitution of 1793, stated that "men are born free and equal in respect of their natural and imprescriptible rights of liberty, property, security and resistance to oppression."[2] Clause 4 defines liberty as "being able or empowered to do anything that is not harmful to others." In general, the exercise of the natural rights of each man has no limits except those ensuring that other members of the society enjoy the same rights. These limits can be determined only by the law, which ought to be the same for all (clause 6).[3]

One notes that equality is not mentioned as one of the imprescriptible rights. Men are equal only in rights and before the law. Abbé Sieyès, one of the drafters of the declaration, proposed two articles which would have made it clear that there could be no liberty if privileges persisted but that equality applied to the domain of rights and not to means.[4] The Constituent Assembly was in complete agreement, but for some reason did not accept the proposal. It thus failed to make explicit what bourgeois equality was meant to imply from the very beginning.

It also becomes apparent that the goals of the French bourgeois revolution were negatively defined—freedom from, not freedom for—without the participants having been aware of this fact. It was somehow assumed that a formally free man would be able to make full use of his freedom to his own benefit. Such negatively defined liberalism—which was to become synonymous with bourgeois liberalism—far from automatically producing equality and brotherhood, tended to destroy them.[5]

Political freedom was to become an enormous advance compared with feudalism. Yet, it was to be used—and misused—by the powerful, not by everyone. At first it represented almost entirely a proclamation and a request, rather than a realization. The development was remarkably slow. The French republican constitution of 1893 remained unimplemented. The American Constitutional Convention of 1787 left qualifications for voting up to the states, and it was only in the middle of the nineteenth century that manhood suffrage was introduced throughout the country. Women were allowed to vote after the First World War. Full voting rights without discrimination against anyone, including blacks, were established in the United States only within the last decade. Thus, in this respect, it took almost two centuries to apply the proclamation of political liberties embodied in the American Declaration of Independence.

It is both instructive and illuminating to observe how slow and gradual was the process of political democratization in England. The demand for manhood suffrage was put forward for the first time during the revolution in the 1640s, by a group of soldiers and civilians known as the Levellers. The Levellers failed. In 1832, slightly less than two centuries later, riots and demonstrations swept the country. Under the popular pressure, the middle class scored a political victory: the Reform Bill of 1832 established voting rights for property owners. At that time members of Parliament were completely subservient to the great aristocratic landowners, who, as one writer remarked, did not even have to issue instructions, so assiduously did "their" members study their every wish before each vote in Parliament. The ten-year-long Chartist agitation for the extension of voting rights was defeated in 1848. Two decades later, in 1867, most of the skilled workers in towns were enfranchised, and in 1885 voting rights were extended to rural workers. In 1911 the House of Lords lost veto power, but it retained a considerable delaying power until 1948. Women were not enfranchised until 1918, and even then only those older than 30 years of age were allowed to vote. This restriction was removed in 1928. In 1945 double votes for property holders and university graduates were abolished. The voting age was lowered to 18 only in 1966. The House of Lords and the monarchy still exist. According to investigations by Laski[6] and Nightingale,[7] during the time up to the end of the laissez-faire phase of capitalist development, no more than about 1,000 families ruled British society, holding the leading positions in it. Commenting on this situation, Karl Mannheim concluded: "Sociologically speaking, England has been a political democracy run by an oligarchy which has gradually expanded its basis of selection."[8]

Although the gradualness was less elaborate, the pattern of political liberalization was similar in other countries. Throughout most of Europe, labor unions had to fight for suffrage. By the end of the nineteenth century, more than one hundred years after the French and American bourgeois revolutions and more than two hundred years after the English revolution, universal suffrage existed in no country in the world, and manhood suffrage was established in only a handful of countries. If we define conventional democracy as male suffrage, secret ballot, and responsible government, then it is hardly a century old.[9] If we insist on female suffrage as well—as we should—it is much younger. Women acquired voting rights in some of the developed bourgeois countries only after the First World War;[10] in France, Belgium, and Italy, after the Second World War; and in Switzerland in 1971. And yet, the right to vote represents just one necessary, and by no means sufficient, condition for a meaningful democracy. Even at its most successful, bourgeois democracy came to mean a political life dominated by political parties, and political parties are dominated by party machines and their bosses. The ordinary citizen has the privilege of choosing every three, four, or five years the least undesirable political bosses preselected for him by the ruling strata of the society. Bourgeois democracy is a political system that transforms the *formal* will of the majority into the *actual* will of the *minority*.[11]

Equality before the law, with which bourgeois development really started, was also an enormous advance compared with the arbitrary administration of justice in feudal times. In fact, it represented an indispensable foundation on which political freedom was to be built. Yet it soon became apparent that rich and poor are not treated quite equally in the courts. The former come from the same class as the judge, share with the judge the same values and prejudices, and are able to buy high-quality legal defense. "The bourgeois society," comments Lj. Tadić, "actually recognizes only the private owners and members with full rights though formally it proclaims general equality."[12]

A special case of legal equality is market equality. Here employers and employees, the rich and the poor, are clearly in a very unequal position. "The law in its majestic equality," runs the famous summary of bourgeois equality by Anatole France, "forbids the rich as well as the poor to sleep under the bridges, to beg in the streets and to steal bread." Throughout the nineteenth century, the accumulation of wealth on the one side was accompanied by the accumulation of misery on the other. In England, where industrial revolution occurred first, real wages remained stagnant—and were even falling—in the first half of the nineteenth century, in spite of economic development and productivity growth. That, of course, implied a disproportionate growth of profits and private wealth. At the beginning of the century, the working day was as long as fifteen hours—twelve hours for children. The recurring unemployment was enormous: up to 33 percent for steelworkers, up to 50 percent for textile workers.[13] Slums and ghettos, undernourishment and outright hunger, disease and high mortality, the appalling squalor and wretchedness of a large section of the population in the cities—these were the proletarian side of capitalist industrialization, so vividly described by young Engels[14] around the middle of the century and by Marx in the historical chapters of *Capital.*

In spite of the doctrine of inalienable rights, the working class had no political parties, for workers did not enjoy even the most elementary political right, that of voting. Periodic dissatisfactions were suppressed by the police and army. Workers could not form trade unions because all forms of working class combinations were treated as criminal conspiracies in England and elsewhere. The French bourgeois revolution was in full swing when, in June 1791, the National Assembly passed the Chapelier Law, which rendered illegal workers' organizations and gatherings "directed against the free exercise of industry." More specifically, it held that "workers and journeymen in any art or craft may not make decisions or draw up any regulations concerning what they claim are their common interests. . . ." In the parliamentary debate, Chapelier took pains to prevent possible misunderstandings: "None of us intend to prevent the merchants from discussing their common interests."[15] A few years later England introduced legislation (the Act Against Unlawful Oaths in 1797 and the Combination Act in 1799) which made offenders liable to seven years' deportation. Similar conspiracy and combination laws were enacted in almost every Western European country. Article 415 of the Belgian penal code declared trade union action punishable by two to ten years in jail. In case of dispute between the master and the worker, the employer was accepted at his word, while the worker was obliged to produce evidence in support of his testimony.[16] Until 1883, every Belgian worker was required by law to possess a workbook which was held by the employer and could be annotated by him. New employment could not be obtained without producing the workbook. In France the workbook requirement was abolished in 1890.[17] This oppressive regime was first relaxed in England in 1824–25. Worker combination was made lawful, but its exercise was circumscribed by many legal restrictions. When, eight years later, Owenite unionism began really to matter, however, employers and the government moved in concert to destroy it. Laws against strikes were repealed in France in 1863, and in the Netherlands in 1872. In the United States worker combinations were treated as conspiracies until almost the middle of the nineteenth century. Only since 1871 in England, since 1884 in France, and even more recently in other countries, have trade unions been legalized and workers granted freedom of industrial organization. In the United States unions were finally accepted by employers in the late 1930s; in France, after the Second World War (in the Constitution of 1946).

Lest the reader be left with the impression that brutal and unscrupulous class exploitation belongs only to the last century, let me point out that it survived the initial stages of industrialization and that it is still with us. As late as 1918, the American Supreme Court ruled that congressional restriction of child labor to eight hours a day was unconstitutional. Economic historian Alexander Gerschenkron tells the following story about the imperial city of Vienna (and the same was true for Germany as well) at the beginning of this century:

> the existence of large and rapidly growing working-class districts meant virtual separation in schools of workers' children from those of the middle class. Workers were precluded from entering certain paths which were reserved for those higher up on the social ladder. . . . The first car on Viennese tramways was regularly used by the better-dressed public, whereas workers took their seats in the second and third cars, a practice which to some extent survived even the revolutionary upheavals of 1918. . . . This was indeed a situation of profound alienation of the worker. . . . Its basis was a combination of discriminatory legislation [e.g., on labor contracts], administrative measures, judicial practices and social taboos.[18]

The worst features of class exploitation are now reproduced in many less developed countries throughout the world.

The continuous growth of productivity and the pressures of working class political and professional organizations have gradually led to important improvements, and so today, in the most advanced countries, the horrors of the early accumulation of capital belong more or less to the past. In even the most developed capitalist countries, however, the distribution of income is still very inegalitarian, while the distribution of property is particularly unequal. For instance, in the United Kingdom in 1960, 5 percent of the population owned 75 percent of personal wealth and received 92 percent of all property income.[19] As far as the operation of the system is concerned, it is perhaps more amusing than important to point out that the British upper classes own more wealth than their nation has created so far! Namely, apart from tangible wealth they also own national debt.

Once equality was destroyed, liberty lost much of its meaning, and brotherhood, of course, disappeared. The latter was clearly not an inalienable right that could be included in a constitution. In the bourgeois world there is still a lot of talk about freedom—we have constantly been brainwashed about the free world—much less about equality, and almost none at all about brotherhood. Even to apologetically inclined individuals, it must sound somewhat absurd to associate brotherhood with the capitalist market competition.[20] Nor should this be surprising. The three ideals were proclaimed by the Revolution, not by the victorious bourgeois class. The bourgeoisie believed in private property, the free market, and family inheritance. The three ideals of the French Revolution can still be found together—a strange symbolism—inscribed on the coins of the state of France.

II. Expropriation of Independent Producers and the Concentration of Economic Power

It is now well known that capitalist development leads to the concentration of capital, employment, and power. It is somewhat less known that it leads to the almost complete destruction of individual economic freedom, to the massive expropriation of private producers. An illustration is provided in Table 1. At the beginning of industrial capitalist development in England, the majority of the population were their own bosses. By the end of the liberal capitalist development, close to 90 percent of the working force (if managers and top officials are excluded) had to sell their labor power to employers, private and state. Elsewhere this process developed with a time lag, but the final result was the same.[21]

TABLE 1

Structure of Employment in England and Wales (in percent)

	Late 17th century	1921
Employers	14	4
Employees	34	90
Independents	52	6

Source: W. F. Oakeshott, *Commerce and Society* (Oxford: Clarendon Press, 1936), p. 215.

The process of proletarianization just described is an outcome of capitalist accumulation. The simple figures in the table mask an unending sequence of countless human tragedies, thwarted expectations, frustrated desires, destroyed homes. The capitalist system works like a gigantic iron hand crushing the independent, disciplining the deviant, exploiting the weak, and forcing everyone to submit to the logic of capitalist accumulation. The free play of market forces in competitive capitalism leads to a gradual concentration (growth through accumulation) and centralization (mergers) of production. Independent producers disappear. So do the small firms—or else they grow. The size of the average firm constantly increases. The larger the firm, the more viable it is. There are at least three reasons: the first is technological—(1) a large firm reaps economies of large-scale production; the other two are related to market control—(2) a large firm can control its sources of supply and can influence demand for its products; (3) it is financially stronger and thus less dependent; in particular, it commands the necessary resources to engage in costly research and development. It is really (2) and (3), not superior productivity due to (1), which explain the cancerous growth of large firms.[22] Because of (2) and (3), a large firm can exert pressure on its weaker partners and can manipulate the terms of buying and selling in its own favor. Such market control implies that risks are minimized and that large firms are able to survive periodic slumps. During upswings, on the other hand, mergers and other forms of combination prove profitable. Large firms increase their share of the market in three different ways: by internal growth, by merger,[23] and by competitive elimination of weaker rivals. They also combine to establish trade associations, cartels, and syndicates, and practice other forms of covert or overt collusion. Thus market competition tends to destroy its own basis and is gradually replaced by oligarchic planning by giant corporations.

Large corporations appeared as early as the second half of the nineteenth century in connection with railway construction. After the great depression of the 1870s, they spread to industry. In the United States their appearance was duly recognized by the passage of the Sherman Antitrust Act in 1890. Around the turn of the century, one-tenth or more of all workers employed in manufacturing enterprises in the United States were employed in firms with more than 1,000 employees; in France, one-tenth or more of all workers employed in nonagricultural enterprises worked for firms with more than 500 employees.[24]

Between the two wars, Berle and Means startled competition-obsessed economists by establishing the fact that, in 1929, no more than *200* of the largest American corporations controlled about one-half of total nonfinancial capital, whereas the other half was controlled by *300,000* smaller firms. In view of this disproportion in numbers, the effective market control of the largest firms went far beyond one-half of the economy. Interlocking directorates worked in the same direction. This implied that out of a population of 125 million, about 2,500 individuals directly or indirectly controlled the operation of the larger part of the enormous American economy.[25] Since 1929 the firms have, of course, continued to grow. While in 1929 some 100 of the largest corporations owned 44 percent of fixed assets in manufacturing, this percentage increased to 58 percent in 1962.[26] In Britain the largest 100 manufacturing firms increased their share of net output from 10 percent in 1880 to 26 percent in 1930 and to 50 percent by 1970.[27]

A new phenomenon has appeared recently: business planning on a worldwide scale by gigantic corporations. Although the export of capital started at an early stage, only after the last world war did world trade come to be dominated by a small number of giant multinational corporations. In 1969 the sales of each of the three largest corporations—all of them American—were greater than the gross output (gross national product plus intermediate goods) of any of some 120 sovereign nations.[28] It has been estimated that by 1985 some three hundred companies will control about 75 percent of the capital assets of the capitalist world. The key industries, such as automobile manufacture, computing, and chemicals, will each be effectively controlled by four or five multinationals.[29] The reasons for the multiplication of transnational corporations are techno-economic and institutional. If, instead of exporting commodities, the output capacity itself is located in a foreign market, transportation costs can be reduced, cheaper local raw materials, energy, and labor can be used, and output can be adjusted to local demand. Further, by operating in several countries, the corporation can secure its own sources of supply and can use the advantages of a larger market. But perhaps the major advantage is institutionally determined. The corporation can escape unpleasant government controls and, by manipulating internal prices, declare profits where taxes are lowest.[30]

As usual, quantitative growth resulted in qualitative changes. First, individually owned enterprises have been replaced by joint stock companies. There are at least two reasons for this. One is that the corporations were simply outgrowing the financial possibilities of single families. The other is that death duties (introduced in Britain in 1894) made it increasingly difficult to perpetuate family control from generation to generation. On the other hand, capital gains either were not taxed at all (capital gains taxes were not levied in Britain until 1965) or were taxed at rates substantially below income tax rates. Thus, it paid to liquidate family interests through company flotations. As a result, ownership became separated from managerial control. Of the 200 largest nonfinancial American corporations, only 12 were family firms in 1929 and none at all in 1963. In an additional 57 firms in 1929 and 23 in 1963, control was exercised on the basis of majority or minority ownership of stock. Some 88 firms were management controlled in 1929, and 169 firms in 1963.[31] In Britain, management control in the 50 largest mining and manufacturing firms increased from 50 percent in 1936 to 72 percent in 1951.[32] Second, management has become largely an autonomous and self-perpetuating oligarchy. Finally, corporations tend to generate necessary funds internally. This provides at least two advantages. On the one hand, transaction costs and uncertainty of new capital issues in the stock market are avoided. On the other hand, shareholders prefer this policy because capital gains are taxed at much lower rates than the distributed dividends. Self-financing makes corporations financially independent, and management remains in full control of funds. As a consequence of this triple change, competitive capitalism was transformed into *monopoly capitalism.*

The term is somewhat ambiguous. In this case, "monopoly" does not mean complete control of sales. In many industries three or four firms control two-thirds or more of total output; only in exceptional cases does a single firm dominate. Thus, strictly speaking, the reference should be to oligopoly,[33] not monopoly. The term *monopoly* might still be employed, however, in the sense that the demand curve is downward sloping, which means that the firm is no longer a price taker as under competition. This situation is due to the large size of the firm and the differentiation of its product. But there is more to it than that. Once an entire industry is controlled by three or four giant firms, competitive price cutting is a very dangerous affair. It may—and did, when in the early days inexperienced partners experimented with it—result in a general disaster. Thus, planning and coordination are in everyone's interest. Cartels and other forms of open collusion are usually curbed by antitrust laws. But tacit collusion is possible and is widely practiced. Firms study each other carefully and know very well what they can do without provoking retaliation. Prices are established so as to reflect common interest. No consultation is necessary. Tacit collusion is expressed most conspicuously in price leadership: the acknowledged leader takes initiative in changing prices and other firms follow suit. As a consequence, oligopolistic behavior begins to resemble very closely that of the monopoly. Statistical evidence indicates that oligopolistic prices fall substantially less than competitive prices in a depression and that profits of large firms and of firms in oligopolistic industries generally are larger than those of smaller firms and those in more competitive industries.[34]

Capital concentration and centralization both provoked and enabled labor centralization. Faced with the economic power of employers, workers organize themselves into unions. In order to be effective, unions must be large organizations, and they grow until they reach the absolute limit of nationwide associations. At this stage, monopoly labor is facing monopoly capital. Each fights for a larger share in the national cake. This conflict is, of course, obvious. What is less obvious is that the two monopolies have vital interests *in common.* In the early days of capitalism, labor unions were a mortal threat to the profits of small entrepreneurs. Thus, state power was used to outlaw them. The giant corporation is sure of profits and fears only the destructive consequences of disorderly behavior on the part of workers. If an organization is willing to respect management prerogatives and guarantee labor discipline, the corporation should be only too glad to negotiate a deal.[35] Contemporary labor contracts state explicitly that strike action is forbidden without the approval of the union. "Today," comments Staughton Lynd on American arrangements, "the worker who 'wildcats' can expect to be dismissed with the assistance, indeed at the insistence, of the union."[36] And so labor unions came to be integrated into the system. Wages rise and profits do also, while corporations are able to plan and to minimize risks.[37]

III. The General Pattern of Capitalist Development

Capitalism is based on competition and constantly produces monopoly. It is founded on market and constantly generates attempts to destroy market, to internalize all its decisions. Corporations strive for vertical integration in order to control prices and other conditions of supply. Horizontal integration is established in order to eliminate competition in the selling markets. A high degree of self-finance—preferably 100 percent—insures independence from financial markets. High-pressure advertising is used to mold consumer preferences, even to create needs that otherwise would never have emerged. The filing of restrictive patents or vexatious lawsuits and exclusive collective rebates provide barriers to entry. Ever-expanding corporations try to internalize all decisions concerning production, buying, selling, and financing. This amounts to total planning. However, even if two hundred firms dominate an entire economy and each of them is rationally planned, something is still wanting. The *economy* is not planned. Nothing in the system guarantees the sufficiency of aggregate demand, the stability of prices and, consequently, the absence of periodic slumps. This was demonstrated very persuasively by the world economic crisis in the early 1930s. The state had to step in to fill the gap in the planning process. Soon Woytinski, Wigforss, and Kalecki, on the social democratic side, and John Maynard Keynes, on the other, showed how this could be accomplished. And capitalism acquired yet another epithet: it came to be called *state capitalism.* The two world wars helped to speed up the process. Both government and business learned to cooperate in the joint venture of controlling the economy and the society.

A brief historical digression may prove useful. State interference in the capitalist process did not occur for the first time in the interwar period. Nor did monopolies emerge only after the 1870s. Capitalism, in fact, started with both. Its first, preparatory stage is known as *commercial capitalism.*

In Western Europe, this stage lasted about two hundred years, until the early eighteenth century. In order to expand trade and create new manufactories, merchants asked for—and were granted—monopolies. Young national states, growing more centralized until they reached the stage of "enlightened absolutism," searched for new sources of revenue. Trading companies, conducting business under very precarious conditions, needed state protection. The symbiosis between commercial capital and the state was a natural outcome. Royal manufactories in France under Colbert are a particularly illuminating case. But the expansion of trade was bound to undermine restrictions and monopolies eventually. By the end of the seventeenth century, regulated companies ceased to be the dominant form of organization in foreign trade. In the early eighteenth century, the putting-out system began to be replaced by factory production. The stage was set for the Industrial Revolution, which began in the 1760s with a perfected steam engine and improved textile machinery. Soon *industrial capitalism* was in full swing, destroying the remaining trade barriers.

Its competitive stage ended with the great depression in 1873–96—and the rest of the story we already know. When a firm grows relative to a given industry, it reaches a stage where further expansion *within the confines of that industry* reduces profitability. It is then forced to go outside and diversify industrially and geographically. "Thus the typical production unit in modern developed capitalism is a giant corporation which is both conglomerate (operating in many industries) and multinational (operating in many countries)."[38] A small number of such big corporations, aided and coordinated by the government, effectively run the show.

Each of the four developmental stages is faithfully reflected in economic theory. *Mercantilism* is the theory of commercial capitalism. It insisted on the identity of commercial profit and national benefit. The competitive stage of industrial capitalism is spanned by *classical political economy*. Its first heralds were William Petty (*Political Arithmetick*, 1672) and Richard Cantillon (*Essai sur la nature du commerce en général*, 1755). Physiocrats popularized the *laissez-faire, laissez-passez* principle, and Adam Smith the "invisible hand." The last original work in the classical tradition was Karl Marx's *Das Kapital* (1867). It marked at the same time the accomplished beginning of a new, anticapitalist thinking and development. The marginalist revolution of Jevons, Menger, and Walras in the 1870s and the theories of imperfect and monopolistic competition of the early 1930s (Joan Robinson and E. Chamberlin) delimit the era of neoclassical economics. It started with the theory of competition and ended with the theory of monopoly. In 1936 Keynes's *General Theory* appeared. Keynesian economics is still with us. And so is state capitalism.

Other classifications are also possible—for instance, a three-stage division into commercial, industrial, and postindustrial capitalism. Since I am concentrating on the last stage, I found it convenient to lump competition and monopoly into one single laissez-faire stage and contrast it with the last, regulated stage. But the four periods described above seem so well demarcated historically that they must enter into any conceivable developmental classification. They illuminate the dynamics of the system. They also demonstrate the acceleration of development: each stage becomes progressively shorter. Table 2 summarizes the discussion. For the sake of completeness I add the transition period from feudalism to capitalism, of which more later (chapter 14, section IA).

We can now resume our analysis of state capitalism.

TABLE 2

Classification of Capitalist Development

Transition from feudalism:	Petty commodity production, mid-fourteenth to mid-sixteenth century	
First regulated stage:	Commercial capitalism, until the mid-eighteenth century	
Laissez-faire stage:	Competitive, until 1870s	
	Monopoly, until 1930s	Industrial capitalism
Second regulated stage:	State, until 1970s	
	Transnational (?)	Postindustrial capitalism, transitional (?)

The rapidly increasing role of the state is well indicated by the share of government spending in the gross national product. Around the turn of the century, this share amounted to 5–10 percent in the advanced capitalist countries. It did not increase substantially before the world crisis.[39] Since then, it has risen rapidly, however, and in the 1970s reached one-third, or even 40 and 50 percent as in Scandinavia and the Netherlands. This is already a large enough mass of resources to be used effectively for stabilization purposes. A large public sector, in fact, fulfills two different stabilization tasks: since government purchases are not subject to spontaneous market fluctuations, they provide an island of stability against cumulative waves in upswings and downswings; apart from that, fiscal and monetary weapons can be used to produce countercyclical effects.

Within the government sector, special significance attaches to defense expenditures. In the American case, these expenditures almost double government purchases. This led to the creation of what is known as the military-industrial complex. As noted by President Eisenhower, who can scarcely be considered a radical, its "total influence is felt in every city, every statehouse, every office of the Federal Government." Opposition to taxation somehow melts away when money is spent on armaments. Thus military expenditures help to sustain aggregate demand. And more than that. They "provide underwriting for advanced technology and, therewith, security for the planning of the industrial system in areas that would otherwise be excluded by cost and risk."[40] So a modern capitalist state has a certain stake in military expenditures. But this role should not be overstressed. Space competition can effectively replace the arms race in this regard. So can direct financing of research and development. It might be noted that military expenditures are small in the Federal Republic of Germany and negligible in Japan, while these two countries achieve substantially higher rates of growth than the United States.[41] In general, the larger the total public sector, the less important are military expenditures.

In addition to the traditional Keynesian prescriptions, the acceleration of technological progress was shown to be one of the tasks of the modern capitalist state. So is the provision of trained and educated manpower. The state also participates in investment and engages directly in production. The capital-intensive infrastructure—roads, railways, airlines, energy supply—as a rule is provided by the state. The state bails out failing corporations, subsidizes unprofitable industries, and guarantees export risks. When necessary, it regulates wages and prices. In general, whenever the corporate system fails, the state steps in. Hence the appellation for the system in question: *state-monopoly capitalism.*

There is one important thing that a national state cannot accomplish. It cannot plan on an international level. The corporation can transcend national boundaries, the state cannot. The current crisis of the international economic order reflects this fact. Since modern economies are highly interdependent, national planning cannot prevent business fluctuations unless economic activities are coordinated on a world scale. The internationalization of planning is a likely next stage in institutional development. It may therefore be characterized as *transnational.*

Big business implies big labor; both of them imply big government. In a capitalist setting, the government is based on political parties. Parties, like unions, are bureaucratic mediators. Workers cannot negotiate or strike without unions. Deputies cannot vote or act without the permission of the parties. In order for the government to be effective, it must be stable. In order to stabilize it, the number of political parties is gradually reduced until all of political life is dominated by two major parties.[42] Further, there is a strong tendency for these two parties to link themselves with the other two monopoly groups and to represent their interests. Thus, it is likely that there will be a "conservative party" favoring the interests of private capital and a "labor party" supported by trade unions.

Four giants dominate the social scene in state-monopoly capitalism: organized capital, organized labor, and two political parties. Insofar as the political parties clearly identify themselves with the two antagonistic social interests, the oligopoly of four reduces to a duopoly. But even if this identification does not take place, it is still the fact that human affairs are conducted by gigantic organizations. Business managers and state officials are organization men.

Technostructures[43] and bureaucracies are instruments of organizational control, of coordination and regulation. Groups that have access to the commanding positions of such organizations wield enormous power. Together with competition and the laissez-faire market, individualism is disappearing under a heavy weight of organization. In fact, the life of every individual is regulated by some organization over which he has little or no control. Because of this overwhelming importance of organization, I propose to denote the modern stage of capitalism as *organized or regulated capitalism.*

The last two stages of capitalism are quite clearly separated by the interwar period. The laissez-faire stage ended with the First World War. Organized capitalism was fully established after the Second World War. Between the two wars, political instability, economic stagnation, world economic crisis, and the emergence of fascism marked the rather turbulent evolution of one stage of capitalism into the other. In what follows, we shall focus attention on the latter stage, on organized capitalism. At this stage, as we saw, the state plays an exceedingly important role. In this respect, it bears a certain similarity to another modern social system in which the state plays an even more significant—and, for all practical purposes, absolute—role. This system is less well known and so requires the somewhat more detailed analysis to be given in the following chapter.

2

Etatism

At the time they wrote the *Communist Manifesto*, its authors were separated from the French Revolution by a period exactly as long as the one separating the present author from the October Revolution. Now as then, the new social system is mature enough to allow a systematic analysis and an evaluation.

To facilitate understanding of the analysis that follows, let us begin by providing a provisional definition of etatism. A society will be called *etatist* if its ruling strata profess the basic tenets of traditional socialist ideology, such as the elimination of private productive property and the emancipation of the exploited classes, but revise the socialist approach in regard to one crucially important aspect: the role of the state. Socialists have traditionally viewed the state as an apparatus of repression. It consists of a *government over people* which should be replaced by the *administration of things* (Saint-Simon, Engels). "In order to assert themselves as individuals, the proletariat must overthrow the state" (Marx and Engels, *German Ideology*). All government officials should be paid workers' wages and should be recallable at any time (Marx, Lenin). All political posts must be only temporary (Bebel, Lenin). Complete control over the political process should reside with the population, and the state should gradually wither away (Proudhon, Engels). For that to happen, decision making must be decentralized and based on communes and associations (anarchists, Paris Commune, Marx). Bourgeois democracy, with its many social constraints, will be superseded by a much more meaningful social arrangement in which the freedom of every individual is the precondition for the freedom of all (*Communist Manifesto*). Only the most complete freedom of thought makes possible the constant progress that is a vital principle of the society (Bebel in *Future Society*, Rosa Luxemburg).[1]

In an etatist setting, all these ideas are replaced by a totally opposite ideology in which a strong, centralized, authoritarian state becomes the main pivot of society. All economic and political power is concentrated in the hands of the ruling political organization, which openly claims the monopoly of political power. In 1930, Stalin explained this revision "dialectically" by asserting that, in order to wither away, the state must first grow stronger;[2] this corresponds closely to another "dialectical" discovery—namely, that, with the building of socialism, the class struggle is bound to become more violent. "The destruction of classes is not achieved by extinguishing the class struggle but by intensifying it. The withering away of the state happens not through the weakening of the state power, but through its maximal strengthening. . . ."[3] At the Eighteenth Congress of the Communist Party in 1939, Stalin attacked the well-known proposition by Engels concerning the development of the state. Engels maintained that the first act by which the state appears as a representative of the entire society—the socialization of the means of production—is at the same time its last independent act in the same capacity. The intervention of state power in social relations becomes superfluous in one field after another and gradually disappears. Stalin claimed that this approach was inapplicable in the Soviet Union because it was the only existing socialist country, encircled by a hostile capitalist world. Since then, the capitalist encirclement has been broken up; countries in which capitalism has been eliminated include one-third of the world population—and yet the same theory is still fully accepted.[4]

Thus, in short, etatism is a blend of traditional socialism and authoritarian state. How this incongruous combination came about and what its consequences are, remain to be explored. To do so, let us turn back to the first half of the last century.

I. False Antinomies

The spectacle of the needless misery that early capitalist accumulation inflicted on the powerless and practically outlawed working classes could not but create strong reactions. That is how socialist movements emerged in the nineteenth century. Having lived in the reality of unscrupulous exploitation, people began to lose faith in the ideals of bourgeois revolution. The society must have gone wrong somewhere. It was quickly discovered that liberty, (legal) equality, and private ownership generate not brotherhood but capitalist exploitation. Analytical minds soon arrived at a consistent theoretical solution that can be summed up in the following three propositions: (1) Private ownership is the major cause of economic inequalities. Economic inequalities lead to political inequalities and generate class exploitation. Thus, a fundamental precondition for a classless society is socialization of the means of production. (2) Laissez-faire markets generate periodic slumps and unemployment. In order to secure work for all members of the community and to make rational use of the available resources, the society should establish central planning. (3) Since, at the time, workers did not enjoy even the most elementary political rights, a reformist social transformation did not seem feasible. Thus a violent revolution appeared to be the only available alternative. "The Communists . . . openly declare that their ends can be attained only by the forcible overthrow of all existing social conditions" (*Communist Manifesto*).

At the level of application—that is, when it was accepted by broad political movements—the theory just sketched received a characteristic psychological twist. Socialists became socialists not for theoretical reasons, but because they strongly opposed the oppressiveness of bourgeois society. Like any spontaneous reaction to something one dislikes, the socialist critique tended to become a naive, straightforward negation of bourgeois institutions and values. Once again the basic approach was a negative one. This time it was not the feudal barriers but the bourgeois institutions that had to be destroyed in order to emancipate humanity. Whatever existed was wrong and had to be replaced by something opposite. It was often overlooked that bourgeois society was not only bourgeois but also a result of the entire development of the human race up to that time. Thus a thorough analysis of the society was required—an analysis directed at the precise identification and clear distinction between more fundamental behavioral patterns and accidental phenomena characteristic of the bourgeois phase of development. Instead, the attitudes and reasoning tended to be as follows.

—Capitalist exploitation is based on private property. Thus private property must be abolished and replaced by public property. Continuing to think in terms of inherited bourgeois legal categories—an owner is a natural or juristic person—socialist ideologues and their followers could visualize public property only as state property. And so it happened that the percentage of productive capital owned by the state came to be regarded as the most appropriate index of the development of socialism in a particular country.

—A (laissez-faire) market generates periodic slumps, unemployment, inefficient allocation of resources, and alienation.

Thus the *market* as such has to be abolished—again there was no awareness that there could be any but a capitalist market—and replaced by the administrative allocation of resources. Market was identified with a special, laissez-faire, form of capitalist economy and was absolutely opposed to—that is, conceived as incompatible with—planning.

—In an economy without market there was no place for money. In his *Future Society*,[5] the German labor leader Bebel expressed this idea in a very simple—and simpleminded—fashion: "where there is no capital there are no commodities and so there can be no money." The conclusion has been widely accepted, and there have been many attempts to eliminate money, to introduce "moral incentives,"[6] etc. Closely related to money is interest, which was treated exclusively as a nonlabor income—a sort of usury as viewed by the Catholic church in the Middle Ages. Thus interest had to be abolished. For a long time socialist ideologues remained—and many still are—unaware of the allocational function of interest. And so it did not occur to them that interest as private income can and must be abolished, while interest as a price for the use of social capital ought to be retained.

—Ruthless and egotistical *individualism* (generated by private property and unbridled competition) creates an inhuman environment characterized by the state of *Homo homini lupus*. Thus individualism is wicked and must be replaced by *collectivism*, in which the interests of society reign supreme and individuals are expected to subject themselves to the verdict of society. The society is—and can only be—represented by the state.[7] Closely related is the observation that *private initiative* based on bourgeois liberalism caused exploitation of the poor by the rich. Thus private initiative and liberalism are antisocialist and must be replaced by strict *governmental control* and supervision. Next, individual initiative is spontaneous. Thus *spontaneity* is bad. It results in dangerous expressions of petty bourgeois passions, disorganizes society, and leads to anarchy. Consequently, it must be replaced by *conscious*, all-embracing *control* by the state, which ensures standardized behavior. From here it is but one step to a more or less complete negation of individual autonomy, particularly in a society with little material wealth, a phenomenon already observed by Marx and described as primitive or crude communism:

> This communism, which negates the *personality* of man in every sphere, is only the logical expression of private property, which

> is this negation. Universal *envy* setting itself up as a power is only a camouflaged form of cupidity which re-establishes itself and satisfies itself in a different way. The thoughts of every individual with private property are *at least* directed against any *wealthier* private property, in the form of envy and the desire to reduce everything to a common level; so that this envy and leveling in fact constitute the essence of competition. Crude communism is only the culmination of such envy and leveling-down on the basis of a *preconceived* minimum. How little this abolition of private property represents a genuine appropriation is shown by the abstract negation of the whole world of culture and civilization, and the regression to the *unnatural* simplicity of the poor and wantless individual who has not only not surpassed private property but has not yet even attained it.[8]

The list of such false, though consistent, antinomies can be prolonged at will. They have become cruder and more intensive since the Revolution in Russia because that country was backward and, as the only one of its kind, fully encircled by threatening capitalism, it developed a strong defensive impulse so that anything from outside was considered as *prima facie* antisocialist. Thus relativity theory, gene-determined biology, and econometrics were bourgeois inventions, unscientific as such and not to be accepted in a proletarian state. And, quite consonant with Marx's description of a regression to unnatural simplicity, abstract art, jazz, experimentation in literary expression, and atonal music have been considered decadent and thus forbidden. Instead, socialist realism—as the style was christened—with what are really petty bourgeois horizons and taste, and its state-glorifying educational purpose, was prescribed as the only proper art for the working class.[9]

One of the antinomies, fully developed only after the Revolution, had tragic consequences. It follows directly from the negation of personality described above and concerns political democracy. Democracy, as a bourgeois invention, must be bad as such; it protects wealthy classes and leaves the proletarians poor and exploited. Thus it ought to be replaced. By what? By the "dictatorship of the proletariat" as a form of socialist democracy. This somewhat ambiguous phrase (replacing the term "rule of the proletariat" used in the *Communist Manifesto*), which Marx partly inherited from Blanqui[10] but gave a different content, was misused—not always consciously—to create one of the greatest mystifications of the century. The concept was *intended* primarily as a sociological category describing the class character of the political system, and implied a contrasting of rule in favor of the proletariat, which represented the great majority of the population, with rule in favor of the bourgeoisie (bourgeois dictatorship), which, like any ruling class, represented only a small section of the population. The phrase was *used* primarily by the ruling parties in its original Blanquist version to justify political dictatorship.[11] That was not difficult, for in the revolutionary labor movement, under conditions of political repression, there was a strong current of thought and action oriented toward dictatorship pure and simple. Even before Blanqui, Babouvists considered a "dictatorship of the revolutionary leadership." In his *Guarantees of Harmony and Freedom,* Weitling observed that a large group of French communists "incline to a dictatorship, because they well know that the sovereignty of the people . . . is not suited to the period of transition from the old to a completely new organization."[12] In 1848, in Prague, Bakunin developed plans for a regime "with unlimited dictatorial powers"[13]—which resembles Lenin's 1920 formulation of "an authority based on violence and not restricted by anything." In 1864 Bakunin produced a document for his secret organization, founded in Italy, in which he ordained: "All members of the national Junta are appointed by the central directorate, to which the national Junta owes absolute obedience in all cases."[14] After the successful revolution, his organization was to exercise "invisible dictatorship."[15] As far as Blanquists are concerned, their attitude is perhaps best described by Friedrich Engels: "From Blanqui's assumption, that any revolution may be made by the outbreak of a small revolutionary minority, follows of itself the necessity of a dictatorship, not of the entire revolutionary class, the proletariat, but of a small minority that has made the revolution, and who are themselves previously organized under the dictatorship of one or several individuals."[16]

The Marxist approach is, of course, very different. The following dialogue will clarify the issue. Commenting in 1891 on the draft of the Erfurt Program of the German Social Democratic Party, Engels wrote: "If one thing is certain it is that our Party and the working class can only come to power under the form of the democratic republic. This is even the specific form for the dictatorship of the proletariat."[17] Once again Stalin, and with him the Communist Party of the Soviet Union, disassociated themselves from the views of Engels and of the socialist movement in general:

> Before the Second Russian Revolution (February 1917), the Marxists of all countries assumed that the parliamentary republic

> was the most suitable form of political organization in the period of the transition from capitalism to socialism. . . . Engels' authoritative statement in his criticism of the draft of the Erfurt Program in 1891, namely, that "the democratic republic . . . is . . . the specific form for the dictatorship of the proletariat" left no doubt that the Marxists continued to regard the democratic republic as the political form for the dictatorship of the proletariat. . . . What would have happened to the Party, to our revolution, to Marxism, if Lenin had been overawed by the letter of Marxism and had not had the courage to replace one of the old propositions of Marxism . . . by the new proposition concerning the republic of Soviets. . . .[18]

Stalin got his way rather easily. An interesting historical paradox may be observed: a symbiosis between masochistic intellectuals and power-thirsty rulers. In a poor and unjust society, intellectuals—themselves a privileged group—tend to develop an acute feeling of guilt, which is then relieved by unconditional submission to the autocracy of the "revolutionary leaders." The phenomenon has been worldwide. And Stalin knew how to exploit it.

Once democracy was courageously transformed into dictatorship, other consequences followed by logical necessity. Bourgeois democracy implies several political parties; consequently, socialist democracy can imply only one party. Under the bourgeois-type reasoning of the socialist-communist ideologues, it was impossible to visualize a *no*-party arrangement. Eventually the vicissitudes of political development led not to elimination of the imperfections of *bourgeois* democracy, but to the rejection of *democracy* as such. The quest for democracy began to be described scornfully as anarcholiberalism, as a petty bourgeois weakness that a disciplined communist must not tolerate.[19]

A very special political system evolved. The Polish Marxist Wlodzimierz Brus has described it as totalitarian and noted its four major characteristics:

1. the domination of the bureaucratic apparatus over formally elected bodies throughout the entire political structure;
2. the replacement of meaningful elections by appointment of candidates for party, state, and union posts from above by the higher levels of bureaucracy;
3. a leading role for the party, interpreted as the complete subordination of all other institutions to the party apparatus and total prohibition of all independent political initiatives;

4. the monopoly control of mass media, including universal preventive censorship.

"Thus in all areas of social life," concluded Brus, "members of society are confronted by an all-powerful state apparatus and are reduced to atomised individuals deprived of political and legal means of expression or control."[20]

II. The Religious Structure of Consciousness

In the foregoing section, we saw how mere negation did not change the framework of bourgeois reasoning. Mere negation remains within essentially the same structure of consciousness. Suppose, now, that a socialist revolution occurs in a backward, prebourgeois society. One might expect that in such a case not only bourgeois, but even prebourgeois attitudes will be found to be described as socialist. And, indeed, this is what happened.

Characteristic for the prebourgeois world is a religious structure of consciousness.[21] By this I mean a prerational and nonrational mode of reasoning oriented toward *authority*—not toward evidence—and based on *beliefs*—not on facts. In addition, the objects of beliefs are treated as *sacred.* The authority-beliefs orientation produces an attitude of mind that is not simply irrational but has the same pattern as that of religious sects. The cognitive component is supplemented by two others. First, there is an identification with the leader or the organization. One's own personality is immersed, dissolved in the object of worship. Second, as a consequence, the latter is treated as sacred. Every religion implies a clear distinction between sacred and profane. And vice versa: whenever a person, an organization, or an idea is placed outside the reach of criticism, it is placed in a sacred realm that implies religious attitudes.

Since the first socialist revolutions occurred in backward countries, the ensuing socialism was pervaded by religious consciousness and is reminiscent of the religiously oriented societies in the Middle Ages. Marx and Engels expected the coming of an authentic human society. What emerged was a reified and ideologically alienated "socialism." They and their followers insisted on scientific socialism. What emerged was a very different theological socialism. This theological socialism continues to be called "scientific." Why theology is masquerading as science is rather obvious: (a) "truths" have greater motive power than mere subjective "beliefs";[22] and (b) "scientific ideology" provides a justification for, and so an efficient defense of, established interests. Why this theological masquerade is possible is not so obvious and will be the subject of the ensuing analysis.

A. Ecclesiasticism

Theology, of course, implies religion of one kind or another. It may be remarked that the postrevolutionary ruling parties have not been religiously oriented but, on the contrary, are atheist. Indeed, they have been atheist, and quite militantly so. But *a*theism means a negation of theism, and thus their proponents remain captives of theism. Atheism was "prescribed as a *dogma* to the members," as Marx observed long ago concerning Bakuninists.[23] The antireligious zeal required of party members has in common with its counterpart the fact that it is related to religion and that it is a zeal. Atheism can be—and has been—preached with as much religious fervor as any other religion and is often accompanied by all sorts of superstitious beliefs, just as are some of the more primitive religions.

The religious characteristics of parasocialist ideologies and movements have been noticed many times by now. Let me quote, as an illustration, two statements by two very different men—Bertrand Russell, the English philosopher, and Julius Nyerere, the African statesman. Russell points out that "the Jewish pattern of history . . . is such as to make a powerful appeal to the oppressed and unfortunate at all times. St. Augustine adapted this pattern to Christianity, Marx to Socialism."[24] The conclusion is tempting but hardly correct. The basic reason for the similarity is to be found not in the psychology of the oppressed as such—sympathetic members of privileged classes, leaders, and the population at large shared the same psychology—but in the religious frame of mind that requires transcendental concepts of faith, not rational analysis of social interdependencies, in order to achieve salvation (as the resolution of social conflicts was visualized).[25]

Nyerere restricted himself to describing what he observed, but he did so with great precision:

> There is . . . an apparent tendency among certain socialists to try and establish a new religion—a religion of socialism itself. This is usually called "scientific socialism" and the works of Marx and Engels are regarded as the holy writ in the light of

> which all other thoughts and actions of socialists have to be judged. Of course, this doctrine is not presented as a religion; its proponents are often most anxious to decry religion as the "opium of the people," and they present their beliefs as "science." Yet they talk and act in the same manner as the most rigid theologians. We find them condemning one another's actions because they do not accord with what the priests of "scientific socialism" have decided is the true meaning, in modern terms, of books written more than 100 years ago. Indeed we are fast getting to the stage where quarrels between different Christian sects about the precise meaning of the Bible fade into insignificance when compared with the quarrels of those who claim to be the true interpreters of Marxism-Leninism![26]

One could quote a number of authors that come to similar conclusions. But none of them explores the problem in any detail. In what follows, we attempt to fill this gap.

A religion needs a church. This role is fulfilled admirably by the ruling party. The church never makes mistakes, neither does the party. In the well-known *History of the All-Union Communist Party of Bolsheviks,* prepared under Stalin, there was recorded not a single instance of a wrong decision made by the party in its entire history of several decades. Members of the party err, but not the party.[27] When the secretary of the Czechoslovak Communist Party, Rudolf Slánský, and other leaders were accused of treason and executed,[28] party chief Klement Gottwald was asked who could be trusted after that. He answered: "Trust the party."[29] When Khrushchev denounced Stalin as a criminal in 1956, he did not direct a single word of criticism to the party in whose name all the crimes were committed.

The church must have its high priest. This role is filled by the head of the party, called the chairman or secretary general. Like the Pope, the chairman is infallible. He never errs—at least as long as he is in office. He is never criticized publicly. In fact, any attempt to criticize him is considered a serious political offense, a mean act of a sworn enemy of socialism, and the offender is appropriately punished. Even a private criticism in a letter to a friend may earn one a ticket to the GULAG Archipelago, as was discovered by the young officer Aleksandr Solzhenitsyn.

The chairman is a man of genius, often considered the fourth classic. His speeches, reports, and toasts are published in voluminous books and studied at party gatherings and in schools. For more simpleminded persons, selections of writings are prepared—such as *Questions of Leninism* by Stalin, or the little red book of quotations from Mao by Lin Biao (a "hidden enemy," as was discovered later)—in the form of compact catechisms published in millions of copies. The chairman is not only a genius but also an honored and beloved leader and a lord of his people.[30] His portraits are found in classrooms, offices, shop windows, and even the private premises of more devout citizens. They replace the Christian crosses and king's portraits of former times. The country is planted with his statues while he is still alive; streets and cities bear his name. Postage stamps carrying his portrait are issued. His birthday is a sort of national holiday. When the great leader passes away, his body may be embalmed—as in Moscow or Sofia—and exhibited in a glass coffin for the benefit of the faithful citizens. They come in great numbers to pay homage to their deified leaders.

Where there is one great leader, there must be many small leaders. We find a strict hierarchy in the Kingdom of God, with its various categories of saints and angels down to the worst sinners in Hell. And so it is on earth as well. In the Middle Ages the hierarchy was based on birth; in the age of etatism, it is based on merit—whatever that may be—and is equally strict. In the twelfth century the nun Héloïse wrote to Abélard, her former lover and husband who had become a monk, that she was surprised when, "abandoning customs and natural order," he put her name before his. "When we write to superiors or to those equal to ourselves," she reminded him, "order and civility require that their name be put in front of ours; yet, when we turn to inferiors, the order of names must respect the order of dignity."[31] This statement may appropriately be placed over the entrance door of any bureaucratic office. It is a rule whose nonobservance is punished severely. When reading a newspaper, one need only note the order of names to know what relative (political) rank has been assigned to particular persons. From slight changes in the rank listing of names, political analysts deduce far-reaching changes in policies.

B. Religious Consciousness

At this point it will be profitable to draw attention to some observations about religious consciousness already made by Emile Durkheim. Whenever we encounter great concentration of power, insisted Durkheim, the reason should be sought not in the special position of the rulers but in the nature of the society over which they govern. The individual superiority of a particular chief plays only a secondary role. It explains why he, rather than someone else, holds power—not why power is concentrated.[32] Power is concentrated because consciousness is religiously structured. There are at least two reasons for this. Whenever a community shares certain powerful beliefs, these beliefs inevitably acquire religious characteristics. They instill the same awe as religious beliefs.[33] Since revolutions generate extremely powerful emotions and beliefs, they represent a very fertile ground for the emergence of religious attitudes.[34]

The second reason is to be found in what Durkheim calls the mechanical solidarity of a less developed society. In such a society—which generates "primitive communism" as described by Marx in the quotation above—social masses consist of equable elements, which implies that a collective type is very developed and that individual types—products of the social division of labor, which leads to "organic" solidarity—are still in their infancy. The person does not belong to himself; he is a sort of thing at the disposal of society.[35] Inevitably the psychic life of society is religiously structured.[36] One's first moral duty is to be like everyone else, to abstain from anything personal or individual regarding beliefs or behavior.[37] Where the society has a religious, superhuman property—whose source is to be found in the appropriate structure of consciousness—this property is transmitted to the leader, who stands out high above the common people. The concentration of power is not the result of a need for tough rule; it originates from a collective consciousness[38] and the power is great because the collective consciousness is very developed.[39]

A special feature of a religious environment is extreme hypertrophy of punitive law. Anything—that is, any nonconformity—can be considered a punishable offense, from an inappropriate hairstyle in ancient Sparta to deviant sexual behavior in almost all societies right up to our own days. But particularly numerous are religious offenses. Offending (i.e., criticizing) authorities, making public (and private) speeches against proclaimed doctrines, disagreeing with the established order and instituting organized attempts to change it—all belong here. We immediately recognize that all these crimes represent normal political activities in a developed society. Yet in a religious environment they are offenses. Durkheim was therefore correct in noting that by far the most important contraction of punitive law was caused by the disappearance of offenses against religion.[40] Surprise is often expressed concerning the heavy penalties for political delicts as compared with criminal ones in etatist societies. The foregoing analysis ought to contribute to an explanation of this phenomenon. Even in such an enlightened environment as ancient Athens, sacrilege earned nothing less than capital punishment.[41]

Before we proceed, it will be useful to add two notes of clarification in order to avoid possible misunderstanding. The phenomenon I am analyzing here is *collective* not *individual* consciousness. There have been and always will be individuals with religious feelings and mystical experiences. They are neither to be reproached nor to be praised for being what they are. A poet and an accountant, a metaphysical philosopher and an insurance agent differ tremendously. And it is good that they do. This makes for a variety in life, and also makes it easier to staff various jobs with appropriate individuals. Yet the same percentage of mystics in the active population is compatible with widely different types of collective consciousness depending on the collective experience as expressed in the level of development and the social system. Second, the similarities between the (early) church and (early) communist parties originate not only from the similar structure of consciousness, but also from similar revolutionary attitudes. Both were organizations of the oppressed revolting against the mighty of the world. The mobilizing slogan, "Those who do not work should not eat," which one hears continuously associated with the labor movement, belonged originally to Saint Paul. Jesus is reported to have said that the Kingdom of Heaven belongs to the poor. Saint Ambrose of Milan (340–397) declared that it was nature that created the right of common property, and violence that created the right of private property.[42] Similar quotations could be supplied from non-Western churches as well. Such attitudes are due to the fact that the early Christian church (before it became the dominant church and a part of the establishment) and the early communist parties (before they became ruling parties well entrenched in power) faced revolutionary social situations and reacted similarly. Such early revolutionary traditions may be utilized by political movements to establish legitimacy and for other tactical purposes. They are *not,* however, the object of analysis in this chapter.

C. Secularized Religion and the Role of the Devil-Enemy

The church must have a God. This is History. The party, under the leadership of Chairman X, knows and interprets the

Laws of History and leads the toiling masses toward the paradise of a bright future.

Where there is a God, there must be a Devil as well. The Evil One appears in various disguises. Satan, Beelzebub, witches, antichrists, those possessed by the Devil, seducers, heretics, demons, evil spirits, wicked persons generally, belong to his kingdom. It is of particular interest to note that anything new—a new tool, a new discovery, new art—was often described as the product of the Devil, and innovators were highly suspect and occasionally punished for witchcraft or sorcery. In an etatist setting, the Devil is called the Enemy (though the term *enemy* was often used in medieval scholastic literature as well). Since, all officially claimed successes notwithstanding, life is still rather unpleasant and there are many failures, someone must be responsible for the fact that the brilliant ideas of the infallible leadership are not appropriately implemented. Since the leadership cannot err, the burden of responsibility is assumed by the Enemy. The Enemy is generally not identified; the term usually does not refer to concrete persons. It is simply a personification of everything evil. Therefore one speaks mostly not of the enemies but of the Enemy. If a minister of the interior wants to stress the plurality of enemies, he will use the phrase "members of the enemy."[43] The Enemy also appears under various disguises even more numerous than those of the medieval Devil. The Devil-Enemy is embodied in wicked individuals such as right and left deviationists, revisionists, antiparty elements, provocateurs, saboteurs and wreckers, cosmopolitans, dogmatists, left and right opportunists, technocrats and bureaucrats, bourgeois elements, imperialist agents and lackeys, counterrevolutionaries, hirelings, sectarians and splinter elements, careerists and conspirators. He may also appear as hyphenations such as krypto-kulak, anarcho-syndicalist, anarcho-liberal, and left-sectarian. Followers of the wrong leaders—Trotskyites, Stalinists, Maoists, revisionists like Khrushchev[44]—represent a particularly dangerous segment of the Enemy (not all of them, of course, in the same environment). On the basis of public utterances of authorities and newspaper reports, lists of two or three scores of varieties of the Enemy can be compiled. Ordinary criminals are rarely, if at all, referred to as the Enemy. The Enemy has great functional value in an etatist environment. His existence is, in fact, the only justification for the politocracy's claim of leadership. Without the Enemy, the politocracy would lose its raison d'être. If the Enemy did not exist, he would have to be invented.[45]

The Enemy thus has important mobilizing and legitimizing functions. He has another functional value as well. Since the Enemy is neither defined very precisely nor clearly recognizable—yesterday's hero may become today's enemy—anyone may be declared the Enemy depending on the vagaries of party politics. That makes the existential situation of individuals insecure, indeterminate, unstable, precarious, and full of anxiety. In such a situation, the individual is ready to acquiesce, to conform, to follow. Consequently, the chances for effective manipulation are highest.[46] The appeal to sanctified authority will serve the purpose.

In addition to God and the Devil, the church will have a holy writ and, hopefully, four evangelists. The holy writ is referred to as the science of Marxism-Leninism.[47] The term "science" is a linguistic equivalent for "faith," since it cannot be superseded or disproved by another science.[48] While the Comintern was alive, the four classics-evangelists were Marx, Engels, Lenin, and Stalin. After his death, Stalin was largely denied the status of a classic and was replaced by the appropriate local evangelists. The church ceased to be fully universal and, applying the medieval principle of *cuius regio eius religio,* local churches acquired a certain degree of autonomy, occasionally even full autonomy. The existence of a Bible makes it relatively easy to settle controversial issues. Copernicus was wrong because the Bible said that the sun rotated around the earth. It suffices to discover an appropriate quotation. The empirical evidence is irrelevant because it cannot disprove the statement of a classic.

The church has special schools for priests: seminaries. Party activists and prospective functionaries are educated in special party schools. Theological exegesis is replaced by an ideological one. The difference between theology and other aspects of ideology, remarked Djuro Šušnjić, is that theology refers to Heaven and ideology to the future.[49] Pure faith is periodically determined and defined by ecumenical councils. The general party line is periodically determined by party congresses.[50] Both are sacrosanct.

D. The Doctrine of Partiinost'

The main point of religious faith, in the sense used here, is that there is only one God and only one truth. Since religion is about good and bad, a religious man is basically intolerant. If Judaism and Christianity had been equally respectful, there would have been no need for the crucifixion of Christ.[51] A deviation from orthodoxy is called heresy in theological lingo and revisionism in party terminology. In either case, it cannot be tolerated and revisionists are purged. Occasionally, even the terminology is identical. Thus, opponents within the same creed are called renegades.[52] "The adversary simply for daring to contradict at once became a traitor, an opportunist, a hireling," remarked Ignazio Silone, Italian writer and party activist. "An adversary in good faith is inconceivable . . . ."[53] Disagreement and criticism are hostile activities, and that is why, according to official pronouncements, there are so many enemies in "classless" etatist societies.[54]

Throughout the Middle Ages religion was identified with the society and politics. The founder of scholasticism, Saint Anselm (1033–1109), archbishop of Canterbury, proclaimed: "Credo ut intelligam" [I have faith in order to know]. What he probably meant was that faith precedes knowledge.[55] Successive generations, aided by his other remarks, interpreted the idea in a much less sophisticated and much more pragmatic way, and made it serve the needs of the time. If a thought contradicts the revealed faith, it is not a correct thought; if it were, it would not have contradicted. Philosophy, which represented the science of the time, was proclaimed *ancilla theologiae.* It is true that as early as the fifteenth century Nicoletto Vernia, professor at Padua, expressed the opinion that scientific truth is independent from theological truth. Yet, several centuries passed before this idea was generally accepted. Theological socialism reversed this trend by proclaiming that the two cannot, and must not, be separated—that every truth is ideologically determined truth,[56] and that scientific research must be guided by political considerations. This is known as the doctrine of *partiinost'* (party-mindedness, i.e., ideologically determined reasoning and activity implying unconditional submission to the party leadership). The doctrine is usually associated with Stalin and the Stalinists but, in fact, is both older and much more widely accepted. As Trotsky formulated it, "one can be right only with the Party and through the Party" (see note 27).

In its more extreme form, this doctrine may seriously impede the development of science and technology. As mentioned earlier, for some time in the Soviet Union relativity theory, Mendelian genetics, modern sociology, and cybernetics were considered products of bourgeois decadence. The otherwise valid observation that scientists—and everyone else—tend to be biased because they are conditioned by their social experience and position, is turned on its head. The correct proposition, as formulated by the Austrian communist Ernst Fischer[57]—that a class is progressive if the truth corresponds to its interests—is transposed by his colleagues into: something is true if it favors the interests of the "progressive" class.[58]

In an absolutely politicized life, all activities are subordinated to political considerations. Thus *partiinost'* applies not only to politics proper, but also to science, the arts, professions, everything. Candidates for university appointments must profess official ideology and recognize the leading role of the party;[59] mere scholarship and moral integrity will not suffice. Science used to be *ancilla theologiae,* and so were the arts, as was explicitly decided by the Council of Trent in 1563. In more modern times, they have become *ancillae politicae.* Thus it is natural to see party leadership determining which art is socialist and which is not. It is also natural to see the "socialist state," following the practice of the Catholic church (which in 1559 established an Index Librorum Prohibitorum),[60] select for the benefit of its citizens books that cannot be brought into the country or read without special permission.

A special feature of *partiinost'* is the constant rewriting of history. Only the future is known with certainty; history changes all the time. This implies the old Roman institution of *damnatio memoriae*—becoming a nonperson.[61] It also has its counterparts in the Middle Ages[62] and in totalitarian ideologies.[63]

E. The Suppression of the Individual Self

The ruling party is organized like a monastic order. Since it is a militant organization, it is particularly similar to militant monastic orders, such as the Society of Jesus founded in the sixteenth century.[64] Jesuits are a strictly centralized order; the general congregation of the order holds the supreme power. The latter elects the general and can also depose him. The monks take a special vow of complete obedience. The consequence of this obedience is the acceptance of any job assignment. The ruling party is similarly organized, and the principle of organization is termed democratic centralism. What that means is explained unambiguously by Mao Zedong: "The organization must be placed above the individual, the majority above the minority, the higher party functionaries above the lower, and the central committee above the entire party. That is democratic centralism in the party."[65] Members of the order, as well as members of the party, are encouraged to report questionable acts committed by their colleagues and themselves. The rules of the order, and the practice of the party, require complete subjection of individual will and individual opinion to that of the organization.[66] The so-called party line cannot be questioned, it can only be followed.

This suppression of individual will for the sake of some transcendental goal is, of course, a well-known religious phenomenon. But it can also be found in other prebourgeois environments as a political requirement. Moreover, what seems appropriate as a religious duty turns out to have monstrous consequences when it becomes a political necessity. Erich Fromm quotes illuminating statements by two Nazi (National Socialist, as they called themselves officially) leaders, Hitler and Göbbels. In *Mein Kampf* Hitler declared that an Aryan "willfully subjects his ego to the life of the community and, if necessary . . . sacrifices it." Göbbels said: "To be a socialist means to subject the concept of *I* to the concept of *you*; socialism is sacrificing an individual for the wholeness."[67] Soviet Politburo member Lazar Kaganovich stated on one occasion that a Bolshevik must be "ready to sacrifice himself for the Party. Yes, ready to sacrifice not only his life but also his self-respect and sensitivity."[68] All this was well summed up by Benito Mussolini: Believe, Obey, Fight!

Individual self-denial is closely related to party-mindedness. The two are mutually consistent, have a common origin, and imply the destruction of ordinary morality. In the socialist literature, the two requirements were first formulated explicitly by the Russian anarchists, Bakunin and Nechaev. Paragraph 1 of their *Revolutionary Catechism*—the appellation is clearly not accidental—states:

> The revolutionary . . . has no interest of his own, no cause of his own, no feelings, no habits, no belongings; he does not even have a name. Everything in him is absorbed by a simple, exhaustive interest, a single thought, a simple passion—the revolution.

In paragraph 4 our authors declare that a revolutionary

> despises public opinion; he despises and hates the existing social ethic in all its demands and expressions; for him, everything that allows the triumph of the revolution is moral, and everything that stands in its way is immoral.[69]

This mystical self-denial has serious consequences. If an individual is so completely dissolved in his party, if he has completely surrendered his spiritual freedom, then he can bear no personal responsibility for his activities. Anything can happen. Bacílek, minister of security in the Novotny government in Czechoslovakia, explained this position very persuasively:

> I supported the thesis that the decision of the party was the highest law. At the land conference in 1952, I said that the party determines who is or is not wrong. In this way I only described the actual state of affairs. I could not bear all that responsibility. . . . After all, I only obeyed the party.[70]

One can believe or not believe, but one cannot criticize God. Since the church interprets the will of God, one cannot oppose the church—and remain in it. To oppose a party that cannot sin is not a political but a moral act; it is morally wrong, it is a sacrilege. If one commits a sin of this sort, one must confess publicly. Since 1926, when Zinoviev, Kamenev, Trotsky, Piatakov, Sokolnikov, and Evdokimov published a statement in *Pravda* admitting mistakes and repenting them, through the Chinese Cultural Revolution and the arrest and recantation of the Cuban poet Heberto Padilla for writing counterrevolutionary poetry, public recantations of personal beliefs have become customary. The Catholic church invented the same procedure many centuries ago. Not only Jesuits arranged public admonitions in which participants were reproved before peers and superiors one by one, but the church insisted on the public admission of sins by the leading personalities of the time. The case of Galileo is perhaps the most famous. The Sacred Inquisition accused him of approving of the theory of Copernicus and, at the same time, of being a poor Catholic and acting deceitfully. Galileo was willing to "renounce, damn, and hate" his "errors and heresies," but he begged the judges not to force him to state that he was a poor Catholic or doublefaced. The same happened at the Moscow trials in the 1930s—except that Galileo was spared while Bukharin and his colleagues were executed. In general, the victims of Catholic and party inquisitions, whether acquitted or executed, were willing to admit any error or crime except that of insincerity or faithlessness to their respective sects. To admit the latter would have destroyed them morally and psychologically, regardless of the punishment inflicted upon them.

A state organized along the principles described is likely to appear as a theocracy. Calvin's Geneva of the sixteenth century may be taken as its prototype. In his *Institutio religionis christianae* of 1536, Calvin rejected reason and proclaimed the

Scriptures as the guide of human conduct. State officials and election candidates were chosen in keeping with ecclesiastical requirements. "Correspondingly," commented Barrington Moore, "the church supervised the doctrinal 'loyalty' and acceptability of the secular officials. . . . It was regarded as a conspiracy to speak in opposition to the list of candidates presented by the clergy."[71] If the word *church* is replaced by the word *party*, the description applies perfectly to the modern etatist state. In 1925 Stalin made clear that the party was "the supreme ruling force of the state."[72] "Like the Bolsheviks," Moore concluded, "the true Calvinists had a deadly fear of error and its social consequences, believing every error must be nipped in the bud."[73]

F. Functional Considerations

One might argue that, in certain environments and from a certain point of view, theological socialism is functionally more expedient than scientific socialism. If all knowledge is determined existentially—as Karl Mannheim argued[74]—then in an extremely heterogeneous society there is no possibility of meaningful communication among constituent groups. No consensus is possible. An illiterate peasant and an educated city dweller normally cannot communicate; the former is a subject, the latter a citizen. Add to that class interest, and the result is irreconcilable class conflict. Class conflicts can be partially resolved and consensus achieved by gradual homogenization of the society through a continuous, more or less violent, class warfare. That was the bourgeois path of development. But consensus, which is crucial for an orderly social life, can also be established by faith. In such a case one does not need to understand, one believes. That is how medieval societies operated. That is also how the ruling groups in etatist societies, utilizing the inherited religious structure of consciousness, established consensus based on faith in charismatic leaders and institutions.[75] Empirical proof of the viability and efficiency of this strategy is to be found in the political stability and high rate of economic development in contemporary etatist countries.

Once consensus is transferred to the extrarational sphere, all logical difficulties disappear; in other words, any contradiction may be tolerated. Christian love for every human being—"Love thy neighbor as thyself"—is logically incompatible with brutality, exploitation, and war. Christian slaveowners,[76] Christian feudal lords and war commanders represent a *contradictio in adjecto*. Yet, these contradictions exist without difficulty—represent, in fact, the rule; and, once dead, the noble persons mentioned are ceremoniously buried in Christian churches. Similarly, socialist equality is incompatible with an authoritarian hierarchy, absence of personal freedom, and power politics. Authoritarian people's government, democracy without disagreement, scientific ideology, and similar institutions or concepts are, of course, logical impossibilities but are at the same time very real. Religious and rational minds work differently.

A "scientific ideology" not only successfully reconciles logical contradictions, but also vastly expands (the illusion of) knowledge of the world. Describing his own Polish environment, Leszek Kolakowski observed:

> The 1950 Marxist knew that Lysenko's theory of heredity was correct and that Hegel's philosophy was an aristocratic reaction to the French Revolution, that Dostoevsky was nothing but decadence and . . . also that the resonance theory in chemistry was reactionary nonsense. Every 1950 Marxist knew these things, even if he had never learned what chromosomes were, had no idea in which century Hegel lived, never read one of Dostoevsky's books, or studied a high school chemistry book. To a Marxist all this was determined by the Office.[77]

A person not troubled by contradictions and in possession of absolute knowledge has a feeling of complete security that gives him a distinct advantage over his fellow citizens. He appears quite superior compared with the wavering, confused, and ignorant people around him. This helps to explain the popularity and success of the "scientific ideology."

The medieval man was a member of a church and of a corporation; he was not an individual. If a serf, he was even more insignificant. The names of medieval architects and artists who created significant works of art were not recorded. The society was fully authoritarian. The father in the family, the feudal lord and king in civil life, the Pope or another high priest in religious life, and God in Heaven kept the world together. An individual was not only insignificant but, by assumption, sinful. The legal rule was that the accused was guilty until his innocence was proven. (The French bourgeois revolution reversed the rule, but the same rule applied in Vishinsky's and Solzhenitsyn's Russia.) As late as the sixteenth century, the majority of educated people believed that a democratic republic was attractive only for grumblers and subversive elements. Even in the eighteenth century there was scarcely any author who believed that as large a country as France could survive for long as a republic.[78] And their skepticism seems to have been justified. Similarly, today the toiling masses are held to be incapable of political self-government and self-determination.

Apart from a few exceptions, republicanism and political democracy were achievements of the nineteenth century, made possible by successful bourgeois revolutions. The revolutions shook the old society thoroughly. *Liberté* and *égalité*—at least at the market place—made possible the development of individual personalities and responsibilities. Slowly but thoroughly, the market corroded old institutions and old consciousness. In order to function properly, the market required strict legality. In order to be successful, businessmen had to act rationally, calculating gains and losses and maximizing the positive balance. The interference of the state was neither desirable nor necessary, except in its role as nightwatchman and protector of national business interests abroad. Thus the scope of political authority was reduced considerably. And so was the scope of religious authority. The church was separated from the state and relegated to the private sphere. Money has no religious beliefs. Education, the arts, and science were secularized. The new rising class needed positive knowledge in order to prosper. After old authorities had been destroyed, the struggle of various social and political groups for their interests produced political democracy—limited and class-biased, to be sure, yet fundamentally different from political arrangements in the Middle Ages, unthinkable only two centuries earlier.

Having been delayed in their economic and social development, contemporary etatist societies have not passed through the rationalizing experience of bourgeois development.[79] In Russia, the oldest of the etatist societies, serfdom was abolished only a hundred years ago, and tsarist autocracy only sixty years ago, by the Revolution itself. (In Scandinavia, for instance, serfdom scarcely existed at all. In England and a number of Swiss cantons, it was abolished five centuries ago. In Germany and Austria-Hungary, however, it survived until the revolutions of 1848, and between the two world wars these three countries passed through unpleasant political experiences.) None of the etatist countries (with the exception of Czechoslovakia) had any longer experience with political democracy. The leap from a prebourgeois to a postbourgeois world produced the type of consciousness described above. The persecution of party members produced the same effect.[80] In a semireligious environment, revision of the original socialist theory with respect to the state was not accidental. It should have been expected. The state and the party were needed to replace the king and the church. As time passes, modern technology, universal literacy, and the mounting importance of science are bound to exert a rationalizing influence on the consciousness. Charisma will be replaced by a matter-of-fact approach. For a bureaucratic apparatus to function, personal arbitrariness of the chief must be replaced by legal formalism of the rules, and that must generate rationalizing effects similar to those of the capitalist market. Increasing affluence of individuals will contribute to the development of their self-respect, self-assurance, and individual emancipation. After all, etatism is not a successor of capitalism, not a more advanced social system. It is an alternative mode of social organization that has to achieve essentially the same task: the development of productive forces and social consciousness up to the point where socialism becomes possible.[81]

III. A New Social System

A. Counterrevolution from Within

The reasoning and the attitudes underlying the false antinomies described in section I have two general characteristics in common. One is that socialism is defined as a simple negation of capitalism, and hence only in relation to capitalism. As such it remains necessarily within the horizon of the bourgeois world. The second is that goals have been displaced by means. Socialism is no longer primarily a classless society in which individuals are able to develop fully their personal faculties, in which repression is replaced by social responsibility, and the freedom of every individual becomes a precondition for the freedom of all—but rather a state-owned, centrally planned economy and one-party polity. Yet, once all the stated ideas were implemented after the successful October Revolution in Russia, almost everyone—on both the Left and the Right—accepted the new order as a socialist order. Not an ideal one, to be sure, but basically socialist. The trends described in Table 1 were used as empirical proof of the soundness of the approach. By concentrating capital and expropriating producers, capitalism paves the road to socialism. All that a victorious socialist revolution need do is expropriate the remaining 4 percent of employers—in the purists' view, also the 6 percent of independents—and organize the entire society as one big, centrally planned firm. Everyone becomes a worker, a proletarian; classes are abolished; and the society becomes socialist.

Although almost everyone called such a system socialist, not everyone accepted such socialism as desirable or as producing the expected results. Anarchists[82] and syndicalists were critical long before such a system had a chance to be established. As early as 1891, commenting on the draft of the Erfurt Program of the German social democracy, Engels added that extending state property meant combining the power of economic exploitation with that of political oppression. Serious Marxists and individual humanistically oriented social scientists were able to predict the developmental consequences of the system right from the beginning.[83] Russian revolutionaries were also aware both of the critiques of their strategy and of its inherent dangers. In a book published in 1921 and used as a party text, Nikolai Bukharin—the leading party theoretician—discussed R. Michel's contention that, under socialism, administrators will have as much power as the owners of wealth under capitalism. Bukharin argued that the contention rested on the false assumption that the masses will remain eternally incompetent. In the future society, with education and culture accessible to everybody, "there will be a colossal overproduction of organizers, which will nullify the *stability* of the ruling group." In the next sentence, however, Bukharin qualified his optimism:

> But the question of the *transition period* from capitalism to socialism, i.e., the period of the proletarian dictatorship, is far more difficult. There will inevitably result a *tendency* to "degeneration," i.e., the excretion of a leading stratum in the form of a class germ. This tendency will be retarded by two opposing tendencies; first, by the *growth of productive forces*; second, by the *abolition of the educational monopoly*. The increasing reproduction of technologists and organisers in general, out of the working class itself, will undermine this possible new class alignment. The outcome of the struggle will depend on which tendencies turn out to be stronger.[84]

After half a century of historical experience, we know that the stratifying tendencies have been incomparably stronger. And since hierarchy was adopted as the basic principle of social organization, this comes as no surprise. Besides, if one thinks a little more carefully about what was said, one is bound to conclude that such a socialist society, though clearly different from a bourgeois one, *does not* transcend the latter's limitations.[85] It is created as a negative mirror image of the capitalist society. It is capitalism in reverse. As such, it is not socialism but *etatism*.[86]

Much more is involved, however, than the last paragraph seems to imply. We have been witnessing one of the greatest dramas in human history. In one single determined attempt, with enormous effort and at the price of innumerable sacrifices, one large society tried to liberate itself from backwardness and misery; to smash the chains forged by history, tradition, and vested interests; to emancipate itself and so also humanity. Such a revolution could not proceed in terms of piecemeal reforms or be based on a leisurely analysis of resources and tasks. It could not stop halfway. It could embrace only the most noble, the most advanced, and the most dignified ideology the epoch had produced—that of socialism. And it could not stop before socialism was attained. The hopes of millions of oppressed, exploited, and humiliated human beings throughout the world depended on the success of the October Revolution. It had to succeed, even if it did not—even if it could not! Other revolutions would follow. It was supremely important to keep hope alive. One day we shall have socialism—a society of brotherhood, without classes, in which oppression and exploitation will be eliminated forever. No amount of sacrifice was too great for that goal to be achieved. And it will surely be achieved, for socialism is the only alternative available once capitalism is destroyed.[87] This is roughly the human meaning of etatism, the meaning that includes hope, sacrifice, and disappointment.

History turned out to be different. Its verdict was simple and brutal. As far as I can see, it contains three main lessons. First, there is no simple determinism in human affairs. Apart from capitalism and socialism, other alternatives are possible as well. In the case of Russia, material backwardness conditioned a mentality that, as noted earlier, "has not only not surpassed private property but has not yet even attained it." Thus, accumulation—of means of production for the society and of objects of consumption for oneself—became a primary goal of the new society displacing all other goals. Because of continual threats from the hostile capitalist world outside, the inherent authoritarian tendencies of a society whose only previous political experience had been tsarist autocracy were enormously strengthened. Political autocracy was the most likely outcome. Accumulation plus authoritarianism implied an omnipotent state. And so the etatist alternative became a historical fact.

The second lesson consists in an apparently contradictory proof that a successful revolution may fail. Earlier, it was assumed that the only real danger after revolution would be a possible counterrevolution. It was also implied that counterrevolution meant restoration. Thus, all attention was focused on consolidating and strengthening the positions of power. That again implied an overdevelopment of the state apparatus with all its power mechanisms, such as bureaucracy and the secret police. The experience of Stalinist systems showed that keeping the power was no guarantee that socialism would succeed. In fact, absolute power turned out to be just as counterrevolutionary as successful bourgeois counterrevolutions. It generates counterrevolution but not necessarily restoration.

Finally, the third lesson also provides a refutation of misplaced determinism. It is undoubtedly a fact that socialism meets the *objective* (occasionally called "historical") interests of the working class more than any other available alternative. From that fact, however, it does not follow that the working class *must necessarily* be a bearer of socialism. It may support various systems. It is hardly open to doubt that contemporary Soviet workers support the Soviet system[88] and reject the American, while American workers support the American system and reject the Soviet. The former is etatist, the latter capitalist. On the other hand, authoritarianism may be based on any social class. Traditional authoritarianism is based on the upper class (aristocracy in the last century in Europe, landowners and the bourgeoisie in Latin America). The middle class provided support for fascism in many countries. The working class supported Stalinism and Peronism, which spread to a number of nations. The latter is an anticapitalist populist and nationalist movement usually aligned with the army. We shall discuss it later in some detail (see chapter 14, section IIB).

There will probably be little disagreement that a system in which the state plays an absolutely dominant role is well described as etatist or statist. It is less evident, however, why etatism should be considered an independent socioeconomic system, separate from capitalism or socialism. In this respect two tendencies can be observed: the reduction of etatism either to capitalism or to socialism.

Once it had been realized that the new society had failed to achieve the socialist goal, it was natural for socialists to refuse to consider it socialist. Since in the inherited deterministic scheme only two systems were known, if a society was not socialist it could only be capitalist. And because of the dominant position of the state, the system was termed state capitalism. Many radicals all over the world—Soviet dissidents included—share this view. The socialist revolution only appeared to be successful. In fact, Stalin and his associates, assuming dictatorial power, carried out a bloody counterrevolution, and so the system degenerated into state capitalism. The fundamental characteristic of the system is that the state owns all capital, and employs workers and extracts the surplus value in the same way as private capitalists.[89]

The view just described may be criticized on the grounds that it implies an unwarranted assumption: namely, that a state-dominated class society is necessarily state capitalism. It is easy to find historical cases where this was not so. For instance, in ancient Egypt the state owned the means of production—at that time, these were primarily land and irrigation installations but also included artisan shops—yet it was clearly not a capitalist state. Economic characteristics (central administrative planning), social characteristics (no private wealth, different social stratifications), and political characteristics (special features of communist parties) make etatism basically different from capitalism. Later we shall have an opportunity to substantiate this conclusion by comparative analysis. In addition, capitalism—private or state—implies the existence of capitalists. It is somewhat difficult to identify capitalists in etatist societies.

The second view—identifying etatism either with socialism or, at least, with the first, statist, phase of socialism—is much more widespread. The crucial test for socialism is the nonexistence of social classes, of governors and governed, of order givers and order takers. We shall see later that etatism does not pass this test, and so the first variant is easily eliminated. The second variant is more sophisticated. It starts from the observation that capitalism cannot be transformed into socialism overnight. There will be a transition period, initiated either by a parliamentary victory or by a victorious revolution, in which the state will nationalize all means of production and carry out necessary institutional changes. This is state socialism, the initial phase of socialist development. This conception, plausible as it is, is open to the following objections: (1) state ownership is not a necessary transitional stage between capitalism and socialism; (2) complete state monopoly of economic and political power is not a precondition for transition; (3) if state socialism is a transitional period, it will be short, with a clear tendency present for the role of the state to be reduced to its proper dimensions and for typically socialist institutions to be developed. In contemporary etatist societies, this is not the case. What might have been a transitional, state socialist, period crystallized into a well-established system that shows no tendency toward basic structural changes.

At this point, we may note that, though Marx himself never conceived of a separate social formation coexisting with capitalism—which I denoted as etatism—he nevertheless postulated the criteria that unmistakably identify such a formation. His basic indicator is the control of the surplus labor of producers. "The essential difference between the various economic forms of society, between, for instance, a society based on slave-labour and one based on wage-labour, lies only in the mode in which this surplus-labour is in each case extracted from the actual producer, the labourer."[90] In any hierarchically organized society, the ruling elite is in a position to extract and control the surplus labor. The basic difference between a society based on capitalist wage labor and one based on etatist wage labor lies in the mode in which surplus labor is extracted: in the former case, private property, and in the latter, state property, determine this mode. The state not only insures the reproduction of production relations but also, and first of all, the reproduction of relations of domination and hierarchy. Such a self-reproducing state, which has swallowed the entire society, determines—as Henri Lefebvre pointed out—the etatist mode of production.

B. The Consequences

The strange combination of socialist and antisocialist features of etatism produced a similarly strange combination of results.[91] Let us start with those due to socialist ingredients.

There can be no doubt that etatism has enormously developed forces of production. In the early 1930s, when the entire capitalist world was undergoing its worst economic crisis, the Soviet Union launched its first five-year plans and achieved development rates previously unknown in economic history. After about half a century of persistently high rates of growth, a once backward, semifeudal economy was transformed into a modern economy ranking second in the world in terms of productive power. The launching of the sputniks was a symbol of this transformation. Similarly impressive was the economic development of other etatist countries.

Economic development may result in an increasing inequality of income distribution, in a widening of the gap between the haves and the have-nots. But it can also be used to improve the position of the formerly underprivileged. It is the latter that has occurred in etatist societies. The empirical evidence for this is provided by a recent investigation I conducted into the basic welfare of the common man in various countries.

Basic welfare was defined as the availability of three basic goods: life (measured as life expectancy at birth), education (measured as the number of university students relative to the population), and health (measured in terms of medical services, that is, the relative number of physicians and hospital beds). In order to eliminate differences in economic development, the sixty most highly developed countries were ranked according to gross national product per inhabitant and these rankings were compared with the rankings of social indicators. If the latter rankings are higher—that is, the resulting difference is positive—then the society in question provides its common members with more basic goods than other societies. The best result for each indicator was ranked as 1, the worst as 60. Countries were classified into three groups: etatist countries, welfare states (advanced capitalist countries with labor governments in power for long periods of time), and other advanced capitalist countries. The results are shown in Table 3.

TABLE 3

Basic Welfare of the Population in Etatist and Capitalist Countries

	GNP 1970 (1)	Life expectancy (2)	Education (3)	Health services (4)	Basic welfare (5)	Difference (1)-(5)
Etatist countries[a]	26.6	24.4	25.7	16.3	22.1	4.5
Welfare states[b]	11.3	11.9	15.5	13.6	13.7	−2.4
Advanced capitalist countries[c]	7.0	10.3	13.4	18.3	14.0	−7.0

Source: B. Horvat, "Welfare of the Common Man in Various Countries," *World Development,* June 1974, pp. 29–39.

[a]Including: German Democratic Republic, Czechoslovakia, USSR, Hungary, Poland, Romania, Bulgaria, Albania, Cuba

[b]Including: Sweden, Denmark, Norway, New Zealand, United Kingdom, Finland, Israel, Austria

[c]Including: United States, Canada, France, Australia, Federal Republic of Germany, Belgium, Netherlands

A comparison of the rankings shows that in etatist societies the broad masses of the population live longer, receive more education, and enjoy much better medical care than would occur generally under alternative social arrangements at the same level of economic development. Their basic welfare (average rank, 22.1) is higher than their per capita income (average rank, 26.6). It is the other way around, however, with the other two groups of countries. If we compare the welfare differences, then, on the average, etatist societies lead in terms of basic welfare of the population by 6.9 positions (4.5 + 2.4) in front of welfare states and by 11.5 positions in front of more traditional capitalist societies. These differences are somewhat exaggerated because the etatist group is less developed than the other two, and our measuring device is slightly biased in favor of less developed countries. Yet they are sufficiently great to reflect real differences. It may be concluded that concern with the welfare of the masses in etatist countries was not an empty slogan.

This conclusion is strengthened if we consider comparative income distributions. The available data are still very crude and not strictly comparable, but they do indicate the order of magnitude of the differences. We can take the Gini coefficient of inequality (the ratio between the area above the Lorenz curve and the total area of the triangle; the coefficient ranges from 0 to 1, the larger the coefficient the greater the inequality) as a measure of average inequality of income distribution, and the share of the top 5 percent in total income as a measure of the income span. The results are shown in Table 4. On both scores there is again a marked break between etatist and capitalist groups. Within the latter group, the labor regimes have clearly succeeded in improving income distribution and in reducing the difference between the highest income level and the rest.

TABLE 4

Size Distribution of Income

	Gini ratio		Percentage share of top 5 percent	
	Spread	Median	Spread	Median
Etatist countries[a]	0.19–0.26	0.21	9.2–12.2	10.9
Welfare states[b]	0.33–0.47	0.36	13.3–20.9	15.1
Advanced capitalist countries[c]	0.32–0.52	0.40	13.7–24.7	17.4

Source: S. Jain, *Size Distribution of Income* (Washington, D.C.: World Bank, 1975). The data are for the last available year from the interval 1962–72. Most coefficients refer to households, and the remainder to income recipients; Polish and Bulgarian data refer to workers, Hungarian data to the popultion.

[a]Including: German Democratic Republic, Czechoslovakia, Hungary, Poland, Bulgaria

[b]Including: Sweden, Denmark, Norway, New Zealand, United Kingdom, Finland, Israel

[c]Including: United States, Canada, France, Australia, Federal Republic of Germany, Netherlands

In order to achieve a perfectly egalitarian income distribution, it would be necessary to redistribute and give to poorer sections of the population about 16 percent of the total income in the etatist countries, but double that much—about 30 percent—in the advanced capitalist countries. It is of some interest to note that property income raises the Gini coefficient by no more than 0.03 to 0.06[92] and that therefore the basic difference in the inequality of distribution comes from the inequality of earned incomes.[93] Thus, in general, etatist societies have become more egalitarian. And this is the legacy of socialist revolution. We shall discuss the additional evidence in the section on etatist stratification.

The political side of etatist life has been very different. Soviet scientist Andrei Sakharov informs us that, in the Soviet Union during Stalin's rule, between 10 and 15 million people were imprisoned by the secret police and sent to labor camps.[94] In the 1930s, two decades after the Revolution, the prison population of the Soviet Union was *twenty times* larger than that of, for example, the United States.[95] After the occupation of eastern Poland and the small Baltic states in 1940, tens of thousands of Poles, Lithuanians, Latvians, and Estonians—primarily intellectuals—were deported and killed. Entire nations (Crimean Tartars, Volga Germans, Meskhetians, Kalmyks, and others) were deported. Millions were executed or died. It is still hard to understand how such monstrous crimes could have been committed in the name of socialism. The Russian writer Aleksandr Solzhenitsyn (in his novel-chronicle)[96] and the Yugoslav communist Karlo Štajner (in his memoirs)[97]—both imprisoned in camps for years—provide an account of the meaningless sufferings of victims reduced to the position of slaves, of the meaningless brutality of prosecutors who have lost basic human qualities, of the infernal character of the GULAG,[98] the gigantic enterprise of repression, which, had it not been real, would have required the imagination of a Dante to be described.

All this has been explained simply by the "theory" of increasing class struggle. It is already difficult to see why—after the members of the former ruling class have already left the country during the Revolution—an entire 10 percent of the population should have been so violently opposed to socialism that they had to be physically removed or destroyed. But the theory breaks down completely when those who carried out the Revolution are proclaimed class enemies as well. Sakharov states that in just the years 1936–39, more than 1.2 million Communist Party members—one-half of the entire membership—were imprisoned.[99] Only 50,000 were set free again; 600,000 were shot. Some 1,108 out of 1,962 delegates to the Seventeenth Party Congress were killed, and so were 98 out of 139 members and deputy members of the Central Committee.[100] The highest political body of the Soviet Union was the party Politburo. It was created in October 1917 under the chairmanship of Lenin. Up to 1951 some 27 leaders had been members of the Politburo. At one time or another, a number of them were accused of counterrevolutionary activity, murder, terrorism, treason, espionage, acts of diversion, or attempts to undermine the military power of the country. Out of the 27, 6 died, 12 were executed or murdered, and 1 committed suicide just before arrest.[101] Stalin apparently intended to get rid of 2 of the remaining 8, according to the report of Nikita Khrushchev at the Twentieth Party Congress.[102] Since almost half of the top party leaders were executed and about half of the party members were imprisoned, one would have to conclude that one-half of the revolutionary avant-garde were class enemies. That, of course, is a strange conclusion. A more commonsense interpretation is that all this had nothing to do with socialism and a lot to do with the unscrupulous fight for absolute power, unconstrained by any moral norms. More precisely, a fight for absolute power under the conditions of totalitarianism—the latter originating from a combination of religious structure of consciousness and modern technical efficiency.

Stalinist terror was oriented not only against persons who were actively opposed but against potential adversaries as well, and also against the population at large in a sort of preventive fashion. All independent persons, all those who owed their positions to their own revolutionary activities, represented a potential danger and had to be destroyed. They were replaced by new people who owed everything to the dictator and were completely dependent. Out of twenty-one members of the Central Committee who were elected at the Sixth Party Congress in 1917 and led the October Revolution, the only one to remain alive after the Great Purge was Joseph Stalin. Leading army commanders were equally dangerous and had to be exterminated (three out of five marshals, thirteen out of fifteen commanders of the first and second rank). In addition, 90 percent of generals and 80 percent of colonels lost their posts.[103] The resulting military disorganization contributed to the easy victories of the invading German armies. It appears that, if "wreckers," "imperialist agents," and "fascist spies" existed at all, it was Stalin and his henchmen who fit the description best. Stalin was soon to sign a pact with Hitler—a pact with a secret addendum.

Foreign communists were not spared either. Before the Stalin-Hitler agreement on the partition of Poland, the Polish Communist Party was dissolved and its leaders summoned to Moscow and massacred. Many Hungarian, Yugoslav, Bulgarian, and German communists perished in the purges. After the rapprochement with Hitler, some of the surviving German communists were handed over to the Gestapo. The purges—partly the result of purposeful design and partly the consequence of a self-reinforcing "revolutionary" hysteria—together with the development of a universal system of spying and preventive denunciation, not only intimidated the population, but also destroyed the moral and ideological bonds that united various social groups. The society was reduced to a conglomerate of individuals. Civil society disappeared; all that was left was the state and the subjects. The physical destruction of revolutionary cadres, together with millions of innocent people, renders the counterrevolution carried out by Stalin's regime the bloodiest counterrevolution in history. Its nature could hardly be expressed more appropriately than in an act of sinister symbolism performed by the Soviet government itself: the assassin of Leon Trotsky—who, among the leaders of the October Revolution, was second only to Lenin, and Lenin died soon after the Revolution—was decorated as a hero of the Soviet Union!

These internal developments could not but be reflected in external relations as well. The Cominform attack on Yugoslavia corresponds closely to the attitude of the United States toward Cuba. A few years later, it was followed by an armed intervention in Hungary which resulted in the destruction of Hungarian workers' councils. In 1968 the troops of the Warsaw Pact occupied Czechoslovakia and destroyed the beginnings of socialist development in that country. Ten years later Vietnam, itself a victim of a terrible war, attacked its smaller neighbor, Cambodia. Political and, occasionally, military confrontation between the Soviet Union and China has become a permanent affair. In 1968 Czechoslovak student Jan Palach burned himself to death in Prague because of the brutal destruction of freedom in his country by the "socialist" armies. Four years later the Lithuanian student Romas Kalanta set himself afire in a square in Kaunas exclaiming: "Liberty for Lithuania!"

Police repression is necessarily followed by a moral disintegration of the society. Universal distrust, mutual spying, lack of regard for personal dignity, and denunciation institutionalized as a nationwide system are characteristic of such a society. Political police become the supreme moral authority. Philosophers in all countries and at all times have tended to cultivate critical reasoning and a humanistic approach to societal problems. Not so under etatism. In 1962 four leading Soviet philosophers—all members of the Academy of Sciences and of the party—who in the 1930s were instrumental in physically destroying a group of their younger colleagues, explained their attitude in the following way: "Naturally, we were horrified then and felt revolt about that. We believed, rightly, that the fact that security organs had initiated measures against them proved they had committed grave crimes against the Soviet fatherland. If it is taken into account that, like the majority of party members, we trusted the security organs and held their activity at that time to be right and necessary, then our position and attitude against those jailed as enemies of the people becomes understandable."[104] This explanation should not be considered cynical; it is genuine. In 1978 a textbook on "Marxist" ethics was published in Hungary in which it was stated that a man, regardless of compulsion, must never kill his mother unless she becomes a class traitor![105] Among those arrested were the wives (Kalinin, Molotov, Kusinen), sons (Mikoyan, Kusinen), and brothers (Ordzhonikidze) of top Soviet officials, some of whom were Politburo members. Yet they never protested publicly, and did not even offer their resignations; they approved the jailing of these "enemies of the people," desperately stuck to their bureaucratic posts, and continued to glorify Stalin. Great purges in the 1930s were preceded by Central Committee sessions at which members unanimously condemned their former colleagues before their trials and tried to outdo one another in abusive language and requests for brutal punishments.

It may seem that after Štajner and Solzhenitsyn, nothing new could be said about the moral atmosphere of the purges and the GULAG. This is not true, however, as the following story—on which I happen to have first-hand information—will demonstrate. During the war the famous Hungarian philosopher György Lukács was living in Moscow. His stepson, an engineer, also emigrated to Moscow. Unfortunately, the young man spoke German, which was sufficient evidence for deportation to a concentration camp. Lukács tried to use all his connections with high-placed bureaucrats to save his stepson, but in vain. In 1945 some sort of official celebration was arranged for Lukács. He used the opportunity to ask the most distinguished party official present for help. The man proved to be responsive and said that, as usual, the next Wednesday he would be playing bridge with Beria. If Beria happened to win, he might be in a good mood, and then the issue of the stepson could be raised. The cards were good to Beria, the name of Lukács's stepson was mentioned, the chief of the MVD lifted the telephone receiver—and the Hungarian engineer was released from the camp! One is reminded of Emperor Nero's Rome.

The ridicule of political democracy and the extolling of power, coupled with state ownership and missionary zeal, very naturally produced a totalitarian state. "The latter," wrote Leszek Kolakowski, noted Polish philosopher and former party member, "consists in the constant tendency to destroy all the existing social ties and all spontaneous crystallizations of social life, and to replace them with state-imposed organizations. In the perfect totalitarian society no form of human activity—economic, intellectual, political—is allowed unless planned or permitted by the state, and human individuals are considered the nationalized property of the state."[106] Being totalitarian, this state resembles the Fascist state. But etatism is not fascism, which belongs to another social genus. Political similarities should not obscure fundamental systemic differences. Ancient and modern political democracies are in many respects similar, but the respective social systems are clearly different. Also, Fascists insisted on race, glorified militarism, and appealed to unconscious and irrational motives. Stalinists and their other etatist brethren extol class, insist on political domination, and direct their propaganda to rational motives.

To evaluate all these developments, one must choose the proper standard of comparison. It makes little sense, for instance, to compare the Soviet Union of the 1930s with the England of the same time. The comparison ought to be made with England at the time of the Industrial Revolution, when broad masses of the population had no political or social rights, lived in squalor and misery, and suffered the oppression of the powerful. Since then, England has changed tremendously. And Russia is changing too. It is highly unlikely that Stalinist atrocities will be repeated. Some other etatist countries—Hungary, Czechoslovakia, Bulgaria, Romania, Albania—had their own Moscow trials, mostly staged with the help of GPU agents,[107] but these were unusual episodes (except in Albania). China is a much more backward country than Russia was in 1917, and yet it avoided mass imprisonment, execution, and the creation of a GULAG.

Thus, in the future one can expect a relaxation of political coercion and the development of more humane relationships. Although a powerful state and centralized state control of economic and other activities is always potentially dangerous, it need not necessarily generate a politically oppressive system. In Sweden, for instance, state control and interference is much more pronounced than in the United States and in most other countries. Yet an attempt to measure the degree of political democracy in various countries alloted Sweden an unequivocal first place; the United States was eighth among the ten countries studied.[108]

In conclusion, unfortunate historical circumstances—utter backwardness; military interventions, constant threats, and international isolation of the country; pathological personality of the leader; lack of traditions or experience of political democracy; absence of an adequate economic and social theory of socialism and adherence to an antisocialist political theory—determined to a large extent all the monstrosities denoted today as Stalinism. Etatism need not necessarily have produced Stalinism. Etatism is compatible with much more democratic political systems.

Yet socialism is totally *incompatible* with Stalinism, as it is with the totalitarian state and any other system of political oppression. The cult of personality, as Stalinism is euphemistically called, is not a mistake or a deviation that can be repaired by changing personalities. It belongs to a *structurally different system.* If classlessness is the test for socialism, then political domination must be eliminated just as must any other form of domination.

3

Social Stratification in Capitalism and Etatism

I. Social Class

We can conveniently begin our analysis with the concept of social power. This is the most general concept in the stratification framework,[1] and as such it will enable us to derive other analytical categories and to describe the observed relationships. By *social power* I denote the ability to mobilize resources necessary for the operation of a social system by making decisions that affect the lives of other persons in an important way. What is important is evaluated by those concerned. The definition is designed to reflect both the functional and the conflict aspect of power. Power is *functional* because it is necessary for the operation of a social system. As such, it is not a zero-sum-game concept. In other words, it is *not the case* that there is a fixed amount of power in society—or in a social subsystem—which can be distributed among participants such that the greater the share of one group, the smaller the share of another. Total power may be increased or decreased—that is, all participants may simultaneously acquire more or less power—depending on the institutional arrangements.[2] Insufficient power may render the achievement of a particular set of tasks impossible. From the fact that power is necessary for the operation of the system, however, it *does not* follow that a particular small group of people must appropriate this power—which is a conclusion invariably drawn. Power may be divided, decentralized, and deprofessionalized. The last possibility implies that a division of labor in which a small group of people specializes in the professional exercise of power is not a natural necessity but a historically determined and changeable social arrangement.

Power clearly is not the only possible choice for the basic analytical category in an examination of stratification. If one assumes that social systems are determined by economic forces, as did Marx, then property appears to be the main vehicle of stratification. If one gives primacy to political forces, as did Mosca and Pareto, it becomes natural to talk of the ruling class, political authority, and the circulation of elites. Power is a more general category, however, and contains property and authority or rule as special cases. They simply become economic and political powers. Thus, whatever the property and authority hypotheses can explain, the power hypothesis can explain also—and better too, for, as we shall see, it can also account for certain additional phenomena.

The foregoing considerations indicate also why power is a potential source of conflict. Social systems may be designed in various ways, to promote various interests. Groups with more power are more capable of protecting their interests compared with less powerful groups. In this sense power is a relational concept. If two men possess the same amount of power then, in relation to each other, they have no power. It is usually clear from the context whether power is meant in an absolute or a relative sense. In the analysis of stratification, the concept will normally imply "excess power" in relation to someone else.

Since excess power is unidirectional, it generates hierarchy. In a society with an unequal distribution of power, groups with more power have the privilege of affecting the lives of those with less power. In this way the society becomes stratified, and upper strata are able to impose their will upon lower strata. If this will is guided or determined by self-interest, as conceived by the bearer of the will—which is surely a realistic assumption about human behavior in a stratified society—then *imposing the will* implies *exploitation.* Exploitation may be defined as "any socially conditioned form of asymmetrical production of life chances," where the latter mean "chances of an individual for sharing in the socially created economic or cultural goods."[3] The exploited groups will not be happy with this state of affairs, and their members will try to defend themselves and even to fight back. This is known as the *class struggle,* which reflects the *fundamental social conflict* between order givers and order takers, between the rulers and the ruled, between the governors and the governed, between the dominant and subordinate groups, between the oppressors and the oppressed, between the exploiters and the exploited.

Power can be classified in various ways. An obvious one is to classify it according to the means used. An individual may be forced to comply, or he or she may be lured into compliance. The latter may be achieved by the use of material rewards, nonmaterial status symbolizing rewards, or persuasion. Thus control over the behavior of other individuals may be achieved by physical means of coercion, by economic means of remuneration and deprivation, by symbolic means of remuneration and deprivation, and by normative means of manipulation. In the first case, the ruling group uses brute force; in the next two, utility-generating assets; and in the last, ideas. Consequently, power can be coercive, economic, symbolic, and persuasive.[4] This is at the same time the order of oppressiveness of power felt by the average individual. This order may be symbolized by imprisonment, monetary incentives, honors and decorations, and brainwashing.

The difference between symbolic and persuasive power is generally overlooked. The former consists in the allocation of nonmaterial, status-generating, symbolic rewards such as decorations (particularly in the army), publicity (from the factory wall bulletin to the national mass media), titles (such as "sir" in England, or "hero" in the Soviet Union), gradations in rank (uniforms, office decorations, or types of official cars), access to prestigious gatherings (mostly empty celebrations) and places (clubs, holiday resorts), roles in public events (standing on the platform), etc. Persuasive power refers to the manipulation of information and ideas. Since both represent psychological oppression (as opposed to physical or economic oppression), they are usually lumped together as persuasive, normative, manipulative, or moral power. Closely related in some countries is the ideological insistence on "moral" incentives as more noble and fundamentally different from material incentives. "Moral" incentives are supposedly socialist, while material incentives are capitalist. Yet both incentives are precisely that—incentives—and have nothing to do with genuine moral feelings. Those who are able to manipulate incentives—either material or "moral"—are in the possession of remunerative or utilitarian power.

In this study the focus is not on power as such, but on social power. For this reason, I find it more convenient to apply a somewhat different classification corresponding more closely to the actual forms of institutionalized social power. I shall distinguish *political, economic,* and *manipulative* power. The relation between these three types of power and the corresponding means for achieving compliance can be represented schematically in the following way:

Means of achieving compliance			Types of power
I. Physical coercion (force)			Political
II. Incentives:	(a) status generating	utilitarian	Economic
	(b) material	ideological	Manipulative (Persuasive)
	(c) normative		

Political power is best known and is usually implied when reference is made to power. The essential feature of this form of power is that it is based on the use, or the threat of use, of physical force. Such power can be used as a stick—and then we speak of coercive power; or it can be used as a carrot—and then it is symbolic power. It is not by chance that status symbols such as ranks and decorations are used more intensively in the foremost coercive organization—the army—than in any other organization.

The second form, *economic power,* traditionally has been the main object of social analysis by Marxists. In a bourgeois society economic power tends to dominate and to mold political institutions and the cultural environment.[5] Economic power is based on the ownership or control of productive wealth (means of production), which serves as an instrument of power relations. It is thus indirect, rather than direct. The order takers are formally free not to take orders, and in theory they may set up their own businesses. But for that they need money, proper connections, good credit standing, and adequate education. Besides, the modern bourgeois society is organized in such a way that only about one-tenth or so of the active population can become employers or independent producers of goods and services. The remaining eight- or nine-tenths *must* take orders from those who control the process of production or, more generally, from those who control the social process of work.

Manipulative power is less conspicuous than the other two forms of power and also less known. It is even more indirect than economic power and consists in control over the minds of other people. It is perhaps best exemplified by the achievement of Menenius Agrippa, who in 503 B.C. offered to rebellious plebeians the fable about the parts of the body in revolt against the belly. More generally, every society is a moral community, and the ruling norms are defended by the same sanctioning agencies and those who control them. In other words, "every society honours the conformity that sustains it, i.e., sustains its ruling group."[6] Thus, as Marx once remarked, the ruling ideas of a society are the ideas of its ruling class, and the order takers are induced to believe that their position is quite natural. Both Aristotle[7] and the slaves believed that slavery corresponded to human nature and was beneficial to both parties: the master needed someone to do the work and the slave someone to give orders. In the modern bourgeois setting, the same idea is expressed in the theory of entrepreneurship: exceptional individuals, called entrepreneurs, hire labor (not even workers!) and other factors of production and organize firms in which they issue orders to the benefit of everyone concerned. Again, as in Aristotelian times, both managers and workers believe that this is the only natural state of affairs.[8] The same ruling class ideology is also reflected in the theory, generally accepted in etatist societies, that it is the historical mission of the vanguard party and its leadership to issue directives and lead the proletariat in the interests of the latter. Those who possess the manipulative power can persuade others that it is in their interests to do things that may actually be detrimental to them. One particular institution that specializes in persuasive power is the church. (In etatist countries the church has been replaced to a great extent by the Agitprop of the ruling party.) One can paraphrase Marx in noting that the dominant church has always been the church of the dominant class. In some economically advanced countries—Scandinavia, for instance—even today the dominant church is the state church.

Unlike political and economic power, manipulative or persuasive power is less independent and derived more from the other two forms of power. Only one social group is potentially an independent source of persuasive power: the intelligentsia. Since, however, education is a privilege in a class society, a large number of intellectuals come from families that belong or are closely related to the ruling class. Those with a different class origin are usually bribed with the money, titles, and positions that an intelligent ruling class is prepared to give to able and ambitious newcomers. Thus the progressive or reforming potential of intellectuals is reduced drastically. Yet, what remains is still a very important source of change—particularly because intellectuals, by being intellectuals, possess the ability to transcend their class origins and not infrequently do so. Since latent interests need articulation in order to become manifest—class *an sich* needs consciousness to become class *für sich,* as Marx would say in his Hegelian language—progressive intellectuals have played a very crucial role in creating the ideology of the exploited class. It suffices to mention Marx, Lenin, and Mao.[9] As larger and larger segments of society gain access to higher educational establishments, the independent persuasive power of intellectuals is likely to increase.

Once power is applied, it becomes coercion.[10] Three forms of power generate three kinds of coercion. Political power is used physically to coerce others to comply with the orders of the power wielders. Its secondary means is the allocation of status symbols in order to induce compliance. The state, with its repressive apparatus, is the institution designed to achieve both tasks. Economic power coerces through hunger. It gives to a person the choice: either comply or be deprived of a decent standard of living. Unlike political power, economic power tends to remain concealed;[11] bourgeois ideologues thus are offered a splendid opportunity to present the free *market* society as a *free* society. Political power uses primarily the stick, economic power primarily the carrot. Some time passed before bourgeois society learned that the carrot may be more effective than the stick. Thus, it was only after 1834 in England that special laws no longer compelled poor people to work, since a more efficient method for establishing work—and political—discipline had been discovered.[12]

Manipulative power is used to coerce psychologically. Teachers are hired to mold the minds of the younger generations. The creators of culture are paid to produce culture that corresponds to the needs and tastes of the ruling class. Entertainment industries control leisure time. Mass media are licensed, subsidized, and so on, according to selective criteria. Political parties and business interests spend huge amounts of money on advertising campaigns, on propaganda of one kind or another, on the incessant brainwashing of the public. Churches—religious or secular—fight for the soul of the individual. Charismatic leadership is a specific form of coercive persuasion.[13] Thus advertising, indoctrination, propaganda, withholding information or providing selective information, and charismatic leadership are means of coercing the minds of people into conformity. All these manipulative activities may be decentralized and loosely coordinated by funds the ruling class is willing to spend in order to safeguard its economic, political, and status interests. Or they may be strictly controlled by a ruling class that has monopoly of political power. In either case, the apparently weak and unoffending manipulative power turns out to have formidable strength. By captivating the minds of people, it induces them to serve the ruling class and believe that this is in their best interests.

Often the following question is asked: if there is really a fundamental class conflict in society and the exploited class is so much more numerous, why don't they—particularly under conditions of modern bourgeois political democracy—depose the rulers? We can now give a straightforward answer to this question: because the political, economic, and ideological pressures are so strong that the subordinates do not perceive any other viable alternative.

The unequal distribution of power generates two other important social inequalities: unequal consumable wealth (and/or expendable income) and unequal social prestige. The qualifier *consumable* is used to indicate that we deal here with only one of the two different dimensions of wealth that are usually confused and dealt with indiscriminately. Namely, wealth can be used to exercise power over the labor of others (when it becomes capital and belongs to the power space), or it may be transformed into objects of consumption and enable the owner to adopt a certain life-style. A clear separation of the two dimensions of wealth not only has important analytical consequences but also reflects straightforwardly the process of functional differentiation that has taken place in real life. Since the power dimension of wealth has already been taken into consideration, it remains to draw attention to the life-style dimension. This dimension may conveniently be denoted by *standard of living*. While life-style implies more than standard of living, the latter determines the former. High income and, consequently, a high level of consumption make possible education and the formation of tastes and manners that then characterize a specific style of life.

Social prestige depends on the system of values and on the functional importance of the work a person does. It is determined in large extent by the amount of economic or political power a person commands, but it also depends on descent and occupation as such. Judges in England, university professors in Germany, creative artists in Poland, scientists in the Soviet Union, and physicians in Yugoslavia and the United States are at the top or close to the top in terms of social prestige, though their political or economic power is rather low and income varies between moderate and quite high. In general, prestige is an increasing function of education and knowledge. An independent source of positive or negative prestige is the social status of the family into which a person is born. Though under normal conditions prestige is a consequence of power and income, it is also a value precondition for the two. "If the distribution of honour failed to match the distribution of material advantages, the system of inequalities would be stripped of its normative support. . . . the prestige order serves to stabilize and legitimize inequalities by harnessing notions of social justice in defense of existing class privileges."[14] If a social group begins to lose social prestige—because, for example, it ceases to perform functions considered socially important—it will soon lose power and wealth.

Inequalities of power, income, and prestige in a society tend to be highly correlated. The cumulative distribution of desirable values generates objective incompatibility of the interests of various groups and subjective consciousness of conflict.[15] That is why a group of persons who occupy a similar position with regard to some form of power, standard of living, and social prestige constitute a *social class.* Within limits, the three factors are substitutable for each other. This is particularly true for various forms of power, which are relatively easily transformable one into another.[16] But it also holds for the other two factors. The degree of consistency of the three factors is reflected in the social status a person enjoys. The persons who comprise the core of a dominant class will be characterized by high values for each of the factors and will thus have high social status. Too great discrepancies among the factors may render a person déclassé.[17] The similarity of position with respect to the three most desirable social goods makes for a sense of affinity that generates the consciousness of being a separate class.

Social class, characterized by the three factors just described, is determined by the role of a large group of individuals in the social organization of work. The social organization of work includes both economic and political activities. Within micro-organizations—business firms, government agencies—social classes are separated by lines of authority. Outside them, they tend to be segregated by place of residence, circles of friends, cultural milieu, and marriage.

Beside this general definition of the concept of class there is also another, specific meaning often attributed to the concept. In the latter meaning, class—as an open group—is contrasted to *caste,* which is a closed group whose membership is rigidly hereditary, and to *estate* or *order,* which is a group with distinctive rights and duties established by law. There is also a third, largely uncritical, usage of the concept of class which relates class to the existence of private productive property[18] and associates it exclusively with the capitalist society. Thus, in its general meaning, class refers to a large social group in a stratified society, whatever the nature of this society. In its specific meaning, class is used to denote specific characteristics of social groups found only in specific societies (with reference to the ownership of wealth, or to openness). If this meaning were made exclusive, we would have to find a different word to describe the products of stratification in an etatist society. Analytically, this does not seem necessary. Theoretically, it might be actually misleading. Caste, estate, and class belong to successive social orders. Capitalism and etatism, on the contrary, are contemporaneous. Moreover, the *differentia specifica* for the three concepts is a different degree of openness, not wealth or some other factor. Both capitalist and etatist stratification are based on achievement, not on ascription, and thus both types of societies are open. Consequently, the concept of class should be used in the etatist context as well.

Since a social class is legally an open group, individuals born into a particular class need not necessarily remain in it. The more open a society is, the higher is the degree of vertical social mobility, i.e., mobility over class boundaries. The main instruments for upward social mobility are the accumulation of wealth, the conquest of political office, and education. Not surprisingly, they are but the appropriations of various forms of social power.

II. Social Stratification in Capitalism

To understand the process of social stratification in a particular society, the best one can do is to analyze the social situation with regard to its basic productive units. "If purposeful productive activity is the basis of human existence," declared Miroslav Pečujlić, "then power . . . over the conditions of work is a factor that essentially determines position in the process of production."[19] Power over the conditions of work implies a hierarchically organized process of production and an existentially important division of labor.

The basic productive unit in bourgeois society is the firm. The firm is a typical hierarchically structured organization: the owner or his representatives are located at the top, the staff in the middle, and the operatives at the bottom of the hierarchical pyramid. Since all firms are organized in the same way, there is a natural tendency for the same strata of different pyramids to get in touch, to be linked together, to develop and defend common interests. In this way stratification within the basic productive unit is transferred to the society at large (see Figure 1).

Such stratification across the society produces three well-known classes: the ruling class, the middle class, and the working class.[20] Let us start our analysis with the least clearly defined of the three—the middle class.

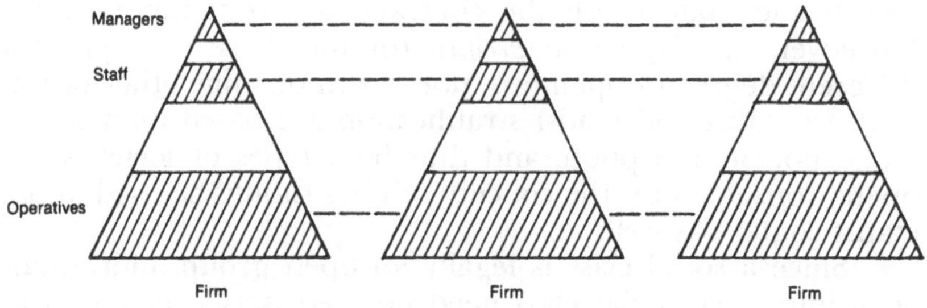

Figure 1. *Stratification in capitalist society.*

The old, early-nineteenth-century middle class consisted of artisans, small merchants, and richer peasants. Their common characteristic was some ownership of productive property. Marx and socialists expected that economic development and capitalist competition would largely wipe out these groups, and that society would become polarized into a small capitalist class and a large working class, the latter including the great majority of the population. The old middle class indeed dwindled, but there was no polarization because a new middle class appeared and expanded tremendously. The new middle class was the result of functional differentiation. Ownership was separated from management, and within management functions were differentiated into order giving and basic policymaking, professional activities, control, and supervision. For this reason Ralf Dahrendorf, following the Austrian Marxist Karl Renner,[21] with justification terms the new middle class the *service class* (*die Dienstklasse*).

The service class consists of two separate strata. The higher stratum is composed of professionals; the lower one includes white-collar clerical and administrative employees. That the professionals are associated with top management should be obvious. But why clerks, who receive orders from superiors and perform more or less routine jobs, are different from workers and ought to be grouped together with professionals, is less apparent and requires special explanation. As usual, the explanation is a historical one.

Historically, the basic social cleavage occurred between manual and nonmanual work. The free man in ancient Greece, the mandarin in China, the gentleman in modern England, the hidalgo in Spain, or a member of the ruling class anywhere in the world never has been supposed to dirty his hands with manual work. In Greece, for instance, the word *school* meant "leisure," and education was clearly intended for the leisure class. Physical productive work was imposed upon slaves because it brutalized the mind and made man unfit for the practice of virtue. In Judeo-Christian tradition, work is toil and represents punishment for sin. Until quite recently in human history, very few people knew how to read and write, and even today the majority of the world population is illiterate. Thus the knowledge of writing and the use of books conferred a special social status. Since clerical jobs required literacy—and left the hands clean—they carried higher social prestige.

Not only has clerical work been a result of the differentiation of managerial (and of governmental) functions, but salaried employees have also remained in closer contact with the employer, which gives them a position of authority. In general, clerical occupations are characterized by delegated authority. As a result, the employment situation of salaried employees is different from that of workers. They enjoy greater security of tenure and have substantially better promotion opportunities. Their working week is shorter. Their salaries normally increase with length of service and experience, while manual workers may even suffer a decrease of their earning power in the second half of their productive life.[22] Salaried employees enjoy fringe benefits not extended to workers (sick pay, more favorable pension schemes, longer holidays). The amenities of work (meals, sanitation, work environment) are better. The incidence of unemployment is lower.[23] For all these reasons, nonmanual salaried employees tend not to create unions, associate themselves with the interests of the employer and are considered by him to have common interests, and develop corresponding social values that integrate even routine white collar workers into the service class.[24] In politics, they opt for conservative parties.[25]

Since the service class associates itself with the ruling class, the three-class structure of society reduces itself to a dichotomous structure: the working class and the others. The dividing line falls between manual and clerical, or wage and salaried work. Until about the First World War, the two strata were sharply separated in European societies: manual laborers and clerical workers were two separate classes with no social intercourse.[26] In the last half-century, however, the line has widened into a zone, a kind of buffer area. Most mobility involves movement into and out of this zone, but not beyond. Social mobility across the dividing line or zone into another class itself is severely impaired. The language of the working class reflects these facts. In Britain, it is *them up there* and *us down here;* in Switzerland, *ceux qui sont en haut* versus *ceux qui sont en bas;* in Germany, *die da oben* and *wir hier unten.* A number of empirical studies have established this dichotomous class division.[27]

We can now proceed to a brief investigation of the capitalist ruling class. It would clearly be incorrect—though it is often done—to identify managers, or owners, or rich people with the ruling class. It would be equally incorrect—though it is equally often done—to exclude them on the grounds that membership in the ruling class implies the possession of political power, while managers specialize in running a business, not in governing the state. Perhaps the most appropriate approach would be to consider the mediating concept of an elite. An *elite* may be defined as the group with the highest social status within a larger functional group.

Under feudalism the determination of the ruling class was rather simple. The same group of people governed, ran the estates, administered justice and the rudimentary public services, and commanded the armies. As T. H. Marshall noted:

> The feudal aristocracy was literally the governing class. The modern capitalists are not. . . . the capitalist is using in the economic field a power that is partly political, in that it is derived from the laws and institutions of the society. If a class is strong enough to secure or to preserve those institutions that favour its activities, it may be said to be "governing" to that extent.[28]

This observation may be elaborated further.

In capitalism four different and separate functional groups have been established. One of them is involved in business, while the remaining three manage state affairs. They are: business executives; politicians; public administrators, characteristically called civil servants; and military personnel. Within each group a small elite exercises control. Four specialized elites perform the four separate functions that have been differentiated out of the original governing function. Thus, in modern capitalist society four functional elites—top businessmen, political leaders, high-level civil servants, and military commanders—comprise the ruling class. Not all elites need be equally developed in all countries. For example, the military elite plays an insignificant role in a country like New Zealand or Canada. Because of the spoils system and the absence of a comprehensive career civil service, particularly at the higher levels, an administrative elite has not developed in the United States. But all capitalist countries have a well-developed business elite, which is the dominant elite in the sense described by Marshall above, and a political elite that, with the advent of the welfare state and the need for government interventions in order to preserve full employment, gains increasingly in importance.

At any one time a person belongs as a rule to only one elite. But movement from one elite to another is both frequent and easy. Businessmen become ambassadors and politicians. Military commanders enter the government or become presidents of states. Former government members and retired generals enter the boards of directors of large corporations.[29] This continuous circulation of individuals among governing elites helps to preserve the appropriate class values and class consciousness. These values and this consciousness are formed at an earlier stage, since the candidates for membership in the elite are recruited mostly from ruling class families[30] and are educated in the same exclusive schools,[31] where they get to know each other; they marry within their own class and, by belonging to the same clubs and charitable and cultural organizations, socialize within their class. They frequent exclusive summer resorts and engage in exclusive recreational activities such as fox hunting, polo, or yachting, which keeps them separate from other fellow citizens and makes them feel superior.

When compared physically and culturally, the ruling and the working classes appear as two different races. Members of the ruling class are taller,[32] live longer,[33] receive much better medical care,[34] are incomparably better educated,[35] and even speak a slightly different language.[36] Describing American high society—though any other "high society" might have been chosen instead—Suzanne Keller writes:

> They attend old private preparatory schools and go to the right college where they belong to the right clubs. Informal socialization is rigidly augmented by formal training among the young—riding, dancing school, and some modern version of the grand tour, climaxed by annual coming-out parties and debuts that signify the maturing of a new generation. They intermarry and frequent the same clubs, the same shops and the same friends. They wear their badge of membership as clearly as the general his uniform. . . . They are taught the values of self-control, subordination to the rules of the caste, good manners, and noblesse oblige. . . . Outsiders may not always recognize them but they recognize each other, able to tell at a glance whether a particular style is the result of the effortless assumption of a status held from birth, or the hard-won shell acquired and maintained only by incessant vigilance.[37]

In view of what has just been said, a distinction must be made between the ruling class in its specific (bourgeois) sense and the power elite. Although the two overlap to a large extent, this overlap is not complete. The class is characterized more by ascription, the elite more by achievement. This contrast is only relative, however, since the ruling class is open to new entrants; and unless they are grossly incompetent, members of the power elite will not be forced to leave. The ruling class may have functionless members not "involved in anything more relevant than raising horses, riding to the hounds, or hobnobbing with the international 'jet set.' "[38] But if too many ruling class members cease to perform ruling functions, their class will soon cease to be ruling. Thus, in normal situations ruling class families will utilize their monopolized access to the strategic elite positions of the society and fill the vacancies with their own members. On the other hand, if a person of lower class origin succeeds in reaching a position in the power elite, he will not necessarily become a member of the ruling class. He must be able to keep this position long enough, accumulate sufficient wealth,[39] and acquire the appropriate life-style before he is accepted and finally assimilated. Thus, at any one time some members of the ruling class will not belong to the power elite and some members of the power elite will not belong to the ruling class.

The discrepancy between the ruling class and the power elite will tend to disappear as achievement increases in importance as compared with ascription. For that to happen, private productive property must be abolished. This occurs in etatist societies, to whose stratification processes we now turn our attention.

III. Social Stratification in Etatism

Capitalist development has passed through several stages: In the competitive stage, the owner of a firm was at the same time an entrepreneur. Later, ownership became increasingly divorced from managerial power. This divorce becomes complete in etatism, where productive capital is owned by the state and is controlled and managed by a bureaucratic apparatus.

State bureaucracy is organized hierarchically, of course. A typical bureaucratic structure looks like a pyramid with a tiny top and a large base. Instructions flow in only one direction—

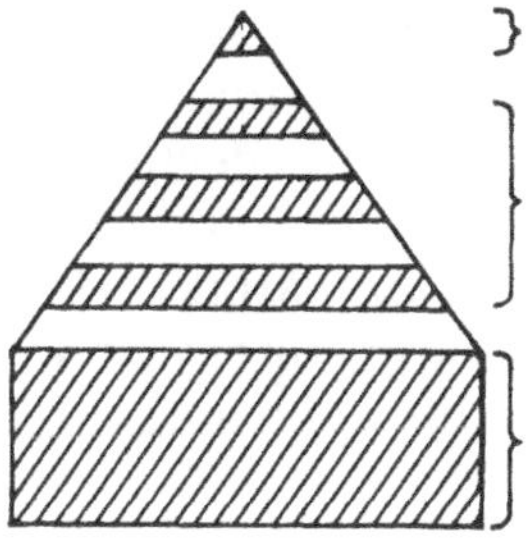

Figure 2. *Stratification in etatist society.*

from the top downward—and are imperative in nature. There are two loose ends: the top, where hierarchical relations disappear in the sense that there are no superiors; and the bottom, where they disappear in the opposite sense, namely, that there are no more inferiors. No direct communication exists between the top and the bottom of the social pyramid. Since it is part of a consistent system, the bureaucratic management in every particular firm must also be organized hierarchically. Thus, we again get capitalism in reverse. The stratification is direct and therefore more precise and effective than in capitalism. And the whole bureaucratic superstructure is opposed to the workers' base, on behalf of which it rules.

The functioning of the system is relatively simple. Edward Kardelj, Yugoslav politician and political theorist, has described it succinctly as follows: (1) directives are issued from the supreme organs of the state machinery to the lowest organs; (2) these lowest organs transmit orders to each individual; (3) superiors exercise strict control over inferiors; (4) tasks are assigned; (5) failure to perform these tasks is punished.[40]

Many layers of bureaucratic authority require a rather large differentiation of income in order to make the system work properly. Thus, the ratio of the differential state wage scale increased from 1:1.8 after the revolution to 1:40 in 1950.[41] Since almost no empirical studies regarding class structure have been carried out by Soviet social scientists, since very little empirical research has been conducted in other etatist countries, and since these governments do not publish the necessary data—a highly significant fact in itself—it is impossible to quantify the relationships. Such empirical evidence as is available suggests that the general pattern of class stratification is similar to that found in capitalism. The basic class division between manual (proletariat) and nonmanual (bureaucracy) work has been preserved.[42] Again this is reflected in the working class vocabulary, in which *my* [we] denotes the proletariat and *oni* [they] refers to the order givers. Miklós Haraszti, a Hungarian poet who worked as a milling operator in a tractor factory, described the feelings of his colleagues on the shop floor as follows:

> In every place of work . . . *them* means the same thing: the management, those who give the orders and make the decisions, employ labour and pay wages, the men and their agents who are in charge—who remain inaccessible even when they cross our field of vision . . . *them* transcends the walls of the factory and encompasses everything which is above, far away, outside the power of whoever is speaking. *Them* are all those upon whom he depends in an elusive and indefinable way: those from whom he receives this or that; by whom he is ordered about . . . officials from organizations, politicians, television producers, doctors, policemen or officials at the football ground. . . . dropping *them* is the first sign that someone really wants to start climbing the ladder.[43]

Inquiries conducted by Soviet sociologists indicate that just as high a percentage of Soviet citizens as of citizens of capitalist countries do not want to be workers or peasants, and that a large majority of workers would not like their children to become workers. Since the present level of technological development requires a substantial amount of manual labor, however, the society has to establish a selective mechanism. Its most important tool is education, and recruitment into education is conducted on a class basis. N. A. Aitov found that proletarian children achieve an average level of education of 7.66 grades, whereas those born into the families of white-collar employees achieve 12.22 grades.[44] While 86 percent of the children of urban white collar workers with higher education and between 45 and 64 percent of the children of manual workers enroll into higher schools, only 10 percent of farm youngsters have the opportunity of doing so.[45] In fact, peasants are the most underprivileged group in this society—and they exact revenge by maintaining low production. The differentiation continues at the university level, where grades are correlated with social origin.[46] The more prestigious the school, the higher the social background of those enrolled. Schools providing training for work abroad are the exclusive preserve of the elite. Competitive entrance examinations exist, but well-to-do parents hire coaches for their children. It was found that up to 85 percent of the students admitted to certain institutions had received such private instruction.

As always, those at the top of the social pyramid enjoy various privileges. Since an etatist economy is based on central planning, money plays a less important role and crucial privileges are granted in kind. They are linked directly with position on the bureaucratic ladder and include vacations at exclusive holiday resorts, access to special medical treatment or treatment in a closed system of hospitals, clinics, and dispensaries,[47] residence in lovely apartments, the use of official cars and of expensive state property [*dacha*], enjoyment of exclusive hunting privileges and other exclusive recreational activities. In a capitalist country, we are likely to stumble upon road signs with the inscription PRIVATE ROAD. In an etatist country, access to a region containing country houses for the bureaucratic elite or to an exclusive hunting ground is prevented by road signs reading FORBIDDEN. Guards may also be present. Privileges further include access to a network of exclusive shops that carry imported commodities and other items not generally available. In the Soviet Union this is known as *Kremlëvskii paëk* [Kremlin ration]. Contrary to what occurs on the market, here goods of superior quality are offered at reduced prices. One is also exempted from the ubiquitous queues. A car is delivered, for instance, in two days instead of in two years—the length of time for which ordinary citizens must wait—and at roughly half the price. Members of an etatist elite are often supplied with personal drivers, domestics, gardeners, nurses, etc., and of course have expense accounts. In all trains, airlines, hotels, theaters, football stadiums, and other recreational facilities, a certain number of places are reserved for the "authorities." Thus, all one need do is to prove one's bureaucratic standing and a ticket is ready. Special stipends are available for pupils at party schools,[48] and additional salaries not subject to taxes are granted to those of sufficiently high rank.[49] Officials cannot be brought to court without the permission of higher authorities, and they are able to remain outside the reach of justice in cases where others would be punished.[50] The highly valued opportunity to travel abroad (to Western countries) is open to members of the elite and rather restricted for the "masses." Foreign press information, not otherwise available, is summarized in special bulletins and put at the disposal of a highly restricted number of persons. In short, there appears to be a well-designed and comprehensive system of fringe benefits that make the life of officials much easier and more comfortable than that of the "masses." Besides, as Mervin Matthews observed, "the psychological significance of permitted access to goods, services and even information denied to 'outsiders' must be a powerful cohesive factor and success symbol among the groups on whom the leadership most relies."[51] The leadership and the masses are kept apart, and it is made quite clear—at least in practice—that they belong to different social classes. Since this contradicts the professed ideology, the privileges are hidden.

It was pointed out that the class division is similar to that under capitalism. But it is not the same. Some important differences are found. Anticapitalist revolutions failed to destroy class society and to establish socialism, but they did upgrade the social status of the manual worker, particularly of the skilled worker.[52] As a result, manual workers and lower, routine categories of nonmanual workers exchanged places on the stratification scale. This is also reflected in wages: clerical and office workers in Soviet industry receive wages 19 percent lower than those of manual workers.[53] Thus the basic, historically inherited manual/nonmanual division is transformed into a more consistent division that is based on education and separates workers performing "brainwork" from workers carrying out routine operations, regardless of whether they wear blue or white collars. As a result, there is substantially more mobility over the dividing zone between manual and nonmanual labor. The difference in life-style between the blue collar worker and the routine white collar worker is still visible to a certain extent, but this should not obscure the basic division between the intelligentsia and the working class. As usual, there is also an intermediate buffer group of those whose work is not expert, but neither is it manual nor completely routine. The division between the intelligentsia and the working class is clearly perceived by the population[54] and represents a meritocratic modification of the old class division between manual and nonmanual work. The same process is already visible in capitalist countries, where, particularly in large corporations, lower categories of white collar workers get fired in the same way as their blue collar colleagues.

Perhaps the best indication of the upgraded social position of workers is their substantially greater access to the educational facilities of the society. Table 5 indicates that clearly. In all countries shown in the table, workers constitute about one-half of the active population, but their access to university varies widely.

TABLE 5

Percentage of University Students of Working Class Origin in European Countries, c. 1960

Etatist countries		Welfare states		Traditional capitalist countries	
Soviet Union	39	United Kingdom	25	France	8
Poland	32	Norway	25	Netherlands	5
		Sweden	16	West Germany	5
		Denmark	10		
		Austria	8		

Sources: Soviet Union: M. Matthews, *Class and Society in Soviet Russia* (London: Penguin, 1972), p. 297; welfare states and traditional capitalist countries: F. Parkin, *Class Inequality and Political Order* (New York: Praeger, 1971), p. 110; Poland: D. Lane and G. Kolankiewicz, *Social Groups in Polish Society* (London: Macmillan, 1973), p. 129.

Access to educational facilities of course promotes social mobility. There is also another powerful vehicle of social mobility—the ruling party. Although workers do not represent the largest group in the party (they constitute between 30 and 40 percent of the membership and are thus several times less well represented compared with the intelligentsia), the party is an elite club that provides opportunities for social advancement nonexistent under capitalism. As a result, the upward mobility of working class children into the elite occupational strata is twice as great in the Soviet Union as, for instance, in the United States.[55] Individuals with a working class origin represented more than one-third of the Soviet governmental apparatus and Politburo/Presidium membership in 1966. In the American government, the corresponding proportion is several times smaller. The Swedish government, on the other hand, shows a larger working class base.[56] A caveat is in order, however. Such comparisons must not be misinterpreted. The greater presence of persons of working class origin in positions of authority indicates greater social mobility but, by itself, says nothing about the policies the authorities will follow. A bourgeois remains a bourgeois whether conducting his private business, joining the government, or simply living a comfortable life on his estate. A worker *ceases* to be a worker when he becomes a manager or a minister. Even a government composed entirely of *former* workers would not be a *workers' government;* least of all would it represent the dictatorship of the proletariat.

The improved social position of women represents the second important change in the direction of greater social equality. The status of women has risen both in the family[57] and in the society at large. The participation of women in the labor force is much higher in etatist than in capitalist countries. In the Soviet Union, 72 percent of all physicians, 68 percent of teachers, 63 percent of economists and, in general, 52 percent of all professional employees are women. Women represent 28 percent of the members of the Supreme Soviet and 20 percent of the party membership—but only 9 percent of members of the Academy of Sciences, and directors of industrial enterprises, and 3 percent of Central Committee members,[58] and hold no positions in the Party Presidium.

In contrast to the positive trends with respect to the status of workers and women, a negative development regarding farmers must be pointed out. In a respectable bourgeois society, anyone without private property is treated as an outcast; the same treatment is accorded those *with* private property in an etatist society. To have a state summer house with a large garden is a matter of honor. To have one's own house with a plot of land to till is a vestige of the bourgeois order and provokes social contempt. Thus peasants, either private or collectivized, are discriminated against; their wages are substantially below workers' wages; their standard of living is lower. They are several times less well represented in the party compared with workers. In the Soviet Union they cannot travel outside the kolkhoz without a passport, which is kept by the management; they have difficulty in moving to the cities. Their children have an appreciably smaller chance of becoming educated. The position of agricultural worker is held in the lowest esteem of all the seventy-four occupations examined in 1974.[59]

Let us now examine the position of the bureaucracy. Here we immediately encounter the view that the etatist bureaucracy or its ruling elite cannot be considered a social class. Social theorists as different as conservative French sociologist Raymond Aron and Yugoslav Marxist sociologist Miroslav Pečujlić hold this view. In an oft-quoted lecture, Aron observed that "all workers become the employees of a single employer—the State," and concluded that, "in this sense it is perfectly true that there are no classes in a society of the Soviet type." He accepted the official etatist view that "every member of the population has his share in ownership, since the means of production belong to the community, and everyone is a wage earner because all incomes are derived from work." But he also claimed that individual incomes may remain as unequal as in a class society, and political inequality is likely to increase.

> Inequality in political power is in no way eliminated or diminished by the abolition of classes, for it is quite impossible for the government of a society to be in the hands of any but a few.
>
> This minority has infinitely more power than the political rulers in a democratic society, because both political and economic power are concentrated in their hands. . . . Politicians, trade union leaders, public officials, generals and managers all belong to one party and are part of an authoritarian organization. The unified elite has absolute and unbounded power. All intermediate bodies, all individual groupings . . . are in fact controlled by delegates of the elite. . . . A classless society leaves the mass of the population without any possible means of defense against the elite.

Aron conceded that in theory a different, decentralized, and pluralistic classless society is possible, but under present circumstances it is extremely unlikely. He concluded:

> The classless society would abolish the proletariat in name and the capitalists in fact, but above all it would abolish the distinction between the various groups and would superimpose a unified elite upon an undifferentiated mass. This transformation could not result in the end of the alienation of labour, and consequently of all alienation, but in the substitution of the single opposition between the masses and the elite for the countless antagonisms in democratic societies.[60]

Thus Aron tells us that a *classless* society involves perhaps the same *economic inequalities,* certainly incomparably larger *political inequalities,* strong *alienation,* and an *antagonistic social relationship* between the dominant elite and the subordinate masses. Unless the concept of class stratification is stripped of all its commonsense meaning, this set of propositions represents a rare example of inherently contradictory reasoning. Since, however, the lecture seems to convey the message that a class society is *better* than a classless one, the *logical* contradictions involved appear understandable. So are the frequent uncritical quotations of what was considered an ingenious analysis.

More serious is the analysis by Pečujlić. He also pointed out that bureaucracy has a monopoly on government, yet it is based not on its own property rights but on a delegation of rights. "It is precisely this separation of property from management that is the historical basis for the formation of bureaucracy and for its differentiation from a class. The bureaucracy does not have its own economic basis founded on personal property and thus it has no historically lasting and stable place in the production process as a class."[61] If the ruling class is by definition connected with personal property, then, of course, bureaucracy is not a class. But this is a trivial remark and reduces to the semantic problem of finding a new term to denote class in an etatist society. We have already dealt with that problem. If, however, it is meant to imply that under etatism no classlike vertical stratification exists, then it contradicts empirical evidence. What Pečujlić really wants to say seems to be that bureaucracy is forced to become more functional than traditional social classes. If it fails to provide adequate services, it will be overthrown at once, because it does not have an independent base of its own.[62] Some authors, like S. Stojanović, have tried to reconcile the Marx-Weber economic theory of class with the social phenomena observed in etatist societies by pointing out that bureaucracy appears as a collective owner of the means of production.[63] This is formally correct, but requires an unnecessary extension of the concept of ownership. Also, unlike other collective ownership, such as that of the church, this one is not recognized *de jure*. The other possibility for reconciliation is to broaden the concept of property in a slightly different way. Thus, for instance, in managerial capitalism Ralf Dahrendorf distinguishes property in the narrow sense (legally recognized right of ownership) and property in the broad sense (control of the means of production).[64] Yet, it is clearly both simpler and more appropriate to consider power relationships—not property relationships—as an ultimate source of social stratification.

Pečujlić also mentions inheritance as an essential element of private property and consequently of social class. Here again one must be careful not to commit the same mistake of identifying class in general with class in a capitalist society. What matters is not the inheritance of wealth as such but of social position. In a slaveowning society slaves, and in caste-differentiated societies people born into particular castes, inherit their social position directly and completely without being able to do anything about it. In feudalism a serf—and even more so a yeoman or a burgher—has some opportunity to rise above his class. Bravery in war and the purchase of freedom or of a noble title are obvious devices. The ruling class position—membership in the aristocracy—is still completely hereditary, as a rule. That is changed substantially in capitalism, however, where one inherits primarily wealth and only secondarily social position. In etatism social inheritance is relaxed even further. One inherits the opportunity to occupy certain positions in the bureaucratic hierarchy. This opportunity is reflected in differential access to educational establishments, as illustrated previously by the ratio of 1:8.6 against peasant children (if the averages could be replaced by data for the top and bottom strata, this ratio would increase substantially) and in differential access to positions of authority (sons and daughters of trusted party workers are assumed—usually with justification—to become equally trusted officials). It is not the jobs but the social position that is inherited. The sons of top political leaders need not become top political leaders, but can be army generals or ministers or influential editors. And the same applies to the offspring of lesser politocrats. They may be allocated to various jobs provided they remain within the established elite. The only thing that is highly unlikely is that they might join the "ruling" working class.

An etatist society is more open than a capitalist society, and the inheritance of class position is further relaxed. But inheritance there is.[65] As usual, the family is the main vehicle of inheritance.

The family provides the necessary cultural and social background for success in life. The families of the privileged class equip their children with more socially relevant knowledge and stimulate the development of substantially higher aspiration levels.[66] Such children stay in school longer, attend more prestigious schools, and get better grades. If they are not particularly gifted, private coaches will be hired to help overcome the critical educational barriers. Since parents are members of the party, children are also likely to become members, and that makes their careers smoother and obstacles more easily removable. If father is a powerful official, he of course has powerful friends and many opportunities to secure more favorable starting positions for his offspring. An uncle will do as well, and then we have a system of "to each according to his uncle" as Serge Kolm defines nepotism.[67] Finally, the wisely arranged marriage plays its traditional role too. Above a certain level, one tends to marry into one's own stratum,[68] and it is desirable that the bride also be "a communist" (that is, a party member) or at least from a good family (i.e., that her parents be party members). The possession of educational and technical qualifications means the possession of valuable resources, of intangible but highly effective capital. This type of capital is as inheritable as the tangible variety.

Family conditioning is not the only social conditioning available or practiced. Party schools[69] replace private schools and clubs in generating the appropriate ruling class consciousness. Communists are a special brand of people, intone the assigned party texts, and the party never sins. One chooses friends from one's own stratum or upwards, if possible. "Outsiders may not always recognize them, but they always recognize each other": by giving words a slightly different meaning (for instance, one is always "responsible," that is, one unquestionably obeys), by using appropriate shibboleths at appropriate times (i.e., various symbols of loyalty), by mentioning casually their close relationship to those who hold power ("our comrades," "comrade X told me . . ."), and by showing in innumerable other ways—but always spontaneously, unlike the ambitious outsider—that they belong to the ruling establishment.

The behavior of an individual in a society depends to a great extent on how he or she is socialized to behave. Socialization is "the process by which individuals acquire the knowledge, skills, and dispositions that enable them to participate as more or less effective members of groups and the society." [70] The three major agencies of socialization are the family, the school, and the peer group. Since the members of an etatist upper class tend to live a life segregated from the rest of the population—they live in high-quality apartments in segregated residential areas and in country houses in special districts, they shop in special shops, frequent special clubs and holiday resorts, tend to intermarry, and send their children to prestigious schools—all three socialization agencies work in the direction of class segregation. They tend to produce an appropriate class consciousness. Equipped with that consciousness, individuals are ready to assume elite positions in the society.

Even if etatism implied a theoretically pure case of meritocracy, that would still mean social stratification. But, of course, it is far removed from ideal meritocracy; and social stratification is an obvious and established fact. All three ingredients of class differentiation are present: power, income and, as long as the ruling class enjoys legitimacy, social prestige as well. In fact, these elements are so closely correlated and so intensely present as to make the politocracy a better integrated and more coherent ruling class than the bourgeoisie.

The bureaucratic pyramid is not a homogeneous structure. It consists of two different parts: the top leadership, where primary power resides, and the bureaucratic apparatus, which holds delegated power and performs the functions of a service class. We also have a very simple clue to discover who belongs where. This is *nomenklatura* in the Soviet Union, and cadre lists elsewhere, which name "those whom the system itself regards as being important enough to require the special attention of the Central Committee's organization department."[71] Not surprisingly, we can also identify four elites: political, economic, administrative, and military. Here, however—unlike in capitalism—the political elite is dominant and plays an integrative role. The ruling elite is much more unified than its capitalist counterpart: top managers, high government administrators, and military commanders are all party members. The leading personalities of the four elites are usually members of the party Presidium, where supreme power is concentrated. The ruling elite does not hide the fact that it considers the governing of the country as its proper job. After the December 1970 crisis, when Polish workers took to the streets to protest the government's economic policy, the head of the Polish party, Edward Gierek—a former mine worker—was reported to have said: "You work well and we will govern well."[72]

What seems to emerge from the foregoing analysis is the following stratified structure of an etatist society. The ruling elite, which may be called the politocracy, is comprised of full-time party officials and top bureaucrats (civil and military). Cadres circulate constantly and systematically between technical (bureaucratic) jobs and political (party) positions. In this way the cadres acquire the necessary technical and political experience to rule the society. Nominally party offices are elective, but actually the organizational bureau or its equivalent makes sure the right people are allocated to the right places. The lower echelons of the bureaucracy—that is, below the leadership level—represent the etatist service stratum. The rest—the large majority of the population—are the masses: workers and the most inferior stratum, peasants. Forced labor plays the role of the etatist lumpenproletariat. The (historical) role of the elite—of the vanguard—is to lead; of the masses, to be led. This fundamental "division of labor" is clear, consistent, and rigid.

Whereas the capitalist ruling class is a result of the interdependent operation of various stratification mechanisms in an environment with few formal and visible—and many substantial and invisible—political constraints, the etatist ruling class is a result of purposeful political design whereby political monopoly is vested in the ruling party.[73] Membership in the party is usually for life. The party is frankly proclaimed to be a vanguard party, the social elite whose historical mission is to transform the society according to a design known to that elite. As such it tolerates no opposition since, by definition, no one can be more qualified to interpret properly the interests of the working people and to find adequate solutions for social problems. This monolithic organization of etatist society explains an apparent paradox: namely, that such a society is at the same time more open and more rigidly stratified.[74]

In conclusion, let us contrast some of the properties of capitalism and etatism. In capitalism, political power is derived mostly from economic power. In etatism, this relationship is reversed. In the former society, the state is in the final analysis ruled by a plutocracy; in the latter one, the economy is ruled by a politocracy. As their respective names already indicate, in capitalism the working class is subject to capital; in etatism, to the state. The two dominant classes are the bourgeoisie and the politocracy.[75] The former includes managers and other ruling elites as well as the service class; the latter comprises the political leadership and the bureaucracy. In capitalism, income is derived largely from one's place in the economic hierarchy. In etatism, income is derived from one's place in the political hierarchy. An equivalent of economic exploitation in capitalism is political hegemony in etatism.

The stages of capitalist development are separated by deep economic crises (1870s, 1930s), and the development proceeds in business cycles. The stages of etatist development will very likely be separated by deep political crises, and etatism certainly experiences political cycles (the Moscow trials in the 1930s; the Cominform blockade of Yugoslavia in the late 1940s; the death of Stalin followed by the workers' demonstration in Plzeň and the workers' rebellion in East Berlin and culminating in Poznań and the Hungarian uprising in 1956; the occupation of Czechoslovakia in 1968, which prompted the development of Eurocommunism; the Great Leap Forward and the Cultural Revolution in China). Capitalist economic crises are followed by political changes (the appearance of fascism, the New Deal). Etatist political crises prompt economic reforms. But the basic characteristics of the system remain preserved.

In governing the society, the capitalist ruling class uses primarily economic coercion, followed by pressure to force minds into conformity and, finally, by political coercion. In etatism ideological coercion[76] is followed by political coercion, with economic coercion occupying last place in the sequence. Since political coercion is personal, it is felt as more oppressive than impersonal economic coercion, and thus etatism appears more repressive than capitalism. As a consequence of the differential importance of various types of coercion, capitalism is characterized by economic insecurity, etatism by political insecurity. These two types of insecurity have been the two main organizational devices for establishing and maintaining stratified social orders in the two systems.[77] As economic security increases, capitalism begins to crumble with inflation, lack of work discipline, and irresistible requests for participation in decision making as concomitant manifestations. Political security in an etatist country corrodes party political monopoly—as demonstrated in Czechoslovakia—and leads to similar requests for the transformation of social relations. But before this happens, both systems remain stratified, class systems. In both systems the proletariat is an exploited class. The main difference between the two systems is to be found in the fact that exploitation is exercised and social power distributed by predominantly economic means in capitalism, and by predominantly political means in etatism.

4

Alienation and Reification

I. Alienation

In its original sense as used by Hegel and Marx, the term *alienation* referred to a divergence between human existence and human essence. Existence refers to the actual existence of an individual in the world. Essence is what the individual can be potentially. A man is alienated if his existence is divorced from his essence.

What the essence of man is, what his human potentialities are, represents the subject matter of philosophical anthropology. Yugoslav philosopher Mihailo Marković voices a widely shared opinion when he describes the essence of man as a free, creative, fully developed, and socialized being. Yet this is clearly a normative (philosophical) and not a positive (scientific) statement. Similarly, we could follow Brazilian educationist Paulo Freire and delineate the essential difference between man and other species of animals by observing that man can change the world and reflect about the world, himself, and his activities in the world, while animals are unable to separate themselves from their actions and are thus beings of pure activity and not of praxis.[1] A Marxist would express the same idea by declaring that man is a being of praxis.[2] As such, he is free since he can choose consciously among different courses of action that are objectively given. And if he can be free, he ought to be free, for otherwise he loses his essential human property. Thus self-realization and self-determination are characteristic for non-alienated existence. That man is not what he ought to be, and that he ought to be what he can be, is another normative element in the philosophical approach to alienation.[3]

The approach just sketched is often thought idealistic and utopian; surely man is a somewhat different animal. Yet serious Marxist social philosophers are far from that naive. Mihailo Marković points out that man is a contradictory creature. Man has always endeavored to enlarge his freedom—yet he also invented slavery. The most distinctive characteristic of man is his creativity—but he has also proved to be horribly destructive.

Man is a social being, a product of society, and cannot exist normally without society—but he can also be selfish, possessive, and power hungry. He is certainly a rational being—but precisely our own epoch has demonstrated how frightfully irrational he can become. This makes one pose the question: "Which are the constitutive characteristics of human nature that we should prefer and whose predominance in the future we should secure by our practical action in the present?"[4] The answer, of course, is normative. But once we define our value criteria, the course of action is clear: one should help to develop the positive features of human nature and try to control and constrain the negative ones. There is little doubt that a large gap exists between the actual position and the possible achievements in this respect. This, then, is the root of the "distinction between what man *appears* to be and what he is *able* to be, between the *actuality* and *potentiality* of the human being," the distinction described by alienation. "A social philosophy which fails to make this distinction, which assumes that man *is what prevails in his actual existence* is condemned to end as an ultimate ideological justification of the existing order."[5]

Thus, in an integrated approach to social theory, one cannot avoid value judgments. On the other hand, it is easier to reach an agreement if the propositions are cast in such a form as to be falsifiable. It will therefore be desirable to minimize the normative component. Scientists are more likely to agree than philosophers. But a price will have to be paid for the greater possibility of agreement.

Apart from its philosophical aspect, the phenomenon of alienation also has a sociological and a psychological aspect. In line with the purpose of this study, we shall concentrate on the sociological aspect. One possible approach is to follow Gajo Petrović and conceive man's essence as his historically given human possibilities. In this case alienation will imply that man is alienated from the realization of his historically created possibilities. And to say that man is not alienated from himself will imply that he has reached the level of his potentialities and that by realizing them—without ever having exploited them completely—he constantly creates new potentialities.[6] Historical, sociological, and psychological research may provide us with a knowledge of the possibilities that men wish to realize.

It is clear that such an approach would require a separate study of its own. It would also require an author with a different professional background (though, in a certain sense, this entire study is nothing but an exploration of presently given human possibilities). Thus it is desirable to try to find a shortcut. Again, Marx can serve as a guide. The shortcut is provided by using labor as the basic analytical category.

If, in order to satisfy their needs as they evaluate them, people have to work substantially more than they would otherwise prefer, the situation can be described as one of acute scarcity. A situation of acute scarcity has characterized the entire history of class societies until our time. In such a situation the conditions of productive work become existentially important, and economic relations determine to a large extent other social relations. Even more than that. Through work man became a human being. Through his practical activity man changes objective reality—nature and society—and transforms it into human reality, i.e., into a result of human work. In this way man also transforms the conditions of his own existence and so changes himself as a species. The social process of work becomes a process of self-creation.[7] And anything that has a negative impact on the process of work must have a negative impact on its result, self-creation. Man is prevented from realizing his human possibilities. He is alienated. Thus, we can undertake the analysis of alienation by exploring the conditions under which productive work is performed in various socioeconomic systems.

It is often stated that the concept of alienation is inherently philosophical and that it cannot be used as a scientific concept. This is the position of Joachim Israel, who in the work quoted above suggests that it be abandoned and replaced by the concept of reification. Similarly, Ralf Dahrendorf claims that, regardless of how much sense the alienation of the industrial worker may make in philosophical terms, "it has no place in empirical social science, since no amount of empirical research can either confirm or refute it."[8] Such claims are based on a methodological misunderstanding. First of all, the gap between the actual and the achievable is a matter of observation and positive knowledge. In this sense alienation is a refutable proposition, since in principle it can be shown that there is no way of improving upon the actual position. Second, the concept of alienation implies a hypothesis about certain important consequences of the observed gap. Here it is good to remember that not all scientific propositions can be proved directly. Very often they represent theoretical hypotheses that can be refuted or proved only indirectly, by considering the consequences. If a hypothesis turns out to be barren, it will be rejected. If, however, it proves fruitful—which means that it makes it possible to organize our knowledge about empirical phenomena, that it leads to a consistent explanation of observed acts and generates additional fruitful hypotheses—it will be retained until a more powerful hypothesis is formulated or newly discovered facts cannot be accommodated within the old theoretical framework. In this sense, alienated labor has proved to be an extremely fruitful hypothesis.

The social process of work has three components: people, their activities, and the product of their activities. Each of these elements can be alienated. Thus the phenomenon of alienation can conveniently be analyzed in terms of three different processes: the alienation of labor, the alienation of the product of labor, and the alienation of a person from other people and the society.

1. *The alienation of labor* occurs when the worker is alienating his labor power by selling it to the employer. The sale normally results in the exchange of labor power for money, but need not. The mere existence of the employer-employee relationship is a sufficient condition for alienation. Once the employer disposes of the labor of the worker, the labor becomes external to the worker, separated from his personality; "he does not fulfill himself in his work but denies himself, has a feeling of misery rather than well being, does not develop freely his mental and physical energies but is physically exhausted and mentally debased.[9] The worker therefore feels himself at home only during his leisure time, whereas at work he feels homeless. His work is not voluntary but imposed, *forced* labour. It is not a satisfaction of a need, but only a *means* for satisfying other needs." This is reflected in one of the fundamental assumptions of bourgeois economic theory—namely, that work is disutility. "Its alienated character is clearly shown by the fact that as soon as there is no physical compulsion it is avoided like a plague."[10] In an etatist factory labor is equally alienated, of course. What happened is well described by Miklós Haraszti, who gives an account of his own experience as a worker in a Budapest factory: "I discovered a change in myself. My interest in materials and ways of economizing my strength is first coloured and then dominated by an obsession about making money. I surrender to an offensive unspoken but all powerful taboo: never approach work to make it more exact, easy, enjoyable or safe."[11]

Alienated labor is treated as a commodity, as a factor of production, on a par with other factors of production. The price for the use of labor power is determined on the market. The value of a worker is calculated as the value of a productive asset: it represents the discounted value of the income stream during productive life. The difference between a worker and a slave is that the worker owns his labor power and hence can engage in marketing himself, while the slave is a commodity marketed by someone else. Occasionally people literally market themselves, not only their labor power. This is true of salesmen and saleswomen, commercial travelers, bureaucratic careerists, and prostitutes. They sell their personalities—smiles, personal charm, thoughts, or bodies—in order to increase commodity turnover, whatever the commodity involved may be: a new product, obedience, or love. If the worker is educated, the value of his "human capital"—to use modern economic terminology—is increased; educated slaves were also more expensive. In short, alienation of labor implies the estrangement of the creative capacities of the worker, their transformation into an object, a commodity, which is then appropriated by someone else. The worker plays no part in deciding what to do or how to do it, and this is a fundamental break between the individual and his life activity.[12] This *self-alienation* is the basic aspect of alienation.

2. *Alienation of the product of labor* is a direct consequence of the alienation of labor. "The product of labour is labour which has been embodied in an object and turned into a physical thing; this product is an *objectification* of labour. The performance of work is at the same time its objectification."[13] Once the labor is sold, all its products are appropriated by the employer. The products of labor now stand "opposed to it as an *alien being,* as a *power independent* of the producer."[14] By appropriating the product of labor, the employer appropriates also the surplus value, that is, the difference between the value of the product and the value of the labor power. Accumulated surplus value increases the economic—and social—power of the employer and creates the conditions for further exploitation of labor. The master, however, is not secure either. Once the product is alienated from the direct producer, it tends to escape control altogether, to start living an independent life, to become an autonomous and threatening force. Men produce commodities and create markets, and then the impersonal forces of the market begin to dominate their social relationships. Men create parties, unions, states, and then these institutions begin to live their separate lives, avoiding the control of their creators. Thus, in a more general sense, once the first sin of self-alienation is committed, man's creations tend to confront him as alien and threatening powers.

3. When man alienates his life activity and his products, he is bound to *alienate himself from other men.* The product of

labor appears as capital, that is, as command over labor. The society becomes stratified into hostile social classes. Competition and class hostility render most forms of cooperation impossible. Alienated members of a society appear as competing egoistical individuals, as proletarians and capitalists, as workers and bureaucrats, as oppressed and oppressors, rulers and ruled—not as human beings.

Alienation affects both the ruling and the subordinate class. "The possessing class and the proletarian class express the same human alienation. But the former is satisfied with its situation, feels itself well established in it, recognizes this self-alienation as its *own* power and thus has the *appearance* of a human existence. The latter feels itself crushed by this *self-alienation,* sees in it its own importance and the reality of an inhuman situation."[15]

According to Marx, three conditions in capitalist society are partly the cause and partly the consequence and expression of alienated labor. They are: private ownership of the means of production, the division of labor, and exchange. Since this proposition is contained in the *Manuscripts,* which were not intended for publication, one is not surprised to find it rather imprecise and ambiguous. Thus the following conclusions may be—and have often been—derived: the abolition of private productive property will end alienation; since technological development increases the specialization of work, the division of labor is bound to remain forever and so is alienation; the existence of market exchange of any kind implies alienation. These three conclusions, besides being inconsistent, are patently wrong. Thus, the conditions for alienation must be determined both more precisely and more generally.

The sufficient conditions for the alienation of labor appear to be as follows:

1. Labor power is marketed as a commodity. As long as that is the case, there can be no self-determination, which is the negation of alienation.

2. There is a division between manual and mental labor. This division is determined primarily by the development of the productive forces. As long as it exists, some labor will be experienced as forced labor. The present level of economic development already makes it possible to give the majority of the population a university education and to eliminate most of the harmful and degrading work.

3. Work and political activities are organized hierarchically in a manner that generates great concentration of economic and political power. This may also be considered as a special

case of the division of labor: namely, the division between professional order giving and order taking, between decision making and mere execution.[16] In fact, this condition is at the same time necessary and sufficient, because conditions 1 and 2 cannot obtain without generating condition 3 as well.

If commodity labor is eliminated, other commodities may remain and the market may be used as an allocational device without at the same time being an institution that causes alienation. If education is equally accessible to everyone and the work situation is changed so as to make work enjoyable, labor will cease to be a means to something else, and will not be experienced as forced labor. Finally, if the concentration of power is eliminated, class alienation will cease to exist as well. That makes possible the gradual establishment of genuine social control of the products of productive labor, as well as of man's creations in general.

The absence of these three conditions is clearly necessary for the elimination of alienation. Whether it is also sufficient remains to be seen. Since experimentation in the social sciences is generally impossible, sufficient conditions cannot be established in advance. They can be found *ex post facto*, after the historical process has completed itself. One can perhaps consider the negation of the three conditions as sufficient in the sense that, once it obtains, the process of alienation will be reversed and the process of disalienation initiated.

It is easy to see that all three conditions of alienation pertain in contemporary capitalism and etatism. Labor power is a commodity sold to the employer—private or state; the division between manual and mental labor has definite social consequences; and classes are generated by the unequal distribution of power.

II. Reification

The process of work results in the objectification of labor. Man appropriates the objective world and makes it his own, human, by objectifying himself in it. When this objectification proceeds under special, alienating conditions, we encounter the phenomenon of *reification*. The term was first used by the Hungarian philosopher György Lukács in the early twenties[17] and has only recently gained somewhat wider acceptance, particularly among Marxist humanists.

Reification denotes a state in which the relations between persons are expressed and experienced as relations between things. Social relations lose their social character and become mystified as technological, exchange, or administrative relations. Men evaluate each other as they evaluate objects. Their consciousness becomes reified. "Human beings become means for each other, means which can be exploited for achieving certain ends. But—and this is one of the central points in Marxist thinking concerning reification—the very phenomenon does not appear to the individual as something abnormal, as something 'alien to his nature.' Instead, the process of reification acquires a characteristic of a 'natural' relationship."[18] Marković points out that the concept of a reified social situation in which its actors acquire, experience, or are ascribed the characteristics of things can be applied to three different levels: "(I) objects (human behaviour under certain historical conditions actually obtains thinglike properties: work becomes repetitive, political life formalistic, society ruled by alienated social forces); (II) theory about objects (in the search for objective knowledge, individual, subjective features of human behaviour must be kept aside); (III) meta-theory (when critical consciousness about the limits of our objective methodology is absent and when our intellectual instruments become too frozen and hardened)."[19] As we proceed, we shall examine reification at all three levels.

The process of reification occurs somewhat differently in capitalism and in etatism. Let us start with capitalism. Here the universalization of market relationships plays the crucial role. If one can sell one's labor power, one can sell practically everything. In a vivid description of this fact, Marx points out in *Poverty of Philosophy* that

> everything, which up to now has been considered as inalienable, is sold as objects of exchange, of chaffering. It is the time in which objects, which earlier have been conveyed, but never exchanged, have been given away but never offered for sale, have been acquired but never been bought: virtue, love, conviction, knowledge, consciousness and so on, the time which, in a word, everything has been transformed into a commercial commodity. It is the time of general corruption, of universal bribery or, in the language of economics, it is the time when each object, physical as well as moral, is put on the market as an object of exchange to be taxed at its correct value.[20]

If everything is marketable, the market begins to play a special role as a universal standard of evaluation. Thus the structure of bourgeois consciousness will be basically determined by the universality of market relationships. This is reflected in everyday language: someone tries to "sell" his ideas or refuses to "buy" another's opinion. As usual, Marx had already noticed this phenomenon. In reality as well as in language, exchange relationships become the basis of everything else: *propriété* and property mean both ownership and trait; *valeur*, value, *Wert*, commerce, *Verkehr* "are the words used both for commercial relations and for characteristics and relations of individuals as such."[21] In a more subtle—and also more profound—way, *having* replaces *being*. Individuals say that they *have* problems, sleeplessness, or an unhappy marriage, instead of saying that they feel miserable, cannot sleep, or quarrel with their wives. Modern man *has* everything: car, house, profession, children, marriage, problems, angers, relationships—and, if all this is not sufficient, he also has a psychoanalyst. He *is* nothing.[22]

Freedom is measured by the extent to which "impersonal market forces" are left to operate without outside interference. Thus bourgeois consciousness confuses market freedom with human freedom. Economic efficiency (the so-called Pareto optimum) will be derived from (idealized) market relationships. First-year students of economics are taught the theorem which proves that a free market achieves the best allocation of resources—labor included. *Human capital* (!) calculated as a discounted stream of wages has already been mentioned. Academic economists analyze the size of the family by treating children as consumer durables and calculate appropriate demand elasticities. *Market* profitability tends to be the crucial criterion for *social* desirability. Enormous differences in income and wealth are explained and justified by differences in marginal productivity. The lack of employment opportunities, business fluctuations, and the low rate of economic development, with their concomitant social costs, are justified by demand and supply conditions. Demand and supply are seen as objective forces that have nothing to do with the social system and that change market conditions just as natural forces change meteorological conditions. The fundamental social relationship between an employer and an employee remains hidden behind the labor market. Private labors appear as components of social labor only through the exchange of products of labor. Consequently, social relations among producers do not appear as what they are but as commodity relations among persons and social relations among things. Most social phenomena are traced back to and evaluated on the basis of commodity relationships. In the religious world, the products "of the human brain appear as independent beings endowed with life, and entering into relations both with one another and the human race." In the economic world the products of labor—commodities—play a similar role. This similarity induced Marx to label the fundamental aspect of reification *commodity fetishism.*[23]

It will be of some interest to substantiate the above analysis by at least one concrete example of reified thinking. For this purpose, I have selected a book by the Austro-Anglo-American economist F. A. von Hayek, *The Constitution of Liberty.*[24] This choice is motivated by the fact that Hayek is an economist of considerable professional reputation, that he has also acquired a reputation as a champion of human liberties by showing much keener interest in social problems than most of his professional colleagues, and that his book was well received and his thinking has had a considerable following.[25] Thus it is clearly interesting to find out what are the limits of reified freedom. The argument of this representative bourgeois liberal can be summed up in the following eight points:

1. For some reason the exploited masses are dissatisified with their position. Alienation is felt as oppression. Hayek does not use this terminology and is unaware of its meaning, but he has the same phenomenon in mind when he argues: "It may indeed prove to be the most difficult task of all to persuade the employed masses that in the general interest of their society, and therefore in their own long-term interest, they should preserve such conditions as to enable few to reach positions which to them appear unattainable or not worth the effort and risk."[26] A difficult task indeed!

2. "That the freedom of the employed depends upon the existence of a great number and variety of employers is clear when we compare the situation that would exist if there were only one employer."[27] If freedom is to be enhanced, the employer-employee relationship must be abolished—this is an obvious conclusion arrived at through commonsense reasoning. That the number of employers must be multiplied is a conclusion of a reified bourgeois mind. In other words, freedom consists in the free choice of a master (see point 4).[28]

3. The alienation of labor is, of course, the most natural state of a producer. "There can be little doubt . . . that employment has become not only the actual but the preferred position of the majority of the population, who find that it gives them what they mainly want: an assured fixed income available for current expenditure, more or less automatic raises and provision for old age."[29]

4. The market is impersonal, the unequal distribution of power does not matter, and selling one's labor power is an

exercise of free will. "It is not power as such—the capacity to achieve what one wants—that is bad, but only power to coerce, to force other men to serve one's will by the threat of inflicting harm. There is no evil in the power wielded by the director of some great enterprise in which men have willingly united of their own will and for their own purposes."[30]

5. While subordination to the authoritarian rule of management is treated as free will, the insistence on workers' solidarity is conceived as coercion. "It cannot be stressed enough that the coercion which unions have been permitted to exercise contrary to all principles of freedom under the law is primarily the coercion of fellow workers."[31]

6. The really mortal sin of the unions, however, consists in their obstruction of the operation of the market. "If unions have in fact achieved much less by their wage policy than is generally believed, their activities in this field are nevertheless economically very harmful and politically exceedingly dangerous. They are using their power in a manner which tends to make the market system ineffective. . . ."[32]

7. If market rationality happens to conflict with human rationality, the latter must give way. "It may seem harsh, but it is probably in the interest of all that under a free system those with full earning capacity should often be rapidly cured of a temporary and not dangerous disablement at the expense of some neglect of the aged and mortally ill."[33]

8. Finally, and quite consistently with our previous analysis of the conditions of alienation, Hayek concludes: "The recognition of private property is thus an essential condition for prevention of coercion. . . ."[34]

It may be of some interest to add yet another set of quotations, which come from Hayek's latest treatise[35] and represent a perfect example of commodity fetishism. Hayek admits "that the manner in which the benefits and burdens are apportioned by the market mechanism would in many instances have to be regarded as very unjust *if* it were the result of a deliberate allocation to particular people. But," he argues, "this is not the case. Those shares are the outcome of a process the effect of which on particular people was neither intended nor foreseen by anyone when the institutions first appeared. . . .To demand justice from such a process is clearly absurd. . . ." In other words, "in a free society in which the position of the different individuals and groups is not the result of anybody's design . . . the differences in rewards cannot meaningfully be described as just or unjust." Thus his "basic contention" appears to be "that in a society of free men whose members are allowed to use their knowledge for their own purposes the term 'social justice' is wholly devoid of meaning or content. . . ." Consequently, the quest for social justice, which implies interfering with the verdict of the market, is not only undesirable; it is meaningless!

Reified reasoning encompasses a much larger area than the above examples would suggest. Market rationality and strict calculability mold the structure of consciousness in a very specific way. Social consciousness becomes "one-dimensional," focused exclusively on directly given facts, immersed into and reduced to the factual, and unable to transcend it and consider the potential.[36] The one dimension left is in fact the economic dimension, the production of commodities evaluated in money terms. Other dimensions have been repressed. "Western man," writes Walter Weisskopf, "has thus become alienated from 'parts' of himself because the multidimensionality of his existence has been reduced to the dimension of technology and economy. Western society requires the individual to choose without values (repression of the normative); to work without meaning (repression of the spiritual); to integrate without community (repression of the communal dimension). One could add: to think without feeling (repression of the affective) and to live without hope, myth, utopia (repression of the transcendental dimension)."[37]

Much of what has been said about reification in the bourgeois world applies to the bureaucratic world as well. But here the source of reification is different: it is not the universalization of market relationships but the universalization of bureaucratic relationships; man is not reduced to a commodity but to the office he holds. Even Lukács noted that bureaucracy was a source of alienation. Bureaucracy gives rise to an adjustment of way of life and work, and consequently of consciousness, to the basic conditions of etatist society (Lukács talks of capitalist society), similar to that made by the proletariat in capitalism. Formal rationalization of law, state, and administration implies a similar decomposition of social functions into their elements, and similar consequences for consciousness as arose when labor was separated from the individual capacities and needs of the operative in the factory. A bureaucrat is role bound and as such alienated from himself.[38] But Lukács was not aware that the effects generated by the bureaucratic structures in capitalism appear with much stronger force in etatism (which he identified with socialism), where bureaucratic relationships become universal.

Let us again introduce our subject by a quotation from Marx:

> Whatever I can do, what the office can enable me to do, what becomes my own by means of the office, that is my Self, myself as the incumbent of the office. My power is just as great as the power of my office. The properties of office are *my* properties, my essential qualities, since I am the incumbent. Therefore it is by no means my individuality that determines what I am and what I achieve. As regards my individuality, I am halt, but office lends me 24 feet—so I am halt no longer. I am a sinful man, without honour, conscience or spirit; but office is honourable, and so its incumbent must be; office is the greatest good, so its incumbent is good likewise; office allows me to dispense with the efforts of dishonesty, and thus I pass as honest; I am lacking in spirit, but office is the real spirit of all things—how, then, should its incumbent be lacking in spirit?[39]

This passage describes in etatism a direct counterpart for the capitalist commodity fetishism. I proposed to label this phenomenon *office fetishism.*[40]

The paragraph by Marx quoted above, in which he refers to office fetishism—without mentioning the term—may come as a surprise to some familiar with the works of Marx. Had not Marx always been talking exclusively about money, commodity, and market relationships as the primary conditions of alienation? Yes he had; the surprise would have been justified. I played a trick with the paragraph: I simply replaced the original words *money, buy,* and *owner* with *office, do,* and *incumbent.* The fact that the meaning of the paragraph has been perfectly preserved shows that the Marxian analysis of alienation is equally applicable to an etatist society.

Thus, just as commodity fetishism represents a tendency to view relations between man and man as relations between commodities, office fetishism means hiding actual human relations behind the veil of impersonal bureaucratic rules, a mystification of the activities of office holders. The judgments of the market are infallible and so are the judgments of an official with respect to his subordinates. The holding of office confers upon the incumbent the qualities of being cleverer, more honest, more reliable (politically or otherwise), more intelligent—in short: *superior* to all individuals placed lower in the office hierarchy. The parallelism, of course, goes even further. Both the free market and bureaucratic structures have their separate lives, which cannot be brought under conscious control. The most impressive demonstration of this ultimate alienation is to be found in the historical fact that the proletarian revolution was fought in order to establish socialism and resulted in etatism.

III. Some Psychological and Moral Consequences

Since "to be reified" means to acquire or to be ascribed the characteristics of a thing, and since, whatever his nature, man is certainly not a thing, the divergence between human existence and human potentialities is bound to generate very definite psychological and moral consequences. As a result the entire society, not only its individual members, becomes sick. Mihailo Marković has summarized as follows the features of reification in capitalist and etatist societies:

> When all means of production are owned by a small elite, when the aim of production is maximization of profit, when all other possible criteria of evaluation are subordinated to efficiency, when, consequently, the highest possible degree of division and professional specialization of work has been introduced, then individual work loses all human qualities and becomes as repetitive, frozen and stereotyped as that of any animal. Work loses any subjective meaning; the worker is transformed into a living machine, into a thing. One meets the same phenomenon in political life whenever the monopoly of political power is in the hands of a privileged minority and real decision-making takes place behind closed doors. Then mass-meetings, elections and public debates become empty rituals, where the ordinary individual is present but does not really count: he is reduced to a mere object.[41]

The market in capitalism and the state in etatism destroy human beings and transform individuals into commodity producers and masses.

Under modern conditions, alienated labor in factories and bureaucratic structures becomes a fragmented labor. Individuals perform only minute, repetitive, and meaningless fractions of the total work, over which they have no control. Work is deprived of any intrinsic reward; it is purely instrumental. The worker does not determine his own work but performs the tasks set before him simply in order to exist. Man is reduced to an instrument of his own existence, which makes this existence meaningless. The sheer size of modern productive and political institutions makes an individual powerless. He is just a cog in an enormous mechanism; he has no power, no freedom, no autonomy while in society. Only when, in his leisure time, he escapes into the seclusion of his private existence, can he hope to regain some of his human faculties. Since human faculties are essentially social, however, this escape ends in new frustrations. Behind the veil of commodity and office fetishism, market and state appear as impersonal forces—modern substitutes for divinities—and render the individual completely helpless. A man is thus reduced to an object manipulated by other persons and dominated by impersonal forces. One-dimensional thought does not perceive alternative possibilities. Thus diffuse feelings of meaninglessness, powerlessness, and helplessness appear to characterize capitalist and etatist societies.

These feelings generate three additional second-order effects. It is hardly possible for a human being to live a life deprived of meaning, characterized by complete subordination to other human beings, and reduced to an object of blind social forces. People will rebel, and so there are outbursts of deviant behavior. Some people will collapse under the stress of their inhuman existence. Thus, neuroses of one kind or another are likely to become a characteristic sickness of a deeply alienated society.[42] This explains the famous empirical findings of the lack of interest in participation among workers and of the general political apathy among citizens. The former is then used as a proof that workers really do not want workers' management, which therefore should not be established. Concerning the latter, it is often argued that political apathy is really an essential precondition for the smooth operation of political democracy. If everyone had active political interests, there could not be any orderly government!

A society would be unable to function if everyone were either deviant, or neurotic, or resigned into complete apathy. Thus the major escape mechanism is of a different kind. It operates outside the production sphere and outside the political sphere, in the only sphere where man still feels at home—the sphere of consumption and during leisure time. Thus bourgeois and bureaucratic man are reduced to a species known as *Homo consumens.* If man is alienated in his productive and political roles, however, it is rather natural to expect that his consumption activity will appear in an alienated way as well. That, in fact, is the case.

When other avenues to meaningful life are blocked, people try to establish self-respect and self-determination as consumers. In the first place, this implies the acquisition and accumulation of things. People learn to evaluate themselves through the exchange value they possess and "perceive themselves as having use-value as human beings through the exchange-value of things they own."[43] An expensive or new model car, a color TV, a summer house, a yacht, etc., are not bought in order to satisfy real needs—less expensive models or renting when necessary may satisfy needs equally well or better—but in order to impress neighbors and clients. In the United States a successful lawyer is expected to drive a Cadillac or the equivalent, and so an unsuccessful lawyer is forced to buy a Cadillac, or he runs the risk of losing his clients. An American sociologist tells the story of a manager of a large bank who did not buy the make of car that was in vogue at the time. Instead, he bought a cheaper automobile, which he personally preferred. This action, however, led to a distrust of his bank's stocks.[44] Poorer residents of a neighborhood may install TV antennas on the roofs of their houses even if there are no TV sets inside. In etatist countries, and in bureaucratic structures in general, the furnishings of one's office, an official car with or without a driver, dachas, and other consumer durables are a direct reflection of social status and a measure of life success. People buy books which they do not read, pianos on which they do not play, jewelry which they do not wear, and paintings which they do not enjoy—sometimes do not even see. Instead of providing one of the deepest human satisfactions, art is becoming a status symbol or a means of capital accumulation. Carefully compiled compendia instruct the rich on how to invest in art. Wealthy individuals then buy paintings and sculptures, or hire someone to do it for them in an expert way, and lock them in the safe deposit boxes at their banks.

The accumulation of things that satisfy imposed and not real needs is just one aspect—and perhaps not the most important one—of the alienated consumer. The other is consumerism. *Homo consumens*

> is the man whose main goal is not primarily to *own* things, but to *consume* more and more, and thus to compensate for his inner vacuity, passivity, loneliness and anxiety. In a society characterized by giant enterprises, giant industrial, governmental and labour bureaucracies, the individual, who has no control over

> his circumstances of work, feels impotent, lonely, bored and anxious. At the same time, the need for profit of the big consumer industries, through the medium of advertising, transforms him into a voracious man, an eternal machine who wants to consume more and more. . . . New artificial needs are created and man's tastes are manipulated. . . . The greed for consumption . . . is becoming the dominant psychic force in present-day industrialized society. *Homo consumens* is under the illusion of happiness, while subconsciously he suffers from boredom and passivity. . . . He mistakes thrill and excitement for joy and happiness, the material comfort for aliveness; satisfied greed becomes the meaning of life, the striving for it a new religion. The freedom to consume becomes the essence of human freedom.[45]

These behavioral traits are less visible in etatist societies because of their greater material poverty. But competition with the West and the determination of the ruling class to preserve power—which requires focusing on consumption to keep the subordinate satisfied—are bound to generate consumer reification of life there too.

In order to function, the society must mold the character structure of its members so that they want to do that which they have to do and are satisfied with the conditions imposed upon them. An alienated person likes his alienation. And economic theorists, simpleminded and socially conditioned as they are, make the sovereignty of alienated consumers the cornerstone of their economic theory. But social character, defined as "that particular structure of psychic energy which is molded by any given society so as to be useful for the functioning of that particular society,"[46] is more than simply consumption conditioned. Let us, therefore, explore some of the more important character traits reflecting the modern conditions of alienation.

The displacement of living by consuming leaves a definite imprint on the value structure of the society and generates a specific vision of the world. In the West the world is seen as a place inhabited with competitive little creatures, each carrying an enormous ledger in which he or she carefully records all gains and losses with the aim of maximizing the positive balance. Man reduced to an accountant worrying only and exclusively about his balances—this is the anthropology of utilitarianism which provides the philosophical foundations of modern bourgeois economic theory, and of most social theory as well. Because of a much wider divergence between theory and practice, which we shall discuss in a moment, in etatist societies utilitarian hedonism is not so obvious. Here man is visualized as an incumbent of an office, an official who renders his labor and his loyalty to the state and acquires in return access to the pool of consumption goods, honors, and power. Here the ledger is more politically colored, but the principle is the same.

If an equivalent exchange is the basis of all activities, then every individual is isolated from all others, and sacred egoism becomes the fundamental motivational principle. Other men are treated as means and not as ends. Concern about other people's lives is proclaimed methodologically illegitimate (the happiness or welfare of two individuals cannot be compared) and unnatural (altruism is not realistic). Again, this is modified in an etatist setting, where the state decides what is good for everyone, thus keeping individuals apart while solving the problems that must be solved. The well-known psychological phenomenon of identification, whereby the individual associates himself with the position of another and acts accordingly[47]—which serves to resolve the contradiction between egoism and altruism—is ignored. Altruism is depicted as requiring self-sacrifice, the giving up of oneself. Yet the bookkeeping life of either private or state accountants is not particularly exciting or satisfying. "Life is meaningful and valuable," comments Polish philosopher Marek Fritzhand in discussing Marxian anthropology, "only when it is lived intensely and thoroughly, only when the human being can realize himself during his lifetime by developing all his human abilities and satisfying all his human needs. . . . Man can only achieve real happiness and perfection when he associates his own happiness and perfection with those of others."[48] Once the present conditions of alienation are overcome, we can expect a new morality to emerge. "The morality of human beings in this new society will not be alienated morality which makes an *obligation* of mutual love, treats love as *self-sacrifice,* as contrary to real interests of the individuals. According to the new morality, love is a natural phenomenon of human life, it is *self-affirmation* of man in his relation with other people."[49]

In both capitalist and etatist societies,

> from childhood on, true convictions are discouraged. There is little critical thought, there is little real feeling, and hence only conformity with the rest can save the individual from an unbearable feeling of loneliness and lostness. The individual does not experience himself as the active bearer of his own powers outside of himself into which he has projected his living substance. Man is alienated from himself, and bows down before the works of his own hands . . . before the state, and the leaders of his own making.[50]

In an illuminating analysis of modern society—the lonely crowd—David Riesman shows how the other-directed man, deprived of personal convictions and values, becomes a dominant type of man.[51] He is a complete conformist, sensitized to the expectations and preferences of others and psychologically guided by feelings of diffuse anxiety. The etatist variety of lonely crowd is a bureaucratically structured collectivity. The collectivistic man also suffers from permanent anxiety; he is not socially integrated into the group but remains alone, and thinks and works according to slogans and directives. In both societies people lose the capacity for spontaneous contacts and base their relations on calculated returns for whatever they do.

In several of his books, E. Fromm analyzes the social mechanisms that produced the observed behavioral characteristics just described.[52] Since the consciousness of one's personality is the product of one's practical activity, and since under the conditions of reified existence—where individuals are hired by private and state employers—this activity is transformed into a relationship among things, the personality becomes alienated. Things do not have personality. An individual ceases to be an individual and adopts the personality which, in the expectation of others, he must have. Once one's own personality is lost, the only possibility for regaining one's identity is conformity. In order to be accepted, one has to do what everyone else does; one must not be different; one must not remain outside or go beyond standards and stereotypes; one must not insist on what is correct but only on what is expected, accepted, and acceptable. Right is what the crowd feels is right. Right is what the state says is right. As individuals, we are minute particles of the crowd and the state; as such, we have no power, no significance—no personality. We are completely dependent on the general mood of the crowd, on the orders of the state. Any divergence from accepted standards, any deviation from the party line, creates a feeling of extreme anxiety. Anxiety can be relieved only when conformity is reestablished.

If the source of our personal identity is outside ourselves, then we are likely to be dominated by this outside force. In particular, we feel strong and secure, relieved from anxiety, even happy, when we identify ourselves with powerful masters and subordinate ourselves to their authority. This is the genesis of the authoritarian character structure, so widespread in our time. As an individual, I am insignificant. But as a part of something big—a state, a nation, a party—I am also big. Thus, in order to prevent my own degradation, I must defend the authority. Fascism, Stalinism, colonialism with its atrocities in Vietnam, Algeria, and Portuguese Africa, reflect some of the consequences of the authoritarian character structure.

The authoritarian structure of society, characteristic especially of etatist societies, naturally develops an authoritarian structure of consciousness. The latter gives rise to a personality structure that, according to Rade Bojanović, manifests the following traits: submissiveness; respect for hierarchical relationships; opposition to the subjective and the imaginary; respect for power, discipline, and authority; rigid reasoning and infection with stereotypes. How far the reification of consciousness has progressed in these societies is illustrated by the fact that, in party compendia, exactly the characteristics enumerated above are said to be distinctive of the revolutionary personality. To realize this, we need only change the terminology appropriately. Instead of descriptions such as Bojanović uses, we substitute the following terms with the same meaning: "responsibility" for "submissiveness"; "democratic centralism" for "bureaucratic hierarchy"; "petty bourgeois subjectivism" for "feelings and imagination"; "revolutionary discipline" for "unconditional obedience to superiors"; "party line" and "Marxism-Leninism"[53] for "absence of reasoning." "An authoritarian way of thinking," continues Bojanović, "requires complete inclusion into the collective and into hierarchical relationships. It completely negates independence and individuality. It is characteristic for such people that they are ashamed when they talk about personal problems. . . . Escape from one's own personality . . . from any individuality . . . lies at the basis of an authoritarian personality."[54]

Whenever the unity of human personality is somehow destroyed and some parts of it alienated, we observe a special phenomenon that may be called *Homo duplex.* The same man is subject to authoritarian rule as a producer and is free as a consumer. The same man is a tender father to his children in his private capacity, and a cruel murderer of other children in his official capacity, as, for example, when he is "pacifying the rebel territory." Perfectly reasonable men are ready to commit callous and brutal acts, if told to do so by an authority.[55] Private thoughts and official pronouncements often differ. And so forth. Although he exists in capitalism as well, *Homo duplex* is particularly characteristic of etatist societies. This is due to the fact that there is an especially wide gap between the socialist ideals proclaimed by the ruling class and the actual social practices in which it engages. Thus as a rule, and not only occasionally, words and deeds will diverge. One of the results is the curious phenomenon of a language in which words have double meanings: one linguistic and one practical. In order to be able to communicate properly, one must know both meanings. *Homo duplex* speaks this special language, which directly reflects the alienation of the real meaning from the appearance. How translations are carried out was illustrated by the above example in which negative character traits were transformed into positive ones by calling submissiveness, responsibility; hierarchy, democratic centralism; and respect for power and authority, revolutionary discipline. Similarly, a military occupation (as of Czechoslovakia) is called "international aid to brotherly people" or "solidarity" (as the Vietnamese intervention in Cambodia). "Proletarian internationalism" means unconditional submission to the Soviet Union, while genuine internationalism is known as rotten "bourgeois cosmopolitanism." Moral values are attacked by calling truthfulness "opportunism"[56] and moral integrity, "petty bourgeois." The denunciation of fellow citizens is identified with patriotism, and the secret service holds a place of honor in the society. Political opportunism and the absence of all ethical principles is denoted as "the class approach."[57] "Administrative measures" means repression (such as incarceration without due process). "Revolutionary legality" means the absence of legality or illegality. "Progressive" or "reactionary" refers to support or opposition to the Soviet government. Current political views are the criteria for what is "scientific," while pragmatic measures of the Soviet state are denoted as "objective laws of history." To become "a comrade" means to join the ruling party or obtain a commanding position and abstain from comradeship. "We" in fact means "them."[58] In Moscow streets huge posters with two slogans are exhibited next to each other: "All power belongs to the people" and "We shall carry out everything the party demands." Logical consistency would require that the second slogan be rephrased: "The party shall carry out everything we demand." Since this is not done, consistency is preserved by reinterpreting the first slogan to mean: "All power belongs to the party, which acts on the people's behalf." This dictionary of moral-political alienation could be expanded at will, but the foregoing sample of doublets will suffice.

Nowhere are the official and the private sphere as strictly separated as in etatism, and hardly anywhere are spontaneous social relations more thoroughly destroyed and the society more decomposed into isolated individuals. "Man may be more or less aware of his alienated condition," remarked Yugoslav philosopher Vranicki, "but the end result is the division of his personality against itself and the formation of *Homo duplex*. As a man, he does not feel himself to be part of the broader community. As an official being, he does not feel himself a man."[59]

We have reached the end of our inquiry. The two contemporary class societies are characterized by profound alienation. As a result, human relations tend to disappear and to be replaced by objects and functions. The commodity man and the office man are the creatures we meet in everyday life. These reified creatures think in a reified way, behave accordingly, and enter into reified relations. Their life goal is not to develop their personalities in order to enjoy life as fully as possible, but to accumulate and command; in other words, the goal is not to *be* but rather to *have*—things and offices. They are unable to establish spontaneous human contacts: in capitalism, money associates with money—even dances with money;[60] in etatism, office associates with office; and in neither of them does the person associate with the person. "At this stage, the question is no longer: how can the individual satisfy his own needs without hurting others, but rather: how can he satisfy his needs without hurting himself, without reproducing, through his aspirations and satisfactions, his dependence on an exploitative apparatus which, in satisfying his needs, perpetuates his servitude? The advent of a free society would be characterized by the fact that the growth of well-being turns into the essentially new quality of life. . . . Freedom would become the environment of an organism which is no longer capable of adapting to the competitive performance required for well-being under domination, no longer capable of tolerating the aggressiveness, brutality and ugliness of the established way of life."[61]

PART TWO

Searching for an Alternative

Theory is only realized in a people so far as it fulfills the needs of the people. . . . It is not enough that thought should seek to realize itself; reality itself must force its way toward thought.

MARX, *Contribution to the Critique of Hegel's Philosophy of Right* (1843)

The criticism of religion ends with the doctrine that *man is the supreme being for man* . . . with the *categorical imperative to overthrow all those conditions* in which man is an abased, enslaved, abandoned, contemptible being.

MARX, ibid.

5

Historical Laboratory: A New Social System in the Making

I. Introduction

The world in which we live is very imperfect. We may try to improve it. If we do, it is very natural to proceed in the following way: first, we produce a blueprint for a good society in which the manifest evils of the present society will be eliminated; next, we introduce national central planning into the affairs of the society; and, finally, we ask its members to follow certain rules designed to increase their welfare or happiness. That is why socialist thought has shown a distinctly centralistic orientation throughout its history: from Thomas More (1478–1535) and Tommaso Campanella (1568–1639) to Comte de Saint-Simon (1760–1825) and Etienne Cabet (1788–1856) in its utopian phase; and from the Internationals and the social democratic parties in the nineteenth century, to Lenin, the Comintern, and the Communist parties in the twentieth in its second phase, when practical applications were attempted.

Only very much later, in the nineteenth century, in connection with the advent of liberal capitalism, did social reformers begin to question the desirability of a centralist order. If the good society means maximum freedom for each individual, then clearly the elimination of the state and complete decentralization is the goal to which one should strive. William Godwin (1756–1836), to a certain extent Pierre Joseph Proudhon (1809–65), Mikhail Bakunin (1814–76), Prince Peter Kropotkin (1842–1921), and modern anarchists developed this line of thought.

So far anarchists have failed to implement their ideas on a national scale, and so their teaching may be considered as remaining in the utopian phase. Centralists, or state socialists, have been successful in a number of cases. The resulting social system, however, tended to deviate considerably from what had been expected: instead of socialism, centralizers produced etatism.

To a certain extent connected to, though by no means identical with, the centralist orientation is elitism. If you know what is good for the people, you are entitled to tell them what they should do. Saint-Simon—like Plato—believed that knowledge should rule and that great industrialists are natural leaders of the industrious poor (here he differed from Plato, for philosophers did not appear of great avail in an industrial setting). Lenin and modern communists vest all power in the vanguard party, which is supposed to lead the less conscious majority to a better society. In a backward society with a high percentage of illiterates—to mention just one dimension of retarded development—elitism may make good sense. On the other hand, anarchists rely largely on voluntary goodwill and the sense of justice of individuals guided by the ultimate rule of reason.

The third dichotomy in socialist thinking relates to the means by which the new society is to be achieved. In the first half of the nineteenth century, trade unions were illegal in most of the developed countries of the time and universal suffrage existed in none of them. The working class was subject to brutal exploitation and suffered needless misery inflicted upon them by capitalism. It was hopelessly naive to believe that the ruling class would voluntarily abdicate from its privileged positions and allow a classless socialist system to be built. Thus the only realistic way to carry out social reforms was to force the ruling class by violent means to undertake changes, or to overthrow the entire system in a single blow through an eruption of the revolutionary energy of the exploited masses. In fact, nineteenth-century Europe passed through an unending series of violent social upheavals and revolutions. The first theoreticians and practitioners of revolution were Gracchus Babeuf (1760–97) and Louis Auguste Blanqui (1805–81). Since legal means of radical social change were barred, illegal ones had to be employed. Small, well-organized conspiratorial groups, representing a conscious minority, would seize power at an appropriate moment and lead the oppressed masses into a fight for the overthrow of the present exploitative order. The doctrine of *minorité consciente* was later widely accepted by revolutionary syndicalists. In its mature form, it was elaborated into the theory of a (clandestine) workers' party preparing the revolution and establishing a dictatorship of the proletariat. The Russian October Revolution represents the most successful application of this theory. Ché Guevara and the contemporary Latin American Tupámaros are the latest practitioners of a more primitive version of Blanquism. It remains to be added that some groups of anarchists—who often had nothing to do with socialism—believed in the necessity for violence. They indulged in individual terrorism, carrying out "propaganda by deeds."

In the second half of the last century, political liberties were greatly extended in the developed countries of Europe; trade unions were legalized, and the first mass workers' parties emerged. It appeared possible to change society peacefully. Soon peaceful reformism was born, as distinct from the earlier ideology of revolutionary violence. Louis Blanc (1811–82) and Ferdinand Lassalle (1825–64) were among the first practicing politicians to rely on the state to carry out reforms. In the later years of his life, even Engels became a convinced reformist (at least with regard to Germany, though he acknowledged a possible need for revolutions in some other countries): "The irony of world history turns everything upside down. We, 'revolutionaries,' 'rebels,' we advance immensely better using legal means than illegal ones or by a rebellion."[1] Through social inertia the social democratic parties of the Second International (1889–1914) continued to profess ideas of revolutionary violence, but they were already completely reformist. More than that, they became part and parcel of the establishment, and, when the First World War broke out, all of them voted in the parliaments for war credits in support of the war efforts of their national bourgeoisie.[2] That, clearly, was in complete contradiction to their professed socialist ideals. As a result, a split occurred in the world working class movement. A new Communist International was established, reformism was declared a treason, and the need for violent revolution proclaimed again as the only acceptable tenet of socialist faith. Thus, the exclusive insistence on reform or revolution became the basic distinction between social democrats and communists. Bitter political fights ensued, and in the process the two approaches developed into actual tenets of faith, completely divorced from the historical circumstances that may render one or the other approach practically relevant. The confusion is further increased by the frequent current usage of the terms *revolutionary* and *reformist* in the sense of "radical" and "gradual" or "progressive" and "reactionary." Greek dictatorship called itself "revolutionary," while the Swedish government will no doubt apply the word "reformist" to its affairs.

The three theoretical and tactical dichotomies—centralization versus decentralization, state dominated by a conscious minority versus anarchy (in its original sense as a society without government), and revolution versus reform—reflect the trial-and-error type of development of socialist thought and socialist movements. *Ex ante* all of the six naive, extreme alternatives seem very natural approaches to be tried out. *Ex post,* after two centuries of experimentation, none of them appears to be leading to the proclaimed goal. Clearly, a more sophisticated theory is required. In all likelihood, such a theory will include these six alternatives as components, though not in an eclectic fashion. It is important to discover what history can teach us in this respect.

The sections that follow are not intended to provide a condensed history of socialism with all its detours, frustrated attempts, and mistaken ideas. Rather, the aim is to distill from such an indiscriminate history only those ideas and developments that seem to be leading toward socialism conceived as a self-governing society.

In the building of a self-governing society we can distinguish four waves of events—waves that are partly successive and partly superimposed upon each other. First come the visionaries, whose conception of a better society, though utopian in terms of immediate practical implementation, becomes realistic and relevant in terms of later historical development. Next, people associate into groups and social movements emerge. The third wave produces practical attempts to establish a new society. Finally, a new establishment is gradually built up.

II. Visionaries

The second half of the eighteenth century witnessed the advent of a new, capitalist society. The new society generated a new class conflict, and very soon the exploited class obtained its first intellectual defenders. Not quite conscious defenders, to be sure—for, as Engels observed, at first they claimed to emancipate not a particular class, but all humanity at once. The most developed countries of that time—Britain and France—supplied the most remarkable among them.

Robert Owen (1771–1858), the first and perhaps the most outstanding of the reformers, conceived of the future society as a federation of cooperative communities governed by producers. He owed some of his basic ideas to John Bellers, a Quaker, who in 1696 suggested the establishment of colleges of industry in which the poor could pool their efforts and work for themselves instead of for the rich. A college or corporation would include three hundred laborers engaged in all sorts of useful trades and would make labor and not money the standard of value for all necessities. Bellers' primary goal was to make it possible for the unemployed to work.

Owen was the son of a poor Welsh ironmonger and began to earn his living at an early age. His ideas were developed over two decades spent as the manager of a large cotton mill in the Scottish village of New Lanark, during which he improved the housing of his workers, organized education for their children, reduced working time from fourteen to ten and a half hours, abolished child labor, introduced a type of unemployment insurance, and, in general, anticipated by more than a century the treatment workers would later receive on a national scale. In 1824 Owen went to the United States. He bought an estate in Indiana and established New Harmony, the first experimental cooperative village. Its statute reads like that of a contemporary Israeli kibbutz. The experiment did not prove a success; nevertheless, eighteen more communities were formed in the next few years. Owen left his sons in New Harmony and returned to Britain, where he became involved in the trade union movement. The movement had just emerged from illegality and had begun to stimulate the formation of cooperative workshops. Owen's ideas inspired the cooperative movement and later, in 1844, a group of his disciples founded the Rochdale Pioneers cooperative society. In the meantime Owen induced the recently formed Builders' Union to lay plans for taking over the entire building industry through a Grand National Guild of Builders, thus eliminating private contractors—an anticipation of the future schemes of French syndicalists and British guild socialists. The Grand National Consolidated Trade Union was formed in 1833–34 in an attempt to unite the entire working class for a direct onslaught on the capitalist system, which was to be replaced by a system of workers' management. But employers and the government reacted quickly, and in a few months Owenite unionism came to an abrupt end.[3] Even before this defeat, however, the once popular "philanthropic Mr. Owen," as he was known in establishment circles, was expelled from "good society" and branded as a sinister individual intent upon destroying the established order of church and state. On his deathbed he told the minister who visited him that his ideas had not been accepted because they had not been understood, and because he had come before his time.

Charles Fourier (1772–1837) came from a middle class merchant family and was himself a clerk and commercial traveler.

He lived in a less industrialized environment and therefore laid more stress on the proper organization of agriculture. In contrast to Owen, Fourier believed that human nature was unchanging. Thus a social environment had to be created to fit it. For this, the best organization was self-governing *phalanstères* comprised of around 1,600 persons who would cultivate about 5000 acres of land. Since all the wrongs in agriculture were caused by the private ownership of land, land had to be collectivized in a phalanstery. Industrial establishments should be widely dispersed and located in agricultural phalansteries in order to eliminate the differences between the city and the village. Work had to be transformed from an unpleasant activity performed for fear of hunger into something attractive. This could be achieved if workers changed occupations from time to time, attaching themselves to an occupational group according to current interests. In addition, hired labor would be abolished. The income of a phalanstery would be used to cover the costs of production and social overhead (board and lodging, medical care, education, etc.); the remainder would be devoted to the remuneration of talent, capital, and labor. Phalansteries were to be federated under a coordinating governor known as an omniarch.

Fourier was very much concerned with individual freedom. The French Revolution had proclaimed political liberties but did not provide the poor with material means to make use of them. When a poor man expresses an opinion contrary to the opinion of a rich man, he will be persecuted even if his opinion was justified. Thus it appears that freedom is reserved for the small minority possessing wealth. Freedom is illusory if it is not universal. There can be no full freedom if people are economically dependent. That is why the phalanstery guaranteed the right to work and provided material security for its members. Once this was achieved, the state might disappear, for the absence of opposing interests would make coercion unnecessary. The deplorable state of social organization was due, in Fourier's opinion, to the stupidity of mankind. After they discovered the truth, future generations would be grateful to him for their great happiness.

Fourier advertised for rich philanthropists to finance the establishment of phalansteries, and every day expected the unknown guest at the lunch table in the restaurant where he took his meals. None ever came. Yet, after his death his disciples did raise money and established a number of cooperative communities, most of them in the United States, where the social climate was very favorable for this sort of venture. Between 1843 and 1853, forty phalansteries were founded. In Owenite communities, income was distributed in equal shares; in Fourierist communities, members who brought in more capital or showed greater ability participated more in the income of the community. Both types disintegrated with equal speed, the most successful surviving a decade or so.[4]

Another Frenchman, *Louis Blanc* (1811–82)—a lawyer and journalist—decided to explore another possibility. A moderate and a disbeliever in violent revolution, Blanc thought that the state could be made the agent for social reforms. In his famous book *L'organisation du travail* (1840), he argued that only the state could protect the weak members of society. Key industries, banks, insurance, and railways ought to be nationalized. The government must undertake to regulate national production, and should supply capital for the creation of *ateliers nationaux*—national workshops—in the most important industries. The government would appoint the directors of these workshops in the first year, and afterward workers would choose their own directors. The capital subscribed would be interest bearing and there would be no profit. Blanc accused the Fourierists of practicing capitalism because they assured a permanent share in product to suppliers of capital. The distribution of income, at first unequal, would gradually become more and more equalized. Blanc's ideal was an egalitarian society in which personal interest merged into the common good. This he summed up as *à chacun selon ses besoins, de chacun selon ses facultés* [to each according to his needs, from each according to his abilities]—the idea that later, in Marx's hands, became famous as the formula of communism. National workshops should establish a real fraternity within the country and, by gradual evolution, transform international relations and lead to a peaceful organization of humanity.

The Revolution of 1848 brought Blanc unexpectedly into government. His colleagues were unsympathetic to his projects, but had to tolerate his presence because they hoped he would help keep the workers quiet. Soon, however, they tricked him out of the government and made him president of the Commission de gouvernement pour les travailleurs, known as the Luxembourg Commission. The commission was to study workers' problems and report on what steps should be taken. Victor Considérant, the chief disciple of Fourier, also took part in the commission. Needless to say, however, the commission had neither the money nor the power to act. In a speech in March 1848, Blanc asked for a true social revolution that would lead to the achievement of the ideal *de produire selon ses forces et de consommer selon ses besoins* [to produce according to their powers, and consume according to their needs].[5] The commission prepared the draft of a law stipulating that one-quarter of all profits should be accumulated in a reserve fund. These various reserve funds would form a fund of mutual assistance to be used in case of need. In this way a large body of capital would be accumulated—capital that did not belong to anyone in particular but rather belonged to all. The distribution of this capital would be controlled by a council.[6] In the meantime the government acted on its own and discredited Blanc's chief project by establishing national workshops as relief agencies in which unemployed workers were assembled to perform useless work or even no work at all—the main idea being to keep them off the streets in those turbulent days. After the Assembly declined to consider Blanc's proposal for the creation of a Ministry of Labor, he resigned. His commission disappeared. He was accused of rebellion against the Assembly and soon sentenced to deportation. In that same year of 1848, Louis Blanc was compelled to leave his country and could not return for more than twenty years.

When Blanc became a member of the government another associationist, Philippe Buchez (1796–1865) became the president of the Constitutional Assembly, though he was soon removed from that post. Buchez, a doctor of medicine, anticipated Blanc's main idea. In 1831 he founded an association of cabinetmakers that served as a model for later producer cooperatives. Buchez believed that associations could provide a means of creating the new society within the womb of the existing one.[7] He undertook to reconcile religion and social progress and so initiated the development of Christian socialism.

Louis Blanc demanded universal suffrage to enable workers to compel the state to set up national workshops. The German workers' leader Ferdinand Lassalle, influenced by Blanc, came to the same conclusion in the 1860s. Lassalle expected the state to provide capital and credit that would enable workers to organize production cooperatives, dispense with employers, and appropriate for themselves the whole product of their collective work.

The appearance of self-governing workshops in France, in association with the work of Louis Blanc, influenced a group of English Christian socialists who formed the Society for Promoting Working Men's Associations and succeeded in establishing several workshops. In Hungary, Blanc's ideas were followed by Jozsef Kritovics, who advocated the introduction of manhood suffrage and the establishment of self-governing national workshops whose initial capital was to be provided by the state. Lassallean influence was considerable in Hungary in the late 1860s. All developments were criticized severely by Marx, who considered it both absurd and treasonable to expect the emancipation of the working class from the bourgeois state.

Given the historical conditions of the time, Marx was right, as the complete failure of Blanc's and Lassalle's attempts amply demonstrate. Yet, somewhat more than a century later, the Chilean government was providing capital for self-managing agricultural cooperatives, and the Peruvian government was also supplying capital to worker-managed agroindustrial and industrial enterprises. Blanc's mutual reserve funds, administered by industrial councils, were introduced in the Yugoslav economy under the same name and were used to cover the losses of collectives encountering difficulties.

A complete vision of self-governing society was described for the first time in the voluminous writings of *Pierre Joseph Proudhon* (1809–65). Proudhon was born in Besançon, the birthplace of Fourier. The only proletarian among the visionaries, he was a man with great intuition but very little formal education. His father was a cooper and a domestic brewer; his mother, a peasantwoman. Proudhon was apprenticed in the printing trade, became a press corrector, and educated himself by studying the volumes he corrected. Later he taught himself bookkeeping and engaged in various business ventures. As a young printer in Lyon, he set in type the new version of Fourier's major work, *Le nouveau monde industrial* (1829). The Revolution of 1848 brought Proudhon into the National Assembly, together with Buchez, Blanc, and Considérant. But Proudhon's political activities soon landed him in jail, where he remained for several years. After the publication of his book *De la justice dans la révolution et dans l'église* in 1858, he was charged with "attacking the right of the family, outraging public and religious morality and disrespecting the law." To avoid persecution he emigrated to Belgium, where he remained until 1862.

Like Fourier, Proudhon set for himself the task of completing the unfinished work of the French Revolution. The French Revolution had failed, he held, because it was limited to political reform; liberty and equality had to be extended to the economic sphere, to establish *economic democracy.* In a way similar to Fourier, Proudhon derived the institutions of the good society from the characteristics of human nature. The supreme principle is *justice.* Justice is given, along with labor, and together they represent an unchanging feature of human nature. From the principle of justice are derived the ideals of *liberty* and *equality.* Liberty is the fundamental precondition for justice. Thus the social order should be structured so as to enable every individual to enjoy full freedom. All people, endowed with identical reason and eager to preserve dignity, are equal before justice. Consequently, the development of consciousness determines the pace of social development as well as relations among men. When a man comes to know his true nature, external coercion to maintain discipline becomes unnecessary. If wealth is distributed approximately equally, people can cooperate in the society without the interventions of an authoritarian state. The way to abolish the state is to dissolve it in its economic organization and to decentralize it by transferring all power to local units, the communes. In both cases the principal instrument is the contract as the basis for reciprocal justice, which precludes the violation of anyone's freedom. This means that each man is free to make arrangements with other men as he pleases, provided this is done on the basis of free bargaining.

Economic organization, based on free contracting, leads to *mutuellisme:* equitable exchange, equalization of business conditions, and equitable cooperation of individuals with personal freedoms preserved. The institution responsible for such an economic organization would be the Banque d'échange, the only central institution that would remain in Proudhon's society. The bank would determine the labor value of commodities and issue the appropriate receipts to producers. (One recognizes the old naive idea of labor money suggested already by Owen, and by anticapitalist economists John Gray [1799–1850] and J. F. Bray [1809–95]. It was to be resurrected in the Spanish anarchist collectives in 1936–38, after the Campuchian revolution, and elsewhere.) There would be no money and credit would be reduced to "exchange in which one partner gives his product at once, while the other supplies it in several installments, all without interest."[8] Since production would be carried out at the order of the consumer, supply and demand would be in equilibrium. Large private productive properties are clearly incompatible with the system of reciprocal justice and ought to be abolished. But small private property is acceptable. When technological conditions required the employment of many workers, private property would be replaced by collective property of workers' associations. Workers would come together to set up enterprises on the basis of contracts stipulating mutual rights and obligations. The initial capital would be provided by the Exchange Bank. When a worker left an enterprise, he would take with him a certain amount of money, corresponding to his past labor. Individual producers and associations would federate themselves into industries and into a national economy on the basis of contracts. The national economy would be an agroindustrial federation. Contrary to Louis Blanc's formula, reciprocal justice, reflected in equitable exchange, requires that the reward for work be proportionate to service.

Mutualism in the political sphere is federalism. A commune would be created through a contract among a certain number of family heads. Communes would be federated into provinces and states. The decisions of central organs would become obligatory only when accepted by the communes. Proudhon considered traditional representative democracy as unsatisfactory because it represents the rule of the majority, which restricts the freedom of the minority. Also, no man can really represent another. Thus all individuals should participate in political decision making, and there can be no hierarchy in the political organization of the society. The most important central political organ would be the Assembly of the confederation. It would be composed of provincial delegates, who at the same time would be representatives of communes. The delegates would elect an Executive Commission, which would carry out the decisions of the Assembly. Political parties would be superfluous in such a system in which citizens retained their sovereignty.

In short, the new social order would be based on mutualism in economics and federalism in politics. In this way nonearned incomes and exploitation would be eliminated, social classes abolished, and social revolution achieved. Equilibrium among various individual interests, brought about by mutualism, represents a new social order that needs no coercion for its maintenance. Looking now a century back, one can conclude that Proudhon's vision was a remarkable anticipation of a modern—and still, to a certain extent, future—self-governing society. Proudhon touched on all important aspects of this society. But his handling of the problems was hopelessly naive, confused, and often just plainly wrong. The idea of labor money was economically untenable, and when an Exchange Bank was created, it soon went bankrupt. Collective ownership is incompatible with income based on labor only. So is gratuitous credit. The equilibration of supply and demand is an immensely more complicated affair than Proudhon even suspected. So is the functioning of the state. Free bargaining does not automatically eliminate the inequality in and abuse of political power, and so forth. Proudhon's solutions to the problems were inadequate or wrong partly because it was inherently quite difficult to solve the problems of a late-twentieth-century society in a mid-nineteenth-century environment. But it is also true that many mistakes were at least partly avoidable and were due to his deficient and unsystematic training. Proudhon extensively discussed questions of economics, political organization, philosophy, and law with no background of learning in any of these disciplines. Therefore it is hardly surprising that Karl Marx was one of the first and most outspoken critics of Proudhon. At the beginning, Marx and Proudhon were friends. They held in common certain fundamental ideas such as the withering away of the state, the elimination of unearned incomes and exploitation, the disappearance of money, and the creation of a classless society. But Marx, a man of great learning, soon found Proudhon's professional ignorance—and intellectual arrogance (a quality that frequently accompanies it)—utterly irritating. In 1847 Marx wrote a book-length critique (*Misère de la philosophie*) of Proudhon's views, particularly the economic views expressed in the latter's book, *Philosophie de la misère,* published a year before. Marx complained that Proudhon treated economic categories as eternal ideas instead of approaching them as theoretical expressions of historical conditions in production corresponding to a certain level of development of material production. He found Proudhon's knowledge of political economy—whose critique he undertook—partial and totally insufficient. In an article written in 1865, after Proudhon's death, at the request of the newspaper *Social-Democrat,* Marx scathingly described Proudhon's "self-boasting and conceited tone, particularly that always unpleasant chatter about science. . . . This is accompanied by the clumsy and disgusting pretention to scholarship of a self-taught person."[9] By "chattering about science," Proudhon also coined the famous expression "scientific socialism."

What Marx found wrong in Proudhon's confused and unprofessional writings must have appealed to other less learned men—in addition, of course, to the inherent value of his ideas. Proudhon's influence was predominant among Parisian workers in the 1850s and 1860s. In the early days of the First International, Proudhonists controlled its French section. The French cooperative and trade union movements were also influenced by his ideas. The Paris Commune of 1871 was dominated by Proudonists and Blanquists, and the former were responsible for the economic decrees of the commune. Proudhon was the first to introduce the word *anarchism,*[10] and his international influence was greatest among anarchists. Proudhon's ideas can be found as well in the guild socialist thinking at the time of the First World War. It is also of some interest to record the revival of Proudhonism a century later in a completely different environment. Although Proudhon is practically unknown in Yugoslavia—except in the utterly negative version presented by Marx—the official thinking of the 1960s and 1970s and some institutional solutions bear a striking resemblance to several of Proudhon's ideas. The enterprise is conceived as an association based on a contract among workers. Mutualism at higher levels is reflected in bargaining among associations, termed *samoupravno sporazumijevanje* [self-management agreement] when bargaining is sectoral, and *društveno dogovaranje* [social compact] when bargaining is general and involves state authorities. The "right to past labor," guaranteed by the Constitution, sets forth a worker's stake in enterprise capital apart from current wages. In political thinking, the withering away of the state and of political parties is accepted as a goal. Federalism is the main principle of political organization. The communes enjoy great autonomy, and the relatively small federal states retain sovereignty, at least in principle. The federal government is an Executive Committee of the Assembly and is called so. It cannot act before the constituent states have agreed as to a particular decision. Directly elected representatives are to be replaced by the delegates of work associations and of local political bodies.

After Proudhon's death—at the beginning of the final third of the nineteenth century—the time for conceiving utopias had already passed. The problems to be solved were of an immediate and very practical nature. Yet utopian schemes and ideas continued to appear. Two interesting books deserve brief mention: *News from Nowhere* (1891) by W. Morris, and *Freiland* (1890) by T. Hertzka.

William Morris (1834–96), an artist and an activist in the British socialist movement, described in his book—as he himself put it—the kind of society in which he would feel most at home. Instead of just commodities produced for the market by workers in an alienating environment, everything made ought to be "a joy to the maker and a joy to the user."[11] The state would wither away when the minds of a sufficient number of people had been changed to enable them to lead the masses toward a free association. Social and economic life would be based on the spontaneous activities of relatively small groups.

Theodor Hertzka (1845–1924), an Austrian Jew born in Budapest and by profession a journalist, is the only alien in the

Anglo-French company of visionaries. Like others, Hertzka detested capitalism. But the way to destroy it, in his opinion, lay neither in engineering violent revolutions nor in appealing to the government to carry out reforms. The former repelled him, the latter he found futile. He would lead a group of pioneers into an area still uninfested by capitalism—in his novel *Freiland,* he chose the highlands of Kenya—where they would set up self-governing communes. The perfectly free movement of labor and capital would eliminate all unearned incomes and exploitation. Each worker would be free to choose where to work; because of diminishing returns, this would equalize incomes and eliminate rent and profit. The system would be closed by the introduction of gratuitous credit provided by the community, which would eliminate interest. The prosperity of Freiland would induce one country after another to adopt the same social system. It need hardly be mentioned that the economics—and politics—of Hertzka are utterly naive. Yet in his insistence on the perfected market as one of the instruments of social organization, Hertzka foreshadowed so-called market socialism, which appeared in the next century. In 1893 Hertzka announced the first Freiland expedition, to set sail the next year from Hamburg to Africa. But the British authorities refused to grant passage to Kenya, thus killing the project. In his own days Hertzka attracted a considerable following, chiefly among intellectuals. Freeland associations were formed in a number of continental countries, Great Britain, and the United States. Hertzka's book is said to have influenced Australian Labour leader William Lane to lead five hundred pioneers to Paraguay, where in 1893 they established the colony of New Australia. After six years, internal dissension and the unfavorable climate brought this experiment to an end.[12]

The visionaries cleared the ground. They provided the conceptual framework. They or their followers even invented the very word *socialism.* It was in November 1827 that *Co-operative Magazine*, founded by Owen's followers in England, used the term "communionists and socialists" to denote adherents to Owen's doctrine. For Owen himself, "social" was the opposite of "selfish." In February 1832, the Saint-Simonist journal *Le globe*, whose editor was Pierre Leroux and one of whose journalists was Auguste Blanqui, introduced the word *socialisme.* The next year, in the essay "De l'individualisme et du socialisme," Leroux successfully popularized the new term.[13] The word *communism* was coined in the secret revolutionary societies of Paris between 1834 and 1839. After the publication of

Étienne Cabet's *Voyage en Icarie* in 1840, the word *communism* was used mainly to designate his theory. By 1848, when the *Communist Manifesto* was published, socialism tended to be associated with various utopias, and so the term *communism* was chosen to refer to the working class struggle.

III. Movements

By the middle of the nineteenth century, the primitive accumulation of capital had already been accomplished in the most advanced countries, the Industrial Revolution had been carried out, and the development of a new social order was in full swing. In the ideological sphere, isolated individuals were to be replaced by broad movements. The new social order, capitalism, generated a new exploited class, the industrial proletariat. Numerous strikes, industrial warfare, and illegal trade unions demonstrated the gradual emergence of its class consciousness. There was a pressing social need to provide a theoretical explanation of the dynamics of the new order and a moral need to provide a defense for its victims. Both were superbly accomplished by *Karl Marx* (1818–83) and *Friedrich Engels* (1820–95). Thus, historically, *Marxism* appears as a theory of the emancipation of the emerging working class. Since the proletariat is the exploited class, by emancipating themselves workers will emancipate the society at large; they will destroy the class society and establish socialism. Consequently, socialist movements appeared to be essentially working class movements, where "working class" refers primarily to the industrial proletariat.

Around the middle of the last century, political democracy was still in its infancy, voting rights were severely restricted, and trade unions were not legal. The state was completely dominated by the propertied classes, which showed no desire to allow their privileges to be infringed in the least. Thus no political channels existed for even small social reforms to be carried out, not to speak of radical changes. Radicals could see only one instrument of social transformation: a violent revolution foreshadowed by the great French Revolution. And, indeed, the history of the nineteenth century in Europe is characterized by a great number of revolutionary upheavals in many countries.

Very naturally, Marxism is primarily a theory, and an ideology, of the *revolutionary* emancipation of the working class, as a result of which "the proletariat will be organized as a ruling class" (*Communist Manifesto*). In order to fight the bourgeoisie successfully, the proletariat ought to be well organized. Hence the need for political centralization and for disciplined political parties. Once workers' parties were formed in the second half of the last century, they generally accepted Marxism as their ideology.[14] As a consequence, the first two Internationals were dominated by Marxism.

Yet, Marxism is a (critical) theory of capitalism and its destruction, not a theory of socialism. Even in his first writings, Marx declared (and that was intended as the program of *Deutsch Französische Jahrbücher* of which he was an editor in 1844): "If the designing of the future and the proclamation of ready-made solutions for all time is not our affair, then we realize all the more clearly what we have to accomplish in the present—I am speaking of a *ruthless criticism of everything existing*." Marx wrote on socialism only rarely and unwillingly—mostly when pressed to do so. He thought it utopian to write on a society that did not exist. Besides, it was unnecessary. Since capitalism could be replaced only by socialism, all that mattered was to find the ways and means to destroy capitalism. The future men will be no less intelligent than we, Engels added, in deciding what to do next. There were pressing current problems to be solved; thus idle speculation about the future might be positively harmful by distracting attention and energy from the important daily tasks. The latter pragmatic attitude was prevalent among the political leaders of the social democratic parties. As a consequence, organized socialist movements were very little concerned with socialism; their energy was absorbed in fighting capitalism and exacting small improvements when possible. Even worse, fighting a stronger enemy, they unwittingly adopted his attitudes. And when the great day eventually arrived, the day after a victorious revolution, they could do no better than simply turn the bourgeois society upside down. They did not know how to replace it by a basically different society. Instead of socialism, etatism turned out to be the next social system.

These historically determined contradictions have caused great confusion in the evaluation of Marxian socialist thought. It is therefore necessary to clarify this point by letting Marx speak for himself.[15] As a twenty-five-year-old youth, then a bourgeois radical, Marx was enthusiastic over the idea of human liberation:

> Man, who would be a spiritual being, a free man—a republican. Petty bourgeoisie will not be one or the other. . . . What they want is to live and multiply. . . . that's what animals want. . . . Man's feeling of his own values, freedom, should be awakened in the breast of these people. Only this feeling . . . can again make of society a community of men for the realization of their greatest aim: a democratic state.

In its mature form, the same idea appeared seven years later in the *Communist Manifesto*, written together with Engels:

> In place of the old bourgeois society, with its classes and class antagonisms, we shall have an association in which the free development of each is the condition for the free development of all.

Many years later Marx explained (*Critique of the Gotha Programme*, 1875) that

> freedom is when the state is transformed from an organ that is dominant over society into an organ that is completely subordinate. . . .

Engels naturally agreed, and elaborated (*Anti-Dühring*, 1878):

> When there is no longer any social class to be held in subjection; when class rule and the individual struggle for existence based upon our present anarchy in production . . . are removed, nothing more remains to be repressed, and a special repressive force, a state, is no longer necessary. The first act by virtue of which the state really constitutes itself the representative of the whole of society—the taking possession of the means of production in the name of society—that is, at the same time, its last independent act as a state. State interference in social relations becomes, in one domain after another, superfluous, and then dies out by itself; the government of persons is replaced by the administration of things. . . .

The last phrase is, of course, a reproduction of the famous Saint-Simonian idea. And the beginning of the paragraph reminds one of Proudhonian anarchism. While the entire passage implies that an authoritarian political system—a dominant coercive state—is by itself a proof of the existence of a class society, not a few modern political movements which call themselves Marxist derive an exactly opposite conclusion: namely, that "taking possession of the means of production" and operating them by appointed state officials is the essence of socialism! It will not be surprising that the two men who held the ideas quoted above greeted the Paris Commune of 1871 enthusiastically. "The Commune," Marx wrote,

> at the very beginning had to acknowledge that the working class, coming into power, could not rule with the old state machinery . . . that it had to secure itself against its own deputies and employees, proclaiming that all of them, without exception, were dispensable at any time.

Nor is this all:

> The Paris Commune had, of course, to serve as the source for all the large industrial centres of France. As soon as Paris, and other centres, were brought into communal administration, the old *centralized* authority had to be replaced in the provinces by *self-managing* producers. [Emphasis added]

Decentralization does not mean particularism:

> The unity of the nation was not to be broken, but, on the contrary, to be organized by the Communal organization. It was to become a reality by the destruction of the state power which claimed to be the embodiment of that unity but which wanted to be independent of, and superior to, the nation itself. (*Civil War in France*, 1871)

As to the worker-producer, Engels explained ten years later, "the worker is free only when he becomes the owner of his own means of production," where ownership is to be interpreted in terms of social, not state or collective, ownership.

It follows that Marxian socialism means the destruction of the authoritarian state, communal decentralization, and producers' self-management. This is very different from the way in which many people, both sympathizers and adversaries, interpret Marxism today. But this does not deny the fact that Marx and Engels were also centralistically oriented, and that they thought, or implied, that individual freedom in self-governing socialism can be achieved by centralistic means, primarily by central administrative planning that would eliminate market, money, and commodity relations. No doubt, historical experience makes clear that Marxian means and ends were not fully consistent. No doubt, too, if Marx and Engels had lived to see later developments, they would have changed means, not ends.

When faced with the choice, many of their vulgar followers did the other way round.

In 1864 representatives of English and French trade unions (the latter were still illegal and existed under the guise of friendly societies), together with exiles from various countries, established the International Working Men's Association in London, later to be known as the First International. Marx wrote the *Founding Manifesto*. The *Manifesto* surveyed economic and social developments since the Revolution of 1848 and, among other facts, recorded that in England and Wales three thousand persons received annually an income larger than the aggregate income of all agricultural workers. More important for our purpose is Marx's evaluation of cooperative work. The *Manifesto* pointed out that, though cooperative work is important in principle and useful in practice, it would never be able to stop the expansion of monopolies nor alleviate the burden of misery. In order to liberate the working masses, cooperative labor had to be developed on a national scale, which required national means of finance. But the owners of land and capital would use their political privileges to prevent this from happening. The same idea was expanded somewhat a year later in Marx's instruction to the delegates of the General Council to the Geneva Congress of the International. The merit of the cooperative movement was seen to lie in the fact that it indicated the possibility for replacing the existing system, in which labor was subject to capital, by a system of association of free and equal producers. But the latter could be achieved only after producers assumed state power.

The issue of producers' cooperatives was discussed at the Geneva (1866), Lausanne (1867), and Brussels (1868) congresses of the First International. The first of these congresses declared its support for the promotion of producers' cooperation, but stressed the inadequacy of voluntary cooperation as the basis of the social system. The second called on unions to support cooperatives by investing in them and by providing moral support. The third congress pronounced in favor of cooperative ownership in manufacturing aided by gratuitous credit through mutual banks—an influence of Proudhon—and for communal ownership of land cultivated by agricultural cooperatives. Cooperatives were also discussed at the Copenhagen Congress of the Second International (1910). Yet the resolution spoke only of consumer cooperatives; no mention was made of producers' and agricultural cooperatives. Lenin suggested an amendment declaring that cooperatives would be able to play a socializing and democratizing role only after the expropriation of capitalists, but the amendment was rejected by a large majority.

At this point, it may be useful to evaluate the role of cooperatives in socialist development. The first French and first Owenite producers' cooperatives were conceived as an instrument of social transformation. So, to a large extent, were the two hundred—mostly unsuccessful—cooperative mills, mines, shops, and factories organized by the Knights of Labor in the 1870s and the 1880s in the United States. Yet producers' cooperatives, in a capitalist environment, turned out to be a failure. Except in agriculture, they either degenerated into capitalist partnership or joint stock companies or just disintegrated. Cooperatives encountered insurmountable difficulties in obtaining the necessary credit—hence the many attempts to set up various kinds of mutual banks—and, because of their egalitarian distribution of income, could not attract the best managerial personnel. If, in spite of both handicaps, they survived in the competition, the founding members tended to treat newcomers as hired labor, which of course signaled the beginning of the end. As for consumers' cooperation, there was nothing particularly socialist about it. By the 1850s in Britain, it had lost its connection with the Owenite new society. When the better-paid skilled workers could afford to invest in cooperative societies, they were interested primarily in direct benefits: unadulterated goods, fair prices, dividends on purchases, and safe investment—a list of goals to which any good bourgeois would subscribe. To make things even worse, cooperatives occasionally were used to prevent any socialist development. Germany is a case in point. Here the conservative promoter of cooperatives, Victor Huber, treated them as an alliance between the traditional order and the workers against the claims of the bourgeoisie, while the well-known liberal cooperative organizer, Hermann Schulze-Delitzsch, expected them to strengthen free enterprise by educating working class entrepreneurs.

One of the characteristics of the last years of the First International was a continuing struggle between Marxists, who favored political action and centralization of the organization, and anarchists, who opposed both. At the Hague Congress (1872), which was the last, anarchists and federalists were greatly outvoted. The defeated minority then decided to reconstitute the International (the attempts failed) on the basis of complete decentralization and to keep separate meetings in the future (which they did). At the Geneva (1873) and Brussels (1874) meetings, Belgian labor leader César de Paepe (1842–90) was the principal speaker in favor of workers' self-management. Workers' groups, he contended, ought to produce under the supervision of local communes. The commune would own the land and main capital assets. Every worker would participate in political decision making by giving delegates imperative instructions. Communes would be joined into a confederation.[16] One recognizes the influence of Proudhon, whose ideas had been absorbed into the anarchist teachings of the time.

Anarchists can be divided into individualists, and collectivists or anarchocommunists. The former are few—among them Max Stirner in Germany and Benjamin Tucker in the United States—and have nothing to do with socialism. The latter are many—Bakunin, Kropotkin, Réclus, Jean Grave, Emil Pouget—and advocate some sort of utopian libertarian socialism. They demand the abolition of private property and would replace the coercive state with a free federation organized from below. In the 1890s anarchocollectivists reemerged as revolutionary syndicalists, who organized a working class movement of considerable importance. Syndicalism also had a utopian precursor of a different kind—the only woman in our gallery of visionaries, Flora Tristan (1803–44). In 1843 she published her most important work, *L'union ouvrière*, in which she advocated small annual contributions by all workers to a fund for the emancipation of labor, the conversion of workers' unions into something like a self-governing corporation, and the international cooperation of workers. The latter became the first published project of a Workingmen's International.

Syndicalism developed in France from a rival trade union movement started in the late 1880s in opposition to the Fédération nationale des syndicats, which fell under the influence of the Guedist Parti ouvrier. Weak French unions of that time were disrupted by five contending socialist parties fighting for union support. In such a situation, political neutrality seemed the best policy. The movement aspired to establish local trade union federations, called *bourses du travail*, which would serve as labor exchanges under trade union control and as trades councils engaging in propagandist, organizing, and educational activities. In 1892 the Federation of Bourses was set up. Three years later, Fernand Pelloutier (1867–1901) became its secretary. Pelloutier laid the foundation for the movement, which attracted all those who, like himself, were disillusioned with the fights of the quarreling socialist factions and advocated revolutionary working class activity independent of political parties. Syndicalists wanted to place the management of industry in the hands of trade unions. Trade unions were to be federated locally into labor bourses, which would establish a monopoly of labor, take over the ownership of industries, and run them under local self-governing communes. Syndicalists repudiated parliamentary action, relied on a "conscious minority" instead of on thoroughly organized large unions or parties, and hoped to achieve their aim by a general strike. These characteristics of the movement—which were an obvious rationalization of a situation in which union members were few, financial resources lacking, and bargaining rights nonexistent—explain at once why the syndicalists came to be detested equally by employers and by orthodox unionists; why, by disorganizing it, their action inflicted damage on the working class movement;[17] and why they failed to realize the goal of workers' management.

In 1902 the federations of bourses and of industrial unions were amalgamated into the Confédération generale du travail (CGT). In the next four years, the industrial militancy of the French syndicalist unions reached a peak, provoking strong action by the government and a great consolidation of employers' organizations; as a consequence, syndicalists were forced to retreat, and after the First World War their ideas were basically modified. A not insignificant role in this process was played by the fact that, due to the war, unions multiplied their membership and developed into large bureaucratic structures. An important legacy of syndicalism was well summarized by Hubert Lagardelle, leader of Le mouvement socialiste group which rallied to the side of syndicalists against the parliamentary socialists: "Syndicalism had always laid down as a principle that bourgeois institutions will be eliminated only in proportion as they are replaced by working class institutions."[18]

French revolutionary syndicalism prompted the development of industrial unionism in Anglo-Saxon countries and of anarchosyndicalism in other, primarily Roman, nations. In the early 1870s, the Italian anarchist Giuseppe Fanelli introduced Bakunin's ideas to groups of workers in Madrid and Barcelona. From that time, anarchism exerted continuous influence in Spain. After the Marxist-Bakuninist split at the Hague Congress of the International in 1872, the Spanish section of the International remained predominantly anarchist. In 1916, the Confederación nacional del trabajo (CNT) was formed and patterned after the French CGT. The goal was *el comunismo libertario*. Twenty years later, Spanish anarchosyndicalists had an opportunity to test their ideas in practice, at the time of the Civil War.

In Italy an anarchosyndicalist movement developed out of local labor chambers. In 1912, the Unione sindicale italiana was formed. It had its predominant influence in Milan and Turin, where it played the dominant role in the occupation of factories in 1920. In Germany, the anarchosyndicalist Freie Arbeiter-union Deutschlands (FAUD) developed from anticentralist opposition in German unions established in 1897. Anarcho-syndicalist unions struck roots in Argentina, and also in Sweden after the defeat of the general strike in 1909.

The variant of syndicalism that spread to the United States became known as *industrial unionism.* The organization responsible for it was the Industrial Workers of the World, created in 1905 through a fusion of the mining and lumbering groups of the Far West, and the Leonite and other groups of the Midwest and eastern states. The IWW was against orthodox unions and reformist socialists, and held that the basis of working class policy should be a revolutionary class struggle for the complete overthrow of capitalism and the conquering of political power by organized workers. On other important questions, IWW members were split into several factions ranging from anarchists, who were completely opposed to political action, to the followers of Daniel De Leon, who advocated political action by a revolutionary party working in alliance with revolutionary unions. De Leon (1852–1914) was a lecturer in international law at Columbia University and considered himself a Marxist. He joined the Socialist Labor Party in 1890 and soon became its leader. De Leon saw clearly the need for a strong union and for political organization. He and his supporters thus overcame two basic weaknesses of syndicalism. But continuing factional fights prevented the establishment of an efficient organization. The IWW was based to a large extent on ill-paid immigrant workers and failed to strike firm roots in the American working class. Revolutionary unionism was more a result of lawlessness in the newly opened mining and lumbering areas of the Far West—where bitter industrial warfare raged—than an expression of lasting forces of American society. As such, it was gradually driven back and replaced by orthodox unionism. In the meantime, it provoked even more violent reaction than had syndicalism in France. A number of federal states enacted laws making the propagation of syndicalist doctrines a criminal offense. A reflection of this frame of mind is the judicial murder of two immigrant workers, Sacco and Vanzetti, in Massachusetts in the 1920s. The IWW was weakened even further after the First World War, when many members left the organization to join the newly founded Communist Party.

Syndicalism and industrial unionism spread to Australia, Canada, Mexico, Ireland, and some other countries. Industrial unionism was pioneered in Britain by James Connolly (1870–1916), an Irish labor leader, who was later executed by the English for his part in the uprising of Easter 1915 in Dublin. After a campaign to spread the ideas of Daniel De Leon, Connolly split from the existing Social Democratic Federation in 1903 to form a new Socialist Labor Party named after its American equivalent. The influence of these ideas was soon reflected in the famous manifesto of Welsh miners, *The Miners' Next Step* (1912),[19] which proclaimed the goal of the "mines to the miners" in opposition to the official union policy of nationalization. The state, the Welsh miners argued, would be no less tyrannical than private employers and a good deal more powerful. What was required was a militant industrial policy of pressing for ever increasing wages and improved conditions until mines become unprofitable for the owners. Then they will be taken over and organized under the workers' control. If other workers pursue a similar policy, the capitalist system will become unworkable, and the road will be cleared for social revolution.

Britain also produced an autochthonous movement, *guild socialism*. This somewhat strange name arose by historical accident. In 1906 A. J. Penty, a Christian socialist architect who hated capitalist industrialism, wrote a book called *The Restauration of the Gild System*, in which he advocated a return to medieval handicrafts. Soon afterward, S. G. Hobson turned Penty's ideas into something very different—workers as masters of the means of production and guilds as the agencies for running industry—which became the basis of the new movement. The most mature formulation of guild socialist ideas is to be found in the writings of G. D. H. Cole (1889–1959).

Cole quoted three fundamental assumptions of the movement: (1) essential social values are human values, and society is regarded as a complex of associations held together by the will of their members; (2) it is not sufficient for the government to have only the passive consent of the governed, for the ordinary citizen to enjoy little more than the privilege of choosing his ruler; the citizen should be called upon to rule himself, the society ought to be self-governing; (3) democracy applies not only to politics but to every form of social action. It is not poverty, but slavery and insecurity that are the worst evils of contemporary society. The position of a man in daily labor determines his position as a citizen. Without industrial democracy, political democracy can be only a pretense. "The essence of the Guild Socialist attitude lies in the belief that society ought to be so organized as to afford the greatest possible opportunity for individual and collective self-expression to all its members and that it involves and implies the extension of positive self-government through all its parts."[20] For this purpose, the omnicompetent state with its omnicompetent parliament is utterly unsuitable. Guildsmen invoked Proudhon, Kropotkin, and William Morris against the view that all political issues can be resolved only through a concentrated political power. No man can truly represent other men. The citizen must choose someone to represent his point of view only in relation to some particular purpose or group of purposes, i.e., in relation to some particular function. This *functional democracy* leads to a pluralist society in which there is no single sovereign and in which power is distributed among functional groups.

Production is to be carried out by state-chartered guilds of workers based on trade unions. "A National Guild would be an association of all the workers by hand and by brain concerned in the carrying on of a particular industry or service, and its function would be actually to carry on that industry or service on behalf of the whole community."[21] In addition to the producers' organizations or economic guilds, there are to be three more functional organizations: consumers' organizations or cooperatives and collective utility councils; civic service organizations or civic guilds (for the professions excluding the ministry); and citizens' organizations or cultural and health councils. In contrast to these four functional organizations, there is to be one communal organization with two major tasks: (a) coordinating functional bodies into a single communal system; and (b) coordinating bodies operating over smaller areas with bodies operating over larger areas. All functional bodies are represented on the communal boards, and all these representatives taken together represent the commune.

The commune will have five tasks to perform: (1) it will allocate local resources and to a certain extent regulate incomes and prices; (2) it will serve as a court of appeal for the conflicts of the functional bodies; (3) it will determine the line of demarcation between functional bodies; (4) it will decide on matters concerning the town as a whole, such as the construction of a new town hall; (5) it will operate the coercive machinery. "The national co-ordinating machinery of Guild Society would be essentially unlike the present state, and would have few direct administrative functions. It would be mainly a source of a few fundamental decisions on policy, demarcation between functional bodies . . . and of final adjudication on appeals in cases of disputes. . . . Into the National Commune. . . . would enter the representatives of the National Guilds, Agricultural, Industrial and Civic, of the National Councils economic and civic, and of the Regional Communes. . . . "[22]

Functional representation in the political sphere leading to political pluralism and a severe reduction of traditional state authoritarianism, and self-management in all work organizations—this is the essence of guild socialism. This is also the essence of the self-governing organization of a truly socialist society.

Guildsmen initially comprised a group of intellectuals, some of them Oxford dons. Only after 1912 did the movement begin to attract workers; it became widely influential after 1914. In 1915, the National Guilds League was formed. It exerted great influence on the shop stewards' movement and on several unions. The experience in the shop stewards' movement, on the other hand, induced J. M. Paton to formulate the policy of *encroaching control*, of progressive invasion of capitalist autocracy.[23] By gradually assuming the controlling functions in industry, workers would deprive the owners of active or useful participation in the industry from which they drew their incomes. Owners would be reduced to a useless appendage, to be swept away relatively easily at the time of final transition. Atrophy of the functions of the possessing class would destroy its moral claims to its rights; the "busy rich" would change into the "idle rich" and then would be "expropriated." The other policy of transition advocated by guildsmen was the capture of the state by the working class in order to take industry under public ownership. After that, Parliament would hand over the task of administration to the national guilds (former trade unions) within the terms of a parliamentary charter.

Neither policy really worked. During and after the war, a number of small guilds were created. The most important was the movement to reorganize the building industry as a national guild in which employers were to become salaried administrators, subject to election by the workers employed—a remarkable resurrection of the Owenite building guild of 1834! At first the building guilds were quite successful, which Cole explains as due to the fact that ordinary housebuilding requires almost no fixed capital and that there was a heavy demand for houses. Guilds charged lower prices, rendered services of higher quality, and attracted the best workers. In the first postwar depression in 1922–23, however, the movement collapsed, and a year later guild socialism as an organized movement was dead in Britain.[24] Some of its key workers joined the Communist Party. Immediately after the war, national guilds leagues spread to South Africa, Australia, and Japan—but then also died out.

IV. Revolutions

If the first wave brought into existence individual socialist ideologues and isolated groups, and the second gave rise to organized movements, the third wave produced the first realizations. Broadly speaking, the European revolutions of 1848 mark the time when the working class emancipated itself and asserted itself as a separate social class. It might be supposed that, in the revolutions which were to follow, the working class would attempt to establish industrial self-management and, perhaps more generally, social self-government. Let us examine this hypothesis in light of the events that actually took place.[25]

The era of proletarian revolutions began with the *Paris Commune* of 1871. Self-government has two fundamental components: functional and territorial. From the very beginning the commune developed both of these components. Politically it developed a fully participatory democracy. In the industrial sphere, the commune passed a decree by which industry was to be reorganized on a cooperative basis and enterprises run by workers. The positive experience of the Paris Commune, the heroism of its citizens, and the tragic outcome of their fighting inspired many individuals—Marx and Lenin, among others—groups, and entire movements. In particular, eighty years later it exerted great influence, through the writings of Marx, on the development of workers' self-management in Yugoslavia. Though Yugoslav institutional arrangements and social theory reflect many ideas contained in Proudhonism or guild socialism, there is no historical continuity here; these ideas were not known in Yugoslavia and were discovered anew. Marx's evaluation of the commune was well known, however, and influenced thinking and action in a most direct manner.

The next in time was the *Russian Revolution* of 1905. It produced soviets, a specifically Russian institution of revolutionary power. Since the soviets were to play a great role in future revolutionary developments, a brief description of their origin is in order. In January 1905, after a strike, troops killed

1,000 workers and wounded 5,000 more demonstrating in the streets of Petrograd. This set in motion a wave of strikes throughout the entire country. In May 30,000 workers in the textile center of Ivanovo Voznesensk stopped working and elected delegates to an assembly of 151 members. This body assumed not only the conduct of the strike but also political power and created its own militia and court. That was the first soviet. Others soon followed, the most famous of which was the Petrograd soviet acting under the leadership of Trotsky. In October, 2 million workers participated in a general strike. Soviets then existed in some fifty-odd cities: workers elected delegates who gathered together in city soviets. The first workers' demands were traditional unionist demands concerning wages and working conditions. But these were soon surpassed by more radical demands, such as the eight-hour working day, which became largely political after the October general strike (an end to autocracy, creation of a constituent assembly, freedom of speech and assembly). The tsar was forced to grant concessions, and promised the guarantee of civil liberties and establishment of a parliament. As soon as the situation was again under control, the soviets were liquidated, and most of the concessions taken back.

As we have seen, the soviets developed out of strike committees with the participation of political parties. Their appearance was completely spontaneous, and bore no relation to any established theory or political strategy; yet they look as if they were the outcome of industrial unionism. The functional and territorial-political components of self-government are still undifferentiated in a soviet. But the tendency is for the latter to predominate, and, during the general strike, soviets became local executive authorities largely replacing the municipal authorities.

Both the Paris Commune and the Russian Revolution were crushed, and workers' self-government did not survive them. The destiny of the second Russian revolution, the *Great October Socialist Revolution* of 1917, was different, however. The chain of events was started by a strike of Petrograd female textile workers on February 23 (March 8 according to the new calendar). Four days later, a soviet was created as a joint organ of Petrograd workers and soldiers. The number of members—delegates of factories and of military units—soon reached 2,000. Order no. 1 of the soviet, most of whose members were soldiers, was that all military units should set up committees composed of representatives elected among the lower ranks. A month later Lenin wrote his famous *April Theses* urging that the bourgeois-democratic revolution be transformed into a socialist one. His battle cry was: Power to the soviets! Land to the peasants! Peace to the people! To which the workers soon added: Factories to the workers! In the same month, at a Bolshevik conference, the Ural delegate Sverdlov reported that in his region workers had taken over some factories and that it was believed that the soviets would have to assume management of the factories if the owners refused to operate them. On May 23 the provisional government issued a decree that legalized *factory committees* but attempted to limit them to consultative bodies. Factory committees soon transcended these limits, however; in particular, when there was danger of a factory close-down, they would assume the management of production. Such workers' takeovers have since become a typical form for the spontaneous introduction of self-management and have been practiced in many countries. In Latin America, they have become known as *las tomas de fábricas*.[26]

The peasant soviets appeared somewhat later, but by the summer of 1917 there were already four hundred of them in existence. In May the First Congress of Delegates of Workers' and Peasants' Soviets opened in Petrograd. The congress proclaimed the confiscation of large estates and workers' control in factories. In the same month, the First Petrograd Conference of Factory Committees took place.[27] Lenin presented a resolution arguing that workers' control represented the only way to avoid economic disaster. The resolution carried by a great majority, and the conference elected a Council of Factory Committees. After the conference Lenin explained his position more precisely by pointing out that workers' control meant control by the soviets and not "the ridiculous passing of the railroads into the hands of railwaymen, the leather factories into the hands of leather workers."

During the night of October 24–25, (old calendar) the uprising in Petrograd brought the Bolsheviks to power. The Second Congress of Soviets, then in session, decided that all power in all places should pass into the hands of the soviets of workers', soldiers', and peasants' deputies. The Soviet Republic was born.

Two weeks later the new government issued the "Decree on Workers' Control." Councils for workers' control were to supervise the entire operations of enterprises, and their decisions were to be binding for all workers. From then on, this promising development was to take a very different course.

Factory committees were to be responsible to local councils of workers' control, whose members were to be chosen from factory committees, trade unions, and workers' cooperatives. Local councils were subordinated to an All-Russian Council of Workers' Control. Since the old Central Council of Factory Committees, which grew out of the congresses of factory committees from May to October, was still in existence, the new organization implied a duality of leadership. More than that. The two bodies interpreted workers' control very differently. The Central Council issued a *Manual* explaining that the decisions of factory committees were binding on the administration of firms and that noncompliance might be punished by sequestration. The instructions of the All-Russian Council, on the other hand, reserved management for the owner and barred factory committees from confiscating the enterprise under any circumstances. A bitter controversy ensued. One of the most outspoken critics of the Central Council's approach was the Bolshevik trade unionist A. Lozovski, who in his book *Workers' Control,* argued that it "abolished the entrepreneur" and made the factory committee "the boss of the given enterprise," and pointed out that such transfer of factories to the workers was "not only not socialism but, on the contrary, a step backward, a strengthening of the capitalist mode of production, albeit along new lines."[28]

The debate was soon streamlined by practical measures. On December 1 the Supreme Economic Council was created. It abolished the All-Russian Council of Workers' Control and made the control function a component of the overall task of regulating the economy. It coordinated a network of local economic councils [*sovnarkhozy*]. Thus one rival body was eliminated.

Bolsheviks were now arguing that there was no need for separate workers' organizations after the conquest of power, as in the time when factory committees exerted workers' control and trade unions organized the struggle against the bourgeoisie. In January 1918, the First All-Russian Congress of Trade Unions decided to transform factory committees into primary trade union organs. This device—killing workers' self-management by unionizing it—would later be used in other countries as well. And so would the justification given by Larin at the meeting of the All-Russian Council of Workers' Control: that "the trade unions represent the interests of the class as a whole whereas the Factory Committees only represent particular interests."[29] The decision did not pass unopposed, however. At the Second Congress of the Comintern many delegates continued to treat factory committees—the organizations of direct producers—as more revolutionary than trade unions, which operated through leadership. Yet the congress approved the amalgamation of the two. In March the Central Council of Petrograd Factory Committees disappeared, absorbed by the *sovnarkhozy* of the northern industrial region.[30] In *Immediate Tasks of the Soviet Power,* Lenin wrote that it must be learned how to harmonize the tumultuous democracy of the working masses with iron discipline at the work place, with absolute submission to the will of one single person—the Soviet leader—in the process of work. He claimed that "the revolution demands, precisely in the interests of socialism, that the masses *unquestionably obey the single will* of the leaders of the labour process." These views were not left unchallenged. In April 1918, V. V. Osinsky wrote in *Kommunist* that the construction of the proletarian society was to be achieved "by the class creativity of workers themselves, not by ukazy of 'captains of industry.' . . . Socialism and socialist organization must be set up by the proletariat itself, or they will not be set up at all; something else will be set up—state capitalism."[31]

In May and June large sectors of the national economy were nationalized. At the same time, the First Congress of the Soviets of the National Economy was held. The congress decided that, in nationalized enterprises, management committees be composed of workers' representatives elected by trade union members (one-third) and of members appointed by the regional or supreme council of the national economy (two-thirds).[32]

The shift from workers' committees to union control continued in 1919 and reached a climax at the Eighth Party Congress in March. The famous point 5 of the new Party Program proclaimed:

> The organizational apparatus of socialized industry ought to be based in the first instance on the Trade Unions. . . . Participating already . . . in all local and central organs in industrial administration, the Trade Unions ought in the end actually to concentrate in their hands all the administration of the entire national economy. . . . The participation of the Trade Unions in economic management . . . constitutes also the chief means of the struggle against the bureaucratization of the economic apparatus. . . .[33]

A French syndicalist would have scarcely any complaint. Yet proclaiming does not necessarily mean implementing. The next party congress, held a year later, marked the turning point. The raging civil war, with its concomitant shortages and sabotage, required—or at least so it appeared—the strict centralization and military organization of all of social life. Preobrazhensky and democratic centralists attacked the idea of one-man management. Shliapnikov, the former commissar of labor, called for a separation of powers between the party, soviets, and unions. Lenin insisted that the party could not agree that political leadership alone should belong to the party and economic leadership to trade unions. His view prevailed. It was argued that management by individuals does not infringe upon the rights of the working class or of the unions because the class may exercise its rule in various forms depending on expediency. For it is the ruling class at large that appoints persons for managerial jobs.[34] How true!

Tensions mounted. Crucial events spilled after one another in rapid succession. The climax was soon to be reached. In March 1920 Kropotkin, who lived in Dmitrov, wrote his first letter to Lenin. It contained a warning: "One thing is certain: even if the dictatorship of the party were an efficient means for the destruction of the capitalist system . . . , *it is an enormous obstacle to establishing socialism*" [emphasis in original].[35] Lenin neither replied nor understood the warning.[36] In July 1920, Trotsky wrote:

> it would be a most crying error to confuse the question as to the supremacy of the proletariat with the question of boards of workers at the head of factories. The dictatorship of the proletariat is expressed in the abolition of private property in the means of production, in the supremacy over the whole soviet mechanism of the collective will of the workers and not at all in the form in which individual economic enterprises are administered.[37]

Shliapnikov, Aleksandra Kollontai, and a number of trade union leaders formed an oppositional group called the Workers' Opposition. The Opposition demanded workers' self-management under the control of the unions. The party could not recall the candidates nominated by the unions. Too late!

At the December Plenum of the Central Committee, Bukharin produced a resolution on industrial democracy. Lenin reacted furiously by pointing out that industrial democracy gives rise to a number of utterly false ideas and might be understood to repudiate dictatorship and management by individuals. At a party meeting on December 30, Bukharin tried to build a bridge between official party views and the Opposition, but was again rebuked by Lenin. Shliapnikov, a metal-worker and the leader of the Opposition, asked that an All-Russian Producers' Congress be convened to elect the central management of the entire national economy.[38] On January 25, 1921, *Pravda* published a set of theses on the tasks of the trade unions prepared by Shliapnikov and thirty-seven union leaders. Theses 15, 17, 18, and 20 called for the members of the unions actively to participate in the management of the economy; for that purpose, they would elect workers' committees, which would form the basic organizational cells of particular industries. These committees would manage the firms under the guidance of the unions. Somewhat more than a month later, the sailors of Kronstadt (a town and naval fortress near Petrograd) rebelled. Cold and famine provoked discontent in Petrograd. The Civil War was over, and workers expected the promises of the Revolution to be fulfilled. On February 24, strikes broke out. On February 28, the crew of a battleship voted a resolution—later widely accepted—that demanded new elections for the soviets, freedom of speech and of the press for workers, peasants, and all socialists, the right of assembly, and the liberation of socialist political prisoners. The Provisional Revolutionary Committee was formed at a mass assembly on March 2. On March 7, the government launched a military attack against Kronstadt. The next day the Tenth Party Congress opened in Moscow. With the Civil War having ended only three months earlier and Kronstadt sailors calling for the "third revolution of the toilers," the delegates perceived the new state to be in grave danger. Unity was extolled. Factional rights were abolished. By March 17, the rebellion was suppressed in blood. Shortly afterward, the Workers' Opposition was declared illegal and was crushed. The trade unions soon were required to operate primarily as an instrument for persuading workers to fulfill production tasks. Former factory committees were replaced by production cells, which in 1923 developed into production conferences encharged with consultative functions and the primary task of increasing production. Workers soon became disillusioned, and the conferences withered away without ever being formally abolished.[39] The last remnants of workers' control lingered for some time in the managing triangle: director–party secretary–chairman of the trade union committee, with the director becoming more and more important. In the late twenties, Stalin removed even these remnants and in truly Weberian fashion proclaimed that the essential condition for discipline and efficiency was for the director to exercise absolute and complete control over the enterprise and to be subject only to orders from above. *Edinonachalie* [one-man management]—already foreshadowed by Lenin, who asked for an absolute submission to the will of one single individual—was adopted as the basic principle of social organization. Significantly enough, after a short while the gap between workers' wages and managerial salaries widened by several times. Workers' control was dead for the time being.

The Russian Revolution had a strong impact on revolutionary fermentation in other European countries. Soviets sprang up all over Europe. National conferences of soviets were held in Austria, Germany, and Norway in 1918 and 1919. Several thousand workers' and peasants' councils were organized by various political groups in Poland. In other countries, such as England (in Leeds in June 1917) and Switzerland (in Zurich in January 1919), soviets appeared sporadically. With a lag of a decade, they spread to Asia, where they were organized by Chinese communists and appeared in the 1930 uprising in Indochina. Workers proved able to exact constitutional and legal reforms and occasionally to assume (temporarily, of course) management of their factories. In a way, the most dramatic event was the *Hungarian Revolution,* which gave birth to the Hungarian Soviet Republic in spring 1919. Lenin sent greetings. As early as October 1918, workers' and soldiers' councils, mainly under socialist leadership, had begun to be formed in Budapest and some other places. In large factories management passed into the hands of factory workers' soviets. The Soviet government was brought to power in March 1919 by an action of the Budapest council of workers' and soldiers' deputies. The government nationalized industry and trade, and entrusted management to production commissars and factory soviets. The Soviet Republic immediately encountered strong internal and external resistance and exacerbated the situation by committing grave mistakes in adopting a rigid and dogmatic course and allowing arbitrary treatment of people, particularly in the villages. The civil war began. Hungary was attacked by the Romanians and the Czechs. After 135 days of existence, the Hungarian Soviet Republic was crushed by the combined efforts of French, Romanian, and Yugoslav troops and a small army of Hungarian emigrants. Romanian troops entered Budapest in August, and, with the arrival of Admiral Horthy in November, the white terror began. Instead of toward socialism, Hungary was heading toward fascism.

The situation was hardly less revolutionary in another country defeated in the war, *Germany.* But, unlike Hungary,

Germany was a much more developed country, with a long tradition of working class movements and a well-organized Social Democratic Party professing Marxism and advocating the revolutionary transformation of society. Yet, when the occasion arrived, the old theory proved wholly inadequate, and the main body of the party failed to move. Developments were spontaneous and forms of organization unexpected. The revolutionary movement was triggered by the refusal of the fleet in Kiel to leave the harbor for an attack on the British fleet in November 1918. The authorities reacted, of course, and hundreds of marines were jailed. The marines requested that their comrades be liberated and captured the naval bases on November 3. The next day, soldiers' councils were formed. A day later, councils of soldiers and workers met and a general strike was proclaimed. On the same day, a general strike burst out in Hamburg, and on November 6 the council of workers and soldiers assumed power. Developments were similar in Lübeck, Bremen, and other harbors. The dynasty was overthrown in Stuttgart, and on November 7 in Munich as well. Here a council of workers and soldiers assumed power and proclaimed the Bavarian Republic under the leadership of Kurt Eisner, member of the Independent Social Democratic Party formed in 1917. Over the next two days, the Revolution spread to several more provinces. On November 10, a new government was formed in Berlin consisting of two groups of Social Democrats: the right-wing majority socialists and more radical independent socialists. On the same day, the new government proclaimed that its task was "to realize the Socialist program." Friedrich Ebert, former saddlemaker and successor to Bebel as leader of the Social Democratic Party, became head of the government and, later, of the state. An assembly of councils of workers and soldiers in Berlin, representing the revolutionary movement of all of Germany, elected an Executive Committee of the councils and declared support for the government. On November 23 a joint committee of the councils and the government proclaimed political power to be vested in workers' and soldiers' councils of the German Socialist Republic. Twenty-two German monarchies perished.

On January 10, 1919, the Socialist Republic of Bremen was formed. It lasted for twenty-five days until federal government troops entered the city after a fight. The revolutionary ferment was strongest in Bavaria. On February 15, Eisner was forced to resign, and four days later the Congress of Councils—at the initiative of the majority socialists—decided to dissolve and return power to the Landtag in Munich. Just before the

Landtag opened, however, on February 21, Eisner was assassinated. Tensions increased immensely. During the night of April 6–7, the Bavarian Councils Republic (Räterepublik) was proclaimed. It lasted until May 1, when it was destroyed by the Freikorps, created and led by former imperial officers and sent by the socialist federal government. Hundreds of insurgents were murdered. "The uprooting of the Munich revolutionaries," commented G. D. H. Cole, "and the establishment of military rule which ensued, destroyed Bavarian socialism and made the city into a stronghold of counterrevolution in its most extreme forms."[40] It was Munich where Hitler started his sinister career, and his Putsch in 1923 heralded what was to come ten years later. Early in the same year, when the two councils republics were destroyed, an uprising that developed out of a protest strike in Berlin was quashed by Gustav Noske, the majority socialist commander-in-chief, with the help of the Freikorps. A year later, the Reichswehr was sent to put down the workers' revolt in Ruhr. What was supposed to be the workers' government was persecuting workers all over the country.

With the outbreak of the November 1918 Revolution, a universal call for socialization swept the country. Workers, intellectuals, civil servants, and even the bourgeoisie expected that socialization would save the country from chaos. Capitalism as an economic order seemed to have collapsed. Socialism provided the only hope for escaping complete social and economic disintegration. But what should a socialist economy look like? No one knew. How should the popular request for socialization be implemented? No one knew that either.[41] The Social Democratic Party had existed for half a century but, apart from a few platitudes, party theoreticians had never bothered to produce a program of social and economic transformation. Back in 1892, in connection with the party's Erfurt Program, chief party theoretician Karl Kautsky had written: "Few things are . . . more childish than to demand of the socialist that there be drawn a picture of the commonwealth which he strives for. . . . Never yet in the history of mankind has it happened that the revolutionary party was able to foresee, let alone determine, the forms of the new social order which it strove to usher in."[42] This idiotic dogma was faithfully adhered to. Thus, when the Social Democratic leadership were unexpectedly catapulted into government, they did not know what to do. But at least they knew what they did not want to do. Like their Bolshevik colleagues in Russia, they were determined to prevent the strengthening of the Rätebewegung (councils movement). Under pressure from below, a Committee for Socialization (Sozialisierungskommission) was appointed on November 24 under the chairmanship of Karl Kautsky. The committee met, but could not decide how to go about socialization. The bourgeois economists on the committee—Ballod, Lederer, Schumpeter, Wilbrandt—turned out to be more radical than the party and union representatives.[43] What the committee did was later described succintly—and approvingly—by one of the participants, Joseph Schumpeter, as follows:

> The idea that managers of plants should be elected by the workmen of the same plants was frankly and unanimously condemned. The workmen's councils that have grown up during the months of universal breakdown were objects of dislike and suspicion. The Committee, trying to get away as far as possible from the popular ideas about Industrial Democracy, did its best to shape them into an innocuous mold and cared little for developing their functions.[44]

In December 1918, the National Congress of Councils met in Berlin. The leading party economist, Rudolf Hilferding, read the paper "Socialization and Economy." Hilferding complained that Social Democrats had expected to come to power during a slump, with warehouses full of unsold merchandise, and then they would know what to do. Instead, they inherited a country destroyed by war, hungry and impoverished. In order not to discredit socialism, the best that could be done was to let the bourgeoisie carry out the job of rebuilding the economy. Thus, there could be no question of workers taking over factories. That would create anarchy. The fewer the obstacles, the faster would be the recovery.[45] The congress, dominated by majority socialists, voted to hand over power to the forthcoming Constituent Assembly as soon as possible. The decision was carried out in February 1919, when the Assembly met in Weimar. In the meantime, the Social Democratic government allowed two Spartacist socialist leaders, Karl Liebknecht and Rosa Luxemburg, to be murdered by the Freikorps. It looked as if the Revolution had been brought under control and that more orthodox parliamentary methods would accomplish the necessary social changes.

Yet the ignorant caution of Hilferding, Kautsky, and their colleagues and the irresponsible brutality of the government did discredit socialism. In June 1920, the elections brought defeat to the majority socialists and a right-wing party took office. The consequences were in fact much worse than this change in government might suggest. Ignorance and inactivity not only fail to contribute to the solution of difficult social problems, but can aggravate the situation beyond repair. And German problems—with the old society breaking apart, the economy disintegrating, and the victorious powers humiliating the nation politically while imposing an economically unbearable burden of reparations—were as difficult as could be imagined. A capable leadership would have turned these difficulties into a source of mass mobilization and social transformation. Not, however, the government of Fritz Ebert. The obvious precondition for any constructive action was the elimination of antirepublican, compromised, and dubious elements from the army, police, and officialdom. The strong antimilitarist and antimonarchist sentiments of the time would have rendered such measures both possible and popular. However, they were even not contemplated. Instead of allying themselves with the socialist forces, Ebert and his government relied on the "forces of order." Ebert personally made a secret arrangement with the General Staff while the government dismissed the left-wing chief of the Berlin police and authorized Noske to purge the country of socialists by using the bands of Freikorps. The economic policy of majority socialists was no better. Apart from the intricacies of socialization, which were far beyond the capacity of the government to deal with, in terms either of social theory, professional economics, or ideological commitment, the economic situation required that at least three obvious measures be immediately undertaken: banks be put under public control to prevent the flight of capital; cartelized industry be put under public control to prevent the concentration of irresponsible power; and the landed estates be broken up in order to destroy the power of the notoriously reactionary Junkers. These three measures contain nothing specifically socialist; every decent bourgeois government would have carried them out; Meiji restorationists did it. But the Social Democratic government of a party that had preached social reforms for half a century did not do it; the measures were even not seriously discussed. Capital was leaving the country, while the foreign exchange deficit mounted, unemployment increased, and inflation galloped. By November 1923, the value of money was practically destroyed. On November 20, one dollar was worth 4,200,000,000,000 marks. Workers were embittered, the middle classes ruined. Speculation blossomed; fortunes were amassed. Employers ignored the constitutional rights of the workers. Junkers and the military began to play the old game. Wealthy industrialists were about to begin financing the Nazi Party. The Revolution seemed definitely defeated.

Not all hope was lost, however. In the 1928 elections there was a substantial swing to the left. Social Democrats and Communists gained considerably, while all other large parties lost votes. As the strongest party in the Reichstag, Social Democrats formed a coalition government with Hermann Müller as chancellor and Rudolf Hilferding as minister of finance. Soon the world economic crisis set in. The government had to act. What did it do? One could have expected that Social Democrats and Communists—both seemingly faithful to the old Marxian slogan, "Proletarians of all countries unite!"—would have combined forces, at least nationally, to fight unemployment. Yet, they hated each other more than they hated either the capitalists or the Nazis. Communists remained in active opposition together with the Nazis. As for the government party, any positive action was paralyzed by doctrinaire intraparty fighting about whether they should act as a *Klassenkampf Partei* [class struggle party] or *Staatspartei* [state party]. In the end Müller, failing to secure the support of his own party, resigned in March 1930. This signaled the end of the Great Coalition and the beginning of the end of German parliamentarism. The Social Democrats had forfeited their great historical chance.

It is of some interest to relate a parallel story that is much less known. A few months after Hilferding became minister of finance, Vladimir Woytinsky, a capable economist, became the chief economic adviser of the German unions. The economy was rapidly sliding into deep crisis. Woytinsky developed a counterdeflationary program that called for public works, easier credit, and monetary expansion in order to create new jobs and additional purchasing power. This was a set of policies that would later be rediscovered and theoretically elaborated by Keynes. By 1931 Woytinsky had succeeded in convincing the union leadership as to the correctness of his program. But Hilferding (no longer in the government) was opposed and continued to support the traditional deflationary policy. In a beautifully dogmatic fashion, Hilferding (who was originally trained as a physician) argued that depressions "result from the anarchy of the capitalist system. Either they must come to an end or they must lead to the collapse of this system . . . [no] programme can mitigate depression."[46] Party leadership sided with Hilferding.[47] By September 1931, the number of registered unemployed had reached 4.3 million; in spring 1932, about 8 million workers were unemployed. A year later, Hitler assumed power.

A comparison is forced to one's mind between the Russian and the German revolutions. While Russians had daring and capable leadership but lacked the necessary economic, political, and cultural maturity for socialism, in Germany it was the reverse. Here the leadership was clearly incapable of coping with the tremendous tasks of a social revolution. Incapable and unwilling. The bourgeois intellectual Lenin did everything to flare up the revolution. The worker and union organizer Ebert employed the imperial army to contain it and destroy it. If the German Revolution had succeeded, it might have helped Russian revolutionaries to avoid some of their fatal mistakes. On the other hand, if the Bolshevik terror had not discredited revolutionary socialism, if the Comintern had not inspired a meaningless uprising in Germany, and its policy of "the worse—the better" and "social fascism" had not rendered impossible any policy of cooperation between Communists and Social Democrats, then the Germans might have behaved more sensibly. And if the two revolutions had cooperated, they could have triggered revolutions elsewhere, for the entire continent was like a volcano ready to erupt.[48] As it happened, the failures of these revolutions fed upon each other. With an ominous consistency reminiscent of ancient Greek tragedies, and with unshaken, ignorant dogmatism, Russia was heading toward Stalinism and Germany toward fascism. Trotsky, Bukharin, and many other Russian revolutionary leaders were murdered at Stalin's orders. Hilferding, Thälmann, and a number of other German socialists, both Social Democrats and Communists, perished in Nazi prisons and concentration camps.

Spontaneously formed soviets and works councils in Germany (which will be discussed in greater detail later) stimulated extensive controversy regarding their proper role and functions. Even a movement, known as Rätekommunismus (councils communism), was brought into existence. Its chief theoreticians were Anton Pannekoek (1873–1960), a Dutch astronomer and later a member of the Dutch Academy of Sciences, and Otto Rühle (1874–1943), a German teacher. Rühle was a member of the Reichstag, voted with Liebknecht against war credits, and during the November Revolution served briefly as chairman of the United Revolutionary Workers' and Soldiers' Council in Dresden. The doctrine of councils communism was never formulated precisely. With the subsiding of the Revolution, the movement faded away, though some isolated groups exist even today in Holland and France. The doctrine is based on four major ideas. The power hierarchy at the work place is to be eliminated by introducing workers' self-management. Political parties are a bourgeois invention and represent a concentration of power; thus parties must be banned and parliament replaced by a system of soviets. The proletariat, organized at the work place where it exists as a class, is to build the political organization from the base upward by electing recallable delegates. (The latter idea was introduced into the Yugoslav Constitution of 1974.) Such an organization serves both to prepare the Revolution and to facilitate the takeover of the economy and the state.

Under the impact of the Revolution, workers' self-management acquired two other important advocates: philosopher Karl Korsch (1886–1961), member of the German Communist Party; and the philosophically trained labor leader Antonio Gramsci (1891–1937), one of the founders of the Italian Communist Party. Korsch, close to an industrial unionist position, combined orthodox Marxism and syndicalism. He argued that, during the political transition period characterized as the dictatorship of the proletariat, proletarian associations of labor should be established in every shop, in industries, and in the entire economy on the basis of industrial democracy; the resulting system of councils would put the state power in its service.[49] A consideration of Gramsci's thought brings us to the next center of revolutionary turmoil, Italy.

Though victorious in war, *Italy* found itself on the verge of a revolution. In the elections of 1919, Socialists won 2 million out of a total of 5.5 milion votes. The left-wing leadership of the party proclaimed that the next step would be the creation of a socialist republic and the establishment of a proletarian dictatorship. Workers began to occupy the factories, and peasants in the south appropriated the uncultivated estates of absentee landlords. In August 1919 at the Fiat center in Turin, an assembly of workers, furiously dissatisfied with the existing *commissione interna,*[50] succeeded in forcing it to resign, and for the first time elected shop stewards, who constituted a factory council.[51] In the same year and in the same city, Gramsci established the weekly *L'ordine nuovo.* Searching in Italian tradition for an institution that could serve as the embryo of future soviets, Gramsci and his group advocated the establishment of workers' councils. Gramsci was one of those labor leaders who realized clearly that trade unions did not transcend the framework of bourgeois society. But, unlike Lenin, he thought that only workers' councils could create a new consciousness among workers and help to build a new structure of production relations. He also understood the need for a differentiated—functional and political—approach to self-government. In one of the first articles in *L'ordine nuovo* (June 21, 1919) the opinion is expressed that the slogan, "All power in the factory to workers' committees," under which workers must begin to elect their representative assemblies, ought to be combined with the slogan, "All state power to workers' and peasants' councils." Naturally enough, such ideas did not appeal to the trade union bureaucracy, and it prevented the spread of workers' committees outside Turin.

In August 1920, a long strike of metalworkers in Milan was followed by a lockout. Workers retaliated by occupying factory after factory. Even before that time, factories were occasionally taken over by workers, who would continue to work without management. Now most factories in Milan and Turin were occupied. But the entire action was not adequately prepared, and it soon collapsed under the combined pressure of employers and the government. The government promised reforms, but after negotiations were over and factories were returned to the owners, it gave up the idea of passing a law on workers' control. In the face of the workers' claims for a greater share in the control of industry, employers became restive; they began to consolidate their organizations and by the summer of 1919 a number of big industrialists had started financing Fascists as the force most likely to check the working class movement. On August 31, 1922, a general strike called by the unions failed, and the middle classes began to look more favorably toward the Fascists. In October of 1922, Mussolini marched on Rome. A few years later fascism was firmly established in Italy. Gramsci was caught and sentenced to twenty years in jail.

The next country chosen by history was *Spain*. For more than a decade after the First World War, Spain passed through a period of extreme political instability in which intervals of almost no government alternated with military dictatorships. The days of old monarchy had clearly gone. But the country did not seem ripe for a democratic bourgeois republic. Nevertheless, a republic was proclaimed in 1931; military mutiny followed a year later. In 1933 the government suppressed a broad anarchist movement, and a year later a strong popular movement in Asturia was put down by armed forces. In such an atmosphere, left-wing parties were able to win an absolute majority in the February 1936 elections. As early as July, General Franco began a military mutiny in Morocco. The Civil War began.

In the early months of the Civil War, effective power was exercised mainly by local workers' committees. Even the army was made up mostly of workers' militia. All over the country workers took over abandoned factories; and peasants, deserted estates. Workers elected committees to run the factories, and peasants established communes. The collectivization of land was far more widespread because it encountered less resistance. The communes were really communist organizations, and money was often abolished. The committees were composed mainly of militants of the trade union confederation, the Confederación nacional de trabajo (CNT). The CNT was largely under anarchist influence, kept aloof from party politics, and proclaimed as a goal a society organized as a loose federation of free local communes. Its influence was strongest in Catalonia, and it was exactly here where the famous Decree on Collectivization and Workers' Control was issued in October 1936. The decree called for the collectivization of all enterprises that employed more than one hundred workers, those that had been abandoned or whose owners had joined the rebels, as well as those in which three-fifths of the workers desired collectivization. In collectivized enterprises, management was in the hands of workers represented by enterprise councils. Private industry was to be managed by owners subject to the approval of a workers' control committee. The enterprise councils would elect directors and would include government inspectors whose duty it would be to insure compliance with the law. Coordination of the activities of individual enterprise councils and the task of drawing up plans for various industries would be entrusted to general industrial councils composed of representatives of the enterprise councils and trade unions, as well as technicians appointed by the government. Under the conditions of the Civil War, this scheme had little chance to be tried out as envisaged. Besides, not only the enemy but also the supposedly socialist government itself—as in Russia and Germany—was opposed to workers' management and tried to destroy it. Somewhat more than two years later, the Spanish Revolution collapsed. The *comunismo libertario* of the CNT Saragosa Congress in 1936 was replaced by a fascist dictatorship. The lesson to be learned from the Hungarian, German, Italian, and Spanish experiences seems to be that unsuccessful or half-successful revolutions are likely to generate fascist dictatorships.

The Second World War generated new revolutionary upheavals and, with them, new attempts at workers' self-management. The *Yugoslav Revolution* of 1941–45/48, which will be discussed in greater detail later, produced the first successful implementation of an integral system of workers' self-management. Just as the Russian Revolution influenced developments in other countries, where many imitations of soviets arose, the Yugoslav Revolution popularized workers' councils, which were set up in a number of countries.

The Yugoslav influence was perhaps most strongly felt in *Algeria,* where, as a result of the National Liberation War (1954–62), favorable conditions for social change were created. As before in Russia, Hungary, and Spain, workers and peasants occupied the abandoned estates and establishments of French colons. *Comités de gestion,* established spontaneously in the summer of 1962, were supported by UGTA unions as the basic democratic form countering the autocratic tendencies of the FLN (National Liberation Front) leadership. The first elections were held in September 1962, and as early as October a decree was promulgated legalizing *comités de gestion* in vacant agricultural estates. The next year the celebrated March Decrees established management committees as a keystone of Algerian socialism. The Yugoslav formula was adopted: all full-time workers constituted a general assembly and, in enterprises with more than thirty workers, elected a workers' council. The council elected a management committee. But many members of the state and party machinery were opposed to self-management. Step by step, the state apparatus increased its control over the activities of enterprises. Their funds came to be held and administered by state agencies. Finally, the committees were dissolved, except in agriculture, and enterprises were integrated into *societés nationales.*[52] Self-managing enterprises of the Yugoslav type were replaced by public corporations patterned on the French model. Once again self-management degenerated into etatism. But the idea was kept alive. A new start was made in 1974 when workers' assemblies were elected in state enterprises. The assemblies have mostly consulting rights, however.

Postwar events in the most developed Eastern European countries have many characteristics in common. All these countries were liberated by the Soviet Army. In all of them, various forms of workers' management appeared spontaneously near the end of 1944 or the beginning of 1945. *Betriebsräte* reappeared in East Germany. Factory committees were legalized in Hungary in February 1945. In the same month, a decree on factory councils was passed in Poland. In Czechoslovakia, a 1945 decree established enterprise councils. In nationalized firms, the highest organ of management was a board consisting of elected workers (one-third) and representatives of authorities appointed in consultation with the unions (two-thirds).[53] By 1948 communist regimes had consolidated their power, and workers' management soon disappeared in all these countries—replaced by a *Gleichschaltung* on the Soviet pattern.

After Stalin's death, a new revolutionary tide swept these countries. Stalin died in March 1953; in June, Czechoslovakian workers demonstrated, demanding greater participation in factory management and free elections. Two months later, the workers of East Berlin rebelled. For the third time within a generation, Hungarians attempted to establish workers' management. In April 1956, the Petöfi Circle was formed by young communist intellectuals in Budapest. It soon became a center of criticism and protest. By September, workers had become active and began to demand "genuine workers' self-management." By the end of October, the country was on the brink of a revolution. Spontaneously created workers' councils were legalized in November 1956. According tc the law, the council, elected by the workers, was to manage the enterprise and take binding decisions on all important matters. Territorial workers' councils would not only coordinate the activities of enterprise councils, but would also serve as organs of political power. That was particularly true of the Budapest Workers' Council.

The Russian military intervention put an end to this development. Within a month, the central council and all regional workers' councils were dissolved. Unlike in the 1917 Revolution, when Hungary was greeted enthusiastically by Lenin as an ally, in 1956 it was treated as an enemy. This was not accidental, nor was it the first time such a thing had happened. In 1917 both countries were experiencing socialist revolutions. In 1956 the etatist Soviet Union crushed socialist revolution in Hungary—just as in 1848 feudal Russia crushed the Hungarian bourgeois revolution. After the defeat, enterprise workers' councils continued to exist, and a device tried previously was applied: trade unions were urged to assume the leading role. In 1957 workers' councils lost their independence and were replaced by factory councils, which were consultative bodies under the leadership of unions. The chairman of the trade union committee was an *ex officio* chairman of the factory council. On November 17, it was officially announced that all remaining workers' councils were to be abolished forthwith.

In *Poland,* after the Poznań upheavals in June 1956, workers' councils of various forms were created in a number of enterprises. In November a law was passed stipulating that a workers' council elected by all workers would manage the enterprise and approve the nomination and dismissal of the general manager. Yet, as soon as the situation was again under control, the authorities encroached on the rights of workers' councils, which found it more and more difficult to operate. A new law passed in 1958 explicitly stated the principle of *edinonachalie,* or one-man management; self-management was replaced by co-participation. The workers' council, trade union committee, and party committee together represented the conference of self-management. The conference was entitled to make proposals, but all decisions were to be made by the director.

Czechoslovakia lagged behind by about a decade. But, when the time arrived, the Czech attempt appeared most promising, for industrial democracy was developing within a mature political democracy. The first elements of self-management appeared in 1966 together with the economic reform. But the development was successfully checked by the existing etatist regime. The Prague Spring brought a fundamental change. After the old Stalinists had lost power, in the first months of 1968, self-management became the major subject of discussion in newspapers and journals, and at factories. Preparatory committees for future workers' councils [*podnikove rady pracujicich*] began to be established all over the country. In June, the trade unions gave support to this initiative and in fact established two-thirds of all preparatory committees, which soon existed in half of the industrial establishments. The government announced that a law on socialist enterprise, which was to settle all matters concerning self-management, would be promulgated by the end of the year. Conservatives, of course, were opposed. Representative of their views was a document circulated among party members and prepared by two members of the party Presidium for its session on the fatal night of August 21. It declared that the creation of workers' councils generated "the danger that the anarchist and anticommunist elements will gradually acquire the most important position in the councils and use them to weaken and destroy the positions of the party, trade unions, and economic agencies in the production process. Bearing in mind transformations occurring in the structure of management, this fact could have very great consequences."[54] Russian leaders shared this view, and there is some sinister symbolism in the fact that, on the very night when the document was to be discussed at the party Presidium, troops of the Warsaw Pact invaded Czechoslovakia. One of the first political requests of the occupying power was the dismantling of the workers' councils. Preparatory committees and workers' councils continued to exist for some time, however, occasionally operating illegally. The announced law on socialist enterprises was withdrawn in the summer of 1969. The dissolution of the most important council—that of the Škoda factory in Plzen—on November 12, 1969, marked the end of workers' management. The old etatist system was reestablished.

We can now summarize our findings. In the first century of socialist revolutions, all but two of them produced attempts to establish self-government. The two exceptions—the Chinese and Cuban revolutions—could probably be explained by the very specific nature of these revolutions.[55] China, for example, is a very underdeveloped country. Military coups and national liberation wars that claimed association with socialism and might be regarded as revolutions occurred in some undeveloped African and Asian countries, but these, too, failed to produce workers' management. It seems that, in addition to social revolution, a certain minimal level of development is also a necessary condition for workers' management. On the other hand, it should be noted that Chinese agricultural communes and industrial revolutionary committees went rather far in increasing the participation of ordinary peasants and workers. In a more liberal post-Mao environment, the trend is likely to continue toward more pronounced self-management. As far as Cuba is concerned, the country has been living under conditions of siege. In such a situation, decentralization does not appear as an obvious arrangement. Another Latin American revolution, the Bolivian Revolution of 1952, promptly produced *control obrero* [worker control] in nationalized enterprises. Thus, historically speaking, socialism and self-government appear to be synonymous.

It has frequently been stated that, wherever workers' management was attempted, it failed. In a sense this is true. After its frustrated attempts, a country would lapse back into capitalism or etatism. But the inference that, because of this failure, workers' management must be regarded as an unrealizable utopia, is clearly false. During no historical period have new social institutions been established successfully at a single stroke, without bitter fights against vested interests and without many failures. What is significant in the events we have reviewed is not the failure to achieve the goal, but the continued attempts *despite* all failures.

V. Establishment

The three waves described so far could not fail to exert great influence and modify that relatively stable and sanctified pattern of social life denoted as the *establishment*. The establishment itself began to change, and this is the fourth and most superficial layer of the historical trend we have set out to investigate.

Various kinds of workers' and works councils (the former are composed of workers only, while the latter include employers' representatives as well) are as old as the trade union movement itself. These councils or committees dealt with complaints, welfare work, and conditions of employment. They were always advisory; the employer reserved the power to make the final decision. But for a long time they occurred only sporadically.[56] They did not represent an institution. Similarly, labor legislation dealing with some forms of workers' participation in factory organization—almost exclusively confined to welfare matters—can be traced back to the end of the last century in several countries (Prussia and Austria, for instance).[57] These were also sporadic events, and the extent of workers' participation was insignificant. The first landmark in the history of workers' participation in management was reached in the First World War and the Russian Revolution.

During the war, in order to enhance war production, the British, French, and German governments sought—and obtained—the cooperation of the unions. As a result, various forms of management-worker cooperation developed. The events that occurred in these countries are so significant that they warrant a more detailed discussion.

The three years preceding the outbreak of the war represent one of the most disturbed epochs in British industry, according to J. B. Seymour, historian of the Whitley councils. At the commencement of the war, a hundred strikes were in progress.[58] It was during this period that syndicalist influence was at its strongest in Britain, and in 1912 miners and the largest of the four railway unions accepted the demand for the complete control of industry by workers. It was also during this period that the future shop stewards' movement was announced (Glasgow engineers' strike, 1912).

Before the war, shop stewards were minor officials appointed by the union from among the men in the workshop to see that union dues were paid and that newcomers were organized. They had no power to negotiate over grievances, nor were they officially recognized by the management. Then came the war—which, as pointed out by C. G. Renold, who watched events through the eyes of an employer, "was not felt by workpeople to be 'their' war. . . . It was regarded by large sections as a capitalists' war and the restrictions, controls and hardships were resented accordingly."[59] It suffices to add that when, under the Treasury Agreement of 1915, trade union leaders voluntarily pledged themselves not to sanction strikes during the war, the dissent of the rank and file was certain. The big Clyde engineers' strike early in 1915, in which the strike committee disregarded superior union officials and won the strike, set the pattern and initiated what became known as the shop stewards' movement.[60] Shop stewards' committees, comprised of representatives of all the workers in an establishment, spread throughout the country. Local delegates of the establishments in a given area made up workers' committees, which became federated into an unofficial nationwide workers' committee movement. This spontaneous development resembled very much the appearance of soviets in Russia, and so it is quite natural that, after the February Revolution in the latter country, soviets became popular in Britain. The Leeds conference of June 1917, mentioned earlier, called for the formation of workers' and soldiers' councils.

Syndicalism, guild socialism, the shop stewards' movement, the increasing number of working days lost by strikes despite all restrictions—2 million in 1915, 2.5 million in 1916, 5.5 million in 1917—this alarming situation called for government intervention. In October 1916, a commission known as the Whitley Committee was appointed to examine methods for securing permanent improvement in industrial relations. The following year the Whitley Committee produced its scheme of employer-worker cooperation. For each industry, a national joint council and district councils were to be formed to bring together employers' organizations and unions. Joint works committees in individual establishments were to provide a recognized means of consultation between management and employees. But the scheme as a whole failed to work, except in government departments: "The employers, as a body, have never favored the scheme. . . . The trade unionists, frightened by the shop stewards' movement, appear to shrink from giving authority to any rank-and-file movement and away from the central organizations."[61] Out of about a hundred works committees formed in response to the Whitley Committee recommendations, only one-half were still alive by 1929. After the war the government rejected the demands of miners and railwaymen for nationalization and self-government. The first post-war recession, which began in 1921, killed the shop stewards' movement and guild socialism.[62] The situation was again normalized, and the capitalist machine could work as before. But not quite; the seed had been sown.

In France, during the First World War the Socialist minister of war initiated the establishment of enterprise committees composed of workers' representatives in factories producing war materials. The committees disintegrated after the war. The German government also created workers' committees during World War I (1916), with the expressed goal of contributing to a better understanding between workers and employers. Unlike Britain and France, Germany was defeated in the war, and events there took a different path. Defeat, coupled with the tremendous influence of the Russian Revolution, produced a German Revolution in 1918. Workers' and soldiers' councils sprang up all over the country. Badly frightened, employers were ready to go very far to escape full-scale socialism. And so it happened that in July 1919 Germany became the first capitalist country to promulgate a constitution that included among the "fundamental rights" of citizens the following one: "For the purpose of safeguarding their social and economic interests the wage-earning and salaried employees are entitled to be represented in workers' councils for each establishment, as well as in regional workers' councils organized for each industrial area, and in a federal workers' council."

On the basis of the Constitution, a law was passed in 1920 making works councils (*Betriebsräte*) compulsory in all establishments with twenty or more employees. The councils were to supervise the operation of collective agreements, to enter into agreements on conditions of work and subjects not regulated by wider agreements, to monitor hiring and dismissal, and also to advise the employer on how to improve efficiency and organization. Constitution and laws are dead letters, however, if they are not backed by active social forces. The German working class movement of the time was deeply divided both in its trade union and in its parliamentary section. The majority, who held power, were undetermined, compromising, and hesitating. The state bureaucracy was hostile. The unions were critical and helped to kill the bill regulating participation above the firm level. This gave employers a breathing space. The results of the revolution were gradually undermined—with the slump of 1924 playing a not insignificant role—and then liquidated. The process came to an end in May 1933, when both trade union and works councils were abolished—an event that marked the advent of fascism.

As for other European countries, it suffices to mention that, during 1919 and 1920, laws on enterprise councils or workers' committees were passed for similar reasons in Austria, Czechoslovakia, and Norway. In Yugoslavia, the law on the protection of workers (1922) provided for the election of workers' commissioners (*radnički povjerenici*) from the shop floor, whose task it was to protect workers' interests and cooperate with the employer. The attitude of the employers and trade unions very soon reduced this provision to a mere formality. With the lag of a decade, and after a period of strikes, a similar solution was reached under the Popular Front government in France in 1936; shop stewards (*délégués ouvriers*) were recognized and given the right to meet with management every month. In the United States, a somewhat different type of union-management cooperation regarding production problems was begun on one of the railways in the 1920s when the union wanted to reduce costs in order to secure work for railway shops. Other firms and unions tried out similar ideas until the 1929 depression, which killed experiments of this kind. A decade later the steelworkers' union developed quite successful cooperation plans in a number of small steel and steel products firms. The steelworkers' scheme survived the war and continued to operate in some thirty firms.[63]

In the United States the first works councils were established around the turn of the century. By 1926 they existed in more than four hundred companies, including large firms such as Bethlehem Steel, General Electric, International Harvester, and Westinghouse. But they did not multiply. Curiously enough, the legislation of the 1930s, sympathetic to the unions, prevented the development of works councils. Union leaders called them "company unions," and in 1937 the Supreme Court outlawed the works councils because they belonged to "employee associations instituted, controlled or influenced by employers." Apparently "class collaboration" was not desirable. Thus American legislators and union leaders unwittingly adopted "the correct class approach" of the European radicals. We shall later have an opportunity to discuss the consequences.

The second landmark in the development of workers' participation in management was occasioned by the Second World War. Just as the First World War, it initiated a cycle, though on a much larger scale. Again governments sought the cooperation of workers in order to enhance war production, and joint production committees were set up in various countries (Britain, the United States, Canada). Again Britain was victorious and Germany defeated; and there was spontaneous development in the former, while legislative measures were taken in the latter. Again British miners expected to attain self-government; they got joint consultation instead. But there were also several novel features, the most important of which was large-scale nationalization in some countries and full-scale nationalization in a number of others (Eastern European and Far East Asian nations). And in all nationalized industries, joint consultation between workers and management was introduced as a matter of course.

In Britain two national agreements drawn up during the war set the pattern for the establishment of joint production committees. The committees were to have an advisory role and were to provide an outlet for the regular exchange of views among employers on welfare and production matters, subject to the qualification that the terms and conditions of employment were to be dealt with by unions on behalf of the workers. In 1947 the National Joint Advisory Council recommended to employers' organizations and unions that joint consultative machinery be set up where it did not already exist. The recommendation was followed, and soon there were several hundred committees in existence in Britain.

In West Germany, the legislation of the Weimar period was not only revived but pressed a step further: from joint consultation to co-determination (*Mitbestimmung*). In the two basic industries—coal, and iron and steel—unions have achieved parity for workers' representatives in the supervisory board (*Aufsichtsrat*), a body that appoints the board of management. Moreover, one of the (generally) three members of the management board—the personnel director (*Arbeitsdirector*)—is to be nominated by the union (law of 1951). In other industries workers' representatives are still in the minority, although this minority (one-third) may be larger than during the Weimar period. Works councils (*Betriebsräte*), representing both wage and salary earners, must be elected in all establishments employing no less than five permanent employees (law of 1952). In order to promote cooperation between the works council and the employer, in establishments with more than a hundred employees an economic committee (*Wirtschaftsausschuss*) must be formed, to which each side appoints half the members.

In France, a law passed in 1946 made it compulsory for industrial concerns employing more than fifty workers to establish a works committee (*comité d'entreprise*) representing manual workers and technical grades. Every act of major management importance must be subject to agreement by the committee. If there is disagreement, the case must go to arbitration.

Also in 1946, unions and the employers' association in Sweden reached an agreement under which enterprise councils were to be created in firms with twenty-five or more employees. The task of these councils may be described broadly as joint consultation on all important matters. It is of some interest to record that, in 1923, when a royal committee headed by E. Vigforss proposed the formation of similar joint production committees, both unions and employers opposed the idea, and nothing came of it. By 1950, following the Second World War, enterprise councils had been set up in 2,650 firms employing 600,000 workers.[64] Similar joint consultation committees were introduced in Norway (1945) and Denmark (1947) on the basis of union-employer agreements, and in Finland (1946) by a special law. In Austria, works councils were established again by law in 1948 and were granted the right to participate in management, which had not been the case in 1919. In Belgium, enterprise councils (*conseils d'entreprise*) were created by law in 1948, and in the Netherlands similar councils (*ondernemingsraad*) were established in 1950. Somewhat later, in 1966, internal enterprise commissions (*commissioni interne d'azienda*) were set up in Italy. Various forms of joint consultation were developed in Eastern European etatist countries as well. In the Soviet Union attempts were made in 1957 and afterwards to resurrect the defunct production conferences, and eventually, in 1973, a decree was passed to that effect.

In a number of other countries, the prewar practice of joint consultation was continued after the war as well, or, where it did not exist, was introduced for the first time. In 1951 the International Labour Office registered more than thirty countries with *permanent* organs of workers' participation in management. Practices varied, but these bodies had one important common feature: with few exceptions, they were confined to joint *consultation*. Yet, this was just the beginning. Over the next two decades, the participation movement grew stronger and gained new ground. Development proceeded invariably toward co-determination, occasionally even with parity representation.

After the Second World War, the movement for workers' participation in management spread to non-European countries as well. Algeria has already been mentioned. During its first year of independence (1947), India passed an act stipulating that the appropriate state government could require an employer to establish a works committee consisting of representatives of employers and workmen and serving a consultative function. In 1957 a scheme of voluntary joint management councils was launched based on the idea that "in a socialist democracy labor is a partner in the common task of development. . . . There should be joint consultation and workers and technicians should, whenever possible, be associated progressively in management."[65] By 1969, about 150 joint management councils and 3,133 works committees had been set up. Pakistan requires a worker representative on the management board of all firms employing more than fifty people. In Bolivia a decree on joint councils was passed in 1960 and, after the Revolution, another decree on workers' control in 1963. In Tanzania advisory workers' committees were established in 1964, and workers' councils were introduced into public enterprises in 1970. In Turkey, Egypt, and Syria, participation has been introduced in public enterprises. A law passed in Venezuela in 1966 provides for the representation of workers on the governing boards of state-dominated undertakings. Zambia, the Democratic Republic of the Congo, and other countries have experimented with various forms of participation.

A special type of syndicalism developed in Israel, a country with a mixed economy dominated by the public sector. Here the trade union federation, Histadrut, is the largest industrial concern in the country, accounting for one-fourth of national employment. Histadrut proved—though it looked impossible before—that unions can act simultaneously as bargaining agents and as employers. In 1945 Histadrut established joint production committees comprised of worker and management representatives in its own enterprises, and negotiated an agreement with the private manufacturers' association to encourage production committees in private firms. This attempt proved unsuccessful, however, because of managerial resistance and worker apathy. The effort was renewed in 1956, with the adoption of the Joint Council Plan, which was to provide in-plant control over all business except wages and benefits. The idea was to establish co-determination, but what finally emerged was joint consultation.

The other special feature of the Israeli economy is the kibbutz. The word *kibbutz* comes from the Hebrew word *kvutzah*, meaning "group." The first kibbutz was founded in 1909. Kibbutzim began as rural communal settlements but later moved into manufacturing as well. They produce about one-third of the agricultural output and slightly less than one-tenth of the industrial output of the country. Kibbutzim vary in size from 40 or 50 members to as many as 1,000, though most have between 250 and 500 members. They represent the most radical form of self-management in existence today. The aim is the complete identification of the individual with society. All members participate in decision making, management is shared on a rotational basis, and members' needs are supplied by communal institutions on an egalitarian basis. Kibbutzim employ less than 4 percent of the active population, however, and this share appears stagnant.

Like most kibbutzim, Chilean *asentamientos* are agricultural settlements. They were established on land acquired by the agrarian reform in 1964–70 and, after a transitional period of several years, developed into self-governing cooperatives with indivisible property. In this country, in the manufacturing sphere, a spontaneous movement developed—disregarded and disliked by both the government and the Opposition, as well as by the unions—which represents genuine workers' self-management. Since 1968 workers have been occupying, one after another, enterprises that were abandoned by their owners, that were or were about to become bankrupt, or that simply failed to operate successfully. Workers assume management, continue production and, as a rule, avoid bankruptcy and improve business results. By 1972 one hundred such *empresas de trabajadores* had been established, employing about 10,000 workers. In the meantime, the government and the unions reached an agreement to establish joint consultation machinery with elements of co-determination in the public sector. The military coup brought this development to an end, but new worker-owned firms are being formed each year.

Chile's neighbor, Peru, also carried out an agrarian reform and established self-governing peasant cooperatives. The new military government, which overthrew the civilian government in a 1968 coup, acted in a very unorthodox and unmilitary way. The government stated its social philosophy in roughly the following terms: Western capitalism has created unbearable social differences, slowed economic development, and turned the country into an economic colony. Thus capitalism, however reformed, is unacceptable. Eastern communism has created a totalitarian society in which the political freedom of the working people has been destroyed or severely limited, and is therefore equally unacceptable. Fortunately, these are not the only two alternatives, as people once believed. The third alternative, self-governing society—*democracia social de participación plena*, as Peruvians call it—is the alternative for which one should opt.

Large-scale nationalizations, the establishment of agricultural cooperatives, and self-management in the sugar industry were the first steps. With regard to private industry, the government applied a very original idea: firms were obliged by law to put a certain percentage of profits each year into an indivisible trust fund operated by the employed workers, who represented a work community, or *comunidad laboral.* As the share of capital belonging to the *comunidad laboral* increases in the total capital of the firm, the voting rights of workers' representatives in management increase proportionately. This scheme, applied intelligently and efficiently, implies nothing less than the use of capitalist mechanisms themselves for the expropriation of capitalists. But the country encountered unexpected economic difficulties. President Velasco Alvarado, initiator of the reforms, was removed, and the expansion of the worker-managed sector came to a halt.

It remains, finally, to record the first successful attempt to establish workers' self-management on a national scale. The Yugoslav Revolution was made possible and was reinforced by the National Liberation War in 1941–45. Since partisan warfare requires a great amount of local initiative and resourcefulness, the first organs of local self-government and the first self-managed partisan factories were organized as early as 1941. The first five years after the armed phase of the Revolution were decisive, however. A law passed in 1945 provided that workers' commissioners (*radnički povjerenici*), as legal representatives of workers, establish contact with management, government agencies, and union branches with the task of protecting the social and economic interests of the workers and aiding the advance of production. The major portion of the economy was nationalized the following year, and nationalization was completed in 1948. In the meantime, workers' commissioners ceased to exist, and instead trade union factory branches obtained the legal right to put forward proposals to the management. This represented a retreat from control to consultation—a dangerous step backward very reminiscent of the Soviet development during 1917–20. As early as 1949, however, there was a new change: in a number of factories, consultation between the management—mostly people who had taken an active part in the Revolution themselves—and workers came to be introduced spontaneously. At the same time, the fierce attack of the Cominform, launched in the middle of 1948 and continued over several years, acted as a force to help check the polarization process. In December 1949 the government and the trade unions jointly issued an instruction on the formation of workers' councils as advisory bodies. Councils were elected in 215 larger enterprises. Soon other enterprises asked to be given the same privilege, and by the middle of 1950 there were already 520 councils in existence. In June 1950, the National Assembly passed a law transforming councils from advisory into managing bodies. The working collective of every enterprise elects a workers' council (*radnički savjet*), which, for as long as it enjoys the confidence of its electors, serves as supreme policymaking body in the enterprise. The council elects its executive body, the managing board (*upravni odbor*), which is concerned with the day-to-day implementation of the council's policy, its actual execution, as well as the job of routine coordination of enterprise activities carried out by the general manager and the expert administrative and technical staff. The perennial management-worker antithesis was not eliminated at a stroke by this piece of legislation but conditions were created for its resolution. By 1950, it had already become abundantly clear that, in general, bureaucratic organization results in inefficiency and undesirable social relations, and thus the introduction of workers' management cleared the ground for the series of institutional changes that were to follow. Subsequent development in other spheres of social life, in turn, strengthened the new organization of industry. Self-government of producers was extended beyond the immediate work place in that all representative organs, from local councils up to the Federal Assembly, were given a second chamber—a *council of producers.* In 1953 the Constitution was changed to take account of the new social institutions. *Workers' management had became a part of the establishment.*

The Yugoslav solution should not be regarded as the end of a process, but rather as a promising beginning in the development of a genuinely self-governing society. By now self-management appears to be reasonably well established at the enterprise level in Yugoslavia. What remains is to extend it to other levels and, in particular, to develop an equally new political system, appropriate for a self-governing society.

VI. Evaluation

Historically and logically, there are two approaches to workers' participation in management: one negative, containing; the other positive, constructive. The former developed first and has been based on the following reasoning and behavior. Employers and workers represent two social classes with antagonistic interests. Higher profits imply lower wages, and vice versa. Thus, a normal state of affairs is a class war conducted by more or less civilized means. On that basis, trade unions were created as fighting organizations of the working class. In radicalized situations, when class tensions are intensified, traditional collective bargaining is supplemented by a request for *workers' control.* "Workers' control" may thus be used as a term describing the negative, containing approach to participation. Its historical origins were analyzed in the section on revolution. It refers to the aggressive encroachment of trade union or unofficial groups on management powers in a capitalist or etatist framework. By the strength of their organizations, workers exact concessions from employers. They do not make positive proposals regarding the conduct of business—because they are not asked to, this being a prerogative of the management; they do not assume any responsibility—because the firm is not their property; they determine what *cannot* be done, thus limiting the arbitrary power of the employers, and they try to maximize their share in the cake. As long as there is capitalism (or etatism), there cannot be cooperation. Since capitalism cannot be abolished overnight, such an attitude is often instrumental in perpetuating capitalism. A modern advocate of radical workers' control, E. Mandel, has stated its four main goals as: (1) access to financial documents (Open the books!); (2) control of the system of remuneration; (3) control of the speed of work; and (4) control of dismissals and refusal to close down works. "We require full control and the right of veto for the workers. But we reject even an atom of responsibility for the capitalist management of the enterprise."[66] According to this view, co-determination and self-management is possible only under socialism.

Although the interests of employers and workers are basically opposed, they are not totally so. There are some areas—for instance, welfare, safety, and health questions—where interests are not opposed and cooperation is possible. Thus, while bargaining about wage rates and conditions of work will remain reserved to the trade unions in most cases, workers on the spot will begin to participate in decisions concerning noncontroversial matters. In this way, negative control will be supplemented by constructive participation. Participation passes through three stages: *joint consultation*, *co-determination*, and *self-management.* The first stage leaves the capitalist and etatist framework intact, but provides an important psychological attack on the managerial autocracy. The second stage already implies a share in power and represents the beginning of the end. It is important to realize that the first two stages are transitional and consequently highly unstable.[67] Stability is achieved during the third stage, which is possible only under socialism. Most of the developed countries, both capitalist and etatist, find themselves in the first stage. By 1977, however, nine nations (West Germany, Sweden, Norway, Denmark, Austria, the Netherlands, France, Luxemburg, and Spain) had laws requiring labor representation on the supervisory and management boards of major companies—which is already co-determination. As a rule, this is still a minority representation, but strong pressures are exerted toward parity and beyond.

In evaluating the development of workers' participation in management, the following five aspects of the problem seem important.

1. The *motivation* for setting up joint consultative machinery falls into four distinct categories. Revolutionary pressure from below compels employers and the government of the day to relax the managerial authoritarianism. Because it is the result of a strong clash of interests, the outcome of the fight must be legally sanctioned to remain permanent (although legal sanctions often prove to be a fiction). The German case is typical here.

Next, during modern totalitarian war, governments are vitally interested in stepping up production and therefore devise and advocate schemes of joint consultation to bridge the gap between employers and workers. This case is typified by British and American practice. With respect to the latter, the International Labor Office study noted: "The general purpose of the Labor-Management Production Committees was to raise the quantity and quality of output for war production by the joint effort of labor and management in each war plant." The extent to which this purpose was achieved can be seen from the following evaluation in the same study: "While there seems to be little doubt that the committees made a substantial contribution to plant output, a number of the committees did not aid to as great an extent as had been expected. . . . "[68] Some 5,000 committees were established in plants with war contracts. Most disappeared with the end of the war.

The third type of motivation is that of individual employers who are not forced *by law* to adopt joint consultation, but adopt it primarily on economic grounds. This point is illuminated by the following statement of C. G. Renold, himself an employer who introduced successful joint consultation in his firm: "In the first place the point should be made that the whole development had its origin in a very practical need—the need felt by the management for closer contact with its men in the interest of smooth working."[69] This need appears when the concern outgrows one-man management.[70] It becomes urgent under the turbulent conditions of war and industrial unrest. And once the works' council is set up, it is likely to continue to exist in the ensuing period of military and industrial peace. War has another effect as well: it increases the self-consciousness of the exploited classes and humanizes the members of higher social strata, thus providing a psychological bridge between them.[71] Then there are also a small number of employers who are interested in joint consultation for its own sake, because they regard it as a humanizing institution. This Owenite type of employer, practically nonexistent in earlier times, is likely to multiply to the degree that adverse social pressure—on the part both of their equals and of the establishment as a whole—decreases. The example of individual employers, the recurrent interventions of government, and the constant improvement in the educational level of workers, gradually create an atmosphere in which joint consultation becomes an indispensable part of the managerial routine. Exactly this seems to be happening in Britain today, as demonstrated by the appearance of yet another type of employer: in the majority of firms visited by the National Institute of Industrial Psychology research team, "joint consultation seemed to be regarded as an up-to-date technique for improving management-worker relationships."[72]

The fourth type of motivation is of rather recent vintage. In Britain and Italy, for example, employers urge unions to assume management responsibilities as a means of preserving labor peace. When companies in a depressed economy are only marginally profitable, even a short strike may knock them out of business. Thus, according to a spokesman of the Confederation of British Industries, co-determination is viewed as a last resort to reduce the number of industrial disputes in order to improve competitiveness on the world market.

Competition is the essence of capitalism; accordingly, there is nothing to stop capitalist firms from competing, even in improving relations with workers. This sounds paradoxical, but so are the conditions of full employment under capitalism. Clearly, if pursued consistently, such a competition must eventually lead to the destruction of capitalist relationships; but this will be nothing more than a parallel to Schumpeterian "creative destruction," the destruction of profits by competition initiated to increase profits.

Nationalized industries and nationalized economies represent a separate case, in which joint consultation is an indispensable minimum to make the system work at all—that is, to make them socially acceptable. The only development one can visualize is a constant increase in workers' participation in management, either granted by the governing bureaucracy or won by the workers through revolutionary means.

2. What happens to the *discipline* in an organization where executive authority is undermined because everyone has the right and the opportunity to question the validity of commands from above according to his own set of criteria? This is the very question our Weberian-minded generation will ask in connection with the practicability of workers' management schemes. For, is it not true that an efficient organization requires obedience, where obedience is defined as following "such a course that the content of the command may be taken to have become the basis of action for its own sake"?[73]

In fact, however, the literature on joint consultation and workers' management,[74] including the most detailed studies, gives no indication of any "problem of discipline." I can do no better than to quote two employers' testimonies: "When I first took the step of introducing joint consultation on a very broad basis into my own works," wrote G. D. Walpole, "I was told by most of my fellow employers that I was selling the pass to the enemy, and that the first result would be that works discipline would go to the devil. I have found, on the contrary, after two years' experience, that works discipline has improved almost out of recognition, and that every other legitimate interest of ownership has also been catered for in a measure which four years ago I would not have believed possible: production is up, absenteeism is down; wastage is reduced, and valuable time is saved."[75] C. G. Renold explained the mystery of this phenomenon: "The need to base managerial authority on reason rather than on arbitrary power—as is implied in the whole philosophy of joint consultation—has enhanced that authority."[76]

It is hardly necessary to add that the same applies with even greater force to a system based on the philosophy of self-government. An International Labor Organization mission in Yugoslavia found in 1960 that, "while the self-government machinery for labor relations has curtailed the former powers of the supervisory staffs, it would not appear to have impaired their authority. . . . It has undoubtedly strengthened the position of the collective vis-à-vis the management, but it does not appear to have undermined labor discipline."[77] In Chile it was found that worker discipline improved after the introduction of self-management.[78] Self-government substitutes understanding for obedience, the agreement for the exercise of arbitrary power. By eliminating capitalist or bureaucratic duality and polarization of interests, it reduces tensions and improves coordination.

3. The *success* of joint consultation has been quite limited so far, and we shall examine the reasons for this in a moment. According to McKitterick and Roberts' evaluation of the German works councils of the Weimar period, the councils "were useful in protecting the workers' interests, but achieved virtually nothing in the way of genuine participation in management." Regarding postwar development, the authors declared: "Where workers' councils exist the general experience has been that the employees take a keen interest in their activities. . . ."[79] In Britain broad masses of workers are still apathetic, but four-fifths of workers' representatives in councils support the institution and show a keen interest in it. It is also significant that the experience in joint consultation has induced chief executives, senior management, and workers' representatives to take a more favorable view than they originally held about joint consultation in 37, 48, and 58 percent of cases, respectively, and a less favorable view only in 9, 5, and 1 percent of cases.[80]

4. Next, there is the problem of the *fundamental relation* between capital and labor. These two opposing sides are reflected in the very term *joint* consultation. The initiative on the part of the employer to introduce joint consultation in his firm is not infrequently a deliberate attempt to anticipate and check the development of unionism.[81] But even if this is not the aim, joint consultation increases loyalty to the firm, and this loyalty and loyalty to one's class are two different, indeed conflicting, allegiances.[82] Joint consultation produces workers' leaders who are not trade union officials and so are outside the grip of the "machinery." Clearly, unions will not be enthusiastic about partnership proposals and frequently will oppose them. If, on the other hand, a union or shop stewards seek to participate in joint committees, employers will fear infringement of their own prerogatives. The hopelessness of the situation lies in the fact that *both* sides are right in their fears. With employers basically opposed to surrendering their arbitrary power and unions ba-

sically unwilling to assume responsibility for the organization of production—because they gain nothing and lose their independence, as well as their grip on the membership's loyalties—the status quo is likely to be prolonged and potential changes prevented. The logic of the situation is such that unions act in virtual collusion with employers against workers, a collusion that becomes overt in more turbulent times.[83] This sheds new light on the events we have surveyed: formidable social forces have been and will be opposing workers' participation in management.

5. The trade union paradox represents an illustration of the working of *bureaucratic structures.* In order to protect themselves in a world of polarized interests, a world whose institutions are against them, workers build strong bureaucratic organizations: unions and parties. Once these organizations are built, they acquire their own separate interests different from the interests of those who support the whole structure. There is nothing ethically wrong in this; it does not happen because the leaders are wicked. The development is perfectly natural and, to a certain extent, inevitable. The way out of the impasse is logically easy. The organization must first be used to eliminate the fundamental cause of the polarization of interests—in this case, the private control of production. Then the bureaucratic principle of organization must be replaced by self-government. Actual unions and socialist parties, however, are unlikely to follow this course straight away on their own. Having become a part of the establishment with a clearly defined role in it, they are not prone to leave the life of routine and rush into the uncertainties of full-scale socialization. Self-government, on the other hand, is an idea so alien to the spirit of bureaucracy that it is clear it will encounter vigorous resistance.[84]

The situation, however, cannot remain completely unchanged. There is no reason to believe that business cycles have died out. But there is some cause for believing that the governments of industrial countries in the second half of our century cannot afford to tolerate heavy unemployment without risking major social upheavals. By curing the slump, the first decisive element of change is introduced into the process: the increasing degree of social control. The welfare state is its symbol. Uninterrupted full employment has a thoroughly anticapitalist effect, however: it generates competition in the improvement of management-worker relations. For employers are vitally interested in avoiding labor turnover, in escaping strikes, and in overcoming resistance toward the introduction of new processes, while workers feel secure and for this reason are actively conscious of their rights and possibilities.[85] By raising the status of workers, employers gradually surrender their autocratic power, and so their social function loses its content. In this way a second element is introduced into the process: the increasing degree of workers' participation in management. It is unlikely that the process will always develop smoothly. In the case of revolution, however, the trend is even clearer.

In the 150 years that have passed since the first Owenite experiment in New Lanark, relations between employers and workers have been constantly changing. These relations are reflected in the character of meetings between employers and employees, which, as the British National Institute of Industrial Psychology aptly described it, "over the last 150 years shows a historical development from deputation and negotiation to consultation."[86] And, we may add, to direct management in the end. This last phase of development supersedes the two-sided nature of the meetings and unifies the interests of all concerned in the institution of self-government.

The past five decades have produced joint consultation on a large scale. During the last twenty years, the first attempts have also been made to go beyond mere consultation. German co-determination is a case in point; so is Peruvian full participation. Individual firms have also begun to move toward co-determination or even to a state of genuine workers' self-government.[87] A communitarian movement appeared in several European countries following the example set by the watch-case firm of Boimondau in Valence, southern France.[88] These self-governing *work communities*—a term that at first sounded rather strange, but that was later to become a legal, even constitutional term in Yugoslavia (*radna zajednica*) and Peru (*comunidad laboral*)—went beyond producers' cooperatives by treating productive property as indivisible social property, by eliminating wage labor, and by aspiring to the full development of the human potential of their members. Less ambitious and less demanding socially, but more viable economically, was the Mondragón project, a system of Basque cooperatives begun in 1956. It proved that, with proper institutional arrangements, producer cooperatives may not only survive without degeneration but also expand rapidly even in an environment like Franco's Spain.[89] The attitude of the Catholic church changed. The 1961 encyclical *Mater et Magistra* of Pope John XXIII declared: "Moving in the direction set by our predecessors, we also feel that the aspirations to participate actively in the life of enterprises they form part of and work in is legitimate in workers. . . . the exercise of responsibility by workers in productive organizations, besides responding to the legitimate claims peculiar to human nature, is also in harmony with historical development in the economic, social, and political fields."

Participation is not only more desirable, it is also economically more viable than traditional authoritarian management. Econometric measurements indicate that efficiency increases with participation.[90] Bankrupt or moribund capitalist firms in Britain, the United States, Latin America, and elsewhere are revitalized when they are transformed into worker-managed enterprises. When specific economic problems are encountered and traditional policies fail, worker management is attempted as a solution. The Turkish government tried to improve the performance of the notoriously unprofitable state-owned industries by introducing worker participation in management. In northern Sweden, the government policy of industrialization failed because private firms would receive government subsidies, move into the area, and then pull out again, claiming that business was unprofitable. It was natural to conclude that worker-managed firms should be set up and be given subsidies because they would not leave. In France, participation is considered as the only alternative to the growing bureaucratization of the economy. In Britain, where the opposing forces of capital and labor have reached a stalemate, an awareness is gradually being formed that the traditional industrial organization must be replaced with something very different if the slide of the economy is to be arrested. Under pressure from their members, trade unions have begun to change their attitudes. In revised laws or union-management agreements, the scope of joint consultation has invariably been increased. Co-determination has been introduced in the social welfare sphere and occasionally beyond it. There is little doubt that the world is moving toward a socialist, self-governing society at an accelerated pace.

6

Comparative Organization and Efficiency

Our historical analysis revealed a very clear tendency for society to develop in the direction of self-government. In order to understand this tendency, we must identify the factors that determine it. There are at least three such factors: organizational feasibility, improved economic efficiency, and desirability of the new social order. The society that is historically possible, more desirable, and potentially more efficient than the available alternatives is also historically necessary. "Necessary" in this context indicates a high probability that such a society will eventually be established. But high probability is not the same as absolute certainty, and "eventually" may turn out to be a very long process. Two consequences follow: if our analysis is correct, self-governing socialism is not a utopian dream but a realizable project. Yet it will not be accomplished automatically. In a human society, events occur as a result of human action. Socialism may be achieved sooner or later and may have different features depending on how adequate this action is. A basic precondition for successful action is a good theory. The following analysis of the three determining factors of the movement toward self-government will lead us to an operational definition of socialism. Once that is settled, the foundations are laid for a meaningful theory.

I. Comparative Organization

A. Capitalist Organizational Model

Two general principles underlie alternative organizations of productive units and entire societies: hierarchy and participation. The first generates classes and, in modern times, capitalist or etatist social orders. The second implies classlessness and is the organizational precondition for socialism.

These two organizational principles are not simply logical categories capable of formal manipulation. We cannot simply choose one or the other regardless of the social context. Thus, again, it is necessary that we undertake a brief historical analysis. Historically, the hierarchical principle is the earlier one and, of its two manifestations, capitalist organization is the older.

Feudal society was a society of dependence, a prototype of a paternalistic order. The serf was totally dependent on his lord; he was obliged to work for and obey him. The master, on the other hand, had his own duties: to defend the village, to help in time of distress, to provide guidance. It is only too natural that during the early development of capitalism this paternalistic ideology of dependence should prevail. Even such a social reformer as Robert Owen was profoundly paternalistic. The ruling class, the aristocracy, viewed it as the duty of the higher classes to assume responsibility for the lives of the poor.

> The lot of the poor, in all things which affect them collectively, should be regulated *for* them, not *by* them. They should not be required or encouraged to think for themselves, or give to their own reflection or forecast an influential voice in the determination of their destiny. It is supposed to be the duty of the higher classes to think for them, and to take the responsibility of their lot. . . . This function . . . the higher classes should prepare themselves to perform conscientiously, and their whole demeanor should impress the poor with a reliance on it, in order that, while yielding passive and active obedience to the rules prescribed for them, they may resign themselves in all other respects to a trustful *insouciance*, and repose under the shadow of their protectors. The relation between rich and poor should be only partly authoritative; it should be amiable, moral and sentimental: affectionate tutelage on the one side, respectful and grateful deference on the other. The rich should be *in loco parentis* to the poor, guiding and restraining them like children.[1]

As the primitive accumulation of capital proceeded, this ideology became an obstacle to capitalistically efficient business operations. Entrepreneurs needed highly mobile workers, a reserve army of unemployed, and employment at minimum cost. Thus they did not want to be bothered with the private problems of workers and their families. It was discovered that obedience could be secured by more efficient means than physical compulsion and the ideology of natural responsibility. That means was hunger. As early as 1786, Rev. Joseph Townsend wrote:

> Hunger will tame the fiercest animals, it will teach decency and civility, obedience and subjection, to the most perverse. In gen-

> eral it is only hunger which can spur and goad them [the poor] on to labour; yet our laws have said they shall never hunger. The laws, it must be confessed, have likewise said, they shall be compelled to work. But then legal constraint is attended with much trouble, violence and noise; creates ill will, and never can be productive of good and acceptable service: whereas hunger is not only a peaceable, silent and unremitted pressure, but, as the most natural motive to industry and labour, it calls forth the most powerful exertions. . . . The slave must be compelled to work; but the freeman should be left to his own judgement and discretion; should be protected in the full enjoyment of his own, be it much or little; and punished when he invades his neighbours' property.[2]

Thus personal freedom, law, and order were required to make possible uninhibited capitalist exploitation. One further step was necessary to render the new ideology fully consistent: obedience was to be secured and exploitation accomplished on the basis of free consent as expressed in contractual relationships. A few years later, in 1795, the conservative political theorist Edmund Burke formulated the doctrine with precision and clarity:

> labour is a commodity, and as such, an article of trade. . . . When any commodity is carried to market, it is not the necessity of the vendor, but the necessity of the purchaser, that raises the price. The impossibility of subsistence of the man who carries his labour to a market is totally beside the question in this way of viewing it. The only question is, what is it worth to the buyer.[3]

The medieval social consciousness was still too strong, and Rev. Townsend's advice as well as Burke's conclusion were not followed immediately. Quite to the contrary. In 1795, the justices of Berkshire established by their ruling what came to be known as the Speenhamland Law. It ensured the "right to live" by outdoor relief to those workers who earned less than a subsistence income. "No measure was ever more universally popular," observed Karl Polanyi. "Parents were free of the care of their children, and children were no more dependent upon parents; employers could reduce wages at will and labourers were safe from hunger whether they were busy or slack; humanitarians applauded the measure as an act of mercy even though not of justice. . . . "[4] Yet its popularity soon began to wane. The "right to live" was not quite congruent with capitalism. It destroyed its "harmony and beauty," as Townsend predicted. The measure which began as aid-in-wages in the interest of employees turned into the use of public means to subsidize employers. Wages fell since the pool of labor was sufficiently large, and the difference between wages and the minimum income was covered out of public funds. Low wages adversely affected productivity, and that of course provided an additional reason for employers not to raise wages above the minimum set by the scale. Both the drop in wages and the drop in productivity destroyed the morale of the workers, who lost their self-respect and sank to the status of paupers. By 1834, human and social degradation was so widespread that anything seemed better than wage subsidies, and Speenhamland humanitarianism was replaced by the cruel rationality of the Poor Law Reform Act, whose effects were to occupy the attention of Marx and Engels and their socialist friends for years to come. The right to live was superseded by the right to compete on the labor market, to sell one's own labor as any other commodity.

Ever since those days, bourgeois political scientists and economists have treated labor as a commodity and employment as a buying and selling relationship. If someone were poor, that was his own fault. Either he had not worked hard enough, or he had failed to comply with the dictates of an impersonal market. No one bore any responsibility. That was a natural state of affairs. Similarly natural was the hierarchy of social relations: like any other buyer, the employer had the right to dispose of the commodity—i.e., labor—he bought as he found fit. This implied that the employer issued orders and the employee was expected to obey.

The role of the state in the economic process was reduced to very moderate dimensions. It was to guarantee law and order and stay away from production and the employment of labor. Complete freedom of action for the capitalist entrepreneur was considered the ideal—and, in economic textbooks, most efficient—arrangement. It came to be known as a *laissez-faire* arrangement.

The development described so far produced a typical pyramidal structure of authority in the firm. The owner-employer was located at the peak and the workers represented the bottom of the pyramid. Orders flowed in one direction: from top to bottom. This structure proved to be highly unstable, for the following reasons.

If workers were personally free and employers were not responsible for the living conditions of the workers, then the organic unity of feudal society was definitely broken, and two different, separated, independent—and hostile—groups emerged. Society began to be polarized into two new social classes: proletariat and capitalists. Feudal society was obviously a class society as well. But there the political, legal, and ideological means for successful organization of the exploited class were not available. The very needs of capitalist development created such means, however, and soon they were being used. In 1848 Marx and Engels wrote their *Communist Manifesto.* In the same year the English liberal economist John Stuart Mill described the new state of affairs in the following terms:

> Of the working men . . . it may be pronounced certain that the patriarchal or paternal system of government is one to which they will not again be subject. That question was decided, when they were taught to read, and allowed access to newspapers and political tracts; when dissenting preachers were suffered to go among them, and appeal to their faculties and feelings in opposition to the creeds professed and countenanced by their superiors; when they were brought together in numbers, to work socially under the same roof; when the railways enabled them to shift from place to place, and change their patrons and employers as easily as their coats; when they were encouraged to seek a share in the government, by means of the electoral franchise. The working classes have taken their interests into their own hands, and are perpetually showing that they think the interests of their employers not identical with their own, but opposite to them.[5]

Workers began to organize themselves into political parties and trade unions. Within industry, the existence of unions implied a counterstructure built on the same workers' base. Thus the complete organizational model of a capitalist firm constituted a double pyramid (Figure 3): to the power of the employer, workers opposed the countervailing power of the union. The competitive struggle on the market was supplemented by the competitive struggle between employers and unions. Management began to accept the legitimacy of the unions. Labor was a commodity and unions were to bargain about its selling price. The structure was closed, the social situation stabilized, and unions ceased to be revolutionary.

This development was preceded by another which occurred a decade or so earlier. If labor were just a commodity, it should be treated accordingly. Once the price was set, the labor commodity was to be combined with other commodities in the production process. "Scientific management" was born.

Scientific management concentrated on the organizational structure and treated the worker as a dehumanized bundle of muscles and nerves. Its founder, Frederick Taylor, epitomized

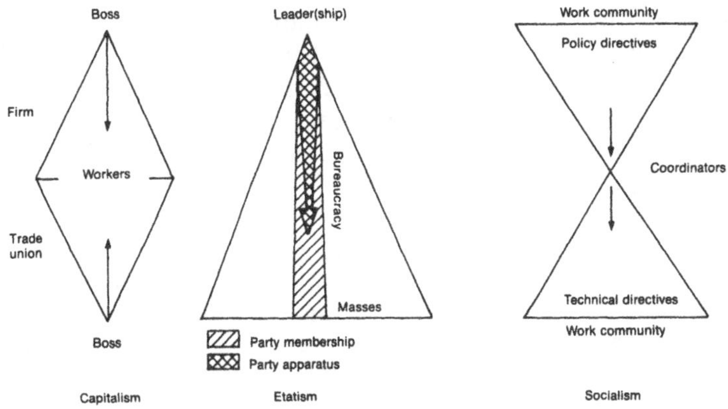

Figure 3. *Organizational models of capitalism, etatism, and socialism.*

the approach in a bit of advice that was to become famous: "For success, then, let me give one simple piece of advice beyond all others. Every day, year in year out, each man should ask himself, over and over again, two questions. First, 'What is the name of the man I am now working for?' and having answered this definitely, then 'What does this man want me to do, right now?' "

The First World War and the Great Economic Crisis of the early 1930s—euphemistically called a depression—represent the end of laissez-faire capitalism. A literate, educated, and politically experienced working class was no longer prepared to accept being treated as commodity labor. Unions developed into national organizations with great economic and political power. Keynesian economics required systematic state intervention. Firms grew in size and owner-entrepreneurs were gradually replaced by professional managers, who themselves were formally employees of the firm. Competitive laissez-faire capitalism evolved into organized, state-monopoly capitalism. Resources continue to be allocated *through* the market, observes Andreas Papandreou[6]—but no longer *by* the market.

These changes implied changes in managerial ideology and in employment relations. "Scientific management" was running into difficulties. It was discovered that workers were not merely commodity labor and hired hands, but also human beings. As such they resented hierarchy and meaningless work.

Neither, however, could be avoided. Without hierarchy, the entire social system would collapse. Therefore it was announced that efficiency required hierarchy, which was proclaimed as an inherent part of management prerogatives and as such excluded from union bargaining. On the other hand, an attempt was made to substitute for interesting work by showing an interest in the worker. In this way the commodity-labor approach was replaced by what came to be known as the human relations approach. Bendix described the salient features of the new approach as follows:

> By the 1930's this awareness of workers as human beings was widespread among American employers. Failure to treat workers as human beings came to be regarded as the cause of low morale, poor craftsmanship, unresponsiveness, and confusion. Management was accused by its own spokesmen of neglecting to give to the employee "what every human being asks of life: respect for his personality, his human dignity, an environment that he comprehends, and the assurance that he is progressing." . . . Since it was difficult at best to encourage the workers' creative interest in their jobs, employers frequently were reminded to create a sense of satisfaction among their employees. "Treat workers as human beings. Show your interest in their personal success and welfare." That is, if the work holds no interest, show your interest in the workers.[7]

This, of course, is very different advice from that given by Frederick Taylor. The needs of early capitalist development made personal freedom mandatory. Similarly, late capitalist development required civilized treatment of workers in order to avoid disruptive discontent. But the human relations approach meant little more than the skillful manipulation of human sentiments in order to preserve the profitability of business operations. And it seemed to work, at least for a while.[8] A successful manager was defined as one who could control his emotions, while subordinate employees and workers could not do so. Personality salesmanship and human social skills were what is really implied and required. Since human dignity and social hierarchy are incompatible, the newly discovered interest in workers as people was just a new form of the old paternalism. This paternalism has been developed further into an all-pervasive ideology of organized capitalism due to the giant size of corporations, the giant size of unions, the complexities of the modern state, and the apparent need for important decisions to be made by an informed elite. The common man does not participate in decision making. At best, he is allowed to ratify his leaders' choice.

In the 1950s the human relations approach fell into disrepute. Unions had been hostile all along anyway, and the workers were no longer willing to remain the objects of thinly veiled manipulations. New approaches such as "job enrichment" and "human resources" had to be tried out. The latter can be described as follows: In contrast to the traditional human relations models, management's task is seen not so much as one of manipulating employees to accept managerial authority as of developing a "partnership" or "family" of employees, with each member contributing according to his or her abilities and interests to the organization's goals.[9] Thus the circle of historical development of capitalist organization is closed. Capitalism began by destroying the social and emotional bonds of traditional—i.e., feudal—organization; it seems to end by trying to reestablish these bonds by supplementing the free contract with the emotional relationships of "family" and "partnership." Maslow's recently developed theory of human needs (which will be discussed in greater detail in chapter 15, section I) was utilized to design policies for exploiting untapped human resources. If people want to be creative, responsible, and self-directed, the job of management is to create an environment in which all "family" members will contribute to the limits of their ability. If that means the participation of subordinates, let them participate.

Now, in a hierarchical system subordinates remain subordinates even with participation. Unions remained hostile, perceiving the humanization movement "as a management power play, as evidenced in the prevailing non-union status of the 'humanized' enterprises and the anti-union or union substitution rhetoric of the theory's practitioners."[10] Unions do not reject self-determination in work, but they do not interpret it as individuated self-actualization. Since the latter is obviously utopian in the modern capitalist enterprise, unions insist on collective self-determination, which clearly implies strong union organizations.

Unions have thus remained workers' organizations. Very strict limits had to be imposed upon their activities, however, if the system were to be preserved. "Industrial peace," observed Papandreou, "has been achieved . . . in the advanced capitalist world—on terms which amount to the assimilation of organized labour leadership into the ruling coalition, on terms acceptable to those who have the focal control."[11] Union democracy, resembling a "one-party state," is severely limited. Since their return to the shop would mean a substantial lowering of living standard and social status, and is regarded as humiliation and failure, union leaders try to restrict democracy as much as possible and, in fact, remain in office for life. The double pyramid in Figure 3 can now be given a final interpretation. In times of conflict, the bosses of the two bureaucratic organizations—the firm and the union—negotiate a settlement. Countervailing power in capitalist societies can be organized only in terms of hierarchical bureaucratic structures. The interests of these bureaucracies and their bosses are not necessarily identical with the interests of those whom they represent. In fact, the powerful groups of all bureaucracies in a capitalist society have one overwhelming interest in common: the preservation of the status quo, of the establishment.

Thus countervailing power is strictly limited by the untouchability of the establishment—that is, by the basic interests of the ruling class.

B. Etatist Organizational Model

Britain is the oldest capitalist country. Consequently, the development of capitalist organization is best investigated by studying British socioeconomic development as we did in the preceding section. Similarly, the Soviet Union is the oldest etatist country, and as such will provide us with useful empirical material for a study of etatist organization.

The economic development of Russia was delayed by about a century as compared with that of Western Europe. Its first two railway lines, comprising about 1,000 kilometers, were not completed until 1850. At that time the country contained no more than 2,800 shops employing some 860,000 persons. Many of the employed were not industrial workers but serfs. The liberation of serfs was initiated by law in 1861, but it was many years before the process was completed. The state was autocratic, and in this respect the continuity has remained unbroken until the present day. Lack of experience in political democracy meant that people were treated as subjects, not as citizens. Trade unions were repressed. The first congress of trade unions was convened only after the October Revolution. The slow process of industrialization was dependent on governmental support and supervision for about two centuries. For these reasons, the paternalistic ideology of the earlier feudal society was still very much alive when the Revolution broke out in 1917. Actually, the Revolution was a direct consequence of the fact that tsarist autocracy had survived so long into the modern era as to have become incompatible with further social development.

During the Revolution, the national economy gradually became disorganized to the point of complete breakdown; production was drastically reduced, discipline and responsibility were seriously weakened. In 1918 Lenin urged that courts be used to inculcate labor discipline and that, at the place of work, workers must observe iron discipline and comply unconditionally with the orders of one man, the Soviet manager.[12] We have already noted (chapter 5, section IV) how this nipped workers' self-management in the bud. After the Revolution, Russian society lived for two more decades in a state of siege. This was due partly to hostile bourgeois encirclement. But the atmosphere of siege and insecurity was also created deliberately by Stalin and his propagandists in order to justify internal repression. The final result of this peculiar combination of circumstances was a foregone conclusion. The tsar and the aristocracy were replaced by the state and a new elite. The new bureaucracy inherited the virtues and vices of the tsarist officialdom. The power of the state grew unchecked until all of social life was regulated and controlled by the state. In this way an etatist system of organization was developed.

The etatist model comprises a monolithic structure based on the principle of *edinonachalie,* or one-man management. Directives flow in one direction, from the top of the social pyramid to the bottom. Polish economist Bronislav Minc has noted that state ownership of the means of production carries four consequences: production takes place at the state's account; the state manages and controls production and distribution; there is a need to protect public ownership from the encroachments of group ownership; and the state appoints the organs managing production and distribution.[13] Minc consistently identified society with the state, using the terms interchangeably, since he was unable to visualize society as other than state run or state controlled. The absence of any checks and safeguards that could produce countervailing power is generally explained and justified by the claim that classes and conflicts are absent from such a society. Consequently, everyone is placed where he belongs, and any disagreement or opposition is crushed as dysfunctional and antisystemic (counterrevolutionary, in the respective political jargon).

It is taken for granted that there must always be the leaders and the led. The latter are the toiling masses. The former are the technical experts who are talented. "Communism is impossible without management," writes F. B. Sadykov, "but managing the toiling people [*rukovodit' trudovym narodom*] is the obligation of those who are most talented, . . . who possess deep knowledge of the various spheres of production, who are acquainted with the newest achievements of science and technology, people of high culture and intelligence."[14] The ideologues of the system are aware, of course, that hierarchy can generate a conflict of interest. But Sadykov easily disposes of the problem: "The difference in the official position of leaders and the toiling masses in fulfilling the production function does not generate contradictions between them because, in keeping with their objective position and vocation, the leaders take care of social interests and fight for the welfare of the people."[15]

Etatist social scientists not only insist on hierarchy but are also aware that their managerial hierarchy is the same as, for instance, in capitalism. How, in the absence of an atmosphere of critical scientific inquiry, the problem can be explained away is shown by the philosopher I. Volkov, a section head at the Institute of Marxism-Leninism of the Party Central Committee:

> Under socialism the system of societal management is externally similar to those that existed in previous formations: management is carried out in a state form; there is a particular stratum of persons engaged exclusively in the performance of the respective functions. On the gnoseological plane, this is precisely what makes possible the fabrications . . . of the ideologists of anticommunism and of various opportunists. In reality, no matter how the apparatus of management in socialist society is formed and functions, and no matter how externally similar it is to that existing under capitalism, the *essence* of management, of the relations of management, has a qualitatively different character than under capitalism, being defined by the specific nature of the social structure of socialist society.[16]

(Incidentally, note the meanings attached to the words *anticommunism* and *opportunists* and compare them with our analysis in chapter 4, section V.)

According to socialist tradition, the state is an apparatus of repression, and its role should be reduced to a minimum. Marx and Engels urged and expected a withering away of the state. Not so the etatist theoreticians, who envisage an increased role for the state even in postsocialist society. Thus N. A. Feliforov points out:

> in the period of communist construction the functions of the socialist state, as a central organ of management, increase. The state administers all processes of communist construction: the building of the material-technical basis of communism, the transformation of the socialist social relations into communist ones, spiritual development, the education of the Soviet people.[17]

Far from being a shortcoming of the particular social order that Feliforov calls socialism, this etatist organization is seen as its main advantage:

> The greatest advantage of socialism as compared with all preceding social systems consists in the fact that here society develops as one single, complete system, uniting (on democratic principles) economy, politics, spiritual life. In order to achieve this unity, centralized management of all spheres of society is indispensable.[18]

The organizational principle underlying this model is called democratic centralism. The meaning of the centralist component ought to be clear by now. The other, democratic component is described in terms of a rather confused paternalism, an etatist variant of the human relations approach: it "is expressed in the methods of training and the activities of management organs, in the increased attraction of the toiling masses to direct management, in their broad initiative and creative self-activity in building a new society."[19] What happens when this creative self-activity deviates from the directives of the center is left unexplained. Miloslav Formanek, expressing the views of the postoccupation Czechoslovak establishment, argues that "democratic" means that which serves socialism and the people. The obvious question as to who evaluates the people's interests is not tackled, but the answer is implied in the ensuing text: "Socialist democracy in Czechoslovakia gives maximum equality, freedom and rights to workers, peasants and intellectuals, applying at the same time repression against the minority, bourgeoisie and its influence."[20] Thus, whoever opposes may conveniently be proclaimed a bourgeois or under bourgeois influence, and so repression is justified.

In order to function, the model described so far needs an elite. This role is fulfilled by the ruling party. "The basis of the successful functioning of the Soviet state and other organizations administering social processes lies in the managing and directing role of the party."[21] Formanek argues that the leading role of the party is an expression of socialist democracy, because the party realizes the people's interests. Quite consistently, the internal hierarchy is then projected into the international realm: "The country has become a powerful constituent part of the world socialist system led by the Soviet Union."[22] The author wants to say that the country has become a satellite. The party, explains Yampol'skaia, is an organization that "not only expresses the will of the progressive strata of the people, its vanguard, but also actively influences the formation of the general all-people will."[23] The will of the party and the general will coincide, and there can be no divergence between the interests of the party and the interests of the people "because people's interests—these are also the personal interest of the communists." "The Communist Party selects leaders from its own ranks first of all."[24] This is a new organizational element, and it will be useful to take a closer look at it.

Without the party the social pyramid, with two loose ends, would be highly unstable. Position in the hierarchy cannot be justified by birth or tradition, or by success in a competitive market; it can be based only on (political) merit. In a centralized—and hence authoritarian—setting, there is need for a special screening mechanism whereby relative merit can be determined. The party fulfills this role. As a consequence, it functions as a bolt running through the pyramid from top to bottom and holding all the strata together (see Figure 3). The party recruits its members from all social strata and represents—in relation to alternative hierarchical arrangements—a comparatively efficient channel of upward social mobility. This mobility proceeds through two stages. First, candidates for party membership are selected in a particular environment. After they have become members, in the second stage the most promising leaders are selected for various professional party jobs. Once a member of the party apparatus, a man or woman can climb quite fast, regardless of his or her origin, providing the climber is reasonably able and acts in strict accordance with the relevant norms (the chief of which is absolute conformity).

This relatively high social mobility strengthens the party's grip on society. One is reminded of Marx's description of the medieval Catholic church: "The fact that the Catholic church in the Middle Ages formed its hierarchy out of the best brains in the land, regardless of their estate, birth, or fortune, was one of the main means of strengthening priestly rule and holding down the laity. The more a ruling class is able to co-opt the best minds of a ruled class, the more stable and dangerous becomes its rule."[25]

According to official ideology, the party is the party of the working class, an instrument of the dictatorship of the proletariat. In practice this is not so; and by the very nature of things, it cannot be so. For instance, in the Soviet Union workers represented 57 percent of the party at the time of the Revolution and only 36 percent a decade later. A political elite is always a ruling elite and, as such, is small and is recruited primarily from higher social strata. In fact the simplest way to discover the hierarchy of social strata in an etatist society is to determine the share of party membership belonging to particular strata. Table 6 shows such a breakdown for the Communist Party of the Soviet Union.

TABLE 6

The Composition of the Communist Party of the Soviet Union, 1966

Social category (overlapping)	Total size of category (in millions)	% of category who are party members	% of category in total party membership
Executives, administrators	1.2	76	8
Engineers	4.4	40	15
Intelligentsia	11.2	36	38
Workers	51.0	9	37
Collective farmers	30.0	7	16
Trade, services, other office workers	14.4	4	4

Source: K. W. Deutsch, *Politics and Government* (Boston: Houghton Mifflin, 1970).

The higher up the social group, the greater the percentage of its members who belong to the party. More than three-quarters of the bureaucratic strata are party members. Less than one-tenth of workers and peasants belong to the party. In 1967, workers represented 54 percent of the population and only 38 percent of the party membership.[26] Engineers are placed relatively high, which is consistent with the technocratic view of society expressed by Sadykov as quoted above. Even this statistical picture is misleading, however. The real decisions are made not by party members but, in conformity with the principle of democratic centralism, by the party apparatus. Members are primarily a transmission mechanism; functionaires make decisions. At the Twenty-third Party Congress in 1966, out of 4,943 delegates, only 23 percent were workers and 11 percent peasants. In the Central Committee (360 members) elected at that congress, the share of workers and peasants dwindled to insignificance.[27]

Another way of looking at party membership is in terms of population groups classified according to the level of education achieved. The five educational groups show the following party saturation (measured as the share of each group who are party members):[28]

7% of those with an eighth-grade education or less
11% of those with incomplete secondary education
18% of those with complete secondary education
22% of those with complete higher education
46% of those with a postgraduate degree

The more educated a person, the more likely he is to become a party member (or vice versa). Among the best educated, every second man or woman is a party member. The political elite is at the same time an educational elite.

We may summarize our findings.

Unlike in capitalism, where different organizational principles are applied in the polity (democracy) and the economy (autocracy) and at the macro (market) and micro (administration) levels, etatist organization is fully consistent, and the same rules apply everywhere. They are called the Leninist principles of management and can be described as follows:

1) the unity of political and economic leadership as expressed in the leading role of the party;

2) democratic centralism, which, as in any bureaucratic system, means that managerial personnel are always appointed by the higher authorities and never elected; for the same reason they are also always accountable upwards to their superiors and never to those whom they manage;

3) one-man management, which, according to one Soviet writer, means that "the leadership of each production unit . . . is assigned to a single executive who is endowed by the state with the necessary rights to manage and who bears full responsibility for the work of the given unit. All individuals working in the unit are obliged to fulfill the instructions of the executive."[29]

In the etatist organizational model, the hierarchical structure is closed by a special device that connects the top and bottom of the pyramid—the party. In addition to performing the integrative role of keeping the structure together, the party is also an instrument of power. The party dominates society; the party apparatus dominates the party; and the supreme party leadership, composed of professional politicians, dominates the party apparatus. W. Brus observes that it is not the party congress that elects the Central Committee, it is the Central Committee that elects the congress. Unlike in capitalism, the political and power pyramids coincide and are in fact identical. The entire society is organized as one single monolithic pyramid, internally stratified but kept monolithic by the party. According to the etatist theoretician Feliforov, quoted above, this is its greatest advantage over all preceding societies.

C. Socialist Organizational Model

As has already been mentioned, a socialist organizational model must be structured so as to eliminate hierarchy, which inevitably generates class stratification. This is achieved by closing the organizational structure in a very specific way: no countervailing power, which generates competing bureaucracies; no party bolt, which gives rise to one single omnipotent bureaucracy; but the combining of management and work by the same people—that is, self-management. The capitalist and etatist organizational models can be described as double and single pyramids; the socialist model was dubbed a "sandglass" by my students (Figure 3). We can also say that, whereas capitalist organization implies a duality of power, while in the etatist model the power structure is monolithic, in socialism it is genuinely pluralist. Finally, we may characterize the three models in terms of ownership: capitalist organization is based on private ownership, etatist organization on state ownership, and the socialist model on social ownership.

At this point, the concept of hierarchy ought to be clarified. Hierarchy refers to two very different social phenomena which are very closely related in the prevailing social practice. They must be clearly distinguished, however, if hopeless confusion is to be avoided. Hierarchy may imply coordination or control. In the latter case, it is power based and handles otherwise unresolvable conflicts. In the former case, it is power neutral with no conflicts of interest. The coordinating hierarchy is a product of the division of labor and as such is eternal. The conductor will always conduct the orchestra. The controlling hierarchy is a product of class struggle; consequently, it is a social phenomenon and will tend to disappear with the disappearance of exploitative social relations.

Like many other relationships, hierarchy may be formal (referring to means) or substantive (implying the results). The failure to distinguish these two also leads to frequent confusion. The two aspects of hierarchy are not necessarily positively correlated. The reduction of formal hierarchy may lead to an increase of informal hierarchy. This happens, for instance, when the number of levels of hierarchy is formally reduced or eliminated—everybody decides on everything—which creates a chaotic situation in which informal cliques gain the upper hand.

The sandglass model is based on the observation that there are two fundamentally different spheres of activity or decision making. The first is concerned with value judgments, and consequently each individual counts as one in this sphere. In the second, technical decisions are made on the basis of technical competence and expertise. The decisions of the first sphere are policy directives; those of the second, technical directives. The former are based on political authority as exercised by all members of the organization; the latter, on professional authority specific to each member and growing out of the division of labor. Such an organization involves a clearly defined coordinating hierarchy but eliminates a power hierarchy.

In a self-managed socialist firm, all workers participate in policy decisions. Once a policy decision is reached, it becomes a directive for the management. The management acts as an executive committee of the working collective and implements policy decisions by translating them into the day-to-day operations of the firm, into technical decisions based on professional competence. Each firm is an association of individuals. So is each institution, each work organization, and each local community. The economy is an association of firms, society an association of associations.

Once the sandglass model of organization is socially accepted, we may expect that both the perception of what is desirable, and actual relations and behavior will change substantially. Productive life is democratized and alienation reduced.[30] Managers become coordinators and are not perceived as a group that ought to have more power than the workers. Contrary to traditional expectations, however, although managers are stripped of their authoritarian power, the total amount of power available for solving the problems increases. Workers do not feel less satisfied with their pay or their position compared with the "managers." The ratio of top to bottom salaries is reduced several times. Mobility *opportunities* are high, but *aspirations* to move up the hierarchical ladder, to the extent that it still exists, are weak. Agents of control are no longer primarily supervisors—though they, too, have a function—but peers. And the main technique of control is not rewards and punishments but social criticism and approval. Generally, we shall expect socialist production relations. And, in fact, the various traits enumerated are not merely a matter of reasonable expectations; they have already been discovered through empirical research.[31]

In a society organized along these lines, the antinomies described in chapter 2, section I, disappear as false. There is neither private nor state ownership, but social ownership. There is no exclusive reliance either on the market or on planning, since they are complementary, and the market becomes a planning device *sui generis*. Money and interest become pure instruments of economic regulation. There is neither individualism nor collectivism but full and free development of the personality of each cooperating individual. There is neither private initiative nor governmental dictate but individual initiative in organizations of associated labor. There is neither (bourgeois) democracy nor (bureaucratic) dictatorship but self-government.

At this stage of our inquiry, I cannot elaborate on the statements just made. They will be explained and proved as we proceed. Here it suffices to contrast the institutions and theoretical categories of a socialist society with those of the two class societies. Socialism is not only different; it is fundamentally unlike the two alternative social orders of our time.

II. Comparative Efficiency

The term *efficiency* as employed here means the best possible use of the available resources. If "the best" relates to economic welfare, then we speak of economic efficiency. The present chapter deals with economic efficiency. In the economic sense, the available resources are material and human resources. Different social systems use the available economic resources with varying degrees of efficiency. In this respect we are interested in comparing the performance of capitalism, etatism, and socialism.

Economic efficiency—or inefficiency—can be discussed conveniently in a micro- or a macroeconomic context; that is, as it relates to individual productive units or to the national economy as a whole. It has been observed that, in capitalism, the firm is organized rationally, but the system is macroeconomically inefficient because of business fluctuations, unemployment, and lack of coordination of economic activities. On the other hand, it is said, etatism is rational at the macroeconomic level, but irrational—i.e., inefficient—at the level of the firm because of the stifling effects of bureaucratic organization. While these observations are not incorrect, neither are they complete. They take capitalism (private ownership) and etatism (state ownership) as the only two standards of reference. It will be shown that both these systems are microeconomically as well as macroeconomically inefficient.

A. Inefficiencies of Capitalist Organization

Given the available resources, the desired goal in a capitalistically organized economy is less than what is objectively possible. The system's inefficiency is observable at both levels—that of the firm (micro) and that of the national economy (macro).

The firm. The basic cause of inefficiency is to be found in the fundamental social conflict between employer and employees. Class conflict generates at least five types of inefficiency.

1. Since the worker is not working for himself but for someone else—for a master—his work effort is not optimal. He lacks the appropriate *motivation.* This fact has received rigorous empirical documentation over the last half-century. In the late 1920s, a Harvard Business School professor, Elton Mayo, and his group conducted sociological research at the Hawthorne Works of the Western Electric Company in the United States. It was found, for instance, that there was no correlation between the dexterity and intelligence of a worker and the product of his work. The potential ability of a worker is transformed into an actual economic effect only if an appropriate motivation exists. The study found that workers worked substantially below their capacity and that, no matter what the incentive scheme invented by the employer, the productivity of work was controlled by an informal consensus of the working group.[32] The Second World War seriously impaired the legitimacy of the authoritarian capitalist order. Work below capacity became noticeable even without special studies. In 1959, American sociologist Daniel Bell observed: "The most characteristic fact about the American factory worker today . . . is his lack of interest in work."[33] This lack of interest is manifested in absenteeism, high labor turnover, and poor work discipline—all of which have been getting worse since Bell made his observations. In an interview in 1974, Leonard Woodcock, one of the less conservative among major American union leaders, noted characteristically:

> The fact that absenteeism in the last five to seven years has doubled indicates that it is not necessarily a plant-related business, because there hasn't been any particular change in the way the work is done now as against seven years ago. . . . Strangely enough, the rise in absenteeism took place, not only among assembly-line crews but also in plants where working conditions are not based upon assembly-line technique. . . . We really don't know what the reasons are. We just don't know.[34]

But we do know what the reasons are. Let me conclude this American dialogue—and similar French, English, Swedish dialogues could be constructed—by quoting William Halal of American University in Washington:

> Because bureaucracies typically offer work roles which are highly specialized, the resulting routine jobs offer insufficient interest and challenge to satisfy the more sophisticated workers of today. Also, the authoritarian, centralized form of leadership employed in bureaucracies is increasingly unacceptable and often results in a sense of oppression because employees are prevented from effectively influencing their working lives. As a result, problems of worker alienation have become widely experienced phenomena among many groups of employees, including most blue and white collar workers and even middle managers.[35]

In order to control workers more efficiently and to reduce the costs to themselves of replacing existing labor and training new workers, employers introduce ever-finer division of labor and specialization of tasks, together with an assembly-line technology that dictates the pace of work. As a consequence, work is deskilled, workers' autonomy reduced, job satisfaction destroyed, and workers' dissatisfaction and resistance enhanced. More and more often, strikes erupt for reasons other than wage demands.[36]

2. In order to extract labor from the worker, the employer must undertake close *supervision* of his work. People have a natural inclination, as Demsetz[37] put it, to refrain from work when they are not supervised by the master. In the managerial literature, one man is considered able to closely supervise between three and ten other men. At a lower level of routinized work, the ratio between superiors and subordinates may be as high as 1:30. In a firm with, say, 4,000 workers, there may be eleven layers of authority.[38] Clearly, the supervision costs are enormous. Besides, income inequality is necessarily increased. If compensation increases by 25 percent for each increase in rank, the top salary will have to be twelve times greater than the average worker's wage. On the other hand, more than a century ago the English bourgeois economist John Stuart Mill realized that, in a socialist farm or factory, the worker is supervised not by his master but by the entire community of which he is a member.[39]

3. In an authoritarian setting, the impulse toward *innovation* is weakened. There are at least three reasons. Since the worker is treated as an operative, the necessary social atmo-

sphere is lacking, and innovation is considered to be the business of the staff. Innovation premiums, however designed, do not prove to be very effective. Next, since the real benefits of innovations go to "them," why bother? Finally, the foreman, who is the normal intermediary between worker and management, may—and generally does—have his own careerist reasons for belittling the capacities of the workers under his command. An innovating worker is proof of the foreman's inferiority. More generally, new ideas are simply dangerous and thus unwelcome. They may disrupt the existing equilibrium of status and power.

4. In a corporation, the connection between managerial behavior and *sanctions* has largely been destroyed. Managers make mistakes and shareholders are punished. The process of replacing inefficient management is slow and ineffective. The market's most radical verdict—bankruptcy—is socially a very costly affair.

5. Finally, *bargaining procedures* are costly and absorb time and energy. In order to protect their interests, workers must organize unions; the upkeep of union machinery involves, of course, real cost. So does the maintenance of employers' organizations. Strikes and lockouts constitute a manifest waste of resources. Instead of spending their time and money fighting each other, the people involved could engage in more rewarding productive work. The problem is well summarized by P. Chaulieu:

> If a thousand individuals have amongst them a given capacity for self-organization, capitalism consists in more or less arbitrarily choosing fifty of these individuals, of investing them with managerial authority and of deciding that the others should just be cogs. Metaphorically speaking, this is already 95% loss of social initiative and drive. But there is more to it. As the 950 ignored individuals are *not* cogs, and as capitalism is obliged up to a point to develop them, these individuals will react and struggle against what the system imposes upon them. The creative faculties which they are not allowed to exercise on behalf of a social order which rejects them (and which they reject) are now utilised against that social order. A permanent struggle develops at the very kernel of social life. It soon becomes a source of further waste. The narrow stratum of order-givers has henceforth to divide its time between organising the work of those below and seeking to counteract, neutralise, deflect or manipulate their resistance. The function of the managerial apparatus ceases to be merely organization and soon assumes all sorts of coercive aspects. Those in authority in a large modern factory in fact spend less of their time in organization of production

than in coping, directly or indirectly, with the resistance of the exploited—whether it be a question of supervision, of quality control, of determining piece rates, of "human relations," of discussions with shop stewards or union representatives. On top of all this there is of course the permanent preoccupation of those in power with making sure that everything is measurable, quantifiable, verifiable, controllable, so as to deal in advance with any counteraction workers might launch against new methods of exploitation.[40]

At the level of the *national economy*, one can distinguish the following sources of inefficiency.

1. Class antagonisms prevent the optimal use of available human resources. There is a tremendous *waste of talent*. The society's educational, cultural, and medical facilities are not used by those who would benefit most from them; the differential access to these facilities is provided in accordance with the class position of the candidates. This problem was touched upon in chapter 3, sections I and II, and merits further discussion here. In prewar England graduates of the so-called public schools (privately financed schools charging tuition fees) represented 2 percent of the population; but their chances of governing the country—that is, of becoming members of Parliament—was 115 times greater than that of pupils who did not have access to these privileged establishments.[41] On the other hand, "while nearly all the children of the larger business and the professional classes who possess ability have the opportunity of higher education, the corresponding figure for clerical and commercial employees is approximately 50 percent, for skilled wage-earners 30 percent, and for unskilled wage-earners 20 percent."[42] In the United States, a country with more universities than any other country, 58 percent of the ablest one-tenth in terms of intelligence quotient did not receive a college education in the 1950s.[43] Such percentages clearly also reflect the level of economic development and will improve as the level of development increases. But at any given level of development, substandard children of the privileged classes receive education at the expense of bright children of the exploited classes.[44]

When, in a wealthier society, education becomes more widely available, the ruling classes still manage to discriminate. In the United States the families of major business executives produce as many business leaders as the *entire* labor population, while the families of business owners produce twice as many.[45] The son of a business executive or owner of a large business has about a 12 times greater chance than the son of an unskilled or semiskilled worker of becoming a successful businessman, and a hundreds of times greater chance than the farm laborer's son, for whom it is virtually impossible to penetrate into the business elite.[46]

2. Closely related to the previous point is the fact that the privately owned economy generates an *irrational distribution of income.* It is irrational because a more equal distribution of income—such as would be possible in a different institutional setup—would increase economic welfare. But it is irrational for yet another reason: it lowers the potential productive efficiency of the economy. The volume of production—and, for that matter, of consumption—depends on the efficient use of all resources, including labor resources. Now, labor resources *are not given,* they have to be built up, and they can be built up in various ways. The most efficient solution is achieved when the *health, education,* and *creative will to work* of a population are maximally enhanced. Adequate shelter, proper diet, and medical attention not only produce healthy bodies—an asset in itself—but, as psychological investigations have established beyond any doubt, they also foster intellectual development. A more equal distribution of income, since it is likely to increase the standard of health, is desirable on economic grounds. The same applies to education. If the market system is left to operate uncontrolled, it will lead to a waste of talent, because not the most promising children, but the children of parents able to pay, will get educated. The problem of education is not exhausted by the matter of school attendance, however. It has much broader implications in terms of the sharing of the entire cultural tradition of a given society. Again, greater equality of income is conducive to the construction of a more efficient labor force and, conversely, inequality *reduces* social mobility, which, from the economic viewpoint, is as undesirable as any other reduced mobility of resources.

3. Since basic decisions about the activities of a firm are made by a handful of individuals on the board of directors, *social control* is practically *impossible.* A firm may engage in collusive practices; it may use its international business network to hide profits, circumvent regulations regarding capital export, etc. (as multinational corporations do all the time); it may remunerate the management in a more or less arbitrary way;[47] and it may engage in various activities that are not strictly illegal but are socially harmful. Untouchable "commercial secrets" provide a cover for all these activities.

4. A privately owned firm has every incentive to grow beyond the optimal productive size. The bigger the firm, the stron-

ger it is financially. This implies that it can command credit and control market. Thus, *oligopoly* and *monopoly* are natural tendencies. And that, of course, leads to a maldistribution of resources.

5. Private ownership imposes definite *constraints on social planning*. Uncoordinated economic decisions result in business fluctuations, unemployment, and a tremendous waste of material resources. As a consequence, the rate of economic development is lower than would otherwise be possible. Endemic inflation is the newest form of economic instability and the newest consequence of private ownership. In the last three decades, really large-scale unemployment has become politically intolerable. Moreover, in a situation of relatively full employment, unions are strong enough to increase their share of the social cake. For the same reason, employers are strong enough to shift that increase onto the general public and preserve profits more or less unchanged. As a result, prices rise. If profits are reduced, the rate of growth diminishes. If wages are kept low—and occasionally unions are used as an instrument to achieve exactly that—private wealth increases. The resultant vicious circle is usually resolved in inflation.

6. Closely related to the previous point is the waste that occurs in the business process, even under conditions of full employment. Since profits are made by selling commodities and services, *high-pressure advertising* becomes an indispensable component of the production process. For the firm to survive, its share in the market must be secured; if the market does not exist, it must be created. This implies large advertising expenditures, expense account entertaining, bribery if necessary—as the international Lockheed affair vividly demonstrated—the maintenance of an excessive number of sales outlets, expenditures on public relations and lobbying, the maintenance of showy office buildings, and business litigation. The cost of swollen finance, insurance, real estate, and legal services ought to be added.[48] The social costs of artificially created needs, of an irrational consumption structure, and of ecological damage are hard to measure but ought to be included under the same heading.

7. The conflict of interests between labor and capital requires a complicated, delicate, and costly process of *reconciliation by the state*. The state must incur huge supervision costs in order to reduce the damage arising from speculation and antisocial behavior on the part of private capitalist groups as described in points 3 and 4. Since the primary distribution of income in a capitalist setting results in gross inequalities—with the con-

sequences mentioned in point 2—the state must intervene by heavy taxation (in the most favorable case). But heavy taxation also involves certain real costs, apart from administrative costs. For example: (a) it weakens the incentive to work; (b) it invites dishonesty and tax evasion and thus affects public morality; (c) however complicated, it can never be perfect, and substantial legal loopholes will remain; these are exploited primarily by the wealthier segments of the population.

B. Inefficiencies of Etatist Organization

An etatist system will display all the inefficiencies characteristic of a bureaucratic system. Evaluating the situation in his country in a speech to the party congress in 1952, Malenkov enumerated some of them: fear of reporting defects to superiors; concealment of the truth about local affairs; laxness in securing action; overindulgence in giving orders; gross nepotism in making appointments.[49] In order to make possible a comparative analysis, I shall classify these and other inefficiencies according to the same scheme applied to the capitalist system in section A. We begin by considering what happens at the level of the *firm*.

1. Since an etatist society is also stratified, it will be characterized by similar motivational defects as exist in capitalism. It is well known that devices such as the courts, jails, and forced labor are occasionally employed to cope with the lack of workers' discipline and with managerial failures.[50] So we can presume that interest in work is not great. Ota Šik, former Czechoslovakian vice-premier in charge of economic affairs, described the situation in his country as follows: "Shoddy work produces an ever-increasing number of rejects; absenteeism and pilfering are on the increase. Many workers . . . supplement their earning by doing odd jobs 'on the side' for private individuals."[51] Productivity is also likely to be low because management lacks operational autonomy in conducting business affairs.

2. As new tiers of hierarchy are added outside the firm, additional supervisory costs must be incurred on top of those within the firm. Describing the Hungarian situation in 1956, János Kornai noted that supervision and control were exercised, in the first place, by industrial directorates and the ministry that governs enterprises. Next came the Ministry of State Control and, for more important enterprises, the ministerial council, and planning and statistical bureaus. The party ought to be included as well. And "in suspicious cases, the police or state

prosecutor's office [would] pursue inquiries."[52] The control authorities busied themselves by administering penalties to managers at various levels for all sorts of offenses. Thus, Hungarian directors have been penalized for offenses such as negligent warehouse management, failure to visit the ministry in person to discuss a payment of excess wages, failure to reduce the number of technical personnel by a single man, nonobservance of the prescribed norm of raw material utilization, and nonadherence to planned holiday periods.[53] In 1966 there were 84,000 legal regulations that dealt with the framework of executive decisions in Poland.[54] Thus there is plenty of scope for breaking the rules, which necessitates a rich assortment of supervision and controls.

3. Regarding innovations, Kornai observed that enterprises do not try to develop new products because that is not advantageous to them. Neither are they eager to exploit technical inventions or adopt new processes introduced by other establishments. Since any improvement is immediately incorporated into the next annual plan ordered by the government, any possible advantages are quickly lost, and a higher level of productivity becomes obligatory. Because of this double reluctance to change the established technology, enterprises must be ordered from the center to introduce innovation. "The drafting and supervision of the multifarious instructions and orders which this gives rise to evidently necessitates the establishment of central staffs and so a large administrative machine concerned with technical development is born."[55]

4. The next type of inefficiency is somewhat different. Bankruptcy as a sanction for managerial failure is out of the question. But the sanction applied is faster and more effective than in a capitalist firm because the general manager is not his own boss. The criteria employed are different, however. A manager is expected primarily to be politically efficient. This means that he must reliably carry out all the commands of the higher authority; he must unconditionally obey. The manager is in fact a bureaucrat. He is afraid of independent decisions. Consequently, the operational efficiency and innovational capability of management are seriously reduced. The manager becomes neurotic when instructions fail to arrive. He then delays decisions. He is irresponsible because he reacts to rules and commands, not to problems. The result is waste, which increases with the complexity of the economy. Since the market plays practically no role, the major device for controlling managerial efficiency is fulfillment of the production plan. This means that

managers are motivated to conceal their production possibilities in order to avoid the imposition of a taut plan. Since other managers behave in the same way, the entire economy is working below capacity. Besides, the quality of products is notoriously poor.

5. An etatist economy avoids bargaining costs and there are (almost) no strikes. But a trade union bureaucracy exists, and substantial costs of indoctrination, propaganda, and policing are incurred.

6. Unlike the capitalist firm, the etatist firm suffers from an additional, sixth type of inefficiency due to its lack of economic autonomy. As a result, it cannot make proper use of a decentralized market and a price system. The market is a mechanism for communicating information. As Friedrich von Hayek observed correctly, centralized decision making requires the aggregation of information.[56] In the process, many relevant details are necessarily lost. Statistical aggregation requires standardized data and the lumping together of items that differ in quality, location, and other particulars; efficient decision making requires that all specific differences be taken into account. There is no reconciliation between the two requirements in a centralized setting. Moreover, the longer the information channels, the more distorted the final information is likely to become. So centralization implies substantial *loss and distortion of information*, which must be filtered through various layers of the hierarchy; in other words, it implies a tremendous waste of the knowledge available to society. We may add two other consequences. Since the firm is completely dependent on sources of supply controlled by some central authority, it will try to accumulate labor, raw materials, spare parts, and other goods beyond any current need in order to make sure that the necessary supply is available. As a result, etatist firms experience chronic overemployment (and hence low productivity of labor) and have huge inventories (which could otherwise be used productively).[57] On the other hand, the firm is motivated to satisfy the plan, not the consumer. This also increases inventories (of unwanted goods) and creates endemic discrepancies between the structure of demand and supply. In capitalism goods are available but money (the effective demand) is scarce; in etatism it is the other way around: money is available but goods are scarce.

At the level of the *national economy*, etatism fares much better regarding the first three inefficiencies.

1. The waste of talent is smaller because of universal access to education and higher social mobility. On the other hand, the

requirement of strict political conformity seriously reduces the possibilities for the full use of available talent.

2. Income distribution is more egalitarian.[58]

3. There are no trade secrets or private speculations. Collusive practices are much weaker and consist primarily in various deals outside the regular planning channels.

4. With respect to the fourth inefficiency, the situation is somewhat specific. Instead of monopoly and private firms, there is a total monopoly of the state. As a result, the structure of consumption is distorted. Also, for obvious reasons, bureaucracy has a preference for large firms. So there is a conspicuous lack of small and very small enterprises that cater to the specific needs of the population and are often useful innovators.

5. While the lack of autonomy on the part of the firm is the principal shortcoming of an etatist organization, *central planning* is its principal advantage. Central planning makes possible speedy mobilization and rapid reallocation of resources. The balance between saving and investment, as well as the volume of accumulation, can be secured in advance. There is no unemployment. Inflation is easily controlled. Business fluctuations are reduced considerably. But the rigidity of administrative planning prevents the planners from exploiting all the possibilities for efficient coordination of economic activities. It is estimated that 25 percent of all working time is lost due to the malfunctioning of the supply system.[59] "Clumsiness and protraction of decisionmaking, poor coordination of participating activities, frequent changes in the plans, reallocation of investment limits and fading of responsibility for the effects of investment are well-known weaknesses of investment allocation under direct planning."[60] When the formal channels do not function, illegal practices develop. Firms employ the services of special supply agents called *tolkachi* [pushers] to locate sources of supply and arrange the deals. Since the actual market does not work well, it is often replaced by the black market, while bribery becomes almost universal. It ranges from exchanging favors, to buying scarce materials from truckers on the highways as they transport the goods of their enterprises, to sending pecuniary and nonpecuniary gifts to influential persons.[61] Bribery reduces administrative rigidities but destroys morality and, with it, normal incentives and productivity.

Next—and this is a parallel to the fifth capitalist inefficiency—informational distortions, hierarchical rigidity, and the consequential barriers to communication make for low adaptive potentials on the part of national bureaucratic organizations. The system begins to react only when great damage has already been done. Thus etatist systems are characterized by an unending sequence of crises. The crisis, Michael Crozier has remarked quite aptly, is an integral part of a bureaucratic system because only a crisis makes possible the necessary adaptations.[62]

6. Because of central planning, *advertising drives* and *financial intermediaries* are largely irrelevant.

7. The last macroeconomic inefficiency—the need for and the resulting costs of *state arbitration*—is very much greater in etatism. The state initiates everything and controls everything.[63] For this it needs a huge administrative and repressive apparatus. There are also the specific costs of the state monopoly, as represented by the monolithic organizational pyramid. Since absolute conformity is required, heterodox social innovation is blocked. There is only one truth: that contained in the party line and proclaimed by the party Presidium. While the options are relatively simple and obvious—as would be the case in a less developed country—the cost of monolithic orthodoxy is relatively low. The advantage, on the other hand, is substantial: the entire nation can be effectively mobilized in the pursuit of certain targets such as the elimination of hunger and the achievement of economic development. When the tasks become involved and the options cease to be obvious, however, an exclusive orthodoxy will reduce the possibilities for successful development. We have noted the defect of rigid central planning. A natural move would be decentralization. But genuine decentralization would lead to a pluralist society and so destroy the entire order.[64] Consequently, an etatist establishment faces very narrow limits within which it can experiment. And orthodoxy is a condition for survival.

C. Comparative Efficiency

The capitalist economy is based on private ownership. The resulting autonomy of the firm makes for relatively high microeconomic efficiency. But the lack of coordination at the national level generates macroeconomic waste. Etatist economy is based on state ownership. The resulting central planning improves macroeconomic efficiency, but it also generates great waste within the firm. It is not at all obvious, on a priori grounds, which of the two systems is more efficient overall. The problem may be approached in the following way.

If efficiency is measured by the output obtained from available resources, then the most meaningful indicator of the overall economic efficiency of a social order is the rate of growth in output that it can achieve. The preceding analysis would indicate that etatism is likely to be more efficient in less developed countries and less efficient in advanced countries. Statistical studies confirm this expectation.[65] The rate of growth of less developed etatist countries (with the exception of Cuba) is substantially higher than that of comparable capitalist countries. At the level of development of the Soviet Union, etatist countries approach the general trend line; beyond that level, they seem to fall below the trend line.[66]

An analysis of the structure of the rate of growth would reveal additional interesting information about the economic profiles of various social orders. Due to the lack of data, such studies are still extremely rare. Table 7 summarizes the results of a study by Bela Balassa and Trent Bertrand in which they compare five European etatist countries (Bulgaria, Hungary, Poland, Romania, and Czechoslovakia) with four capitalist countries at approximately the same level of development (Greece, Ireland, Norway, and Spain), as well as with Yugoslavia.

TABLE 7

Rates of Growth of Output, Factor Inputs, and Factor Productivity in Manufacturing Industries in Countries with Different Socioeconomic Systems, 1953–1965

	Annual rates of growth			
	Output	Capital	Labor	Combined factor productivity
Capitalist economies	7.1	6.3	2.5	3.3
Etatist economies	8.7	8.1	4.1	3.0
Yugoslavia	11.8	7.5	6.7	4.7

Note: Unweighted averages. Constant-returns Cobb-Douglas production function is used with labor elasticity $\alpha = 0.65$.
Source: B. Balassa and T. S. Bertrand, "Growth Performance of Eastern European Economies and Comparable Western European Countries," *American Economic Review*, May 1970, p. 316.

Etatist countries at the middle level of development achieve a higher rate of both output and factor inputs. The latter implies larger accumulation and substantially more employment. Factor productivity increases at a somewhat lower rate. One may conclude that the higher rate of growth is due primarily to larger investment and faster increase in employment. It can be conjectured that the exhaustion of labor resources at a higher stage of industrialization will lead to the increasing substitution of labor by capital, a reduction in the elasticity of substitution, a decrease in combined factor productivity, and a consequent reduction in the rate of growth. These are the general effects of industrialization. Superimposed upon them are the effects of the system's rigidity, which depresses factor productivity.[67]

There are only a few etatist economies in existence today, and therefore statistical comparisons must be interpreted with caution. There is no socialist economy in existence, so these statistical comparisons are not possible. Since the Yugoslav economy comes closest to a self-governing organization, it may be taken as an approximation to a socialist economy. According to Table 7, Yugoslav performance is consistent with our expectations. But one case is not statistically significant and can be taken primarily as an illustration.[68] Apart from growth and productivity, basic welfare (for a definition and data see chapter 2, section IIIB) and income distribution are also indicative of systemic differences (Table 8).

TABLE 8

Basic Welfare and Income Distribution

	Basic welfare differences	Income distribution: Gini ratio	Income distribution: Percentage share of top 5%
Advanced capitalist countries	−7.0	0.40	17.4
Welfare states	−2.4	0.36	15.1
Etatist countries	+4.5	0.21–026[a]	10.9–12.2[a]
Yugoslavia	+5.0[b]	0.25	12.7

[a]Bulgaria and Poland
[b]+10.0 on the basis of World Bank data.

The data in general, and the income distribution data in particular, are very crude, and the latter at best make possible only a ranking rather than an evaluation of absolute distances. Besides, income distribution is a function of level of development and of inherited regional differences, which are much greater in Yugoslavia than elsewhere. To achieve at least partial comparability, only Poland and Bulgaria are considered among etatist countries, and workers instead of households are chosen as the statistical population. Taking all this into account, we may conclude that basic welfare is perhaps higher in Yugoslavia than in etatist countries, while income distribution is about equally egalitarian.

Still another systemic test is possible. Yugoslavia is also a country that has experienced all three basic contemporary socioeconomic systems within the time span of a single generation. It passed through a capitalist market economy before the war, it established a centrally planned economy after the war, and it has been pioneering in the self-governing economy since then. This sequence of three different systems within a relatively short period of time offers a precious opportunity for analyzing the comparative efficiency of these systems, since the other variables are kept as nearly constant as is possible in an economic analysis. The relevant results are shown in Table 9.

TABLE 9

Rates of Growth of Output and Factor Inputs and Measures of Factor Productivity in Manufacturing, Mining, Construction, and Crafts in Yugoslavia, 1911–67

	Annual rates of growth			
	Output	Capital	Labor	Combined factor productivity
Capitalism, 1911–40[a]	3.7	3.2	1.5	1.5
Etatism, 1940–54[a]	5.9	10.0	4.8	−1.0
Self-management, 1954–67	10.3	7.8	4.4	4.4

Source: B. Horvat, "Technical Progress in Yugoslavia," *Economic Analysis*, 1968, p. 48.
[a]Excluding the war years 1914–18 and 1941–45.

The productivity growth of 1.5 percent per annum during the capitalist phase of development corresponds to that of contemporary Latin American economies. Compared with the capitalist market economy, etatist central planning increased the rate of capital and employment growth by three times. Since output growth lagged behind, the change in total factor productivity was negative. If Yugoslavia had continued to practice central planning, it would have become positive, of course, as in other etatist economies. The most likely interpretation of our data is as follows. The introduction of central planning speeds up growth, but, by increasing inputs relatively more than output, it lowers productivity as compared with alternative economic systems. Subsequently, the combined productivity of the inputs may grow at relatively high rates, but at any one time its absolute level is lower than in comparable economies belonging to the other two systems. The self-management period appears to be a sort of synthesis of the positive features of the preceding two periods. Employment continues to grow about as fast as under central planning. But output expands much more rapidly, so that productivity growth achieves rates beyond anything known before.

So far, empirical data more than confirm our expectations. In 1965, however, there was a change. In an effort to speed up economic and political decentralization, an ill-prepared reform was carried out. It initiated extremely complex social processes whose analysis is outside the scope of the present study. I shall confine myself to only the bare essentials. Economically, the reform was based on the naive idea that "the working collectives know best what is good for them." That implied the dismantling of government investment funds and specialized federal banks; the reform resulted in the removal of most levers of effective planning and exclusive reliance on monetary policy (at first extremely restrictive). Generally, the reform meant a revival of the nineteenth-century laissez-faire economic approach. No wonder that the economy immediately plunged into recession, and that within two years the rate of growth of industrial output fell below zero. As a consequence, the country encountered rapidly increasing unemployment—for the first time in its postrevolutionary history. Politically, the reform implied an approach reminiscent of traditional liberalism. That led to genuine decentralization but also contributed to the development of a national-state ideology in the six republics constituting Yugoslavia. If one remembers that the country was unified only within the lifetime of the present generation; that it is composed of many nationalities; that it comprises three parts which used to belong to three different world cultures—Roman Catholic West, Orthodox East, and oriental Moslem South—and that the difference in economic development between the most advanced and the least developed component nations, as measured by per capita output, is as great as 6:1, then it will come as no surprise that economic failures and national-state ideology soon revived the dormant nationalist antagonisms and generated a veritable explosion of political passions.[69] To economic recession was added political instability.

These trends were reversed in 1971 by a political action that arrested the process of democratization and replaced the laissez-faire market with para-state arrangements known as social compacts.[70] The country was stabilized politically, but it lost its pioneering drive and enthusiasm. Economic performance improved slightly, but the rate of growth remained substantially below the former achievement and below the objective possibilities, even when allowance is made for the world inflation and recession after 1972.[71] The heritage of the preceding period was a transformation of the state organization into a sort of confederation. The federal government cannot pass any important economic decisions at all without the unanimous consent of the appropriate interstate committees composed of representatives or premiers of the state governments. Eight national banks decide jointly on monetary and credit policies. Custom duties are practically the only independent source of federal revenue. Thus fiscal policy proved impossible and is in fact nonexistent. In general, all economic policy—both in its formulation and in its implementation—is overburdened with clumsy political negotiations that render it inefficient, because economic decisions are not based on professional analysis and cannot be carried out on time.

The country is passing through a maturation crisis. All sorts of ideas are being tried out. All sorts of political compromises among various forces have been struck. A good indication of what is happening is the fact that two constitutions (in 1963 and 1974) and fifty constitutional amendments have been adopted within a time span of eleven years. Yugoslavia is still the only worker-managed economy in the world, and the pioneers never travel a smooth or particularly efficient path. In spite of this, the country has achieved relatively high economic prosperity and political stability. If a lesson is to be drawn from the Yugoslav example, it is probably that the transformation to self-government is relatively easy and simple at the level of the work organization. The introduction of self-management is likely to speed up growth but does not automatically guarantee a continuation of the same trend. The real problems are associated with macroeconomic and macropolitical organization. Here the solutions, both theoretical and practical, are yet to be worked out. But, although we do not know the solutions at the moment, our analysis has indicated—if we are allowed to follow the methodological guide of mathematicians—that the solutions do exist.

A more general comparative analysis is possible if we derive the relevant consequences from the specific features of the socialist organizational model. In a self-managing group of workers, *motivation to work*, and consequently *productivity*, are likely to increase. Many studies have shown that participation increases productivity even in a capitalist environment.[72] *Supervision costs* are reduced.[73] The factors constraining the *innovational* impulse are removed. *Sanctions* for bad management are relatively fast and adequate. The income of the working collective depends on the performance of the firm. So the effects of poor management are felt immediately and those responsible for losses can be fired. Since capital is socially owned, it is easy to institutionalize managerial help to firms in difficulty and to avoid bankruptcy. Finally, even if *strikes* do not disappear, they become very rare and economically insignificant. And whatever the function of the unions may be, it is certainly not that of negotiating wages with employers, since employers no longer exist.

At the national level, *education* becomes available to everyone, and the barriers between social strata are eroded; as a result, mobility across occupations is increased. Income distribution is substantially more egalitarian than under any other alternative system.[74] *Social control* is maximally effective—and the possibility of managerial abuses drastically reduced—because management operates before the watchful eyes of the workers' council and the entire working collective. It is both impossible and illegal to keep socially important decisions secret. Contrary to *monopolistic* tendencies elsewhere, the concentration of capital is discouraged. The working collective in a labor-managed firm is not inclined to overexpand the firm by mergers because it then loses control over the firm's affairs. On the other hand, because of the different social organization, financial power is no longer so important. A competitive firm can neither be bought nor owned. Thus, a labor-managed economy is likely to operate much closer to the textbook model of the competitive market. Social ownership *implies planning,* but *does not eliminate the market.* Consequently, the labor-managed economy achieves exactly what Hayek considered to be impossible: an alternative form of organization in which genuine autonomy on the part of the firm is rendered compatible with *ex ante* coordination of economic activities and full use is made of the existing knowledge while losses due to market failures are avoided. Planning and social property render financial speculation almost impossible and substantially reduce the scope of wasteful advertising. *Interventions by the state* are minimized since decisions are automatically controlled at every stage, and taxation is simple because of egalitarian income distribution.

We may sum up our findings. Etatism succeeds in mobilizing economic resources but at a low level of efficiency. Capitalism achieves higher efficiency, but leaves substantial resources idle due to business cycles. Neither of the two systems has a clear net advantage—or, at best, the possible advantage is a function of the level of development. Socialist economy implies a market and autonomous, self-managing productive units. Consequently, a socialist firm can do anything a capitalist firm can do productively. The socialist economy, based on social property, also implies social planning. It can thus achieve all the productive effects that a centrally planned economy can. Since it is at least as efficient as each of the alternatives, and capable of achieving something else besides, it is more efficient.

Socialist organization of the economy is, of course, not an unmixed blessing. It increases efficiency by solving many old problems, but it also creates new ones. As we proceed, we shall be able to consider some of these problems, as well as to elaborate and place into historical perspective the findings of the present section.

7

The Desirability of Socialism

I. Value Judgments

Modern science, including social science, insists on value-free analysis. In this respect, two types of statements can be distinguished. *Statements of fact* refer to the properties of objects. These statements can be either true or false. *Value judgments,* on the other hand, are statements about the state of mind of the person who makes them. They cannot be falsified and, as such, ought to be kept outside the science. Instead of referring to them as true, we justify them by calling them fair or just or desirable. When I say, "Socialism is good," I make no statement about the properties of socialism—it would remain completely unaffected even if I thought it were bad instead. I simply express my own evaluation of the object called socialism. I say, in effect, "I like socialism" or "Socialism is desirable." This evaluation is neither true nor false. Anyone can contradict me without committing either a logical or a factual error.

It is surely of great importance to distinguish clearly between factual statements and value judgments. A failure to do so is bound to result in hopeless confusion. Yet it is one thing to distinguish between the two aspects of the description of reality and another to claim that value judgments can be eliminated from scientific analysis. The latter is simply impossible. In fact, the entire science is based on a value premise; this value is called *truth.* Truth is the aim and fundamental criterion of every scientific inquiry. But there is no logical reason why this should be so. Clearly, without truth as a criterion science would become meaningless. But why do we need science, after all? It may be shown that science and value judgments are inseparable in a more general sense. Science requires thinking; but thinking is not a purpose in itself, it implies willing. When a man thinks, he intends to do something, he wills something.[1] Thus, it is in the nature of things that factual statements cannot be value neutral.

To analyze human activity, we need to distinguish among its various aspects. No assumption of schizophrenia is implied here, however. Various aspects may differ, but they are not independent nor totally separated. They belong to the same *human* activity. Whatever we do, it is always related to both facts and values. In a certain sense, the value dimension is a specifically human dimension; take it away, and you destroy human existence.

Although value judgments are made in every scientific inquiry, there is something special about value judgments in the social sciences. Here our interests—occasionally existential interests—are at stake. Consequently, in the social sciences value judgments, mostly implicit and hidden, are likely to distort factual analysis to an incomparably higher degree than in the natural sciences.[2] Max Weber, who himself strongly insisted on the distinction between values and facts, also pointed out that values intrude into our analysis at two points: they determine the subject matter we select for investigation, and they influence our judgment about the cause of a specific event. This position has been criticized on the grounds that natural scientists are similarly influenced, though admittedly to a lesser degree, and that the problem is really practical and not logical. "Accordingly," Ernest Nagel remarked,

> the undesirable difficulties that stand in the way of obtaining reliable knowledge of human affairs because of the fact that social scientists differ in their value orientations are practical difficulties. The difficulties are not necessarily insuperable, for since by hypothesis it is not impossible to distinguish between fact and value, steps can be taken to identify a value bias when it occurs, and to minimise if not to eliminate completely its perturbing effects.[3]

The difficulties are somewhat greater than those implied in the quotation from Nagel. There is no simple frame of reference within which every scientific inquiry is conducted. In order to discover regularities and causal relations, we must simplify the world. For this purpose we build models. What is true within one model is not necessarily true within another model. A class of models with basically similar properties comprises a paradigm. The paradigm is our essential vision of the world. Within a given paradigm, Nagel's analysis can certainly be applied. But two different paradigms usually cannot be translated unambiguously into one another. The ambiguity is generated by the initial difference in value positions. In social sciences, the choice of a paradigm is determined basically by the social situation and, in the final analysis, by class position.[4] After a point, a neoclassical and a Marxist economist, a conservative and a radical sociologist, can hardly communicate. The discussion typically ends in some sort of deadlock such as the following: "If we assume A, B, and C, then Y follows," one participant explicates his model of inquiry. "But A, B, and C are meaningless assumptions, and so Y is irrelevant" is the reaction of the other participants in the discussion. What is meaningful or meaningless depends on the paradigm one accepts, and the latter is, of course, determined by the values one holds. A drastic though widespread case is what I called reified thinking. Nobel Prize winner Friedrich von Hayek was shown to be one of its more distinguished representatives (chapter 4, section II).

Let me now point out certain additional complications. Value cannot be true or false, but neither is it arbitrary. Value is subjective, but it is also objective. Value is different from fact, and yet it is not devoid of cognitive content. Values are values because they satisfy certain human needs. To the extent that these needs are socially determined, values are not only individual but also social. The objectivity of values consists in the congruence of individual desires and wills. The objectivized value becomes a norm of a group and, as such, a request upon the behavior of the individuals in the group. The evaluation is subjective, but the validity is objective. Perhaps a more adequate way of describing this phenomenon would be to denote it as intersubjective. The intersubjective validity of a value judgment corresponds to the objective validity of a positive statement.

The cognitive content of a value judgment is especially important. If I say that socialism is good, and *if it is known* that I resent class exploitation and that I advocate political freedoms and an egalitarian distribution of wealth and power, then I am making a statement about socialism itself, not only about my state of mind. In other words, on the basis of my statement, and the knowledge of my values, an observer can infer the properties of socialism. Moreover, this statement may also be true or false. It may happen that societies referred to as socialist are neither egalitarian nor free. In this case, I am simply mistaken in my judgment. Thus, in order for a value judgment to be meaningful, its factual basis must be true; in other words, the implied state of the world must correspond to the actual state of the world.

Since values are about needs, and subjectively felt needs depend, among other things, on our knowledge about our real needs, our true selves, and about the possibilities for satisfying them, there is an interaction between valuations and knowledge.

Our knowledge of facts enables us to make a prognosis about the possible outcomes of alternative courses of action designed to achieve desirable ends. This prognosis then exerts feedback on our initial valuations. Paul Streeten describes four different ways in which analysis and prognosis modify programs.[5] (1) Better information renders programs more consistent and thus more effective. (2) The facts discovered may activate value standards that previously were only implicit or even absent. (3) Better knowledge about facts may help to clear up confusions about one's own desires. Rationalizations and pseudo-interests will then give place to the knowledge of real interests. (4) Divergencies between words and deeds, action and belief, may become apparent.

The interaction between scientific analysis and valuations does not imply that value judgments can be *proved* in the same way as factual statements.[6] But it does imply that, by rational argument, people can be *persuaded* to change their programs and modify their valuations.[7] The purpose of the present book is to achieve exactly that. The process of persuasion can be carried quite far, until it reaches the rock bottom of real interests. After that point, the coordination and social integration of individual programs is continued through a sociopolitical process.

There is an elegant way to minimize the complications generated by value judgments. We have noted that a basic difference exists between value judgments and factual statements. Thus, all we have to do is to observe what people actually desire. Next, we investigate the compatibility of their desires and, in our case, self-governing socialism. If the compatibility is not satisfactory, we try to design a better alternative. Apart from the value connotations of the terms *satisfactory* and *better*, even this procedure involves a basic value premise: namely, that it is good to satisfy human desires. But why should this be so? A misanthrope may conceive of a system that inflicts pain on human beings. We may reformulate our task in a value-free fashion by simply providing an answer to the following question: Which of the possible social systems would most fully meet the suitably defined, observed fundamental valuations of the majority of mankind? In other words, which of the possible social systems comes closest to the ideal of a good society? Before we proceed, we have to consider the question of what constitutes a "good society." This will enable us to continue with our comparative analysis of the three social systems in the sphere of values.

II. Two Versions of Utilitarian Ethics

The idea of a good society obviously is historically determined. Different communities will have different ideas of how society ought to be organized. Basically, two approaches are possible: (1) One or more supreme goods are postulated. The aim is to maximize these goods. Whatever helps in achieving this aim is desirable. (2) Appropriate behavior is postulated. Then any aim compatible with the rules of accepted behavior is good, or at least not evil. The distinction is the familiar one between teleological and deontological ethical theory. In the former, good is defined independently and what is right is derived from the aim of maximizing good. In the latter, right is defined and then good is derived (but not in a deterministic fashion).[8] Thus, right and good are two fundamental ethical concepts.

It is obvious that a teleological ethic will have great appeal in a bourgeois society. Born in the battles against religious mysticism and the ascribed privileges of the feudal order, bourgeois society emphasizes achievement and rationality. Rationality implies a minimization of sacrifices in achieving a given objective or a maximization of desirable effects within the constraints of available resources. The acceptance of rationality as an important value leads to scientific discoveries and rapid economic development. Economics, after all, is nothing but the maximization of gains and the minimization of costs. Maximization of gains extended to ethics leads to teleological ethics.

If there is a multiplicity of ends-goods, there is no easy way to maximize them. A solution can be achieved only on an intuitive basis that escapes quantifications and objective tests. To a quantitatively oriented bourgeois mind, this was not very appealing. Therefore, it was thought that one single end ought to be selected and proclaimed the supreme good. Very naturally, this supreme good was found in *utility*. Bourgeois utilitarianism of course has its predecessors in similar ethical approaches of similar earlier social situations. Greek eudaemonism and hedonism are two such examples. The former proclaims happiness, the latter pleasure, as the supreme good. It is also true that utilitarianism is not the only ethical school in bourgeois societies. Yet never before has utilitarianism been so pervasive, and no other contemporary theory is as widely accepted. In a system in which economic values and exchange relationships are dominant, all other values become purchasable and thus quantifiable. Jeremy Bentham's "moral arithmetic" is then the most adequate reflection of underlying valuations. "Completely meaningless reduction of all those various human relationships to a *single* relationship of utility," Marx and Engels declared, "this obviously metaphysical abstraction originates from the fact that in the contemporary bourgeois society all relations are practically subordinated to only one abstract money-trade relationship."[9]

The crude utilitarianism of Bentham was later theoretically refined; crude hedonism has been replaced by a colorless maximization of the satisfaction of rational desires. Economic theory has achieved a particular perfection in the utility calculus: cardinal utilities have been replaced by ordinal utilities, and in this way interpersonal utility comparisons have been completely avoided. Yet all this only helps to make clearer the social basis of this ethical theory. Society is visualized as a conglomerate of isolated individuals who behave like utility-maximizing machines. The only recognized social requirement is that no individual be made worse off in the process than he was initially (the so-called Pareto optimum). Whether the initial situation itself is good or bad is beyond legitimate scientific inquiry.

The older, cruder, cardinal utilitarianism adopted the maxim of the greatest happiness for the greater number.[10] The maxim was first propounded in the early eighteenth century by the Glasgow moral philosopher Francis Hutcheson. His disciple was Adam Smith, the founder of classical political economy and a moral philosopher himself. Smith's ethical theory differed from that of his teacher. Nevertheless, he demonstrated that in a bourgeois society the greatest happiness for the greatest number is realized as a matter of course, through the operation of market competition. By pursuing their private interests, individuals maximally enhance social welfare. A far echo of Smith's apology is the modern welfare economics "theorem" which states that perfect competition maximizes economic welfare. Every bourgeois economics student is expected to be able to reproduce this proof that he lives in the best of all possible worlds.

The universality of the exchange relationship is a sufficient but not a necessary condition for utilitarianism to become the dominant ethic. All that is necessary is a sufficiently alienated society in which the supreme good is sought outside man himself. Thus, bureaucratic rationality can be expected to generate utilitarian ethics as well. This is in fact the case. The two ethics are not exactly the same—in the bourgeois world the individual is confronted with the society, while in the bureaucratic world the collectivity is juxtaposed to the individual—but they generate the same frame of mind: conformism adopted with a view toward maximizing the accumulation of utilities (material goods and the levers of power). Utilitarianism is usually conceived as individualistic, which is a reflection of its historic origin; yet it can just as naturally be interpreted collectivistically. All that need be done is to apply to the society the principle of choice for one man, which is what bureaucracy is doing all the time. Thus, there is "no reason in principle," observes John Rawls, "why the greater gains of some should not compensate for the lesser losses of others; or more importantly, why the violation of liberty of the few might not be made right by the greater good shared by many. . . . For just as it is rational for one man to maximize the fulfillment of his system of desires, it is right for a society to maximize the net balance of satisfaction taken over all of its members."[11] If we replace "society" by "state," the quotation is transformed into a typical justification for anything etatist rulers undertake to do. This is not a new discovery. It has been observed a number of times. The Yugoslav moral philosopher Miladin Životić quotes the recent Soviet book *Scientific Communism* (1965) ("Even in communism the will of one man must be subordinated to the will of the entire collective") to illustrate how the utilitarian principle that the social purposefulness of an action is the measure of its value leads to subordination of the individual to the collectivity.[12] The Australian philosopher Eugene Kamenka points out:

> The socialist's [read: etatist's] vision of society, as Rosa Luxemburg once said of Lenin, is the capitalist's vision of a factory, run by an overseer. The conception of economic planning, Schumpeter has pointed out, is a capitalist conception: the capitalist manager is the prototype of the socialist administrator. Both depend in their ideology on the commercial morality of utilitarianism: on the conception that all things can be treated and assessed as means to ends and that ends can be reduced to a common measure.[13]

Is it really so surprising that once again we find etatism turning out to be a kind of capitalism in reverse? The existence of class relationships in both cases generates the same mode of reasoning and the same basic value orientation.

III. An Ethics of Justice

The preceding discussion indicates that utilitarianism is unlikely to become the dominant ethics of socialism. Is there an alternative? If so, what? To answer this question, let us look at the valuations of social groups at the crucial junctures of historical development, when they appear as real subjects of history. I have in mind revolutions and liberation wars.

What motivates revolutionaries and patriots to risk their lives? Surely not a utility calculus. Neither are bourgeois revolutionary barricades erected in order to establish market competition, nor are workers and peasants fighting for nationalizations or central planning. If there is any single, all-pervasive value that motivates revolutionaries and patriots to heroic deeds, it is the ideal of justice, the quest for a just society. Since socialism can be established only as a result of a genuine revolution—which may be both gradual and nonviolent, however—a socialist society is likely to develop an ethics of justice.

Technically, this is a nonteleological ethics. *Summum bonum* neither is, nor need be, defined. Individuals are not reduced to businessmen maximizing their net profits. Neither are they subordinated to an authoritarian collective will. Human life is allowed to be as varied as possible. Plurality of values is taken for granted. If man is an end unto himself—which is a value position whose history can be traced from the Bible to Kant to Marx[14]—justice is not a constraint but a precondition for an authentic human life.

While a long sequence of utilitarian theories has been developed, there are, surprisingly (or is it?), scarcely any elaborated theories of justice. Only recently has the first such theory been produced by the Harvard moral philosopher John Rawls. This fact justifies a brief critical examination of Rawls's theory.

The first obvious question to ask is: Why is justice selected as a foundation of societal ethics? Rawls's answer appears to be: because it is reasonable to select justice and also because a theory of justice overcomes some of the difficulties (information requirements are less demanding, strains of commitment are weaker, and so on) of the utilitarian ethics. The second part of the answer is of secondary importance and need not concern us here. The first part appears contradictory at first sight: a value cannot be justified by a logical or factual analysis; it is either axiomatic or justified by another value. Let us see how Rawls himself copes with this difficulty.

The fundamental values are introduced into the analysis as derivatives of an intuitive notion of human nature. The moral decisions to be made express our nature as free (including free to enjoy private property), rational, and self-interested persons. Not unexpectedly, human nature happens to have all the crucial characteristics of a bourgeois liberal. Yet Rawls realizes that his bourgeois moralists will hardly be able to reach the kingdom of justice by themselves, and so he imposes two important principles on their attitudes: the principle of fairness, and another which he calls the Aristotelian principle. Justice, for Rawls, is a legal or political counterpart of the ethical concept of fairness. The latter implies that formal, or negative, freedom is insufficient and so unacceptable unless complemented by positive, substantive freedom. It also implies that the fundamental rights of no person can be impaired for the sake of increasing the sum total of utilities. The Aristotelian principle means that "human beings enjoy the exercise of their realized capacities (their innate or trained abilities) and this enjoyment increases the more the capacity is realized or the greater its complexity."[15] This principle points in the direction of the Marxian philosophy of praxis, although Rawls is unaware of that. Consequently, the rich possibilities of the praxis principle are left unexploited.

Following the contractarian tradition, Rawls places his stylized bourgeois liberals in an initial situation where they participate in a social game that is supposed to produce just arrangements. This attempt fails. In a class-ridden society, no consensus is possible, and consequently the principle of fairness is inapplicable. Rawls is therefore forced to sink a veil of ignorance whereby the participants are deprived of their personal histories and a knowledge of their social positions and prospects. He describes the procedure adopted as follows.[16] Suppose we have a well-ordered society defined as one that is effectively regulated by a public conception of justice, whose members are free and equal moral persons and whose basic social institutions generate an effective supporting sense of justice. Which conception of justice is most appropriate for such a society? Obviously, the one that would be agreed to unanimously in a hypothetical situation in which the members of the society are fairly situated with respect to one another. This hypothetical situation is the original position.

Principles of justice as fairness are those that free and rational persons concerned with furthering their interests would accept in an initial situation of equality. The test of fairness consists in the possibility for mutual agreement. A rational person is considered "to have a coherent set of preferences between the options open to him . . . he follows the plan which will satisfy more of his desires rather than less and which has the greater chance of being successfully executed."[17] In the initial situation, all participants are equal and free, as a result of the amnesia of the parties in the original contract. Everyone is deprived of the morally irrelevant information. No one knows his place in the society, his class position or status; the parties do not know to which generation they belong, and so information about natural resources and technology is not available; one's place in the distribution of abilities, intelligence, and strength is also unknown; finally, participants do not know their own conception of good and are unaware of their deeper aims and interests and of their special psychological propensities. The reason for this psychological amputation is Rawls's desire to force participants to act autonomously in the Kantian sense; that is, the principles of their actions are chosen by them as the most adequate possible expression of their nature as free and equal rational beings. If social position, or natural endowments, or special preferences influence the actions of a person, he is acting heteronomously. "The veil of ignorance deprives the persons in the original situation of the knowledge that would enable them to choose heteronomous principles."[18] This is not quite true, however. As Robert Wolff has observed, Kantian autonomy requires that the choice of principles be motivated by the idea of the good and not by rational self-interest. Thus, what Rawlsian noumenal bourgeois are doing may be termed generalized heteronomy.[19]

In the situation in which "all are similarly situated and no one is able to design principles to favour his particular condition, the principles of justice are the result of a fair agreement or bargain."[20] These are the principles:

1. Each person is to have an equal right to the most extensive liberty compatible with a similar liberty for others.

2. Social and economic inequalities are to be arranged so that they are both: (a) to the greatest benefit of the least advantaged; and (b) attached to positions and offices open to all under conditions of fair (not formal!) equality of opportunity.[21]

The first principle regulates political life and postulates equal citizenship. The second principle regulates economic life and postulates conditions where the deviations from equal economic distribution are justifiable. A measure of the benefit of the least advantaged is provided by an index of social primary goods defined as things that individuals are presumed to want whatever their final ends and other desires. Primary goods include rights, liberties and opportunities, income and wealth, and the social bases of self-respect. The first principle has priority over the second; there is no tradeoff between liberty and economic welfare. The basis for this priority is to be found in an asymmetry in the satisfaction of human needs. Once basic material needs have been satisfied, the marginal significance of further economic and social advantages diminishes relative to the interests of liberty—the marginal utility of wealth diminishes, while the marginal utility of liberty increases due to the Aristotelian principle—and, beyond a certain point, it becomes irrational to choose a lesser liberty for the sake of greater economic welfare and the amenities of office.[22]

Equality of opportunity is to be fair, i.e., substantive, not merely formal. Capitalism and etatism are social systems that include formal equality of opportunity—as contrasted with feudalism, for example—and will be excluded as such (though not by Rawls himself, as we shall see in a moment). Taken together with the other principles, point 2b also eliminates meritocracy. Meritocracy may be envisaged as a system based exclusively on the principle of equality of opportunity—a sort of idealized etatism—without regard to the resulting great disparities in the level of living, power, and privileges.

The most interesting and really novel is principle 2a, which Rawls calls the difference principle.[23] Its meaning is as follows. If we take as a standard the equal distribution of economic and other (political and organizational powers, etc.) goods, inequalities are introduced only if this is to everyone's advantage. If we start from an existing distribution, a change ought to be carried out if and as long as the welfare of the worst-off representative man can be increased, and then each higher position's condition is maximized in lexicographic order. "In order to treat all persons equally, to provide genuine equality of opportunity, society must give more attention to those with fewer native assets and to those born into the less favourable social positions."[24] More generally, "to regard persons as ends in themselves in the basic design of society is to agree to forego those gains which do not contribute to their representative expectations. By contrast, to regard persons as means is to be prepared to impose upon them lower prospects of life for the sake of the higher expectations of others."[25]

Taken together, "the two principles are equivalent . . . to an undertaking to regard the distribution of natural abilities as a collective asset so that the more fortunate are to benefit only in ways that help those who have lost out."[26] Rawls is aware that this conclusion will not necessarily be accepted on the basis of his artificial model of initial amnesia. Therefore, early in the analysis he warns: "A conception of justice cannot be deduced from self-evident premises or conditions or principles; instead, its justification is a matter of the mutual support of many considerations, of everything fitting together into one coherent view."[27] Rawls wants to design a kind of moral geometry. In doing so, he reverses the procedure of a mathematician. Instead of starting from self-evident axioms and deriving the theorems, Rawls starts from intuitive notions of justice, as exemplified in the two principles, and tries to derive the principles from which these notions could be deduced. Thus the consistency between the assumptions and the conclusions is what makes the content of *A Theory of Justice.* But it is also more than that. The search for consistency and the elimination of contradictions and conflicts leads to a clarification of initial insights and to their modification. Eventually this process brings the abstract principles and our intuitive notions of justice into what is termed reflective equilibrium. If our conviction of what is just can be deduced from a set of abstract principles, then it is also to a certain extent justified, because these principles, being poorer in content and therefore more general, will be more readily accepted.

Every step in the derivation of the above theory has been questioned, and every major conclusion criticized. For our purposes, I shall confine my criticism to but a few essential points. The weakest link in the entire structure is, of course, the initial situation. It does not correspond even remotely to any real world situation. If it is replied that this was not the intention and that the initial situation is a purely logical construct, a *Gedankenexperiment,* then we encounter an insuperable difficulty when the theory is to be applied. There is a basic contradiction in the general argument. As John Charvet observed, Rawls assumes that people are engaged in a well-established system of human practices and as such have human attributes. But it is also assumed that all are equal in power and ability, and that no one knows his position in the society, which means that the participants cannot be engaged in social practice at all and, in fact, are not human.[28] It would have been simpler and more consistent to assume from the very beginning that human beings prefer equality and have a sense of justice. A reasonable justification for the latter is provided by Rawls himself:

> the capacity for a sense of justice and the moral feelings is an adaptation of mankind to its place in nature . . . for members

> of a species which lives in stable social groups, the ability to comply with fair cooperative arrangements and to develop the sentiments necessary to support them is highly advantageous, especially when individuals have a long life and are dependent on one another. These conditions guarantee innumerable occasions when mutual justice consistently adhered to is beneficial to all parties.[29]

The priority of political liberty is supposed to be an expression of the expectation that men will recognize one another as free and equal rational persons. If we rigorously deduce the implied assumptions of this priority, we must conclude that either the cost of political liberty in terms of material wealth becomes infinite at the margin, or the "production possibility frontier"—to borrow a technical term from neoclassical economics—is such that, after a point, political liberty and economic wealth cease to be substitutable and become complementary. The first assumption represents a value judgment; the second is an empirical hypothesis. Neither can be derived rigorously from Rawlsian premises.

The most interesting derivation from the initial situation—the difference principle—does not really follow with any necessity. It is plausible, but it is not the only basis on which fair agreement among contracting parties is possible. Analytically, it implies an infinite risk aversion. Rawls explicitly deprives his participants of any knowledge about their risk preferences. But then he goes on to indicate several reasons why they should be risk averters. In the initial situation, they choose the rules that are to govern their lives forever. Thus they are bound to be extremely cautious. Besides, the parties want the effects of chance to be regulated by some principle, for otherwise natural talents and social contingencies of life threaten the relations between them as free and equal moral persons. Because the maxi-min principle is applied, no one benefits from natural and social contingencies unless everyone's position is improved. Every abstract principle, however, if applied consistently, leads into an impasse, and so does the maxi-min principle. Why should an infinitesimal damage to the interests of the least advantaged group be socially or morally more important than an alternative great benefit to the rest of the society? The possible future hardships can be satisfactorily averted if the initial contract specifies a certain minimum of basic needs that must always be satisfied.[30] Robert Nozick suggests another possibility. If the participants are egalitarian minded and assume that the worst-off group gains a slight benefit, then it may be preferable to choose the principle whereby "an inequality is justified only if its benefit to the worst-off group . . . is greater than . . . the cost of the inequality."[31] Obviously, other alternatives can also be envisaged.

As for implications, Rawls fails to realize a truly fundamental one. He notes that "the main problem of distributive justice is the choice of a social system," but at the same time states that "the choice between a private-property economy and socialism is left open; from the standpoint of the theory of justice alone, various basic structures would appear to satisfy its principles."[32] All that need be done is to manipulate subsidies and taxes (notoriously biased),[33] restrict monopoly (notoriously ineffective), and the like. For Rawls, for example, "the unequal inheritance of wealth is no more inherently unjust than unequal inheritance of intelligence."[34] The imposition of inheritance taxes in accordance with principle 2a copes with the problem. Rawls is unaware of the fact that a social system cannot be "chosen" without a fundamental change in social relations.[35] In fact, given the system, the choices are predetermined. Even if the two principles were written into a bourgeois constitution and applied conscientiously—which clearly is a fantasy—the inequalities necessary for the operation of the system, so as to benefit the least advantaged, would be considerably greater than under socialism. Rawls is not alone, of course, in taking this position. In his time, Aristotle considered slavery a potentially just system. It was to the advantage of the slave, he maintained, to have a master. Similarly, Saint Thomas Aquinas was persuaded that feudalism—with some minor corrections—was a just system. After all, it was ordained by God. Both of them would have considered that to be born a slave or a serf is inherently no more unjust than to be born stupid. We have here a welcome illustration of our introductory discussion of the social limitations of scientific analysis. But the nonneutrality of social analysis has yet another aspect. As Wolff remarked,[36] John Rawls wrote a book that was intended as a philosophical apologia for an egalitarian brand of liberal welfare-state capitalism. What Rawls actually did was to prove convincingly that justice was incompatible with the society in which he lives. If capitalism and etatism are incapable of securing justice (as understood by contemporary mankind), and we *accept* justice as an important social goal, then the two systems *ought* to be destroyed (not necessarily by violent means) and replaced by one that incorporates this goal. Thus, regardless of the intentions of its author, *A Theory of Justice* has revolutionary implications, and that justifies our interest in it.

IV. The Just Society Operationalized

We can appropriately preface our inquiry by the following quotation from Rawls:

> Justice is the first virtue of social institutions, as truth is of systems of thought. A theory however elegant and economical must be rejected if untrue; likewise laws and institutions no matter how efficient and well-arranged must be reformed or abolished if they are unjust.[37]

While I accept this initial position—with the correction that, in a historical context, justice and efficiency are positively correlated—in the ensuing analysis I generally part company with Rawls. The basic difference between our two approaches is that I apply the idea of social contract not to a mythical original situation, but to actual everyday life. This implies a fundamental change in social relations. It also implies a very different theory. I propose to proceed as follows.

We have already identified a universal quest for justice in societal affairs. Now we have to examine more closely the content of the ideal of a just society. An analysis of revolutionary movements reveals three fundamental values common to all of them: freedom, social equality, and human solidarity. The great French Revolution proclaimed these three values explicitly and with great precision as *liberté, égalité,* and *fraternité.* A century and a half later, the General Assembly of the United Nations passed the Universal Declaration of Human Rights, whose Article 1 reaffirmed the same three revolutionary ideals: "All human beings are born *free* and *equal* in dignity and rights. They are endowed with reason and conscience and should act towards one another in a spirit of *brotherhood*" [emphasis added].[38] In the civilized world, these three values are generally accepted as ethical norms—accepted, but not practiced.

It is immediately obvious that the historical tricotomy of values corresponds to the one suggested by Rawls, and he himself is aware of this. Freedom is reflected in the first principle; equality in principle 2b and partly in principle 1; and solidarity in principle 2a. The first two values found their way into bourgeois constitutions (as political liberties and equality before the law); the last one did not, apparently because it could not be operationalized. It is a great credit to Rawls that he showed that it could be. A natural interpretation of the concept of brotherhood/solidarity is to refrain from having greater advantages when this is not to the benefit of those who are less fortunate. This, clearly, is incompatible with the acquisitive individualism of a bourgeois order. It is also incompatible with the meritocratic elitism of an etatist order.

It is natural to ask: Why do human beings insist on freedom, equality, and solidarity? One possible answer is to attribute these three qualities to human nature as derived from the history of mankind. In fact, the "human" may be defined so as to imply the possession of a sense of justice as specified in the three values. It is a fact, however, that human beings practice not only justice, but also injustice; they are not only constructive, but also destructive. To this one may add that, on balance, the constructive component prevails because it assures the survival of mankind. Since the instinct of self-preservation seems to be inborn in all animals, a value orientation that satisfies this particular existential need is likely to prevail.[39] Thus, *ceteris paribus,* an ethics of justice is more likely than an ethics of injustice.[40]

Basically there seem to be three different visions of human nature: (1) religious—man is projected into the mystical world of God; (2) utilitarian—man is projected into the external world of utilities; (3) humanist—the focus is on man himself, on his generic being (as Marx would say), on mankind. The first two imply fundamental alienation. They can be cruel, as demonstrated by religious wars and primitive capitalist and etatist accumulation. They imply individual egoism as the basis of human nature and are unable to explain altruistic motives. Altruism is thought to be ordained by God, or by the party, or to be simply a camouflaged utilitarian egoism. In Kantian language, the first two visions see man as a means. The last one sees him as an end in himself. The gap between an alienated, means-oriented world and a disalienated, mankind-centered world is really the gap between a class and a classless society. In the latter, individuals are economically, politically, and socially free. The traditional distinction between egoism and altruism—reflecting the inimical confrontation of the individual and the society—loses its meaning. Compared with mankind, an individual is tremendously limited. More than that. Because of the narrow limits of his individual lifespan, only a few of his potential abilities can be fully developed. Thus, a precondition for the complete development of the personality is that everyone else have the same chance; I can live my human life fully only if everyone else can do the same. This is Marx's (*Early Texts*) principle of *mutual completion.* It "leads to the species-life, to the truly human life" as contrasted with the bourgeois ideology of competition, that is, of mutual exploitation.

Our next task is to investigate the exact relationship among the three components of justice. The first two are clearly complementary. If *everyone* is to be *free,* everyone must be *equally* free. My liberty must be consistent with the liberty of others. The reverse is also true. Equality implies freedom. If some are less privileged, then they are, to that extent, unfree. Equal freedom implies free equality. In an abstract sense, the same interrelationship does not apply to solidarity. One could envisage a society of free and equal individuals in which there was no solidarity or brotherhood among them. But that would not be a human society. Without human solidarity, inequality and unfreedom would immediately reappear. Thus, solidarity makes (substantive) freedom and equality possible. Freedom and equality make solidarity necessary.

The logical analysis may be supplemented by a historical one. Historically the three values have had different meanings in different societies. Kautsky held that the meanings depend on the position taken toward property and production. Equality meant an equal distribution of goods in primitive Christianity and an equal right to property in the French Revolution, whereas under socialism it would mean an equal right to use the products of social labor; freedom meant, respectively, idleness and the free use of one's property in the most profitable way in the first two societies, and would mean the reduction of necessary working time under socialism.[41] Though one might not quite agree with Kautsky—for instance, bourgeois equality means primarily equality before the law, while socialist freedom and equality have deeper meanings than he realized, and the social is not identical with the economic—it is certainly true that these values have been historically determined. But changes in values are not arbitrary. And in this sense the historical analysis can be extended as follows.

We live in a stratified society in which social classes exist and the (great) majority of the society's members are in some important sense (economically) exploited and (politically) oppressed. This majority accepts the values of liberty, equality, and solidarity. On the assumption that each human being is to count as one (which is one aspect of equality), these values may be considered as relevant social values. Equality may be interpreted as social equality, equal life chances; freedom is to mean freedom of self-determination. It follows that equality implies freedom, which is, in fact, one of its own dimensions. Similarly, freedom implies equality, because only by overcoming class stratification can the freedom of the oppressed majority be increased. Here we encounter a difficulty generated by our realistic assumption that the society is socially stratified. Increased freedom for the majority—due to greater equality—may reduce the freedom of the privileged minority that controls the allocation of scarce values such as authority, status, rights, wealth, income, etc. Consequently, we have to balance greater freedom for some against reduced freedom for others. The principle of equality, as already mentioned, solves the problem. We can also look for a general solution that will take us into the realm of philosophical anthropology. Namely, an exercise of economic and political power over fellow citizens against their interests and will (otherwise, it would not be an exercise of power but simply administration) subjects the privileged minority to an alienating experience that is humanly degrading for the power wielders themselves. In order to avoid this process of dehumanization—a life in which the creative potentials of human beings are either undeveloped or distorted—the privileged minority ought to opt for greater equality. The case is strengthened by invoking the principle of mutual completion. Human powers are countless, and a man cannot be considered fully human if he does not develop them. But this is an immense task far beyond the reach of individual persons. As an individual, man is severely limited, and he needs other individuals to complete him. Even a group will not do. The task cannot be solved short of engaging mankind. Men are humanized through each other's help with all class, national, and other dividing lines destroyed.

It appears that freedom, equality, and solidarity are necessary conditions for societal justice. If one component is absent, the other two collapse and justice is destroyed.[42] They are also sufficient conditions. If they are present, the society will generally be considered just. This conclusion requires a qualification. Justice is a relative concept, relative to some standard. A society will be called just if it lives up to its historically given possibilities. Thus, there may be lesser or greater degrees of freedom, equality, and solidarity, and a final stage of perfection can never be reached. But whatever improvements are made, these three components—being complementary—move together. Contrary to what is generally believed, in a given society there can be no tradeoff, no substitution among them. The purported examples of such a tradeoff that are generally cited show, upon closer scrutiny, that what is being substituted is one *kind* of freedom (say, political liberties) for another *kind* of equality (say, regarding economic goods), or the freedom of *some* persons for the equality of *others* (say, two different generations). These are genuine problems, of course, as are the problems of substituting one kind of *equality* for another kind of *equality*, or the *freedom* of some persons for the *freedom* of other persons. But in no case do we trade overall freedom for overall equality. A more equal and less free society, or vice versa, is an impossibility. If, in spite of that, choices of this sort are suggested, the explanation is usually to be found in the realm of ideology and class interests.

So far, our discussion has been conducted on a highly abstract plane. If a just society is to be designed, we must first operationalize the concept itself. Since each of the three components of justice implies the other two, we can simplify our task by selecting the aspect of justice that can be operationalized most effectively. Solidarity is clearly not the one. Even when operationalized by Rawls, it is not easily measurable, nor is it easily applicable. How do we know who is worst off, and how much each group is affected? Liberty is a possibility. It has already been partly tried out by Harold Laski. Laski defines justice as equal opportunity for self-realization.[43] This implies equality, for "my realization of my best self must involve as its logical result the realization by others of their best selves."[44] It also implies liberty, which is a product of rights, of the "eager maintenance of that atmosphere in which men have the opportunity to be their best selves."[45] Liberty has three aspects.[46] *Private liberty* is an "opportunity to exercise freedom of choice in those areas of life where the results of my efforts mainly affect me." Religious freedom and adequate legal protection are two illustrations. *Political liberty* means effective participation in the affairs of the state. Finally, *economic liberty* consists in a secure and reasonable income. This approach is obviously intended to prepare ground for the design of a political system. It could be elaborated to cover the entire social system. Upon reflection, however, one is bound to conclude that the results will not be entirely satisfactory.

We are thus left with the third aspect of justice—equality. The principle of equality has a long and distinguished tradition. Roman lawyers, following the Stoics, proclaimed: *Omnes homines, iure naturali, aequales sunt.* Many centuries later, the idea was echoed in the European Enlightenment. In religion, equality is characteristically transferred to the other world: all men are equal in the sight of God. Significantly, the socialist tradition has always focused on equality, as if socialists have surmised that equality is best suited for practical application. And so it is.[47] While liberty may mean many things, including the freedom to make profits, equality is much less equivocal. Unless equality is defined in purely formal terms, remarked Ernest Bloch,[48] equality (and brotherhood) is either socialist or it is not equality.

In spite of "natural law," equality is not natural. People are not *naturally* equal. In fact, they differ very much in terms of abilities, needs, and interests. This diversity is doubtless desirable. Thus, the quest for equality implies equality in some special, social sense. Equality means equality of opportunity. Rights, whatever they are, must be effective, not merely formal; they must be transformed into opportunities. Members of the society must enjoy equal freedom to lead life according to their own choices. In this sense they must have socially equal life chances. A life chance depends also, of course, on personal qualities such as health, innate abilities, and purposeful work. Social equality then implies that life chance is not basically modified by a person's position in the society (such as being born into a particular group) or by the manner in which the society is organized (as, for example, when the market discriminates against the poor). An equality-based socialist society is an achievement society; but it is more than that. Achievement is accepted only under the conditions of equal chances. And it is modified by the principle of solidarity, which adds the dimension of needs.[49]

All this may be accepted as a lofty ethical ideal, but is it practicable? or is it yet another utopia? I propose to operationalize the principle of social equality in the following way.

Every person engages in a number of typical activities in his social life or, to put it differently, plays different roles in the society in which he lives. If, in each of his roles, every person has equal chances and equal rights, and receives equal treatment, then surely the society must be equitable. Now, there are just three fundamental social roles in this sense: each of us is a producer, a consumer, and a citizen.[50] Thus, equality must be secured in production, in consumption, and in the social sphere.

Equality of producers implies equal access to the productive capital of the society. Consequently, productive capital must be socially owned—not state owned. Social ownership implies two fundamental consequences. Within any group of people whose work is organized for the purpose of earning for a living, any individual producer has the same right to participate in decision making as any other. This means self-management—a conclusion we have already reached by means of a different route in our earlier discussion.

The second consequence is social planning. In order to make rational use of social productive capital and in order to reduce uncertainty enough so that self-management decisions produce the expected consequences, the activities of productive units must be coordinated on an *ex ante* basis, which is the essence of planning. It is important to realize the difference between bureaucratic or administrative—usually called central[51]—planning and social planning. The former implies imperative coordination—coordination based on orders—and destroys the autonomy of the firm. The latter implies economic coordination—coordination based on economic interests—aimed at achieving the desired *global* proportions and leaving each *individual* firm full autonomy—and responsibility—for decision making. It is clear that, in this case, planning is a precondition for the genuine autonomy of working collectives. Without social planning, they would become victims of haphazard forces of an uncontrolled market.

Since, in an economy of scarcity, the greater part of our conscious life is connected with productive work, producer's equity is vital for a humane existence.

Equality of consumers implies an equitable or just distribution of income. Again, equitable does not mean a mechanical equality, for in a world of scarcity such a distribution would be considered manifestly unjust and, as such, would cause a drastic reduction of output and economic welfare. The lazy and the industrious cannot obtain the same reward—our sense of justice tells us. An individual ought to receive from the society exactly as much as he contributes to the social output. And this is the well-known principle of distribution according to work. It is also one of the corollaries of the postulate of social capital. Capital cannot be considered social if someone derives income apart from and above—and another, consequently, below—his labor income. We get a wholly consistent theory in which the equality of producers implies the equality of consumers and vice versa.

The theory needs an important amendment, however. The principle of labor income cannot be generalized. In a socialist society education, the preservation of health, and access to cultural activities cannot be determined by the earning capacity of a particular individual or his family. This would lead to a perpetuation of social differences, and social differences result in a class society. Besides, the requirements for producers' equality would be violated. Unequally educated individuals cannot be equal as producers. Equal education is clearly one of the basic preconditions for the equality of producers. So is equal access to the medical and cultural facilities of the society. It follows that the principle of distribution according to work—and, consequently, market and exchange activities—must be abandoned in that section of personal consumption which makes basic contributions to the development of personal capabilities. Here the exchange principle of distribution according to work must be replaced by a nonexchange principle of *distribution according to needs.* This is how the principle of solidarity comes into play.

The socialist economy uses the market because this is the most efficient means available for achieving the targets of producers' and consumers' equality. But it is neither a laissez-faire nor a universal market. It is a market strictly regulated by social planning. And it is supplemented by an important segment of nonmarket activities whose importance grows with economic development.

Finally, *the equality of citizens* implies an equal distribution of power and a meaningful participation in political decision making. This requirement is not satisfied—and in principle cannot be satisfied—in even the most developed bourgeois democracies. Political equity is possible only when productive and consumptive equity have already been achieved. But it is also a precondition for genuine equity in the field of production and consumption. Private property and class differences make equal distribution of power impossible in a capitalist society. The enormous concentration of political power makes genuine producers' and consumers' equality impossible in an etatist society. Party bureaucracies—either one or more—are not compatible with an associationist society. Even the concept of democracy is no longer fully satisfactory: in addition to the rights of the majority, the society will have to safeguard the rights of minorities as well. Let us denote the political framework that satisfies these requirements as *self-government.*

It is hardly necessary to add that the three equities cannot be achieved totally in the real world. They serve as standards and criteria. The available experience shows that contemporary societies can go very far in satisfying these standards. In a socialist polity, they must be treated as fundamental rights of citizens.

The three basic requirements have had an interesting history in connection with socialist thought and socialist movements. They were discovered at different stages of development and have never been stated explicitly as a complete set of conditions for consistent socialist theory and practice. First to be discovered was the principle of distribution according to work; it was made popular by Marx and is widely accepted today. It was only after the Second World War that Yugoslavia demonstrated that self-management can be applied on a national scale and that it represents an indispensable component of a socialist society. In contrast to the quite satisfactory knowledge and important practical experience regarding socialist production and consumption, we still do not know, even in theory, how to achieve an equal distribution of political power. Thus, the equality of citizens turned out to be the hardest nut to crack. Consequently, politics—not economics—appears to be *the* problem of socialist society.

The equality of producers, consumers, and citizens provides the basis for a socialist society conceived as a just society. The only operational way to find out what is just in each particular instance is to give everyone an equal chance to participate in the evaluation. Socialism is a participatory, self-governing society.

PART THREE

The Design of Self-governing Socialism

The philosophers have only *interpreted* the world, in various ways; the point, however, is to *change* it.
MARX, Eleventh Thesis on Feuerbach (1845)

In place of the old bourgeois society with its classes and class antagonisms, we shall have an association in which the free development of each is the condition for the free development of all.
MARX AND ENGELS, *Communist Manifesto* (1848)

8

Equality of Producers

I. Social Property

Production implies appropriation. The end result of production—the product—always belongs to someone. Thus, from the point of view of an economic system, *property relations* are *production relations* and vice versa.

In the world of commodity production, property relations are legally regulated. This process generates *rights of property*. The legal theory of property rights was already fully developed in Roman law. The basic ideas have been changed only insignificantly. The Romans conceived the rights of property as an unlimited, absolute, and exclusive power of a person over a thing. Bourgeois law replaced the concept of power with the concept of subjective rights authorizing a person to treat a thing in a certain way. At the time of the French Code Civil of 1804, which represents a landmark in the development of bourgeois law, property rights were defined as *ius utendi, fruendi et abutendi* (the right of usage, appropriation of benefits, and disposal of a thing). In both the Roman and bourgeois interpretations, property means excluding others from control over a thing.

Elaborating on Roman-bourgeois legal theory, the socialist tradition distinguished three types of property: private, cooperative, and state. In this respect, the landmark was provided by the Soviet Civil Code of 1922. Its paragraph 52 enumerates the three types of property mentioned above. The first type is characteristic of a capitalist system and, in a postrevolutionary society, is said to represent vestiges of the past. As such, it ought to be destroyed as fast as possible. The second, higher form of property is unstable under both capitalism and socialism, and represents a transitional category. State property is considered to be the highest form of property and, as such, provides the foundations for socialist production relations.

On the basis of our previous analysis, it is not difficult to realize that the theory of state-socialist property is yet another instance of misplaced bourgeois reasoning. There is no basic contradiction between private and state property. True, the first can be considered a subjective right, while the latter may be juxtaposed as an objective right. Yet, this implies only that individual owners are replaced by functionaries. Consequently, private property generates capitalism, and state property generates etatism—both of which are class systems. In this sense, the two systems are similar, and both of them are at the same time fundamentally different from the third—socialism. If socialism is to be defined in terms of property relations—which, bearing in mind our introductory remark, is perfectly legitimate—it ought to imply a new and different category of property. Let us call it *social property*. What is the content of this concept?

Socialism conceived as a self-governing society implies that there exists no particular class of owners of the means of production, either individual or collective. Everyone is equally an owner, which means that no one in particular is an owner. The specific feature of the Roman-bourgeois concept of property—the exclusion of others—is not applicable. If no one is excluded, then everyone has equal access to the means of production owned by the society. As a consequence, property confers no special privileges.

It is clear that social property, as just defined, cannot be fit into the traditional legal framework. Any attempt to do so encounters considerable difficulties. Thus, it may be argued that social property *is* property because it implies usufruct and sale. It may be argued just as plausibly that it *is not* property because there is no disposal right and no traditional exclusion of others. One may contend that social property belongs to the sphere of *public* law, since such property clearly is not private. But one may also argue that it belongs to the sphere of *private* law, since it is clearly not state property. Roman-law-based legal theory obviously was not designed for a classless system. It will have to be changed along with other elements of the superstructure.[1] But this is not our concern here. All we have to do is give a precise meaning to the concept of social property. I propose to achieve this by considering the legal, social, and economic aspects of social property.

From the *formal legal* point of view, property is a bundle of rights and obligations concerning a thing that has economic value. In the case of social property, we can recognize two fundamental rights and one obligation. The rights are:

1) to use, change, or sell commodities, including means of production;

2) to reap benefits from the use of productive assets (usufruct).

The fundamental obligation is:

3) the value of productive assets must not be diminished whatever the source of original finance.

The three legal principles enumerated are necessary for the legal regulation of economic relations among *autonomous* producers' collectives.

In terms of *social relations*, productive property implies command over the labor of other (propertyless) members of a class-structured society. Thus, Marx very appropriately defined capital as productive property generating exploitative production relations based on the command over the labor of others. In this sense, both capitalism and etatism are exploitative, and capital can be both private and state. In a classless socialist society, property implies the absence of control over and exploitation of the labor of others. It is clear that the ownership of consumer goods (including consumer durables) is compatible with this requirement; so is family production, as well as the legal definition of productive property given above. The absence of exploitative relationships implies the following three fundamental rights:

1) every member of society has the right to work;

2) every member of society has the right to compete for any job, according to his personal capability (consistent with the specifications of the job);

3) every member of society has the right to participate in management on equal terms.

If any of the three rights is violated, social property is not fully social and, consequently, socialist production relations are not fully—or perhaps not at all—developed.

Economically, social property implies the negation of the very essence of property in presocialist societies—the appropriation of income from property. Capital income cannot be appropriated either privately or collectively. If, as before, we define this aspect of social property positively, we can add the following fundamental right/obligation:

—every member of society derives economic benefits exclusively from his work and none from property.

This right (to the product of his work) and obligation (nothing but the product of work) serve as a basis for the application of the principle of distribution according to work. This principle, in turn, generates consumer equality (to be discussed in the next chapter).

The economic aspect of social property has been, and continues to be, equally often misunderstood as the social one. Both socialists and nonsocialists keep on confusing formal legal and economic ownership. (Legally) private property is juxtaposed to social property and (legally) nonprivate property is juxtaposed to private property. This sort of reasoning leads to the conclusion that every nationalization represents a step toward socialism and that the existence of private artisans and farmers is incompatible with socialism. That complete state ownership has nothing to do with socialism ought to be almost self-evident by now. It remains to be shown that peasants and artisans are (potentially) just as much "socialist elements" as those working in (legally) nonprivate sectors. To see this, one must make a clear distinction between legal title and economic substance.

One of the first to make this distinction clear and precise was Alexander Bajt.[2] Bajt drew attention to the fact that legal title and economic ownership not only are not identical but often diverge substantially. For instance, the legal owner of a house is the person who holds the legal title. If rents are controlled and tenants cannot be evicted, the partial (or even full) economic owner of the house is the person who lives in it and so reaps the benefits from the property. Similarly, an individual peasant may own land legally. If he cannot employ outside labor, however, and the rent of the land is absorbed by a suitably designed tax, the economic benefits of land belong to society.[3] On the other hand, social property may be legally established in a country but, at the same time, workers in some industries may earn substantially higher incomes than those in other industries (as happens, for example, in Yugoslavia). This difference in incomes or the relative size of nonlabor income in privileged industries reflects the degree of privatization of social property.

The above analysis has important policy implications. Contrary to the traditional view, legal expropriation is neither a necessary nor a sufficient condition for socialism. It is not sufficient because total legal expropriation may and has produced nonsocialist systems. It is not necessary because what matters is not the expropriation of legal titles but the expropriation of economic benefits arising from the control of property. Since family production was found to be fully consistent with the social aspect of social property—and now we see that this is true of the economic aspect as well—it may be concluded that small-scale family businesses are compatible with socialism in general. As for the legal aspect, legal obligation 3 given above may be relaxed as inappropriate. Thus, under socialism we may, following Bajt's suggestions, distinguish two types of social property: collective and individual. All the rights and obligations enumerated apply to the former. The latter is more restrictive, concerns only family businesses, and lacks some of the characteristics because they are inappropriate (legal obligation 3) or inapplicable (social rights 1 and 2).[4]

We may summarize our discussion by concluding that social property represents a special type of property with distinct legal, social, and economic characteristics that make exploitation impossible. In this context, exploitation is defined as: (a) command over the labor of others; and (b) appropriation of nonlabor income. Alternatively, social property may be said still to be property in the legal sense (a bundle of appropriately defined rights and obligations) but no longer in the social or economic sense (no privileges accruing to persons on the basis of property). The latter implies that legal property cannot be transformed into capital.

II. Workers' Management: Principles of Organization

Industrial democracy, like any democracy, is a political concept. A business firm run by workers is not only an economic organization but also a political organization. The implications are twofold. First, the most complete and direct self-management is possible only at the enterprise level, so any study of self-management appropriately begins with an investigation of workers' management. Second, what happens in enterprises is of fundamental importance for social relations in the society at large.

The organizational/political goal of a socialist enterprise is to maximize democracy in decision making together with the efficiency of implementation. Traditional organizational theory considers this double goal to be inherently contradictory. It is considered equally as contradictory as a coupling of market and planning. A socialist organizational theory will treat the two goals as complementary. This has to be shown.

The maximization of democracy may be defined to mean that the opinion of each member of a work community is weighted exclusively by its objective importance for the decision at hand. Thus, the decision reached would be independent of the subjective motives and interests of any particular member. At the same time, it would be as efficient as possible. Maximum democracy would imply maximum efficiency.

As attractive as the solution just sketched might appear at first sight, it is really no solution at all. It is an empty tautology like, for instance, the neoclassical theory of value. Democracy is simply defined in such a manner as to imply efficiency. We have no indication of how to achieve one or the other and make them compatible. They have been made compatible by definition. Thus, we have to search for a more meaningful approach.

In reality, there are two essential problems to be solved. First, who evaluates the objective weight of a proposition? Second, what is the objective weight of a value judgment? The answer is that democracy must be determined by the *mode* of decision making, not by the *quality* of decisions. Now the tautological identity disappears, and we can postulate the following six organizational principles for a labor-managed enterprise. The first two guarantee democracy; the next three, efficiency; and the last makes the two goals compatible.

1. Absolute maximum democracy is achievable when the work community consists of only one member. When others join, the freedom of decision making necessarily becomes limited, and technical complexities increase. Besides, distinct possibilities arise for cliques and coalitions to form, with a consequent manipulation of group opinion. Even if this does not happen, it is still possible to have a genuine diversity of interests that causes two subgroups to emerge. The majority may then tyrannize over the minority; it may disregard and overrun the legitimate interests of the minority. For all these reasons, basic work groups should be sufficiently small and homogeneous so as to make possible face-to-face interactions, informal communications, and interpersonal contacts among members. In such a primary social group:

a) the participation in decision making will be direct;

b) the process itself and the decisions reached will be transparent;

c) because of the homogeneity of the group, unjustified and permanent imposition of majority will is unlikely;

d) because of (a) through (c), the possibilities for the manipulation of opinion are limited.

We can now derive the first organizational principle: the basic organizational unit is not the enterprise but the work group, with the characteristics described above. I shall call it the *work unit.* A work unit is not only a group of workers but also a definite subsystem in the production system known as the enterprise. In this capacity, as the smallest functional unit, it will be referred to as an *economic unit.* A work unit may be further subdivided into work teams, which assume various production and other tasks.[5] Work units are federated into a *work community*; economic units, into an *enterprise.*

2. Whenever the decisions of a work unit affect substantially the interests of other work units, the right of decision making ought to be delegated to the next higher level. This is the justification for establishing a *workers' council* as the second-level decision-making body.

Efficient management implies: (a) correct decisions; and (b) efficient implementation. The organizational principles that follow are intended to satisfy these two conditions.

3. The individuals and organs making decisions should bear responsibility for these decisions. In other words, rights must be matched by sanctions.

4. The implementation of decisions—executive work and administration—is a matter of professional competence, not of democracy.

5. Principle 4 implies the separation of two different spheres of activity: the interest sphere and the professional sphere. The former consists of policy decisions, the latter of professional work and administrative routine. Policy decisions are legitimized by political authority; executive and administrative work, by professional authority. The former represent value judgments; the latter, technical implementation. In the interest sphere, the rule of one man, one vote applies; in the professional sphere, vote is weighted by professional competence.

6. Since political and technical decisions cannot be neatly separated—and neither can work units be made perfectly homogeneous nor the entire work community sufficiently small—there is always a possibility for individuals and groups to abuse power. Therefore, special safeguards should be built into the system. This implies the institutionalization of control and conflict solving, as well as the institutionalized defense of individual interests against the inconsiderateness of the group and of collective interests against the misbehavior of individuals. The offenses to be adjudicated are those of the operatives, of the work coordinators, and of the legislators.

III. Workers' Management: Organizational Chart

If the six principles outlined in the preceding section are applied, the organization of the labor-managed enterprise will follow that depicted in Figure 4. It is immediately apparent that the figure is nothing but an elaboration of the sandglass model of organization (see Figure 3). The upper section falls into the policy sphere, the lower into the sphere of technical implementation. Since we are dealing with a political system, we can also make use of traditional political theory and speak of a separation of powers. Legislative power is located in the upper part of the structure, executive power in the lower. Apart from that, and in keeping with organizational principle 6, there is adjudicative power as well, located on the left in the central portion of the figure.

In principle, all decisions are to be made always at the lowest possible level. Only when decisions affect the interests of other work units will they be made at the level above the work unit. Most of the decisions that affect the daily lives of workers can be made at the work unit level. These are the decisions concerning job assignment, work conditions, social priorities, distribution of the surplus, employment and dismissal, conflict resolution, and so on. Empirical research reveals that these are exactly the problems workers insist on including within the realm of direct participation in decision making.[6] Other policy decisions may be delegated to the central legislative organ, the *workers' council*. There is, however, a class of vitally important decisions that are made by neither the workers' council nor the individual work units, but by the entire work community at a general meeting or by referendum. These are decisions regarding merger, radical reorganization, heavy investment programs, passage of the constitution and various ordinances, and similar matters. In such cases, the majority vote of every constituent work unit may be required.

When a new worker joins the enterprise, he signs a "social contract" whereby he associates his labor with that of the rest of the work community under the existing constitution and ordinances.

Work units will range somewhere between ten and two hundred members depending on the size of the enterprise and the complexity of the production process. A work unit takes decisions in plenum. It elects a chairman, who represents the

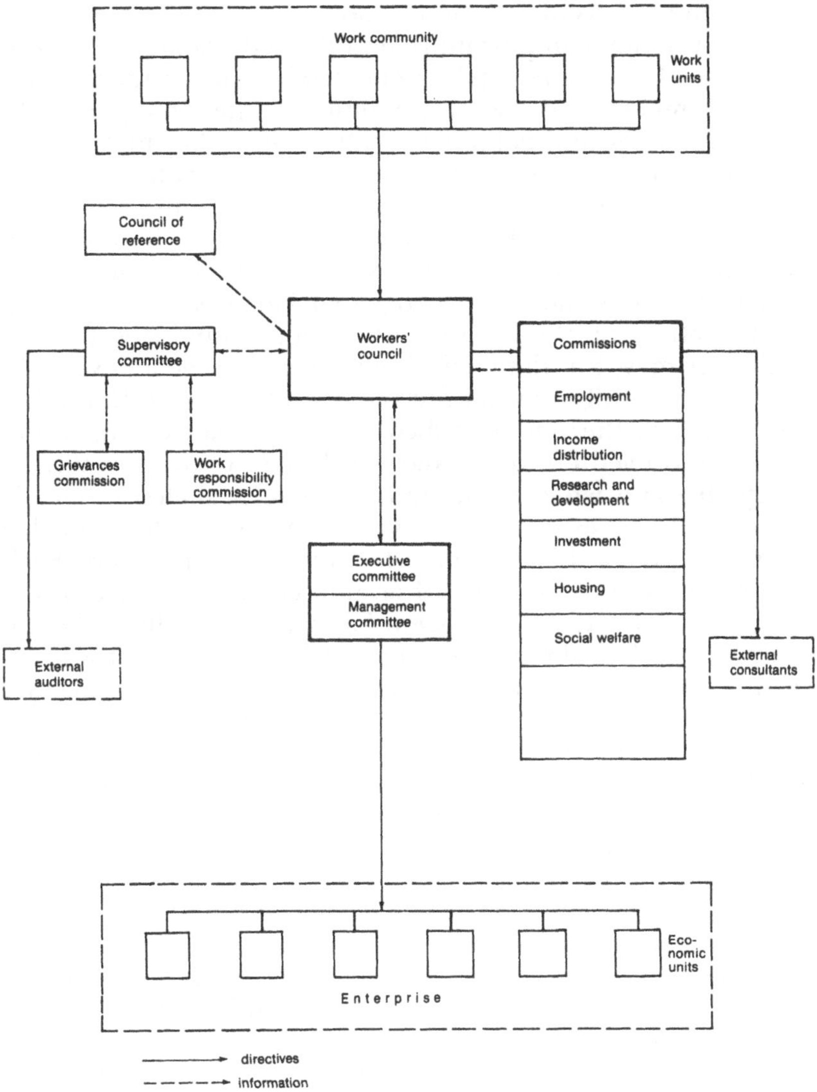

Figure 4. *Organization of a labor-managed enterprise.*

unit on the workers' council. In addition to work unit chairmen, who represent "sectional interests," the workers' council also includes commission chairmen, who represent "functional interests." The latter are elected by general vote. Since every member of the council is individually responsible for a particular set of activities (either political or technical), principle 3 is satisfied.

Commissions of the council have only advisory power, yet they play a vitally important role in the self-management process. They bridge the gap between professional managers and other members of the work community. They integrate technical knowledge and political considerations. They make it possible for practically everyone to be involved in management, at least at the stage of preparing the decisions. Thus, not only is technical knowledge tapped, but also precious social experience is gained, which improves understanding and communication and helps to reduce inherited social barriers. An unskilled worker sitting on the income distribution commission for several years may, for all practical purposes, become an expert in the field. He will know all the reasons why wage differentials were fixed in the way described in the ordinances, which decisions improved efficiency and which did not, what is socially acceptable and what is not, and so forth. A skilled mechanic sitting on the investment commission may prove to be a valuable source of practical information for investment planners. Such people become repositories of accumulated knowledge of the firm's activities. If a commission happens not to have the appropriate technical expertise in a particular matter, it will engage a consulting firm from outside. While decision-making organs are elective and based on rotation of membership—the term of office normally being two years—membership on commissions depends on personal preferences; it need not be limited in duration and, for the more technical commissions, it need not be elective. There is plenty of scope for an individual to specialize in some particular aspect of enterprise management. This not only contributes to efficiency but also satisfies the need for active personal involvement.

The workers' council passes decisions on the basis of recommendations made by its commissions and committees. The most important committee is the *executive committee*, which replaces the former management board. The general manager—perhaps better called the general work coordinator—who serves as chairman of the executive committee, is appointed by the workers' council. The chairman of the workers' council is an ex officio member of the executive committee. Other members are departmental heads and the enterprise's secretary, who are appointed by the workers' council upon recommendation by the manager. Work units appoint their own economic unit managers in agreement with the general manager. Making managerial personnel maximally acceptable to both the workers and the general manager obviously enhances efficiency. It is of some interest to note that the "federal" units will be doubly represented in the management structure of the enterprise: chairmen sit in the workers' council and managers sit in the management committee. The chairman is a politician, a specialist in good work relations; the manager (the work coordinator) is a technician, a specialist for work tasks. If both of them enjoy the confidence of the workers (and have compatible personalities), the work unit is likely to be politically democratic and economically efficient.

The general manager usually is appointed for a period of four years. His appointment is conditional upon presentation of a satisfactory development program. Once a program is fully elaborated and accepted by the work community, it becomes a sort of internal law. Both the council and the manager and his staff are obliged to implement it. This means that the workers' council must provide full political support (or initiate the procedure for a change of the program), and the executive committee bears full responsibility for the realization of the program (principle 3). The executive committee and the workers' council may disagree. Then the general manager may tender his resignation or bring the dispute before the general electorate—that is, before the entire work community and its work units (since the workers' council has only delegated decision-making power). The general manager is also responsible for the legality of all enterprise activities and, therefore, is obliged to veto unlawful decisions of the workers' council. On the other hand, at the beginning of each business year, the debate on the business results of the preceding year and on the plan for the following year ends with a vote of confidence concerning the executive committee. If the members of the council conclude that poor business results do not justify further confidence in the management, the management committee will have to be changed, and the general manager may have to resign even if his term of appointment has not expired.

In every human group, conflicts are bound to occur and some individuals may abuse their power or fail to live up to their responsibilities. Therefore, every system of government—self-management included—needs to perform two additional functions (apart from legislation and administration): the functions of adjudication and of control.

There are two types of conflicts between individuals and the collectivity: (a) an individual may be harmed by an action of the collectivity (or by a decision on its behalf); and (b) the interests of the collectivity may be impaired by the irresponsible behavior of an individual. Since these are two different types of conflicts, it is advisable to set up two different organs: a *grievances commission* dealing with the first type of conflict and a *work responsibility commission* dealing with the second. The former may be elected by all members of the work community, since it must enjoy the full confidence of all individuals. The latter may be elected by the workers' council, since it must enjoy the confidence of the legislators. Both commissions are fully independent in their work. Any member of the work community may introduce a case before either of the commissions. Note that the second commission replaces the former disciplinary commission. Yet, in the present setting, it is not only the superiors who initiate adjudication by the commission of a particular breach of discipline. The "superiors" themselves may also be brought before the commission. On the other hand, they have the right to make use of the grievances commission when they themselves feel harmed.

The two commissions act in the same way as do courts: they apply rules as established by the constitution and use precedent, creating in this way some sort of common law. They cannot change the rules or insist on their own preferences. Since the rules, however perfect, are always rigid, occasionally the need for a modification or reinterpretation arises. For this reason, it may be advisable to give the workers' council the role of a court of appeals. If the workers' council itself is the defendant, then the commission is the court of last resort within the enterprise. Yet even then an appeal can be made, in this case to an outside organ called the Public Attorney for Self-Management (to be described in greater detail in chapter 10).

The chairmen of the two commissions are ex officio members of the *supervisory committee*. The supervisory committee is an organ of workers' control and supervises all managerial activities. Since conflicts provide first-hand information about poor management, it may be useful to establish a link between the commissions and the committee. The chairman of the committee, and possibly additional members as well, are elected either by a general vote or by the workers' council. The committee makes recommendations to and prepares reports for the council, but is otherwise independent. In order to work efficiently and to react in a timely way to changing business conditions, the management must be given certain discretionary power. Yet this power, like any power, may easily be abused. Therefore, an institutionalized control is needed. The supervisory committee serves this function. It has access to all documents and may scrutinize any managerial decision. At least once a year, the committee engages external auditors to prepare an evaluation of the business results for the business debate mentioned above. The committee, however, acts not only as an instrument of control and an unpleasant critic of management, it can also serve as a powerful instrument of support to an energetic and enterprising management. An active management is likely to generate resistance among more sluggish members of the community. To rationalize their discontent, they may begin to spread rumors questioning the appropriateness, legality, and so on, of certain managerial actions. The only efficient way to fight rumors is to bring the issue into the open and confront it with facts. Rumors may be fought—or hidden abuses discovered—in yet another way. Any information passed to the supervisory committee is considered confidential and may not be disclosed until and unless it is found to be true. On the other hand, the committee may ask for information from, and inspect the books of, any department or organ in the enterprise. Thus, if an individual sees an indication that something vicious has been done, but he is not sure, he will inform the committee. If his surmise proves correct, damage will be prevented. If it proves wrong, an honest man's reputation will have been preserved unblemished and an unnecessary conflict avoided. The importance of a vigorous supervisory committee for good human relations in an enterprise can scarcely be overrated. Such a committee will help to minimize conflicts.

Conflicts may arise not only when rules are not adhered to or legitimate interests are not honored, but also when parties disagree on the interpretation of the rules. Or, as in a novel situation, there may be no rules at all. Then someone must decide what is correct or fair. This is the role of the *council of reference*,[7] which is a combination of a constitutional court and an arbitration board. Any worker can contest the legality of any decision regardless of whether or not he is personally involved. Any organ may contest the legality of a particular act of any other organ. Alternatively, before an important decision is made, the need may arise for a competent interpretation of the rules. Such cases are referred to the council, whose decisions are binding. The council also supervises elections.

Since satisfactory adjudication requires good knowledge of the enterprise's organization and experience in management, it may be a good rule to make election to adjudicative organs contingent upon previous service in advisory commissions and the workers' council. In general, all elected members of self-management organs retain their productive jobs. Only the chairman of the workers' council may be required to quit his usual job during his term of office, for in somewhat larger enterprises his responsibilities may require full-time engagement.

The above organization is not a copy of any particular enterprise, though it shows quite a few similarities to the actual organization of Yugoslav worker-managed firms. The organizational chart is based primarily on my first-hand experience as, successively, a member of various workers' councils, a member of many commissions and committees, a general manager, and a member of an adjudicative organ over the course of some fifteen years. It is designed for a medium-sized enterprise. In a small enterprise, the management structure will be simplified; in a large one, there may be several tiers of management with plant, enterprise, and firm workers' councils. It is important to realize that the same organization applies, *mutatis mutandis,* to *any other work organization.*

There is no reason why only business firms should enjoy the privilege of self-management. In a socialist society, whenever individuals associate their work in order to earn their living, they form a work organization based on self-management. The hierarchy is replaced by cooperation and the three—or, rather, four—governmental functions are appropriately institutionalized. There is one important complication regarding the present organizational chart that needs to be mentioned. Some work organizations may be of special societal interest; that is, their activities may affect other segments of the society in an important way. Consequently, full autonomy might not be desirable. In such a case, a *board of trustees* may be introduced into the structure. The members of the board will consist of representatives of the work community as well as representatives of the particular societal interests in question.

Worker management can function properly only if it is fully public. Consequently, prompt and adequate information regarding everything that is going on is vitally important. The decisions of all organs should be published in the enterprise bulletin, and the minutes of all meetings should be accessible to every individual member.

The participatory organization is technically somewhat more complicated than the traditional hierarchical organization. It cannot be established overnight. A period of learning is required. In the meantime, various difficulties, which are analyzed in the next section, will have to be overcome. At first sight it appears that costs are increased in terms of the time required. And, indeed, a naive and inexperienced approach to self-management may result in heavy losses in efficiency if meetings replace productive work. In a normally functioning system, however, a substantial overall gain is likely to be realized. A hierarchical system only appears to operate rapidly. It is true that orders can be issued quickly and then must be carried out. But such procedures generate unwanted side effects, and a great deal of successive activity is wasted on coping with these side effects.[8] Participation requires a special preparatory stage in which all interested parties are informed about the intended action and their views are solicited. Once agreement is reached, the decision is implemented without resistance, and the desired results are achieved more expeditiously.

Doubt is sometimes expressed about the applicability of self-management to particular production organizations. Our discussion of organizational design shows that it is universally applicable. The same cannot be said, however, for the traditional hierarchical organization. Universities and research institutes are obvious examples. But even enterprises using the most advanced technology cannot be run in the traditional way. If routine production is replaced by individual projects—which is likely to be more and more characteristic in the technotronic age—then organization becomes multidimensional, and the one-dimensional line of authority becomes simply inapplicable. Each project involves various departments and requires various staff services to be integrated. William Halal, an American professor of management, certainly was not exaggerating when he wrote:

> the evolving post-industrial society will virtually eliminate most physical forms of labour and instead will concentrate on the "information" industries. The prevalent fields of employment by the close of this century will include research, computerization, services, communications, education and the like. These technologies involve dramatically different features from those with which existing organizational forms have been designed to deal. The component tasks associated with the "info-comm" technologies are so unique that programmed routines are often inappropriate. Interaction between various parts of a problem makes it difficult to separate into specialized jobs; and the uncertainty involved in such, as yet, poorly understood processes makes prediction of outcomes far more problematical than it is for processes involving the repeated execution of similar tasks.[9]

Unstructured problem solving cannot be routinized. As a consequence, great demands will be laid on creativity and innovation. In addition, the rapidly changing environment requires that the organizational system be opened. Some of the activities that managers used to control by the internal authority system begin to fall outside the system. The need for greater adaptability and for the establishment of temporary organizations to deal with specific problems requires a different type of coordination. Traditional bureaucratic organization, with its ranks and programmed role expectations, becomes meaningless or at least dysfunctional.[10] Thus, it will have to be replaced by something that is technologically more appropriate.

Once again we reach the familiar conclusion: advanced technology and advanced social organization go together. Thus, self-management is not only compatible with the developmental trends in technology. Meaningful participation is in fact indispensable for the normal functioning of a postindustrial society.

IV. Potential Problems under Workers' Management

Attempts to introduce workers' management have been met by three standard objections. It was said that self-management would erode discipline, that workers' councils lacked competence to act as a board of directors, and that workers would distribute all the profits in wages, thus reducing the growth potential of the economy. None of these prophecies proved to be correct.

The first objection implies that workers' management will destroy hierarchy (correct), that without hierarchy there can be no authority (incorrect), and that without authority discipline is bound to disintegrate. The reasoning is based on a confusion between two types of authorities—one coercive and the other professional. Coercive authority disappears with hierarchy, while professional authority remains and is even enhanced by self-management. Empirical research has shown no decrease in work discipline[11] and has indicated that the effective power of both workers and management increases. An international comparative study concluded:

> Participation in decision-making by workers has a direct bearing on the influence of workers as a group, which has implications in turn for the personal influence, trust and responsibility felt by workers. Where workers trust management and feel a sense of responsibility in the plant, they are likely to be responsive to

> the influence attempts of managers and managers are therefore likely to be influential under these conditions. Plants where workers participate in decisions tend therefore to be characterized by a relatively high level of control according to members. The enhanced influence of workers under these conditions does not have the effect of reducing the influence of managers since the trust and responsibility felt by members provide a basis for sustaining the influence of managers if not increasing it.[12]

Concerning the effectiveness of the decision making on the part of workers' councils, our discussion of organizational design shows that this supreme policymaking body can utilize all information and knowledge existing in the firm. The council is in an incomparably better position to contribute to the operation of the enterprise than its capitalist twin, the board of directors. What the board—mythologically described as representing the interests of the shareholders—really does is well described by Robert Townsend: "They meet once a month, gaze at the financial window dressing (never at the operating figures by which managers run the business), listen to the chief and his team talk superficially about the state of the operation, ask a couple of dutiful questions, make token suggestions (courteously recorded and subsquently ignored), and adjourn until next month."[13] By contrast, those who participate in the meetings of a workers' council are manual and intellectual workers who live with the firm, who are familiar with its problems, and who are existentially interested in the correct decisions.

As to the third objection, growth depends not on profits but on investment. And, if anything, there have been chronic overinvestment tendencies in the worker-managed economy. This is explained by the higher marginal efficiency of investment due to lower risks and less uncertainty about the future.

The three objections remind one of the fundamental objection Adam Smith raised two centuries ago to the joint stock company: "The directors of such companies . . . being the managers rather of other people's money than of their own, it cannot be well expected that they should watch over it with the same anxious vigilance with which the partners in a private copartnery frequently watch over their own. . . . Negligence and profusion, therefore, must always prevail, more or less, in the management of the affairs of such a company."[14] Smith thought that only private owners could conscientiously manage their enterprises; the separation of ownership and management was bound to produce negligence and profusion. Contemporary ideologues know from experience that this is not so, but they insist that only authoritarian management can do the trick. They expect negligence and profusion to be caused by the separation of productive coordination from policy decisions.

It was not difficult to dispose of these three pseudoproblems. Yet, there is a host of real problems that must be carefully examined.

1. *Waste of time in discussions.* Participatory management is characterized by what might be termed "the unanimity syndrome." A great reluctance is found to decide an issue by vote. It is felt that there should be one best solution acceptable to everyone. If people disagree, they will try to persuade each other until consensus is reached. Now, if a meeting is poorly prepared, if the participants do not have adequate information and did not have time to think about the issues involved and carry out informal consultations beforehand, if the technical and legal background of the issue is not clearly and precisely formulated—all of which is likely to happen in the early stages of workers' management—the meetings are likely to last for hours, even for days, with all sorts of irrelevant issues being discussed and with the final decision being more a result of exhaustion on the part of the participants than of real progress in coping with the issue. Thus, preliminary discussion in the advisory commissions that prepare the proposals, and expert legal and technical advice from the managerial staff are indispensable preconditions for reducing the discussion time to what is really necessary to reach consensus.

2. *Violation of organizational principles 3, 4, and 5.* The distinction between legislative and administrative work is not clearly perceived, nor is responsibility pinpointed. Since management is what managers do, self-management appears at first sight as managerial work. There is therefore a spontaneous tendency to interfere with the day-to-day administration of the enterprise. This puts the general manager in a delicate position, and he may respond in several different ways.

a. A *passive or incompetent* manager can easily avoid any responsibility by letting the workers' council assume all risks.

b. A *demagogue* will build his position on his apparent willingness to obey always and unconditionally—regardless of the damage caused by inappropriate decisions.

c. A *manipulator* will let the workers' council decide on trivialities and on issues requiring technical competence that the council members do not possess in order to make them rubber-stamp his own decisions while avoiding any personal responsibility.

d. A truly *dedicated* and potentially efficient manager may be accused of usurping self-management rights. After a couple of disappointing experiences of this sort, the frustrated manager is likely to evolve into one of the preceding three types.

In this context, all decisions can be classified into four categories: strategic decisions, tactical decisions, professional decisions, and routine decisions. Self-management is concerned primarily with strategic decisions; tactical decisions should be left mostly to the executive committee; professional work and routine administration should be carried out in a routine way by the respective staff without outside interference. Failure to distinguish between these four categories of decisions results in general organizational confusion.

In fact, the problem of decision making is even more complex. In the early stages of self-management, there is a pronounced tendency to concentrate on just making the decisions. This looks like an obvious sign of power and authority. Yet decision making has at least five stages, and taking the decision is just one of them. If the other four are not controlled, mere decision taking amounts to very little in terms of power and may have definitely negative effects in terms of efficiency. Modifying somewhat the approach of Ivan Paj,[15] we can describe participation in strategic decision making as shown in Table 10.

TABLE 10

The Process of Strategic Decision Making

Stages of decision making \ Decision participants	Work community	Work unit	Workers' council	Executive committee	General manager	Professional staff	Advisory commissions	Individual members
	1	2	3	4	5	6	7	8
I. Initiative (definition of the problem)	x	x	x	x	x	x	x	x
II. Preparation of decision (elaboration of variants)				x	x	x	x	x
III. Taking of decision (selection of a variant)	x	x	x					
IV. Implementation of decision				x	x	x		x
V. Control of implementation (and possible corrections)	x	x	x	x	x	x	x	x

There are five stages of decision making and eight decision participants. In the first and the last stage, everyone participates. The third stage is reserved for self-management organs, for the legislators. Yet, they will exercise their authority properly—that is, democratically and efficiently—only if the remaining twenty-five elements of the decision-making matrix function properly. In particular, the fourth stage reflects organizational principle 4, which states that executive work is a matter of professional competence.

3. *Misconceptions about control.* This is closely related to the second problem. Self-management naturally implies control of all managerial activities. It is then naively thought that control is exercised most efficiently by direct participation in all decisions, including administrative, professional, and routine decisions.[16] This leads also to the interference already mentioned in problem 2 above. Treating tactical and routine decisions as strategic and denying any discretionary authority to the executive committee have the following consequences.

a. Business is conducted *less effectively* because managers cannot react immediately to changing business conditions. They first have to ask that a meeting be convened in order to get an ex ante endorsement for the intended action. Since members of the workers' council are production workers, they cannot be called for meetings irregularly and at any time. Thus, decisions will be delayed, while, in the meantime, conditions might change and the intended action become meaningless. If decisions are not delayed, then the manager is acting illegally, which increases his frustration and erodes the system.

b. The idea that management can be controlled in this way is an *illusion*. What distinguishes managers from other members of the community is neither higher intelligence (anyone may be more intelligent), nor better education (research workers are better educated), nor higher status (elective officers carry high social status). It is familiarity with the work they do, accumulated experience and, occasionally perhaps, special talent for this sort of job. Thus, no amount of education can replace the necessary amount of properly digested information. And information cannot be digested at a meeting called on short notice. In brief, managerial work (tactical, professional, and routine decisions) is professional work and ought to be treated as such. Amateurism is of no avail to anyone and does great harm to all.

c. Because of points (a) and (b), control not only fails to be achieved; it is easily avoided and replaced by rubber stamping.

Efficient control may be achieved in the following way:

(a) by evaluating overall business results; if they are good, management is probably good; if they are poor, management has to give a satisfactory explanation;

(b) by comparing policy decisions with implementation; in other words, by evaluating specific results;

(c) by handling grievances.

4. *Direct violation of organizational principle 3,* that is, a divorce between decision making and responsibility. This is a very common phenomenon. Everyone is eager to decide, but no one is willing to assume responsibility. I became aware of this fact by studying the behavior of my own council, which consisted of highly educated people. On several occasions, the council tried to force me, as the director, to undertake (or not to undertake) certain actions when I knew definitely that this would be harmful to the institution. After I had failed to persuade the council to accept my proposals, I offered to carry out the decision of the majority under the condition that the council assume responsibility for the outcome and that the work community be informed about this in advance. I thought this was a fair deal and was quite surprised when my offer provoked an outburst of discontent. I was told that the council may make any decision whatever and that the director is obliged to carry it out at his own risk. My subsequent offer to resign was decried as blackmail. Since this was not an isolated episode,[17] I came to the conclusion that inherited authoritarian attitudes are so deeply ingrained that they are unconsciously carried into self-management. The council holds power. Whoever holds power has the right to issue binding orders. Whether these orders make sense is irrelevant; they must be carried out. An attempt to evaluate them negatively is a challenge to the authority of the council and cannot be tolerated. In other words, power is not power if it cannot be arbitrary. A good reference council may help in cases of this sort. And, of course, general, scientifically based education regarding self-management is quite indispensable.

5. *Popularity-based or inconsistent decisions.* This problem is closely related to problem 4. When self-management is centered on the third decision stage and, consequently, decisions are not well prepared, the outcome of a debate depends very much on the prevailing mood of those present. If at the next meeting the membership is somewhat different, or the mood is changed for whatever reason, the earlier decision may be reversed. Since the council is sovereign in the sense described in point 4, this

is not considered inappropriate. On one occasion, the council allocated an unfinished apartment to a person who was first on the priority list. Soon afterward, the man was drafted, and somewhat later another worker applied for the apartment. Now, the council allotted the same apartment to the second man. By the time the apartment was finished, the first man had returned. The manager—a passive type—informed the council innocently that he could not issue two titles to the same apartment. The continuation of the story can easily be imagined. Another case illustrates inconsistency on the part of the council coupled with a refusal to bear responsibility or be bound by its own decisions. I find it startling even today. Within the institute there was a Computer Center that could not cover its costs. We decided to introduce an incentive scheme whereby the members of the center would share in all positive or negative differences in business results compared with those of previous years. Improvement did not appear very likely and, in any case, the incentive percentages were very modest. The new manager of the center turned out to be an exceptionally capable man, however, and at the time of the annual business debate, the center could boast of phenomenal improvements. Instead of giving full recognition to what had been achieved, the council decided to ignore its own decision of a year earlier, proclaimed the incentive scheme inapplicable, and distributed the surplus in an arbitrary fashion. No amount of arguing that *pacta sunt servanda* for everybody, including the council, could stop the disastrous decision. We did not know that they could do so well, was the answer, and it cannot be tolerated that they should earn more than others. The center lapsed into losses again. After a few more decisions of this sort, feelings of uncertainty and insecurity began to spread throughout the work community.

6. *Misconceived justice and misplaced solidarity*. If managers are superiors, it is evident that they may behave unjustly and inflict harm on individual workers. From this follows a recognized need for due process in handling grievances. If workers rule, however, this need is not so obvious. If some wrong is done a person, he appeals to the workers' council and his grievance is redressed by his colleagues. This attitude explains the tendency to let the workers' council deal with everything and to neglect institutionalized resolution of conflicts. As a result, grievances are dealt with in an arbitrary fashion, falling among the last items on long agendas of an exhausted council. Less vocal, less persistent, less popular, and less powerful workers are likely to receive no redress. The council's justice appears very disappointing. Embittered workers then turn to trade

unions and to the regular courts, or go on strike—which of course destroys the very essence of self-management. Not only does harm done to individuals remain uncorrected, however, but damage to collective interests also remains unpunished. This may be termed misplaced solidarity. Railwaymen responsible for railway accidents are not fired unless they are convicted in courts. Cashiers imprisoned for embezzlement are employed again in the same job. Managers convicted of felony again become managers.

7. *Impossibility of neatly separating political and administrative work.* Education means power. Information means power as well. Since managers are likely to be better educated than workers (for the time being) and better informed about the firm's affairs than anyone else, they will hold more power than some other groups. This power can be, and frequently is, abused. How naive attempts to exert control by participating in administrative decisions can backfire was explained above. What can be done to cope with the problem? Empirical research reveals certain interesting facts that are not quite consistent with the expectations. The wielders of arbitrary power tend to be general and departmental managers. Their victims are skilled workers in small work organizations and experts in the larger ones. The hostility of hegemonic cliques toward skilled workers and experts reveals their professional inferiority. Indeed, further sociological research has indicated that managerial groups with a lesser degree of education are less inclined to cooperate with other groups, less ready for critical communication, less interested in correct information, and more sensitive to hierarchical differences. In short, the less competent a manager is, the more arbitrary and aggressive he is likely to be. He must form a ruling clique, since this is the only way to retain power. And if, for some reason, political criteria play an important role in the selection of managers, incompetent managers will tend to form political alliances with the centers of power outside the enterprise, which will exert stifling effects on both worker management and efficiency. Arbitrariness in personnel policy has also been found to be highly correlated with poor organizational development of the work organization.[18] Once again we reach the conclusion that strict professionalization of (executive) management is a necessary precondition for successful self-management. The other precondition is a fully developed and consistent organizational structure.

8. *Fragmentation due to decentralization.* According to the first organizational principle, the economic unit is the basic organizational unit. If an enterprise is treated as a federation of

economic units, internal organization is likely to be rather complex and requires experience and professional knowledge in order to be handled appropriately. Internal decentralization is practiced in capitalist firms as well, and there is a body of professional literature on its various aspects. The relevant knowledge exists and can be usefully applied. Yet, this does not reduce the complexity of the problem; besides, capitalist literature is frowned upon. The spontaneous amateur reaction to the problem is to ask for economic autonomy of economic units. If work units are to be self-governing, they must have financial independence. This will be achieved if the economic unit has its own bank account and sells its services to other units at market prices. (The head office is jointly financed, of course, and there are some joint funds at the level of the enterprise.) As a consequence, economic units begin to behave like separate firms. Since, by the very nature of things, some units cannot operate as separate firms (such as an accounting department or a specialized repair shop), those that can (which produce finished products to be sold on the market) are in a privileged position and begin to exploit their advantages. The enterprise disintegrates into quarreling constituent parts. And if the integrity of the firm is preserved, decentralization turns out to be mere window dressing.[19] The mistake committed is obvious. An enterprise is an enterprise precisely because its internal organization is based on nonmarket principles. The market stops at the gate of an enterprise. If it is introduced inside, the enterprise disintegrates. The self-governing autonomy of an economic unit can be preserved by appropriate budgeting, but again this requires adequate professional knowledge.

9. *The multiplication of conflicts.* The fragmentation described in point 8 is likely to increase the frequency of conflicts. This is what happened in Yugoslavia after a poorly designed institutional reform that established the so-called basic organizations of associated labor. An international study comparing one Yugoslav and one English company indicated that conflicts were three times more numerous in the Yugoslav enterprise.[20] Yet, even in skillfully designed self-managing organizations, it would be utopian to expect conflicts to disappear. The opposite is more likely to happen. As the authors of the study just cited have hypothesized, conflicts should be more frequent when power is more equally distributed; not much conflict is expected when the power distance between the groups is great. This hypothesis is supported by the finding that, in the English enterprise, the groups involved in conflicts came mainly from the

same hierarchical level, while in the Yugoslav firm they were hierarchically close to one another. Generally, the more equal the distribution of power, the greater is the uncertainty and the more conflict-ridden is the organization. The uncertainty caused by democratization may have integrative or disintegrative effects. In the former case, more numerous conflicts contribute to greater flexibility, greater responsiveness, and quicker crystallization of conflicts, which leads to improved efficiency. In the latter case, both interpersonal relations and efficiency may be disastrously affected. The self-management organization is thus very conflict sensitive. Consequently, an appropriate organizational design and methods of conflict resolution appear extremely important for efficient decision making.

10. *Misuse of democratic procedures by individuals and groups in furthering their private interests.* Even if all six organizational rules are observed and the institutional framework is perfectly designed, self-management still may not function properly. While *formally* observing statutes and ordinances, rules and bylaws, individuals and groups may misuse the decision-making rules and kill their democratic *substance.* Anyone familiar with committee work is perfectly aware of that. What follows is a brief, systematic account of my own empirical observations over several years in a self-managed work organization with highly educated participants. The account is not exhaustive, but it gives a fair idea of the disruptive potential of such practices.

1. An individual or group initiates the consideration of an unpleasant problem. The opposition tries to block the initiative. The simplest and most primitive action is to fail to include the request on the appropriate agenda. The explanation given might be forgetfulness, misplacement of the file, the need for preliminary consultations with other bodies.

2. If the request reaches the agenda, it is not preceded by the necessary informational material. Without adequate information, the council or the committee refuses to discuss it.

3. The subject is put at the end of a long agenda. By the time it comes up for discussion, everyone is exhausted, and the meeting is adjourned or the quorum is no longer available, and so consideration is postponed. The same device may be used to elicit the desired decision. When, through exhaustion, the potential opponents have left, the clique members who remain may more easily press for a favorable decision.

4. If the first three obstacles are overcome, decision making may be disrupted by a clique in yet another way. All that is necessary is for several people to raise completely meaningless

issues and create confusion. As a result, either the decision taken will be confused or meaningless, or decision on the issue will be further postponed. The same trick may be applied when a new statute is being prepared and the responsible committee is obliged to answer all suggestions or criticisms, which it tries to avoid.

5. The decision is taken but somehow is not recorded in the minutes or is formulated ambiguously.

6. If no other device works, the executive officer may simply fail to implement the decision. In order to react, one must find the appropriate minutes and criticize the man or the body publicly. Not many are likely to engage in such an activity.

7. A more elegant way is to wait for a while and then to return the issue to the self-managing body for reconsideration because "it was not clear how one should implement the decision." Since new people are likely to be present and a new mood prevail, the new decision is likely to be slightly different, which provides a welcome opportunity for further confusion. If possible, the reconsideration is timed so that the original initiator is not present at the meeting (he is ill or is away on business).

8. A well-known trick is to proclaim the issue so important as to require special study by subcommittees set up for this purpose. By the time the subcommittees are formed and the issue is considered, it has already become irrelevant.

9. If there are several self-management bodies, the executive officer may circulate the issue among them, pretending not to know under whose jurisdiction it falls. The resulting confusion is usually sufficient to kill the project. The same device can be used when one wishes to impose an unpopular decision: one raises the issue with various bodies until one of them is willing to consent. Care must be taken, however, to start with the lowest authority and move upward.

10. If there is a legal deadline by which something has to be done, the issue, project, or statute is prepared for discussion on the last day. In this way no substantial revision is possible.

There is clearly plenty of scope for the activities of undemocratic and power-seeking individuals. The more decision-making bodies there are (chair, senate, council, assembly in the case of a university department) and the more regulating bylaws (twenty-eight in the same case), the greater are the possibilities for misusing self-management. If the statutes, bylaws, and rules are prepared hastily, they must be revised frequently and again reconciled. One soon gets completely lost in the resulting pile of paper. Those engaged in executive work, whose duty is to sit for all meetings, have a definite advantage over the rest of the work community. They are not only better informed but can also guide the decision-making process so as to prevent undesirable decisions and elicit desirable ones. When paperwork piles up, full-scale research might be needed to find out what was decided, when, and by whom. It is thus quite crucial that the organization be simple and control well institutionalized. The major remedy, however, is the development of a self-management culture, which can be achieved only with time, education, and active participation.[21]

11. *The dangers of inefficiency and etatism.* If managers form cliques, injustices are not corrected, economic units fight each other, and meetings last *ad nauseum*, then workers' management will not be very idyllic. Far from disappearing, alienation may in fact increase. Human relations will markedly deteriorate. Efficiency will decline. Faith in self-management will be shaken. Workers will spontaneously turn toward government. Instead of solving their problems by themselves, they will ask the government to intervene. That provides a mass social basis for etatism.[22] Unsuccessful socialism degenerates into etatism.

We may now conclude our discussion of producer equality. It is clear that worker management is no panacea. It creates its own problems, which are by no means insignificant. If they are not handled with the utmost care, the society runs great risk of ending up under etatism.

Self-management is a radically new social organization. People raised in and conditioned to another system cannot change overnight. In particular, individuals are not used to evaluating other individuals' views objectively and do not readily tolerate decisions taken without them by their peers. From this issue the mistakes in organization discussed above. But even if organization is appropriate in principle, it still may not necessarily work. Not everything can be regulated. In fact, overregulation has negative effects just as does misregulation. What is required is mass experience and social adaptation. Only after appropriate customs and traditions have been formed can such an organization be expected to work properly. *Quid leges sine moribus?* It is good to be reminded that early capitalism required decades to rid itself of such barbarous practices as corporal punishment and police intervention in labor relations. Once the first generation has passed through self-management experience from kindergarten age onward, the society will be in much better shape to handle the eleven problems revealed by social practice so far.

The present analysis also indicates factors that facilitate the development of worker management. They are the following:

a. Long industrial tradition. Skilled workers show a markedly more positive attitude toward self-management than unskilled workers. Industrial workers take division of labor and professional competence for granted.

b. Long tradition of political democracy. Since self-management is a political process, the relevance of this condition is obvious.

Conditions (a) and (b) can be replaced—I do not know whether wholly or only partly—by a genuine social revolution that raises the level of social aspiration and generates willingness to make sacrifices for a cause.

c. High wages that provide for the satisfaction of essential needs. Since existential risks are reduced, people are not so greedy and are more willing to get along with others. Competition can more easily be replaced by cooperation.

d. Short working week, which provides sufficient free time for participatory activities.

e. High educational level, which reduces barriers in communication.

It is clear that these five conditions, taken together, imply a high level of economic development. This is, of course, the old Marxian conclusion that the most developed countries are potentially the most ready for socialism. Yet, since social development is not deterministic, existing potentials may or may not be used. That is why workers' management need not—and did not—appear first in a highly developed country. On the other hand, a low level and rate of development are likely to kill workers' management even if, for some reason, it appears.

One last remark needs to be made. The obstacles to the development of genuine workers' management are truly formidable. But this is no reason for despair. On the contrary. If we are interested in a more humane social system—which is what socialism is supposed to be—then workers' management is the most powerful instrument of social transformation at our disposal. It provides a daily training ground for the development of socialist production relations and a meaningful political democracy.

9

Equality of Consumers

I. Distribution According to Work Performed

Since the time of Proudhon, and particularly since Marx authoritatively reproduced the Proudhonian dictum[1] in his *Critique of the Gotha Programme* (1875), distribution according to work has been generally accepted as *the* socialist principle of distribution. What is meant is really distribution according to the product of work. It seems natural to consider just exchange as requiring that each person receive from the society as much as he or she contributes to it (more precisely, some proportion of the productive contribution, since there are social costs that must be covered jointly). This has been considered such an important principle that it often has been used as an economic definition of socialism. It is therefore rather strange that, so far, this principle has not been subject to a rigorous analysis. There is a lot of talk about distribution according to work. There is practically no analysis to tell us what that should really mean.

One of the reasons for this state of affairs is the fact that the results of individual work are to a considerable degree socially determined. It seems rather difficult to establish an objective basis that will enable us to disentangle individual and social components of productivity and remunerate only the former. In order to do exactly this, I propose to proceed as follows.[2]

In the general case, the output of a particular commodity depends on two groups of factors that may be denoted as labor and nonlabor factors. We wish to remunerate the former but, in order to do so, we must specify the latter as well. Moreover, for allocational purposes, we have to "remunerate" the latter also. Evaluating the importance of a factor in the overall productive result means attaching a value weight to that factor. Thus the task of distributing income according to work performed implies establishing a theory of price formation in a socialist economy. For our purposes, only a rudimentary sketch of such a price theory will suffice.

The labor component consists of two separate factors: (a) *individual work;* and (b) *collective work.* These factors may also be called (a) *direct work*; and (b) *entrepreneurship.* The former requires individual rewards, the latter collective rewards.

Individual or *direct work* has been well described in the literature and so requires little elaboration. The result of individual work is determined by two different causes: (1) intensity and duration of work; and (2) skill. Now, skill depends partly on innate talents and partly on learning, the latter being a result of learning effort as well as of educational opportunities open to the worker. If, in order to avoid *reductio ad infinitum,* we ignore the fact that aspiration levels, value patterns, etc., depend on family background and immediate social environment and thus are socially determined, we can distinguish three different elements in the factor "direct work." An individual is fully responsible for the intensity and duration of work and for learning effort. Talent is an exogenous gift of nature. Differences in educational opportunities are socially determined. Thus, strictly speaking, the distributional principle is applicable only to the first element. Talent requires special treatment. Educational opportunities ought to be made equal for everyone.

In a capitalist or etatist firm, the owner or his representative is an entrepreneur. In a labor-managed firm, the society is the owner, and all the workers are society's representatives. They appear as a *collective entrepreneur.* Entrepreneurship as a factor of production reflects the fact that work is not performed in isolation. As a rule, it is organized and performed collectively. Entrepreneurship consists of three different elements.

1. First, the workers must somehow establish work relations in their firm. They may quarrel or cooperate. Work atmosphere may be favorable or unfavorable to productive efforts. Human groups in the firm may be integrated or disintegrated. The emotional and physical energy of the collective may be expanded in productive efforts or wasted in mutual accusations and copings with personal and group conflicts. Experience shows (and one would hardly expect anything else) that work productivity is a very sensitive function of the human relations existing in a collective.

2. The second element is of a more technical nature. Entrepreneurship implies coordination of all activities. Coordination has to be carried out at several levels, starting from the level of the economic unit and ending at the overall level of the firm. Coordination entails technical coordination, control, and supervision.

3. The third element consists in decision making under uncertainty, including innovation. The working collective bears the responsibility of the decisions made. In case of success, everyone will share in the surplus; in case of failure, everyone will suffer his share of the loss. The basic ingredient of entrepreneurial decision making is a constant stream of innovations. Economic growth implies continuous increase in productivity, and that implies innovation. Those who fail to innovate fast enough will see their wage bill lag behind the general trend. If the innovational failure is more serious—for example, if the quality of the commodity produced ceases to satisfy consumer requirements—the working collective will suffer losses, and the wage bill will shrink in absolute terms. In the opposite case of high productivity growth, personal income will rise faster than the national average.

Thus entrepreneurship is determined by *human relations,* by *organization of work* and the *creativity* of the working collective. Consequently, the personal income of every particular worker has two ingredients. One reflects his own individual contribution (wages). The other is the result of the collective efforts of his firm (share in surplus, or profit, due to innovational activities). The undistributed part of profits remains in the firm and is used to finance investment.

We may summarize. Wages plus distributed profits represent personal income. Personal income plus undistributed profits represents labor income. The practical procedure for determining labor income is to find total income and deduct nonlabor income.

Nonlabor income consists of various types of rents. The best known, of course, is land rent. Technically, it can be absorbed by taxation according to the cadastral revenue of the land. Cadastral revenue is established on the basis of the quality of land and the average conditions of production. Differences in cadastral revenue are taxed away. Surplus produced above the cadastral revenue is a result of work and innovational activities, and is retained by the farmer or the farming collective.

Closely related is *urban rent.* By studying demand and supply relations in a particular locality, it is not difficult to establish the equilibrium price of the land or of its service per unit of time. The imposition of an appropriate tax rate will absorb the rent.

There is long practical experience on how to extract *mining rent* by an appropriate system of royalties.

A very different type of rent is represented by capital income, or *interest.* Since capital is scarce and socially owned, the working collective has to pay a price for the privilege of using it. In an idealized textbook case, the marginal efficiency of investment would be equalized throughout the economy, and the equilibrium interest rate would be set so as to equalize the demand for investment with the supply of available investment funds. This investment is financed out of borrowed funds; the interest is included in the annuity for the repayment of the loan. This is why some economists insist that, in a labor-managed economy, all investment must be externally financed.[3] But there is no real need for that. In fact, it would be rather dangerous, for the autonomy of the working collectives would be reduced and the power of financial institutions and government offices increased. All that is required is that the same interest rate be charged on investments financed out of internal funds. These interest charges, however, may well remain in the investment funds of the firm.

The types of rents described so far are well known, and there is an enormous literature on them. One type of rent, however, has not been discussed in the literature. I call it *technological rent.*[4] It should be pointed out that what is meant is not the technological rent of one particular innovational activity. That rent is well known. Rather, the term stands for the fact that in any period of time objective innovational opportunities differ widely from one industry to another. In the last two decades, productivity increased slowly in the textile industry and rapidly in electronics. There is nothing that textile workers can do to reverse this trend. Thus, if productivity increases were taken as a criterion for distribution according to work—as the Yugoslav trade unions have advocated—the personal income of textile workers would have increased slowly, that of electronics workers rapidly, and in neither case would the distribution of income be related to the actual work performed. In order to distribute income according to work, technological rent must be taxed away. Technically this is not difficult to achieve. Since the basic conditions generating differences in productivity increase change only very slowly, past trends can be extrapolated into the future for the next couple of years. On that basis, and with corrections for relative price changes, we can assess the tax. In fact, the basic principle is the same as that of the tax on cadastral revenue.

The reason why technological rent has not been discussed in earlier theoretical literature is to be found in the unrealistic

neoclassical assumptions of perfect mobility of factors and instantaneous adjustments. Under such assumptions, technological rent cannot logically appear. As soon as the relative profitability of an industry increases, labor and capital will move into it, depressing the prices of its output. At the same time, the supply of other industries will be reduced. Thus, in the enough, prices are rather sticky downward, and increased investment speeds up technological progress, which leads to even larger differences in productivity increase. As a result, technological rent stays for many years.
vestment speeds up technological progress, which leads to even larger differences in productivity increase. As a result, technological rent stays for many years.

After all enumerated rents have been eliminated, there may still be some nonlabor income left. A monopoly or monopsony position of a firm—whatever the reason—is likely to generate an additional monopoly rent. Monopoly rents tend to be highly volatile and, unlike the other types of rent, cannot be determined objectively. Monopoly rent may be both positive and negative (e.g., windfall losses). The only instrument for the absorption of a monopoly rent is a general purpose, progressive taxation. This is a very crude instrument, since in some firms it will not eliminate the entire monopoly rent, while in others it may affect labor income. Yet, these distortions are likely to be quantitatively insignificant, for the following reasons.

1. Because of strong decentralization forces and because of substantially greater openness of business activities, labor-managed firms are less monopolistically inclined than their capitalist counterparts.

2. As will be shown later, the monopoly power of an industry can be controlled. Thus, industrywise, monopoly rent will be eliminated. It is true that individual firms escape objective control. But it is also true that individual firms are not likely to remain permanent monopolists. Windfall gains and losses tend to hit the firms in a stochastic fashion. Thus, an averaging tendency will occur over a somewhat longer period of time. If every firm is a bit of a monopolist at some particular time during the relevant period, no firm stands out.

3. Social planning increases the stability of the market and consequently reduces windfall gains and losses.

4. Since capital is socially owned, there is no need to tax *undistributed* profits. Thus, an efficient working collective may avoid penal progressive taxation by not distributing the surplus in wages but investing it instead.

A lucky collective will react similarly, perhaps putting the undistributed surplus in the reserve fund, which will help it to cover possible windfall losses sometime in the future. In this way the workers themselves will carry out an evaluation—at least partly—of monopoly rent.

5. Monopoly, or residual, rent is closely related to risk bearing, and the latter is socially limited in socialism. Although windfall gains cannot be measured precisely, the order of magnitude is roughly known, and there are strong informal social forces restricting an excessive increase in personal income. Very low incomes cannot be tolerated either. A firm suffering heavy losses will either be liquidated and its workers reemployed elsewhere, or else it will be helped out. In the meantime, incomes cannot fall below a guaranteed minimum. But the working collective has to pay a price for the failure to manage society's capital efficiently. The price consists in a temporary suspension of self-management. In a textbook world of perfect certainty, monopoly rent cannot appear. In the real world, it appears all the time; but in a reasonably organized, self-governing economy, it does not matter very much.

One last point remains to be made. The elimination of rent does not necessarily imply that rent income must be siphoned off from the firm. All it implies is that it cannot be distributed as personal income. It may in fact be desirable to leave, say, interest, technological rent, and mining rent in the firm to stimulate technological progress or meet heavy investment requirements.

II. The Determination of Labor Income

The problem of determining labor income will be solved in two steps. We must determine first labor income for the entire working collective and then personal income for every member of the collective.

To solve the first task, the economy will be divided into techno-economically homogeneous industries, each comprising a score or more of plants. The number of plants must not be too small, for then statistical regularities cease to be operative. If it happens that there is just one or only a couple of plants in a particular industry, the solution of the income distribution problem becomes more complicated, and it may be necessary to negotiate each case individually through the machinery of the chamber of trade or the trade unions.[5]

Within each industry, individual firms will operate at very different levels of efficiency. Variability in efficiency will be reflected in variability of labor incomes. Under normal conditions there is nothing to complain about, for differences in efficiency are caused by differences in entrepreneurship, and our distributional principle requires that entrepreneurial work be rewarded.

The overall labor incomes of different industries must not vary, however. It is practically impossible that all working collectives in the electronics industry are more industrious or efficient than all working collectives in the textile industry. For statistical reasons, the average labor income, weighted by formal skills, must be approximately the same for all industries. Possible differences ought to be absorbed by appropriate policy instruments that eliminate rents through various types of taxes or affect the input and output prices through regulatory devices in investment and foreign trade. It is of some importance to realize that a socialist market cannot be a laissez-faire market. It must be very strictly regulated. But this regulation is not arbitrary and cannot be left to the whims of the government of the day. The regulation ought to establish equal business conditions throughout the economy following a clearly defined and constitutionally guaranteed principle. Thus, the government becomes an integral part of a socialist market or, perhaps more correctly formulated, the market appears as a device of conscious social planning. Each firm remains completely autonomous—which, of course, is a crucial precondition for self-management. The labor-managed economy comes closer to the textbook competitive model than a capitalist economy can ever do. And yet working collectives remain within the accepted socialist framework at all times. Clearly, social planning transcends price planning. There are a number of other components of social planning that make it possible to convert the market into a planning device. But, for the purpose at hand, we need not elaborate on this important question.

Once income is distributed among collectives, it remains to distribute it within collectives. First of all, a part of income is set aside for investment purposes and for various collective funds. Self-management bodies decide on that. The remainder—that is, the bulk of income—is distributed among individual workers. What criteria are to be used?

Two aspects of work can be distinguished: work generates products and incurs costs.[6] More productive work is more valuable. Also, more difficult, responsible, dangerous, unpleasant, unhealthy, and complicated work, requiring long training and learning efforts, is more valuable. Just how much more valuable depends on the valuations of the supplier of work and his fellow workers. They are influenced, of course, by general supply and demand conditions, by tradition, and by valuations of the larger community. But the actual decisions about the wage differentials are made by the sovereign working collective. They are the result of a process of deliberations, negotiations, and mutual persuasion. It is an iterative and, under normal conditions, a converging process. As a rule, at the start the individuals consider their jobs more important or difficult and their work more valuable than do their colleagues. In the end, some agreement is reached and is recorded in the statute of the firm.

The reasons for the convergence of the process are rather simple. Every member of the collective has a stake in the just distribution of income. And "just" is what people consider to be just. A worker—more usually, a class of workers—who consider that their jobs have been undervalued, will work below their capacity, and this will reduce the total income of the collective. If their feeling of injustice is very strong, it pays their colleagues to increase their wage rates. In the neoclassical tradition, one might say that it pays to increase the wage rate until the marginal dinar of additional wages just generates the marginal dinar of additional income. In practice, this requirement seems to be satisfied automatically. The productive behavior of a worker seems to be discontinuous: he distinguishes only two regions of wage determination, the unacceptable and the acceptable one. A point in the latter region may not be fully satisfactory, but that does not influence productive behavior. Thus, in the unacceptable region—wage rate too low—the disruptive effects of dissatisfaction are always higher than the increases in wage rates necessary to reach the acceptable region. Perhaps the following rule can be formulated: keep increasing wages until the acceptable region is reached. And this is what seems to be happening. Workers find the established wage differentials acceptable but consider their jobs slightly more valuable.

An equilibrium wage rate may be reached from the other side as well, by extending the acceptable region downward. This is the result of the social persuasion process. It is a well-known empirical finding of social psychology that individual valuations are forcefully molded by social valuations. What is just is what the group considers to be just. As a result, the lower limit of the acceptable region will tend to be rather uniformly established, and the quoted neoclassical requirement satisfied for all workers and not only for the marginal one.

One general effect of social valuations is worth noting. This is egalitarianism. Income differentials are substantially smaller in a labor-managed firm than in a capitalist or etatist firm.[7] The differentials are being constantly reduced with the economic development of the country. Various types of manual work are evaluated higher than before. The so-called manual, as well as monotonous, tedious, and unpleasant work, are considered to incur additional costs and consequently are evaluated higher. Changed social relations generate changes in values. A rapid equalization of educational opportunities gives an additional impetus toward egalitarianism.

It is always possible that the structure of wage differentials, as established by the collective, will remain unacceptable to some members. They are then free to leave, and often do so.

Although working collectives are autonomous, they are not isolated. Since capital is socially owned, every vacancy must be publicly announced, and the best applicants must be accepted. The free movement of labor brings about uniformity in wage differentials. This has important allocational consequences.

So far, we have been discussing the case in which the supply and demand of particular kinds of labor are just about equal. If they are not, there is a disequilibrium, and rent is bound to appear. Technological progress creates new jobs with special skills that for the time being are in short supply. For instance, in the initial phase of computerization of a country, programming specialists are likely to be scarce. Thus, firms will compete for programmers and their wages will rise above the level considered appropriate for a job with similar characteristics. When the necessary number of programmers has been trained, their wages will go down until they reach the lower limit of the acceptable region. In the meantime, programmers will enjoy a personal monopoly rent.

Opposite is the case of an oversupply of a particular kind of labor. The redundant workers will have to be retrained, or reallocated to similar, less valuable jobs. In a poorly organized economy, they may even become unemployed. While the adjustment process lasts, the redundant workers earn negative rent.

Personal rent may also be permanent. Extraordinarily gifted scientists, managers, artists, and sportsmen are very rare.

If they were to be rewarded according to their productivity, their incomes would be intolerably high. At the same time, the just acceptable income that would induce them to work at full capacity is relatively moderate. In a textbook case, gross income will be set as high as the market can bear, and the difference between the market income and the just acceptable income will be taxed away as a personal monopoly rent. In this way, net income will be equalized with just acceptable income. In practice an Einstein will get a rather moderate gross income because there is no way to measure the value of his productive contribution; nor does it matter. What matters, both socially and personally, is to make it possible for a scientist to develop fully all his talents. In the entertainment business, gross income will be higher—because movie firms and football clubs compete in a different way—but not as high as the market can bear because public opinion will impose certain upper limits that are socially tolerable. On the other hand, the tax on personal rent will not be 100 percent but only sharply progressive, approaching 100 percent in the upper limits.

Again, there is an opposite case. The productivity of physically and mentally handicapped will be too low to provide them with the means for a decent life. A subsidy, that is, a negative income tax, will be used to fill the gap.

III. On Allocational Efficiency and the Optimum Distribution of Income

In the normal case, with the demand and supply of labor just about equal and personal monopoly rents absent, the specifically socialist market solves the problem of income distribution according to work performed. That implies certain allocational consequences. When a working collective engages in determining the structure of wage differentials, the workers have some notion of the differential productivity of different types of work. But nobody knows how to measure the productive contribution of an accountant, or a secretary, or a foreman. Nor is that measure the only ingredient of a just wage. Once wages have been determined, they become costs to be added up in building the value of the firm's output. This value may be just in tune with the market demand, or deviate from it. If it is below the market valuations, the firm will earn extra profits and expand its operations. If it is above the market prices, the firm will have to reduce its costs or change its production program.

How much does all this satisfy the conditions for efficient allocation of resources?

The only reasonably elaborated theory about the efficient allocation of resources available at the moment is the neoclassical theory. According to the tenets of this theory, labor will be allocated efficiently if in every use its marginal value product is equal to the wage rate, which is uniform throughout the economy. It is thought that marginal equality assures that there is no other allocation of labor which could increase output. If marginal products differed, a reallocation of labor from firms with lower marginal product to those with higher marginal product would increase the value of total output. Thus, the absence of a more productive alternative is the definition of efficient allocation. It is clear that in our system it is theoretically easy to satisfy this requirement. One simply has to follow the attitude of neoclassical economists and assume that throughout the economy wages are equal and only the profit component of personal income varies with variations in productivity. But this is not very enlightening. One may reasonably assume, however, that three market forces exert strong equalization pressures on personal incomes (wages plus distributed profits). These forces are: among industries, the entry of new firms; among firms within the same industry, the free movement of labor, including the organizers; among workers with the same skill throughout the economy, an exodus from the firms and industries in which a particular skill is undervalued and a press of applicants in places where it is overvalued, together with the generally accepted principle that equal work should be equally remunerated.

Before we proceed, let us look at how neoclassical theory is applied to the capitalist system.

One immediately notices an inherent contradiction in the corpus of neoclassical theory. In one of its branches entrepreneurship is proclaimed to be a factor of production, in another branch it is treated very differently from all other factors (land, labor, capital). The rate of remuneration is equal to the value of the marginal product for all factors, except for entrepreneurship, which somehow gets the residual. This is then forgotten, and the allocation is proclaimed efficient. But it is clear that the particular distribution of entrepreneurship at any given time is fortuitous and that a different distribution could perhaps increase social product.

Next, the marginal equality requirement applied to another factor—capital—involves circular reasoning. Since the quantity of capital has no existence independent of the profit it yields, the proposition that the marginal value product of capital is (or should be) equal to its rate of interest (or profit) is devoid of any meaning. Now, if two factors do not get priced according to their marginal productivity, there is no theoretical ground to assume that the "correct" pricing of the third factor—labor—would generate higher output than pricing based on some other principles. Besides, the postulated marginal equality formula requires a very special production function in order to be possible. Only a linear homogeneous production function makes the sum of remunerations of factors equal to the product. Since there is no reason why all production functions ought to be linearly homogeneous, marginal equalities will lead to surpluses or losses and the actual wages—and other factor returns—have to be established by bargaining. This is what happens and is also the reason for the existence of unions. Finally, marginal equalities are—and can only be—expressed in value terms, and values depend on the distribution of income. Since neoclassical theory has nothing to say about the optimal distribution of income, efficiency considerations in the Pareto spirit do not take us very far. Thus neoclassical theory breaks down without repair, and we have to find another standard for evaluating the efficiency of the socialist system. The obvious thing to do is to compare it with the actual capitalist system.

Take entrepreneurship. In a socialist economy, entrepreneurship—though of a different type—is also unequally distributed. But here the institutional framework makes it possible for the society to extend entrepreneurial help to less efficient firms. Consequently, social capital is used more efficiently through a partial redistribution of entrepreneurship, which is impossible under capitalism. A smaller degree of monopoloy leads to additional improvements.

The problem of wages is slightly more complicated. In the textbook neoclassical economy, all wages are equal because of efficient competition; they are also equal to the marginal value or marginal revenue products—since entrepreneurs maximize profits—which implies that marginal products are equalized throughout the economy.[8] Empirical research reveals that this assumption is an illusion. Wages differ substantially not only from firm to firm but also from industry to industry. And it is obvious that the manager of a very profitable firm will pay his workers more in order to avoid labor troubles. In our theory of the socialist firm, we start from the observation that marginal products and wages differ from firm to firm (but *not from industry to industry*, at least not wages). In an abstract world that implies inefficiency, for if a worker is moved from a firm with low marginal productivity to one with high marginal productivity—i.e., from an inefficient to an efficient firm—total product will increase. In the actual world of nonmalleable capital, the problem is posed somewhat differently. In equilibrium, it may be assumed, all workers are employed and all firms are operating at minimum average cost, but average cost differs from firm to firm. Moving a worker from a low- to a high-efficiency firm would only slightly increase the "net output" of the latter but would have disruptive effects on the output of the former. As a result, total output would decrease. The same observation may also be formulated as follows. When the plant is operated below capacity, marginal product is approximately equal to average product and to the wage. At capacity level, marginal product is sharply reduced. Consequently, in order to achieve an optimum, every otherwise viable firm must fully utilize the available capacity.

The foregoing discussion indicates that there is no neat solution to the problem of efficient allocation as soon as we leave the abstract textbook world. At the level of the firm—and from the point of view of the firm—neoclassical recommendations are more applicable. As a convenient approximation, a socialist firm may perhaps be taken to equalize marginal cost and marginal product for each resource, including labor. The aspiration wages, determined at the beginning of the year, will serve as accounting wages for that purpose.[9] Production function limitations are mitigated by treating profits as a residual. Then wages and marginal product will be equal in every firm but both will differ for different firms. In this respect socialist firms resemble capitalist firms. In terms of the allocation of entrepreneurship and its smaller degree of monopoly, a socialist economy is more efficient than a capitalist one. Since the workers are not only laborers but also entrepreneurs, the socialist and capitalist firms are basically different. When a worker moves from one firm to another, the production functions of the two firms do not necessarily remain unchanged because of the entrepreneurial capacity that the worker carries with him. Entrepreneurship implies innovation, and innovation means changes in production functions. Since such changes cannot be known with certainty, we simply cannot say that moving a worker from a firm with low wages to a firm with high wages would increase total product. At the national level, we may treat both labor and entrepreneurship as factors with residual effects and apply marginal equalities to nonlabor factors only. The policy rule will then read as follows. The cost of capital is exogenously determined by the planning authority, which sets the appropriate interest rate. Firms employ resources (labor included) so as to equalize marginal cost and marginal revenue. In the case of labor, marginal cost is determined by the aspiration wage, which serves as an accounting wage for the relevant period. With the assumption of diminishing returns to entrepreneurship, the society ought to allocate entrepreneurship so as to reduce differences in efficiency among firms.

Larger society must also intervene in the distribution process when it comes to the two opposite tails of the distribution of ability. This will be done by introducing positive and negative taxes. Now the principle of distribution according to work tends to be interpreted not in terms of productive contribution but in terms of work effort. Talents and handicaps are fortuitous, not related to individual work effort, and ought to be largely disregarded.

Let us now explore the conditions under which the distribution of income may be considered optimal. Optimal distribution of income requires: (a) efficient production (output must be produced before it is distributed); and (b) just distribution. The former presupposes inducement to work at full capacity. Since such an inducement is socially determined, it is never discussed in the neoclassical literature but is simply assumed to exist. The second component has been proclaimed as intractable to scientific treatment because it involves interpersonal utility comparisons that seem impossible. And, indeed, a laissez-faire market (or a governmental decree) cannot achieve an optimal distribution of income; consequently, optimal income distribution is inherently impossible in a capitalist or an etatist setting.[10]

In socialist economics, the inducement component is discussed right from the beginning. Since the worker (a) is working for himself and not for a boss, and (b) participates himself in the determination of the wage rate, there are incentives to work at full capacity. The distribution component requires an additional comment. Assume that, *ceteris paribus,* the marginal utility of income is diminishing (a generally accepted assumption) and that consumers are in some fundamental sense similar. Then any change that makes the distribution of income more egalitarian and does not affect productivity adversely will increase the welfare of the society. In the limit, income will be distributed equally. But long before the limit is reached, productivity will be affected. Those who feel that they do not get a just reward will reduce their productive effort and total output (income) will shrink. Formally, we may face the following problem: the transfer of an additional unit of income from more productive to less productive members of society will increase social welfare; at the same time, because of dissatisfaction, total output will decrease and, consequently, income and welfare will be reduced. How do we find the point where the welfare gain due to redistribution is exactly equal to the welfare loss due to reduced output—which is the point of maximum welfare and which, consequently, determines the optimum of the income distribution?

From the point of view of a benevolent despot—traditionally assumed tacitly by welfare economists when discussing possible improvement in income distribution—there is no answer to the question posed without engaging in interpersonal welfare comparisons, which leads to an impasse. Fortunately, however, in the institutional setting of a socialist economy, the benevolent despot problem is irrelevant. Here, wage differentials are determined—and, consequently, income is distributed—by a process involving the most direct interpersonal welfare comparisons. Once the members of a working collective have agreed on a just income distribution, there is no other distribution that could increase their welfare. Arriving at a just distribution implies a complete evaluation of the welfare of every member of the group. If it were thought possible to increase the welfare of the group, the group would have proceeded to do it, and that would then be the optimal distribution. It is impossible, in a normal human group, to consider that injustice contributes to welfare.

The solution of the optimum distribution problem proves possible because the actors themselves engage in interpersonal welfare comparisons and make the relevant decisions. Neither the capitalist market nor the etatist bureaucracy can do that.

IV. Distribution According to Needs

Equal opportunity for a producer implies equal opportunity in developing one's innate talents. Differential access to educational or health establishments would render equality among producers a sham. Consequently, health services and education ought to be exempted from the exchange relationship and distributed differently from the purchasing power of individuals. In general, anything that substantially influences the development of individual capabilities must be exempt from the exchange criterion and subject to the needs criterion. Let me elaborate.

The entire social product may be divided into two parts: market (or commercial or profit motivated) product and nonmarket product. The latter can further be subdivided into the part with welfare content (e.g., education) and the part that plays the role of social overhead (e.g., judiciary). The market output of goods and services can be—and should be, since this is the most efficient solution available—organized on the basis of exchange, which implies distribution according to work. Nonmarket output calls for a different organizational principle. In fact, these are tautological statements until we identify the market and nonmarket parts of social product. Of the latter, it is only the part with welfare content that interests us here. In its consumption aspect, I shall call it *collective consumption,* reserving the term *public consumption* for the nonwelfare part.

If class stratification is to be avoided, distribution must be organized on the basis of work contribution; for this reason, socialists insist on distribution according to work. If private productive property exists, part of the social income will flow to property owners *qua* owners, and that will provide the basis for the emergence of a class of capitalists. If the state monopolizes productive property, then part of the social income will flow to state officials, the distribution will correspond to the structure of social hierarchy, and this will provide the material basis for the emergence of a class of bureaucrats. For socialism to be established, all nonlabor income must be eliminated. Even this, however, will not quite do. If prosperous families can buy better education and health for their children, all members of the society will not be equal at the start, while equity is the essence of socialism. Thus, again, personal income will not depend exclusively on personal efforts but also on extraneous factors such as the wealth or wisdom of one's parents.[11] For this reason, even strict distribution according to work is not sufficient for a socialist society; it must be supplemented by distribution according to needs whenever this has an important bearing on the development of the talents and personal faculties of individual members of the society. Whether one has a large or a small car does not really matter because both will take one wherever one wishes to go. If a person has only primary education and has had no chance to attend a university, or if he had suffered from malnutrition in childhood, he will be fundamentally handicapped in his life. Let us note, in passing, that the requirement that every individual be given equal opportunity is not only social justice—the socialist principle of equity—it is a principle that coincides with the maximization of economic efficiency, since the available store of social talent will be maximally exploited.

The following activities contribute to the building of personal capabilities:

(1) education;
(2) medical care;
(3) social welfare;
(4) culture;
(5) physical culture;
(6) environmental conservation and creation.

These six personality-building activities ought to be organized on a nonmarket basis. This implies that both the supply and the demand side should be organized in a way different from that for market activities. Here we are concerned only with the demand side. As for the supply part, I should like only to draw attention to the distinction between provision and production: collective provision of a good does not imply production by a public body. Let me also make a terminological suggestion. *Collective good* refers to nonmarket output with welfare content. Its essential characteristic is that it contributes to the development of individual faculties. There are at least six broad categories of collective goods. *Public good* refers to nonmarket output without a welfare content which represents a social overhead cost (judiciary, police, army, public administration).[12]

Classical economists did not have much to say about demand. They talked of *use value,* which was subjectively determined, and there was little, they thought, one could say about subjective valuations. Neoclassical economists demonstrated that even use value can be analyzed. In fact, under the name of utility, it became the center of their interest. Individual consumers and their preferences would determine aggregate demand; the individual firms and their costs, aggregate supply; and a perfectly competitive market would lead to a Pareto-optimal equilibrium. We know now that this drastic simplification was very far from what was actually happening. Let us again stick to the demand side. Even in the market sector, demand has more than one dimension: apart from an individual consumer, there is the society, which encourages or prevents (as in the case of drugs) certain consumption, and there are experts who produce norms of accepted quality (e.g., for evaluating medicines, testing consumer goods, or working out national standards). In the nonmarket sector this tridimensional demand space—containing the consumer, the expert, and the society—is absolutely essential. The preferences of the individual consumer occasionally are even completely disregarded (as in the case of vaccination) or reduced to yes/no answers (as when the doctor suggests an operation). The society decides on the size of the market. Experts perform some sort of rationing, replacing the role of prices.

Like everything else in economics, the need has a social dimension. While individual consumer demand depends on the consumer's preferences restricted by his budget, collective demand depends on needs restricted by the resources available to the society. (In both cases, demand is modified by changes in relative prices.) We may imagine a social preference map in which individual consumer demand can be compared to collective demand, and various components of collective demand can be compared to each other. Applying the conventional criterion of equalizing the utility per unit of expenditure, the society divides the available consumption goods and services between individual and collective consumption. This is done by means of a political process about which we know very little and expect to be educated by political scientists (who, however, prefer to leave us waiting). We know even less about what should be done to improve the efficiency of the process. Finally, the distribution of resources to various activities within the components is carried out mostly by experts.

Although collective needs in a poor and in a wealthy society may in some sense be equal, the needs revealed or backed by resources or, simply, collective consumption, will differ and in general will be an increasing function of the level of development. In the early stages of development the share of compulsory consumption (vaccination, primary education) is likely to be great. Later, collective consumption will extend to goods and services provided free of charge (or at subsidized prices) by the society while individuals will continue to exercise free choice (university education, museums and arts galleries, theaters and sports fields). The provision of collective goods is often likely to follow a certain priority schedule, rather than marginalist calculation. Thus (except for relatively short transition periods) social programs are not likely to be oriented toward eradication of one-half of malaria and three-quarters of smallpox cases, or to the maintenance of 80 percent literacy and 1 percent university education, but rather to the complete elimination of infectious diseases and toward attainment of complete literacy regardless of the fact that other medical and educational needs have not yet been satisfied.[13] Thus, there seem to be certain socially determined standards and it is not deemed acceptable to tolerate consumption at lower levels.

We reach the conclusion that every society will decide—through some sort of efficient or inefficient political process—on the share of collective consumption in social product. The poorer the society, the lower, *ceteris paribus,* the share. But no matter how high it may be, collectively financed goods and services will not satiate potential demand. Thus collective consumption will be supplemented by individually financed consumption of personality-forming goods and services. To the extent that this happens, the equity principle of socialism will be violated. Except in textbooks, one cannot prevent this encroachment of private use of collective services (high officials or wealthy people will have access to better hospitals and will receive better treatment; family influences cannot be eliminated; corruption and nepotism will emerge, etc.). Even if one could prevent by force all individual purchases of collective goods, that would clash with the socialist principle of free development of every individual. The welfare of the society cannot be increased by reducing the choices (that have no adverse externality effects) of its members. It follows that the best solution is to provide a certain limited market for nonmarket goods as well. The limits of this market will be determined by the existing social ethic and are likely to be narrower in a socialist society than in other contemporary societies. This inconsistent but unavoidable market is likely to shrink as society gets richer and moves closer to socialism. Thus it would appear difficult to build socialism in a poor society.

Once the volume of collective consumption has been decided, goods and services are distributed among individuals according to needs. What the needs are is determined either (a) by the individuals themselves (mostly in the spheres of culture, physical culture, and environment enjoyment; and partly in education, medical care, and social welfare); (b) by experts, in cases of compulsory consumption or when consumers are not competent to decide (as with children, insane people, patients); or (c) by both, when the proposal of an expert has to be accepted by the individual (surgical operations). The determination of needs is always carried out within a given social framework.

In conclusion, the principle of distribution according to work performed must be complemented by the principle of distribution according to needs. In terms of goods, this implies that pure consumption goods will be distributed on an exchange basis as market goods. Ability-developing goods will be distributed on a nonmarket basis. As regards productive contribution, the work principle will fully apply only to producers falling within a certain ability range, socially considered as normal. Outside that range, positive and negative corrections will be made. It was mentioned in section II that these corrections may be interpreted as complementing the criterion of "work contribution" by "work effort." In the context of the present section, it may be interpreted as complementing the work criterion by the *need* criterion. This interpretation is particularly appropriate when applied to disabled persons.

Consumer equality implies that personal effort determines variations in income. This is the normal case and can be applied to a great majority of producers whose abilities are considered to fall in the normal range. Those with subnormal abilities—due to physical or mental causes—must first be brought to the consumer starting level before the work principle can be applied. In the extreme case of lunatics or total invalids, the entire personal income consists of negative income tax, and the work principle is completely replaced by the needs principle. One may note that all societies somehow care for their disabled. But in class societies this is charity; in socialism it is income and is consistent with the fundamental premises of the system. For socialism is not based on individual egoism. Neither is it based on altruism or idealism, which are defined in relation to egoism and thus do not transcend the bourgeois world. Socialism is simply based on the social responsibility inherent in unalienated human relationships.

10

Equality of Citizens: The Decentralization and Deconcentration of Power

Every social system consists of several interacting subsystems. Different authors define these subsystems differently and for different purposes. Marx speaks of material, social, political, and spiritual life. The latter three aspects of life belong to the superstructure and are determined by the first one, the mode of production or the economic structure.[1] The most popular contemporary classification—that of American sociologist Talcott Parsons—is not entirely dissimilar. Parsons contends that all social systems must solve four basic problems: the development of disposable resources to increase the system's capacity to cope with its environment; the achievement of goals; the integration of individual actors into the larger system; and the maintenance of the value pattern over time in order to stabilize the system in the face of pressure to change institutionalized values through cultural channels. Thus, Parsons distinguishes four primary subsystems with their corresponding organizations: the adaptive subsystem (economy), the goal-attainment subsystem (polity), the integrative subsystem exercising normative control (law as norms, political parties), and the pattern-maintaining subsystem, with its corresponding institutionalization (family, schools, and churches).[2] Economist Kenneth Boulding has talked of the threat system (politics), the exchange system (economics), and the integrative system (affection, love, and similar sentiments).[3] One may perhaps add that these systems involve three different types of relationships: coercive, utilitarian, and normative. One might also note that normative relationships are characteristic of so-called primitive societies, coercive relationships of precapitalist societies, and utilitarian ones of the mature capitalist societies.

Daniel Bell describes society as an amalgam of three realms: social structure (which consists of economy, technology, and the occupational system), polity (which regulates the distribution of power and adjudicates the conflicting claims of individuals and groups), and culture (which is a realm of expressive symbolism and meanings concerned with human existence). Each realm is ruled by a different axial principle (defined as an organizing frame around which the institutions are developed): economy is governed by functional rationality, polity by legitimacy, and culture by the desire for fulfillment and enhancement of the self. In the economy, decisions are reached by technocratic rationality; in the polity, by bargaining or by law. Utility and efficiency provide clear rules for economic innovation and change; in culture, there is no unambiguous principle of change.[4] The three realms "are not congruent with one another and have different rhythms of change; they follow different norms which legitimate different, and even contrasting types of behaviour. It is discordances between these realms which are responsible for the various contradictions within society."[5]

For our purposes, it will be convenient to realize that each society, including the socialist one, faces three different tasks: (1) the provision of means for survival and, more generally, the development of resources in order to achieve ever greater mastery over nature in satisfying human wants; (2) the overall coordination of tasks and conflict resolution; and (3) the integration of individuals into society. Thus, we can distinguish three fundamental subsystems that we call economy, polity, and culture. The first two subsystems can be subject to a purposeful design and therefore are investigated in the present study. The third one, culture, is largely a product of spontaneous activity and will not be discussed here.

This decision is not immune to objection, of course. Culture is not a mere *Überbau* (superstructure). The three subsystems are obviously interdependent. Culture both determines economic and political organizations and is determined by them. Culture provides values that generate political goals leading to the mobilization of economic resources. And contrariwise: economic development generates changes in institutions and values. If our task is to be manageable, however, it must be simplified. What I propose is to take the existing culture for granted for the time being and consider economics and politics as crucial instruments of social change. With this in mind, economic and political systems are to be designed so as to enhance as much as possible a genuinely free, unfettered, spontaneous cultural development. More precisely, on the basis of an analysis of human needs (chapter 15), I assume that modern economic development generates institutional changes characterized by the demand for self-management. Self-management begins to be treated as a fundamental human right.[6] As a consequence, self-determination becomes one of the basic values or, perhaps, *the* basic value of the new culture. Cultural changes then reinforce political and economic changes, since the new value system has mobilizing effects and renders legitimate the use of force against deviants. Eventually, some sort of new equilibrium is reached. This new equilibrium is self-governing socialism.

We have already dealt with the two basic aspects of economics—production and distribution—and will come back to the subject in chapters 12 and 13. Thus we can now proceed to the design of a socialist political system.

I. The State

The characteristic feature of political relations is that they involve power in one way or another. People living in a society are bound to disagree. Such disagreements follow certain patterns and can be settled in various ways. If the way in which they are settled is determined largely by the relative power endowments of the contestants, then we can identify the relationships as political ones. In order to distinguish political relationships from other power relationships (in the family, club, etc.), we associate them with the various levels of global society. Thus the management of societal tension and conflict resolution are the first function of a political system. In this sense, politics is responsible for "law and order." But this is only one of its functions. Define authority as legitimized power, and legitimacy as compatibility with the values prevailing in the community.[7] Then the other two functions of a political system consist in the authoritative specification of social goals and the equally authoritative mobilization of people and resources to implement the chosen goals. These two functions imply that politics is not only about conflicts but also about coordination. In all three cases, the decisions made and implemented are binding for a society.

The main political institution is the state. The state is a social organization that has a monopoly on the legitimate use of physical force within a given territory (Max Weber). Every power is backed by sanctions. But not every political relation implies physical coercion. This is a characteristic only of the state, which is just one of the constituent parts of the political system. The other political organizations—political parties, pressure groups, nonparty political associations—do not have this property. In a class society, state power is naturally used to secure and protect the privileges of the dominant class.

The modern state is based on law. Law is a normative order of human behavior backed by state power. The latter, on the other hand, is an expression of a coercive order sanctioned by law.[8] In this sense, law reflects the will of the dominant class.

It would be of some interest to discuss briefly two celebrated and equally controversial Marxian concepts: the dictatorship of the proletariat[9] and the withering away of the state. If the legal system and the state are organized so as to benefit the dominant class, then, in capitalism, the state functions as a dictatorship of the bourgeoisie regardless of the forms of political ritual. What a proletarian revolution is supposed to achieve is a reversal of conditions so that the state can begin to function as a dictatorship of the proletariat. It is obvious that, in this context, "dictatorship of the proletariat" is not the reverse of "democracy," but the reverse of "dictatorship of the bourgeoisie."[10] Since the proletariat is much more numerous than the former ruling class—the proletarian movement is that "of the vast majority in the interest of the vast majority"(*Communist Manifesto*)—the proletarian state is able to implement political democracy to a much higher degree. The Paris Commune of 1871 provides a case in point. Marx called it "the government of the working classes" and Engels referred to it as "the dictatorship of the proletariat."[11] The commune, as is well known, introduced universal suffrage, recallable representatives, rotation of functionaries (who were to receive workers' wages), and mass political participation. As already mentioned (chapter 2, section I), Engels later added that the democratic republic was a specific form of the dictatorship of the proletariat.

When Lenin analyzed the texts of Marx and Engels, he also generally followed the logic of their reasoning as sketched above. He spoke of an "enormous extension of democracy," of the state after the socialist revolution as "the most complete democracy."[12] Yet later, when he was in a position to apply the theory to the actual Russian environment, Lenin made a radical right turn and defined the "scientific concept of dictatorship" as "an authority based directly on violence and not restricted by anything, by any law, by any rule."[13] "The revolutionary dictatorship of the proletariat," wrote Lenin in a book against Kautsky, "is an authority maintained by the proletariat by means of force over and against the bourgeoisie, and not bound by any laws."[14] Leon Trotsky fully shared this opinion.[15]

These utterances must not be exaggerated, however. They were made in the heat of a battle for survival. What mattered was organization and determination, not legal hairsplitting. When he was dismissing laws and rules, Lenin probably had in mind the inherited tsarist legal structure. It was absurd to think that the old laws and codes should first be revised and only then action undertaken. Lenin and Trotsky relied on what they considered to be the class instinct and the justice of their cause. Nevertheless, even the most benevolent interpretation cannot hide the fact that the *regime* was becoming dictatorial. And whatever the personal intentions of Lenin and Trotsky, this change was not a transitional phenomenon but was to become permanent and, as such, justified by their followers.

Thus, in application, the sociological meaning of dictatorship was easily replaced by its political meaning, and the idea of a (proletarian) class rule was replaced by the idea of a specific (dictatorial) political regime; and this has become the generally accepted meaning of the term in etatist countries and in the pseudo-Marxist literature. The original ideas of Marx and Engels were brushed away as a petty-bourgeois weakness.[16] Rather early, the entire line of reasoning—together with its practical implementation—was brought to its logical consequences by G. Zinoviev: "Every conscious worker must understand that the dictatorship of the working class cannot be realized otherwise than by means of its advanced guard—the Communist Party."[17] If any doubt was still left, Stalin made sure to dispel it: the leadership of the state "passed *fully* and completely into the hands of *one single* party, into the hands of our party, which does not share and cannot share the ruling of the state with another party. This is what we call the dictatorship of the proletariat" [emphasis in original].[18]

The state, as an instrument of legitimized violence by the ruling class, is surely not necessary in a classless socialism.[19] This conclusion caused great confusion. In bourgeois thinking, it is dismissed as utopian. In etatist thinking, it is endlessly postponed until the "higher stage of development." The consequences are similar: state power increases. The root of the confusion is to be found in the dual role of the modern state: it is an instrument of repression, but it also provides public services. Public services are rapidly expanding and will continue to do so. It is only the repressive function of the state that is supposed to wither away. Expressed in the terminology of Saint-

Simon and Engels: government over men disappears; the administration of things remains and expands.[20]

Yet even this last statement is not quite precise. Society will have to be protected against criminals. Thus police and some sort of penitentiary system are likely to remain with us. But they will not be used against the "enemy," either internal or external. Political repression will wither away. In fact, from the Marxist point of view, in modern societies the degree of political repression *ceteris paribus* is the most reliable measure of class exploitation and distance from socialism.

Three important social institutions—family, property, and state, all three already selected by Engels—seem to have displayed similar developmental trends. In a patriarchal family, *pater familias* is not simply the head of the family, but has absolute power over the family; in a sense, he owns his family, and he can punish—even kill—his children and often his wife or wives. Historical development gradually imposes limits to his exclusive power until it finally disappears and all family members are treated equally. Similarly, in Roman times property was absolute; nonowners were excluded. If property rights were restricted at all, the restrictions had to be justified, not the exclusiveness of the ownership. Again, development has gradually eroded exclusive property rights, and in a socialist society it is exclusiveness that must be justified, while the sharing of (productive) property is assumed. Finally, in the Middle Ages a prince was the owner of his estate. This implied the possession of both property rights and political rights. In the late sixteenth century, the patrimonial rights of the king were formulated as the doctrine of sovereignty. Public law was later based on this doctrine. The monarch, having the right to issue orders, was the bearer of sovereignty. And sovereignty meant absolute and permanent state power, i.e., the exclusion of everyone else from making political decisions. Bourgeois revolutions replaced the monarch by the people. People's sovereignty inaugurated a process of gradual inclusion of citizens into the management of state affairs. The more inclusive is state power, and the more democratic is the political process, the less it is naked power and the more it is an institution providing public services. Three centuries after Jean Bodin, his compatriot Leon Duguit replaced sovereignty with public service as the basis for public law. In his opinion, rulers have no subjective rights to state power but only the duty to use this power for the organization of public services. All wills are equal. Public law is no longer a set of rules to be applied to the relations between state power and the subjects, but a set of rules regulating public services.

Similarly, laws are no longer the orders of a sovereign state but the statutes of public services.[21] The change in approach is obvious. And changes in legal theory naturally reflect changes in actual relations. Subjects are transformed into citizens, the exclusiveness is reversed and, by becoming more and more inclusive, the old state begins to wither away.

A society building socialism can radically diminish the role of the state in at least three different ways: (1) (some) public services can be organized on a nongovernmental basis; (2) state administration, adjudication, or orders can be partially replaced by market, arbitration outside the courts, public opinion, and professional ethics; (3) conflicts can be reduced by generating appropriate information about past (statistics, scientific research) and future (social planning) events.[22] What remains is the area of state activity proper. Here we want to establish reliable social control of the state. Operationally, this implies an effective decentralization of state power.

II. Separation of Powers

The absolute power and arbitrariness of monarchs and the privileges of aristocracy clearly are incompatible with a capitalist organization of the economy. Thus, one might have expected that the first bourgeois revolutions would not only establish parliamentary governments, but would also undertake to decentralize power and introduce some order into the operation of state affairs. This was indeed the case, and with no exceptions. The decentralization of power came to be known as the doctrine of the separation of powers. It emerged in seventeenth-century England during the period of its bourgeois revolution.[23]

In order to safeguard liberty, government must be divided into three separate branches: legislature, executive, and judiciary. This division can be accomplished because every branch has its own special function. The three branches of government (in the modern formulation by G. Almond) deal with rule making, rule application, and rule adjudication, respectively. Each branch is staffed with different people. In this way, each branch functions as a check on the other two, and no single group of individuals can control the state.

Influenced by contemporary English writers, particularly by Locke, whom he misunderstood,[24] Montesquieu gave the doctrine its best-known formulation:

> When the legislative and executive powers are united in the same persons or body, there can be no liberty, because apprehensions may arise lest the same monarch or senate should enact tyrannical laws, to enforce them in a tyrannical manner. . . . Where the power of judging joined with the legislature, the life and liberty of the subjects would be exposed to arbitrary control, for the judge would then be the legislator. Were it joined to the executive power, the judge might behave with all the violence of an oppressor.[25]

Montesquieu's ideas were eagerly accepted on the other side of the Atlantic and were soon absorbed into the first American constitutions in 1776 (Virginia) and 1778 (Federation). These, in turn, influenced French revolutionary constitutions a decade and half later. In the next century, the separation of powers became a universally accepted doctrine throughout the bourgeois world.

Yet the rigid identification of government branches with government functions did not survive the test of practice. It was therefore modified by the doctrine of checks and balances. Each branch was given the power to exercise some degree of control over the others. In the American setting, the Supreme Court may proclaim a law void on the grounds that it is unconstitutional; the legislature may impeach the president; and the president may veto legislation. In Europe, administrative tribunals check the arbitrariness of bureaucrats. These checks, however, did not prevent the executive from emerging as the dominant and by far the most important branch of government. The evolutionary trend seems to be still in the same direction.

Separate from the issues of domination is the fact that branches cannot be organized efficiently on purely functional lines. Their activities are to a certain degree multifunctional. Rules are made not only by the parliament, but also by civil servants and judges (common law). Rules are applied not only by the executive, but also by the courts. Courts are not only judicial but also administrative organs (they register mortgages and other encumbrances on real property, settle estates, register companies). Judicial decisions are made not only by judges, but also by civil servants and parliaments (amnesty). The latter also engage in various elections (of federal government, federal court, army chiefs as, for example, in Switzerland).

Nevertheless, the doctrine of separation of powers is essentially a sound doctrine. It needs only a slight reformulation to fit practical requirements. We may proceed as follows. The government—or, in a socialist framework, self-government[26]—is a very complex activity. In order to be carried out, it should be decomposed into elementary activities. This is the familiar principle of division of labor. Every administration involves at least three different activities: rule making, rule application, and rule adjudication. Thus, there is a need for specialization in these activities and for the organization of three specialized administrative branches. Each branch is formally multifunctional, yet each of them is an ultimate authority in its field of specialization. Rules made by the executive (many times more numerous than parliamentary ones) and judges cannot contradict the constitution and parliamentary laws. Rules can be applied by courts only if the executive carries them out. Judgments by civil servants and parliaments are subject to the verdict of the courts. Finally, we must recognize the fact that the same functions may be performed by two different institutions, if the objectives are different (as in the case of recruitment); also, that separate branches may have—perhaps, ought to have—separate constituencies.

So much for the traditional doctrine. Now we encounter a much more important and difficult problem, however. It is obvious that every administration implies the three elementary activities mentioned. But are they the only ones? The answer depends partly on the objective properties of the administrative process and partly on the political goals set by the society.

We have already encountered the problem of control. In every interdependent system—and the three-functional government described above is certainly one—the functioning of the system exerts a certain controlling influence on the functioning of its components. Yet, as every systems engineer knows, this is far from sufficient. If we want optimal results, we must build special controlling devices into the system to prevent any substantial departure from the optimal regime. In the political field, this implies the institutionalization of control.

We now have four branches of political administration. Their actions are not predetermined; they depend crucially on the people with whom they are staffed. Thus, recruitment into political and administrative roles is the next elementary function. In discussing this function, we must turn for inspiration to a Far Eastern Montesquieu, the Chinese revolutionary and statesman Sun Yat-sen. Drawing on the ancient historical experience of his country, Sun suggested a five-branch structure. The first four branches coincide with the four enumerated above, while the fifth is called the examination branch. Its task is to "examine the knowledge and the abilities of the candidates for the civil service."[27] Sun noted that a similar system had already existed for a long time in England,[28] and so it will come as no surprise that Harold Laski, the English political scientist, was a strong advocate of it. Laski contended that (1) civil servants must be appointed by persons other than those in the cabinet or its subordinate political posts, and (2) appointment rules must be formulated so as to reduce to a minimum the chances for personal favoritism. Laski believed that these conditions would be satisfied if the competition for posts were open and if candidates were selected by a commission whose members could be removed only under circumstances similar to those for a judge.[29] But it did not occur to Laski to denote the recruitment function as one of the fundamental functions of government. Besides, recruitment into administrative positions is only a minor part of the problem. The major part is recruitment into political positions.

If the government is conceived as the executive council of parliament, then the executive function will have to be separated from administration proper. The former requires political qualifications, the latter professional ones. We thus reach the conclusion that public administration is the sixth and last function of self-government. To complicate the matter slightly, let us note, as does E. Pusić, that public administration is further differentiated into authority and service.[30] The former reflects the conflict component and the latter the coordination component of politics.

Let us summarize our findings. Self-government implies six distinct functions:

Legislative—promulgating general laws;
Adjudicative—applying the laws to particular cases;
Executive—giving effect to the decisions of the first two branches;
Administrative—implementing the orders of the executive authority and applying the laws;
Control—overseeing the activities of the other branches;
Recruitment—supplying personnel for the other branches.

It now remains to try to design appropriate institutions that will be responsible for the six activities enumerated.

III. Institutionalization of the Six Functions of Self-Government

I shall assume that we are concerned with a reasonably developed self-governing society. The "transition period between capitalism and socialism" has already been left behind.

Economic development has progressed beyond the poverty line, and society can afford to provide a reasonably comfortable living for each of its members. In other words, the present Western European level of economic and cultural development is assumed. In order to avoid, or at least restrict, the influence of particular individual experience and personal prejudices, the design of institutions will be limited to the bare essentials. Besides, a detailed institutional design can be meaningfully undertaken only for a particular community and in a concrete historical situation.

1. *Legislature.* If each of us plays three fundamental roles, it may be desirable that we be represented separately in the legislative assembly in each of the three roles. On the other hand, a separate representation of consumers may not really be necessary. The interests of consumers are sufficiently close to the interests of citizens so that joint representation appears sufficient. Besides, we have another institution to take care of consumers' interests (see item 5 below).

We can distinguish two different categories of interests: territorial and functional, or quality of life interests and productive interests. The latter correspond to producers' representation and the former to consumers' (and citizens') representation. Thus, the Commonwealth Assembly will consist of at least two houses, a House of Citizens and a House of Producers.[31] Members of the House of Citizens will represent their regions, while members of the House of Producers will represent their branches of production. Each house will decide independently in the area of its specialization. As far as decisions on issues of common interest are concerned (for example, the annual budget, the development plan, the election of the government, etc.), both houses will participate and will decide by a majority vote in each. Finally, by a majority vote each house may proclaim any issue to be of common interest.

Since each house represents only partial interests, it may appear to some desirable to establish a third house to deal with common national interests. This in unnecessary, however, for common national interests will be safeguarded by the interaction of the two houses. A special arbitration procedure must be set up for cases where the two houses disagree.

A problem arises, however, if constituent regional units differ greatly in size and also vary ethnically and economically. The principle of safeguarding minority interests requires that each region have the same say—that is, the same number of representatives. Commonwealth interests, on the other hand, may occasionally clash with regional interests as determined in this way. Consequently, we may need a Senate and a House of Representatives. The complications of the American and other double-house systems are not really necessary, however. Under specified conditions, the majority of the representatives of a region may proclaim an issue to be "a regional issue" or "a minority issue," and then the decision can be reached only by interregional consensus. Certain issues may be defined in advance as regional issues; for example, development plans. If this approach is adopted, regional representation in the Assembly may remain unequal since, under the circumstances, representatives do not vote as individuals but as the members of their regional delegations, and each region has just one delegation.

The Commonwealth Assembly makes basic political decisions for the entire country. This is reflected first of all in legislation, but also in general political guidance, harmonization of conflicting sectional interests, and mobilization of national resources. The Assembly controls the activities of the government proper. It appoints various national functionaries and elects the Executive Council.

It would appear that I am subscribing to the doctrine of the unity of power; this must be contrasted with the division of power, not with the separation of powers, which I treat as a separation of functions. In the power hierarchy, the Assembly reigns supreme. There is one constraint, however: laws must be constitutional. This constraint reflects the postulate that the ultimate bearers of power are all citizens, who, as a body politic, adopt the supreme law of the land.

2. *Executive.* The Assembly has various specialized committees that facilitate its legislative and political work. The most important committee is the Executive Council, which replaces the former government. The Executive Council is responsible for achieving the political objectives decided in the Assembly. The council is expected to propose its own program, of course, and also shares in the legislative initiative. After deliberations in the Assembly, the program, or a particular proposal, is either accepted (possibly with amendments) or rejected. If accepted, its realization becomes a political obligation for the Executive Council. Failure to comply with Assembly decisions may lead to a vote of confidence and, if the outcome is negative, to a dissolution of the council.

The president of the council acts as a prime minister. The prerogatives of the president and the rules governing the functioning of the council depend very much on the national temperament and traditions. The council may be elected for a fixed period, and without recall; its members may be reelected if they wish to serve further, and the post of president may be subject to rotation on an annual basis—all as is characteristic of the Bundesrat in contemporary Switzerland. Or the survival of the council may be subject to a vote of confidence; its members may be barred from reelection more than twice in succession; and the president may be elected separately and be substantially more than just *primus inter pares*. In general, strict accountability to the Assembly and collective rather than individual decision making represent characteristics that are more in tune with a socialist environment.

3. *Administration*. Public administration is carried out by civil servants who are professionals rather than politicians. The heads of various branches of the civil service are permanent secretaries in the Executive Council. Civil servants enjoy tenure and cannot be fired unless they are found guilty of gross misbehavior or criminal activities. It is a function of the civil service to apply the law, and in this work it ought to enjoy full professional independence. Its other major function is to implement the decisions of the Executive Council.

It is clear that relations among the three branches ought to be organized so that the Assembly has complete political control, the council has full operational initiative, and the civil service functions with a high degree of professional competence and independence. The council is the link between the legislature and the administration. The council and the Assembly, as political bodies, are motivated by political considerations. The civil service is guided by professional ethics. Such a system needs capable individuals; it does not need professional politicians or traditional political leaders, least of all charismatic leaders. It is also important to note that what we want to achieve is a decentralization of power, not a reduction of power. In fact, socialist society is vitally interested in increasing the total amount of power,[32] since the solution of problems requires sufficient power. For this reason, branches specialize in different fields of activity and enjoy full initiative (coupled with full responsibility).

4. *Judiciary*. Judges administer justice. As a result, wrongs are redressed and/or the offenders are punished. There are four categories of offenders: citizens (individual or associated), the state apparatus, self-government bodies, and self-management bodies. Correspondingly, there are at least four kinds of

courts. Originally courts were established to adjudicate the offenses of citizens (civil and criminal). *Administrative tribunals* dealing with the offenses of state officials are of rather recent vintage. They first appeared after the French Revolution (headed by the Conseil d'état in 1799), but it took some time before administrative law was recognized as a separate legal branch. In Anglo-Saxon countries, this happened only in the twentieth century. Administrative law was developed to establish the legal limitations of administrative discretion. Its first principle is that no administrative measure that imposes a burden on a citizen can be undertaken without legal authorization.[33] Legislators themselves may commit offense when they fail to observe the rules of the basic law, the constitution. In order to prevent this from happening, the courts have the right and duty to undertake the judicial review of legislation, i.e., to decide whether a law of the legislature or an act of the executive is valid under the constitution. This function is usually performed by a special court called the *constitutional court*.[34] This court also arbitrates in conflicts between organs of the state, including federal and state governments. Finally, statutes and ordinances of self-managed work organizations—in other words, their autonomous normative activity—gives rise to a special autonomous law. If the self-management machinery fails to settle a dispute within a work organization, the matter is referred to a special court, which in the Yugoslav Constitution of 1974—by which it was first established—is called the *court of associated labor*.[35] The names and actual organization of various courts obviously will vary from country to country. What is important for our purposes is to establish the four different functions of the judiciary. There are other specialized courts, such as military, economic, or arbitration courts, etc., but they fall into one of these four functional categories.

To administer justice, judges must be impartial. To be impartial, they must be independent. To safeguard their independence, their selection must be free of political influence. Candidates for a judicial office, remarked Laski, cannot possibly put before an electorate a special program or a personal plea.[36] The necessary influence of public opinion is exerted through the jury. More generally, independence implies that a judge must not suffer consequences because of the view he takes. While judges cannot be politically elected, they can be selected and appointed on the basis of merit. This is the job of the Recruitment Board, to be discussed later. There are several exceptions. The public prosecutor's office and the constitutional court are at least partly political organs. Candidates for these jobs ought to be elected by the respective assemblies. Perhaps the same applies to members of the supreme or appellate courts.

Private productive property and bureaucratic power—two extremely important sources of conflict in capitalist and etatist societies—will be eliminated under socialism. This does not mean, however, that conflicts will disappear or that they will become less numerous. The more developed a society, the more differentiated are the various functions and the more complex are relationships among the members of the society. These relationships are regulated by rules, and the interpretation of rules requires certain legal skills. Thus, there is no danger that the legal profession will die out. Yet, if legal advice is necessary—as is, for example, medical help—why should not the bar be socialized, just as is medicine? This was the idea of Harold Laski—nowhere in the world fully implemented as yet—when he suggested that an *office of legal advice* be attached to the local authority served by the court. The office may have a division for providing advice (where an ordinary citizen[37] who suffered damage "could come . . . in the same way as the rich man goes to his private lawyer"),[38] a division for mediation (dealing with slander, libel, and quarrels), and a division for preparing cases for the courts.

5. *Control.* Rudimentary control exists in presocialist societies as well. It has already been pointed out that the interdependence of subsystems implies control. By applying judicial review to legislation, the courts control the legislators. The legislators control the executive, and the latter, in turn, controls the administration. The public prosecutor's office is an organ of control.[39] An extremely important lever of control is public opinion. The essential precondition for genuine public opinion is the availability of adequate information, which will be discussed later.

Apart from the sources of control enumerated above, there are at least two institutions specializing in social control: one in financial matters, the other in everything else. The former is the Social Accounting Service, which controls the financial transactions of work organizations and state organs (see chapter 13). The latter is the Office of the People's Commissioner.

The primitive version of the Office of People's Commissioner is to be found in the parliamentary grievance commissions. These commissions receive complaints from citizens, transmit these complaints to relevant authorities, and urge them to take the appropriate actions. The results are not very encouraging. Besides, a situation in which citizens beg for mercy, which may or may not be delivered, is a drastic expression of alienated state power. Also, why wait for complaints? Why not organize vigorous and *active* control? In this sense, the real modern precursor of the people's commissioner is the celebrated Swedish ombudsman.[40] Though as early as 1680 the chancellor of the king became the first ombudsman, the office of ombudsman in the modern sense was not established until the Constitution of 1809. The *justitieombudsman*, as he was called, was to supervise the courts and administrative agencies and, as such, acted as an instrument of parliamentary control over the activities of government.[41]

The First World War generated antimilitary feelings in Sweden, and the parliament reacted by establishing the *militeombudsman* in 1915 in order to prevent the distrust of military administration. The *militeombudsman* dealt with undue constraints of liberty, unwarranted arrests, and false imprisonment. The institution of ombudsman gradually spread to all Scandinavia and later, after the Second World War, to New Zealand, the United Kingdom, Canada, West Germany and some other countries. In addition to civil and military ombudsmen, ombudsmen to help enforce laws on restrictive trade practices; to protect consumers against false advertising, undesirable marketing practices, improper contract terms, and so on; and to insure the trustworthiness of the press, were created. The Yugoslav Constitution of 1974 established what might be called the ombudsman for self-management (*društveni pravobranilac samoupravljanja*).

By now, the ombudsman's function has been verified historically, and so we may introduce him in our system as the people's commissioner, since this is what he really represents. The Office of People's Commissioner is concerned with legal security in the administrative process. This implies questions such as: Has the person involved in an action been given an opportunity to answer the evidence against him? Are the decisions of administrative agencies founded on sufficient evidence? Have public and private interests been balanced objectively? Has the case been delayed? Have decisions been influenced improperly?[42] Citizens complain to the ombudsman mostly about employment conditions, wages, and pensions, and the refusal of authorities to grant licenses, permits, or concessions. Frequent complaints are lodged against the prosecuting authority for the failure to prosecute an offense, for unsatisfactory investigation on the part of the police, or occasionally for police brutality. In Norway, prison inmates make up a large share of complainants.[43] Danish ombudsmen deal with the following categories of cases: (1) the qualification of an official in the decision-making process; (2) bias on the part of an official; (3) incorrect or incomplete data resulting in harm to the petitioner; (4) failure of an official to specify the reason for a decision; (5) undue delay in the administrative process; (6) arbitrary, unreasonable, or capricious procedure; (7) rudeness or other uncivilized behavior of an official; (8) willful official negligence; (9) other acts of mal-, mis-, or nonfeasance in office.[44] One could enumerate other areas that might need the commissioner's attention, such as: waste of time due to queues and disorder in government offices; failure on the part of public services (governmental and nongovernmental) to honor obligations toward customers; ecological damage; poor quality of consumer goods, etc. The Yugoslav public attorney for self-management protects social property and the self-managing right of workers in organizations of associated labor.

The people's commissioner gathers the information for his activity not only from the complainants, but also from press and other mass media reports and from inspection tours in which he engages on his own initiative. He has access to all offices and all documents, including internal minutes. He can hold hearings or attend meetings of all authorities under his supervision. He is not, however, a substitute for internal and judicial control and for the administrative appellate system, but rather a complement to them. Citizens are first directed to pursue matters through regular channels and only if that fails does the commissioner act. His main concern is with that vast area between strict legality and strict offense or crime. Not everything can be regulated by law. In fact, comparatively few issues can, if the system is to work normally. Thus, there is a plenty of scope for administrative abuse, negligence, imprudence, carelessness, lack of understanding, lack of competence, and untoward behavior. Consequently, most of the commissioner's actions will consist in: (1) informing the appropriate authorities or self-management bodies about the problem and asking that it be settled; and (2) admonishing the offending official to proceed in a given way. The commissioner cannot penalize the culprit himself, but he can (3) order disciplinary action against the offender or, (4) in severe cases, prosecute or order the public prosecutor to bring the case before the court. Ordinary breaches of law are referred to ordinary courts, administrative offenses to administrative tribunals, constitutional evaluation to constitutional courts, and offenses against social property and self-management to courts of associated labor. The commissioner for self-management can (5) temporarily stop the execution of acts of work organizations and of political executives if it would damage social property or self-management rights. Finally, the commissioner may (6) initiate bills in the Assembly.

In order to function properly, the people's commissioner must be independent and accessible. His job is clearly a political one. Thus he will be elected by the Assembly or, preferably, by a general vote of the entire community whose interests he is supposed to serve. His term of office is fixed for a relatively long period, say eight years, during which he cannot be removed. People's commissioners as a body represent the society's Supervising Council, the fifth branch of self-government.[45]

Before we proceed, let me draw attention to a new phenomenon that is largely overlooked—the corporate actor. This will put the role of the people's commissioner in a more general perspective. Why have administrative tribunals and ordinary courts proved an insufficient defense for the citizen's rights and liberties? Because governmental agencies and business firms are corporate actors and, as such, are incomparably more powerful than individual citizens. Until about the fifteenth century, the only corporate bodies that existed—such as the manor, the guild, and the village—wholly contained their members and exercised full authority and responsibility over them. Besides, they were embedded in the feudal hierarchical structure of subordination and superordination. Capitalist development gradually destroyed feudal ties, liberated individuals, and generated corporate bodies able to engage freely in transactions. Instead of containing persons, the new corporate actors contained the resources of their members or owners (firms) or the positions of their incumbents (bureaucracies). This development led to a legal innovation: the creation of a juristic person analogous to the natural person. This legal fiction became a source of trouble because the two "persons" were very different. James Coleman has pointed out that "because the corporation has been viewed as a juristic person, and because the average size and resources of juristic persons relative to natural persons has continually grown, the law has been slow to recognize power differences between corporations and natural persons. Thus a symmetric allocation of rights between corporations and persons can lead in practice to an asymmetric realization of interests."[46] In comparison with individuals, corporate actors command enormously larger resources, are incomparably better informed, and do not feel emotions. For these reasons, the "free" contract between two legally symmetrical persons such as the worker and the firm is a sham. One of the first attempts to eliminate the power difference involved in the free contract was to create trade unions. The resulting power difference can also be compensated, at least partly, by the Office of Legal Advice and the activities of the people's commissioner. The latter was originally concerned only with the activities of government agencies. It has become necessary, however, for his control to encompass the activities of corporate actors throughout the society.

6. *Recruitment.* In order to govern, a political regime needs reliable people in the key positions—totalitarian regimes extend this requirement to all positions—of the political and administrative hierarchy. For this reason, leaderships of states and political parties jealously guard the right of appointing their own followers to political and administrative posts. This state of affairs changes under socialism. Socialist political systems are not about government but about *self*-government. They need not leaders[47] but collective decision-making bodies subject to rotation and recallable at any time. The elimination of class conflict and the educational and economic homogenization of the population make it possible to base the recruitment of personnel on certain objective criteria.

I have already mentioned that ancient China and modern England went very far in staffing their public services with individuals selected by open competition on the basis of merit. It is clear that a socialist country can do at least as well and, one hopes, better. Recruitment boards will be established at various levels of self-management, and will select the candidates for vacant posts in administrative agencies and courts. Board members will be elected by the respective assemblies for a fixed period of time and will not be recallable.

Socialism eliminates class conflicts but not all conflicts; class interests, but not diversity of interests. Conflicts have to be resolved and diverse interests brought into harmony; this requires political decision making, and politicians carry it out. When conflicting interests are involved, objective criteria are not available. Politicians cannot be selected like administrators, they must be elected. We shall consider this problem at length in the next chapter. Election means that the entire population becomes a recruitment board. Yet elections have to be supervised and administered, and this is a legitimate job for our Recruitment Board.

IV. Territorial Decentralization: Deconcentration of Power

There are four fundamental levels of territorial self-government, corresponding to decreasing levels of intensity of emotional attachment or rootedness. A person develops his roots in the place where he or she was born and/or raised. This is the local level. A person is also a member of an ethnic group which inhabits a certain region. If the region is not too big or the ethnic group too small, the two coincide. A person is next a citizen of a national state. Finally, the fourth level is that of the world community.

This fourfold citizenship remains valid even if people leave the places where they were born and the regions where their ethnic group lives. The four allegiance levels make possible a four-stage decentralization of state activities. If we leave out the world level—since international relations are not discussed in the present study—we can identify three forms of state organization that correspond to the remaining three stages or levels. I shall call them commune, state (or region), and federation (or commonwealth). As in Switzerland, citizens have (at least symbolically) three citizenships: that of the native commune, that of the (ethnic) state, and national citizenship.

Decentralization implies that, in principle, decisions are taken at the lowest possible level and are elevated to a next higher level only if they affect substantially wider communities. This means that in defining activities and responsibilities, we have to start from the highest level, for anything that is not explicitly attributed to a higher level is implied to belong to lower levels.

Each level of government has legislative and executive autonomy. The federal constitution, representing the social contract, determines the sphere of competence of the federal government. Whatever is omitted falls under the jurisdiction of the state, which legislates either independently or within the federal framework laws. The function of the state constitution with respect to the local government is similar. The executive is not integrated vertically—except, perhaps, in military matters—and the executive councils are responsible solely to the respective assemblies.

The federation is concerned with defense and foreign relations—in other words, with the relations between the national commonwealth and the rest of the world. It is also concerned with internal coordination. Its Assembly passes framework laws and decides on overall policy measures. The organizational structure of the federation is given in Figure 5.[48]

The figure is self-explanatory and needs only a few words of clarification. The House of Producers is reduced to the House of the Economy, since it is only the economy that needs permanent steering at the federal level. Education, cultural problems, and health can be dealt with at the state level. As far as the general problems of work organizations are concerned, what applies to business enterprises applies to other work organizations as well. Thus the House of the Economy is fully qualified to pass framework laws regulating the activities of work organizations in general.

As far as the judiciary is concerned, there is no particular need for federal courts to be hierarchically superior to state courts, except in one case to be mentioned in a moment. Therefore, they do not serve as appellate courts and adjudicate only cases related to federal activities. Similarly, there is no need for any line of hierarchical subordination concerning the remaining five fundamental state organs. Decentralization implies that the spheres of competence of the federation and the states be neatly separated. The exception mentioned concerns a restricted class of judicial cases whose uniform adjudication is considered of great importance for the basic unity of the legal system of the country. Since the federal constitutional court is the guardian of the basic law of the country, it may also serve as an appellate court for that selected class of cases. Since the federation does not come into direct contact with the citizens, members of the Supervisory Council need not be elected by a general vote. At the federal level, people's commissioners are really parliamentary commissioners.

Similar charts could be designed for the other two levels of self-government, but this is not really necessary. A summary description of state-level organization will suffice. The state is just large enough to represent the basic level of political sovereignty and is not too large to be uncontrollable. The state has the right to leave the federation and join another commonwealth. What the federation does is, in principle, the result of a consensus among the states. The state makes the laws that are

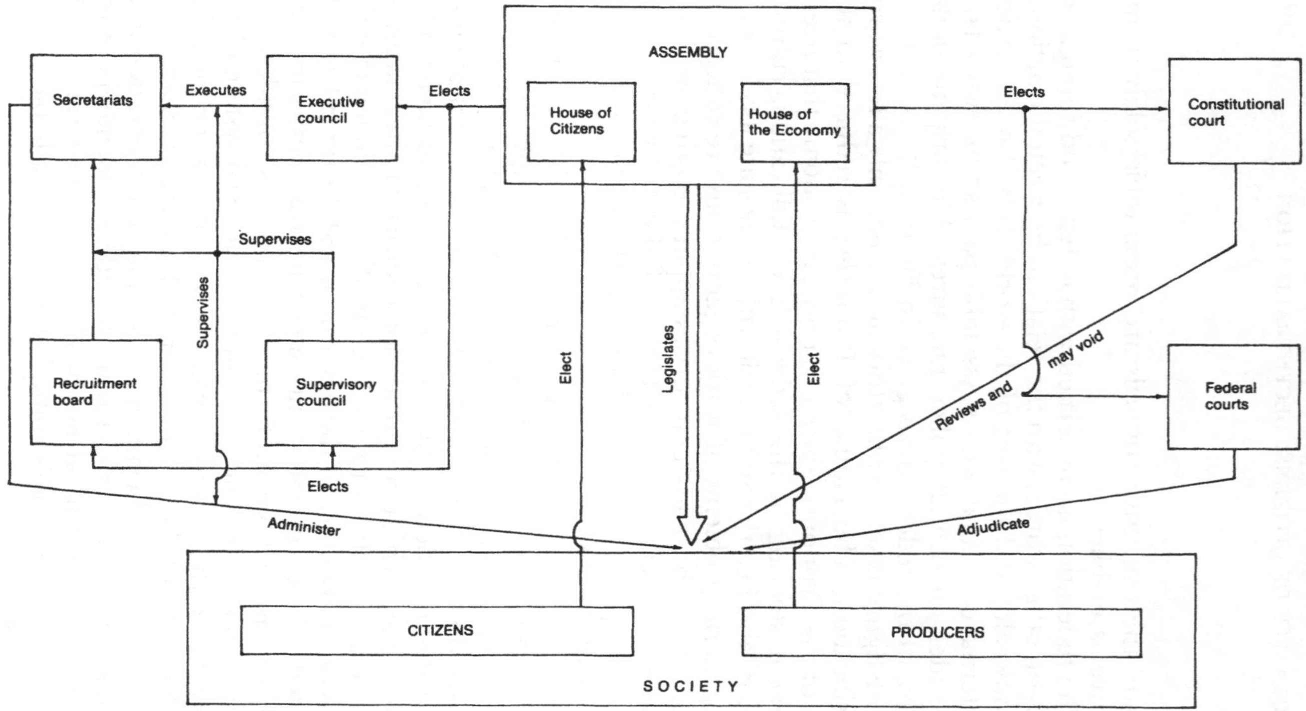

Figure 5. *Organization at the federal level.*

actually to be applied. The state regulates all activities that need state regulation. The state assembly has three houses of producers: for the economy, for education (including science and culture), and for health (including social welfare and physical culture). People's commissioners are elected by general vote and the courts serve as appellate courts.

The position of the commune in the political structure is similar to that of the enterprise in the economic structure. It actually provides public services to the population. Almost all contacts between citizens and the state are those with the commune. This warrants a few more words about this level.

There are four factors that integrate people into a local community: habitation, work place, political jurisdiction, and communication (the transference of messages, objects, and individuals that generates patterned interaction among social units).[49] Not all factors need be present for a local community to exist as a social system. For instance, some persons may reside elsewhere, others may work elsewhere. The same person may be subject to two jurisdictions: as a dweller in one and as a producer in another. In modern times, communication is not limited locally, of course. Yet for most people most of the time the four factors remain operative.

Local communities have passed through a process of transformation, and the same trend is still continuing. Emotional attachment is decreasing. As pointed out by E. Pusić,[50] interests are becoming more differentiated, which means that an increasing number of people participate in an increasing number of "interest circles" (work organization, profession, various societies, ideology). Since many of these circles transgress local territory, the importance of local interests and emotional attachment to the local community decrease. At the same time, the volume of services provided locally increases.[51] In this way, the local community is being transformed from a group of people poor in organizations and rich in emotions into a territorial entity with an increasing number of organized public services accompanied by a decreasing emotional involvement on the part of the inhabitants.[52]

The communes perform three groups of functions. These include: (1) *socioeconomic and coordinating* functions such as planning and coordinating local social and economic development and providing services for the satisfaction of material, educational, cultural, and other needs of the citizens; (2) *sociopolitical and regulative* functions such as those connected with the application of laws, legal titles, and ecological matters; (3) *protective and supervisory* functions such as protecting the citizens' rights and liberties, maintaining law and order, and carrying out social control.

Just as with an enterprise, a commune is too big for direct participation. Thus it is very naturally decomposed into a number of neighborhoods. A neighborhood is concerned with child care, elementary education, basic medical services, shopping and recreational facilities, and other similar problems of importance for the daily living environment.

The neighborhood is not a governmental unit, just as an economic unit is not a firm; it does not have a legislature. It is the primary level of self-government. The neighborhood elects a nonprofessional council and executive committee to take permanent care of local interests. The president of the council is at the same time the president of the committee and is also a member of the communal assembly. Likewise, the president of the communal assembly is also a member of the state assembly. The other members of the two assemblies are elected by a separate vote and become members of parliamentary commissions and committees, including the respective executive councils.

Presidents of the state assemblies, together with the president of the Federal Assembly, can constitute the Presidium of the commonwealth.[53] The Presidium works as a collective chief of state. One of its possible functions is to deal with questions that are proclaimed "minority issues" and are not settled by the regular procedure; this comprises another means of safeguarding regional or minority interests. The Presidium does not vote but decides on the basis of consensus. In case of a deadlock, the constitutional court may serve as an arbitration board.

* * *

The institutional system described above is intended to contribute to the solution of the same double problem at the macro level as the organizational structure of the self-managing enterprise (chapter 8, section III) did at the micro level: maximum democracy coupled with maximum efficiency. The former implies functional and territorial decentralization of power with opportunities open to any individual initiative. The latter implies "strong government," i.e., operational autonomy of the executives at various levels and of the professional civil service. In addition, the control system is designed so as to minimize the abuse of administrative or political power.

11

Equality of Citizens: Socialist Democracy

I. Political Parties

We have already mentioned that a modern political system has several components. Its first component, the state, was discussed in the previous chapter. Its second component, political parties, is the subject of the present section.

Political parties are associations of citizens organized with the purpose of conquering state power by means of recurring elections. This definition implies three different institutions: (secular) state, parliament, and popular suffrage. Political parties are a relatively new societal phenomenon. Throughout history, people have associated themselves into groups which fought for political power. Yet these factions were not parties. One or another—or perhaps all—of the three institutions mentioned had yet to come into existence.

The secular state did not exist in antiquity. Even the term was unknown. Roman law did not develop an appropriate concept of the state. *Civitas* and *res publica* denoted collectivities that were both secular and religious. The Roman Empire and oriental monarchies "were held together by an authority and legitimacy which was basically religious."[1] The term *lo stato* has come to be used only since the Italian Renaissance. Niccolò Machiavelli is credited with introducing it into writings about politics. The Serbo-Croatian word *država* can be traced back to paragraph 39 of the fourteenth-century codex of the Serbian Emperor Dushan.

The precursors of parliaments are the assemblies of estates which emerged in Europe in the fourteenth century and later (*états généraux* in France, *cortés* in Spain, *seym* in Poland). The three estates that participated in the assemblies were the clergy, the aristocracy, and the bourgeoisie (the inhabitants of the bourgs). In Scandinavia, where feudalism was much weaker, free peasants represented the fourth estate. The development of absolute monarchies temporarily halted the activities of estate assemblies. In France, the estates did not meet from 1614 until 1789. Yet, when the king was forced to call the estates into session in 1789, that proved to be the beginning of the Revolution. In the process, the old estate assembly was transformed into a parliament elected on the basis of universal suffrage (1792).

In the United States, the War for Independence led to the establishment of a parliament. In England, Parliament existed even before the Revolution, but asserted its supremacy over the monarch and conquered the right to legislate only after it. In 1688 Parliament established its authority to determine monarchical succession, and in 1707 Queen Anne, for the last time, refused to sanction a law. Parliaments were gradually established in other European countries, but the process was exceedingly slow. Belgium introduced a parliament in 1831, Denmark and the Netherlands in 1848. Sweden replaced its estate assembly by a parliament in 1866.[2] A parliament was established in 1888 in Serbia, in 1890 in Japan.

Once parliaments were created, their members tended to form groups with similar political views, which very directly reflected their material interests. These parliamentary groups were the precursors of modern political parties. Thus, along with parliaments, bourgeois revolutions generated parties. Whigs and Tories emerged in England around 1679. The former took its name from Scottish opponents of the monarchy; they favored an increase in the power of Parliament and enlisted the support of urban and mercantile interests. The latter were named after groups of outlaws favoring Catholicism and the traditional monarchy; they represented a court party and were supported by the majority of landed nobles. The Tories were succeeded by the Conservative Party in 1824, and the Whigs by the Liberal Party in 1832. The two parties preserved the continuity of their political orientations and have remained politically active up to the present.

The second historical pair of political parties, one of which has survived to the present day, was the product of the American Revolution. These were the Republicans (later renamed the Democrats), who held that the power of the federal government should be strictly limited, and their opponents, the Federalists. A few years later, a third pair of political parties followed, spawned by the French Revolution. The Jacobins, who met in the monastery of St. Jacob, represented the radical middle class. Girondists, named after the region of Gironde in Southern France, included wealthy individuals as members and supporters. In Japan, several years after the Revolution, the first political societies emerged, fighting for a constitution, representative institutions, and personal liberties. A few years later, in 1881–82, they gave birth to the first three Japanese political parties.

In France, revolution was followed by restoration. In England, the Revolution was slow to begin with. Thus, in the first half of the nineteenth century, parliamentary democracy was relatively developed only in the United States. At the end of the eighteenth century only 250,000 citizens elected representatives into the English House of Commons. In the first half of the nineteenth century, France had 200,000 voters out of a population of 30 million.[3] Such a restricted suffrage did not pose great problems for election organization. Electoral committees, if they were created at all, were usually dissolved after elections. Local notables retained control of their constituencies regardless of what they did in the parliament. Distinguished members of the upper classes knew each other and did not need special programs or organizations to defend their class interests. It was different in America, however. There electoral committees had to choose candidates and agitate among the electorate, and so had to be more permanent. Besides, the spoils system consolidated their structure. Once electoral committees become permanent, are associated on a national scale, and establish ties with parliamentary groups, full-fledged modern parties come into existence.

In Europe, workers organized into unions and legal or semilegal political groupings and exerted pressure on the upper classes, forcing them to eliminate limitations on suffrage one after another. The process was described in chapter 1, section I. With extended suffrage, here, too, permanent electoral committees became necessary as instruments of support and agitation. On the other hand, the working classes soon discovered that the only weapon they had to fight those in control of state and wealth was an efficient political organization. In the second half of the nineteenth century, two German social democratic parties, soon to be united, set a pattern for social democratic parties all over the world. In this way, the mass political party was born.

There is just one remaining link in the political evolution to be mentioned: the Communist Party. If the ruling class is unwilling to make concessions, gradual social evolution is prevented, and the political opposition can be organized only in the form of a clandestine party. This is what happened in tsarist

Russia. In order to survive, a clandestine party needs strict centralization, rigid hierarchy, and authoritarian leadership. This is how the Bolsheviks organized their party and succeeded in conquering political power. The new Revolution created a new type of party, the Communist Party. The success of the Bolsheviks, which coincided with disgraceful behavior on the part of the social democratic parties during the First World War, gave an impetus to the formation of communist parties all over the world and to the creation of the Communist International. Communist parties are organized according to the principle of democratic centralism, which, in its practical application, means that lower bodies are strictly subordinated to higher bodies; that the minority is subordinated to the majority, but always only at a given level of hierarchy; and that elections consist in ratification of the candidates selected by the superior organs. The basic ideological tenet is that of Rousseau: only in total submission to the community will all find themselves free. This tenet is modified somewhat by an etatist addition: the community will is determined by the party, which, knowing the laws of history, is alone entitled to lead the toiling masses into a better future.[4]

Once parties exist, the political system can consist of several parties contending for power, of two parties, or of just one. There may be an open and organized opposition, or none; a real competition for power, or not. The various relationships are summarized in Table 11.

Experience shows that multiparty systems involving coalition governments tend to be unstable; two- and one-party systems, stable. The explanation lies in the dynamics of party struggle. In order to attract votes in a multiparty system, each party exaggerates its differences from its closest competitors. Each party tends to appeal to a particular group, ethnic and religious animosities are formed, and the nation is fragmented. In a two-party system, parties avoid controversial extremes, mobilize various social groups, and stress common ground in order to appeal to the decisive voters in the middle of the political spectrum. Strictly speaking, this holds true when the distribution of opinions is unimodal. If the society is sharply polarized, which means that the distribution of opinions is bimodal, a two-party system may make the conflict even worse. In a one-party system, the party claims to represent common social interests. The single party may still be quite democratic if it tolerates open discussion and if each seat is contested by several candidates. Finally, except in one-party systems, inde-

TABLE II

Classification of Party Systems[5]

Monocentrism or polycentrism	**Polycentrism of the party system**			**Monocentrism**	
Number of candidates per constituency	Several				One
Existence or lack of institutionalized opposition	Political opposition			No political opposition	
Real competition for power	Real competition for power		No real competition for power		
Party composition of the governing majority	Coalition essential	Coalitions not needed, governments based on the majority of one party			
Party systems	Multiparty system A	Two-party system B	Dominant party system C	Mono-party system D	E

Examples: A—Some Roman countries, Switzerland, Netherlands
B—Some Anglo-Saxon countries, Austria, West Germany
C—Mexico, India (formerly), Sweden (for 44 years)
D—Tanzania
E—Etatist and less developed countries.

pendent candidates are not formally prevented from running for office. Yet the prohibitive cost of financing an electoral campaign makes this possibility scarcely more than a theoretical one.[6] The personal qualities of individual candidates matter very little;[7] party selection is decisive. Even this is not quite a correct description of political realities: it is the party leadership that runs the show.[8]

The political structure described above strongly resembles economic structure. In economic terms, we would talk about oligopoly, duopoly, and monopoly, and a rather elementary analysis would show that the first system is unstable, while the last is stable but undesirable. The fourth theoretical possibility—perfect competition of many sellers and buyers and a political system without party intermediaries—has been proven impossible historically.

Yet it was exactly such economic and political systems that the bourgeois founding fathers—Jean Jacques Rousseau, Adam Smith, and the framers of the American constitution—had in mind. Parties, like cartels—not to speak of monopolies—restrict free choice and generate inefficiencies. The founding fathers never thought of parties, nor did they assign them any place in the democratic system (though for different reasons). The first constitutions do not mention parties. Interest groups or parties increase the chance that some special interests will prevail rather than the general will. The sentiment was so strong that even as late as the First World War it was forbidden in a number of parliaments to make direct references to parties.[9] In political theory, deputies were considered isolated and independent, just as in economic theory firms were considered isolated and competitive; in the real world, however, alienated political and economic powers dominated the society.

II. Recruitment into Political Roles: Elections

Parties represent a disappointment for liberal democratic theory—just as imperfect competition and underemployment equilibrium are for neoclassical economic theory. Even before World War I, Robert Michels, a German sociologist and former socialist, provided a classical criticism of the party organization (and of trade unions).[10] Michels studied his own Social Democratic Party, perhaps the most democratically organized large party at the time. He observed that individuals in a position of authority within an organization cannot be controlled efficiently by those who hold subsidiary positions. The reasons for this are: (1) technical—because of the division of labor in large organizations, certain individuals are given the right to act in the name of the mass membership and become professional leaders; (2) psychological—a widespread sense of need for direction or guidance among ordinary members and a sense of gratitude to those who direct them.[11]

Commenting on Michels's "iron law of oligarchy"—which, of course, is not "iron" but only a strong probability—Seymour Martin Lipset cited the following three reasons why the officers of large-scale organizations have a near monopoly of power:

(1) they control the sources of information, which can be used to secure assent for their program;

(2) they control the formal means of communication with the membership, such as the press, travel, or the organization of meetings;

(3) they are skilled in the art of politics: they are more proficient than nonprofessionals in making speeches, writing articles, and organizing group activities.[12]

Since losing command over their organization means losing what makes them important as individuals, leaders become extremely aggressive when faced with a threat to their authority. Any democratic right is easily suppressed. This attitude is justified by reference to the damage wrought by powerful and evil opponents, by the ever-present enemy. Criticism of the leadership means treachery to the organization itself, and thus to the very ideals it is supposed to serve.

Michels himself concluded that, over a period of time, leaders win recognition for what they claim is their own indispensability and devote themselves to consolidating their own positions of power. Very soon they come to regard the organization and their own role in it as more important than the professed goals of the organization.[13] Michels thus accurately predicted what, half a century later, in its extreme form, would be euphemistically called the "cult of personality."

Political parties might not be very desirable. Yet, if we cannot get rid of them, if they are part and parcel of "modern democracy," then let us understand more clearly what good they can do. This is the prevailing attitude both in the East and in the West. In the West it is asserted mostly simply: "Political parties are the indispensable links between the people and the representative machinery of government";[14] or "Parties are necessary because opinion must be organized if anything resembling representative government is to exist."[15] In the East, the rule of the Communist Party is simply identified with socialism. There is no accepted and empirically tested theory of the functions that parties perform. The Western literature suggests that there may be four main functions.

1. *Political socialization: integration.* In traditional society, the place of an individual was predetermined by his ascribed status at birth. So was his relation to leadership. In modern society, predetermined affiliations do not exist; the individual citizen "is helpless and lost as he confronts in the state a remote, impersonal entity which he cannot understand, with which he can identify only as an abject subject. For men to belong to the commonwealth in any meaningful sense, they must belong to elements of it that are closer, more understandable by them, more amenable to their influence than is the central executive power."[16] One might remark in passing that, in societies in which national integration is most urgently needed—where national identity and community have only to be created—party systems are likely to be the most fragmented and parties act as disintegrating forces.

2. *Political socialization: opposition.* Empirical research shows that children—at least in contemporary Western culture—do not oppose authority. They have to learn how to do so.[17] They do this through a process of political socialization. On the other hand, a conflict of interests leads to disorder and violence, if individuals are not educated to settle their disputes peacefully. Both tasks are performed by the political party. Naturally, authorities are interested primarily in the second task and do not complain when citizens remain too obedient. De Sola Pool provides us again with a good presentation of this point of view:

> a stable commonwealth is promoted by the existence of loyal intermediary groups within it. His majesty's loyal opposition is a factor for stability, not instability. The expression of its dissident views is far less important a fact about its political role than that it guides people as to how dissent should be expressed and binds them into playing the game by those rules. An anomic society which does not foster control by subgroup over the members of the society is headed for turmoil much more surely than one which encourages pluralistic loyalties to various intermediary organizations.[18]

3. *Interest articulation and aggregation.* Gabriel Almond defines interest articulation as a process by which individuals and groups make demands upon political decision makers, and aggregation as a process by which demands are converted into general policy alternatives. "All types of political systems rely heavily on the political party: totalitarian societies as a means to mobilize support; democratic societies, as a channel to articulate and aggregate demands; and transitional societies, as an agency to create and structure new norms of behavior."[19]

4. *Political recruitment.* Apparently some special group of citizens must exist in order for appropriate candidates to be selected for political offices and, in particular, for leaders to be chosen and governments formed.

Since little empirical research has been undertaken in this field, the four functions listed must be considered primarily normative rather than positive. There is probably no disagreement that political parties do socialize, articulate and aggregate interests, and help recruit into political jobs. It is doubtful that they do all this well, however, or even that they play a central role. LaPalombara assigns the functions of political socialization and education as well as of interest articulation and aggregation to legislatures.[20] Concerning integration, Anthony King notes that "parties can hardly be said to be performing a positive integrative function if there exists widespread antipathy or even indifference toward them; rather the reverse."[21] As for interest aggregation, the same author points out that this function "is performed by a variety of structures of which the political party is only one and not necessarily the most important." He concludes that "the most that parties seem generally able to do is to present electorates with highly generalized platforms and with alternative candidates committed to very general policy standpoints."[22] Where leadership recruitment is concerned, at least in America "cabinet officers, not to mention senior career bureaucrats, military officers and interest group leaders, are often selected irrespective of party affiliation and by procedures which have little or nothing to do with party. . . . Even in connection with recruitment to elective offices, the role of party is at least problematical."[23] In the United States parties do not form the government. Even less in Switzerland. Even Britain—generally considered as a paradigm of party government—has, according to Richard Rose, "a political system in which administrative government is much more nearly the case than party government."[24] On the whole, the record does not seem very impressive. Why do parties exist, one may ask, if they function so poorly? The answer is: because their main function has little to do with the functions assigned to them by academic political theory. Their main function is to conduct the political game in an orderly and generally acceptable way so as to support and preserve the bourgeois social order, to uphold its legitimacy. They have performed this function exceedingly well. They have made it possible for the competition among undemocratically chosen elites to be called and considered democracy—more than that, *the* democracy.

In the etatist version, the single ruling party has somewhat different functions. Jerzy Wiatr has described the functions of the Polish Communist Party as follows:

> 1. The party represents and expresses the socialist ideology underlying the entire political system. It determines the fundamental aim and values which constitute the basis for the functioning of the political and socio-political institutions of our country.
> 2. Through the activity of its members in the institutions of state and social organizations, the party harmonizes the functioning of these institutions with the basic goals of the system.
> 3. The party determines the general directions of policy making by the state institutions.
> 4. The party mobilizes a number of citizens to participate in political decision making at various levels of government.

5. The party recruits and educates cadres of political leaders operating within the party as well as in the institutions of the state.[25]

To what extent are the functions of parties in capitalist and etatist societies—assuming that they are really carried out—relevant for a socialist society? Do we need political parties?[26] Let us examine the functions in the order given above. (1) If the *integration* of individuals into self-management structures is carried out from kindergarten age onward, there is no danger of their feeling isolated, lost, or helpless. If the state is accessible and controllable, it ceases to be an alien power, mystical and untouchable. (2) *Opposition* is better learned in everyday participation practice than under the guidance of oligarchical organizations. (3) *Interest articulation and aggregation* need no additional special institutions apart from those already existing: the press and other mass media, research institutes, universities, political societies (such as the Fabian Society), professional associations, and, of course, the self-governing machinery proper. We are thus left with (4) *political recruitment* as the only problem that needs further discussion. As far as the etatist version is concerned, the first four functions described by Wiatr belong properly to assemblies at various levels, since the essential quality of socialism as a classless society is that it cares for all people, not for a particular class of people. The fifth function is the same as in the capitalist setting and represents the next issue of our inquiry.

There seem to be two general principles a socialist society might establish in this field.

1. The selection of candidates for political offices is a prerogative of the voters, not of parties or any other intermediaries.

2. Candidates must have direct access to the electorate. Just as any producer may apply for any job under the conditions of open competition, any citizen may apply for any political office under the conditions of free, secret, and direct ballot. Social property implies equal access to the means of production; socialist democracy, equal access to political positions.

The first principle requires that voters be provided with adequate information. The second principle requires that political campaigns be financed out of communal funds. Both practices have already been attempted, though they have nowhere been developed into a complete system.[27] Bearing in mind these two principles, elections can be organized along the following lines. The constitution and the law specify formal requirements every candidate must meet (such as prescribed age, citizenship, mental health, absence of a criminal record). The prospective candidate obtains a certificate from the Recruitment Board certifying his eligibility and then, in standardized form, sends to the respective newspaper his offer to serve as a political worker. If he receives the required number of signatures, his name is put on the slate. All candidates who pass the signature test—a sort of primary election—are asked to answer the electoral questions formulated by the Recruitment Board. Their answers, along with other relevant information, are published in an *Electoral Guide.* Finally, each candidate is allocated a specified amount of time or space in the mass media and is also given the opportunity to address audiences at publicly organized meetings. If there is too great a demand for a particular means of publicity, the choice is made by lot. The candidate who wins the most votes is elected. If the vote is too fragmented, voting may be repeated for the two most successful candidates. It may seem desirable for several others down the list to remain politically active as well. They may form a delegation, a body of activists advising the elected representative and providing a link with the electorate. The first runner-up may act as a deputy representative.

The procedure described applies strictly to elections for the House of Citizens. In the case of the House of Producers, elections may perhaps be indirect. Candidates for the offices will then be chosen only from among members of workers' councils. Here, too, delegations, in addition to elected representatives, may prove desirable.

The election of legislators is just the first half of the job; the second half consists in controlling them. Representatives cannot be transformed into delegates bound by prior decisions of the electorate, for that would make it impossible to reach agreements in assemblies. They must be free to decide on the spot. In fact, the absence of the party whip is an advantage to be fully exploited in building consensus; it should not be replaced by another whip. Yet, representatives cease to fulfill their role if they fail to represent their voters. It is up to the voters to evaluate the behavior of their representative and, if they feel dissatisfied, they ought to be able to replace him.[28]

Citizens can also control or participate in legislation directly. This is done by referendum or people's initiative. The adoption of a constitution or a constitutional amendment should be subject to obligatory referendum. An optional referendum (concerning a law or a treaty) is held if it is requested by a certain number of citizens, or communes or states. In the same way, a new law may be initiated from below.[29] The recall, the referendum, and the initiative are three instruments of control and direct participation in political decision making by citizens.

This completes the institutional design of the political system. One might ask the pertinent question: Will it function? Swiss experience, which is rather relevant in this context, indicates that it will. Politics can be divested of the glamor that results from uncontrolled or poorly controlled state power. Political activities become an aspect of the social division of labor and nothing more. There is little doubt that, in a socialist society, political power can be effectively deconcentrated and decentralized. Yet, this does not solve all problems. Self-government seems to have its own dangers. One of them is mediocrity. Switzerland has been described—and the Swiss themselves enjoy in quoting the description—as *volkommen Mittel-mässigkeit* (complete mediocrity). Another, and related, problem is conservatism.[30] I leave the further analysis of these problems for a time when we shall have more experience regarding them. For our purposes it suffices to note that both dangers are surely immensely less threatening than the present concentration of power.

III. Participation vs. Liberalism and Collectivism

Political philosophy, which reflected the growth of the new bourgeois order from the seventeenth century onward, developed a characteristic dualistic concept of man. One aspect referred to utility and the other to man's capacities. The first implied that man was a bundle of appetites demanding satisfaction; the second, that he was a bundle of conscious energies seeking to be exerted.[31] The task of political democracy was to provide maximum scope for the latter in order to maximize the former. This task apparently could be achieved in different ways. From the very beginning two different approaches emerged, one individualistic, the other collectivist. Individualists start from the conception of natural rights. Every individual is endowed with these natural rights and should be allowed to pursue his interests as he wishes. Society must not interfere—or, at least, must minimize its interference. These ideas are associated with John Locke, who thought of a relatively small society of privileged citizens in a system of highly restricted property franchise. In a large nation, with democratic rights accessible to all citizens, unconstrained individualism did not appear viable. Therefore, Rousseau replaced it with the collectivistic discipline of a "general will." The state is a natural instrument of the general will. Those who dissent are traitors.[32] Lockean individualism led to political oligarchies in the eighteenth century. Rousseau helped to prepare the French Revolution. Marat read *The Social Contract* to excited audiences in the first clubs of 1788, improvised in Paris parks. Rousseauian collectivism soon found its practical implementation in the Jacobian terror and, somewhat more than a century later, in the Stalinist terror. Less extreme heirs of the two are contemporary bourgeois liberalism and bureaucratic collectivism.[33] The former finds its justification in the reasoning: since everyone is free, an individual's success or failure depends on him. The latter would claim: since we are all equal, the individual's destiny is in his hands. The fallacies of the two ideologies are too obvious to require comment.

Contemporary bourgeois and politocratic political systems are clearly very different. Yet they have one important feature in common: they are elitist. They are based, both theoretically and practically, on the presumption that every society is divided into an elite and the masses. The masses are incompetent, inert, unruly, unreliable, and passive. Their passivity is even considered a precondition for the good functioning of Western democracy. Etatist political practice takes an additional step: it is not sufficient for the masses to be merely passive and abstain from any initiative, they must be "actively passive," that is, they must support everything the leadership does, always praising its unerring wisdom. The masses being what they are, they need an active and creative leadership. Western theory refers to it as an elite; Eastern theory, as the vanguard party.

Traditionally, elites were considered as one of the major dangers to the democratic polity. Modern political theory treats elites as indispensable for democracy. This difference in outlooks obviously is not a result of cognitive progress, it simply reflects the facts of life. Compared with feudalism, the bourgeois order achieved tremendous advances in political democracy. But it also hit the limits imposed by the existence of elites. Now, if "the division into elite and mass is universal," as Lasswell proclaimed,[34] all one can do is to impose certain restrictions on the structuring of the elites. Thus democracy is fulfilled if:

(1) voters are able to choose between competing elites; (2) the elites do not reproduce themselves by rendering their power hereditary but new groups are able to enter their ranks; (3) no single form of power is dominant because support is derived from shifting coalitions; and (4) various elites (business, military, public service, etc.) do not form a common alliance.[35] Even these conditions are fulfilled only quite imperfectly in the most developed bourgeois democracies. In bureaucratic collectivism, most of them are directly violated. What the socialist polity will have to do is to overcome the basic contradiction between elites and the masses; the elitist democracy must give way to one based on participation.

The political philosophy of participation has already been described in the discussion of the just society (chapter 7). Man is conceived as a being of creative self-realization. He can realize his potential fully only if every other man is able to do the same. As already mentioned, both bourgeois and bureaucratic ideologies imply a fundamental division of citizens into the rulers and the ruled, the governors and the governed, the leaders and the masses.[36] Socialist ideology eliminates this division and replaces it with participation. If there are no classes, why should any particular group rule? Why should there be a class of professional leaders? Why should not the "masses" engage in self-government?

The central category of a political system is authority, just as that of an economic system is property.[37] Under socialism both must be socialized. I have defined social property as free and equal access to the means of production (chapter 8, section I). We can define political authority (where authority means the "right to invoke binding obligations")[38] on the part of citizens as free and equal access to positions of political power. That, of course, implies the elimination of political parties. Since they provide obvious advantages to political leaders, parties are not entirely likely to disappear of their own accord.[39] Hence, they must be forbidden. Is this possibly a restriction of liberty? Joseph Schumpeter aptly defined a political party as "a group whose members propose to act in concert in the competitive struggle for political power."[40] Replace the term *political power* by the term *profit* and you get the definition of a cartel. It has been universally accepted that cartels of businessmen must be forbidden. And they are, at least legally. Yet cartels of politicians are left free to operate. Why? Is it not because politics, rather than economics, is really crucial for the perpetuation of class rule? In other words, not the expropriation of private property but the *expropriation of political authority is the necessary and sufficient condition for socialism.*[41]

The "expropriation of political authority" is what we mean when we talk about socialist democracy. Consequently, socialist democracy cannot be reduced to a competitive struggle for people's vote with the aim of acquiring leadership positions—which is currently the most popular definition of liberal democracy.[42] According to the latter view, the primary political act of a citizen is to elect rulers. Again, the division into rulers and ruled is assumed as self-evident. Nor can socialist democracy be based on a separation of private and political spheres. Of course, citizens vote for representatives, but this is neither the primary nor the only political act. "In a participatory or self-managing democracy," writes Australian political scientist Carole Pateman,

> direct and representative democracy are no longer seen as two, separate forms of authority structure. Instead both take their place as two . . . interrelated aspects of *one* democratic authority structure. Thus representation does not necessarily involve *plena potestas*; . . . areas of political authority may be temporarily delegated to accountable representatives, but it is never alienated by citizens. Within participatory democratic practice the citizens no longer emerge periodically from private life . . . to put on their "political lion skins": they have no need to do so because they are participating in the political sphere every day as actual political citizens; political participation, democratic citizenship, is as much a part of everyday life as the individual's private activities.[43]

The elimination of political parties[44] does not imply the elimination of politics, just as the eradication of cartels does not kill the economy but renders the market more efficient. All that need be done is to forbid donations and the selection of candidates by party bosses. In other words, the party machinery and its political monopoly must be destroyed. The disappearance of political parties will not leave a political vacuum. On the contrary, it will make possible intensive political participation as described above. One, two, or several parties will be replaced by a multiplicity of political associations. At least three kinds of such associations may be envisaged: (a) political societies of the Fabian type; (b) promotional or cause-oriented groups such as environmentalists, feminists (or masculinists?), supporters of space programs, societies sponsoring various transportation systems; (c) interest groups representing the specific functional or material interests of their members. This system of political associations is likely to display the following characteristics: (1) Overlapping memberships will prevent the total domination of organizations over members. A person cannot normally be a member of several parties, but there is nothing to prevent him or her from belonging to several political associations. In fact, this is the only way for a variety of interests to be expressed directly instead of being forced into the straitjacket of a single party platform. Once the tyranny of the party is removed, real individual interests can come to the fore. (2) The multiplicity of groups means effective decentralization of power. (3) After a particular goal is achieved, or changes, or ceases to be relevant, the group will dissolve. Thus, most groups will be transient—not permanent, like parties—and so political loyalties will not tend to be inherited. (4) The socialist political system, with its many foci of decision making, is much more flexible than the traditional parliamentary system. The multiplicity of groups makes extra-parliamentary methods even more appropriate and desirable. (5) Because of (1)–(4) it is unlikely that permanent political coalitions—whose preconditions are small number and the possibility for secret deals—would be formed. Thus, after some time the prohibition of political parties will cease to be felt as a political constraint, just as the prohibition of slavery in contemporary society is not considered as a limitation of private or market freedom.

The socialist society, like any other society, will have conflicts. Conflicts are resolved by political means. This implies the formation of interest and promotional groups. Since conflicts will tend to be associated with particular issues and not with the entire existential situation of classes of people, groups will appear and disappear as the issues arise and are eliminated. The society will also have its social movements. But, again, these movements will be promoted by a multiplicity of organizations, and it is unlikely that they could be constrained to two or three rigid machines. In short, the disappearance of political parties turns out to be the precondition for overcoming the present general political passivity and replacing it with a rich and varied political life in which most members of the society—not only political activists—will participate.

IV. Socialist Democracy

Self-management in work organizations and self-government in the community do not imply that people must spend their entire lives running from one meeting to another. Yet experience indicates a very real danger that something of the kind might happen. We have already observed how a naive and primitive interpretation of self-management in the firm may lead to the identification of participation with administration. A similar *quid pro quo* is equally likely in politics. Citizens may be asked to decide on highly involved matters of education, science, or culture with regard to which they lack specialized knowledge and, often, elementary interest. As a result, (a) actual decisions may in fact be made by bureaucrats bearing no responsibility; and (b) time, energy, and motivation for the meaningful political activities of citizens may thus be irretrievably lost. The problem can be illustrated very simply by an analogy. If an owner of a business, who himself is uninterested in business administration, wishes to safeguard his interests, what will he do? He cannot avoid attending some meetings and becoming informed about business results from time to time. But except for this, he will hire managers, accountants, auditors, and others to do the work for him. Workers' councils will do the same. And the same applies, *ceteris paribus*, to politics. Citizens want to specialize in occupations for which they feel special affinities. Only very few will choose public administration as their life occupation. In general, the rational interest of citizens consists in just two components: (a) that political decisions be made in accordance with their preferences; and (b) that administration be efficient. To accomplish this, citizens elect representatives whom they trust and hire professionals for administrative jobs. From time to time they evaluate their representatives and functionaries, and those whose work is found unsatisfactory are fired. In general, self-government means not that each citizen will solve all his problems by himself, but that appropriate agencies of the society are at his disposal to do the job.

The principles described are clear and simple. It is much more difficult to apply them. For that, we need an appropriate institutional system and a set of operational rules. The sixfold functional separation of powers makes it possible for most work to be done on a professional basis, in an orderly fashion, proficiently, and with a minimum input of precious time. Now we shall supplement the institutional system described above by setting forth the operational principles for democratic participation.

1. *Principle of importance.* Participation is called for only in deciding matters of political importance. Minor and noncontroversial issues are omitted. What is important is determined by those affected. This brings us to the second principle.

2. *Principle of affected interests.* Everyone who is seriously affected by the decisions of a government should have the right to participate in that government.[45] The volume of issues falling under the scope of decision participation is further drastically reduced by observing the next principle.

3. *Principle of exception.* Inquiries, interventions, etc., are withheld as long as business proceeds normally. In other words, a large amount of decision-making power may be delegated to representatives and the administrative apparatus without abdicating this power.

4. *Principle of majority.* Decisions are taken by majority vote. This principle eliminates the tyranny of the minority, but not that of the majority. Thus we need an additional principle.

5. *Principle of the safeguarding of minority interests.* Democracy implies not only the absence of oppression by either majority or minority but also the possibility for the minority to become the majority under terms that are equal for all. The guarantee for both is provided by a set of fundamental rights and liberties.

From the 1776 Declaration of Independence and the 1789 Declaration of the Rights of Man[46] to the 1948 Universal Declaration of Human Rights adopted by the United Nations with no direct opposition,[47] and the 1966 International Covenant on Civil and Political Rights,[48] a number of human rights have been universally accepted and now represent the common property of humanity. They are no longer justified as "natural" rights and are no longer derived from "natural" law. It has become clear that these rights are the result of social progress, that they reflect the social consciousness of our epoch. These commonly accepted fundamental rights can be classified into five groups; the first two guarantee personal integrity and the remaining three regulate social intercourse. They can be enumerated as follows.

1. *Life, liberty, and security of person.* This includes freedom from arbitrary interference with privacy, family, home, or correspondence and from attacks on honor and reputation. It also includes freedom of movement and residence within the country and the right to leave the country and to return to it.

2. *Freedom of thought and conscience.* This includes religious freedom as well.

3. *Freedom of opinion and expression.* This includes freedom of speech and press and the right to seek and impart information and ideas of any kind, regardless of national frontiers. It also includes the freedom not to speak and not to listen.

4. *Freedom of peaceful assembly and association.* This includes peaceful manifestations and demonstrations.

The preceding four groups of rights, which represent the result of a long historical process of societal development, may and ought to be fully incorporated into the socialist political system. In this respect, the only important difference between bourgeois and socialist democracy is that, in the former, rights are primarily formal—which in practice works in favor of those wielding economic or political power—while, in the latter, they must be also substantive. In other words, *negative freedoms* from possible barriers to action ought to be supplemented by *positive freedoms* for citizens to do what they wish.[49] The generally high level of education, high living standards, and necessary technical facilities at everyone's disposal make positive freedoms possible.

The right to work, the right to health and educational services, and the right to choice of an occupation are also universally accepted,[50] though it is questionable whether these rights have much substance in most countries. They are economic rights, and they were mentioned or implied in our discussion of producers' and consumers' equality. There is, however, a conspicuous absence of two fundamental socialist rights: the right of self-management and the right of political self-government (and, of course, a more general freedom from exploitation).[51] The reasons are obvious. Another political right is also largely absent and deserves special mention and discussion.

5. *The right of information.* A citizen has the right to receive information about anything that affects his interests. This means access to the documents of his work organization and access to the files of any administrative agency dealing with matters that concern him. More generally, this right implies also that the press, in its capacity as an agency of the society, must have access to all information gathered by the state except in strictly specified cases related to security. The press and other mass media have not only the right to gather information but also the obligation to disseminate it. A self-governing society cannot function if citizens are not fully and correctly informed.

Media of mass communication have become an extremely important lever of political power in modern times. Those who have money and/or control the state can effectively control the mass media. Those who control the mass media can control the formation of public opinion. Ideas are produced, advertised, and sold just as are commodities. Information can be biased, or just plainly false—or not given at all. If we add the effect of commissioned educators, writers, priests, and propagandists of one kind or another, it becomes clear that public opinion can be effectively manufactured. And those who wield power do not leave this opportunity unexploited. A socialist society cannot tolerate this state of affairs.[52]

If we summarize our findings concerning the mass media scattered throughout this chapter, we can conclude that the media perform the following functions:

1. The mass media are the chief institution of nonparty elections. They provide a two-way communication between the voters and the candidates, and serve as an instrument of interest articulation.

2. By discovering administrative irregularities and breaches of law, the media are an extremely important organ of social control.

3. More generally, the media are the most important instrument of (nonstatistical) information gathering, transmission, and dissemination in the society. This includes advertisement information as well.

4. On the basis of points 1–3 and by critical evaluation of legislative activities and administrative practices, the media exert a crucial influence on the formation of public opinion.

The four functions enumerated give the mass media a special role in socialist society, a role that requires appropriate institutionalization. The details of such an institutionalization fall outside the scope of this study. Suffice it to mention that the media, like the courts, must be free of political control and of control by money. Social supervision of the mass media is performed by the respective people's commissioner.

* * *

This completes our analysis of the fundamental problems of socialist democracy. It is important to note that self-government is not a panacea. It creates its own problems and dangers. Under certain conditions, participation may increase oppression, as Arnold Tannenbaum has noted.[53] If minority rights are not properly safeguarded, this is likely to happen rather often. Next, equalization of the distribution of political power does not necessarily imply that actual preferences will be maximized. Election paradoxes whereby less desirable policies or candidates win the majority vote are well known. The path that leads from basic principles to satisfactory technical implementation is neither easy nor fast, particularly in social environments. Also, the equal distribution of power—if institutions are designed in a technically deficient way or social conditions are adverse—may reduce rather than increase a community's power to solve its problems. Yet, if there are definite risks involved in participatory arrangements, there are also enormous possibilities for further progress. Remove participation and these possibilities are destroyed. Oppressiveness may increase, but it need not. Without participation, relations are oppressive almost by definition, even under an ideally benevolent dictator. Preferences *may* not be maximized, but without participation they *cannot* be maximized. Technical efficiency may decrease, but it need not; without participation, however, enormous developmental potentials simply cannot be exploited.

12

Planning cum *Market*

It is still generally believed, both in the East and in the West, by both experts and laymen, that planning and market represent two incompatible forms of organization. In this respect, the neoclassical position is well expressed by English liberal economist Lionel Robbins:

> The alleged advantage of economic "planning"—namely that it offers certainty with regard to the future—depends upon the assumption that under "planning" the present controlling forces, the choices of individual spenders and savers, are themselves brought under the control of the planners. Therefore, the paradox presents itself: either the planner is destitute of the instruments of calculating the ends of the community he intends to serve, or, if he restores the instruments, he removes the raison d'être of the "plan."[1]

According to the vulgar Marxist version of this same viewpoint, the private market implies anarchy in production and generates capitalist relationship, and should be replaced by state planning. Private property can only be—and therefore must be—supplanted by state property, so that autonomous individual decisions give way to central, hierarchically structured decisions of the state.[2]

As we proceed, it will become clear that the paradox and anarchy belong to ideology and apologetics and not to scientific thinking.

I. Market Failures

If consumers are sovereign in their choices, they will spend their incomes on the assortments of goods and services that maximally satisfy their needs. If producers are free in their economic activities, they will combine purchased inputs so as to minimize costs and will produce outputs that maximize profits. The most profitable outputs will turn out to be exactly those that are most valuable for the consumers. Thus, by furthering their individual interests, by maximizing their *private* gains, the actors in the market automatically maximize *social* welfare. This laissez-faire vision of the market, defined by Adam Smith as the "invisible hand," is the basic market model of classical and neoclassical economics.

We know that actual capitalist economies diverge widely from this model. The reasons for the divergence are analytically rather simple. In order to work, the model requires an environment of certainty, availability of full information to the actors, instantaneous adjustments, and divisibility of all commodities. The real world is different; decisions must be made under uncertainty, information is costly, adjustments occur with considerable lags, and investment is often lumpy. As a result, production is subject to business cycles, many people are unemployed, monopolies and advertisement distort price and output structures, and economic welfare obviously is substantially lower than it could be otherwise.

Why has such a misleading model existed for so long? There are at least three reasons. First of all, it serves ideological needs well (think of Robbins!). It "proves" that capitalist systems maximize economic welfare. Second, it serves as a useful methodological device. Economic reality is so complex that it must be drastically simplified to be analytically tractable. The construction of the model and study of the conditions under which it might be valid have helped to build an ingenious economic science. Third, the model may be used as a standard of comparison. This is the use to which I am going to put it. We shall encounter a paradox somewhat different from that of Robbins. It will turn out that efficient operation of the market is possible only in a planned socialist economy! Let us proceed by examining the imperfections and failures of the ordinary market.

1. *Consumers' choices are not correct.* Consumers' choices are often irrational, shaped by habit and custom and lack of knowledge. The use of narcotic drugs and liquors, conspicuous consumption, and the purchase of foods of little nutritive value in relation to the price paid are frequently quoted examples. If medical services must be paid for by the user, health is frequently neglected in favor of some trivial consumption item. Books are bought and read, and theater performances attended only by those introduced to them. Education is appreciated only by the educated. As Maurice Dobbs points out:

> the consumer and his wants are a social product, moulded both by the commodities which enter into his experience and by the social standards and customs amongst which he has been reared. Thus, in shaping the course of development, economic policy inevitably shapes the changing pattern of consumers' wants.[3]

If our choices are socially determined, then we had better consider how to control the forces responsible for this determination and stop flattering ourselves as to how much individual sovereignty we enjoy.

2. *Producers' choices are not correct.* Uncertainty and lack of knowledge generate windfall gains and losses. Even if the prices of current goods are known, those of future goods are not. Hence, the plans of economic agents will be inconsistent, which renders efficient allocation of resources impossible. The concentration of market power generates monopolies, with the accompanying exploitation of consumers and other producers. As Marx and Keynes have shown, the sum of individual gains may result in a societal loss. This happens when, for instance, aggregate saving is greater than aggregate investment. Since demand does not match available supply, production falls and workers become unemployed. The only cure against unemployment and periodic slumps is social planning.

3. *Markets are unstable.* This instability is caused by the special characteristics of products. If supply and demand are very inelastic, as for staple foods, a slight deficit will increase prices sharply and a slight surplus will depress them just as sharply. If the production time is long—as for rubber, coffee, pork, ships—the so-called cobweb cycle tends to develop. And, if indivisibilities are great, as in heavy industry, investment cycles will appear. Consequently, to preserve the smooth operation of the market, the regulation of prices and investment will often be necessary.

4. *Money prices may not exist or may not be applicable.* Even in a universal market economy, not everything has a money price. If I cultivate a beautiful garden, my neighbor will enjoy it too. If I produce unpleasant noise in my garden, my neighbor's satisfaction will be reduced. Since we live in a society, our activities affect our fellow citizens, and often these effects cannot be appropriated. Occasionally, considerable differences arise between real social cost and money cost and between real social benefit and price. Air pollution, occupational diseases, and depletion of aesthetic values may appear on the cost side, while the enjoyment of economic and social equality, security from disease, and employment security will appear on the benefit side. So-called public goods also come under this heading. The cost of providing a public good does not increase at all, or does not increase appreciably, if the number of consumers increases. Alternatively, no individual must reduce his consumption of the good because of the consumption of an additional con-

sumer. Clean air, lighthouses, and national defense are examples. In such cases, the ordinary market mechanism with transactions between buyers and sellers breaks down.

5. *Technological and pecuniary externalities appear.* Here prices are applicable in principle, but production does not react properly, and an uncontrolled price system leads to uneconomic production solutions. Static externalities are to be found in external economies and diseconomies in current production which profit-maximizing firms do not take into account, and in uncaptured effects of new industrial locations. Examples are familiar. If an industry supplier operates under the conditions of economies of scale (as in the steel industry), its expanded operations will benefit the industry purchaser (say, the coal industry) in the form of lower costs. A hydroelectric power station may help farmers by increasing the supply of water, or it may cause damage by changing the climate. An oil refinery may spoil tourism, a chemical factory may kill fish. Two complementary factories at one location are likely to be more efficient than just one, or each at two different locations. In all such cases, prices and the market do not generate rational solutions; the intervention of a planning authority is necessary.

One particular, dynamic externality has so far eluded the attention of market theorists. It is a consequence of the limited capacity of any economy to absorb investment. The marginal efficiency of an additional unit of investment to a particular firm may be high and positive, while at the same time it is negative for the economy as a whole. This happens when organizational strains and resource scarcities reduce the aggregate output of all other firms by more than the increase in output in the investing firm. No market signal exists for the communication of this information.[4]

6. *Social decisions by their nature replace individual decisions.* Two vitally important decisions remain that should be made in every economy and that in a socialist economy cannot be left to the free play of market forces. Every price system will produce a certain distribution of income among the members of the community, and a certain division of social product between the investment and consumption parts. In a socialist economy, the *optimum* is required in both cases.

The above analysis leads to the conclusion that: (a) the price mechanism operates rather inefficiently; (b) it breaks down occasionally in the sphere of production (wrong signals); (c) it most definitely breaks down in the sphere of distribution (since distribution decisions are in principle social, while market organization presupposes decentralized individualistic decisions). This is a rather formidable list of shortcomings. The market seems scarcely acceptable for socialism. When the market goes wrong, all we can do is to introduce planning. If this is so, shouldn't we opt for planning right away and forget about the market?

The answer is No. First of all, the choice is not either/or. Second, we have found (central) planning to be rather inefficient as well (chapter 6). Then, perhaps, a combination of the two—a sort of mixed economy? That would imply an eclecticism for which there is no need. We wish to preserve essential consumer sovereignty because socialism is based on the preferences of the individuals who constitute the society. We also wish to preserve the autonomy of producers, since this is the precondition for self-management. When these are taken together, we need a market. But not a laissez-faire market. We need a market that will perform the two functions just stated, neither less nor more. In other words, we need *the market as a planning device* in a strictly defined sphere of priorities. In order to make it work properly, the six imperfections of the market should be corrected by planning interventions. This, in turn, means that we need *planning as a precondition for an efficient market.* Planning means the perfection of market choices in order to increase the economic welfare of the community. Far from being incompatible or contradictory, market and planning appear complementary, as two sides of the same coin. Neither is a goal in itself. Both are means for the appropriate organization of a socialist economy. How such an organization can be achieved will be explored in the following sections.

II. The Functions of Planning

It is obvious that economic actions must be planned at all levels. For the purpose at hand, we shall concern ourselves with planning on the national level. In doing so, we start from the assumption that, in a self-management market economy, the basic economic decision-making units—the enterprises—are completely autonomous in making their economic decisions. This does not, of course, imply a laissez-faire economy, it does not mean haphazardness, and it does not signify a naive belief in the efficiency of the "invisible hand." We dealt with that in the preceding section. But it does mean that, in coordinating the initiatives of work collectives, planning and economic policy organs can employ administrative, physical control measures only in exceptional cases, and that normally economic instruments are used, which also implies providing relevant information. We assume also that social plans have expert and social components, which are equally important. Plans prepared with insufficient expertise, with erroneous forecasts and mistaken analyses—as happens only too often throughout the world—cannot be transformed into an effective instrument of guidance by any sort of democratic self-management action. On the other hand, even when the most modern techniques of resource allocation and econometric forecasting models are used, the plan will remain without effect if it lacks a social base—which in our case means that it should be adopted in a way consistent with self-management. Planning itself ought to be participatory. By this I mean that plans are formulated at all levels and then are gradually integrated into an overall plan by an iterative process of consultation and negotiation. The remaining disagreements are eventually ironed out through political process in the Federal Assembly.

Attention should be called to the fact that planning does not reduce to the formulation of plans, which is only one—and, at that, the easiest—part of the work; it also includes the follow-up and implementation of plans. In this way, planning and economic policy comprise a unified whole.

A social plan has four basic functions:

1. The plan is above all a *forecasting instrument.* In addition to the normative part, the document of the plan must also contain a detailed analysis of economic trends with equally detailed forecasts. The purpose of every detailed publication of planning forecasts is to provide producers with insights into the most probable economic changes and to provide all the information necessary for them to formulate their own business policy. The planning bureaus that prepare these forecasts bear full professional responsibility for their accuracy and reasonableness.

2. The plan as a forecasting instrument is at the same time an *instrument for the coordination of economic decisions.* Only the part of the plan that relates to state organs is compulsory, and only for those organs. For everyone else, it provides only economic guidance. The social plan is worked out in a participatory fashion, however, which implies prior harmonization of the development progress of various regions, economic associations, and firms. Once the plan is finished, it represents not only a projection of probable change but also a projection of

mutually agreed change. The more successful this preliminary harmonization, the greater the probability that the plan will be fulfilled.

3. On the basis of forecasts of possible development and coordination of the initiatives of elementary economic decision-making units, modern methods of economic analysis, together with consultation with all relevant social agents, should be used to determine which economic changes would be optimal from the standpoint of the country as a whole. When this is determined, the appropriate economic instruments are chosen, their effects are quantified, and their application is adjusted to achieve the adopted social goals most efficiently. These steps comprise another basic function of the social plan: to serve as an *instrument for guiding economic development.*

4. As an elaboration of economic policy, the plan represents an *obligation for the body that has adopted it and a directive for its organs.* Insofar as the social plan is concerned, it represents an obligation of the Federal Assembly and a directive to the Federal Executive Council and the state organs subordinate to it. These organs are obliged to carry out the economic policy formulated in the Assembly or agreed upon by work organizations, states, and consumers. They are responsible for the attainment of the adopted goals—increase in production, increase in employment, maintenance of a favorable foreign trade balance, maintenance of price stability, raising of the standard of living, etc. To aid in realizing these targets, a set of efficient economic instruments is at the disposal of the planning organs. Under normal conditions, these organs bear full political and professional responsibility for any nonfulfillment of targets.

Let me add one technical point. Planning requires continuity. As new information comes along, plans should be revised to make the best use of available opportunities. The result is so-called rolling plans. If medium-term plans cover a period of five years and long-range plans twenty years, then each year the planning horizon will be shifted one more year into the future, preserving a five-year planning horizon at every moment. At the end of the original five-year plan, the long-range planning horizon will be shifted five years into the future, thus maintaining a twenty-year planning horizon for executive decisions.

Traditional election practices are not consistent with these requirements. Continual planning requires continual government. Every year, or every second year, part of the Federal

Assembly retires and a corresponding number of new representatives are elected. In this way, a "revolving" Assembly keeps track of all planning activities. The Executive Council can be fitted into the game at any time.

Social planning not only improves macroeconomic efficiency but also adds a new quality to the economic process. The liberal capitalist economy, based on an uncontrolled market, is a competitive economy. But cutthroat competition is not quite consistent with socialism, which is based on cooperation and solidarity. Both these dimensions are introduced by social planning. Competition is not eliminated, but it is directed toward improving the quality of commodities and reducing production costs, not toward driving competitors out of the market. The competitive firm cannot be bought or subordinated in other ways; it is highly unlikely that it will go bankrupt. Monopolistic behavior is impossible. Financial power is of no great avail, since the market is organized; and sound projects will always receive the necessary finance. Besides, full employment, relative certainty, and fast growth leave sufficient elbow room for everyone. Thus, there will be a strong tendency toward cooperation and division of labor. This, in itself, not only is socially desirable but usually is likely to be economically more efficient as well, particularly when coupled with the intrafirm cooperation inherent in workers' management. Empirical research comparing the behavior of groups organized along cooperative or competitive lines has indicated the advantages of the former:

> the cooperative groups met the puzzle problem more efficiently and contributed in more detail to the analysis of the human-relations problem. . . . Within the cooperative groups there was more differentiation of individual function, that is, more division of labour; in the competitive groups, on the other hand, duplication of effort was considerable, for all were equally on their own to do all that was required. Communication was smoother in the cooperative group. . . . Such experiments as Sherif's and Deutsch's give microeconomic sanction to what . . . has long been clear: That the most effective way of reducing intergroup tensions lies in mobilizing individuals into activities where cooperation is absolutely vital to success—where, in short, it is functional.[5]

Social planning makes cooperation functional and integrates workers' management into a consistent macroeconomic system.

III. Five Types of Regulatory Mechanism

An economy is a large system involving a multitude of feedbacks that have delayed effects and are subject to oscillations. The stabilization of this system and the attainment of optimal performance require that automatic stabilizers be constructed and certain regulative techniques applied. The former entails the development of a system of institutions and norms of behavior; we shall discuss this problem later. The latter concerns economic policy. The regulatory mechanisms that can be used for purposes of economic policy form the subject of the present section.

In comparison with engineering systems, an economy is extremely complicated, and hence the possibilities for completely automatic regulation are limited. The importance of economic policy is thus all the greater. The systems analogy is used to emphasize that, after decisions have been made concerning several basic social dilemmas, the solution of a problem is objectively constrained and little room is left for political bargaining.

By the very nature of the matter, it is the functioning of the system as a whole that should be regulated. Accordingly, the economies of constituent states and communes cannot develop efficiently unless basic macroeconomic decisions are made at the level of the federation. Because of participatory planning, the economic policy of the federation should be based on interstate agreements. These agreements, if they are to be effective, should be institutionalized. One of the most important instruments for the institutionalization of interstate agreements is the social plan.

So far, we have been discussing the market and the plan as the only two coordinating and regulatory mechanisms. They are, however, but two among five such mechanisms. A brief, historically interpreted description of these five mechanisms is given below. As it turns out, economic systems can be classified according to which type of mechanism is dominant in coordinating economic activity.

1. Historically, the first form of economic coordination (in modern economies) was the *laissez-faire market.* The free market served as the means for integrating the earlier fragmented feu-

dal economy into a unified national economy. In principle, the state is outside the economy, and its role is to protect property and permit unlimited private initiative. Since one can sell only what someone else wishes to buy, everyone who wants to make a profit must orient his activity so that he satisfies social needs as well as possible. It is from such reasoning that Adam Smith derived his theory of the "invisible hand": every individual "intends only his own gain, as he is in this, as in many other cases, led by an invisible hand to promote an end which was no part of his intention."[6] Motivated exclusively by personal interests, private producers nevertheless produce precisely those commodities that are necessary, and at the lowest cost of production.

2. The "invisible hand" did not prove to be especially efficient. We have already mentioned why. Periodic crises of overproduction and unemployment alternated for an entire century and a half. Growth was relatively slow (about 2 percent annually, compared with the world average of 5 percent today and of 10 percent in the most rapidly growing contemporary economies). In addition, effective (backed by money) demand is not at all identical with true social demand—it can differ greatly from social needs. Consequently, socialist critics of the capitalist market oriented themselves toward the "visible hand" as the instrument of coordination. State initiative replaced private initiative, and *central planning* replaced the market.

3. The great economic crisis at the beginning of the 1930s brought the capitalist type of economic coordination to the verge of complete collapse. Central planning and expropriation of private property were obviously not an acceptable alternative in capitalist countries. Besides, central planning had severe defects when conceived and implemented as administrative planning. An escape was found in introducing the state only partially into the economy, as an organ of *economic policy*. We may call this solution the "indirect hand."

4. The development of economic statistics, economic analysis, and the technology of gathering, processing, and distributing information enabled economic decision makers to obtain incomparably more relevant information than previously. Insofar as the market represented an information system, this technological progress meant the perfection of the market. There were two aspects to this improvement: (a) up-to-date and comprehensive economic statistics offered economic decision makers complete information about the economic situation, without a delay (whereas the old market gave partial infor-

mation belatedly); and (b) modern forecasting methods permitted a reduction of uncertainty about future wants, and thus former *ex post* decisions were elevated to *ex ante* decisions. Together, they meant that economic decision makers obtained a rather complete collection of the parameters important in making correct decisions; that is, those that would lead to the production of precisely those commodities that could be sold. We can call such improvement of the operation of the market by *organized information diffusion* among economic decision makers an improvement of the "invisible hand." The *enormously increased speed and precision of information gathering and processing,* made possible by electronic computers, has also substantially improved the "visible hand."

5. Finally, the "visible hand" can undergo a further major improvement similar to that of the "invisible hand" complemented by economic policy. This consists in various nationwide *agreements, consultation,* and *arbitration.* These constitute nonmarket means of coordination which are fundamentally different from administrative orders of the state.

These five types of economic coordination—laissez faire, administrative planning, economic policy, production of information, and nonmarket-nonstate coordination—developed in the order stated. But historical sequence is not necessarily identical with hierarchical order or evolution in the biological sense. The individual types of mechanism are complementary; the major problem is to achieve the organizational optimum. Different socioeconomic systems allow different degrees of efficiency of economic organization.

Liberal capitalism is based on the free market, which means that laissez-faire is the dominant principle of macroeconomic organization. Administrative planning is the basis for *etatism,* in which state bureaucrats replace individual entrepreneurs as organizers of production. The Keynesian revolution in the theory of economic policy made it possible to submit market instability to relatively efficient control by the state as an organ of economic policy. Together with the creation of state (public) corporations and the ever-greater use of *ex post* and *ex ante* information systems, this led to the so-called *mixed economies* (or "welfare states") characteristic of contemporary highly developed capitalist countries. Finally, a *socialist economy* should be characterized by optimal use of all five types of coordinating mechanisms in order to maximize the welfare of the members of the social community.

IV. The Behavior of the Worker-Managed Firm

In chapter 6, section II, we studied the comparative efficiency of the worker-managed firm. In chapter 8, we analyzed in detail the organizational problems of the worker-managed firm. In the present chapter, we must inquire into the market behavior of this type of firm. For, surely, if the firm does badly when exposed to market forces, its supposedly superior efficiency must be questioned. That is exactly what the adversaries of workers' management have done. The theory of the worker-managed firm is the only theoretical issue concerning the economics of workers' management that has been subjected to extensive international debate. Ever since Benjamin Ward analyzed his Illyrian firm and obtained some strange results,[7] these findings have been taken as prima facie evidence of the inferior efficiency of the worker-managed firm.[8] Let me briefly reproduce the argument.

Consider a firm with a simple production function with two variable inputs, labor (x_1) and other resources (x_2),

$$q = f(x_1, x_2). \tag{1}$$

There is also fixed cost k, which may be interpreted as depreciation or as capital tax. Profit appears to be

$$\pi = pq - (wx_1 + p_2x_2 + k), \tag{2}$$

where p is the price of output, w is the wage rate, and p_2 is the price of the other variable input. In the neoclassical literature, it is generally assumed that a capitalist firm maximizes short-run profit. Empirical research shows it to be highly doubtful that modern capitalist firms behave in this way,[9] and therefore, in order to be precise, I shall talk of "neoclassical firms." If profit is to be maximized, the first-order conditions are the familiar marginal equations,

$$\begin{aligned} \frac{\partial \pi}{\partial x_1} &= 0, \rightarrow pq_1 = w, \\ \frac{\partial \pi}{\partial x_2} &= 0, \rightarrow pq_2 = p_2. \end{aligned} \tag{3}$$

The second-order conditions are satisfied if diminishing returns are assumed, as will be done throughout.

An analysis of conditions (3) shows that: (a) an increase in product prices increases output and employment; (b) an increase in factor prices decreases output and employment; (c) a change in fixed cost produces no effect, since k does not appear in the conditions; and (d) labor is treated the same as any other resource; there is complete symmetry.

Let us now change the status of the firm and replace neoclassical management by a workers' council. Since wages do not exist, we cannot establish profit. Asking himself what an objective function for the new entrepreneur might be, Ward decided that it should be income per worker:

$$\text{(2a)} \qquad y = \frac{pq - (p_2x_2 + k)}{x_1}.$$

He was not quite sure that the actual Yugoslav firm, to which the theory referred, maximized y, and so he preferred to talk about the "Illyrian firm," which is the term I shall adopt as well. The Illyrian firm is assumed to maximize income per worker, which leads to new first-order conditions:

$$\text{(3a)} \qquad \begin{aligned} \frac{\partial y}{\partial x_1} &= 0, \rightarrow pq_1 = \frac{pq - (p_2x_2 + k)}{x_1} = y, \\ \frac{\partial y}{\partial x_2} &= 0, \rightarrow pq_2 = p_2. \end{aligned}$$

It is evident that the second-order conditions are also satisfied.

We cannot analyze the first of conditions (3a) directly; I shall therefore transform it by rearranging terms:

$$\text{(4)} \qquad q - q_1x_1 = \frac{k}{p} + \frac{p_2x_2}{p}.$$

It is easy to see that the following is true:

$$\text{(5)} \qquad \frac{\partial}{\partial x_1}(q - q_1x_1) = -q_{11}x_1 > 0.$$

A similar analysis now produces the following results: (a) an increase in p reduces the right-hand side of equation (4); in order to preserve equilibrium, the left-hand side must also be reduced, which, according to (5), amounts to reducing employment x_1 and, consequently (by virtue of (1) above), output; (b) an increase in the factor price of other resources has the same effect as in the neoclassical firm; (c) an increase in fixed cost k increases output and employment; and (d) factors are not treated symmetrically, since wages do not occur in (3a) and the conditions are structured differently.

The entire exercise is more clearly surveyed in Table 12.

TABLE 12

Effects of Various Changes on Output and Employment

Type of change	Neoclassical firm	Illyrian firm	Worker-managed firm
Increase in product price	+	−	+
Increase in wages	−	0	0
Increase in the price of material inputs	−	−	−
Increase in fixed cost	0	+	0

The results provide the required proof of inferior efficiency. By treating labor differently from material inputs, Illyrians behave in a strange way and irreparably impair the efficiency of their firms. When product prices in the market increase, they reduce output! The economy is thus hopelessly unstable. When the government wants to increase employment, it must levy a lump sum tax! The higher the tax, the higher are output and employment. Wage policy is of no use, since Illyrians discard wages. Because $y > w$, and q_1 (Illyrian) $> q_1$ (neoclassical), where q_1 is the marginal product of labor, an Illyrian firm employs fewer workers and produces less than its capitalist counterpart. For the same reason, it uses more capital than necessary. Less employment and higher capital intensity imply, for a given time preference, a smaller rate of growth. The latter is further reduced by smaller saving due to the fact that social property makes impossible the instantaneous recuperation of capital at the market rate of interest.

How are we to evaluate the theory of the Illyrian firm and its predictions? Any meaningful theory must pass two fundamental tests: the verifiability of assumptions test and the predictability test. A theory may pass both tests and still not be a correct one. If it fails to pass one or both of them, however, it is surely not satisfactory. If its assumptions cannot be verified, the theory has no explanatory power; if its predictions are wrong, it is simply useless. The latter test is much simpler and more conclusive, and so we may consider it first. For this purpose, we rely on the empirical research concerning the Yugoslav economy.

The theory of the Illyrian firm predicts that an increase in price will reduce output. Nothing of the kind has been observed. Increases in price, as signals of unsatisfied demand, have been followed rather quickly by efforts to increase supply.

The theory also predicts that a reduction in *k* will reduce supply. It is impossible to verify or reject this prediction without a special empirical inquiry. But when the 6 percent capital tax was abolished in Yugoslavia in the 1960s, I did not observe a depressing effect on output—and to my knowledge no one reported anything close to it.

The theory predicts that the worker-managed economy will be labor saving. The Yugoslav experience shows, on the contrary, chronic overemployment in the firms. The government is constantly lamenting the "extensiveness" of production.

Where saving and investment are concerned, the theoretical prediction is again wrong. Internal saving of the firm is modest, but borrowing is enormous, so that the national saving rate oscillates around 35 percent of the gross national product (with government accounting for a negligible share). On the other hand, overinvestment tends to contribute to chronic inflation. And that is what a Keynesian economist, in contrast to a neoclassical, would have expected. The rate of interest has little to do with the time preference. A high marginal propensity to consume is conducive to growth. It is not saving that determines investment; investment generates saving. Social property and planning reduce risks and thus increase investment opportunities. Both reduce interest rates and increase the rate of growth.

It is still possible to save the Illyrian firm by introducing a free entry in the long run together with a number of other modifications, while retaining the basic assumption about maximization of income per worker.[10] It is much simpler, however, to replace the theory by another one, which corresponds more closely to the facts. Besides, there is a universally accepted rule in scientific research which states that, of two theories with equal predictive capacity, the simpler is the preferable.

When I was first challenged by my students to produce an alternative theory,[11] I asked myself not what workers should do, but what we members of workers' councils *actually* did. The answer is the following: At the beginning of an accounting period, the workers' council sets the aspiration level of personal income to be achieved. The aspiration income consists of the last period's income or some standard personal income (*w*) and a change—normally an addition—to be achieved in the current period (Δw). The aspiration income is a function of: (a) expected sales; (b) incomes in other firms; (c) incomes in the preceding and earlier years; (d) labor productivity; (e) cost of living; (f) taxation policy; and (g) longer-run prospects for income and employment expansion.

Since personal income is fixed, what remains to be done is to maximize the residual surplus.

$$\pi = pq - [(w + \Delta w)\, x_1 + p_2 x_2 + k]. \tag{6}$$

At the end of the period, aspiration income is revised upward or downward, depending on the success of the firm. Thus, we must distinguish between two types of income: accounting income ($w + \Delta w$) and the personal income actually paid ($w + \Delta w + \Delta w^*$). Only the former enters the objective function; for all practical purposes it performs the allocation role of the wage rate—without, however, being a wage rate.

A look at equation (6) suffices to persuade one that the mathematical properties of the equation are the same as those of (2): a worker-managed firm will behave like a neoclassical firm and will be equally efficient. The only distinction—yet one that has extremely important social consequences—is that labor is no longer a commodity; it is no longer sold to an employer, and so actually earned personal income does not figure in our table. In interpreting (6), one must not commit the mistake of talking about maximization of profit. The objective function used is correctly described as maximum total income subject to the constraint that accounting personal income be $w + \Delta w$.

It is of some interest to warn against committing another rather common mistake—that of identifying the maximization of surplus with the size of surplus. Maximization does not mean that surplus ought to be great, or even that it must exist. It is perfectly possible for a firm's behavior to be determined by the principle of surplus maximization, while the actual surplus is small or even decreasing—as, for instance, in Yugoslav firms after 1965. How large the surplus will be depends on the preliminary deductions from income, i.e., on aspiration personal incomes. What remains is maximized and that determines the pattern of a firm's reactions to market changes.[12]

Unlike natural science, which is always positive, social science can be normative as well. This provides one last possibility for salvaging the theory of the Illyrian firm. It may be true that actual worker-managed firms use the objective function described by (6), yet this may not be *rational;* it may be that workers *should* maximize income per employed person. Since what is rational in a capitalist environment need not be rational in a socialist environment, we encounter here the difficult problem of identifying the criteria for rationality and for determining system-specific rationality. Such a problem falls outside the scope of the present study. But at least it can be shown that (6) satisfies the criteria of neoclassical rationality. We may imagine workers' councils adopting a long-term plan that maximizes the incomes of employed workers over a collectively chosen horizon. The plan is then broken into a series of short-run plans, one for each accounting period. The resulting personal incomes represent the aspiration incomes for relevant periods.

V. The Optimum Rate of Investment

In section I, item 6, we postulated the need to arrive at the optimum distribution of income and the optimum rate of investment in a socialist economy. The first optimum was discussed in connection with consumer equality. The second will be discussed now. Its importance can hardly be overemphasized.

We saw how the neoclassical paradigm makes the discovery of the optimum distribution of income an impossible task. Similarly, it is impossible to determine the optimum rate of investment under this paradigm, except for classroom purposes. The standard approach is as follows. Fix a planning horizon within which consumption is to be maximized and apply the appropriate discount rates to the consumption stream in order to reduce future consumption to its present value. Choose the investment plan that maximizes consumption, given the constraints. Since any particular planning horizon is arbitrary, and since the utility discount rate cannot be discovered, the entire exercise ends in an impasse. Less critical authors use the market rate of interest as a substitute for the rate of time preference and a measure for the marginal efficiency of investment. But this is grossly unwarranted. As Keynes—and many before and after him—has shown, the market rate of interest is basically a monetary phenomenon and has nothing to do with the social time preference/discount rate. As for the marginal efficiency of investment (*mei*) in a growing economy, it is different for the firm and for the economy as a whole, even if all market imperfections are removed. The two *mei*'s may even differ in sign, as was already mentioned in section I, item 5. At a certain point, the investing firm will still be increasing its output (the individual *mei* is positive), while the disturbance generated will imperceptibly reduce the potential output of every other firm in the system, and the sum total of these small losses will surpass the gain of the investing firm (the social *mei* is negative).

The confusion of the two *mei*'s caused an almost universal misconception about the structural characteristics of the economy. That the marginal efficiency of investment is falling, at least after a point, is commonly accepted, of course. Since, however, *individual* firms stop investing long before their *mei* sinks to zero, it is concluded that the case of *social mei* = 0 implies such a large volume of investment that consumption will have to be drastically reduced. Thus, the starvation level would represent the upper limit of economic growth. This is simply wrong. Under normal conditions, the barrier of maximum growth (social *mei* = 0) is reached while consumption is expanding. All that can productively be done is to increase the share of investment in national product by 1 or 2 percent annually until the ratio of gross investment to gross national product reaches about 0.35 to 0.40, when no further acceleration of growth is possible. Now, small annual changes of 1 percent yield great wonders over a longer period of time. In working on the long-term Yugoslav development plan for 1960–80, I compared two investment alternatives: (a) the rate of investment remains unchanged at 23 percent; and (b) the rate of investment increases by 1 percentage point annually until it reaches 35 percent, and then remains constant.[13] The maximum discrepancy between the two consumption streams occurs in the tenth year and is equal to a one-year delay; in other words, alternative (b) achieves the same volume of consumption in the eleventh year. The two alternatives are equalized in annual consumption in the fourteenth year. If the gain in consumption in the remaining twenty-three years is compared with the consumption sacrificed in the first fourteen years, we obtain a ratio as high as 50:1. Suppose a referendum is held and the population is asked to approve a plan that, in its worst year, calls for a one-year delay in achieving the possible consumption level but, over the life of the plan, promises a gain in consumption fifty times larger than the consumption sacrificed in the early years of the period. It is highly likely that the plan will be accepted.

We now have all the elements to solve the problem of optimum saving and investment. The following assumptions will be made.[14]

1. Consumption is maximized over the life span of the members of the community. This is justified either by holding

a national referendum or by assuming a welfare function which implies that it is better to consume more rather than less over one's lifetime if no real hardships are involved. In reality, some periods of life may be more demanding than others (and, of course, we do not know exactly how long we shall be living). We may admit all that and assume only that deviations in the needs of various individuals compensate for each other so that, on average, the society behaves so as to maximize the consumption of each generation.

2. The community is democratic, which implies that every consumer has one vote. In modern communities, the average life expectancy of individuals alive at any particular moment of time will be somewhere between thirty-five and fifty years. This is, at the same time, the generation's life span with respect to which consumption will be maximized.

3. Since the investment absorption capacity is limited, the marginal efficiency of investment for the economy must fall as investment per unit of time increases. It drops less rapidly if the rate of technological progress is higher, but it falls in any case.[15]

4. In the real world, the uncertainty of outcomes of investment decisions increases with the length of the planning horizon. The long-term development plans worked out so far rarely go beyond a horizon of twenty years, and almost never beyond twenty-five years. This practice implies a belief that future events become so uncertain after twenty to twenty-five years that the programming or forecasting of these events cannot possibly improve present-day investment decisions.

5. It follows that the relevant time horizon for output maximization is twenty to twenty-five years. Consequently, the marginal efficiency of investment must be driven to zero with respect to this time period.

6. Since the life span of every generation is considerably longer than its planning horizon, every generation maximizes not only output but, quite probably, consumption as well. Within twenty to twenty-five years consumption is not maximized, because a part of output is used for investment that is not brought to fruition within that period. When the investment maturation period is short enough, that investment will generate consumer goods—either directly or indirectly through further investment—within the remaining years of the generation's life span.[16] Thus, every generation will maximize its total consumption, if it is taken into account that every newborn baby pushes the end point of the generation's life span further ahead.

These six points lead to a straightforward conclusion: The characteristics of the real world are such that output maximization decisions coincide with consumption maximization decisions if we agree that each generation's consumption maximization is the proper target for a national investment policy. Of course, there is no logical need for us to agree on that. But the target and the assumptions involved seem to be rather realistic—certainly considerably more realistic than the assumptions generally found in economic theorizing.

One word of clarification is perhaps necessary. Consumption maximization is justified as an endeavor to satisfy the material needs of the community as fast as possible in order to increase maximally the realm of freedom of every person. This has nothing to do with the reckless growthmanship that generates the destruction of resources, international tensions, and ecological pollution. These three undesirable effects are not the result of growth as such, but of a specific social organization of growth. Investment may be used for environmental improvement, inventions may be oriented toward the conservation of resources, and increased affluence may be used to help those who lag behind.

Technically, the optimum rate of investment is determined by the point on the investment curve at which the social marginal efficiency of investment with respect to the period of twenty to twenty-five years becomes zero. As already mentioned, under normal circumstances such an investment policy cannot imply a reduction of consumption, not even temporarily. Once put into full operation, it produces a share of gross investment in gross national product of about 35 to 40 percent, and an annual rate of growth of output and consumption of about 10 percent, if recent experience and national income statistics may be trusted.

The point *mei* = 0 cannot be determined directly and rigorously, since repeated experiments under unchanged conditions usually cannot be carried out in economics. This point can be approximated fairly closely by indirect methods, however—for example, by observing changes in the maturation periods of individual investment projects, by examining changes in the average and marginal capital coefficients of total and new investments, by examining changes in capacity utilization, and by comparing national performance with those of other countries. The precision of such methods might not be particularly satisfactory, but are the measurement errors in the natural sciences substantially different?

13

Macroeconomic Organization

I. Four Basic Institutions

As usual, we start with a brief historical survey. The development of market economy was accompanied by the ideology of laissez-faire, by the theory of the "invisible hand," and by so-called Say's law, which postulated that every production not only increases the supply of goods but also creates the demand for them. Violent cyclical oscillations during the entire nineteenth century did not prevent the appearance of neoclassical economics in the 1870s. Neoclassical economics preached automatic stabilization of the economy by marginal adjustment and culminated in an aesthetically pleasing general equilibrium theory developed by Léon Walras. On a more practical level, however, people had already become aware of the problems, and in the second half of the century governments began to regulate monetary affairs by establishing central or national banks. Usually one of the existing private banks was selected and transformed into a semipublic or public institution. By the time of the First World War, it had already become pretty clear that monetary policy was indispensable to stability and that inherent market forces—whatever they were—would not do. But monetary theory was never really integrated into the dominant neoclassical theory. Besides, it was believed that monetary policy was not only necessary but also sufficient.

This illusion was thoroughly dispelled by the Great Slump of the 1930s. Soon Keynes discovered that Say's law was fallacious,[1] and that equilibrium often occurs at an underemployment level. Keynes explained why, under the usual circumstances, monetary policy alone would not be able to transform an underemployment equilibrium into a full employment one. To solve the problem, he introduced fiscal policy into the game.

Explaining *actual* saving by the time preferences of the population has been one of the cherished tenets of neoclassical economics until our time. Economic theorists in this century—like their colleagues in the last century—have not been worried by the extreme fluctuations of "time preferences" as reflected in the negative saving rate during the American slump and the

35 percent saving rate during the Japanese boom. Keynes explained the mystery by showing that in industrialized countries the cause of the low investment rate was not high time preference, but the reverse; in other words, that too much saving was responsible for too little investment. It looked like Hegelian dialectics, but it was in fact hard positive economics. Yet, in their "pure theory" sections, textbooks still determine the *national* saving rate by *individual* time preferences.

Potentially, Keynesian full employment economics was also growth economics because, given the rate of technological progress, the increase in the labor force uniquely determines the maximum possible growth of output—as was later elaborated in the Harrod-Domar type of model building. Actually, however, Keynes never went beyond short-term equilibrium analysis. In his time, economies grew at rates between 2 and 4 percent per annum. Rates between 5 and 10 percent—common in our era—would appear to Keynes and his contemporaries (recall the appeal of the stagnation theory) as unreal, fantastic, impossible, not worth bothering about.

Post-Keynesian economics did little to fill the gap. Soviet-type administrative planning was neither appealing nor efficient in a highly developed country. Yet the problem is rather obvious and can be formulated in two questions: Why shouldn't fiscal policy be used as an instrument of growth? Why shouldn't the government establish a separate investment authority resembling the monetary authority embodied in the national bank?

We are now prepared to proceed straight to institution building. There are many economic institutions, of course. A number of them, and their interlinkages, will be described in the next chapter. But four of these institutions are basic and in fact determine the functioning of the entire system. One of them is concerned with producing plans. The next two apply economic policies designed to implement the plans; one of them deals primarily with short-term adjustments, and the other with long-run changes. The fourth institution settles specific disputes.

1. *The Planning Bureau.* The Planning Bureau is an information-producing establishment. But unlike the Statistical Office, it produces information about the future: forecasts and development plans. The Planning Bureau has no administrative power whatsoever. Its sole function is to do *ex ante* what the market does *ex post,* and to do it much better. In other words, the task of the Planning Bureau is to accomplish *ex ante* coordination of economic activities on the basis of the relevant set of preferences. If the bureau's forecasts are good, the mere

existence of a plan will act as a powerful coordinating device. What is still left can be accomplished by the remaining three institutions.

2. *The National Bank.* The National Bank must supply the economy with adequate amounts of domestic and foreign money. It serves as a lender of last resort and so saves the monetary system from periodic breakdowns. In controlling the money supply, the National Bank also exerts important influence on general economic stability. The control of prices is perhaps the most important task in this respect. Yet control of the money supply must be strictly qualified. The quantity theory of money explained inflation as due to an oversupply of money. Keynes's inflationary gap was not far from this interpretation. And such an explanation is not untrue. Thus, monetary restriction appeared as an obvious remedy. When applied, however, it usually produced contraction of economic activities and unemployment. It was then discovered that inflation can also be generated by structural disproportions, and that monetary policy is powerless to cope with such inflation. The third type of inflation is caused by disproportions in income distribution.[2] This is usually discussed under the heading of cost-push inflation, together with some less important forms. It is clear that monetary policy cannot handle this case either.

An analogy may aid in understanding the function of the National Bank. A car engine cannot run without oil. Similarly, business transactions cannot be performed without money. If the supply of oil is inadequate, the engine may suffer damage and may even break down. Thus, pumping oil into the engine is of vital importance. But if the engine does not run properly, no amount of oil will eliminate the trouble. The engine itself must be repaired. The damage the National Bank can cause by pursuing incorrect policies is much greater than the help it can provide in overcoming difficulties by correct policies. It is an institution of marginal and short-term adjustments.

In addition to prices, the bank can also try to control investment (and aggregate demand) by manipulating discount interest rates. Empirical studies, however, have shown that investment demand is highly inelastic to interest rate changes. What matters is not the rate of interest but profitable investment opportunities (in industrialized countries) or the availability of investment money with reasonable rates for lenders (in developing countries).

3. *The Development Fund.* While the bank alone may not be terribly efficient, in conjunction with a Development Fund it

can produce miraculous results. The fund supplements the monetary operations of the bank by stabilizing investment, aggregate demand, balance of payments, and those prices whose changes were due to structural disproportions. In the long run, the fund is responsible for achieving the desired rate of growth.

The fund's activities replace fiscal policy, which traditionally has been conducted by the Ministry of Finance. This policy generally is so closely tied up with budget policy that theoretical analysis fails to separate the two. Yet the distinction is quite clear. A budget is a device by which the planned activities of government administration and various public services are financed from planned sources. Stabilization, development, and income redistribution activities are extrabudgetary and belong to the fiscal policy sphere. The first two can be handled by the fund, while the last falls exclusively within the province of the Assembly.

If the Development Fund is established as a separate investment authority, certain conditions must be fulfilled. The fund cannot invent new taxes or change tax progression and, in general, cannot affect income distribution among social groups or segments of the economy. But it can manipulate surtaxes so as to equilibrate aggregate demand and supply. The fund operates within the confines of the social welfare function defined by the Assembly. It is responsible for stability and growth under conditions of Pareto-type efficiency. Increasing efficiency without disturbing distribution—this is the goal. Theoretically, this goal is not completely unambiguous, and in practice deviations cannot be avoided. But the situation is not substantially different from that in the monetary field, where the National Bank has come to be universally accepted as an independent monetary authority.

There are four sets of objectives the fund can fulfill: implementation of investment programs, short-term investment in working capital for special purposes, operating subsidy schemes and compensations, influence of aggregate demand and supply (by surplus absorption and deficit spending, replacing former budget surpluses and deficits). Investment finance comes from the repayment of loans, earmarked taxes, and various kinds of borrowing.

In organizational terms, the fund is a policymaking, not a business institution; a financial and not an administrative one. The actual administration of loans is left to commercial banks, and the actual administration of taxes to the Secretariat for Finance. Short-term economic policy requires close cooperation among the three institutions. While the secretariat is preparing the budget, the fund formulates its annual intervention program and the bank prepares financial flow forecasts. The administrative budget, investment intervention program (including subsidies), and financial flows forecasts represent three components of an annual development plan. The annual plans represent operational breakdowns of a medium-term development plan prepared by the Planning Bureau.

4. *The Arbitration Board for Incomes and Prices.* A self-managed economy can work properly only if the outcomes of business ventures are reasonably predictable (assuming that the ventures fit into the general framework of the plan, that they are in no way extravagant, etc.). More precisely, the income earned ought to be the result of work and not of haphazard and uncontrollable forces. The government and its agencies are responsible for assuring that such conditions obtain in the economy.

If uncertainties are too great, work organizations will earn windfall gains or suffer windfall losses. The case of gains is not difficult to handle; the collectives will not complain, and most of the gains will be absorbed automatically by progressive wage bill taxation anyhow. Unjustified losses are an entirely different matter; workers will demand normal incomes, and no automatic negative progressive taxes exist in order to amortize losses. Thus, windfall losses, or unjustified reduction of incomes, are likely to represent a permanent source of political trouble. This is true when the government fails to undertake the appropriate action. It is even more true when windfall losses are generated by deliberate government action, such as fixing the prices of some commodities, introducing import quotas, or abandoning a particular spending program. If nothing is done, the moral basis—and, consequently, the efficiency—of economic policy will be seriously impaired. There will be a tendency to force redress for losses by forming pressure groups, plans will be disregarded, and the government will become overcautious and irresponsible, passing the initiative and the responsibility to the Assembly, which is not equipped to handle day-to-day business.

The proper solution is to set up an Arbitration Board for Incomes and Prices, which will settle the disputes. Since a fairly simple set of rules and criteria can be established,[3] and income and price effects can be measured, arbitration—and not political confrontation in the Assembly—is the right approach. The board is an independent institution, composed of qualified representatives of the relevant interest groups (government, unions, business, academia) and is entrusted to handle complaints against discriminatory measures of government agencies and requests for the establishment of equal opportunity conditions for conducting business. The board can order the government to change a particular policy or measure and/or to compensate the party that suffered losses. Compensations are paid out of the Development Fund.

II. The Federation: Three Basic Functions of Economic Policy

In guiding the economy, the federation has three basic tasks: (1) *equalizing the conditions of economic activity,* without which there is no distribution according to work and monopolistic exploitation arises; (2) viewed from the short run, *ensuring market equilibrium,* without which task (1) is impossible or the autonomy of work organizations is destroyed; (3) viewed from the long run, *ensuring economic growth,* without which tasks (1) and (2) and the building of socialism are impossible.

These tasks are not easy or simple, and so there will be a permanent tendency on the part of economic policy organs to blame others, particularly firms, for economic failures. If mistaken investments occur, the enterprises that undertook them and the banks that financed them are blamed without correcting this phenomenon or dealing with the fact that the production-investment behavior of economic organizations is a function of the economic system and economic policy. If prices rise, firms are blamed for driving prices up. If personal incomes rise faster than the productivity of labor, work collectives are blamed for insufficient social consciousness. If the economy becomes illiquid, exports too little, or imports too much, the firms are blamed for failing to adapt to the intentions of the reform and to adhere to recommendations and political resolutions. While it is understandable from a psychological standpoint, such behavior on the part of governmental agencies is also conditioned by a widespread confusion as to the nature of economic policy and the requirements of the social division of labor. Even if it cannot issue administrative orders, the government is responsible for the performance of the economy because sufficiently powerful instruments of economic guidance are available. On the other hand, the *autonomy of the firm* does not imply any responsibility for the *macroeconomic* consequences of its actions. Work collectives operate under certain conditions that are given to them as parameters for decision making. Taking into account these parameters, they make their decisions led by their material interests. Precisely because the motivation for economic activity comes from material interests, bureaucratic subordination becomes unnecessary and real autonomy possible. But the satisfaction of some partial interests must not harm other partial interests; otherwise, exploitation occurs and this is incompatible with socialism. Whether exploitation will occur or not, as well as whether the decisions of self-managed work organizations will lead to economic equilibrium and growth, depends on the institutions and the parameters of the system. And for that, the organs of the community bear responsibility.

More specifically, the three basic functions imply the following:

1. *Equalizing the conditions of economic activity* means organizing the economy so that all economic decision-making units earn income under the same starting conditions. Insofar as differences in income appear, they will be the result of differences in work and entrepreneurship and not the result of external conditions work collectives cannot control. To achieve an equalization of conditions, it is necessary (a) to ensure stability of the economy; (b) to eliminate administrative interventions and particularly frequent changes in regulations resulting in changes in the parameters of economic activity; and (c) to prevent the formation of monopolies and eliminate gross market imperfections.

The degree of equality of conditions of economic activity is objectively rather simple to determine. The device is the same as that used in determining distribution according to work (chapter 9). The average income of all industries (with a statistically satisfactory number of establishments) should be equal across the economy.

Equalization of economic conditions includes compensations for damages to industries adversely affected by the interventions of the government. It also includes regional equalization of development. It does not, however, preclude favoring or disfavoring certain production when this is an accepted goal of the social plan.

2. In an interdependent system such as an economy, very little can be done independently at individual points. The business success of each individual enterprise is in good part predetermined by the functioning of the economic system as a whole. If that system functions poorly, then the effort of the

collective and the expertise or skill of the enterprise's management cannot assure exceptional business results. In this context, ensuring *market equilibrium* means: (a) achieving full employment of the labor force and other factors of production; (b) stabilizing price; and (c) achieving balance of payments equilibrium. To attain these goals, it is not enough to construct an adequate economic system; suitable anticyclical policy against stagnation and unemployment, on the one hand, and against inflation, on the other, must also be undertaken. The task can be solved by the appropriate combination of monetary, credit, fiscal, and income policies.

3. *Economic development* is the ultimate test of the progressiveness of a socioeconomic system. If socialism is to survive, its rate of economic development must be superior to that of any alternative system. Full employment is not sufficient. Social systems that lag in economic development necessarily decline. On the other side, the world economy models itself according to those systems that expand fastest. Quasi-philosophical debates on whether development is desirable or not are beside the point. The fact is that people want economic development and, if they do not get it, they react violently. The rather fashionable worry that development will lead to ecological disaster is grotesquely untrue: air, water, and so on can be either polluted or purified—it all depends on policy, not on development. The familiar argument of academic economists that growth requires investment, that an increase in investment means a reduction in consumption, and that consumers will not tolerate such reductions, is fallacious. In the economies that are growing fastest, real personal income—and, consequently, consumption—also expands faster than elsewhere. Besides, it was shown earlier (chapter 12, section V) that the maximum rate of growth maximizes the life-time consumption of every generation.

Growth is not identical with development, but it is a necessary precondition for it. Both represent the responsibility of the federation.

III. The Federation: Institutions

A self-managed economy can be visualized as a gravitational system in which the parliament represents the center of gravity and producing units comprise the periphery. There is no physical contact between the center and the periphery. The force of gravity, which insures the stability of the system, consists of material (and nonmaterial) interests of producers. States represent similar gravitational systems that move within the overall system. In this way, the system as a whole behaves as a polycentric system. The analogy should not be carried too far, however; there are also significant differences between a cosmic and an economic system. One of these differences is that, in an economic system, there are five specific types of linkage between the center and the periphery. We have already discussed them earlier (chapter 12, section III). They are administrative, economic-regulatory, market, informational, and negotiation-arbitration linkages. Institutions and linkages taken together provide for the "automatic" regulation of an economic system.

The task of the federation is to integrate the functioning of all subsystems and thus to ensure the overall functioning of the entire system. In carrying out this task, the federation performs the three functions discussed in the preceding section. All three functions require that uniform decisions be made for the entire economic territory of the country. But the uniformity of decisions does not predetermine the way in which they are made. The mode of decision making can be autocratic, oligarchic, or democratic and participatory. In particular, the federation is not identical with the federal government, nor are centralized decisions necessarily characterized by official arbitrariness.

In examining an institutional model of the federation, we can again conform to the historical order in which the coordinating links appeared. We start with the completely autonomous enterprise in the free market and a state that stands outside the economy and concerns itself exclusively with public administration. Since the market is inherently unstable, regulation is necessary. This is the concern primarily (but not exclusively) of the state. Hence, the state establishes a certain number of organs that specialize in various aspects of economic policy. These organs are connected by administrative links and are obliged to execute the directions of the political center. How that center ought to look and how it should make decisions was investigated in chapter 10.

In Figure 6, the box in the center represents the Federal Assembly, whose executive arm is the Federal Executive Council. It deals with three separate sets of problems. One set relates to traditional governmental activity. I call it *public administration,* and it includes foreign relations, defense, and public administration proper. The second set relates to what may be termed

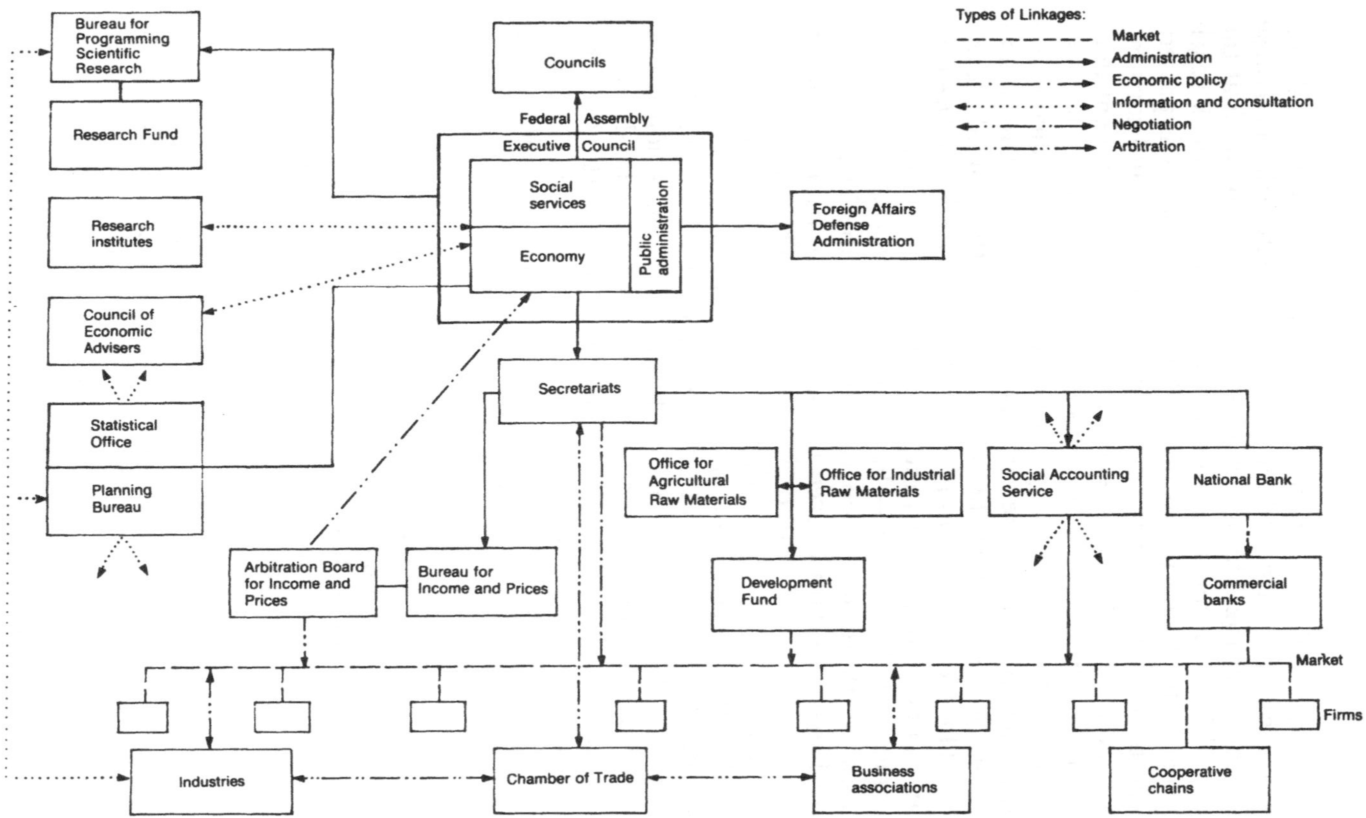

Figure 6. *Federal institutions.*

social services. These include education, medical care, social welfare, science, culture, and the like. It is characteristic of all these activities that they do not require day-to-day regulation at the federal level. From time to time the constituent states reach agreements on specific issues, and a framework law is passed; everything else remains the concern of the states (and consumers) themselves. For this reason, the federal government does not have secretariats for various social affairs but sets up non-administrative coordinating bodies, which may be called councils. What remains is the *economy,* which requires careful and continual regulation at the overall—that is, the federal—level.

The federal government establishes *economic secretariats* to carry out economic policy measures. In a market economy, one segment of the market—the money market—has special significance; therefore, a separate institution, the *National Bank,* which has a certain degree of independence from the Secretariat for Finance, is founded for its control. The National Bank regulates the functioning of the system of commercial banks, which enter directly into the market. The lawfulness of the activity of enterprises and other institutions is controlled most simply by the control of money flows. Each transaction is registered, and periodically routine checks are made by the *Social Accounting Service,* which alone among federal institutions establishes direct administrative contact with economic decision-making units. Such contact occurs because of the SAS's role as inspector; hence, this administrative contact represents not command, but rather checking. At the same time, the SAS is an exceptionally important source of information about business transactions. The computerization of the SAS makes it possible for economic policy organs to have almost instantaneous information about the state of the economy.

The market still would not function well even with the institutions enumerated so far. The economy is constantly subjected to certain shocks that create disturbances individual enterprises and their associations are not able to eliminate. As a result, general societal—i.e., federal—intervention is again necessary. The most suitable form for such intervention is one or more institutions that handle buffer stocks and administer price support programs designed to stabilize prices. The *Office for Agricultural Raw Materials* smoothes out fluctuations in the supply of agricultural products by means of its buffer stocks. In addition, the office conducts a program of protective and guaranteed minimum prices for agricultural products, through which stable and equalized conditions are created for farmers in spite of the great instability of production (agricultural output may easily oscillate as much as ±20 percent). The *Office for Industrial Raw Materials* has a similar task, except that in this case it works to eliminate disturbances that arise mostly because of fluctuations of prices and supply conditions on the world market.

In order for the system described to function well, one more institution is needed to prevent abuses by monopolies—whether state bodies or individual enterprises—that occur inevitably in the market. This institution is the *Arbitration Board for Incomes and Prices,* which, upon the demand of interested parties, will decide on proper incomes and prices. The arbitration board is composed of representatives of work organizations, trade unions (if they exist), institutions of higher learning, and government agencies; they are appointed by the Assembly for a limited period and their decisions are definitive and binding on all, including the government. The arbitration board is the guarantee that government bodies will in fact act to equalize the conditions of economic activity. If the government adopts measures that discriminate against some industry, that industry will turn to the board, which will make an estimate of the damages. If policies applied in the market put an industry in an unfavorable position and the government fails to undertake the necessary corrective measures, the board will determine the facts and designate a deadline for resolving the problem. The board is also a suitable body for determining the level of compensation. If the government has to carry out some important but unpopular measures, it can seek the prior judgment of the board and, with its consent, can overcome the resistance of privileged groups more effectively than otherwise. The board will determine the level of protective and guaranteed minimum prices in agriculture, representative income differentials according to qualifications, etc. In short, arbitration will make it possible to avoid political pressures, unprincipled compromises, and irresponsible decisions, which occur when the solution of the problems described is left exclusively to governmental bodies. The board can rely in its work on an expert body such as the Price Bureau.

The battery of institutions described so far would allow for relatively stable but slow growth. If the rate of growth by some chance were to increase, disproportions would appear, and the resulting structural disequilibrium would cause instability and again reduce growth. In order to achieve high rates of growth, it is necessary to harmonize economic decisions *ex ante,* to apply science to the maximum in developing modern technology and in managing the economy, and to ensure the necessary proportions in productive capacities, both regionally and in individual industries. To specify all this in the social plan is necessary, of course, but not sufficient. We also need a policy device to ensure that planned targets are attained.

A large part of investment has a gestation period of under two years. Thus, if some plants are not built on time and the economy is growing slowly, the insufficiency of supply can be covered without great difficulty by increasing imports temporarily. However, the construction of a large hydroelectric power plant or steel mill, or the opening of a sizable mine, requires five to seven years or even more. In addition, large investment funds are needed for such projects and for the transportation infrastructure. If these funds are not secured on time, if construction is not begun on time, and if the economy is growing rapidly, such large disproportions will appear in the material balance of the country that the balance of payments will be unable to bear them, and the unavoidable result will be powerful inflationary pressure along with a deceleration of growth. Still other negative consequences will follow. On the one hand, the lack of large concentrations of capital will lead to the construction of atomized, unprofitable plants. On the other, attempts to achieve sufficiently large concentrations of capital will lead to the formation of production and financial monopolies outside of social control.

The obvious solution is to establish a *Federal Development Fund,* whose tasks would be: (a) to participate in financing those projects that require an exceptionally large concentration of capital and/or long period of construction; (b) to intervene in eliminating disproportions in capacity when, for any reason, the market fails to succeed sufficiently in balancing supply and demand; (c) to help eliminate regional disproportions; and (d) to provide finance for some other corrections of market imperfections.

The *Federal Planning Bureau* is responsible for *ex ante* coordination of economic decisions. Its function is primarily informational, and it has communication links with the planning bureaus of states and consumer and business associations. Information about the past is collected and analyzed by the *Federal Statistical Office.* A *Council of Economic Advisers* introduces qualified independent economic thinking into government administration. A *Bureau for Programming Scientific Research,* together with a corresponding fund, ensures an orientation toward the types of research that are most useful for the country.

These comprise the major federal institutions. The economy, on its side, also creates some institutions that fill the gap between the market and the federal political center. These include, first of all, *cooperative chains*—usually one large finalizer with many cooperating firms—which represent vertically integrated market subsystems and which lead to a more lasting structuring of the market. There are also *business associations*, with the usual functions of horizontal integration. The task of the *Chamber of Trade* is to harmonize the interests of industries and to influence current economic policy by representing the economy in consultations with the government. Finally, in this scheme *industries* represent a particular type of business association, whose task is to integrate certain functions as well as to preserve the individuality of enterprises. The modern economy does not tolerate atomization but demands integration. Integration through merger, however, means the creation of large concentrations of economic power, the establishment of monopolies, and the liquidation of self-management. A solution to the problem is for enterprises to preserve their business independence and integrate only those two functions for which direct coordination is essential: (a) basic research and development work, which is the precondition for constant technological improvements in a given industry; and (b) the forecasting of supply and demand and effective penetration of the domestic and foreign markets. To achieve coordination with regard to the former, the R&D departments of industries are linked directly to the Bureau for Programming Scientific Research; for the latter, the planning departments of industries are linked to the Federal Planning Bureau. These links are informational and consultative, enabling all parties to keep fully informed and continually to harmonize the majority of decisions or uncover areas of disagreement. When such conflicts do occur, the Chamber of Trade and state executive bodies undertake the task of finding a satisfactory solution. In that way, the system of permanent planning is completed.

IV. The State

The state has a political center and a structure similar to that at the federal level. Functions are divided between the state and the federation in such a way that the federation is responsible primarily for foreign relations (foreign affairs and defense), while the state is responsible for domestic affairs (justice and public order).

Since the majority of federal institutions in the economic sphere are engaged in equalizing the conditions for the conduct of business and stabilizing the market—which can be achieved only by centralized decision making for the country as a whole—the state is freed of these activities. As a result, its institutional structure in the economic sphere is much simpler. In the area of economic development, the basic task of the state is to achieve even development over its territory. A *state development fund* serves this purpose. The state can also accelerate economic development to some degree by attracting investors from other areas and from abroad through tax exemptions and favorable treatment (by solving communal problems, training labor, participating in loans, etc.).

In the area of market stabilization, the state can intervene by creating a *mutual reserve fund*, which is used to cover losses and reorganize unprofitable enterprises. It is desirable, however, not to stop at the redistribution of funds, but to form alongside the funds personnel exchanges or special bureaus for business organization that would offer failing enterprises complete financial, technical, and personnel aid, including replacement of the entire management.

While the function of the state in the economic sphere is, by the nature of things, relatively modest, it plays a rather basic role in the sphere of social services. State bodies formulate and carry out policy in the fields of education, culture, health, etc. The task of the federation, aside from coordination, is only to ensure financially (by grants-in-aid from the federal budget) and legislatively certain minimum health and educational standards for the population of underdeveloped regions. It may be desirable for the state assemblies to have three chambers in the House of Producers, rather than one, as at the federation level. These chambers would specialize in economics; in education, science, and culture; and in health, social welfare, and related problems.

To separate the state from social services in some way—in order to avoid the patronage of political bodies, which is always desirable if possible—*interest unions* may be formed. Interest unions are comprised of representatives of all relevant societal interests acting as trustees. The assembly, by political decision, allocates funds to individual types of services. Interest unions receive these funds and pay them out on behalf of consumers for the services provided by schools, hospitals, museums, etc. Such a system has several consequences: (a) the separation of the state from the final users of the funds prevents autocratic

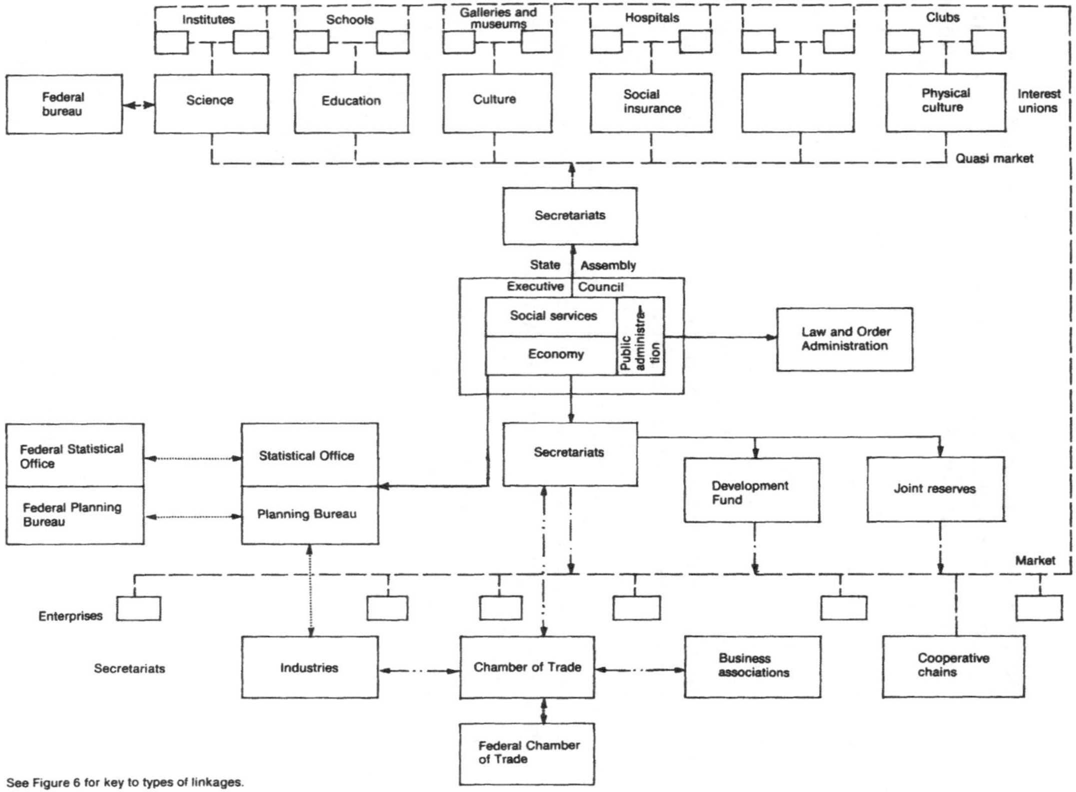

See Figure 6 for key to types of linkages.

Figure 7. *State institutions.*

rule by the administrative-political apparatus in this delicate sphere; (b) work collectives in the sector of social services in principle are placed in the same economic position as work collectives in the productive sector; they do not beg for budgetary grants, they sell their services; (c) the replacement of budgetary financing by contractual agreements develops consciousness of the economic aspects of educational, medical, and other activities, and can lead to more efficient use of scarce resources; (d) in contrast to the market sector, where distribution according to work prevails, in the consumption of social services distribution is based upon need, on the whole. In a socialist society, a young person ought to be educated and a sick person cured regardless of their property or political standing. This communist principle of distribution and the market stimuli to efficiency in production can be reconciled by the system of interest unions. Here unions buy services from producers for consumers in a quasi-market fashion.

There are also direct links between the market and nonmarket sectors. They may not be very important in quantitative terms, but they are very significant in terms of the autonomy of producers and freedom of choice of consumers. Work collectives may purchase the services of the nonmarket sector directly; enterprises may organize social service establishments, participate in interest unions, and establish independent funding for special purposes (corresponding to foundations in private ownership economies).[4]

Universities, educational services, culture, and health are of fundamental importance for the life of a people and are just as fundamental for the building of socialism. Technology is the same in all social systems. Equal or differentiated opportunities for education and for health protection distinguish the classless from the class society. For this reason, while it is the task of the federation to maintain good performance of the overall system, the daily task of the state is to instill socialist content into the system. The political analysis carried out earlier (chapter 10) can only strengthen this conclusion.

V. The Commune

As we move down the levels of state organization, from the federation through the state to the commune, government gradually loses the attributes of political authority and becomes more and more an organization for the provision of public services. The great bulk of public services is provided at the communal level. At the same time, this is the level that comes closest to the conditions of genuine political democracy. The ancient polis finds its successor in the modern commune. Not, of course, in the sense that citizens congregate in the town square to pass laws and discuss war and peace, but in the sense that the commune is autonomous and not a part of a hierarchy, that its functionaries are elected and personally known to its citizens, and that anyone may attend the sessions of the communal assembly, and criticize and raise issues of special concern to him through his neighborhood council. Hierarchical autonomy means that state or federal organs cannot issue orders to communal authorities and the communal constitution cannot be restricted by laws but only by state and federal constitutions. Commune, as polis, is "an aggregate of citizens, or in other words of men possessing access to office and therefore either actual or possible rulers."[5]

Since the commune is primarily an organization serving its members, it may be convenient to define the tasks of the commune in terms of services. In this sense, the commune has five tasks:

1. The first task is the allocation of communal resources in order to solve various *economic* problems. As mentioned earlier, the first of the three citizenships in a socialist state is the communal citizenship. If an individual is left without means of survival, his commune must take care of him. If workers become unemployed, the commune must provide them with the new jobs. The commune guarantees loans for the firms located on its territory. It helps to establish new firms and to attract investors from outside. This concern with economic development is motivated not only by the need to secure enough jobs, but also by the need to obtain funds to finance various communal services. For this purpose the commune has its own sources of taxation, independent from those of the state or the federation.[6] One of the economic responsibilities of the commune is to supervise failing enterprises. If an enterprise suffers permanent losses, the commune may let it go bankrupt. It will rarely permit this, however, because it is then obliged to provide new jobs for the unemployed workers. Thus, the commune normally will bail the enterprise out. In doing so, it will temporarily suspend workers' management, appoint caretaker management, and obtain reconstruction loans from the mutual reserve fund of the state. After the enterprise is put on its feet again, it is handed

over to the workers. To a certain extent the commune also regulates incomes and prices by improving taxes and by operating communal services.

2. If the first task was to provide the jobs, the second is to take care of the minds and bodies of its citizens. The corresponding activities were denoted earlier as *social services*. These include the provision of child-care facilities, schools, hospitals, social welfare institutions, museums, art galleries, theaters, sports fields and other recreational facilities, and the like. Since the commune is self-governed, citizens have full scope for organizing their cultural life and their medical facilities in the way they wish. Full scope, but subject to material constraints. Since in economically poor communities citizens would be arbitrarily penalized, the larger society must intervene with grants-in-aid. These grants are designed to secure acceptable standards of social services with objective economic conditions taken into account. But the community in question may always go beyond these standards by financing extra expenditures out of extra taxes or incurring public debt.

3. The third task is to provide special *communal services*, which represent the basis for material conditions of life in a particular locality. These include housing; electricity, water, and heat supply; transportation and communication facilities; shopping centers; and the like.

4. *Justice and order* are the fourth task. Citizens may wish to have good judges, efficient public prosecutors, and reliable police. Judges are selected by the Recruitment Board, but are paid out of communal funds. The public prosecutor is elected by the communal assembly. The police are subordinated to communal authorities. Passports, documents of citizenship, birth certificates, and other similar documents are issued and administered by communal offices.

5. Finally, the commune must *integrate* all the various activities carried out within its territory into one harmonious whole. For this, it has an assembly, which serves as a court of appeal for conflicts among various bodies, organizations, and interests. The assembly has two houses. The House of Citizens is based on neighborhoods. The House of Producers consists of representatives elected by work organizations. The first deals exclusively with problems under item 4 above; the latter, primarily with those under item 1. Particular issues falling under other headings may come under the jurisdiction of either. In many cases, decisions will be made in joint sessions.

The solution of various problems may require cooperation among several communes. When this cooperation is more permanent in nature, communes will establish associations of communes.

* * *

The institutional model designed in the last three sections is based on my personal planning experience. As such, it is colored by the institutions with which I am familiar. But it is not a copy of any particular economy in existence. Some of the institutions described have yet to be established. The organization suggested must not be interpreted as a ready-made blueprint to be copied directly but rather as a project to be adapted and modified in many ways before it is applied under the enormously varying social, political, economic, and historical conditions in specific countries.

PART FOUR

The Period of Transition

Men make their own history, but they do not make it just as they please, under circumstances chosen by themselves, but rather under conditions immediately encountered, given and transmitted from the past. The tradition of all dead generations weighs like a nightmare on the brains of the living.

MARX, *The Eighteenth Brumaire of Louis Bonaparte* (1852)

The emancipation of the working classes must be conquered by the working classes themselves.

MARX, Preamble of the Provisional Rules of the International (1864)

Co-operative factories furnish proof that the capitalist has become . . . redundant as a functionary in production. . . . In a co-operative factory the antagonistic nature of the labour of supervision disappears, because the manager is paid by the labourers instead of representing capital counterposed to them.

MARX, *Capital,* vol. 3

14

Historical Scenario

I. Doctrine and Reality

A. The "Marxist" Doctrine of Transition

Until about the First World War, the world socialist movement was concentrated in Western Europe and was bred on the revolutionary traditions of the nineteenth century. After the war the movement split into two main currents, one revolutionary and the other reformist. The causes for this schism were to be found in: (a) the rising standard of living and political democratization in the West (which made the revolution unlikely); (b) the victory of the Russian Revolution (which proved that revolution was possible); and (c) the moral fiasco of the Second International (which discredited its successors). The revolutionaries considered themselves Marxists and called adherents of the other current revisionists. Politically, the former were organized into communist parties, the latter into social democratic parties.

Social democrats indulged in day-to-day parliamentary politics and petty reforms, and never produced a coherent doctrine of socialism or the transition to it, beyond the vague phrases of more egalitarian income distribution and social justice. Communists elaborated and applied the received "Marxist" doctrine. I put the term in quotes to indicate that it represents a curious blend of genuine Marxian elements and non-Marxist and anti-Marxist ingredients introduced by Lenin, Stalin, and others. Besides, Marx as well as Engels (who lived longer) changed their views somewhat during their lives in correspondence with changing historical conditions.

Since the revolutionary doctrine is the only established doctrine of transition, and since it became—and has remained—dominant in almost all countries with successful anticapitalist[1] revolutions as well as in a number of workers' parties in other countries, it warrants special attention. Its bare essentials are given in the following set of propositions.

1. Between all social systems, there is a period of transition. But the transition from capitalism to socialism is basically dif-

ferent from all other transitional periods. In earlier times, the new system would develop, so to speak, in the womb of the old system, and the revolution acted as a midwife. Socialism, however, can be created only *after* the revolution. *No* elements of socialism are possible under capitalism. The distinguished Russian economist of the revolutionary period, Evgeny Preobrazhensky, himself a party leader and state functionary, explained the doctrine as follows:

> The bourgeois revolution is only an episode in the process of bourgeois development, which begins long before the revolution and goes on more rapidly after it. The socialist system, on the contrary, begins its chronology with the seizure of power by the proletariat. This follows from the very essence of the socialist economy as a single complex which cannot be built up molecularly within the world of capitalism. While merchant capital could develop in the pores of feudal society, while the first capitalist enterprises could function without coming into irreconcilable contradiction with the existing political structure and property forms . . . the complex of state socialist production can appear only as a result of a breaking through of the old system all along the line, only as a result of social revolution.[2]

At the time this doctrine originated (more than a century ago), it was rather plausible: with trade unions banned, strikes illegal, and no working class political party in existence, socialist reforms were clearly impossible.

2. Since the socialist mode of production cannot emerge under capitalism and no ruling class will willingly abandon its privileges, socialism can be initiated only if capitalism is destroyed by means of a violent revolution. Revolution is a result of class conflict, and so any strategy that generates social tensions and intensifies class conflict is a purposeful strategy. In general, the intensity of class conflict increases with the rise of the proletariat, the latter grows with the extent of industrialization, and so the revolutionary overthrow of capitalism is to be expected in the most developed countries. In the face of historical evidence, this last proposition had to be abandoned in the interwar period and was replaced by the "weakest link" theory: the break of the world capitalist chain occurs at the point of its weakest link.[3] Yet, such a mechanical analogy is hardly consistent with the rest of the theory and certainly leaves unexplained what happens in the most developed countries.

3. Although the timing of the revolution is indefinite, the succession of social systems is fully determinate: worn-out cap-

italism can be replaced only by socialism, *tertium non datur*. Thus, a positive theory of socialism, a design of the new system, is of lesser importance. The only really significant problem is to acquire power in order to destroy capitalism and prevent capitalist restoration.

4. The basic class conflict is that between the proletariat and the bourgeoisie. The latter is interested in preserving the system, the former has an objective interest in destroying it. Thus the transition can consist only in a revolutionary dictatorship of the proletariat. I have already pointed out that by "dictatorship" Marx meant class rule, while in its Leninist-Stalinist interpretation the term has come to mean a dictatorial political regime.

5. Since workers are the revolutionary force, they are predestined not only to destroy capitalism but also to build socialism. They are the only class equipped with a socialist consciousness. As Paul Sweezy, a distinguished American Marxist, has put it:

> These workers were assumed to have acquired, as a consequence of the capitalist accumulation process itself, certain specifically proletarian (and antibourgeois) attitudes and values: solidarity, cooperativeness, egalitarianism, etc. Historically speaking, the proletarian was seen as a "new man" formed by capitalism and possessing the interest, the will, and the ability to overthrow the system *and* to lead the way in the construction of a new socialist society.[4]

Their objective interests can be satisfied only in socialism, and therefore they will fight for socialism. Consequently, "all power to the workers."

6. Now, workers cannot rule as a class. For that purpose they need a political organization, a party. In fact, they need a vanguard party that, knowing the laws of history, will lead the society into socialism. The party, of course, needs a leadership, which acts on behalf of the working class. Since the working class is the bearer of progress, so is its party and the party's leadership. Consequently, no other progressive party can exist. As other parties cannot be progressive, they must be banned. Only one-party political regimes are compatible with the transitional period.[5] For the same reason that it does not tolerate organized opposition, the vanguard party—or, rather, its leadership—refuses to tolerate unorganized, individual opposition either. Whoever opposes the proclaimed party line is a class enemy—that is, an enemy of progress and humanity—and must be silenced.

7. Finally, a centralized political system requires centralized economic management. Private ownership is replaced by state ownership, individual initiative by central planning, bourgeois businessmen by state employees. In this way commodity production, if not eliminated, is at least transformed so as to make alienation and exploitation impossible.

Although not a model of logical perfection, the doctrine just described is reasonably consistent. Thus, whether it is valid or not depends on whether it passes the test of history.

In a critical evaluation of the doctrine, it would be beside the point to try to disentangle Marxian and non-Marxian elements. This would require an exercise in Marxology that is definitely not the task of the present study. What I wish to do is to test the doctrine against the facts. In passing, I shall also comment on some non-Marxian ingredients. Let us follow the same sequence of propositions.

1. If socialism means the expropriation of private productive property, complete proletarianization of the society, state ownership, central planning, job security, and social services—which is how the proponents of the revolutionary doctrine describe their own socialisms—then there is a lot of socialism in contemporary developed capitalist countries. All that must be done is to extend the wage-salary relationship from 80 or 90 percent to 100 percent, to extend the state property from 20 or 40 percent upward by nationalizing the remaining industries, and to strengthen the state planning machinery. Strong workers' parties exist in most of these countries; in some, they control governments and have a majority in the parliaments.

If we judge by the targets set by the First and Second internationals—eight-hour workday, six-day workweek, social and unemployment insurance, paid holidays and vacations, absolute and relative increase in wages, universal suffrage, free education, union organization, and similar others—which have been accomplished by now, we are bound to conclude that the working class is able to improve its position substantially under capitalism and thus to move toward socialism even before the revolution.

Finally, if we consider relative power positions, there is no doubt that the power of the working class has increased enormously since the days of the *Communist Manifesto*. It suffices to be reminded of the powerful unions and the ruling workers' parties. Besides, the development of various forms of workers' participation in management also proved possible—including a small but growing number of firms run entirely by workers.

In short, there is little doubt that the socialist mode of production is developing in the lap of the old system. In this respect, the transition from capitalism to socialism is no different from the transitions between earlier social systems. On the other hand, if either/or dogma—either we have a violent revolution or there is no socialism—were to be adhered to, the consequences for socialist development would be disastrous. In order to be consistent, one would have to wait for the revolution, and many political movements did exactly that. By refraining from constructive socialist activity, they did not promote socialism, but helped to preserve capitalism. The alternative would be to engage in terrorist and other disruptive activities, in order to "raise the consciousness of the masses" and "flare up the revolution." Historical experience indicates that this second method is likely to generate fascism.

An interesting suggestion was made by the Belgian Marxist Ernest Mandel. He pointed out that earlier transition societies were characterized by specific production relations and not just by combinations of the disappearing old mode and emerging new mode of production. The transition from the slave to the feudal society in western and southern Europe (during the fourth to the seventh centuries) passed through a phase of half-free and free peasantry coupled with the liberation of slaves. The transition from feudalism to capitalism in Western Europe in the fourteenth to sixteenth (in Mandel's periodization, fifteenth to seventeenth) centuries went through a phase in which the mass of producers consisted not of serfs and wage workers but free peasants and artisans engaged in nonfeudal, noncapitalist simple commodity production. Let us have a closer look at this transition period.

Its beginning was announced by the peasant uprisings in the fourteenth century—the most important of which were the French Jacquerie in 1358 and the English revolt in 1381—and it ended at about the time of the long revolution in the Netherlands in the late sixteenth century. The whole period was characterized by peasant uprisings (1307 in Italy, 1320 in France, 1323 in Flanders, 1434 in Sweden, the Hussite wars in Bohemia in 1420–34, the peasant uprising in Catalonia in 1462, the peasant war in Germany in 1525). Similarly, the following, formative, period of capitalism—the sixteenth to eighteenth centuries—which I denoted as commercial capitalism, was characterized by bourgeois revolutions: Dutch (sixteenth century), English (seventeenth century), and American and French revolutions (eighteenth century). The decay of feudalism in Western Europe began in the fourteenth century. The revival of trade after the Crusades led to the flourishing of towns and enhanced monetary economy. The latter was reflected in the great concentration of merchant capital and the establishment of the elaborate credit mechanism in the thirteenth and fourteenth centuries. Feudal lords felt an increasing need for money to buy the new and more sophisticated goods. Labor and produce rents were gradually replaced by money rents, which tended to fall with the depreciation of money. Serfs were taking refuge in the towns or were buying their freedom for money—or were even forced to do so. The less efficient manorial system collapsed and was replaced by small-scale peasant agriculture. Petty commodity production expanded in the countryside and in the towns. Its agents, independent farmers and artisans, became the driving force of the bourgeois revolutions during the next period. It is also of some interest to note that the two centuries which I denoted as the transition period between feudalism and capitalism (in terms of the mode of production) are usually described by historians as the time of humanism and renaissance (which is the corresponding ideological superstructure).

The transition society between capitalism and socialism is similarly specific. Mandel believes that it is characterized by a hybrid linking between a basically noncapitalist plan society and the commodity production that corresponds still to bourgeois distribution relations.[6] This assertion is consistent with Mandel's idea of the incompatibility of commodity production and socialism. The analysis of the present study shows that the two are not necessarily incompatible. Mandel's theory can be formulated in a much more convincing form. The fundamental characteristic of the transition society is the enormously increased role of the state in production relations. At the same time, it is obvious that state ownership and planning are both noncapitalist and nonsocialist. In this sense, organized capitalism and etatism may be considered as two forms of the transition society. The former implies transition via political democracy; the latter, via economic security.

2. The erroneousness of the prediction that revolutions will occur in the most developed countries by now has become a commonplace. Through a continuous increase in the standard of living and an equally continuous process of political democratization, mature capitalism has managed to reduce social tensions and avoid revolutions. The interwar period appears to represent a watershed. If anything, the proletariat is growing

less revolutionary and occasionally even becomes conservative (as in the United States, the most developed of all countries). The strategy of stimulating class conflict becomes meaningless and self-defeating. It alienates workers and lends legitimacy to repressive measures. The weakest-link hypothesis can be recast in a more acceptable form in the following way. As a result of capitalist development, the world has become economically integrated. In the process, social antagonisms between workers and employers at the national level have been transformed into national antagonisms between rich and poor nations at the world level. Consequently, social tensions are magnified in the poor countries, and that is where revolutions ought to be expected.

3. In the Preface to *Capital*, Marx wrote: "The country that is more developed industrially only shows, to the less developed, the image of its own future." This is no longer true. If a country such as Tanzania looks to its own future, will it find its image in the Soviet Union? in the United States? or in an as yet nonexistent socialist country—which is what Julius Nyerere and his colleagues would in fact prefer? If there is no strict determinism, then power as such, though necessary, is not sufficient. The design of the new system acquires central importance. The traditional concentration on the question of power has resulted in a number of successful revolutions. Lenin, Tito, Mao, and Castro—to name the most important and the most original revolutionary political leaders—have shown how to seize power and make the revolution victorious. Together with Stalin and a number of others, they have shown how power, once acquired, can be preserved. Given the political doctrines developed and the techniques applied, capitalist restoration is unlikely, and in fact did not occur. Yet, though by now we know quite well how to destroy capitalism, it still remains to be shown how to build socialism.

Proposition 4 involves logical *non sequiturs* that cover gaps in reasoning. It is usually handled in Hegelian terms. The class *an sich* is said to be only potentially a class, with the workers not yet aware of their social position. They become a class *für sich* when they become conscious of their identity and, consequently, of their own interests as opposed to other class interests. Now, if *für sich* is not interpreted as a tautology—which is often done but is not very useful—the "objective interest" mentioned in proposition 4 generates no predictive consequences. First of all, the identity consciousness displayed by the class "for itself" may be either correct or false. An example of the latter is shown by

American workers, who are relatively well organized and engage in a violent class struggle but who believe in capitalism.[7] Or by Russian workers, many of whom believe they are the proprietors of socialist production.[8] Suppose that consciousness is correct; then it becomes a source of objective interests. These are interpreted as objectively determined interests, i.e., as reflecting the entire life situation of a particular social group. Unlike possible subjective or irrational feelings, objective interests are rational or real or true interests, for which the criterion is the concept of human dignity and personal self-determination. In this latter sense, workers may have an "objective" interest in destroying capitalism and yet be unwilling to do so. Similarly, a person may have an objective interest, elucidated by his physician, in engaging in physical exercise and keeping slim, yet he may grow fat and die early, or keep smoking and contract lung cancer. Life situations of this sort are virtually countless. Thus current, or short-term, or subjective interests may easily diverge from objective interests and generate different action orientations; the former are not necessarily determined by the latter. "Objective interests" are often identified with "historical interests," which is an equally ambiguous phrase.[9] It implies an unwarranted historical determinism. It also begs the question of who is to interpret history and how. Any voluntaristic act of a ruling party may be—and usually is—justified by invoking the "historical interests of the working class." Finally, even if objective and historical interests are taken into account, there is still the divergence between individual and group interests to be dealt with. This divergence has been neatly elaborated in connection with the theory of the public good.[10] As a group, workers may vote for free public schools, against the aristocratic second chamber, and for nationalization. Individually they will often, if they can, send their children to exclusive private schools, enter the House of Lords, accumulate corporate stock, and thus help to preserve the old social system. It is obvious that the foregoing sequence of choices among doublets may go wrong at any stage, with the result that workers simply refuse to destroy capitalism, as the majority of German workers did in 1918–19.

Yet this is not the end of all *non sequiturs*. Even if workers possess revolutionary consciousness and are eager to destroy capitalism, it does not follow that they will build socialism—as required by proposition 5. Again, their "objective" interest and their behavior are two different things. Here it will be illuminating to continue the quotation from Sweezy begun earlier.

Challenged to support his interpretation of Marx, Sweezy was unable to do so. "It is easy to cite dozens of passages from the works of Marx and Engels affirming the revolutionary role of the proletariat in the overthrow of capitalism. I have not, however, found any which are specifically addressed to the question of the proletariat's ability or readiness to build a socialist society; and at least some of their formulations, especially those which analyze the effects of the division of labour on the worker, clearly imply a negative evaluation of the proletariat's qualifications."[11] Sweezy found Lenin to hold a similar view. In his book *What Is to Be Done*, written in 1902, Lenin argued that history showed that the working class, by its own effort alone, was able to develop only a trade union consciousness. It is the function of revolutionary intellectuals to carry the worker beyond that point and to introduce socialist consciousness into the proletariat.[12] From a *subject* of the revolution, the proletariat is thus transformed into an *instrument* of the revolution. Besides, a new difficulty arises: if an entire class has a false consciousness, how can we be sure that a small, self-appointed group will have the correct one? It is obviously quite convenient to proclaim the hegemony of a class in order to be able to rule "on behalf" of that class and follow one's own interests, whatever they may be.

If proposition 5 implies the establishment of the familiar "power of the working class"—which it does—then it involves an additional contradiction, as noted by Serge Mallet.[13] The working class can exist only if it is confronted with another, nonworking, i.e., ruling, class. For this reason, Engels could make his celebrated statement that the first act by which the working class rises into the ruling class by appropriating state power is at the same time the act by which it negates itself as a working class. Thus, the phrase "power of the working class" either is meaningless or is used to hide the fact that the working class continues to exist but that power is exercised by someone else. Who that is becomes clear from the following two propositions.

6 and 7. If the role of the vanguard party is not only to rule on behalf of the proletariat, but also to instill a socialist consciousness into workers and teach workers about their real interests, then the bearer of socialism is not the working class but the party and its leadership. Since the bearer of every social system is its ruling class, we arrive eventually at a theory consistent with the facts, though not a theory of socialist transition. If economic centralization is added to political totalitarianism,

what emerges is a system with an immense concentration of power in the hands of the ruling class. We have identified this system as etatism.

In its historical context, the revolutionary doctrine turned out to be a doctrine of building etatism, while the reformist-revisionist approach helped to preserve capitalism. Neither is of any use for our purpose, except in a negative sense. Thus, the task of formulating a theory of transition is still to be accomplished. Before we engage in that exercise, it will be necessary to analyze more thoroughly two social phenomena of fundamental importance to our subject: the revolution and the proletariat.

B. The Revolution

If social improvements do not lead to fundamental changes of the social order, we shall call them reforms. If the change is radical so that the system itself changes, we shall talk of revolution. Two characteristics of a revolution should be noted: (a) there is structural transformation, and (b) it does not occur gradually.[14] By contrast, gradualism and the absence of structural changes define reform. Revolution and reform are not opposed, however, nor are they always even clearly distinguishable. One shades into another. A cumulation of reforms is likely to result in structural changes. A peaceful revolution looks very much like a somewhat more radical reform. Finally, there is nothing in the nature of things to imply that a revolution, as compared with a sequence of reforms, is necessarily either more efficient or more desirable. When I speak of revolution, I shall assume that the structural change was not imposed by a power located outside the society in question.

As just defined, a revolution results in a radical change of dominant values, social structure, production relations, and political power as exercised by various social groups. A revolution may be violent or peaceful. Since radical changes usually require or generate a certain amount of violence, revolution is generally identified with a violent social transformation brought about by civil war. In this study, revolution will mean radical social change; its violent or nonviolent form will be obvious from the context of analysis.

It should also be noted that counterrevolution and restoration are not necessarily identical, as usually implied. A revolution (e.g., socialist) may be defeated by a counterrevolution (e.g., etatist) without that leading to the restoration of the *ancien régime* (capitalism). The Russian Revolution was shown to be a case in point.

History has recorded a score or so of violent bourgeois and anticapitalist revolutions in the last two hundred years. Most of them occurred in this century. We are thus in a much better position than nineteenth-century socialists to derive certain generalizations about revolutions.

1. Revolutions are the result of class conflicts. The exploited classes rebel against the ruling class. But the exploited classes of the old systems do not replace their masters, nor do they build new social systems. The slaves of ancient Rome rebelled occasionally, but never successfully. When the ancient society was destroyed by successive waves of barbarian attacks, slaves did not become the architects of the next, feudal order. Medieval serfs and peasants also rebelled against their masters—occasionally even with success (as in Sweden and Bulgaria)—but they did not build capitalism. The anticapitalist revolutions did not transform workers (and peasants) into the ruling class. Instead, these revolutions, like others before them, tended to produce a new ruling class. These observations are consistent with the statement by Mandel quoted earlier regarding transitional discontinuities between successive social systems.

2. Several of the inferior classes, not just one, participate in the revolution. The class interests of a class that participated in the revolution—or even triggered it—may diverge widely from the eventual outcome of the revolution. The leaders of the revolution often come from alienated groups of the ruling class or from its fringes. The seventeenth-century Puritan Revolution in England was led by the landed gentry. And for two more centuries, political power remained in the hands of the aristocracy. The leader of the revolution, Oliver Cromwell, was a gentleman farmer. But his army consisted mostly of yeomen, tenants, artisans, apprentices, and cottagers. It is among these people that we find the Levellers, who advocated the democratization of government and the leveling of all ranks. The French bourgeois revolution began as an aristocratic reaction, the *révolte nobiliaire,* and was soon radicalized. Its leaders included aristocrats like the Duke of Orléans and the marquises de Lafayette and de Condorcet, scientists like Lavoisier, journalists and, in particular, a great number of lawyers (Robespierre, Danton). In the consecutive assemblies of 1789–1794, nobles and wealthy members of the Third Estate were gradually

replaced by officeholders, lawyers, and professionals. Though at the beginning individual members of the haute bourgeoisie gave some money to finance revolutionary activities,[15] we do not find bankers and merchants among the insurgents,[16] even less industrialists, who were not very numerous anyway (the country had only twelve steam engines at the time).[17] The revolutionary batallions consisted of small artisans, journeymen and shopkeepers, urban proletariat, the so-called sansculottes, and peasants. The dividing line between petite bourgeoisie and workers was not easily noticeable at the time. The radical Jacobin clubs of 1789–95 were comprised of about 60 percent petite bourgeoisie and about 40 percent workers and peasants.[18] They, of course, fought for a society in which their small property would be preserved and secure, in which they would be independent and free and able to support their families without exploiting or being exploited. In a somewhat simplified manner, one might say that the petite bourgeoisie and their allies fought the revolutionary battles and the haute bourgeoisie, which had little to complain about under the *ancien régime*, reaped the economic and political benefits. The Revolution was really completed in 1830, when a popular uprising deposed the Bourbons and the haute bourgeoisie installed the "citizen king" Louis Philippe.

While in France at least the petite bourgeoisie participated in the fighting, in Japan this was not the case; hence its Revolution of 1868–73—characteristically termed the Meiji restoration—cannot easily be called bourgeois, since the bourgeois scarcely took part at all (except individually—most noticeable was the banker Mitsui, who gave financial aid to the anti-Shogunate party). The Japanese Revolution was carried out by the lower ranks of the aristocracy—the impoverished Samurai, who, as a class of warriors, had lost most of their functions during the more than two centuries of peace under the Tokugawa Shogunate. The foreign (Western imperialist) threat played an important role in the process. The merchants, considered inferior by the aristocrats, remained passive. Peasants fought on both sides of the restoration front. Peasant uprisings prepared the Revolution by weakening the feudal order; peasant armies fought together with Samurai armies against the Shogun. But in the early years of the Meiji era, there were 250 peasant uprisings against the new regime. Some Samurai led the Revolution, while other Samurai turned out to be its main victims. Bourgeois reforms of 1870–73 were followed by Samurai uprisings which resulted in a bloody civil war of 1874–77.

The Samurai as a societal group lost their social, economic, and political privileges.[19] The class dynamics of the Japanese Revolution provides a strong warning against naive schematization based on one or two European revolutions.

About half a century later, on another continent, the Mexican Revolution (1910–17) broke out as a result of peasant uprisings. The peculiar feature of the Mexican Revolution is that workers did not join the peasants. Instead, their Red Batallions fought against peasants and helped to save the repressive regime of Carranza in return for the official recognition of trade unions.[20] A year earlier the unions had supported the reactionary General Huerta for patriotic reasons. The peasants were defeated, but many of the demands of urban and rural revolutionaries were later satisfied. The country got a new constitution, extensive labor protection legislation, an expansion of regular education, and land reform, which moved slowly at first but ended with radical changes under President Cárdenas (1934–40).

Although quite different in many respects, with their leaders often belonging to different classes and, in one case, with no bourgeois participants at all, the four revolutions mentioned were clearly bourgeois revolutions, since they established bourgeois social orders in these countries. Similarly, the Russian Revolution of 1917 and the long Chinese Revolution, which triumphed in 1949, were ideologically and organizationally prepared by the revolutionary intelligentsia and carried out by peasants and workers (in Russia). They established new social orders in which the two classes did not become the ruling classes.

3. Revolutions do not break out when the oppression of exploited classes reaches its maximum. They break out when the feasible alternatives to oppressive circumstances become clearly perceived. This usually happens when a period of prosperity is suddenly interrupted by economic or military failures. At that moment, the conflict between the development of productive forces and the inadequacy of antiquated productive relationships reaches a climax and must be resolved.[21] Feelings of frustration and the quest for power—rather than abject misery—are the springhead of revolutionary inspiration. In the sixteenth century, the Low Countries were one of the most prosperous regions of Europe. The attempts of the Spanish Crown to increase taxes triggered a long revolution in 1572. The English Revolution was preceded by dissatisfaction on the part of wealthy London and Bristol merchants, who regarded the attempted tax reform as a threat to their prosperity and

importance. The economic prosperity before the French Revolution was interrupted by a tariff reduction in 1786, which, together with the reduction of exports to Eastern Europe and Levant because of wars in these areas, ruined many textile and metal producers, increased unemployment, and triggered economic crisis. The bad harvest in 1788, the ensuing famine, and the cold winter of 1788–89 added the misery of the poor to the dissatisfaction of the rich. A decade before the First World War, Russian industry was expanding rather fast. Military failures and the enormous sufferings caused by the war triggered the February Revolution in Russia. The Mexican Revolution of 1910 was preceded by two decades of rapid economic development: mineral and sugar production quadrupled, foreign trade and tax revenues increased by ten times. This growth was accompanied by an equally rapid widening of the gap between rich and poor. Finance and trade were controlled by foreigners and the domestic oligarchy. In the countryside, 1 percent of the population owned 85 percent of the arable land, and 95 percent of peasants were left with no land whatsoever. The urban class was prevented from participating in the political system. A revolutionary alliance between the latter and the insurgent peasants was a foregone conclusion.

4. Victorious revolutions are generally triggered by unsuccessful wars that seriously weaken the power of resistance of the old ruling class, or by national liberation wars in which an awareness of the possibility for removing the hated foreign domination generated as well the will for a radical improvement of economic and social conditions. Financial crises due to unsuccessful wars compelled Charles I to convene the Parliament and Louis XVI the Estates-General. Instead of voting additional finance for royal treasuries, the two assemblies moved to limit royal powers. In the process, the two monarchs lost their heads, and the two countries underwent revolutions. The Franco-Prussian War was followed by the Paris Commune; the military debacles of tsarist Russia generated the revolutions of 1905 and 1917. The Western military threat played a role in the Meiji Restoration, while the Chinese Revolution had to fight against Japanese occupation and American intervention. The Dutch (1572–1609) and American (1775–83) wars of independence[22] represented the first in a long series of national liberation wars that, since the Second World War, have led to social transformations in many countries (Yugoslavia, Korea, Algeria, Vietnam, Mozambique, Angola). This fact indicates that the national element in contemporary revolutions is at least as important as the social element.

5. Whatever the circumstances, revolutions are likely to erupt in only a few "innovative" countries, and are also likely to occur in a small number of countries that lag very much behind the contemporary level of development. The ruling class, naturally, is unwilling to abandon power and privileges upon request. In general, before a new system comes into existence, it is not at all certain that it will be viable. Thus, the ruling class—or an imperialist power—indulges in the self-deception that it can preserve the old system and consequently employs brute force in an attempt to do so. As a result, in the pioneering countries the conflict between the productive forces and productive relations explodes into bloody civil war. Once the viability of the new system is established, the ruling classes of other countries have no choice but to follow suit—provided their countries do not lag behind the pioneers too much in their development. Thus, several violent revolutions in pioneering countries will be followed by more or less peaceful transitions to the new system in other countries. Apart from that, in extreme cases of very backward countries, revolutions may prove to be the only means of opening up developmental possibilities and initiating a catch-up process.

6. Since the clear perception of alternatives is so vitally important, intellectuals play a large role in the creation of a revolutionary environment. These are Antonio Gramsci's organic intellectuals, whom "every class creates alongside itself."[23] The process seems to have two stages. First, the general cultural environment begins to change. The leading spirits of the epoch undermine the legitimacy of the existing order. The French Revolution was preceded by the intellectual exploits of Voltaire, of John Locke and Montesquieu, of Rousseau and the encyclopedists. Philosophers and scientists undermined customs and faith by empirical research and rational analysis. The doctrine of natural rights implied that all men are equal. Physiocrats proclaimed the economic principle of laissez faire, laissez passer. Similarly, the Russian and Chinese revolutions were preceded and prepared by socialist utopians, by Herzen and Chernishevsky, by Proudhon and Bakunin, by Marx, Engels, and a host of socialist thinkers, and by the two Internationals. They succeeded in thoroughly undermining the legitimacy of the feudal and capitalist orders. They also produced a minimum set of ideas necessary to prepare and steer the revolution.

In the second stage, this subvertive ideology begins to permeate the receptive social groups. A new and much larger group of revolutionary individuals elaborate and apply the new ideology. Lyford Edwards and Crane Brinton observe that a shift in allegiance of the intellectuals is the most reliable symptom of the coming troubles.[24] In eighteenth-century France, *sociétés de pensée* were informal groups of intellectuals who began by discussing the work of Enlightenment, then turned to political agitation, and finally helped to steer elections to the Estates-General of 1789. Monarchist absolutism was subjected to devastating criticism in the Freemason lodges and the mushrooming political reviews. A similar role was played by Puritan churches in seventeenth-century England, and by groups of populists (*narodniki*), such as Zemlia i Volia [Land and Liberty] and Narodnaia Volia [Will of the People],[25] and "nihilists," anarchists, socialists, and rebelling students in prerevolutionary Russia. Russia is a particularly interesting case because here Marxists—i.e., working class socialists—appeared before workers' organizations and the workers' movement existed. The establishment of the Petöfy Circle preceded the Hungarian uprising in 1956. All these groups were consciousness raisers. Once the importance of social consciousness is clearly grasped, there is nothing to prevent social reformers from disseminating new ideas and engaging in political activities, and so speeding up social transformation. Nothing, that is, except awareness on the part of the ruling class of the explosive potential of such intellectual activities. For this reason, every dictatorship will establish strict control of intellectuals and will ruthlessly suppress any nonconformist intellectual activity.

7. The dynamics of a revolution tend to follow a certain pattern. Even if violent, the revolution usually starts with little bloodshed (French Bastille, Russian October). Soon, however, the class that loses privileges begins to fight back. The revolutionaries are confronted with an "aristocratic conspiracy." A civil war ensues. Passions run high and produce unprecedented heroism and willingness to endure sacrifices, but also unprecedented hatred. At the same time, the movement is radicalized and moves from moderate to extreme positions. The more extreme it becomes, the greater is the need for violence. This process is likely to end in a state of terror. A general fear of being considered too moderate, "too soft," adds additional fuel to the fire of passions. People with moral scruples may be unable to stand the terror and begin to withdraw. In an emotionally charged atmosphere, this can hardly be tolerated. Not only adversaries, but also allies who do not conform completely, are treated as traitors. Caught in such a situation, the French Girondist Vergniaud, executed in 1793, made his famous observation that the revolution, like Saturn, devours its children.

The Russian Bolshevik Bukharin and his colleagues could have said the same. The revolution is "certainly the most authoritarian thing there is," remarked Engels, "it is the act whereby one part of the population imposes its will upon the other part by means of rifles, bayonets and cannon, authoritarian means, if such there be at all, and if the victorious party does not want to have fought in vain, it must maintain this rule by the terror which its arms inspire in the reactionaries."[26] The toll tends to be great. Together with heroism and self-sacrifice, the revolution generates meanness and decay of morals; all sorts of scoundrels search for a promised land. Once the revolution is successfully completed, the resulting political regime is likely to be dictatorial and power obsessed. Terror plus a religious structure of mind produce totalitarianism. To a genuine revolutionary participant, the end result may look like the result of the French Revolution appeared to Gracchus Babeuf who, at his trial in 1797, said to his judges: "My companions and I have groaned over the unhappy result of the Revolution . . . it has merely replaced a band of ancient scoundrels by a band of new ones."[27] If the revolution fails to succeed, it almost invariably ends in fascism (as in Hungary, Germany, Spain, Greece, Chile).

8. In a country with a functioning system of political liberties, there is no likelihood of a revolution. On the other hand, if the ruling class defends its privileges by brute force, the only means of fighting back is to form a clandestine political movement. All revolutions have been preceded by secret societies (in earlier times) or by illegal political parties (since the establishment of the Bolshevik Party). An illegal, clandestine party can be neither democratic nor large. (The Russian Bolshevik Party had no more than 23,000 members at the beginning of 1917,[28] and the Yugoslav Communist Party had about 12,000 members in 1941; in China, at the beginning of 1925, just before the beginning of the long revolution, there were only 900 party members.)[29] Strict centralization and hierarchical relationships are required. The leadership makes all decisions, while the members merely carry out directives. The repressive acts of state authorities and the secrecy of the organization create an atmosphere of mystical devotion and a feeling of messianism. Both exert strong influence toward a revival of religious consciousness, with all the consequences discussed earlier. This consciousness does not, and cannot, change abruptly after the revolution. Thus, a messianic dictatorship rather than a revolutionary democracy is the likely result. To be sure, the

revolution itself quickly raises the aspiration levels of broad national masses, enormously increases their political participation, and provides them with an extraordinary political experience. From this has flowed all the spontaneous attempts at self-government. Yet terror, messianism, and etatist ideology generally proved strong enough to prevent self-government from surviving and developing. There is an additional reason why this happens, a reason already pointed out by a somewhat biased but intelligent observer, Tocqueville: "A people is therefore never so disposed to increase the functions of central government as at the close of a long and bloody revolution, which, after having wrested property from the hands of its former possessors, has shaken all belief and filled the nation with fierce hatreds, conflicting interests and contending factions. The love of public tranquility becomes at such times an indiscriminate passion, and the members of the community are apt to conceive a most inordinate devotion to order."[30]

9. Finally, whether they succeed in implementing the new idea of social justice or not, all genuine social revolutions succeed in destroying the old social system, which has outlived its usefulness, and establishing a new order that makes possible more rapid economic development. Revolutions are veritable locomotives of history. They are followed by explosive economic growth, rich cultural development, and an impressive increase in political power. Seventeenth-century Netherlands and England, eighteenth-century United States and France, nineteenth-century Japan, and twentieth-century Mexico, Russia, Yugoslavia, and China are cases in point. In this sense, anticapitalist revolutions in undeveloped countries, though they failed to generate socialism, were not useless or historically irrelevant. They proved to be powerful instruments for economic growth. Initially lagging behind in economic development, etatist countries have been catching up with the capitalist early starters.

The foregoing historical analysis indicates that revolutions carry great social hazards. Successful anticapitalist revolutions have tended to result in etatism; abortive ones, in fascism. They often involve heavy losses in human lives and saddle the postrevolutionary societies with prolonged dictatorships. The only unequivocal gains are faster economic development and more egalitarian income distribution. Are the gains commensurate with the sacrifices? Shouldn't one advocate reforms instead of revolutions?

Such questions are false questions. Thus, the answers would be meaningless. For genuine social revolutions can be neither engineered nor banned. Nor can deprived people be prevented from rebelling against oppression and tyranny. In certain social situations, violent revolutions are unavoidable. What progressive movements can do is exert a certain amount of conscious control over the revolutionary process. The purpose of the foregoing analysis is not to show that revolutions are bad (since, as a rule, they do not produce socialism) or good (since they accelerate economic growth) but to provide an explanation for the observed characteristics of postrevolutionary societies and for the deep disappointments they generated. If we know the risks involved, we may perhaps be able to avoid some of them. In that event, the dynamics of the revolution may possibly be harnessed to produce more desirable results.

II. The Working Class

A. Revolutionary versus Reformist

The condition for the liberation of the Third Estate was the abolition of all estates. This implied the establishment of a bourgeois order. Similarly, the condition for the liberation of the working class is the abolition of all classes.[31] Since it is not only an exploited class but also the principal producing class of contemporary society, the working class cannot liberate itself without destroying class society as such. This implies socialism. Consequently, the working class is the bearer of socialism. This Marxian reasoning represents a powerful historical generalization. But its simplicity is deceiving and may easily be seriously misleading as well.

It is clear that the ruling class is interested in the status quo. The impetus for change can originate only in the dissatisfaction of the oppressed. Among the latter, the peasants represent the remnants of antiquated systems. The middle class—shopkeepers and artisans—together with the peasants, are being destroyed economically and disappear as a result of capitalist accumulation. It is only the factory workers, concluded the *Communist Manifesto* in 1848—the industrial proletariat—who represent the true revolutionary force.[32] They are the product of the new, most advanced mode of production—industrial production. Two additional characteristics of the industrial proletariat have been recognized. Factory workers are concentrated, disciplined (because of production discipline) and, consequently, easily organized. They do not possess property—unlike peasants—and so they have nothing to lose. These three characteristics make them *the* revolutionary class in contemporary society.[33]

There is little doubt that nineteenth-century European industrial workers were oriented toward revolution—where the term *revolution* implies both radical change and violence. The sociopolitical history of the century, in fact, comprises a long sequence of violence and counterviolence. In 1811–17 English Luddites smashed labor-saving textile machinery in revolt against the emerging capitalist order, which robbed them of what they considered to be their inalienable rights. In 1830, the July Revolution broke out in Paris, and a month later the Belgian Revolution followed. The next year and then again in 1834, there were uprisings of Lyon weavers. English Chartists fought their battles in the decade that followed. Silesian weavers revolted in 1844. The Cracow rising occurred in 1846. In 1848 barricades appeared in Paris, Vienna, and Milan; the next year, in German cities. The revolution swept all of Europe. The Paris Commune of 1871 represented the climax. The Russian Revolution of 1905 was the delayed response of a backward country. After a period of class peace in the last third of the nineteenth century, revolutionary syndicalism and general strikes in the first quarter of the present century began a new revolutionary upsurge. It reached a climax in the two Russian revolutions of 1917 and the revolutionary turmoil in the greater part of Europe immediately after the war. But then the violent, revolutionary actions of European workers came to an end. What happened?

England, the most developed country in Europe, entered the post-Napoleonic era with a sociopolitical organization close to modern totalitarianism. Workers and farmers, the majority of the population, had no political rights. Associations were banned. Spies and agents provocateurs were employed on a large scale. Mock trials produced draconian punishments. Workers' leaders were arrested. Working conditions were abominable. Real wages were low, even falling. Strikes were broken up by police and army. The proletariat naturally rebelled. Local general strikes turned into uprisings. Unions and societies operated illegally or half-legally. Organized resistance culminated in the Chartist movement. And then attitudes changed. The primitive accumulation of capital was more or less complete. New investment could be financed from profits or from the sale of shares (joint stock companies were legally acknowledged in 1855); there was no need for the entrepreneur to squeeze his own income in order to accumulate. Employers were more willing to negotiate. Real wages began to rise—increasing by 70 to 80 percent from 1850 to 1900—and the growing inequality of income distribution was arrested. Workers were no longer treated as dangerous wild animals. Suffrage was gradually extended until it became universal (for men only, of course). Unions were legalized. Eventually, workers' political parties appeared. After 1848, attempts to overthrow capitalism were replaced by a kind of class accommodation and cooperation.[34] Uneasy and antagonistic, to be sure—nevertheless, it was cooperation. This trend was interrupted around the First World War, but since then it has continued more or less unbroken.

On the Continent, the English example was followed with an appropriate delay. In the second half of the nineteenth century, unions were legally recognized in all Western European countries. At the same time, social democratic parties were established in one country after another. The new era was symbolically inaugurated by the creation of the First International in 1864. It was fully established when workers' parties began to form governments, and workers' leaders began to enter the House of Lords or its equivalents. After the Second World War, the continuously rising level of living, the reduced share of manual workers in the labor force, and the proliferation of new job categories were not conducive to a resurrection of the revolutionary spirit. "Once again," points out Paul Sweezy, "as in the period of manufacture, the proletariat is highly differentiated; and once again occupational and status consciousness has tended to submerge class consciousness."[35]

One is led to conclude that workers had a revolutionary orientation when they were too weak to overthrow the system. When their numbers increased, when they succeeded in organizing themselves into trade and political associations, even on an international level—in short, when they were strong enough for the task—they refrained from carrying it out. Why? Apparently, legality killed the revolution. Civic integration helped the proletarians to find the fatherland. If true, is this desirable? The answer will be suggested in the next chapter. In the meantime, let us consider another implication—that of the positive relation between the proletariat and socialism.

B. Different Working Classes

Again, there is very little doubt that the European working class generally has been progressive and, in particular, socialistically oriented. Labor unions organized strikes or threatened general strikes to force the ruling classes to introduce universal male suffrage in Austria, Germany, Belgium, Sweden, and elsewhere. To this extent, Marx's prediction turned out to be correct: in order to emancipate themselves *politically*, workers forced the (Western) European dominant classes to establish political democracy *for all*. In the last century, workers and their parties gave their support to Garibaldi, Kossuth, and the Polish Liberation War. In our century, they greeted the October Revolution, took a stand against Franco in Spain and against Munich concessions to Hitler, and denounced the occupation of Czechoslovakia. Urban workers resisted the appeal of naziism before 1933 better than any other social class in Germany.[36] Workers (Confédération générale du travail and the Communist Party) played the most important role in the French resistance to fascism. All labor, social democratic, and communist parties declared socialism as their ultimate goal.

The working class movement is not entirely progressive. It includes conservative groups as well, which are primarily clerically or nationalistically oriented. The latter follow the lead of their national bourgeoisies. The conservative segment is generally unimportant in Europe. The situation is very different, however, in America. Here conservatism is the rule and socialism a rather rare exception. The American phenomenon requires an explanation.

To protect their interests, workers build two types of organizations—trade unions and political parties. Unions perform two functions: one concerned with conflict resolution, the other with welfare. Unions engage in collective bargaining with employers in order to increase wages, improve working conditions, reduce working time, and prohibit child labor. If necessary, they strike against the bosses. Unions also set up various insurance schemes and pension plans, provide educational facilities, and provide help in time of need. In defending the interests of their members, the unions are clearly adversaries of the capitalist class. The stronger the unions, the greater the concessions of the employers. Yet, in neither of these two functions do the unions transcend the boundaries of the capitalist system.[37] In this sense they are conservative. Only with the appearance of the workers' party does the movement go beyond capitalism and become socialist. This contention received an almost laboratory testing in America.

In Europe the historical appearance of the working class took place in a semifeudal framework. In order to improve their socioeconomic position, workers first had to gain political rights. Fighting for their own interests, workers helped to democratize their societies. Because of their social and political position, their attitude was necessarily progressive. In the United States, on the other hand, political democracy was established before the working class appeared on the scene. Since economic development was rather rapid, workers soon emerged in large numbers. It will come as no surprise to find that as early as 1828 the first workers' party in the world (it was, in fact, locally integrated trade unions engaged in a political campaign) was created in Philadelphia. During the next six years similar parties were organized in sixty-one towns and villages. They stood for free education, the limitation of child labor, a ten-hour working day, the abolition of imprisonment for debt,[38] and the abolition of election tax. In 1832 Andrew Jackson was elected president for the second time and gave support to the requests of the workers' parties. Soon various states implemented one or another item of the workers' programs. The parties disintegrated. Later, at approximately the same time as in Europe, socialist workers' parties were founded in the United States. But they never achieved national importance. The seat of the First International was even transferred to the United States—only to disappear together with the organization in 1876. Since they had been integrated into the political system from the very beginning, American workers felt no need for a party of their own.

The second reason for the absence of powerful workers' parties in America is the abundance of land. Those who were dissatisfied could always leave, move westward, and organize their lives as they pleased. Closely connected is a great geographical mobility. This rootlessness was not, of course, conducive to the development of party and class solidarity. The fourth reason is to be found in the relatively great vertical mobility[39] made possible by the high rate of economic growth and immigration. America was a land of promise. Large masses of immigrants supplied labor for dirty, unskilled, and low-paid jobs. Those who came earlier automatically moved upward. The high rate of immigration meant also that class solidarity tended to be replaced by ethnic solidarity. Ethnic division coincided with different skills—immigrants were largely semiskilled and unskilled—and this intensified the existing conflict between craft workers and common laborers. On the other hand, high vertical mobility made the status barriers less rigid.

Finally, free public schools, a rapidly rising level of living, and the expanding economic and military power of the country generated national pride and identification with the social system. More than 80 percent of the population believe that "the American way of life is superior to that of any other country."[40]

For all these reasons the American working class, while fighting for a larger slice of the national pie, never went beyond that and never acquired a socialist class consciousness.

When, in the early 1930s, the capitalist system appeared to be breaking down and unemployment continued to mount until 15 million people were out of work, socialists and communists—few as they were—tried to organize the jobless for the revolution. But the unemployed were interested in relief and jobs, not in revolution. In the 1932 presidential election American workers did not vote for socialists or communists; their vote went to Franklin Delano Roosevelt (not without expectations that turned out to be justified). This absence of a class consciousness does not mean that class relations were idyllic. On the contrary. American businessmen were savage and ferocious adversaries in comparison with whom the European bourgeoisie appeared almost sentimental. Particularly brutal were the coal operators. Herbert Abel describes how, a year before the elections, coal operators in Harlan and Bell counties guarded the American way of life with terror: "The forces of the coal guards roam the countryside at night, terrorizing the inhabitants. Meetings are broken up with tear-gas bombs, raids are conducted almost every night with their consequent toll of deaths, houses are broken into and property confiscated, the mails are tampered with, the slightest resistance is met with the force of guns."[41] Many people were arrested for "criminal" syndicalism. Outsiders were beaten, thrown out of the county, and subjected to the seizure of property. A notorious gunman was called in and killed several people. Relief was denied to strikers. By the end of 1931, the union was smashed and the operators achieved control over their workers.[42]

In the United States union activities (collective bargaining) were completely legalized only in 1935 with the passage of the National Labor Relations Act under the Roosevelt administration. Employers organized a nationwide campaign to defeat the goals of the act. The records of a Senate investigative committee (the La Follette committee) described the situation as follows:

> The most influential business and financial interests in Los Angeles have deliberately attempted to sabotage the national labor policy of collective bargaining as expressed in the National Labor Relations Act. . . . They engaged in a series of organized con-

> spiracies to destroy labor's civil liberties. . . . They concluded alliances with the local press, local police, local law enforcement officials. . . . Organized conspiratorial interference with collective bargaining included the mass application of the common anti-union devices such as labor espionage, the use of professional strike-breakers, the use of industrial munitions, the blacklist, discriminatory discharge. . . . Behind this vast and powerful movement stood the leaders of business and industry, titular and real, the banking and financial groups, leaders of the local press and until recently many of the public officials.[43]

In coal-mining Harlan County, company guards "persecuted residents and visiting labour organizers. . . . private gangs terrorized union members . . . acting as auxiliaries to the force of privately paid deputy sheriffs," and instigated "a reign of terror directed against miners and union organizers." Hired gangs "repeatedly fired on union organizers, from ambush on public highways, in open country and in their homes. They kidnapped and assaulted union officers and dynamited the houses of union organizers," and at the same time "subverted and corrupted the office of high sheriff . . . through many extraordinary financial favors." In the country districts of California, groups financed by big business interests "proceeded with impunity to perpetuate a system of tyranny" using gunmen, espionage, and violence.[44] Maurice Dobb, from whom I take this selection of quotations, summarized other findings of the committee as follows:

> Leading American corporations spent large sums on the purchase of munitions and made a practice of employing a corp of armed guards for use against strikes and . . . union organizers. . . . the shadowing of an individual at all times and all places so as to amount to intimidation and the planting of spies in every union, with the intent not merely of espionage, but of disrupting the organization and even acting as *agents provocateurs*, were among the less menacing of their activities. They [private police] engaged in assaults upon individuals, the breaking up of meetings and demonstrations and the wrecking of trade union offices.

La Follette himself reported the "usurpation of police powers by private paid 'guards' and 'deputies,' often hired from detective agencies, many with criminal records," as being "a general practice in many parts of the country," and of "areas where no union officer can go without risk of personal violence."[45]

The brutality of class warfare does not necessarily make the exploited class progressive. In spite of many episodes of the kind just described in American labor history, unions remain conservative and are fully integrated into the system. They deal with employers in a businesslike fashion. The material interests of workers are acknowledged as legitimate; in a capitalist society everyone is expected to improve his position through competitive struggle—if he can! In return, the "prerogatives of management" are not questioned. Officials of large unions rank about the same in public opinion as proprietors, managers, and state officials.[46] Instead of in socialism, the American worker believes in private enterprise.[47] In all postwar crisis situations—the cold war, McCarthyism, the intervention in China, racism, the Vietnam war—organized American labor assumed conservative, occasionally reactionary, positions. In some cases racist attitudes can be detected.[48] It was students, intellectuals, bourgeois radicals, Negro activists—and not, as a rule, workers—who protested and who fought. While these groups marched on Washington, destroyed draft cards, and organized teach-ins, workers—with few exceptions— took a "responsible patriotic" stand, supported the government, continued to produce napalm bombs,[49] occasionally refused to load or unload Chinese ships (dockers), and sometimes beat the unpatriotic demonstrators (as did construction workers), while southern workers supported segregation. The existence of class struggle in America is obvious. This struggle is fiercer than elsewhere. But this fact does not necessarily render the working class progressive. It is in universities, not in factories, where progressive America is to be found.

Thus, historically, we can distinguish two different working classes: a progressive one in Europe and a conservative one in America. There is also a third working class to be found in colonial and generally backward countries. In such countries the small modern industrial sector, usually dominated by large foreign firms, represents an affluent island in the sea of extreme rural and urban poverty. Factory and mine workers are often literate and always enjoy an income several times higher than that of agricultural laborers and the great majority of illiterate peasants. In short, the urban proletariat are a privileged class. They can be moved by patriotic and nationalist ideas and will join the national bourgeoisie in the struggle against colonial power or imperialist domination. But they are not particularly interested in the social liberation of the great majority of the population, which lives in abject misery. Since they are in fact a special kind of middle class, these workers live under conditions that do not satisfy Marx's formula for class liberation.

C. The Consequences of Socialization

One further complication can be noted. The economic position of a class does not unequivocally determine its attitudes; nor does an inferior economic status at home render it necessarily progressive. The working classes of developed countries have a definite economic stake in the perpetuation of unequal exchange on a world scale, the victims of which are the working classes of the less developed countries.[50] Workers have more economic reasons to be chauvinistic than the bourgeoisie. Marx himself pointed out (in a letter of April 9, 1870) that "the ordinary English worker hates the Irish worker as a competitor who lowers his standard of life." It has long been observed that workers have a liberal orientation where economic issues are concerned. They favor the elimination of poverty, social security, free education, high wages, progressive taxation, and social equity. This is how they have been expected to behave since the early days of the socialist movement. It was later found, however, that their political attitudes—concerning civil liberties, international relations, etc.—are not quite so liberal. Workers proved to be intolerant, nationalistic, occasionally racist,[51] and ready to support authoritarian regimes. This fact—and history and attitude surveys indicate that it may be regarded as fact—requires explanation.

Seymour Martin Lipset observed that political authoritarianism could be based on any of the three principal modern classes.[52] The upper class was often responsible for traditional authoritarianism as expressed in monarchism. This is well known. That a deeply insecure and frustrated middle class is inclined to back fascism is also relatively well known. Working class authoritarianism runs against traditional sentiments. It has appeared in two forms, which may conveniently be called Stalinism and Peronism. Since Stalinism already was analyzed in the etatist context, let us look at Peronism—an anticapitalist nationalist populism based on an alliance between the army and lower social strata.

General Juan Perón became president of Argentina in 1946 after a coup backed by the army and the workers. Before assuming power, he had been in charge of the labor department, where he was expected to control unions and prevent strikes. Perón used this position to win the support of union leaders. During the time he was in power, Perón nationalized some industries, enacted legislation that improved workers' living standard, increased wages, protected agricultural laborers and tenants, and provided social security. The social and economic rights of the masses were written into the 1949 Constitution. Perón's orientation against foreign imperialists appealed to nationalist officers, the patriotic bourgeoisie, and workers. His main support came from the trade unions, which expanded substantially under his regime and were completely dominated by the peronistas. Perón's alignment with the urban proletariat and impoverished rural masses generated strong opposition on the part of the middle classes, big business, and landlords.

So far there is nothing particularly strange in this story of an apparently progressive leader. Yet, Perón also exalted the strong state, praised Mussolini and Hitler (who, in turn, had "an unconditional respect for Stalin's genius"),[53] and emphasized the dominant role of the leader, whose power supposedly was derived directly from the people. Peronism was scornful of parliamentarism and its "incompetent and corrupt politicians," and had little regard for constitutional legality. In 1955, Perón was deposed by alienated army officers and the church. While in exile, he was shown to have been a corrupt politician himself; this revelation, however, did not diminish the fascination Argentinian workers felt for him. Slightly less than two decades after his downfall, he was triumphantly returned to the country and installed as president. He died soon after and the country was left in chaos.

Peronism was also tried elsewhere in Latin America (as by Getulio Vargas in Brazil), though not very successfully.

Stalinism and Peronism show that workers may be demagogically exploited to act against their historical interests—though perhaps *in favor* of their short-term interests and certainly of their interests as they perceive them. The reason for this is again to be found in the socioeconomic position of the worker, which determines his psychological attitudes. A child born into a lower class—and the proletariat are such a class—is born into a hostile world. The low living standard of the family is not really very important in itself. What matters is that the society will discriminate against him. His mother is poorly educated and has little time for him. A family library is not likely to be available. Thus, he will lack verbal skills. The absence of preparatory family education and of financial means makes access to educational establishments difficult and leads to failures in competitive examinations. The family behavior pattern is likely to be authoritarian; parents apply punishments and have no time for long discussions. At the work place he is expected to obey. In order to succeed, one must do as one is told. The lesson is internalized and the hierarchical social organization is taken for granted. As a child, as well as later, he has little access to sources of information. The prevalent middle class culture is alien to him, and he feels insecure. This feeling of insecurity is magnified by the threat of unemployment. He has little reason to trust society. His personal experience teaches him that power is the only thing that matters. The atmosphere of tension and aggression present from early childhood, accompanied by poor education, is conducive to the development of ethnic prejudice, political narrow-mindedness, and a simplified vision of the world. Most American workers, for example, would not allow communists or atheists to speak at public gatherings, were against putting their books into libraries, and even favored the jailing of admitted communists.[54] The general life situation of the individual makes him intolerant (those who differ must be suspect), submissive toward those above him (otherwise the powerful will take revenge), and suspicious of every change (since it is more likely than not to cause pain). Intolerance toward nonconformity and conformity within a power hierarchy are two sides of the same coin. The lower the socioeconomic status and level of education, the more pronounced are these attitudes.[55] Participation in trade union activities and political parties modifies them and takes the edge off authoritarianism.[56] When trade unions are undeveloped and parties illegal, these attitudes are pronounced. If then a party comes along that provides security, faith, and simple solutions, its attraction will be enormous. Since under capitalism workers are socialized to respect authority, they can be used as a disciplined army to support authoritarian regimes. This is what seems to have happened in the etatist countries. Though the dictatorship is not of the proletariat but over the proletariat, there is little doubt the proletariat supports it (except where it was imposed from the outside).

So far, we have been concerned with workers' attitudes under capitalism. I have no comparable empirical information regarding workers' attitudes in an etatist environment, though they could hardly be different. It would be extremely important to know what happens after the revolution in a setting of self-management. There is just one country where we can study the problem—Yugoslavia. Jozo Županov, analyzing the survey data, found that after one generation of experience with self-management at the factory level, etatist tendencies have deep roots precisely in the working class.[57] Veljko Rus reported on other empirical research in fifteen collectives where the pro-etatist orientation of workers was obvious. More often than other professional groups, production workers held the opinion that strengthening the state was more important for further social development than increasing the power of self-managing bodies or experts.[58] Živko Marković measured the level of socialist consciousness of various social strata by assessing attitudes toward decreasing the power of the state, increasing the role of self-managing organs in work organizations, and self-government as a general principle; he obtained the following indices (where 100 represents the maximum level of socialist consciousness): peasants, 36; workers, 54; intelligentsia, 65. The socialist orientation of the humanist intelligentsia is six points higher than that of the technical intelligentsia.[59] In an ambitious research project directed by Mihailo Popović, which examined the social structure of Serbia, a number of "ideological dimensions" were used to describe social consciousness. It was assumed that values or attitudes such as an orientation toward self-government, openness toward the world, acceptance of social property, and humanism characterize socialist consciousness. Nonmanual workers were found to score significantly higher than manual workers in all these dimensions. Peasants consistently showed the lowest degree of socialist consciousness.[60] Unskilled workers were found to possess the traditional or typical working class consciousness.[61] N. Rot and N. Havelka found a nationalist orientation among high school youth whose parents were peasants or unskilled workers and an internationalist orientation among children of employees with college education.[62] Srdjan Vrcan reported that manual workers are substantially more church- and religion-oriented than intellectuals.[63] In general, the attitudes formed under capitalism persist in a self-management environment, and the ranking does not change within one generation. It should be kept in mind, however, that in general this is the very first generation of workers, since most of them are the children of peasants, and their consciousness has been shaped under the influence of traditional peasant values and attitudes. Since manual workers are less well educated, receive lower incomes, and occupy a lower socioeconomic position compared with nonmanual workers (and, within the group of manual workers, the same is true of unskilled workers and peasants compared with skilled workers), the survey data seem to indicate that increases in the level of education, standard of living, and social status are favorable to the development of socialist attitudes.

The real world phenomenon that we have analyzed is rather far removed from the romantic, almost mythical idea of the working class as portrayed by frustrated bourgeois radicals and propagandized by party demagogues. Such antiscientific romanticism can only do harm, for it prevents the derivation of reliable knowledge from an analysis of empirical facts.[64] The worker is not a born architect of socialism. If that were true, capitalism would not be an alienating and oppressive system. In order to function, capitalism must socialize workers appropriately. And that is precisely what it does—in the family, in the school, at the work place, and in public life. This socialization means the acceptance of hierarchy and obedience as supreme values.

In particular, the worker is not a messiah sent to this world to save humanity. For almost two centuries, workers have been a mercilessly oppressed and exploited human group. But the sufferings they had to endure and the ordeal they had to pass through did not—and could not—lead to a spiritual catharsis and did not turn workers into saints. Religious concepts and ethical evaluations have nothing to do with scientific socialism—and can only prolong the exploitation of the working class. Groups of people behave in certain ways not because they are inherently good or bad, progressive or reactionary, but because their objective or perceived class interests determine their behavior. Experience and empirical studies indicate that solidarity,[65] comradeship, egalitarianism, and fighting discipline are generally characteristic of manual workers. So are authoritarianism, intolerance, and conformity. The two sets of attitudes can be combined in various ways and used for various purposes. We have noted the enormous progressive potential contained in the socioeconomic position of the proletariat. We have also noted the attitudinal limitations of workers, limitations that can be exploited for reactionary purposes. How much of one or the other potential will be actualized—this is not predetermined in advance; it is not written in the Book of History before it happens. All depends on social action; men make their history themselves.

III. The New Working Class

A. Changes in the Structure of the Labor Force

Since the Second World War, the historical scene has changed once again. It became clear sometime before that the prediction of the disappearance of the middle classes was wrong. To be sure, the old middle class did almost disappear. But it was replaced by a new middle class[66] of professionals, technicians, clerical and sales personnel, and government employees, which was rapidly expanding—much more rapidly, in fact, than the working class. A simple but very consistent and pronounced change has occurred in the occupational structure of the active population. In the last century or so, the share of peasants or farmers decreased from more than 50 or 60 percent to less than 10 percent. This made possible an increase in the share of manual workers from 15 or 20 percent to about 50 percent and, at the same time, an increase in the share of the new middle class from about 5 percent to roughly one-third of the active population. When these proportions are reached, the reserves of peasant manpower are practically exhausted, and further structural shifts occur at the expense of manual workers.[67] The share of manual workers decreases, while that of nonmanual workers (should we call them workers?) increases. Similarly, the share of the commodity-producing sectors, even excluding agriculture, decreases, while that of service-producing sectors increases.[68] Labor and social democratic parties react by broadening their class base. From workers' parties they evolve into people's parties. With a lag of a decade or two, the mass communist parties begin to follow the example. A new term is introduced into the political vocabulary: that of the "working people."[69]

These changes in the structure of the labor force must have profound effects on social relations. *If the social group of manual workers shrinks, they cannot provide a basis for the development of a new social system.* Since modern manual nonindustrial workers work under the same conditions as factory workers, we are entitled to extend the concept of the industrial proletariat to all manual workers, and simply speak of the proletariat. The numerical importance of this inclusive proletariat is declining. The share of the industrial sector proper is also shrinking, of course. A social group that is becoming a diminishing minority is unlikely to harbor revolutionary attitudes. They are more likely to adopt the values of the expanding sectors and to set the goal—if not for themselves, then at least for their offspring—of quitting and moving into nonmanual occupations.

A word of explanation might be needed to avoid misunderstanding.[70] The historical working class (industrial proletariat) ceases to be the revolutionary subject. This does not imply that its revolutionary potential evaporates overnight. Nor does it imply a mechanical connection between the size of a group and its consciousness. But it does mean that, given the dynamics of social and technological change, the existing revolutionary potential of the historical working class will diminish, not increase.

The whole idea of the revolutionary role of the industrial proletariat originated from the observations that industrial production was expanding relative to other sectors, since it was superior to traditional forms of production, and that industry was creating an industrial proletariat. In the most advanced countries, neither observation is empirically true any longer for: (1) modern nonindustrial (service) production is no less advanced than industrial (commodity) production and is expanding faster; (2) within industrial (commodity) production, the share of traditional manual labor is decreasing. In order to understand what has happened, we must examine briefly the labor history of the last two centuries. For reasons explained earlier, I shall again concentrate on British labor history.[71]

B. Developmental Stages

At the beginning of the Industrial Revolution, artisans—masters and journeymen—were employed to produce more or less traditional merchandise. These people were often literate and had to undergo a relatively long period of training in the skills of their respective trades. The history of the next century or so of capitalist development proved to be the history of the gradual deskilling of workers and their transformation into factory hands. Our artisans could not know that, but they knew that they had to protect their interests. For this purpose, they combined and formed friendly societies and the first unions. Occasionally—as in the early American unions or in the first modern union in Bolivia, the National Printers' Union of 1905—both owners and apprentices were united vertically in the same union. Thus, until the late 1840s in many English towns "the actual nucleus from which the labour movement derived ideas, organization and leadership, was made up of such men as shoemakers, weavers, saddlers and harness makers, booksellers, printers, building workers, small tradesmen and the like."[72]

The enlarged market favorably affected some of the traditional trades, and so printers, tailors, cabinetmakers, bookbinders, and a few others (in England and not very differently elsewhere) preserved their craft unions until the 1860s and 1870s. The factory system, on the other hand, produced large masses of destitute workers, deprived of civil rights and mercilessly exploited. The gulf between the two groups of workers—the artisans and the laborers—was great indeed. The artisans inherited the estate consciousness, felt that they belonged to the same society as their employers, and tried to preserve their social status and, if possible, increase it.[73] The laborers felt rejected, and they themselves totally opposed the society. "The hordes of factory workers," noted Zygmunt Bauman, "were incapable of setting up stable organizations and rarely made an active appearance in the social area. When they did occur . . . such manifestations, extremely violent, were potentially explosive and imbued with threat of armed revolt and revolution."[74]

Thus, in the first half of the nineteenth century the working class, the proletariat, in the modern sense simply did not exist. It was only beginning to emerge out of a mass of petty producers, semiproletarian outworkers, small traders, and countrymen. All these exploited groups, together with the true proletarians, were called *working people* or the *laboring poor*. Though most workers were dependent on wages for their subsistence, wages were paid not as a price for labor power but as a price for commodities delivered (e.g., pieces of cloth or tons of coal). Closely related was a phenomenon which Hobsbawm denoted as co-exploitation: skilled workers acted as co-employers of their mates and unskilled workers. The engineering employer hired a "piece master," who employed craftsmen, who hired and paid their own laborers. In the cotton industry the capitalist paid a piece rate to mule spinners, who employed piecers and cleaners. And similarly in the mining, iron, pottery, and other industries. "The characteristic structure of an archaic industry such as that of Britain in the early nineteenth century is one in which all grades except the lowest labourers contain men and women who have some sort of 'profit incentive.' "[75] Straight subcontracting survived well into the next stage and began to decline only after the 1870s.

Since unions were not legalized, workers had to fight for political rights in order to be able to protect their interests. In the 1830s and 1840s the artisans of London, the factory operatives and handloom weavers of Lancashire and Yorkshire, and the coal miners of Newcastle and Wales united in the Chartist movement, pressing for universal manhood suffrage. After 1848 the movement collapsed. Thus ended the first period in the development of the new working class.

Around 1850 the construction of railways, the appearance of steamships, and the development of precision engineering resulted in the creation of new skills, and the wage differential between skilled and unskilled workers increased. During this period, it was almost exclusively skilled workers who established trade unions, which in England came to be known as the "new model unions." The first to be founded was the Amalgamated Society of Engineers in 1850. Its executive council soon made it clear that they expected employers not to "regard a society like ours with disfavour. They will begin to understand that it is not intended nor adapted, to damage their interests, but rather to advance them by elevating the character of their workmen, and proportionately lessening their own responsibilities."[76] Masses of poorly paid, unskilled workers were employed to build railways and do dirty and heavy work in the factories and elsewhere. While the journeyman artisan of the former period enjoyed a relatively high social status, the new skilled worker did not have a socially recognized status and wished to achieve one. For this reason, skilled workers accepted bourgeois values, imitated bourgeois habits, and endeavored to dissociate themselves from the rest of the working class.[77] In order to appear financially respectable, they formed relatively well endowed friendly societies and opposed strikes, which could deplete their assets.

The ruling class proved responsive. The Reform Act of 1867 enfranchised all respectable workers. The next year the Trades Union Congress was formed and consolidated the gains of the new unions. The acts of 1871 and 1875 gave the unions the appropriate legal status and the right to picket. In the latter year, the infamous Master and Servant Acts (whereby a worker could be imprisoned for breach of contract) were repealed and replaced by the Employers and Workmen Act (making breach of contract a purely civil affair). It looked as if the class war was over. But this was a delusion.

During the third period, as a result of the mechanization of industrial production, the number of skilled and unskilled jobs was reduced, while semiskilled jobs expanded. Semiskilled workers were employed to mind the machines, a task that called for dexterity rather than craftsmanship. This development culminated in the application of assembly lines and other methods of large-scale production. It was pointless for workers without specific skills to form craft unions, and they set up industrial or even general unions. The new technology required formal technical education for supervisory jobs. Thus, upward mobility was prevented and a gap was created separating the skilled workers from managerial strata. On the other hand, the work force was now much more homogeneous. Both the internal unification and the external separation, observes Bauman, transformed unions from occupational into class organizations. This changed workers' attitudes from deferential to revolutionary. The labor movement also established its separate political arm—workers' parties. Semiskilled operatives needed such organizations more than the artisans. In Europe, and to a certain extent in America as well,[78] the decades after 1900 witnessed full-fledged class warfare, with the appearance of revolutionary syndicalism in Europe and America, general strikes, occupations of factories, and actual revolutions.

After the First World War, labor representatives began to enter bourgeois governments, and workers' parties even formed their own governments. Differences between craft and industrial unions were erased, as were the differences within the working class. This was the period of a mature and unified working class that was able to defend its interests by means of powerful organizations, national unions, and political parties. Yet, these organizations were not used as instruments of radical societal transformation but rather as instruments of negotiation and, occasionally, administration of existing societies. Labor leaders as union functionaries, government ministers, and members of various governmental committees, as well as of supervisory and management boards of large corporations and nationalized industries, enjoyed high social and economic status.[79] If they quit, they did not return to the shop floor, but become civil servants or managers.[80] Collective bargaining and the possibilities for advancement reduced tensions and reintegrated the working class into the social system. Revolution was replaced by reform.

In addition to social and political factors, technological change affected the fourth developmental stage as strongly as the previous stages. The application of science and technology and production on a large scale required an increasing number of engineers and technicians, accountants and financial experts, salesmen and clerks. The proportion of the total labor force *employed in direct production* began to fall. Wage differentials between skilled and unskilled labor and between manual and clerical labor decreased. In Britain, to quote an example, the earnings of male clerks were on a par with those of skilled male workers in 1913; by 1960 they had been reduced to 86 percent of the latter. In proportion to the earnings of unskilled workers, the earnings of clerks dropped from 169 to 128 percent.[81] Workers succeeded in obtaining severance pay, vacations, and company pensions, and were given stock options—all of which used to be the privileges of salaried employees. The sharp dividing line between wage earners and salary earners was gradually blurred. The latter also began to be unionized after unionization had already spread to all manual workers and unions had been confederated nationally. Low-level white collar workers are now likely to be fired before blue collar workers. The salariat is joining the proletariat.[82]

Naturally enough, attitudes began to change as well. The traditional collectivism of manual wage earners has been weakened, and so has the traditional individualism of nonmanual employees. The two groups have converged to what John Goldthorpe and his associates call the twin focus of instrumental collectivism (the acceptance of collective union action as a means of economic protection and advancement) and family-centeredness (the acceptance of the individual conjugal family as a central life interest).[83]

So far, the changes—however important—have proceeded more or less within traditional boundaries. Work remained manual, whether skilled or unskilled. Moreover, though clerks usually have a somewhat higher education, clerical work is a kind of manual work. The next step in technological development, however, is revolutionary. Manual labor as such is replaced by machinery.[84] This is what the advent of automation means. Masses of unskilled, semiskilled, and clerical workers have already been replaced by computerized machinery. Robots begin to take the place of the hands of live workers on assembly lines. The traditional division between manual and nonmanual labor—with the former operating on things while the latter operates on symbols—begins to disappear. At his work place the modern skilled worker reads numbers, charts, and symbols as a matter of course. Engineers and economists, technicians, information-processing personnel, draftsmen, and laboratory assistants enter production in large numbers. Scientists and engineers staff even more important "research and development" departments. Systems analysts, computer programmers, and market researchers fill other departments. Technicians replace skilled workers. The proportion of the total labor force *engaged in manual work*, in controlling automatized machinery with or without clerks, begins to fall—and not only within an industry but in the national economy as a whole.[85] The traditional shops with many individual workers under the command of shop managers are replaced by small, integrated teams consisting of an engineer and several technicians. The hierarchy of power and status is replaced by a structure of specialties and, at worst, by a hierarchy of knowledge.[86]

Technological changes have been accompanied by educational changes. In developed industrial countries, full literacy was achieved long ago. Full secondary school attendance—once an important indication of middle class status as against the lower classes, which reached only primary school, if anything—has also been achieved. Access to a university education has already been provided for up to one-third or more of the population in the respective age group.[87] And when we meet workers and farmers with a college education—as we do nowadays—and when university professors, policemen, and army officers establish trade unions, we are bound to note that the age-old distinction between manual and mental labor has begun to be blurred as well. Diminishing income differentials indicate the same thing.[88] These trends should exert a profound influence on the social consciousness of the respective groups. We shall see in a moment that they do.

C. The New Working Class

Do educated and affluent workers—who often earn more than those in some traditionally middle class occupations—belong to the working or to the middle class?[89] Is the socioeconomic status of the low-paid office worker higher or lower than that of the well-paid worker on the shop floor? Are the large and increasing army of technicians of all sorts to be classified as highly skilled (manual) workers or as elementary skilled engineers? Not long ago, the answers to such questions appeared obvious. Today they are not at all straightforward. Two general answers have been suggested.

First, since the education and level of living of the working class have increased substantially and reached at least the level of the lower middle class,[90] and affluent workers have begun to adopt the middle class style of life, they ought to be classified accordingly. This is the familiar thesis of the working class aristocracy's being turned into a middle class stratum—the embourgeoisement of the working class. The second answer is exactly opposite. If unskilled workers disappear altogether, wages are replaced by monthly salaries, wage and salary differentials are substantially narrowed, and the status distinction between the office and the shop floor is eliminated, then we may begin to speak of a *new working class* composed primarily of skilled and highly skilled manual and nonmanual workers, technicians, and related categories.

The concept of the middle class implies that there is also a lower class. Yet, if the workers associated with advanced technology are promoted into the middle class, there is no lower class left, except for the remnants of former lower classes predestined to disappear. Thus, the first alternative does not leave us with a logically satisfactory classification. Nor is it empirically justified. Goldthorpe, Lockwood, and their associates—as well as other social scientists in other countries—undertook to test empirically the thesis of embourgeoisement and found the evidence to be lacking. They concluded that "assimilation into middle class society is neither in process nor, in the main, a desired objective."[91] On the other hand, if we stick to the traditional concept of the working class conceived as a product of the most advanced mode of production, and bear in mind that every economic system must have its producing class, then the concept of the new working class appears more justified. The way the concept was derived shows that it is not static. As has been observed above, the historical working class passed through four developmental phases, and in each of them it was "new" relative to the historical epoch. Not unexpectedly, these phases correspond to periods in the technological and social development of capitalism. In the process, social differentiation *within* manual labor, based on skill differences, has been gradually eroded. The formation of the contemporary "new" working class implies overcoming differences *between* manual and nonmanual labor, as well as between laborers and workers.[92] The new working class will include more and more social groups until eventually everyone will consider himself a worker—which of course will imply a complete destruction of the original meaning of the concept. At that point, the system will already function as completed socialism.

To avoid possible misunderstanding, let me stress that nothing said above should be interpreted as indicating that the old distinction and dividing lines have already been removed. They clearly have not. Nor will they disappear automatically.

The continuation of class struggle cannot be avoided, and an enormous conscious effort will be required to eradicate the distinctions, which are becoming anachronistic. This is particularly true of the most fundamental of them all—that between supervisory (and nonmanual) and other labor.[93] As mentioned in chapter 3, the main discontinuity in vertical mobility occurs precisely between manual (plus clerical) and nonmanual occupations. The new working class does not exist as yet; it is *in statu nascendi.*[94] On the other hand, the analysis in the present chapter is not oriented toward the past or the present. We are discussing here the problems of a transitional society. Consequently, we need the past only to discover inherent trends, and the present to establish the starting position. Everything else concerns the changes likely to occur in the future.

It is of some interest to realize that Marx faced a similar problem in his time. Contrary to what is generally believed, at the time Marx and Engels wrote their *Communist Manifesto,* a homogeneous industrial proletariat did not exist even in the most developed country, England. The history of unionization showed that very clearly. Maurice Dobb draws attention to the fact (also mentioned in the preceding section) that the conditions of domestic industry and of the manufactory survived into the second half of the nineteenth century. As a consequence,

> the majority of the workers retained the marks of the earlier period of capitalism, alike in their habits and interests, the nature of the employment relation and the circumstances of their exploitation. Capacity for enduring organization or long-sighted policies remained undeveloped; the horizon of interest was apt to be the trade and even the locality, rather than the class; and the survival of the individual traditions of the artisan and the craftsman, with the ambition to become himself a small employer, was for long an obstacle to any firm and widespread growth of trade unionism, let alone of class consciousness. . . . As late as 1870 the immediate employer of many workers was not the large capitalist but the intermediate subcontractor who was both an employee and in turn a small employer of labour. In fact, the skilled worker of the middle nineteenth century tended to be in some measure a subcontractor, and in psychology and outlook bore the marks of this status.[95]

Only at the time of Marx's death had the working class begun to assume the character of a factory proletariat. Then, as now, the theory had to be developed while the respective proletariat was still in the process of being born.

D. New Social Conflicts

The conceptual framework developed above makes it possible to explain some recent events, such as the student rebellion that swept all industrialized countries around 1968; workers and technicians, even engineers,[96] marching together in crisis situations; and the new sources of conflict (such as the lack of satisfaction in work). Let us analyze briefly the first and the last of these three.

Youth has always been radical, and for obvious reasons. Why is this radicalization—particularly among educated youth—much more widespread today than it used to be? The university environment is no more repressive today than in the past. Why do we have student rebellion now and not before, at least not to the same extent? The answer to this question is connected closely with the changing social role of the intelligentsia.

As long as only a few people acquire a university education, and many of them belong to or are associated with the dominant class anyway, the intelligentsia is a special social stratum closely associated with the ruling class. To be sure, outstanding individual intellectuals have played a progressive and revolutionary role in all social systems throughout history. But the majority of their colleagues were happy with things as they were.

Once large numbers of students obtained access to university education, the situation changed fundamentally. It is well known that external motivation is present in the university (more so in America than in Europe, because capitalism is purer and more developed in America) just as it is elsewhere in the system. External rewards consist of status, power, and money. If the number of aspirants is large, only a few who are either especially lucky or particularly gifted can expect to obtain these rewards. The majority of their colleagues will never join the ranks of a privileged social stratum—which is what the intelligentsia used to be in the past—but will get stuck somewhere in no-man's-land, or will be absorbed into the new working class. They will be somewhat better paid than manual workers, but otherwise the difference in their favor will not be great.

Disappointed with their life prospects, young would-be intellectuals rebel. Some of them find the ordeal of years of study and examinations an absurd price to pay for the meaningless life that is to follow. And so the hippie movement with its many ramifications was born. Others do not accept passive resistance. They feel that the social system ought to be destroyed. Not having an appropriate social theory, they often confuse the destruction of the social system and its values with the destruction of university property—assuming the role of twentieth-century Luddites—and with exhibitions of indecency.

If the individual's own life prospects are not satisfactory, he soon begins to question the fundamentals of the social system in which he lives. And so students invariably discover the Marxian world of commodity fetishism and alienation, Marcuse's one-dimensional man, and Fromm's insane society. They begin to rationalize their individual dissatisfactions and become more socially minded.[97] Being themselves victims of an oppressive system, they begin to sympathize with other victims, those of racism and imperialism. In this way the rebellion of students, though motivated by ordinary self-interest—as were all other rebellions in history—becomes one of the most progressive contemporary social movements.

Students, however numerous, are not a class but an age group. They can trigger a social revolution, but they cannot carry it out. In a capitalist, as well as an etatist, setting, the educational system is productive as long as it is repressive, as long as it instills the discipline and obedience necessary for the proper functioning of bureaucratic structures in the alienated world of production. If the educational system is made dysfunctional in this respect, the consequences will soon be felt in the production system.

It is clearly utopian to expect that the university will or should change society directly. But it is not utopian to point out that contemporary society—unlike former societies—cannot live without universities. Thus, universities cannot be closed down for any length of time. If the government is unwise enough to multiply repressive measures, the reaction can be only more violent. In this way a revolutionary feedback has been built into the system.

After their graduation, masses of young intellectuals, already infested with revolutionary ideas, begin their productive life in an environment that has also changed in at least two important respects. First, machines are gradually replacing routine manual work; knowledge and not muscle power is becoming the major productive force. Thus educated labor is the emerging social class that will provide the basic productive services for the society. Second, this is occurring in an environment of affluence in which the struggle for mere physical survival is a forgotten past. If people do not have to worry about food and shelter, they begin to worry about freedom, equality, decent society, and the meaning of life. A self-oriented, money-inspired, gadgetry-motivated life begins to look absurd. The new working class is educated enough to be able to understand the issues involved. Motivated by self-interest, it will be induced to initiate the process of fundamental social change. In the West as well as in the East.

In a relatively affluent society, worry about the meaning of life and work ceases to be a privilege—or a curse—of intellectuals. Less and less, people are willing to accept living as appendages to machines or offices. By merely conceding wage increases, employers cannot eliminate dissatisfaction and revolt, at least not for very long. "The impossibility of living," remarked André Gorz, "which appeared to the proletarians of the last century as the impossibility of reproducing their labor power, becomes for the workers of scientific or cultural industries the impossibility of using their creative abilities to work."[98]

The simultaneous dissatisfaction among students, workers, and the "middle classes" is not accidental. This social fermentation is indicative of a radical change in consciousness. "Seemingly divergent strands," remarked Bogdan Denitch, "massive discontent among students in most industrial societies, a decrease in the independence of professionals, the proletarianization of many technicians and engineers, the increasing militancy of strategically-placed groups of skilled workers—are interconnected. They represent an early phase in the developing consciousness of a stratum in modern industrial societies which can be described as a new working class."[99] This finding should not really be very surprising.

In a sense there is a parallel between the social processes observed by Marx and those observed today. The Industrial Revolution in the nineteenth century created an industrial proletariat, and later development gradually proletarianized the old middle class. The contemporary scientific revolution has created a new working class, which has begun to absorb the new middle class. To the extent that the scientific revolution industrializes agriculture, distribution, services, and administration—in fact, all economic activities—salaried hired labor, remarked Ernest Mandel, is integrated into the proletariat.[100]

There is another historical similarity. The old working class did not serve as a basis for a more advanced system—socialism—though it did perform this function in the collateral system—etatism. This is similar to what happened earlier in history, when transition implied a certain discontinuity, as noted by Mandel. The formation of the new working class marks such a discontinuity between capitalism/etatism and socialism. Here—it is to be hoped—the parallelism ends. What one would expect to happen in the future is not the formation of yet another pair of antagonistic social classes but a society without classes.

15

Searching for a Strategy of Transition

To effect a transition to socialism, we must discover the major vehicle of social transformation. In searching for it, we can conveniently start with a study of human needs. If socialism is to be viable, it must satisfy human needs better than any of the rival systems. If it does, people will be motivated to achieve it. A basis for the present analysis has already been prepared by the examination of alienation, comparative efficiency, and the ethical foundations of socialism in chapters 4, 6, and 7. All we need do is complete the analysis and derive the consequences for a strategy of transition.

Extending slightly earlier anthropological discussion, we may note three aspects of "human nature." Man is, first, a biological or natural being. He is, next, a gregarious or social being. Finally, he has certain specifically or exclusively human qualities. This classification is crude, of course, but will prove helpful. As a natural being, man has biological needs that must be satisfied in order to keep body and mind healthy. As a gregarious being, he has certain psychic or social needs. As a human being, man is a creature of self-creation—by working he changes his environment and himself—and of self-realization—since he has the power of self-creation, he strives to use it; as Aristotle and Marx made clear, every natural being strives to realize its powers and suffers when it is frustrated. Full self-realization is possible only if man is free to use all his powers. From this flows the need for self-determination.

One would expect the three aspects of human nature, and the corresponding needs connected with them, to be not independent, but interdependent. After all, man is a single and not a triple being. One would also expect there to be a certain hierarchy of needs corresponding roughly to the stages of development of the human race.

In line with the general methodological approach in the present treatise, we would like to subject the foregoing propositions to empirical testing. Unfortunately, this can be done only in a very inadequate way. The psychological research on human needs is in its infancy. Thus, the two theoretical attempts to be mentioned will have to be discussed on their own terms.

I. Human Needs

The theory of needs is of very recent origin. The pioneering research into individual human needs was conducted by Abraham Maslow.[1] Drawing upon his clinical experience as well as laboratory experiments, Maslow distinguishes five basic needs. These needs are organized into a hierarchy of relative prepotency: that is, higher needs do not emerge until lower needs have been gratified to some extent. It is probably more correct to describe the hierarchy in terms of intensities rather than existence: all needs are always present, but their intensity varies according to a hierarchical pattern. This pattern can be given as follows:

1. The most prepotent of all needs are the *physiological needs* (for water, food, sex, etc.). Unless gratified, these needs dominate the entire affective, intellectual, and practical activity of human beings.

2. *Safety needs* are next in the hierarchy. These include the need for security, stability, dependency, and protection; freedom from fear and chaos; and the need for structure, order, law, limits.

3. Once relative safety is secured, affective *needs of belongingness* and *love* emerge. Rootedness, stressed particularly by Erich Fromm, belongs here as well.

4. Still further up in the hierarchy are the *need for self-respect* and for *self-esteem*. These needs can be divided into two sets: (a) the desire for strength, achievement, mastery and competence, confidence in face of the world, and independence and freedom; (b) the desire for reputation, status, fame, recognition, attention, importance, dignity, and appreciation.

5. Even if all four of these needs are completely satisfied, the human being will still feel discontented and restless unless she or he can do what *she* or *he*, individually, is fitted for. "What a man *can* be, he *must* be. He must be true to his own nature."[2] Capacities imply motives. The desire to achieve self-fulfillment, to become what the individual is potentially, Maslow calls the *need for self-actualization*. In this need for self-actualization we can easily recognize Marxian human nature treated not as a philosophical proposition but as a problem of empirical psy-

chology. We can likewise recognize Rawls's Aristotelian principle (chapter 7). There is an important asymmetry to be noted here. Gratification of the first four needs reduces the desire for them; but the more the need for self-actualization is satisfied, the more the latter is desired.[3]

It has been pointed out that one of the needs included in the list—safety—is incongruous with the rest. It is like separating food into "food" and "palatability." Clearly, one *needs* food, but one *prefers* palatable food. While the satisfaction of real needs is pursued for its own sake, it is unlikely that mentally healthy people pursue safety for the sake of safety. Safety is simply a precondition, a means, not an end.[4] A similar mistake is made in social product measurement when statisticians add the "output of safety"—i.e., the services of the police and the army—to the output of commodities and services that satisfy consumer wants.[5] A pair of shoes remains a pair of shoes with or without the police. What the police do—if they function properly—is to make it possible for the pair of shoes to be used. We are thus left with four basic needs to be gratified under the conditions of relative safety. The first of these needs relates to mere physical survival. The next two grow out of the fact that people live in societies. The fourth one reflects personality development, which is a specifically human quality.

This leads us to an examination of the characteristics of the hierarchy of needs. Maslow describes a number of them. The following four seem to be of greatest importance.[6]

1. Higher needs represent later phylogenetic or evolutionary developments. The need for food is shared with plants and animals. The need for love is shared with higher apes. The need for self-actualization is not shared with any other organism. "The higher the need, the more specifically human it is."[7]

2. Higher needs are later ontogenetic developments. At birth, only physical needs exist. After some months of life, the infant shows the first signs of affective ties. Still later, the child desires respect and praise. Full self-actualization requires a mature personality; in an alienated world, it may never occur.

3. "The higher the need the less imperative it is for sheer survival, the longer gratification can be postponed, and the easier it is for the need to disappear permanently."[8] Higher needs are less urgent subjectively. Once higher needs have been experienced, however, they do not disappear immediately if the overall level of need gratification is substantially reduced.

4. Higher levels of need gratification mean greater biological efficiency, longer life, better sleep, etc. "Higher need gratifications have survival value and growth value as well."[9]

How do we know that the needs on our list are really basic human needs and are not simply neurotic or socially conditioned? Maslow offers four possible proofs:[10]

1. The frustration of these needs is pathogenic, i.e., it makes people physically and mentally ill.

2. Their gratification, on the contrary, is healthy. This is not the case with the gratification of neurotic needs.

3. Gratification is also chosen spontaneously under free conditions.

4. These needs can be directly studied in relatively healthy people.

If Maslow is right, thwarting gratification of these four basic needs will produce sick individuals. And sick individuals make up a sick society. What the symptoms of sickness are at the societal level, and how such a sick society functions, has been studied especially by Erich Fromm.[11] A society that satisfies basic human needs substantially better than other societies, on the other hand, must in some fundamental sense be a more progressive society.

So far Maslow's original theory of motivation has not been well supported by empirical evidence except with regard to the need for self-actualization. Empirical research into actual life situations has failed to identify five independent needs or to confirm a simple ordering of needs.[12] Attempts have been made to eliminate the overlapping of needs by reducing the number to two or three, and to introduce a more complex ordering while retaining the hierarchy. The most successful revision along these lines has been achieved by Clayton Alderfer.[13] His classification of needs corresponds quite closely to my introductory propositions about human nature.

Alderfer compressed Maslow's five needs into three, which he termed the needs for existence, relatedness, and growth. People must first stay alive; they must relate to each other; and, in order to be human, they must be creative by changing their environment and themselves. Thus existence needs subsume material and physiological desires. When resources are limited, as they are in the scarcity world in which we live, one person's gain is another person's loss. Relatedness needs involve relationships with significant other people and include acceptance, confirmation, and understanding, Here the activities do not represent a zero-sum game; gratification depends on a process of sharing or mutuality. The satisfaction of growth needs "depends on a person finding the opportunities to be what he is most fully and to become what he can."[14]

Alderfer tested his theory in organizational settings. Five out of seven original propositions concerning the functioning of the three-need hierarchy survived the test in more or less revised form. Thus, the following empirically supported theory of motivation emerges.[15]

1. The less existence needs are satisfied, the more they will be desired.

2. Under conditions of low satisfaction of both existence and relatedness needs, the less relatedness needs are satisfied, the more existence needs will be desired. This implies a fixation on material objects in an authoritarian setting with a low level of living.

3. Desire is inversely related to satisfaction at a low level of satisfaction of relatedness needs, and positively related at a high level of satisfaction.

4. When relatedness and growth needs are both relatively satisfied, the more relatedness needs are satisfied, the more growth is desired.

5. Growth is desired more, the less growth needs are satisfied at a low level of satisfaction, and the more they are satisfied at a high level of satisfaction. It was also found that, in a challenging discretionary setting, the more a person was satisfied the more he desired, and the more he desired the more he was satisfied. Thus, a growth-oriented person is likely to become increasingly so.

It follows that the simple deficiency-desire postulate applies unconditionally only to existence needs. The frustration-regression postulate is valid for existence and relatedness needs. The satisfaction-progression postulate applies to relatedness and growth needs. The relative satisfaction of relatedness needs makes growth desirable (proposition 4). Alderfer failed to uncover empirical support for a similar proposition holding that the desirability of relatedness is a function of the satisfaction of existence needs. Other researchers, however, have found some evidence for this proposition. The general hypothesis that the satisfaction of lower level needs activates higher level needs can be justified on the grounds that higher needs become more urgent and the released energy must be applied productively. In the reverse case, when a lower level need is frustrated, energy is absorbed to repair the deficiency and less is available for activities at a higher level.

It is obvious that, while questioning the simplicity of Maslow's theory, Alderfer upholds its essential idea: human needs are objectively identifiable and are hierarchically ordered. The ordering is not rigidly determined. By the manipulation of environmental factors, individuals may be oriented toward lower level needs. And conversely, since all needs are always present, at least in a latent form, individuals may be induced to reach the growth stage faster and experience the self-reinforcing satisfaction-desire process. If Maslow and Alderfer are right, thwarting the satisfaction of basic needs not only makes society sick but also generates the motivation for change. The change implies satisfying basic needs more fully.

How do we find out which society satisfies basic needs more fully? The existence of a needs hierarchy makes possible a simple solution to the problem. A society that better satisfies a higher need *eo ipso* better satisfies all other needs down the list. Consequently, it suffices to show that socialism satisfies the self-actualizing need more than either capitalism or etatism in order to prove that it satisfies all human needs better and is, in this sense, a superior socioeconomic system.

II. Needs at the Societal Level

Before we proceed, one difficulty must be removed. The classification of basic needs from the point of view of individual development is not the same as their classification from the point of view of social system design. We must discover how to transform the multistage scheme at the micro level—physiological, affective, self-esteem, and self-actualization needs, or existence, relatedness, and growth needs—into one applicable at the macro level. As usual, an analysis of historical experience provides the answer.

1. Since physiological or existence needs have a survival quality, neither an individual nor a society can exist if these needs are not satisfied. At the societal level, this category is enlarged to include all *physical needs*, such as food, clothing, and shelter.

2. Once basic physical needs are relatively satisfied, different needs, which we may call *cultural needs*, begin to be felt acutely. People are first concerned with their bodies; next they become concerned with their minds. Education, entertainment, art, and science belong under this heading. Health ought to be included here as well. At the lowest stage, health is often traded for increases in material comforts. It is only after a certain minimum level of living is achieved that health as such becomes of primary concern.

3. The first two stages make for the standard of living. The next two stages make for the quality of life. In a relatively affluent society, people become increasingly concerned with so-called political liberties. *Political needs* (freedom of speech, conscience, assembly, etc.) correspond to Maslow's self-esteem needs and are included in Alderfer's relatedness needs.

4. Finally, in an affluent and politically liberated society, major concern is focused on the growth of the personality, on the full development of the inherent potentialities and capacities of every individual. It is not enough simply to survive, to enjoy life, and to be recognized as a separate and (formally) equal member of the group; it is also necessary to live one's own, self-determined, and authentic life. This *need for authenticity* and *self-determination* corresponds, of course, to Maslow's self-actualization and Alderfer's growth need. It includes affective needs, since personal life cannot be authentic if solidarity, love, friendship, and so on, are thwarted or alienated.

Stages 1 and 4 are the same at both individual and societal levels. Stages 2 and 3 are not. Moreover, the historical evidence is not straightforward. The periodization given above corresponds to etatist development. In capitalist development, political liberties were established before the cultural needs of the broad masses of the population were satisfied. The explanation for this historical indeterminacy is not difficult to find.

The precondition for the development of capitalism was the establishment of a free market. This, in turn, required that the political restrictions of feudalism be removed and political freedoms be made available not only for the aristocracy but for the bourgeoisie as well. The proletariat, on the other hand, could not improve its position vis-à-vis the bourgeoisie unless political freedoms were extended to all members of the society, regardless of their origin and ownership of property. In this way, the class struggle generated political democracy, while cultural needs remained satisfied in only rudimentary form.

Consider now a different historical situation in which, due to a revolution, economic growth is accelerated substantially and the benefits are fairly evenly spread throughout the society. People will now tend to be more concerned with improvements in the standard of living than with politics. This explains the social stability of etatism. It is unlikely, of course, that the absence of political democracy can be preserved for long without overt political repression. But the repression is not a *differentia specifica* of etatism. It exists in capitalism as well. Only there it takes the form of *economic* repression. When, on occasion, the oppressed refuse to tolerate the continuation of economic exploitation, economic repression is immediately replaced with political repression.[16]

As consumption and the cultural level of the population increase, it becomes less possible to prevent the full development of political democracy in an etatist environment. Similarly, material affluence and political democracy lead to a gradual satisfaction of cultural needs (free education at all levels, health insurance, establishment of museums and art galleries, etc.). In this way, both systems converge to a state in which the relative satisfaction of material, cultural, and political needs will generate pressures for radical social change in the direction of self-determination.

III. Work: Its Decomposition and Reintegration

Needs are satisfied by work. This is true not only in the trivial sense that work produces goods and services for consumption, but also in the more important sense that work is an essential human activity. Thus, there will be some correlation between the types of need satisfaction and the types of work. In the first three need-satisfaction stages, work is only instrumental and, consequently, alienated. One sells one's labor power and works in order to achieve something else. Work as such is toil, pain, a cost, something to be avoided. In the fourth need-satisfaction stage, the situation radically changes: work becomes an enjoyment, a need, an end in itself. Let us take a somewhat closer look at this process.

Work is a complex activity with several dimensions. The development of capitalism and etatism is accompanied by a decomposition of work along its various dimensions. The totality is broken up into components, the components become independent, and the process results in alienation. The labor of an artisan or a peasant comprises an undifferentiated whole. The first step in the disintegration of the labor process was to separate the producer from the sources of supply and from the customers. The producer retained his means of production and control of the immediate labor process, but became dependent on and exploited by the capitalist. This was known as the putting-out system. The next step in the process was to separate the producer from the means of production. This was also the most difficult step, and extended over centuries. In Britain, it implied enclosures; in the Soviet Union, collectivization. It meant transforming human beings into appendages of machines, into a factor of production along with other factors such as capital and land. Labor was reduced to manual labor—labor pure and simple—while workers became "hired hands." The producers, of course, refused to work, resisted, tried to combine in order to control their destinies. The owners knew better.

> Combination among workers was visited with brutal punishment, flogging, prison and banishment were the penalties for strikes. Workers were bound for long terms of service, often extending over several years, and were hounded down like military deserters if they left their employment. . . . There was frequently forced recruitment of labour for privileged establishments of all kinds, and parents who did not send their children into industry were threatened with heavy fines.[17]

These methods, characteristic in Europe during the sixteenth through the eighteenth centuries, reappeared in the European colonies in the nineteenth and twentieth centuries.

The separation of the producer from his means of production meant not only a differentiation of labor into free and hired but also its decomposition into manual and nonmanual. The latter type of labor was retained by the owner for himself. Economic development and the ensuing division of labor pushed the decomposition one step further. The owner began to hire persons with the expertise necessary to cope with various production problems in the undertaking, which was growing in complexity. In this way, hired manual labor was supplemented by hired mental labor. The owner retained for himself only entrepreneurship, i.e., overall control and supervision. Eventually, the supreme supervisory labor was also hired, and the owner remained just an owner, pure and simple. In other words, in the last stage of capitalist work decomposition, managers are separated from rentiers; the latter, being pure capitalists, have no productive function any longer. In the meantime, both types of hired labor—manual and mental—are fragmented into simple, routine, tasks requiring no skill or intelligence.

This process of decomposition generating several partial workers had at least three important consequences. First, the sequence of decomposition—manual labor, hired mental labor, and hired supervisory labor—is at the same time the order of socioeconomic position or social strata in contemporary class societies: manual workers occupy the lowest position, business and political bosses the highest. Second, however paradoxical it may seem, up to a point the various strata have a common interest in preserving the existing system. For the ruling stratum, this is obvious. Manual workers, on the other hand, still find themselves in the region of lower needs whose satisfaction is quite compatible with the existing social system. In the United States, this is reflected in the conservative attitudes of the unions, which are oriented primarily toward improvements in material well-being. In the Soviet Union, intellectuals receive little support from the workers in pressing for political freedoms. Since needs are not psychological constants but cultural variables (with a psychological core), this state of affairs may be preserved over long periods of time by artificially inflating lower needs. Third, ownership pure and simple—either private or state—is devoid of the productive function and is becoming growth-inhibiting, which renders it dysfunctional. Functionless or dysfunctional institutions are sooner or later replaced by those that are positively productive. On the other hand, labor pure and simple, i.e., alienated labor, cannot be tolerated any longer once lower basic needs have been relatively satisfied. Thus, the next evolutionary step can consist only in reversing past trends. The decomposition of labor has reached its ultimate limits. What can be expected in the future is reintegration on a new basis. This new basis can consist only in self-determination.

IV. The Fundamental Strategy

How is this reintegration of producers and the means of production, of various components of labor, to come about? What is the social force that will carry it out? The traditional answer is that this social force is the proletariat. We have seen, however, that the proletariat does not transcend the trade union consciousness, that is, it remains *within* the confines of the system of decomposed and alienated labor. This is particularly true if the system leaves sufficient room for the gratification of lower basic needs. Two solutions to the problem have been offered.

The first was put forward by Lenin. Consistent with his idea that the working class is unable to reach a socialist consciousness by its own efforts, he urged the creation of a disciplined party of political activists, headed by revolutionary intellectuals, which could lead and educate workers and would rule by dictatorial methods until socialist consciousness was established. This strategy proved technically efficient but socially self-defeating. It generated etatism, not socialism.

The second strategy is to look for another revolutionary force outside the proletariat. Such a force is found in students, radical intellectuals, and exploited minority groups in developed countries, and in peasants in undeveloped countries. If we temporarily leave aside the problem of peasants, then the second strategy is well represented by the work of Herbert Marcuse. "By virtue of its basic position in the production process," argued Marcuse,

> by virtue of its numerical weight and the weight of exploitation, the working class is still the historical agent of revolution; by virtue of its sharing the stabilising needs of the system, it has become a conservative, even counterrevolutionary force. Objectively, "in itself," labour is still the potentially revolutionary class; subjectively, "for itself," it is not.[18]

While workers are becoming conservative, small and weakly organized groups of militant intelligentsia, cut loose from the middle class, as well as the ghetto population, similarly cut loose from the organized working class, "by virtue of their consciousness and their needs function as potential catalysts of rebellion within majorities to which, by their class origin, they belong."[19] Elaborating this idea to its final consequences, Marcuse ended with an impasse:

> the established democracy still provides the only legitimate framework for change and must therefore be defended against all attempts on the Right and the Centre to restrict this framework, but at the same time, preservation of the established democracy preserves the *status quo* and the containment of change. Another aspect of the same ambiguity: radical change depends on a mass basis, but every step in the struggle for radical change isolates the opposition from the masses and provokes intensified repression . . . thus further diminishing the prospects for radical change. . . . Thus, the radical is guilty—either for surrendering to the power of the *status quo*, or of violating the Law and Order of the *status quo*.[20]

Unlike Lenin's, Marcuse's strategy has not proved successful and clearly never will.

Where do we go from here? Is socialist transformation intrinsically impossible, like squaring a circle? If a particular solution fails, it is always a good rule to look first for the reasons of the failure. Since the (blue collar) working class represents half of the population—and an exploited half at that—no socialist transformation is possible without the working class. Both Lenin and Marcuse would agree with this proposition, and it is, in fact, generally accepted. Here, however, the agreement ends. Where Lenin and the Old Left err—all verbal pronouncements to the contrary notwithstanding—is in treating the proletariat as an *object* of change; in holding that the proletariat must be taught and led. In actuality, the emancipation of the working class must be brought about not by inspired leaders or an elite party but by the workers themselves, and this in the most real sense of the word. Where Marcuse and the New Left err is in a simplified dichotomizing of reality: either law and order or a radical change. Why not use law and order *for* the change?

A historical parallel will clarify the issue. Suppose we find ourselves in a feudal society and contemplate how to speed up capitalist transformation. What do we do? The most sensible thing is to discover the fundamental capitalist institution—the one that essentially governs the system—and try to transplant it into the feudal environment. The institution we are looking for is clearly a universal market, i.e., a free market for both products and factors. The transplantation has its problems, of course, and the social body may reject the transplant. But suppose we succeed. The institution will gradually corrode the feudal structure from the inside and the structure will begin to crumble. If everything can be bought and sold, then feudal estates and aristocratic titles will be soon offered for sale, and the lords will soon prefer to receive money rents from free tenants rather than labor services from their serfs. This thought experiment is not fully invented, of course. To a certain extent European absolute monarchies did in fact behave in the way described. In the process feudal lords lost their power. As Adam Smith observed: "for the gratification of the most childish, the meanest and the most sordid of all vanities they gradually bartered their whole power and authority" and "became as insignificant as any substantial burgher or tradesman in a city."[21]

The fundamental institution of socialism is self-management. The major task of the present study has been, in fact, to examine and validate this proposition. If universal self-management (in both market and nonmarket sectors) is introduced to either capitalist or etatist societies, it will gradually resolve the old production relations and eventually the disintegrating system will have to be replaced by something more compatible with the institution. By participating in management (and in local government), by fighting for a continuous extension of participation until it reaches full self-management, workers learn in their daily lives how to control their destiny, how to overcome fragmentation and decomposition of labor, how to achieve meaningful social equality, how to destroy antiquated hierarchies. They do this without the tutorship of omniscient leaders. They prepare themselves for self-determination. And they use law and order for exactly that purpose. Self-management clearly cannot be established overnight. But neither was the capitalist market. And just as the development of the market, however gradual or irregular, could not be anticapitalist, the growth of participation from its primitive forms of joint consultation toward full-fledged self-management cannot be antisocialist, in spite of the attempts to misuse it for the preservation of the status quo.

The problem of fundamental strategy should not be interpreted in a simplistic fashion. In particular, social systems have a great capacity to incorporate glaring contradictions while continuing to exist and function for very long periods. The capitalist system is characterized by political democracy and private ownership. But ownership implies autocracy at the place of work. The compatibility of political democracy and economic autocracy is rendered possible by the compartmentalization of bourgeois life into separate spheres of activity and of the bourgeois personality into separated, partial beings known as citizen, producer, and consumer. The instrumentality of work, passive consumerism, and formal political liberties keep the spheres separated and the bourgeois individual schizophrenic. It is only after the three separate spheres begin to be reintegrated—which seems to be happening now—that the contradiction between democracy in one sphere and autocracy in the other becomes apparent and must be resolved.

A postbourgeois society is not immune to similar contradictions. A less developed country building socialism may be characterized by industrial democracy and political authoritarianism. Self-management at the place of work and hierarchy outside it are clearly contradictory. The two may be justified during the transition period for reasons to be discussed later (chapter 18). If a conscious effort is not made to resolve the contradiction, however, it may be preserved for a long time. The functional requirements of the system will be met by compartmentalization, which of course implies alienation and delays the development of a socialist society. Self-management is the most powerful vehicle for socialist change available. But it is not a panacea.

Self-management reintegration is possible, and it is facilitated by technological development. Although mass production involving the less sophisticated technology of the capitalist era does not necessarily imply the fragmentation of labor and the destruction of skills, it at least makes them appear rational in terms of cost. In such a situation supervisors are coordinators of work who know all that workers know and a little more. The position of supervisors in the skill hierarchy seems to justify their position in the power hierarchy. The sophisticated technology of the postcapitalist era reverses the trend and contributes to skill creation. Simple production tasks are performed by machines; automation renders work fragmentation both unnecessary and cost irrational. Unskilled work, and later semiskilled as well, begin to disappear. The coordinator is no longer in a position to master all the skills of his collaborators; he must rely on their advice and loses any objective basis for social superiority. The coordinator is now just one specialist among many. Although the new technology does not necessarily destroy the power hierarchy, it makes it seem irrational. Self-management is clearly a more natural organization of production in a situation where muscles are replaced by machines and participants are about equally educated.

Self-management may be introduced by violent (and revolutionary) or peaceful (and reformist) means. It may be attempted in undeveloped or industrializing or developed countries.[22] It can grow up in a capitalist or in an etatist environment. Thus theoretically twelve transition profiles can be distinguished. Not all of them have empirical content, however. For reasons analyzed earlier, a violent revolution is not likely to erupt in a developed country. Besides, it is a historical fact that no such revolution has occurred. This reduces the number of possibilities by two. Next, undeveloped countries are so much dominated by their poverty that the distinction between capitalism and etatism is of lesser importance. This makes for a further reduction of two profiles. Finally, it is generally easiest to build socialism in developed countries and most difficult—if it is possible at all—to effect socialist transformation in the poor, least developed countries. If these two polar cases could be handled, the intermediate case of industrializing countries need not represent special difficulties. Consequently, in the chapters that follow, I shall examine the following three transition profiles: developed capitalist countries, developed etatist countries, and undeveloped countries.

16

Paths of Transition: Developed Capitalist Countries

"The carrying of universal suffrage in England," wrote Marx in 1852, "would . . . be a far more socialistic measure than anything which has been honoured with that name on the Continent. Its inevitable result, here [in England], is *the* political supremacy of the working class."[1] Exactly forty years later, his friend and collaborator Friedrich Engels remarked in a letter: "During forty years Marx and myself have been tirelessly repeating that the democratic republic for us is the only political form in which the struggle between the working class and the class of capitalists may first become universal and then be completed together with the decisive victory of the proletariat."[2]

Today, a century later, all developed capitalist countries have long since established universal suffrage. Most of them are republics, and those which are not are occasionally more democratic than those which are. In England and Germany, the two countries referred to by our authors, workers represent the majority of the population. In both countries, labor parties either are in power or have been so several times in the past. In some other countries social democratic parties have held political power for many years. Yet, in none of them has socialism been established. Nor can that be expected to happen very soon. Both violent revolution and peaceful—and piecemeal—reforms have failed to produce socialism thus far.

Our analysis has uncovered some of the reasons for this. Capitalist development has been fast enough to enable all classes to share—albeit unequally—in the benefits. The ruling class was able to grant substantial political and economic concessions and yet retain the reins of political and economic power. The workers were concerned with lower levels of need satisfaction and failed to develop an effective socialist consciousness. Workers' organizations, trade unions, and parties have to a large extent been integrated into the system and have failed to produce viable radical alternatives. In the struggle for survival, unions and labor parties were forced to build bureaucratic structures that enhanced their power but greatly reduced their socialist potential. In a word, the society was not ripe for socialism.

Yet, Marx and Engels were undoubtedly right when they asserted that the conditions for a socialist transformation are most favorable in political democracies. We now have to investigate how to exploit these conditions effectively. We may proceed in six stages: first, studying the two fundamental preconditions for social change; next, considering the available instruments; and, finally, designing three institutional changes.

I. The Needs Satisfaction Crisis

Whenever a discrepancy develops between the forces of production and production relations, sooner or later the latter will be adjusted. In late capitalist society, this discrepancy is reflected in the failure of the system to satisfy certain fundamental needs. Observing the prolonged misery of the working class, nineteenth-century socialists believed that the system's failure to improve the material standard of living would generate increasing discontent that eventually would result in a revolutionary explosion. This belief proved to be unjustified. It was replaced by another belief, connected with the obvious contradiction between the social nature of production and private appropriation. Observing periodic slumps, many socialists (Louis Boudin, Fritz Sternberg, and, though with a different explanation, Henryk Grossmann) came to believe that capitalism would become increasingly unable to harmonize supply and demand, business cycles would become more violent, unemployment would increase, further accumulation would become impossible, and at some point the system would break down. This did not happen either. The theory of *Zusammenbruch* proved false. The system managed to increase the standard of living substantially, even to reduce the inequality in income distribution. Unemployment and business cycles, though not eliminated, were brought under some control. The rate of growth and accumulation, if anything, increased.

The third widespread belief concerned the colonies. Colonies, it was argued, were indispensable for the normal functioning of capitalism, because they provided outlets for capital and commodity exports (Rosa Luxemburg). Imperialism, as it were, resulted from this need to secure ever-expanding markets. Without them, capitalism could not survive. After the Second World War, colonial empires disintegrated, former colonies won their independence—and capitalism survived, with trade expanding faster than ever before. In general, it was not in consumption or in the barriers to accumulation or in the structure of markets where the system failed to satisfy needs; it was in the work process itself.

In 1969 the Survey Research Center at the University of Michigan conducted a revealing study involving more than 1,500 American workers. At that time the population of the United States enjoyed the highest standard of living in the world. It was found that one out of every four workers under the age of 30 felt dissatisfaction with his work. The share was identical for both blue collar and white collar workers under 30. The percentage of discontented workers was the same for all levels of education. Of the eight top-ranked aspects of work, six were related to the content of the worker's job. Good pay placed only fifth, after interesting work, enough help and equipment to get the job done, enough authority to do the job.[3] The survey was undertaken after it became apparent that work discontent resulted in serious production disruptions, such as wildcat strikes, high labor turnover, absenteeism, poor quality of output, slowdown, and outright sabotage. "The young worker . . . says he hates the job, particularly the monotonous factory job. At times he hates it so much that he will deliberately throw a monkey wrench in the machinery, or turn to drugs to escape boredom. To him, whether the job is better than it used to be or pays more than it ever did and gives benefits is beside the point."[4] Obviously, the affluent, educated worker is no longer prepared to consider his work as purely instrumental in obtaining something else. He wants to engage in *meaningful* work. "The prospect of tightening up belts every two minutes for eight hours for thirty years doesn't lift the human spirit." The young worker feels that "he's not master of his own destiny. He's going to run away from it every time he gets a chance. That is why there's an absentee problem."[5]

Follow-up studies showed a further deterioration of the situation after 1973. Between 1973 and 1977, American workers experienced a marked decline in job satisfaction, intention to stay with their present job, life satisfaction, and overall health. "The decline in overall job satisfaction has been pervasive, affecting virtually all demographic and occupational classes tested."[6] Even the self-employed had a decrement in satisfaction similar to that of wage and salary earners. The decrease in general life satisfaction was more than twice the size of the decrease in general job satisfaction (as measured in terms of number of standard deviations). The worker is no longer satisfied with the collective bargaining that treats him as a "pay category." Neither will he tolerate being "moved" from one job to another or being "put to work" on a machine like another tool without participating in the respective decisions. The system encounters an unresolvable contradiction. Unemployment does not discipline workers any longer; it creates dangerous political ferment. Secure employment, on the other hand, generates the will to control one's own destiny.

Better education and further increase in the standard of living will strengthen these attitudes. So will changes in family life brought about by equalization of the status of women. When a man is the only breadwinner, he will endure any hardships to be able to support his family. He will seek his personal fulfillment through his family. "As long as the money comes in, and as long as the family provider is not threatened, most men will go along . . . with the work routine, however arduous it is. If, however, the man's role as bread-winner grows less vital, the whole fragile bargain threatens to break down."[7] In this respect the employment of women and the free education of children cause a profound change. The marital partners share financial responsibilities, while social insurance and public education make savings for old age, medical treatment, and tuition fees unnecessary. Social relations and the conditions of work, the quality of life, emerge as the most important life concerns.

While workers are becoming more sensitive to how they are treated, employers are becoming more vulnerable. Work discontent is for them a serious danger. Slaves and serfs can operate but the simplest and crudest machines. More sophisticated machinery, invented during the Industrial Revolution, required free wage labor. Similarly, the highly capital intensive plants and automated lines of late capitalist society require a new kind of labor force. The entire assembly line comes to a standstill if one member of the crew is missing. Great damage, out of any proportion to the wage cost, can be caused by poor work in a continuous process plant. Major savings to production costs are no longer to be found in cutting workers' wages. They come from improved yields, reduced waste, and avoidance of shutdowns. If the modern forces of production are to function properly, workers must be responsible and reliable. For that, they must be content with their jobs. This is why employers—regardless of their individual or class preferences—must find remedies for work discontent. And, in fact, they are rather busy experimenting with all sorts of solutions suggested by hired experts. In the United States special legislation was introduced providing for "research for solutions to the problem of alienation among American workers and to provide for pilot projects and provide technical assistance to find ways to deal with that problem."[8]

If work is to become less monotonous and boring, jobs should be rotated, enriched, and enlarged; jobs must be upgraded so as to promise workers a way of transcending deadend jobs; isolated subordinates should be replaced by autonomous work groups, autocratic management by participative management. The "scientific" Taylorist organization of work, whereby complex operations are broken into elementary motions and workers asked to perform these motions like trained cattle, should be abandoned and the trend reversed. Fragments should be reintegrated. The assembly line in a car factory should be broken into separate teams.[9] Billing clerks in a telephone company should be given complete responsibility for certain accounts, rather than a single operation on each account. Piecework should be replaced by teamwork, and work teams should be given some autonomy in work design. Workers should have the authority to control product assembly and the assignment of jobs along assembly lines. Hourly wages should be replaced by weekly salaries. Insulting status differences should be eliminated. The amenities for blue collar workers should be equalized with those of white collar workers. Joint labor-management "quality of working life committees" (as negotiated by the UAW in the United States in 1973) should be set up. In Sweden, the wave of wildcat strikes in the winter of 1969-70 was interpreted as an outburst of accumulated discontent. On the initiative of the unions, the Social Democratic government established commissions to propose legislation to increase the influence of workers in working life. Very soon legislation was enacted whereby employment security was improved, workers obtained minority representation on company boards, and the scope of activities of work place union representatives was increased.[10] Other countries also experienced massive wildcat strikes, and the governments had to react with similar measures.

All these measures have generated certain productivity gains; work discipline has improved, supervisory and management costs have been reduced. They have also contributed to an improvement of working conditions and to a certain humanization of work.

It is good to see capitalists competing to improve working conditions—in sharp contrast to what happened during Marx's time when the sweatshop system, long working day, and low wages were the sources of high profit. Nevertheless, current improvements do not even touch the main source of trouble—the autocratic hierarchy within the productive establishment. Work remains alienated, the worker discontented, and the production system in constant jeopardy.

Since work is existentially important, discontent with work leads to discontent with life. The Michigan survey shows that very neatly. Those who have negative attitudes toward work also have negative attitudes toward life. In both respects, the self-employed report least dissatisfaction. This clearly is due to the independence they enjoy, to the possibility, however small, of self-determination. But the percentage of self-employed is constantly dwindling. Besides, as already mentioned, later studies showed even the self-employed to be affected. Work and life dissatisfactions are increasing. The society is becoming ripe for change. This change will be caused not by material poverty, but by the failure of the system to satisfy the higher, historically determined needs. "That is, the chief accusation against capitalism is no longer that it cannot produce the goods necessary for a decent standard of living, but that it fails to create the fundamental conditions for human freedom and self-expression. It does not permit, at any level, individual self-determination."[11]

II. The Legitimacy Crisis

In the first turbulent postwar year of 1919, William Straker, the Northumberland miners' agent, expressed the following views to the Sankey Commission on the Nationalization of the Mines:

> In the past, workmen have thought that if they could secure higher wages and conditions they would be content. Employers have thought that if they granted these things workers ought to be contented. Wages and conditions have improved; but the discontent and unrest have not disappeared. Many good people have come to the conclusion that working people are so unrea-

> sonable that it is useless trying to satisfy them. The fact is that the unrest is deeper than pounds, shillings, and pence, necessary as they are. The root of the matter is the straining of the spirit of man to be free.[12]

Yet there could be no producer freedom for the miner in Britain, the most liberal of all capitalist states. Strikers were defeated, the mines remained in private hands, and employers' autocracy was reestablished. It is only now, half a century later, that this freedom has generally come to be considered as a fundamental human need. This realization, of course, must have far-reaching consequences concerning the legitimacy of the existing order.

If an order fails to satisfy certain fundamental needs, its legitimacy will be questioned. The legitimacy "involves the capacity of the system to engender and ascertain the belief that the existing institutions are [the] most appropriate ones for society."[13] If an increasing number of people are dissatisfied with work and life, such institutions cannot be the most appropriate. And if the institutions fail to function properly, the value configuration of the community must have changed. This, in fact, is the crucial point. For an increasing number of individuals, existing social arrangements have ceased to be justified. They feel that change is possible and, if it is possible, it ought to be undertaken.

Some fundamental values—such as freedom, democracy, equality of opportunity—may not change, but they gradually acquire a new content and a different interpretation. Consider the concept of democracy. Can a society be democratic if the democracy applies only to political life and stops at the factory gate? Behind the gate, democratic rights are suspended and a repressive autocracy is established. Why should such a duality be justified or tolerated? In 1965 the organ of the German business interests, *Industriekurier,* wrote: "The democratization of the economy is as meaningless as the democratization of schools, barracks, or prisons."[14] A century ago such a pronouncement would not have caused much disagreement. Today, it indicates not that economic democracy is impossible, but rather that corporations are organized like barracks or prisons. And that is simply not acceptable any longer.

Similar reasoning applies to the other values mentioned above. Taking a job with a firm does not appear as a mere free contract any longer. If the firm is organized like a barracks or a prison, then the wage contract implies surrendering one's own personal freedom. Closely related is the treatment of property. It may remain sacrosanct, and yet one may refuse to justify the use of property for the appropriation and disposal of the labor of others. The latter resembles slavery and, as wage slavery, becomes a socially meaningful concept. Democracy and wage slavery are obviously not compatible. As for equality of opportunity between the rich and the poor, or between the weak and the powerful, it sounds like a joke, not like a serious proposition.

The erosion of legitimacy is always accompanied by an erosion of moral standards in public life. A new term—the credibility gap—has come to be used to describe one aspect of this phenomenon. The atrocities of the French military machine in Algeria and American genocide in Vietnam produced deep moral crises in these two countries. The Watergate affair, the ITT subversion in Chile, and the worldwide Lockheed corruption affair are some other instances of the credibility gap.

It is not difficult to indicate the inherent contradictions of the system. Business authoritarianism tends to be extended into political authoritarianism, which of course means the death of democracy. The costs of armaments and repression destroy the rationality of economic calculus. Free business initiative destroys ecological balance and, on a world scale, prevents the development of poor countries. The list can be extended at will.

No social order can be changed if it succeeds in preserving its legitimacy. That is why the erosion of capitalist legitimacy is of fundamental importance for a socialist transformation. It proceeds spontaneously, as in the cases described above. It can also be accelerated. To accomplish this is the revolutionary mission of the intellectuals. On that point Lenin and Kautsky would agree as well. Our study of revolutions has revealed that desertion of the established order by intellectuals precedes successful revolutions.[15] Intellectuals question the legitimacy of the old order, reinterpret values, and create a new consciousness. They explore the alternatives and work out possible solutions. There is no revolutionary movement without revolutionary theory (Lenin).

The system is falling into a kind of moral crisis. The mood of both the ruling and the subject classes is rather gloomy. The general atmosphere is very reminiscent of the decades before the French and the Russian revolutions. After surveying the literature on the American scene, Robert Lane concludes that "there *is* evidence that something about recent history has increased psychological distress and probably depression among the population under age 45." He then adds, more generally, that "there is evidence that people are less optimistic about their own and their country's future, less trusting and less confident that either social problems can be solved or that people in general can control their own fates."[16] Michel Crozier describes the social environment in his own country as follows:

> The system [French administration] is in a moral crisis. Members of the elite no longer have any profound faith in the virtues of the system from which they benefit. Young people criticize the ideology of our social system even if they remain consciously or unconsciously attached to the privileges they draw from it. No longer does anyone have the courage or consciousness to assume sufficient authority, the responsibility of a hierarchic order that is basically aristocratic. The result is that the whole system is crushed more and more by its own weight, and its capacity to develop and pursue social purposes steadily declines.[17]

Similar critical evaluations will be encountered in other mature capitalist countries.[18] People feel increasingly alienated from their own societies, and the established system of values comes under concentrated attack.

Not every attack on established values will undermine the system's legitimacy. It may even strengthen it. Consider the following set of conservative bourgeois values as juxtaposed to the values of the hippie counterculture:

Bourgeois conservative	*Hippie rebel*
Hard work	Leisure
Achieving	No purpose
Decent, straight	Shocking
Growth	Stagnation

Although the hippie also has a case, the naive negation of established values can only generate strong resistance. The old values will be defended and the pseudoradical critique will be dismissed as silly. For hard work may mean the Puritan ethic, and also work for the community. Work, being existential activity,[19] has been valued by all societies, and leisure is certainly not a substitute for but a complement to it. What one would like to do is to increase the spontaneity and creativity of work, not to abolish it. The desire to achieve may be alienating, as when it is oriented toward the accumulation of money and power, but it may also mean perfection in the arts and good craftsmanship. Lack of purpose is certainly not a humanizing alternative. The stupid and hypocritic conventions of the "straight" bourgeois society cannot be fought by frivolity and obscenity but only by genuine decency. Finally, the damaging effects of growth cannot be eliminated by stagnation but by a socially controlled growth.

The hippie or psychedelic counterculture is not likely to provide the basis for social reconstruction, and its negative efficiency is dubious. However, it clearly indicates the legitimacy crisis of the system, now in the cultural realm. "American capitalism," writes Daniel Bell, "has lost its traditional legitimacy, which was based on a moral system or reward rooted in the Protestant sanctification of work." In the Western industrial world, the requirements of the system and the developing cultural trends are contradictory. The system needs functional rationality, technocratic decision making, and a meritocratic reward system; the modernist culture emphasizes hedonism, anticognitive and anti-intellectual moods, and antirational modes of behavior.[20] The corporation wants an individual to be a hard worker, rational, frugal, and interested in a career, while at the same time, by its products and advertisements, it promotes pleasure, irrational spending, and "letting go." "One is to be 'straight' by day and a 'swinger' by night."[21]

This brief description of cultural contradictions and their reflection in pseudoradicalism suggests the following simple rule of positive action. There is no need to deny historical continuity in cultural development. Socialism does not represent a mere negation but rather a new—if one wishes, dialectical—synthesis. Thus, free initiative, responsibility, individual freedom, competition, democracy, and other old values ought to be included in the list of radical political slogans and reinterpreted appropriately. For instance:

—free initiative of associated producers—not monopoly control of corporate oligarchy
—free men in free society—not wage slavery and the rule of plutocracy or bureaucracy
—the genuine democracy of full participation—not a fake democracy for bosses
—self-management—not managerial authoritarianism
—equality of opportunity—not class stratification
—self-government—not party machinery
—competition in the good life—not in exploitation or killing
—respect for the individual personality—not for the possession of property or power
—a culture of fully developed individuals—not the primitivism of crippled moneymakers or officeholders

—production for better living—not for destruction
—expansion of useful output—not of waste and pollution
—greater efficiency—not unemployment and waste of resources

In the 1976 German elections, the conservative opposition fought against the ruling Social Democrats under the slogan, *Freiheit oder Sozialismus* [Freedom or Socialism]. This *Freiheit* was not meant to be exactly the same as the freedom referred to in the present book. But the mere fact that conservatives could mobilize votes under such a slogan—and almost won—indicates that something was wrong with traditional socialism. Both its main variants, social democracy and communism, failed to destroy the legitimacy of the bourgeois order. Bourgeois revolutions produced certain essential individual liberties. The socialist revolution needs neither to deny nor oppose them; it should *transcend* bourgeois freedom. If freedom is to be really meaningful, it must include control of the existential conditions of one's own life. In this essential sense, freedom can be attained better under socialism than under any other alternative system. Thus, the strongest ideological weapon of the bourgeois society can be turned against it and used to mount a powerful attack on its legitimacy. The twenty-ninth thesis announced at the Sorbonne in Paris on the turbulent June 13–14, 1968, proclaimed: "The bourgeois revolution was legal, the proletarian revolution was economic. Ours will be social and cultural, so that man can become what he is."[22]

III. Trade Unions and Socialist Parties and Their Policies

During the long years of class struggle, the working class created two organizations to protect its interests—the unions and the political parties. These organizations can be used as instruments of socialist transformation. One must not forget the limitations of these organizations. Both of them have certain stakes in the old system. Their leadership will not suddenly burst with revolutionary enthusiasm for genuine socialism. But the need satisfaction and legitimacy crises will generate mounting grass roots pressure.[23] Besides, the logic of the struggle is such that each of the combatants must exploit the disadvantages of the adversary in order to achieve domination. In fighting for domination, unions and prosocialist parties will give support to socialist transformation. Let us see how this can be done.

The traditional dilemma—violent revolution or peaceful reform—has by now been resolved.[24] Violence is neither possible nor desirable. Socialism progresses fastest by using means appropriate to its own nature. Hatred today cannot produce love tomorrow. Attitude and consciousness cannot be changed overnight. Change is gradual and is brought about as the transformation progresses. One may perhaps speak of peaceful revolution as the most efficient vehicle for social transformation in late capitalist societies.

There is a more subtle form of the old dilemma, however—not violence; but not cooperation either! Things must be made as difficult as possible for the class enemy. The worse, the better, is an appropriate strategy. Permanent fighting keeps the fighting spirit alive and prevents capitalists from corrupting workers. The gap between the two classes must be left as wide as possible; no bridges, no cooperation, and vigorous opposition will force the ruling class to make concessions and eventually to surrender.

History has not vindicated this strategy. The straining of social relations produces autocracy, not revolution; the preservation of class differences prolongs the life of capitalism and does not promote the development of socialism. Like all negative strategies, this approach reflects a position of weakness, not of strength. It reveals the lack of a constructive alternative rather than the presence of a well-elaborated program of social transformation. If we really know what we want to do, why not make *capitalists collaborate with us* to achieve the task? If, on the other hand, noncooperation and conflict maintenance are proclaimed as the guiding principle, then (a) potential allies will be alienated; (b) disruptive activities will give employers excuses for coordinated repression and intervention by the state: (c) by not assuming the responsibility for participating in management, workers will lose a golden opportunity to learn how to run firms; and (d) as a result of all this, the duration of capitalism is likely to be prolonged unnecessarily. A much better strategy would be to insist on a positive program of socialist reconstruction and let the opposing forces take the blame for obstruction, conflicts, and damage to the economy and the society. This is also a much more difficult task than simply opposing anything the ruling class does. Yet, if unions include the majority of the working population—as they should—and the prosocialist party or parties win the elections—as they certainly can—this is a realistic task. The limits of cooperation and the speed of the reform are then determined by the attitudes of the opponents. The more rigidly they stick to their privileges and the more they refuse to cooperate, the less will they be able to claim legitimacy for their activities and the faster will public opinion swing in favor of socialist construction.

Suppose these two conditions—majority unionization and control of the government—are fulfilled. What are the strategic policies that a labor/social democratic/communist government is best advised to follow? There seem to be at least seven such policies:

1. *A high rate of growth that enhances the affluence of the community.* At least nominally, this is in the interests of everyone. Experience shows that the affluence resulting from growth creates security, and security generates an impetus for change and a willingness to assume risks. Recession, on the other hand, creates insecurity and with it conservative attitudes, a desire to preserve whatever has been achieved, unwillingness to experiment, and a quest for authority that provides security. Rapid growth eliminates unemployment and increases the bargaining position of workers. Job security and affluence orient them toward self-management. Reduced work time as a result of increased productivity has the same effect. If profits increase as well, there is nothing wrong in that. On the one hand, the bourgeois needs an inducement to cooperate, while, on the other, a socialist policy will make sure that these profits are used for socialist purposes. A high rate of growth presupposes a certain degree of social planning, and this also is a socialist measure.

2. *The redistribution of income in order to eliminate publicly recognized poverty.* Public expenditures on social services ought to contribute to a general reduction in standard of living differences as well. The rest is left to direct collective bargaining between labor and capital. In this area, interests are clearly opposed. But the clash of interests has been successfully institutionalized. The gains of the workers and the poor from income redistribution are rather obvious. Employers gain if they avoid strikes. What the reasonable limits are depends partly on the relative strength of each group and partly on public opinion. In spite of the opposed interests, common ground exists. Social services contribute to the effective equality of men and women (making the productive employment of women possible), eliminate the fear of existential risks, and allow the emergence of higher needs.

3. *Free education at all levels to enable every individual to develop his faculties with no limitation but his own effort and motivation.* We have found earlier that education enhances democratic atti-

tudes and increases interest in self-management. In addition, it raises productivity. If the task of redistribution is accomplished by policy 2, and the burden of education is shared by all, policy 3 is difficult to oppose. Party and union schools should provide education in political self-government and participation in business management.

4. *Substantial subsidies for culture.* High-pressure advertising, habit, lack of alternative experience, and pressure to "keep up with the Joneses" in a competitive bourgeois environment where the accumulation of things is a sign of progress and prestige, create what is known as consumerism, i.e., an enormously inflated need for material objects. As a result income, time, and energy are diverted to the satisfaction of the lowest needs, at the expense of higher needs. Man is reduced to only one of his dimensions; he behaves as *Homo consumens*. As such, he is well suited for late capitalism and completely unsuited for socialism. To develop higher needs, man must cultivate his mind. Education is one move, but a quite insufficient one in this direction. It must be complemented by effective access to the culture of the community. Since the taste for things little known must first be developed, "heavy advertising," "competitive pricing," and subsidies are necessary. High-quality fiction must be made so cheap that a taxi driver will be induced to buy it and read it while waiting for customers—as the proverbial Moscow taxi driver is supposed to do. If workers' homes are filled with books, workers' heads will be filled with socialist ideas. Museums, art galleries, and public libraries should be established all over the country and entrance fees abolished. Tickets for drama and ballet performances and musical recitals should be priced to fill theaters and concert halls. Amateur drama, musical, and arts groups should be encouraged, and "houses of culture" built as often as schools and town halls. That this can be done is shown by the experience of some etatist countries. Once mass participation in culture is achieved, yet another precondition for a socialist society will be fulfilled. People who enjoy music, buy paintings, and frequent museums are not likely to be persuaded that the accumulation of gadgets is the prime goal in life. Neither will they consider wage labor and business autocracy as obvious and unavoidable.

These four policies, however important, are designed to create only the preconditions for transition. The actual transition is the task of the remaining three policies. The first is concerned with industrial democracy and the second with the expropriation of capital; the third is a combination of the two.

All three result in a gradual destruction of the basis for class exploitation.

IV. Industrial Democracy

A study of the history of employer-worker relations reveals three development stages. At first employers were absolute bosses, and workers were treated as servants. The employer enjoyed unrestricted power in hiring, dismissing, and fining the worker. Exploitation was brutal, and the relations between the two classes savage. Attempts by workers to set up protective organizations were crushed. Unions were outlawed. When unions were gradually legalized in the second half of the last century, they emerged as the fighting organizations of the working class. They often combined trade and political activities and fought over both industrial and political issues. The First International was created by unions, not by parties. Strikes were used to improve work conditions and extend political liberties. The general strike was considered a suitable means for eventual radical social transformation. An open and ruthless class war raged throughout the entire period. This period is known as liberal capitalism. It ended with the First World War.

Around the turn of the century, political and industrial organizations of the working class were separated and were relatively well institutionalized as parties and unions. After the war, the first workers' parties—in Germany, England, Scandinavia, and elsewhere—came to power. The class war was institutionalized. Employers and workers created national bargaining organizations. This was the beginning of the period of organized capitalism. Unions were integrated into the system. From the viewpoint of the worker, the function of the unions was to secure higher wages and supply social security. From the standpoint of the employers, their function was to keep order on the labor market. Employers came to realize that it pays to collaborate with unions rather than insist on arbitrary power. Two general principles of collaboration were established: (a) unions would restrict their activities to industrial conflicts and avoid political confrontation; (b) management prerogatives could not be subject to collective bargaining. The latter meant that the formerly unrestricted power was replaced by what was considered to be strategic power, and was denoted as "management prerogatives." These included the right to hire, replace, transfer, and dismiss employees and to direct and organize work—as, for example, was neatly formulated in the famous section 23 of the Swedish central labor-capital agreement in 1906, and made an obligatory clause for collective bargaining contracts by the Swedish Employers' Confederation.[25] Joint consultation was compatible with these two principles. The spheres of competence seemed clearly and unambiguously demarcated.

Yet workers have never ceased to consider unions as primarily weapons against exploitation rather than simply instruments for gaining improvements in the standard of living. A new development appeared after the Second World War with the first step toward co-determination in Germany. An *Arbeitsdirektor* (personnel director) was introduced into the top management and labor representatives were seated on the supervisory council. Labor representation on the supervisory council has been moving from minority representation toward parity. The powers of the works councils have been strengthened. Scandinavian countries are following the German example. Multinational European companies seeking incorporation in the European Economic Community are expected to have labor participation in their boards of directors. A Swedish government bill of 1976—exactly seventy years after the appearance of section 23—makes the management of a company, its structure, supervision of work, equipment, working hours, working environment, and so on, negotiable. The erosion of management prerogatives is in full swing. This third stage of employer-worker relations marks the beginning of the transition period.

In 1865 John Stuart Mill wrote, "the relation of masters and work-people will be gradually superseded by partnership in one of two forms: in some cases, associations of the labourers with the capitalists; in others, and perhaps finally in all, associations of labourers among themselves."[26] In this prediction Mill of course was not taken seriously by his bourgeois colleagues. A century passed before examples of the first of his two categories began to appear. Instead of being considered and treated as a servant (the English Master and Servant Act was repealed in 1867) or hired hand, the worker is becoming a partner, a *medarbetare* (co-worker). When the Norwegian law on employee representation on company boards was debated in 1973, even the Conservatives voted for it. The old order is losing its legitimacy; it cannot be defended any longer.

Co-determination implies participation at the shop floor and at the company level. The workers are involved directly in the former, the unions in the latter. Workers are winning the right to participate in the measurement and evaluation of work;

in the determination of time schedules of work and breaks; in the planning of vacations; in job design and the determination of safety measures; and in decisions on transfers to other jobs; They insist on being informed in advance as to intended rationalization measures and on having the right to check management decisions. But participation and autonomy at the work place will not mean very much if workers are excluded from strategic decisions on new organization or technology, investment ventures, or mergers. That is why labor participation in the boards of directors is required. And here unions, spanning entire industries, have great scope for new and completely unorthodox activities.

Unions also participate in "macroeconomic management," in national economic policy determination. In England, representatives of the Trades Union Congress serve on the National Development Council jointly with management. In Sweden, union representatives sit on the Labor Market Board, which also determines the timing of private investment decisions. French unions participate in the National Economic Council, which is involved in planning and the preparation of social legislation, as well as on some thirty modernization committees that set investment, export, and other targets. Dutch unions are represented in the Labor Foundation and the Social and Economic Council, which are concerned with wage and price policies. In Austria, unions participate in the Joint Wage-Price Commission and are also represented in the Chamber of Labor which helps to prepare social legislation.

The institutionalized initiative of the unions is occasionally supplemented—often against the will of the union management—by wildcat strikes and the occupation of factories. The latter occurs when a firm is about to go bankrupt and workers take over its management in order to save the firm (i.e,, to keep their jobs). This is evidence *sui generis* as to the comparative inefficiency of contemporary private management. Outside industry, the participation issue is most evident in the university. In the European tradition, the university is in fact the oldest self-governing institution, but encroachment on its autonomy by state power and the development of professorial authoritarianism have reduced the scope of university self-government. The well-known student revolt of the 1960s reversed this trend. Finally, with the growing unionization of public employees, participation is becoming an issue in public service as well.

Co-determination has been extensively criticized. Some of the critiques are justified, others are simply mistaken. It is said that co-determination serves to discipline the workers to avoid strikes,[27] thus increasing profits. Self-steering groups, works councils, and parity representation induce the workers to identify themselves with the shop or the firm; this sort of local patriotism for the firm destroys workers' solidarity and is nothing but an extended egoism. Members of the supervisory boards become corrupted by their new privileges. They forget whom they represent and behave like bosses, particularly if—as union nominees—they serve on a number of boards. Workers' representatives are torn by double loyalties at the bargaining table: they must press for better conditions for workers and at the same time defend the interests of the company. Unions must refuse to accept any responsibility for production, sales, and profits. Otherwise, they will put in jeopardy their fundamental role as agents of workers' interests. Co-determination is either real—in which case it lures workers away from the unions and weakens union power—or is a swindle. In either case, it is a highly dubious affair.

Co-determination is obviously a very contradictory institution. Yet, every transition is full of contradictions. Attempts to avoid contradiction by preserving organizational purity amount to a conservative defense of the status quo. The corrupting influences of directorial posts may be reduced by rotation, democratic control by the rank and file, and prohibition of multiple mandates. Unions will best serve workers' interests if they promote change. Today, change implies participation. All participation implies responsibility. Egoism cannot be eliminated by alienation. And if work alienation is to be reduced, the worker must become interested in his shop and his firm in order to develop a meaningful interest in his own work. If it is really true that participation increases profits and reduces the number of strikes, it is a highly commendable institution, for it demonstrates that economic efficiency can be improved only by destroying capitalist production relationships.

The trends seem unmistakable.[28] What the unions must do is to press for an extension of participation toward parity—and beyond. In order to make this possible, ownership relations must be changed as well.

V. Socialization of Productive Capital

Capitalism is a social system based on the ownership of capital. This is a banal observation, of course. But it directs attention to one important fact: the ideological justification for the familiar organizational-distributional formula, whereby workers receive wages for their labor and obey the commands of the owners, and the owners receive profits (interest) on their capital and exercise control. To individuals reared in a capitalistic environment, this formula belongs to the category of natural rights and self-evident truths. If the ideological backing is removed, however, if the legitimacy of the system is questioned, the formula suddenly appears quite arbitrary. Why should not workers also participate in profits and in decision making? The nineteenth-century argument was that the owner temporarily abstained from consumption and therefore must be compensated by profits (interest). A simple comparison of the consumption levels of owners and workers makes this argument rather dubious. Currently the standard argument is that the owner bears risks and must be compensated for this.[29] Yet, the worker bears a risk as well—he can lose his job. In fact, his risk is comparatively greater. The owner can spread the risks by acquiring a diversified portfolio of shares, while the worker has just one labor power and one job.[30] As for control over labor, that was a matter of a "free" wage contract. As long as the other party was weak, management prerogatives could not be touched. When power relations changed, however, they became negotiable as well, and thus command and control ceased to be the natural rights of capitalists.

Thus, the issue will not be resolved by theoretical means; it is the changes in social relations that matter in such cases. Two ideological changes can be observed. The worker is becoming a partner in the production process, a co-entrepreneur. Consequently, it is right and proper for the worker to participate in profits and in decision making. On the other hand, the system automatically generates a concentration of wealth and power that is at odds with the professed ideals of democracy.[31] Democratic control can be established by means of participation in management and deconcentration of productive wealth. The latter implies some sort of profit sharing. Thus we again reach the same conclusion. Since co-determination has already been discussed in the preceding section, we shall now turn our attention to profit sharing.

Discussion of and experimentation with profit sharing is as old as capitalism. Profit sharing has been recommended as a device that will make workers loyal to the firm, provide work incentives, and keep away trade unions. What is new in the current developments is an insistence on the *right* to share in profits, the replacement of cash payments by a *distribution of shares* and, finally, the establishment of *collective trust funds* rather than individual appropriation of shares. If a part of profits is paid out in cash, it represents an addition to wages and this is the end of the story. If it is paid out in shares to individual workers, these shares are likely to be sold and, in any case, an increase in the number of very small shareholders does not change anything in the control of industry. Collective ownership, however, makes for a radical change.

France was a pioneer in the field. In 1917, a law was passed establishing *sociétés anonymes à participation ouvrière;* collective funds were to be created by a distribution of shares free of charge to the employees in order to strengthen their position. The situation was not ripe for this innovation, and the law remained a dead letter. Half a century later, in 1967, France became the first country in which profit sharing was made compulsory in firms with more than 100 employees. The money received would be placed in various funds, given as loans to the firm, or used to buy shares in the firm. Only a small percentage of the total amount was used for the last purpose. Though this law contributed to the development of participation, it did not pass the threshold that separates reforms *preserving* capitalism from reforms *destroying* capitalism. That crucial step was made and the pattern set a few years later on another continent. In 1970 a decree was passed in Peru making compulsory the distribution each year of a certain percentage of profits—15 percent in manufacturing firms—in the form of shares into indivisible workers' funds. As the percentage of stock ownership increases, workers' participation in the running of the firm increases as well. Thus, by means of collective ownership the capitalist market itself is used to effect an expropriation of capital. The capitalist rules of the game are used to replace capitalists by workers. More than a century ago, in his *Principles of Political Economy* (book 4, ch. 7), J. S. Mill asked that workers free themselves "not by robbing the capitalists of what they or their predecessors had acquired by labour and preserved by economy, but by honestly acquiring capital for themselves." Today this can be done—though not exactly in the way Mill had in mind.

Apart from outright state intervention, which until recently seemed the only method available, the socialization of private productive capital can be achieved by three different methods, or a combination of them. The Peruvian method, as we have just seen, uses profits to acquire shares.[32] The amount distributed is therefore proportional to the profits earned by the firm. Another method, which we may call the Danish method,[33] adds a certain markup to the standard wage bill. This sum is then converted into equity capital in the firm. In this case, the profits that are distributed are not proportional to capital invested but to "labor invested" as measured by wages. It may be argued that workers and capitalists are owners of two risk-bearing factors of production and that therefore profits should be distributed in proportion to their inputs in the production process, i.e., in proportion to wages and capital[34] or according to some more complicated formula.[35] This theory is just as arbitrary as the one mentioned before, but it is better suited to the changing mood of the times. In practice, however, the consequences are different, as we shall see in a moment.

Finally, it is possible to invest accumulated pension funds in risk-bearing capital. Since these funds are made up of contributions from the workers' wages, the voting shares acquired ought to be used to establish working class control over industry. This method, which is likely to be only supplementary, may be denoted as Swedish. In Sweden, common pension funds (*allmäna pension fonderna*) contain more money than the value of all existing corporate stock; a certain percentage of these funds—as yet rather small—may, according to parliamentary decision, be used for investments in risk-bearing capital.[36]

The main advantage of the Danish method is that it is simpler to administer. Since saving is associated with the wage bill, it may be argued that it is the workers who save and that therefore they ought to control their saving. Next, the markup may be added to wages even in nonprofit organizations. Finally, employers will find it more difficult to evade their obligations. Administratively, the Peruvian method is less efficient. In Peru, employers managed to sabotage the law by showing low profits, or even losses, and by increasing wages in order both to corrupt workers and to reduce profits. Private investments were reduced. Manufacturing firms were combined with service or selling firms to which profits were transferred. Multinational firms represented an especially awkward problem, since they could easily remove profits from the books in any particular country. Wages, on the other hand, must be paid out, and so markups on wages cannot be avoided. But the Danish method has its drawbacks also. It taxes labor-intensive industries more than capital-intensive ones, which means that the former will come under labor control first. Since such firms generally are not the technologically most advanced and most efficient industries, it may happen that an image will be created of workers' management as less efficient. In addition, since wages do not represent a residual like profits, an unprofitable industry may be hard hit (with the value of its shares declining toward zero), while in a highly profitable industry profits may be used for private enrichment. One possible remedy is to differentiate markup according to profitability and/or labor intensity, but this would complicate administration. Next, the initial markup must be small and can be increased only gradually. Even in such a case, however, employers may use it as an excuse for inflationary pricing.

In general, our preliminary analysis indicates that wage bill markup is probably preferable in a less developed country where government administration is not very efficient and the market is far from delicately balanced. Also, in such a country investment resources—profits available for investment—are generally scarce and can be suitably enlarged by a markup on wage bills. In fact, that was the motivation behind the Danish trade union proposal: unions were willing to support larger profits in order to speed up economic growth, provided the workers shared in the control of the new capital. In an economically advanced country, the situation is generally likely to be reversed, and the profit-sharing method might appear more desirable. It is an interesting historical paradox that the pioneers—the Peruvians and the Danes—acted the other way round.

Let us now have a closer look at the profit-sharing method. Since profits represent a residual, this method is neutral with respect to costs, wages, and prices. The only change occurs exactly where it is desired—in the distribution of ownership. If the contribution to the fund is 20 percent of the profits before taxes, dividends and taxes amount to 40 percent, and gross profitability is 5, 10, or 20 percent, it will take 75, 35, and 25 years, respectively, before the fund acquires one-half of the firm's stock.[37] Due to dispersed stock ownership, it is often sufficient to own a small percentage of the stock in order to be able to control the firm. If this share is 20 percent, and other conditions remain the same, workers will acquire control of the firm in 23, 12, or 6 years, respectively. A number of consequences follow. Dispersed stock ownership makes possible the rather rapid establishment of effective workers' control. The higher the rate of profit (and, of course, the higher the share of contributions to the fund), the sooner the control will be established. If, as is generally believed, the capitalist management favors high profits, workers can now agree and collaborate wholeheartedly. The solidarity wage policy of the unions becomes easier and more effective. Since, for technological and demand reasons, profitability varies among industries, solidarity wages—i.e., approximately equal wages in various industries—will result in substantially different rates of profits. But now extra profits will not be pocketed by private capitalists (though they will share too), but will be used to speed up the socialization of the profitable industry. Issuance of new shares may lengthen the transition period. But this effect will be neutralized if the proceeds of the fund (workers' dividends) are used to buy new shares. Pension funds may be used for the same purpose. Since the fund cannot be appropriated, it represents social property. For this reason, contributions to the fund are not taxed. Since they remain in the firm as equity capital, the saving in tax means an increased net profitability and additional investment resources. The capitalist management should welcome this. It is only absentee owners (shareholders) who will protest, because the value of their shares will decline. It may be added, however, that an increase in tax or in the interest rate—which happens all the time—also reduces the value of shares.[38] Anything that reduces the value of the stock increases the relation between the contribution and the stock, i.e., speeds up the relative growth of the fund. The development of self-management often improves business ethics. An effect of this kind can be expected here as well. For tax purposes, the stock held is evaluated below its market value. An undervaluation of stock would mean that more shares would be distributed to the fund, with the consequences just enumerated. Thus, it may pay to be honest.

Workers' participation in management is a request to be judged on its own merit and is not necessarily associated with ownership titles. But in a capitalist environment, the acquisition of ownership may help and may speed up the process considerably. The simplest solution would be to make participation of workers in management and on the board of directors of a particular firm dependent on the stock ownership accumulated in the fund. Once the relative size of the fund makes effective control of the firm possible, the workers' council would take over the operation of the firm. The simplest solution, however, is not always the most efficient one. What one wants to achieve is not simply a redistribution of wealth and power, but an orderly transition to a new socioeconomic system. Two institutions can be instrumental in that process: the unions and the state. Since it is desirable to minimize the use of state power, the formidable task of a radical restructuring of production relations will have to be assumed by the unions. This is surely the most important and the most difficult task in the entire history of unions. To the extent that they succeed, they will render themselves unnecessary, for that will imply nothing less than an emancipation of the working class.

Unions will operate two types of funds. One will consist of a single fund in which the equity stock acquired by labor will be accumulated. This is the Social Property Fund. The second category will consist of several funds disposing of the dividends accruing to the stock owned by labor. These are the labor funds.

The Social Property Fund—one for the entire country—has mostly symbolic importance and is in fact a bookkeeping institution. All shares acquired by labor are deposited here, but the proceeds flow to the labor funds according to an agreed-upon scheme. State corporations and unincorporated firms may be regarded as joint stock companies and shares may be replaced by ownership certificates. The certificates are issued annually in the same relative amount of gross profit as in joint stock companies. This amount is expressed as a percentage share of the firm's capital. These percentages are accumulated in the Social Property Fund and the corresponding dividends (calculated as some average proportion of net profits) are sent to labor funds. According to the capitalist rules of the game, the shares and certificates held by the Social Property Fund generate proportional voting rights that are also administered by the labor funds.

There can be at least three types of territorial (central, regional, and local) and two types of industrial (for the firm and for the industry branch) labor funds. What is the proper function of each of these funds? Since the new task of the unions consists in participating in production decisions, the crucial role will be played by the branch funds. Modern unions, unlike the older craft unions, are also organized on a branch basis, and this will facilitate the task of operating the funds. The funds are managed by elected boards, on which government representatives sit as well. The main task of the branch funds is simply to prepare full-fledged workers' self-management. Workers themselves are familiar with shop floor operations, and so they can participate directly at that level. In order to extend participation to the level of the firm, help is needed from the outside. If this help is not forthcoming, the workers may be manipulated by the old management, or they may make wrong decisions that would discredit self-management. The branch funds, like the branch unions, are familiar with the working conditions of a particular industry. They know its products and its market problems. Thus, they can help directly with advice to works councils. The funds will select candidates for the boards of directors and the top management in collaboration with the works councils. These officials are nominated if and when they are elected by the councils. The branch funds help to work out statutes of the councils and render organizational help. They organize courses in self-management. They use the dividend money to buy new shares, to buy out firms that are about to go bankrupt (if the workers request this), and to set up fully labor-managed firms in their branches. The branch funds may, for the time being, reserve the right to make some strategic decisions such as those regarding the merger or dissolution of a firm, or a heavy investment and modernization program; on all other matters, works councils vote independently at shareholders' meetings.

Participation at the firm level consists initially of three different components. Workers elect their works council, which consists exclusively of workers (blue as well as white collar) and is concerned primarily with problems on the shop floor. The branch funds deal primarily with problems at the firm level. The work community, which comprises all persons employed in the firm—that is, workers *and* managers—operates the firm's labor fund, which represents the results of the work of all. The fund sends an agreed-upon part of the annual dividends of labor-owned stock—say, one-half—to the branch and central funds. The other half is employed according to the preferences of the work community. The work community may use the available resources to buy additional shares in the firm, to give a loan to the firm, to make contributions to a local labor fund, to finance educational, cultural, or recreational activities or institutions, to provide for social welfare purposes, or to increase wages. The decisions on these matters will provide practical experience in collective decision making and will also help to integrate the three components of participation into an eventual single self-management.

The Central Labor Fund is concerned with ironing out regional differences. It intervenes when a massive purchase of shares or other investment proves necessary. It finances research, education, and the dissemination of information concerning labor management. It may fund chairs in labor management and finance graduate courses for managers. It is not sufficient for workers to become educated; managers must be educated as well. If left to themselves, the universities will continue to educate managers for capitalist firms. Consequently, the unions must intervene, and the assets of the Central Labor Fund are best suited to the purpose. The Central Labor Fund may also establish an auditing agency that will provide services to works councils and a management bureau that will serve as a consulting agency, render technical and managerial aid to labor-managed firms, and provide labor-appointed managers for private firms.

After a certain number of years have passed, the voting rights generated by the increasing stock ownership will begin to matter; labor funds will have substantial amounts of money at their disposal and labor-managed firms will cease to be rare exceptions. At this stage, coordinating institutions at the regional level may become necessary. This may require the establishment of regional labor funds. Once the transition period is more or less complete, the labor funds will evolve into institutions of the labor-managed economy described in chapter 13. The central, regional, and local labor funds will be transformed into federal, state, and communal investment funds. The dividends will become the price for the use of social property. The firm fund will merge with the business funds of the firm. Only the branch funds—of central importance during the transition period—will lose their function. They may give birth to branch banks and various research, educational, and other institutions serving the branch. In the meantime, they will have established a practice of branch planning.

VI. Two Issues Likely to be Raised

It may be asked: Why will employers accept a profit-sharing policy that will eventually lead to the expropriation of private productive capital? The answer is that they will not.[39] They will oppose and sabotage the policy as much as they can, but they will realize that the other two alternatives—labor unrest and/or government intervention (assuming the government is controlled by socialist parties)—are even worse. From the point of view of employers, a gradual change that will become substantial only after a number of years—when they will have retired—is vastly more preferable than a sudden unexpected change. In the meantime, the government may be defeated, conditions may change, and there is a chance the policy will be reversed. From the point of view of labor, the transition time is not necessarily fixed; developments may be speeded up by concerted union and government action. The time that will elapse before full control is established will not be lost. Workers will learn how to run the firms. Both parties have a chance to be right. It is exactly the uncertainty in human affairs that makes the policy tolerable. The outcome is not necessarily predetermined. It depends on the involvement of the parties, on human action. In the process, repetition and custom cause relations that are at first shocking and irritating to become familiar and commonplace. In the end, even employers—like Norwegian Conservatives—will vote for workers' management. After all, professional managers, insofar as they are genuinely professional, ought to be able to manage the firms at least as efficiently under workers' councils as under boards of directors and, quite likely, more efficiently.

At this point we encounter another possible question: If labor-managed firms are really more efficient than their capitalist and etatist counterparts, as argued in chapter 6, why do they not outcompete the latter firms in the market? Is not the whole discussion about transition policy misplaced? If labor-managed firms are more efficient, they will expand and socialism will be established in any case. If they are less efficient, the policy aimed at reduced efficiency must be self-defeating. The answer to this question is that a labor-managed firm cannot easily survive in a capitalist environment regardless of its *potential* efficiency. Let me draw a historical analogy.

A capitalist firm, characterized by management hiring of legally free workers for money wages, is clearly more efficient than a feudal estate or an ancient slave factory. After all, that is why capitalism replaced previous social orders and has become the dominant socioeconomic system. Yet, these potentially very efficient capitalist enterprises—together with commodity and money markets—had existed in previous societies and had not prospered. The three main ingredients of capitalist entrepreneurship—mobility of factors, contract law, and property rights—were also present, and yet without much avail. Commenting on this fact, Max Weber wrote: "the specific features of modern capitalism, in contrast to those ancient forms of capitalist acquisition, the strictly rational organization of work embedded in rational technology, nowhere developed in such irrationally constructed states, and could never have arisen within them, because these modern organizations, with their fixed capital and precise calculations, are much too vulnerable to irrationalities of law and administration."[40] It remains to discover what are the irrationalities of capitalism that make workers' management difficult to institute.

A labor-managed firm is similar to a producer cooperative. Most producer cooperatives eventually fail. There are at least three reasons for this:

a. Cooperatives find it difficult to obtain bank and trade credit. They are also discriminated against by private firms in the supply of necessary raw materials and the marketing of their finished products. Capitalist economy behaves like an organism that has undergone an organ transplant: it spontaneously rejects the alien tissue.

b. Cooperative self-management implies a radical reduction in the salary spans for managers. Thus, capitalist firms have no difficulty in bribing away the most capable business administrators—particularly since it is easier to issue commands than to treat workers as equals.

c. Once a cooperative begins to expand, new workers must be employed. In a capitalist environment, this causes social differentiation. The founding members tend to treat newcomers as hired labor. Very soon, the cooperative degenerates into an ordinary capitalist enterprise.

The last observation implies that self-management is behaviorally incompatible with private or collective ownership. It requires social ownership. Thus, we now part with producer cooperatives and consider genuine labor-managed firms.

d. Social ownership means that the right to participate in decision making is derived from employment and not from ownership. That, in turn, implies a thorough overhaul of the entire legal system. Yugoslavia changed constitutions three times in the first twenty-five years of development of workers' management. Because of the inappropriate legal and institutional setting in which cooperatives exist, the most trivial problems, which otherwise would be solved automatically, become extremely complicated; it takes a great deal of time, energy, and ingenuity to sort things out. An alien system generates unnecessary costs.

e. Ideology and vested interests work against the success of cooperatives. In a capitalist setting, a worker-managed firm is deviant. Even well-intentioned business partners and authorities do not know how to treat it. Does it represent a business or a political risk? What criteria should one apply? The trade union finds its position utterly ambiguous. Who is the employer here and who is the worker? What about working class solidarity? What is the role of the trade union in a worker-managed enterprise? Does it have any? Thus, all well-meaning members of the establishment are bound to be highly suspicious. But not everyone is well meaning. Those who are not will be openly hostile. Efficiency improvements even within existing firms will be opposed if they conflict with the ruling ideology and vested interests. "As long as the authoritarian firm makes a normal or reasonable profit, the people in power prefer to maintain the established order rather than create a more efficient but democratic organization. The goals of preserving the existing differences in power, status and income are by far more important values than the over-all efficiency of the firm."[41] It is a simple fact that the efficiency potential in a microeconomic organization can be exploited only if the macroeconomic—indeed, social—environment is changed appropriately.

Changes in the social environment require persistent political struggle. The fundamental strategy of this struggle, as our analysis has indicated, is to do whatever helps human development. For socialism is another word for humanism.

VII. The Role of Producer Cooperatives

Since the days of Robert Owen, social reformers have from time to time advertised producer cooperatives as a suitable means for social and economic transformation. But the history of British and American cooperatives has been quite unimpressive.[42] And nowhere else have producer cooperatives attained more than negligible importance. The reasons for their failures were explored in the preceding section. Thus one might conclude that, though desirable because of their self-governing features, producer cooperatives are not likely to play an important economic role, and thus there is no need to pay special attention to them. This would be an erroneous conclusion, however, for at least three reasons:

1. Contemporary cooperatives seem to be more productive than their conventional capitalist counterparts.[43]
2. In an era of disintegrating capitalism, the social environment is more favorable to cooperative experiments than at any time before.[44]
3. There is no need to perpetuate old mistakes. Cooperatives can be shaped organizationally so as to ensure their survival and expansion.

Cooperatives are usually small- or medium-sized firms. They are established in three different ways: (a) Traditionally, a group of workers would pool their resources and, possibly with an outside loan, would establish a cooperative; as a rule, these are very small establishments. (b) More recently, and increasingly often, workers take over firms about to become bankrupt or to be sold out and run them on their own in order to preserve their jobs;[45] such firms are often larger, and workers are occasionally able to secure communal support. (c) Progressive employers hand over their stock to the employees and the firm is transformed into a co-op; the process of transformation is usually conducted in stages over a number of years.

In what follows, I shall concentrate on case (a), though most of the analysis is applicable to the other two cases as well.

Producer cooperatives provide an intermediary link between privately owned and socially owned firms. They are based on collective property, which is not a very precise category. This provides for organizational flexibility. A cooperative may be organized in such a way as to be indistinguishable from a private partnership firm, or its organizational structure may fall at the other end of the spectrum, where we find the pure worker-managed firm. Because of this flexibility, a cooperative can usually be organized even within a rigid bourgeois legal framework.

The cooperative strategy we are looking for must satisfy two conditions: the firms must be economically viable even in an alien environment; and they must provide for a smooth transition to a socialist economy. If the successes and failures of producer cooperatives in developed capitalist countries are studied, certain regularities can be identified which can be used in designing a desirable strategy. The following seven factors seem to be of crucial importance.

1. *Funding from member contributions.* A person joining the co-op should "buy" his job. The down payment must be substantial in order to be significant, but it should not be so great as to prevent interested individuals from applying. The membership deposit serves three purposes: it is a source of capital; it has educational value as an evidence of commitment; and, in a market economy, it provides incentives for aligning personal interests with the long-term success of the firm. If the applicant does not have ready cash, he may be given a loan or the membership contribution may be deducted from his earnings over a certain period of time. Part of the contribution (in the cooperatives in Mondragón, it is 20 percent) is transferred to the co-op's indivisible reserve account. The balance is entered into a personal account, which may be credited a fixed interest rate annually. Personal balances may not be withdrawn unless the individual leaves the co-op or retires. When a person is entitled

to withdraw his personal balances, he may be paid in debentures or shares and not in cash. Shares are nonvoting but may carry honorific privileges (such as attending the assembly with consultative rights) as long as they are not transferred. In this way, the capital of the co-op is kept intact and the retired member retains an active interest in and preserves emotional ties with the community in which he spent an important part of his active life.

2. *External funding.* Modern capital-intensive technology requires rather high investment per worker. These investment costs cannot be matched by members' contributions. The balance is funded from external sources. For this purpose, the usual financial instruments may be used (loans, bonds, nonvoting stock).

3. *Nonmembers.* Nonmembers are second-class citizens and, in principle, must be prohibited in order to prevent degeneration. There are two possible exceptions. Wage differentials in a cooperative are always narrow. In a capitalist environment, where much larger earnings differentials are found, this might prevent the co-op from securing high-quality managers. Thus, several managerial posts may be reserved for nonmembers and the managers hired as employees. This, of course, reverses the usual procedure in which managers hire workers, but such is the nature of the co-ops. The experience of American plywood cooperatives shows that this can be done. The other exception is seasonal production, where nonmembers are employed to bridge seasonal oscillations.

4. *The supporting structure.* An isolated co-op is not likely to survive very long. National cooperative associations are helpful, but they do not solve the problem. Cooperatives can develop only if they are integrated economically into a sector. The sector need not be large, but it must represent an integrated system. In a national economy, there may be a number of such cooperative systems. For this purpose, cooperatives need what Jaroslav Vanek calls a *supporting structure.* This sheltering organization is a cooperative of the second degree. Since co-ops are usually starved for capital because they lack access to the traditional capital market, the most important part of the supporting structure is the cooperative bank. The bank is a source of investment capital, provides short-term credits, underwrites loans, and provides a market for shares and debentures issued by the co-ops. The two other important sectoral activities are education and the rendering of legal services and management advice together with the provision of managerial personnel. The phenomenal business success of the Mondragón system is

explainable to a large extent by the good organization of its supporting structure, which has all three of these ingredients. As the cooperative sector grows, it becomes possible to guarantee employment by switching labor from one firm to another.

5. *Pension and insurance.* In order to reduce risks, pension and insurance schemes ought to be operated separately. At the beginning, small amounts of insurance money may be channeled into co-op investment through the co-op bank. As the number of cooperatives multiplies and the entire sector grows, a rising percentage of insurance funds may be invested in the sector, thus increasing the availability of investment capital.

6. *Expansion as a precondition for survival.* Technological improvements require continuous reinvestment. Market competition requires an increase in size and financial strength, which necessitates expanding capital investment. It is too risky to rely on external sources for this. Thus, a substantial part of net profits must be earmarked for investment. A certain percentage of profits (in Mondragón it is 20 percent of normal profits and a higher percentage of windfall gains) is credited to indivisible reserve funds. A part of profits is distributed in additional wages (positive and negative), and a part is spent on social and educational projects. The balance, if any, is credited to individual accounts. The indivisible reserve fund of the co-op, financed out of the prescribed percentages of members' contributions and profits, represents the nucleus of social property.

7. *Communal ties.* The cooperative is also a work *community.* It is therefore natural that members will—and should—take an active interest in communal affairs. Part of the earnings will be spent on various communal projects. On the other hand, in times of need, the co-op will legitimately expect help from the local community. One obvious need is for the underwriting of loans.

In all other matters, the organizational principles discussed in chapter 8 apply to producer cooperatives as well. It hardly need be stressed that the basic principle of self-management—one man, one vote—retains full force.

One cannot expect that by following the above seven commandments every cooperative will be a smashing success. It is people and their actions that determine success or failure. But it is possible to say that a contemporary producer cooperative has a reasonable chance of succeeding.

Save in exceptional cases, cooperatives are not likely to be a major, or even a very important, instrument of socioeconomic transformation. Participation in private and state sectors and wage earner funds appear to be much more important. But the cooperative movement can contribute greatly to the creation of an appropriate atmosphere, to consciousness raising, to the delegitimation of private ownership with its social hierarchy and authoritarianism. In addition, cooperatives can solve many individual existential problems. For these two reasons, producer cooperatives form a part of the general strategy of socialist transformation.

17

Paths of Transition: Etatist Countries

I. The Dynamics of Change

Political liberties generally exist in late capitalist societies. For this reason, we can assume that workers have their unions and citizens their parties. We saw that the social trends are such that some of these organizations are likely to opt for socialism. It is entirely realistic to expect that socialist parties will win elections and form governments. Thus, our task was to explore policies that a social scientist could recommend to such governments.

The etatist environment is entirely different. Here political liberties are so restricted that, for all practical purposes, they may be considered nonexistent. Workers do not have *their* unions, nor do socialists have *their* parties. There is no regular possibility for a socialist party to assume power, since there is no regular possibility for such a party to be organized. Intrasystemic opposition (opposition within the apparatus) is rendered, if not impossible, then at least irregular, because of the ban on factionalism. Does all this mean that only a violent revolution—a "political revolution" as Trotsky thought—can change the system and establish a "dictatorship of the proletariat"? Certainly not. A violent revolution is possible, of course, as the Hungarian uprising of 1956 demonstrated. But so is a peaceful transition as attempted in the 1968 Prague Spring.

The problem appears to be immensely more complicated than the simpleminded revolutionaries of 1917 could have imagined. Writing in 1920 about the transformation period, Bukharin voiced a widely held opinion when he claimed: "Under the dictatorship of the proletariat, the question of the 'master' falls aside, since the 'expropriators' are 'expropriated.' "[1] It is true that property was expropriated. But not political power. Dictatorship implies power, and power was appropriated by the new masters. Since at first Bukharin and his colleagues were the new masters, they did not worry. The question of the master fell aside. When they were outmaneuvered in the power game by Stalin, it was too late. And at no time did they have anything resembling a theory of transformation intended to deal with the problem of concentrated political power.

The etatist situation is highly paradoxical. "The Soviet privileged grouping," observes Harry Braverman, "is in the unique and anomalous position, among all the privileged groupings of history, that it must teach the nonlegitimacy of its own privileges and powers over society. By reason of history and ideology, it must either pretend these privileges do not exist or argue in effect that its trusteeship over society is temporary, as over a ward that has not yet come of age."[2] In fact, the ruling class does both: it hides its privileges and insists on its temporariness—though the period of its domination is constantly extended. The state fights socialism while at the same time claims allegiance to it. The party established its monopoly by preventing any socialist movement from appearing, yet at the same time claims to be the vanguard of such movements. This contradictory position is the source of both strength and weakness. Since socialist ideals have an enormous appeal, by using socialist slogans the politocracy supports the legitimacy of its rule. By acting against socialism, however, the ruling class renders itself extremely vulnerable. The etatist politocracy has more power than any other modern ruling class but, as Isaak Deutscher points out, its position is less secure and less stable than that of other comparable classes. Since the politocracy cannot openly behave as a ruling class, it must hide its substance, unlike the bourgeoisie or the aristocracy. "It feels like a bastard of history."[3]

Two consequences follow. The ruling class must generate an unending stream of lies, while at the same time protecting the society from any intruding information about the destabilizing truth. Capitalism admits that it is capitalism; etatism cannot admit to being etatism. It must also remain economically and politically successful. A bourgeois system normally survives an economic debacle or a military defeat; comparable circumstances pose a grave threat for an etatist system. England can grow slowly; Poland cannot. A proclamation by a group of dissidents draws hardly any attention in a bourgeois setting; it frightens the government and almost rocks the regime in a bureaucratic system. Etatism must prove its superiority and infallibility, and must continue proving them.

The custom—more correctly, the necessity—of lying originated in the inability of the leadership to fulfill the promises of the Revolution. After all, etatism is the direct heir of the first socialist revolution. At first, writes Deutscher, the Bolshevik leaders did not try to dress up the difficult position in which the community found itself. They tried to keep alive the hope and courage of their followers by words of truth. But the truth was too harsh to remove the despair. And so it was gradually replaced by consoling lies. The aim was only to mask the gap between the dream and the reality, but very soon the lie was used as a proof.[4] And that turned out to be a road without return. The process was facilitated by the theory of historical determinism. The party was merely executing the orders of history. Since the policy was historically determined, it was not—and could not—be wrong. The party was not responsible for the failures. Consequently, no bad conscience came from lying.[5]

The inability to admit the true nature of the system implies not only the necessity for lying, but also a need to accept certain socialist obligations. We have already seen (in chapter 2, section IIID) that basic welfare—life expectancy, education, and health—is higher in etatist societies than in their capitalist counterparts. We have also observed that etatist societies show a more egalitarian income distribution. In this case, the obligation accepted has been fulfilled, at least partly. In other cases—primarily political—it remains unfulfilled, though proclaimed over and over again. For example, the program of action for the next twenty years, presented at the Twenty-Second Congress of the Communist Party of the Soviet Union in 1961, proclaimed: "The evolution of the socialist organization of the State will lead, gradually, to its transformation into a communistic self-governing republic in which the soviets, the cooperatives and other associations of workers will be united. This process will involve a further development of democracy. . . . The organs of planning and of execution, of economic management and of cultural growth, which today are contained in the apparatus of the State, will lose their political character and become organs of social self-government. The communist society will be a highly organized community of workingmen. . . . The course of history leads inevitably to the extinction of the State." P. Demichev and other Soviet writers declare that this is already taking place "as envisaged by the founders of scientific communism." But then we hear from Demichev that, while the society is becoming classless and the dictatorship of the proletariat has transcended into an all-people state, the leading role of the working class has been preserved![6] What this leading role of the working class means is explained by another author, who argues that "in all stages of the building and development of socialist society, the working class exercises its leading role under the leadership of the Communist Party."[7] Socialist democracy develops further, Demichev declares, while at the same time the ruling role of the party increases! The system containing these contradictions is denoted as "developed socialism in the political sphere."[8] A. K. Belyh makes it clear that socialist self-government means paid, professional, and not always (!) elected officials. The full election and revocability of officials is put off to a future "communist self-government."[9]

In a collectively written book prepared by the Institute of Governmental Law of the Academy of Sciences, one chapter has the heading: "The Increase of the *Ruling* Role of the Communist Party in Society Is a Developmental Regularity of *Democracy* in Developed Socialism" (emphasis added). It is then mentioned that party membership includes about 9 percent of the adult population. The party works out the political line, *directs* and *coordinates* the work of the state and societal organizations, and creates the preconditions for *self-activity* and *creativity*. In Soviet society, forces or organizations opposing their own policies to party rule do not and cannot exist. The entry of Soviet society into the phase of *developed socialism* implies the *development of the class nature* of the state. The ideological functions of the Soviet state are further expanded. The law guarantees the right of workers and employees to participate in production management. This right consists in making suggestions about organizational improvements, and the administration is obliged to consider these suggestions. As for worker management itself, the doctoral collective rejected the idea in disgust, as nothing but an anarchosyndicalist slogan regarding so-called production democracy upheld by contemporary opportunists![10]

In a representative paper published by the Soviet Political Science Association, Boris Topornin argues that "under developed socialism, the sphere of the state's activity considerably expands." Socialism is usually associated with the withering away of the state, and a powerful state is considered a grave danger to individual liberties. But Topornin simply asserts that "the state of developed socialism is distinguished by particular emphasis on the free and all-round development of the individual."[11] These statements clearly reflect the content of the new Soviet Constitution of 1977. For instance, Article 20 declares: "In accordance with the communist ideal—'the free development of each is the condition for the free development of all'—the state pursues the aim of giving citizens more and more real opportunities to apply their creative energies, abilities, and talents, and to develop their personalities in every way." Freedom for citizens means controlling the state. Not so in etatism, where the state controls the citizens and distributes rations of freedoms as benevolent gifts.

The foregoing collection of contradictory quotations summarizes the essential features of the prevailing political ideology: (a) the continuity of the Revolution is upheld verbally; (b) terms are reinterpreted so as to become meaningless; and (c) real change is postponed until some distant future referred to as communism.[12]

Yet, the structure of language—if not of ideology—sets certain limits to the use of words, and human psychology sets limits to the tolerance of unfulfilled promises. Thus, in spite of political monopoly, an etatist state is very vulnerable. It cannot admit free discussion, it cannot open the borders, it cannot grant political freedoms, and it cannot tolerate criticism. It cannot even safely use its troops in the occupation of another country.[13]

At the same time, the revolutionizing influence of modern technology is felt here just as in capitalism. The old, half-illiterate, poor working class recruited from the peasantry is gradually being replaced by a new, well-educated, and affluent working class. In 1970, in Soviet industry one-quarter of all graduates with a technician's diploma were employed in worker jobs.[14] Education is expanding rapidly and cultural facilities are used extensively. Satisfaction of the physical and cultural needs of broad sections of the population is bound to generate a strong request for the next level of need satisfaction—the political one. A caveat is needed, however: this will not happen either immediately or automatically. In a capitalist environment, consumerism delays the emergence of higher needs. In an etatist environment, social atomization coupled with pseudo political activism serves the same function. Technological requirements are less ambiguous. The increasing complexity of technology requires decentralized control and greater independence of workers. It also requires more numerous contacts and closer relations with foreign firms and foreign centers of technological development. Organizational rigidity and isolationism spell backwardness and inefficiency.[15]

The economic superiority of etatism meant higher rates of growth. With a higher level of development, however, this superiority gradually vanishes and, as was indicated in chapter 6, after a certain point seems to turn into inferiority. Political superiority meant monolithic international support. This is no longer the case. Western communist parties feel free to criticize the etatist camp. The Stalinist doctrine of party dictatorship has been abandoned by the most important communist parties outside the camp. The original socialist doctrine of genuine political democracy has been reestablished. Thus, on both scores etatism is on the defensive—except in backward countries—and it is only a matter of time until substantial changes can be expected. Inside the etatist camp, the emergence of the "loyal socialist-democratic opposition," as the most important groups of dissidents call themselves, heralds the new era.[16]

The paradoxical position of etatist countries leads to paradoxical consequences. The more successful the governments—the higher the standard of living—the stronger the grass roots pressure for political reforms. The less successful they are, the less legitimate they are, and the less secure they feel. In either case, the system will have to be changed.

II. What Is to Be Done?

Three-quarters of a century after Lenin first asked the above question, we have every right to repeat it. In view of the discussion in the preceding section, the question may be rephrased slightly: What can be done to speed up the process of transition to socialism? Since organized political activity is not tolerated, it makes little sense to speculate about what might be done if it were. A clandestine Leninist party is not a real alternative either. Once such a clandestine party becomes possible, the system will be on the verge of breakdown anyhow.

A bureaucratized etatist society is socially atomized. Social ties are replaced by bureaucratic hierarchy. Individuals do not have *their* preferences, *their* organizations, *their* private life; it is the state, "the party and the government," that determines everything. Private life is incompatible with bureaucratic collectivity. Those who oppose the state, oppose the collective will and are guilty of immorality. They lose their friends immediately, are treated as enemies, and are socially excommunicated. In a more totalitarian etatist environment, they are arrested and sent to forced labor camps. They cannot count on feelings of solidarity from other members of the community since solidarity presupposes a relatively firm structure of friendship and other ties, and the consciousness of common purpose. Both have been destroyed by police repression and aggressive brainwashing. Thus, before political activity can be initiated, solidarity structures must be created at a more elementary level, in connection with apparently neutral, nonpolitical activities. Once a social restructuring of etatist society starts, it will be the beginning of the end of political hegemony. For this reason, a clandestine political party is neither possible nor necessary. At first, intellectuals may again play the crucial role.[17] In fact, their importance is even greater than in other systems. The reasons are explained by Leszek Kolakowski:

> A system of the Soviet kind enjoys the advantage that it does not have to justify its actions to the public: by definition, it represents their interests and desires. . . . However, it is also exposed to a risk from which democratic structures are immune: namely, it is extremely sensitive to ideological criticism. This means, among other things, that the intelligentsia plays a part that is not paralleled elsewhere. A threat to the intellectual validity of the system, or the advocacy of a different ideology, represents a mortal danger.[18]

In a way, intellectuals have a simpler task than elsewhere; they do not have to work out a basically different vision of the world in order to change the existing consciousness and undermine the legitimacy of the authorities. The vision already exists; it was created by the Revolution, but its meaning was later destroyed. What the intellectuals must do is to restore the original meaning of the words, to render the vision socialist. The rest will be done by the nonrejected legacy of the Revolution.

In fact, there is not only the legacy of the Revolution. There is more than that. The outside world has changed as well. In a somewhat paradoxical way, the outside world helps to contain the counterrevolution inside the camp. The old controversy about the possibility for "socialism in one country" is as relevant as ever, but in the new scenario it is, in a sense, posed on its head. I have already mentioned the radical change in the position of the communist parties in developed capitalist countries. This branch has come to be known as Eurocommunism.[19] While the camp is fully immune to the bourgeois critique, the communist critique is experienced as disastrous. It is possible to begin building socialism in isolation. It is also possible to justify the internal counterrevolution by citing the enormous difficulties and unforeseeable obstacles encountered. It is impossible, however, to withdraw into self-imposed isolation after socialism has been proclaimed victorious. Closely related is the influence of progressive forces in the world community at large. It proves impossible to reject various international covenants concerning human rights. Once such covenants are ratified, they cannot be totally ignored. If this is attempted, it will be met by internal opposition that is fully constitutional and that can be suppressed only by gravely undermining the legitimacy of the regime. The Czechoslovakian Charter 77—and the support it received from communists outside the camp—is a case in point. So is the Soviet Committee for Human Rights and a similar committee in Poland (created in 1977). Thus, what socialists should do in etatist environments is not to engineer violent revolutions but to demand that laws be obeyed and civil liberties be respected.[20] Insistence on legality and the fulfillment of proclaimed goals turns out to be the most revolutionary activity.[21]

Though intellectuals may take the lead, workers are unlikely to remain passive for long. They will react in the traditional field of labor relations: against unfavorable living conditions and then against the bosses. They will go on strike and will organize independent unions. They will soon realize, as did workers during early capitalist development, that unions can function only under a system of political liberties. And then the workers will join the intellectuals in fighting for a common cause. In fact, this scenario is not a mere speculation; such things are already happening. The demonstrations by Polish workers in December 1970 were triggered by a governmental decree that increased food prices. Workers began to demand a number of crucial reforms, such as the democratization of relations at the factory level, the autonomy of trade unions, the abolition of privileges of position, an effective fight against bureaucracy, and the dissemination of information without distortion.[22] In the 1950s and 1960s, a certain number of strikes and worker revolts in the Soviet Union were put down by police and army detachments, and workers were killed or wounded in these actions. In January 1978, the Soviet miner Vladimir Klebanov, together with a number of other workers, established what were termed free trade unions. As in the early capitalist era, most workers were promptly fired and many were jailed. Klebanov and several other workers were interned in a psychiatric hospital.[23] To be fired or jailed for such activity is, of course, the predicament of proletarians in a class system. It is unlikely, however, that such treatment will deter Soviet workers any more than it has their colleagues in other countries and at other times. In February 1978, a group of Polish workers established a Committee of Free Trade Unions in Katowice. The committee was supported by the Movement for Defense of Human Rights.

The workers, and everybody else, will press for self-management.[24] As experience shows, worker management at the factory level may be developed quite far before it begins to threaten political hegemony. Under pressure, the politocracy may rationally choose to yield on that score. The first signs of a development in this direction are already visible. In a speech at the time of the 1965 reforms, Premier Kosygin is reported to have said: "Better management is impossible unless it becomes more democratic and unless the participation of the masses is considerably extended. . . . Every worker should be made to feel that he is one of the owners of the factory."[25] In the second half of the 1960s, Soviet economists and sociologists began to discuss problems of participation.[26] Sociological studies indicated high dissatisfaction among workers with their work and overwhelming support among workers, engineers, scholars, and even party executives (from 89 to 77.2 percent) for the election of lower-level managerial personnel. Only top managers did not seem overly enthusiastic (52.4 percent in favor). Probably for the first time, a Soviet economist, A. Birman, unambiguously declared in an article published in 1969 that socialism is more than public ownership and a high level of production. It makes "indispensable participation of working people in the management of production, of the whole country. But even the word 'participation' is not enough; it is the *exercise* of management by the working people themselves. Socialism is a self-managing—through the state—society of working people."[27] The unavoidable state had to be included in the statement to render it publishable; but Birman makes it clear that he expects workers to be involved, out of "objective necessity," in the hiring and firing of enterprise personnel and the formulation of premium systems.

Thus, worker management is likely to be the initial major breakthrough. We can hardly expect, however, that this will lead to rapid social and political transformation. The effects of negative political socialization, extended over generations, are too strong.[28] It is therefore quite likely that the system will be stabilized for a while.[29] Since worker management may prolong the life of etatism, should we abstain from it? The situation is analogous to that under capitalism, and the answer is the same. We are not interested merely in the destruction of the existing system; our fundamental aim is to build a new, socialist system. The earlier this construction begins and the less social disruption is brought about, the better. Worker management implies a certain autonomy on the part of the firm. This requires decentralization. Decentralization requires legal security. And legal security is a prerequisite for political security.

Worker management also has more direct corroding effects. The Akchi experiment in participatory farming in 1968–70, mentioned earlier (chapter 16, section VI), is the first lonely herald of what is likely to happen. Because it was too successful, it was suspended. But it generated public discussion, which Murray Yanowitch sums up as follows:

> It downgraded the need for a large social stratum of professional managers. It affirmed, in however limited a form, the idea of self-management by "direct producers." It denied that Soviet technological backwardness was the main source of poor economic performance in agriculture. It affirmed the compatibility of an equalitarian income distribution (at least within work teams) with efficient work performance. Perhaps most important . . . was something that was left unsaid. The Party's "mobilizing" and "monitoring" role . . . hardly seemed necessary at Akchi, and its participation in selecting the rotating incumbents of managerial positions was not a structural requirement of the farm's mode of operation. In the language of one of the published commentaries on the experiment, Akchi was an argument for moving from "juridical" socialization of property to a "real" change in relations of production, to the "collective management" of socialized property.[30]

The Akchi attempt failed, but others will follow. There can be hardly any doubt about it.

Once the process of deconcentration of power is inaugurated, it is likely to develop rather fast. Almost overnight the words will acquire their normal meaning. And just as fast the ruling class will lose its precarious legitimacy. Reflecting the Party Program and the Constitution, Topornin and his colleagues proclaim that "the deepening of democracy is the main direction of the development of the socialist state."[31] Under changed circumstances, this may be taken quite seriously. The verbal scaffolding of socialist ideology has been preserved and is ready for use. Etatism ascends into socialism. Czechoslovakia demonstrated how this could happen. Because of the fundamental instability of the mature etatist system, the Prague Spring could have triggered a chain reaction. That is why it had to be nipped in the bud. Czechoslovakia was silenced; but the rest of the world was awakened, and Eurocommunism was born.[32] Etatism can survive only by undermining its own legitimacy and, consequently, its own survival.

18

Paths of Transition: Less Developed Countries

I. The Conquest of Political Power

In the social order denoted as organized capitalism, political democracy is more or less established. To be sure, it is not genuine democracy; it is rather, in the words of Maurice Duverger, plutodemocracy, since political power is based on people (*demos*) and on wealth (*plutos*).[1] Yet certain basic political liberties are quite effectively guaranteed. We saw that in such countries the main problem of transition consists in establishing economic democracy.

In etatist countries, certain welfare preconditions for socialism are quite well fulfilled. Here the main problem of transition consists in safeguarding political liberties, in establishing effective political democracy.

The underdeveloped countries know neither political nor economic democracy. They were either colonies—and thus dominated and exploited by foreigners—or independent states—which implied domination and exploitation by domestic reactionary oligarchies. In either case, the established regimes were oppressive in the extreme, both politically and economically. In addition, the peoples of these countries were poor and uneducated.

We saw how extremely difficult it is to build socialism in advanced capitalist and etatist countries. If this is so, then building socialism in an underdeveloped country must appear hopeless. President Julius Nyerere of Tanzania, who has had to face such a situation, summarized the problems involved:

> With few socialists we are trying to build socialism; with few people conscious of the basic requirements of democracy we are trying to achieve change by democratic means; with few technicians we are trying to effect a fundamental transformation of our economy. And with an educated elite whose whole teaching encouraged motives of individualistic advancement, we are trying to promote an egalitarian society.[2]

If socialism in a politically and economically backward country is an obvious impossibility, why attempt it? The answer is that the question, as formulated, is a false question. If socialism cannot be established overnight, this does not mean that there is no chance to take different routes and that some of them do not lead to socialism much faster than others. Once we discard the deterministic theory of successive stages, we can begin to think in terms of developmental shortcuts. A new African or Asian country may, but *need not,* follow the path of capitalist or etatist development. It may choose a path that leads to socialism much more directly.[3] It is our task now to explore the possible design of such a path. Because of the extreme diversity of countries involved, the discussion can only be very general.

Unlike in advanced countries, in undeveloped countries violent revolutions are possible, even quite likely. Colonial peoples fight national liberation wars that become social revolutions. Vietnam, Yemen, Algeria, Mozambique, and Angola are perhaps the most conspicuous examples. Antiquated monarchies are destroyed by civil wars or by the rebellions of young officers. China, Ethiopia, and some Arab countries are cases in point. The peaceful, "parliamentary" transfer of power provides an exception. Tanzania and Guinea succeeded (so far); Chile failed.

Socialism cannot be gotten as a gift; if it is attained at all, it is achieved through prolonged struggle. As the examples cited above would indicate, this struggle is likely to involve violence, often very brutal. Socialists cannot choose the conditions under which to fight. They can only adapt their tactics and strategy. If violence is imposed upon them, they cannot withdraw. Yet the unavoidability of violence does not imply that violence ought to be advocated. The more violence, the less the chance that victory will be followed by socialist reconstruction. Nyerere has cited the reasons:

> Even the most successful and popular revolution inevitably leaves behind it a legacy of bitterness, suspicion and hostility between members of the society. These are not conducive to the institutions of equality, and make [it] difficult to build a spirit of cooperation between the whole people. In particular, there is always a fear that those who suffered during the revolution may be looking for an opportunity of revenge; there is a memory of injury and bereavement deliberately inflicted, which poisons the relations between men within the society. A violent revolution

> may make the introduction of socialist *institutions* easier; it makes more difficult the development of the socialist attitudes which give life to these institutions.[4]

A feudal or fascist autocracy toppled in a civil war—since the mechanisms for a peaceful transfer of power do not exist—may be replaced by a regime that will nationalize the productive capital but that is unlikely to be able to introduce socialist democracy. The dictatorship of reactionaries is replaced by a dictatorship of revolutionaries, and the latter tends to degenerate into a counterrevolution from within. The history of the Soviet power is illuminating in this respect. Obviously, this is no reason to refrain from fighting the autocracy. But it does demonstrate the vested interests of socialists in a peaceful transfer of power.

Since the transition starts from the existing order, the institutions of that order must be utilized. Thus, a political party will be indispensable. It will often have to achieve a double task; national liberation and social transformation. For this, it must be composed of dedicated political activists. The party needs strict discipline and strong leadership. Consequently, it must be centralized. If the party is driven underground, these conditions apply with even greater force. The type of party best suited for the task is an "organization of revolutionaries" as conceived and created by Lenin.[5]

The party is organized by the revolutionary intelligentsia. The movement it creates has a broad social base. It starts in the city, the springhead of economic progress; but in order to succeed, the movement must conquer the countryside. The peasants represent 70 to 90 percent of the population, and so they are the main revolutionary—or counterrevolutionary—force. When (in capitalism) the peasants own land, they tend to be conservative, loyal to the church and established authority, and resistant to change. This is generally true of the twentieth-century Western European peasantry, but not of the peasants in undeveloped countries (nor of European peasants in former centuries). Here the peasants are economically exploited, politically oppressed, saddled with debts, losing their land to the moneylender and the landlord. The salesman and the mass media inform them of a different world, and the teacher explains to them that their fate can be changed.[6] As a result peasants, with the possible exception of a tiny fraction of rich peasants, are ready for revolution. Contemporary revolutions as different as the Chinese and Yugoslav ones demonstrate that very persuasively.[7]

The working class revolutionary potential is considerably smaller. Workers are few in number, earn income several times higher than that of peasants, and represent a privileged group in a poor society. Unlike nineteenth-century European workers, the workers in contemporary underdeveloped countries are unionized,[8] and the unions take care to integrate them into the existing society. While the landless peasant must attack the ownership of the landlord in order to improve his position, the unionized worker only insists on his proper share in the income of the firm. A socialist party exerting influence on the unions can raise substantially the socialist consciousness of the workers.

The lumpenproletariat consists of poor peasants who moved into the cities and could not find permanent jobs. They live in slums and shanty towns, and in Latin America may represent more than one-quarter of the urban population. They are poor and deprived, but this does not make them progressive. They are often attracted to conservative leaders. Samuel Huntington quotes four reasons for their lack of radicalism: (1) by leaving the village, the migrants feel they have advanced socially; (2) they bring with them rural values and attitudes, such as social deference and political passivity; (3) they are interested primarily in immediate gains in food, jobs, and housing, which they cannot secure by working against the system; and (4) engaged in a fight for survival, they distrust each other, which prevents them from forming organizations.[9] Although not radical by themselves, slum dwellers may be radicalized by a popular and determined socialist party.

Mao Zedong found in China that artisans, small traders, white collar employees, and professionals represented a "reliable ally" of the Revolution.[10] That is probably true more generally. In Latin America, for instance, unions of bank employees proved to be radical strongholds. Mao also included the national bourgeoisie as a temporary ally. Thus, it is only a small oligarchy that opposes national independence and social transformation. It consists of large landowners and wealthy businessmen and politicians acting as the agents of international capital. They must be removed from a position of power. For this task, the party can mobilize the support of virtually the entire population.

Where an appropriate Leninist party does not exist, the task may be accomplished by the army. The army is an organization with strict discipline and single-mindedness of purpose. An enlightened leadership may turn this organization into an instrument of progress. Students and officers are the two most modern groups in the society. If students fail to organize the party, military officers may take over. Because of their training, the officers are nationalists. Because of its function, the army is the most modern sector in the society. Consequently, military officers will assail backwardness and corruption and will advocate efficiency and national integration. If they happen to be involved in the sociopolitical conflicts of the country, they may quickly develop social consciousness, become politicized, challenge the oligarchy, and take the lead in political and economic reforms. The counterinsurgency operations in the countryside had awakening effects on the Peruvian military. It acquired first-hand experience of the appalling conditions of peasant life. The horrible experience of a bloody colonial war prompted Portuguese officers to overthrow the dictatorship. The thousands who were starving while the emperor's court continued with its festivities moved the conscience of Ethiopian officers. In such cases, even if the officers do not have a program of social reforms prior to their ascendance to power, their new responsibilities may turn them into socialist reformers. A number of Asian and African military coups had that experience.

II. Political Stability

The conquest of political power is the first problem to be solved. The choice of a political system is the next. This choice is predetermined by the need for the system to be stable. As Bertrand Russell remarked long ago: "We must . . . seek first to secure government, even though despotic, and only when government has become habitual can we hope successfully to make it democratic."[11] Consequently, "the primary problem is not liberty but the creation of a legitimate public order."[12] Though it is possible to have order without liberty, it is impossible to have liberty without order.

An orderly government is not at all an easy task. A democratic government is even more difficult. High labor productivity cannot be achieved overnight; neither can stable political democracy. Both need gradual accumulation; the former requires the accumulation of capital, the latter that of political experience. In fact, if undeveloped countries have any common feature apart from being poor, it is political instability. Because of it, their fragile democratic structures are destroyed and replaced by dictatorships of one kind or another. It has often been stressed that one of the great achievements of bourgeois development is political democracy. Let us take a quick look, however, at what was happening in the larger part of bourgeois Europe a century and a half after the French Revolution. I have in mind the two decades preceding the Second World War.

The interwar political history of Europe consists of military and fascist coups, a continuous sequence of failures of parliamentarianism, and the wholesale replacement of democracy by dictatorship in most European countries. In the process, European capitalism produced the following gallery of dictators and dictatorships: in 1920, Admiral Horthy became regent of Hungary; in 1922, Mussolini marched on Rome; in 1923, Stambolinski was murdered in Bulgaria and his government overthrown, and the military coup of Zvenov in 1933 and of King Boris in 1934 followed. In 1923, General Primo di Rivera established a military directorate in Spain followed, after several years of parliamentary democracy, by a military uprising of the notorious General Franco in 1936. After two attempted military coups in Greece in 1923 and 1925, General Metaxas established his dictatorship in 1936. In 1926 there was a coup d'état in Lithuania, followed by a sequence of nonparliamentary regimes. In the same year, Marshal Pilsudski engineered his presidential coup in Poland, and after his death in 1935 the dictatorship was continued under the regime of Colonels. In 1927–28, Salazar rose to power in Portugal; in 1929, King Alexander removed the constitution and established his dictatorship in Yugoslavia. Only in 1933, after twenty-one German administrations succeeded each other in fourteen years, did Hitler join the gallery of European dictators. In the same year Dollfus assumed authoritarian power in Austria. Civil war followed, and a few months later Dollfus was killed by the Nazis. In 1938 Austria lost its independence through Anschluss. In 1934 Latvia and Estonia proclaimed a state of emergency and all political parties were banned. The last formally to establish his dictatorship was King Carol of Romania in 1938; but in fact Romanians had lived under conditions of political dictatorship throughout the entire interwar period, whatever the name of the party in power. Parliamentary democracy survived only in those European countries (independent before World War I) in which political democracy, as measured by substantial male suffrage and responsible government, had been practiced for at least one generation—and usually several generations—before the moment of crisis. These were England, France, Switzerland, and the Benelux and Scandinavian countries, to which the formerly dependent Czechoslovakia, Finland, and Ireland ought to be added. These countries also represented the more developed part of the continent (Italy and Germany were exceptions). The only important deviation from the rule[13] was Sweden, where a comparable responsible government probably cannot be dated before 1917. In this country, however, a socialist party was elected to power at the decisive moment, and over the next several decades Swedish Social Democrats managed to turn their country into one of the world's leaders in terms of both political democracy and economic development.

This is not the whole story, however. Even the countries where political democracy survived experienced great political instability. In the period 1919–33, cabinets lasted between one and two years in Norway, Denmark, Sweden, Belgium, and the Netherlands. French cabinets lasted less than six months during the entire interwar period. No wonder that economic development came almost to a standstill.

The interwar experience of the less developed European countries was repeated in the entire underdeveloped world after the Second World War. In the first three decades, successful coups were engineered in nineteen out of twenty Latin American countries. In other words, all surrendered except Mexico, which could build its political system on the reliable basis of a genuine social revolution. The political situation in African and Asian nations is scarcely different.

The reasons are not difficult to find. Economic development and the ensuing mobility destroy old values and social structures without necessarily replacing them immediately with new ones. The first national impulse of every ethnic and social group is to pursue its own interests. Political demagogues have a fertile ground for their activities. Disintegrating forces are strong. And so are tensions. Inequality of income distribution is much greater in the city than in the countryside, and so industrialization increases overall inequality. But the population is less prepared to accept this inequality as legitimate. Education increases the aspiration level. But the satisfaction of new wants lags behind. Political participation develops faster than the institutionalization of the political process. Only around the First World War did the most advanced countries establish universal suffrage, and this achievement followed a century of development. Nowadays universal suffrage is taken as a matter of course, but it does not work everywhere as a matter of course. The strains imposed on the polity are simply too great. And so bargaining and liberal arrangements that do not work are replaced by orders and autocratic arrangements, which do.

It will come as no surprise that under such conditions a one-party system serves the purpose of stability best.[14] If the party in question led the struggle for independence, it will command practically universal popular support, which is a precious political capital with which to start.

It is obvious that a one-party system represents both a danger and an opportunity. The former is described by Frantz Fanon, the latter by Julius Nyerere. Fanon points out that

> the party plays understudy to the administration and the police, and controls the masses, not in order to make sure that they really participate in the business of governing the nation, but in order to remind them constantly that the government expects from them obedience and discipline. . . . The incoherent mass of the people is seen as a blind force that must be continually held in check either by mystification or by the fear inspired by the police force. The party acts as a barometer and as an information service. The militant is turned into an informer. He is entrusted with expeditions against the villages. The embryo opposition parties are liquidated by beatings and stonings. The opposition candidates see their houses set on fire. . . . In these conditions . . . the party is unchallenged and 99.99 percent of the votes are cast for the government candidate.[15]

Such a party, clearly, cannot serve as an instrument of socialist reconstruction.

Nyerere, on the other hand, explores the possibility for making the one-party system more democratic than its rivals. If the dominant party behaves in the traditional way, the leadership will choose the candidates and they will be elected automatically. The people effectively have no choice.

> This means that our procedures are, in practice, endangering both democracy and unity; if the people always acquiesce in the . . . candidate who is submitted to them by the Party machinery, they are losing their effective power over the representative and his actions. If they oppose him, they are in danger of giving sustenance to the enemies of our national unity and bringing into jeopardy the future of the principles which they wish to defend. We have thus come to a position where the maintenance of institutions and procedures which were supposed to safeguard the practice of democracy, and which are appropriate to a multiparty system, in fact eliminates the people's choice of the representative.[16]

The solution was found in establishing a one-party system by law and giving citizens full opportunity to choose their own candidates. In preliminary elections, party delegates at regional conferences screen the list of candidates. The two who receive the largest vote become (in principle) candidates for the general election. Their election campaign is financed by the state. They are free to advocate their own ideas, but they must not attack certain established values of the society such as national unity, religious, ethnic, and racial tolerance, and the like.

A one-party system may be misused. It may be turned into Fanon's rather than Nyerere's type of political system. Yet the choice is not between a one-party and a multiparty system. The choice is between a political system dominated by a bourgeois or etatist party and one dominated by a socialist party.

III. The Economics of Transition

Political stability is one of the basic preconditions for fast and continuous economic growth. Yet, it will not lead to growth automatically. In fact, a politically stable society may have an economy that grows slowly. Rapid growth requires purposeful design. Rapid growth, however, generates forces of instability. On the other hand, there is no hope that socialism will be established if economic growth is slow. There seems to be an inherent contradiction in the pursuit of these various objectives. Our task is to explore the possibility of making the objectives consistent and mutually reinforcing.

Growth means industrialization. In a country where peasants comprise 70 to 90 percent of the population, industrialization means a transfer of the labor force from agriculture into urban occupations. Historical experience indicates (with Yugoslavia perhaps holding the record)[17] that this transfer can proceed at a rate of up to 2 percent per year. Thus, it will take between five and twenty years before the share of the agricultural population is reduced to some 60 percent and the country enters the industrialization phase of rapid growth.

In the initial phase, at the lowest level of development, growth is likely to be slow. The rate of accumulation is low, 10 to 15 percent, while the capital-output ratio is high, perhaps even increasing. The industry mix is unfavorable; slowly expanding agriculture predominates, while the rapidly expanding manufacturing industry accounts for only a few percentage points of gross domestic product. After a while, the basic productive infrastructure will have been built, and the country will reach what Rudolf Bićanić called the threshold of economic growth.[18] There are at least four different reasons why economic growth accelerates in the industrialization phase:[19]

1. The capital-output ratio decreases—the faster the rate of growth, the faster the decrease. In the first two decades of postwar development in Yugoslavia, for example, the average capital-output ratio was reduced from 7.5 to 5. Most of this reduction was due to changes in the industry mix: the share of capital-intensive industries declined.

2. Capital cost per unit of output decreases for yet another and a very different reason. In a stationary economy, all of the investment is used for the replacement of worn-out capital goods. The faster the rate of growth, the smaller the share of replacement in investment, and the lower the replacement cost per unit of output. If the rate of growth is 10 percent per annum, practically all gross investment (more than 95 percent) is used to generate additional output, and replacement cost per unit of output is reduced to one-seventh of its stationary value. The economy behaves as if capital cost were close to zero.[20]

3. The growth of global factor productivity seems to be correlated with the growth of factor inputs. The faster the inputs expand, the faster is the growth of combined factor productivity ("technological progress"). The effects seem to be substantial.[21]

4. The increase in the share of the easily expanding manufacturing industry increases the investment absorption capacity of the economy. In other words, the economy can absorb more investment productively, the marginal efficiency of investment increases (given the rate of investment), and so the economy can achieve a higher rate of growth.

These four effects (some of them partly overlapping) work in the same direction: the faster an economy grows, the easier it is to accelerate growth even further. In the industrialization phase, the share of investment in gross national product may be raised to 30 to 40 percent, in which case the rate of growth will be around 10 percent per annum.

Not unexpectedly, the most difficult is the very beginning. When agriculture is by far the largest producing sector, economic growth depends primarily on what happens in agriculture. The first step is to carry out a land reform that will eliminate parasitic owners and will give the land to those who wish to till it. Large estates should be generally preserved as commercial producers for home and export markets and as nuclei of technological progress. Organizationally, they will be transformed into state or labor-managed farms. Apart from that, the redistribution of land ought to enable all peasant households to become viable producers. Agricultural extension services, price support arrangements, the provision of marketing facilities that will eliminate exploitative middlemen, a cooperation program, and agricultural credit complete the first set of policy measures.

The top priority is to ensure the productive employment of the agricultural labor force, which will result in food self-sufficiency and possibly generate some surpluses. A substantial share of available investment resources will also be used in connection with agriculture. Irrigation and melioration projects will increase the amount of arable area and improve yields. Investment in plants producing agricultural implements, fertilizers, pesticides, and insecticides represents the natural beginnings of industrialization. The emerging purchasing power of formerly subsistence peasant households will provide a mass market for simple consumer goods. The expanding consumer goods industry, together with the industry providing agriculture with capital and intermediate goods, and the construction of roads and railways will provide a market for building materials, metallurgical products, and other producer goods. The increasing output will have to be accompanied by expanding energy production. The industrialization will gradually gain momentum.

To exploit all the growth potential of the country, a central planning machinery will have to be established. Its major instruments will be a national investment fund and the physical allocation of available resources to key projects. Central planning is complemented by regional and local developmental initiatives utilizing local resources.

If a market economy is to be properly guided and controlled, the government must control financial flows and foreign trade. The latter requires strict general supervision and some system of licensing strategically important import and export flows. The former requires full nationalization of banks and insurance companies.

By contrast, a full-scale nationalization of the productive sector of the economy is not at all necessary. Neither is it feasible. Many of the owners—the national bourgeoisie, as Mao called them—will have actively cooperated with the socialist party, possess otherwise extremely scarce know-how, and should not be antagonized by nationalization. Buying out foreign-owned corporations requires financial means that the country needs for developmental purposes. On the other hand, it may prove indispensable to nationalize one or two foreign concerns—such as oil fields or copper mines—that are too profitable and too important for the economic independence of the country to be left outside full national control. As for the rest, parliament may oblige foreign concerns to appoint citizens of the country to managerial positions, introduce co-determination in all firms, and use the Danish method of establishing wage earner funds that will generate additional investment resources while at the same time quietly socializing productive capital. Foreign firms could hardly protest, since the same process will be taking place in their native countries as well.

Thus, in the initial stage, the economy will consist of several types of productive enterprises. A small number of large farms and manufacturing, mining, and transportation firms will be owned by the state. A certain number of producer and consumer cooperatives will exist. Former private estates not taken over by the state will be managed by peasants. A number of small labor-managed firms outside agriculture will be created spontaneously by workers out of failing private firms. Most of the firms will remain private but will be socially transformed by means of co-determination and wage earner funds. Family enterprises—peasants in the countryside, artisans and small traders in the city—which are by far the most numerous, complete this checkered initial property structure.

The coexistence of five different ownership sectors makes the task of running the economy extremely complicated and very delicate. The socioeconomic equilibrium is obviously very unstable. The aim of economic policy is not to preserve the equilibrium of coexistence but to control the dynamics of change. The preponderant corporate and family-owned private sector will tend to impose capitalist development. If this is checked by repressive measures, etatism is the most likely outcome. The state sector is its property base. The labor-managed sector is not only the smallest but the most fragile. A number of years must pass before peasants learn how to run their farms and workers learn how to run their firms. In the meantime, their efficiency may not be high. Wages may be lower than in the private and state sectors, which will tend to drain the best workers and organizers to these latter two sectors. The building of socialism can survive only if the party organization works well. "Red experts" will be sent to farms and worker firms to help them run their businesses, and will work and live together with their fellow workers and peasants. Party members will keep co-determination alive in private firms and, of course, party members will run state enterprises.

The dynamics of the system ought to be clear by now. The resources of the national investment fund will be used primarily to develop old and create new state firms. Co-determination will be introduced into these firms and will help to check etatist tendencies. Co-determination will be generally extended and develop toward full-fledged worker management. The general manager will be appointed by the government and he may be given restricted veto power, but the rest of the organization will be based on labor management. The private sector will also develop and new firms may be established. But the faster the corporate firms grow, the faster they will be socialized. Co-determination will also be extended and will follow, with a lag, the developments in the state sector. Finally, the labor-managed sector will expand, will be supported technically and financially, and will increase its relative efficiency. The three sectors will be oriented to converge institutionally toward one single labor-managed economy. In a generation or so, the task may be achieved.

Worker management is an indispensable basis for socialism. It is, however, not yet socialism itself. The other two ingredients are: appropriate political institutions and a certain minimum level of economic development or productivity. Assuming that the latter is a limiting factor, let us see what kind of time perspective an underdeveloped country faces. If it starts with an agricultural population representing 80 percent of the total, it will need about fifteen years before the phase of rapid industrialization is reached. In the meantime, the output per capita will expand at an average rate of, say, 3 percent per year and by the end of the period will have increased by some 60 percent. If the population increases by 2.5 percent per year, total gross national product will have increased by about 120 percent. In the industrialization phase, the rate of growth may increase to about 7 percent per capita.[22] If the level of economic development prevailing in Western Europe in 1939 is taken as the level under which politically and socially meaningful socialism is possible,[23] then given the assumed rate of growth it will take about thirty years to reach this level. Thus, under somewhat favorable conditions, the transition to socialism in a poor Asian or African country will take about forty-five years. International aid may shorten this interval. The main conclusion one can draw from these tentative calculations is that, even for the poorest countries in the world, socialism is not a distant and unattainable utopia. Those who initiated the transition process may hope to see it completed.

IV. The Politics of Transition

In an undeveloped country, primordial loyalties are high and consensus is low. The possible alternatives are scarcely known to the population. The sociopolitical integration of the country is the task that must be undertaken. Economic and political systems have to be built. The authority needs legitimacy. In a laissez-faire situation, a century of political instability, coups and countercoups, brutal class conflicts, and perhaps civil wars may pass before a stable bourgeois political democracy is achieved. Latin America is a case in point. The social costs involved in such a process are far too great, and the period of time too long to be tolerated. Moreover, the final result falls short of the historical possibilities of our epoch. But there is an alternative route available: the creation of a vanguard party. Its main instrument is socialist ideology. Every society has its ideology. The only (though a basic) difference is that, in this case, the ideology is a product of purposeful design. By socialist ideology, I mean a combination of some fundamental human values and a social theory that makes it possible for these values to be realized. Socialist ideology enables the party to create a broad movement, to bind the community together, to give it the purpose and self-consciousness necessary for socialist reconstruction. Since an ideology cannot be easily changed, once it is firmly established socialist ideology becomes an automatic controlling force for the activities of successive governments and party leaderships. Psychologists claim that childhood experiences exert a fundamental influence on later adult life. History seems to indicate that the ideology of a successful revolution molds the consciousness of many later generations.

The essential role of the vanguard party is to effect the appropriate political socialization. This is the most difficult task to be accomplished in the transition period. We still know very little about the processes involved. If the party fails to do the job, while continuing to remain in power, it will degenerate into a pure power mechanism whose self-perpetuation is its only raison d'être. In such a case, socialization will be replaced by manipulation. It is therefore of some interest to separate very clearly the two processes. In this, I rely on a study by Djuro Šušnjić.[24] As to methods, socializing means teaching others how they can think, evaluate, and act; providing generally accepted facts and criteria; indicating alternatives; getting used to methodological doubts; making reasoned statements; and building rational authority. Manipulation, on the other hand, implies inducing to think, evaluate, and act in a prescribed way; creating artificially an acceptance of what is generally unacceptable; eliminating alternatives; prohibiting doubts on even doubtful matters; condemning without reason; and imposing an irrational authority. In terms of content, socializing means abstaining from the imposition of "correct" thinking; offering ideas; perhaps *unconsciously* spreading fallacies; transferring knowledge; establishing a relation of mutual teaching; and offering truth as a message. The manipulator, conversely, induces others to think what he wants them to think; imposes ideology; *consciously* spreads lies and half-truths; creates beliefs; establishes relations of power; and offers his message as truth. As for purpose, the socializer wants others to know all the essentials about a matter; to increase the knowledge of his subjects; to develop a feeling and a need for freedom and personal dignity. The manipulator, on the other hand, aims at inducing others to believe what he thinks is good for them and restricting the rational options of his objects; for him, freedom and dignity represent inconveniences. The socializer is motivated to explain his positions; to develop the taste and needs of the public; to expand the possibilities of others; and to prepare them for creative self-determination. The manipulator tries to strengthen or change existing attitudes; to exploit the tastes and needs of the masses; to strengthen his power; and to prepare others for trained adjustments. Finally, the consequences of socialization are an open mind and independent thinking; of manipulation, a closed consciousness and dependence. As usual, it is much easier to make a clear notional distinction than to design policies that will promote socialization and prevent manipulation. But however difficult the task may be, it is of fundamental importance to realize that the two attitudes are not identical and that there is scope for rational action.

A sociopolitical system achieves overall societal orientation and conflict resolution in four different ways. Loyalty produces identification with the system and the proclaimed goals. Laws regulate the routine behavior of citizens. Differences in interests are settled by bargaining. In extreme situations, and only exceptionally, the political authority uses force. In this sequence, loyalty is crucial because it gives legitimacy to all other procedures. And loyalty is the outcome of a common ideology. If the sequence is reversed, the building of socialism is bound to fail.

In a more technical sense, the initial phase requires strict centralization. Human and material resources are extremely scarce. Economic and political choices are few and simple. The targets are known, and the problem to be solved is how to catch up with the more advanced countries as fast as possible. What is needed are the political resources of self-reliance and determination to succeed. The obvious strategy is to concentrate the few trained people in government agencies and let them initiate a process of economic growth and educational-cultural development. Yet, the very moment that the new centralized apparatus begins to work and the system is set in motion, the policy should be reversed and a long-run decentralization trend inaugurated. Centralization is a temporary expedient, not a permanent framework. Local and individual initiative works best in a decentralized setting. Socialist arrangements can and ought to make full use of the efficiency gains generated in this way.

It is notorious that economic and political centralization creates vested interests, and it may be extremely difficult to reverse the trend once the bureaucracy becomes entrenched in its positions. Social planners have at least three safeguards at their disposal. The first is local self-government. Centralization at the national level means the centralization of important decisions. This is fully consistent with local autonomy in day-to-day business. Moreover, self-government, once established, has its own vested interests, which will act as a countervailing force.

The second is co-determination. From the very beginning, it will be made clear that co-determination is only the first step. Here unions may play an important role. A program of gradual organizational transformation is worked out and every social plan contains a step further toward self-management. In general, the organizational framework in the transitional period is not a framework of institutions but a framework of change. It is the existence of the ruling vanguard party, consisting of persuaded socialists and dedicated activists, which makes the change easier.

The third safeguard is education. Fast growth requires a rapid increase in educational standards. Socialist ideology insists on education for its own sake. Thus, the two requirements reinforce each other. Historically, relatively high levels of education have sometimes been compatible with political autocracy, as under fascism in Germany and Stalinism in the Soviet Union. But these were different social environments. In an environment of worker management, education reinforces democratization and decentralization tendencies. Earlier it was noted that in underdeveloped countries education generally proves destabilizing. In a country building socialism, education works in the direction of proclaimed social goals and thus has stabilizing effects.

The chief danger faced by an underdeveloped country building socialism is class polarization. Rapid growth generates social stratification. If it proceeds unchecked, then after a while socialism will become an empty word. In the countryside rich peasants will begin to hire their fellow villagers, moneylenders will acquire land in exchange for debts, and a new landowning class will emerge. This process can be checked relatively easily, however. There is no need to nationalize land nor forbid the purchase of land. All that need be done is to establish a landholding maximum that is determined by the amount of land an average peasant household can till without permanently hiring outside labor. The land maximum is gradually increased as the application of new technology increases the productivity of labor. This releases redundant agricultural labor, of course, but industrialization creates new jobs elsewhere. As a result, the distribution of income in the countryside may be made almost ideally egalitarian.[25]

In the city, income distribution will be more unequal because of a threatened brain drain. A socialist country cannot close its borders. And if the salaries of highly educated personnel are too low, they will tend to emigrate. By socializing the managers, worker management makes them more ready to accept relatively low salaries. The same pressure is transferred upward to government bureaucracy.

Factory owners and bankers do not represent a great social danger because they hardly exist. Besides, banks are nationalized, and in factories worker management develops under the conditions of gradual socialization. The main source of enrichment in underdeveloped countries is corruption and the private appropriation of public funds. High government officials receive enormous salaries, which may be two hundred times higher than the average income in agriculture. Thus the main social danger comes from government bureaucrats and political leaders. What can be done to mitigate this danger?

It has already been pointed out that a one-party system does not imply the absence of political choice. Each parliamentary seat must be contested. Ministerial posts must be rotated. Government must be separated from the party. Political leaders must refrain from activities such as renting houses or land and exploiting wage labor; they must have no interests, or retain directorships, in existing private firms.[26] The salaries of leading personnel should be determined by parliament and linked to workers' wages. Finally, the mass media must fulfill their functions of the provision of objective information, documented confrontation of various views, and social criticism—admittedly a formidable list of requirements, but neither impossible nor unknown. If a revolution starts with such a program, it has a chance to carry it out. Historical failures and deviations that can be cited all have been associated with revolutions in which some vital elements of the program were missing.

Once we abandon the laissez-faire approach and opt for a purposeful design of social development, we cannot expect that the goals will be accomplished automatically, by a spontaneous play of social forces. We need a reliable instrument of social steering. This is the vanguard party. Such a party was necessary for a successful struggle for national independence and for the conquest of political power. It was also found necessary for the maintenance of political stability. It is now seen as required for socialist reconstruction. Without it, an underdeveloped country cannot hope to build socialism. Thus, the theory of the vanguard party plays a crucial role in the theory of the transition period.

Like other institutions of the transition period, the vanguard party is subject to rapid change. Unlike traditional political parties, its main purpose is to render itself superfluous as quickly as possible, to destroy itself in order to create a society in which political parties, as power-contesting organizations, will disappear. It begins as a Leninist party, develops into an association of political activists, and eventually disappears. The party does not have a ready-made formula for socialism that need only be put into effect by crushing the resistance of various hostile forces. It is the job of social practice and science (thus, *scientific* socialism) constantly to revise, control, improve, and reconstruct socialist theory. The party itself must perform the following four basic functions (or two pairs of complementary functions): overcoming historically inherited contradictions and integrating the society morally and politically, and overcoming political conflicts within the context of socialism and the construction of a democratic culture.

1. *Overcoming historically inherited contradictions and conflicts.* An underdeveloped country is likely to be ethically and linguistically very heterogeneous. The differences between city and country are enormous; those between intellectual and manual work, equally great. Rapid growth produces rapid social transformation with many disruptive effects. In such a situation of great potential and actual tensions, of incomplete construction of the institutional system, and of rapid and intensive changes, the society requires an organized social force that will act as a stabilizer and will be in a position to control and direct all those complex processes.

2. *Integrating the society morally and politically.* Whereas the first function is confined to establishing mere social equilibrium as the basic condition for the functioning of any social system, the issue is now the establishment of permanent social integration, which is the basis for social self-continuance. It is known that values have an integrative function of this kind in every society. It is also known that values are a historical, or social, category and hence that in a heterogeneous society several systems of values, possibly even conflicting ones, may coexist. Values are an important determinant of societal behavior, but they are not the only one. Societal behavior is a complex system of social reactions of individuals and groups conditioned by inherited and acquired systems of evaluations and ideas, or ethical and existential components of human life, and by personal experience and mode of interpretation of symbolic communication. Even when the objective interests of individual social groups are not in opposition, in a heterogeneous society it is easy for the possibility of communication to be lost—a condition that may then be exploited in various demogogic ways. This possibility becomes a certainty when interests are actually contradictory or the various groups perceive them as such.

Societal behavior is determined by social character. "For any society to exist," Erich Fromm observed "it must mold the character of its members in such a way *that they want to do what they have to do:* their social function must become and be transformed in them into something that they perform out of an internal need, and not by compulsion."[27] Social character internalizes external needs and thus orients the physical, intellectual, and emotional energy of men in such a way as to satisfy the needs of the given socioeconomic system.[28] In this context, it may be useful to distinguish four different character types. We find a *traditionally* oriented character in the countryside, in those small settlements where everyone knows everyone else, where the level of education is low and contact with the outside world weak, and people still live in primary groups. The development of capitalism generated an *individualistic* character. Individuals are isolated, ego-oriented, and emotionally impoverished creatures. Bureaucratic etatism and the relatively prolonged political monopoly of leading cadres, along with the conformity imposed by state security forces, leads to the development of the *collectivist* character and the corresponding mentality. Individuals lack independence and personal dignity, personality is dissolved in the collectivity, obedience and conformity are the chief virtues. In this connection, three important facts may be observed:

a. The transition from one value system to another or, more broadly, from one social character to another, does not take place all at once. During that interval, there is a period of anomie in which the previous standards have ceased to apply but the new system of standards has not yet taken hold or is not yet developed. These are the very dangerous periods of "declining social morality" and "loss of social discipline." They are periods that are all the more dangerous, the more radical is the social transformation. And social transformation is a function of the rate of economic growth.

b. Evidently, none of these three types of social character can serve as the basis for the construction of a socialist society. We must therefore look for yet another, fourth type of social character, which has not existed historically (at least not in fully developed form), but which can, and therefore must, be realized. If autonomous social forces are not subject to conscious social control, their haphazard play is likely to produce either an individualistic or a collectivistic social character, i.e., either capitalism or etatism.

The social character compatible with socialism may be termed the *associative* character. The associative personality achieves full integration with the community—not in an unconscious, unthinking, and hence enforced way, as individuals do in the primary groups of undeveloped societies, but as a free, autonomous personality by means of a conscious choice made possible by the fundamental conditions of his or her existence. The institution that spontaneously produces the preconditions for the formation of the associative character is self-government in all fields of human activity.

In a sense, social character is only another name for social relations. The associative personality is only another name for the socialist personality. The formation of socialist social relations may be slowed or accelerated. Chaotic development is certainly not the fastest. Development will be accelerated to the degree that the society is able to form an avant-garde of associative personalities. Unlike an elite, the avant-garde is not called upon to rule, but to act; it is not differentiated from the "mass," but includes the socially most mature individuals from the various clearly articulated social groups; it relies not on political authority—least of all, on the police—but on moral authority. In this sense, the moral standards of party members play a decisive part in realizing its moral-integrative role.

3. *Overcoming political conflicts on the basis of socialism.* If we examine the history of victorious socialist revolutions, we find a conspicuous absence of restoration attempts. Conflicts there

are, and fierce, but the contesting parties do not question socialism, they question the other group's interpretation of socialism. From the defeated worker opposition group in the early postrevolutionary Soviet Union to the arrested "Gang of Four," including Mao's widow, in China, the most dangerous conflicts arise within the framework of noncapitalist development. Traditional Leninist parties, oriented exclusively toward the conquest of power and believing in one single and simple revealed truth, have been poorly prepared to deal with this sort of conflict. Under the complicated conditions following the winning of power, formal unity proves to be quite inadequate. Real unity requires full democracy, and democracy implies freedom of dissent. In order to be effective, the party must make it possible for every member to express his opinion and then oblige all members to implement the decision of the majority. This was the original meaning of the principle of democratic centralism, before it degenerated into autocratic power of the leadership—to make decisions democratically and execute them centrally. But even in its original meaning, the principle is not sufficient, and its degeneration is almost certain. *The minority must not obstruct action, but no one can force it to renounce its opinion.* Even more, it must have the full possibility to raise the issue again at an appropriate time. All innovating groups—including revolutionary parties themselves—started as minorities. If the party is to survive as a socialist party, debate and the free exchange of ideas must never be halted.[29]

For the party successfully to perform its fundamental function, it must be a firm organization of political activists. In order to be firm, it must be genuinely united. And in order to be united, it must be deeply democratic. This conclusion leads us to the fourth function.

4. *Building democratic culture.* An underdeveloped country does not have centuries of peaceful development behind it as a national state, in which a democratic culture of citizens could be formed gradually. Nor can it tolerate the luxury of extending the process of constructing democratic culture over the coming centuries and thereafter. At the same time, it is obvious that democracy cannot function if citizens do not use their democratic rights in an appropriate way. Either there is no criticism, or criticism degenerates into wild, irresponsible attacks.

Opposition to criticism appeared very early in workers' parties. Characteristic in this respect is the reaction by Engels some eighty years ago: "The labour movement is based on the sharpest criticism of existing society. Criticism is its living element, how can it aim at avoiding criticism itself, forbidding debate? Are we to demand freedom for ourselves only to abolish it within our own ranks?"[30] At the same time, a party, like every bureaucratic organization, *necessarily* generates resistance to criticism (justifying it on the grounds of the general interests of the struggle and the danger of the enemy's exploiting any weaknesses). The more the organization is centralized, the more such resistance is intensified. This applies to a legal party, such as Engels had in mind, but it applies even more to an illegal party, which by necessity must reduce criticism to a minimum. What happens is that the habits formed under conditions of illegality are later carried over into conditions that are radically different.

The absence of criticism is usually explained by saying that no one likes criticism and that those who are its potential targets try with all their might to prevent it. This is only half of the story, however. These mighty individuals are much less an influence on their milieu than they themselves are products of that milieu. The milieu itself is undemocratic, and therefore it does not tolerate different, i.e., deviating, behavior. If a minister of the government is criticized, this will generally be taken as an attack on the regime and on socialism. If the government fails to react to the criticism, then it will be assumed that the person criticized has ended his political career, and that the criticism actually came from official sources and simply represented the announcement of a replacement. In such an environment, individuals are penalized not only when they really criticize, but also when they express some unusual idea that differs from the standard stereotypes.

This does not mean that criticism disappears; it is only transformed. It becomes irresponsible or stays behind the scenes or both. If criticism is discouraged in everyday relations among people, people have no chance to get used to it. Such a situation gives rise to the fantastic, destructive, unproved, and totally irresponsible criticism of individuals and institutions that comes into the open from time to time. Moreover, intrigues, secret reports, and denunciations replace open democratic struggle among opinions. Instead of reading in the newspapers what people think, political leaders must engage police informers to find out.

In a patriarchic milieu, a critical attitude toward government is regarded as a subversion of authority that cannot be tolerated. The patriarchic milieu is not in the habit of evaluating arguments; it is guided exclusively by personalities. In logic, this is known as the fallacy *argumentum ad hominem.* "The lower the level of logical culture and logical discipline of a man's thinking," explains Soviet logician Asmus, "the less able he is to divorce the probative force of an argument from the feelings, sympathies and prejudices it arouses in him."[31] Unfortunately, it is not simply a matter of a fallacy due to poor logical culture. Because of the real social situation, the authority adds to the argumentation such a factual and experience-proven weight that the logical content acquires only secondary importance.

There is still another aspect to democratic culture: initiative. The patriarchic milieu creates authorities in order to use them. To the same extent to which the bureaucrat desires power, the patriarchic milieu imposes it upon him. It is a closed and consistent system. Under it, the citizen does not wish (or does not know how, which comes to the same thing) to make use of his democratic rights. As he once turned to God, he now turns to a "higher instance" for guidance, help, and defense. "I am, for example, forced by the environment to exercise power," declared the secretary of a Yugoslav communal party committee, according to journalist S. Djukić.[32] And since the government administration is technically not very efficient in a poor country, the conservative citizen is in fact pretty much in the right. In order to put into effect the rights guaranteed by law, interventions are required.

It turns out that the questions of criticism and of self-governing initiative do not reduce merely to "allowing criticism" or "guaranteeing initiative by regulation," although these are crucial preconditions, of course. Since we have to deal with a sociopsychological structure cemented by traditions, little will be accomplished by such passive permission. On the other hand, criticism can do great harm in an uncritical milieu. In a milieu not educated to criticism, even the most reasonable criticism may be interpreted incorrectly and thus lose its meaning. Socialism is inconceivable in a milieu where citizens have not learned to make full use, with complete responsibility, of their civic rights. Civic rights cannot be exercised in a milieu in which the cult of authority exists, in which there is no criticism. And there can be no criticism in a milieu where citizens do not exercise their rights. The bureaucratic-patriarchic ring can be effectively broken only by a political force that is at least partly outside it. That force is the vanguard party.

The furtherance of critical attitudes and self-governing initiative, as the basis for the development of democratic relationships and the education of citizens in the exercise of their political liberties, is one of the most important tasks of the party. Party members will accomplish this task most effectively if they first develop democratic culture fully in their own ranks.

A Postscript

The realm of freedom actually begins only where labour which is determined by necessity and mundane consideration ceases; thus in the very nature of things it lies beyond the sphere of actual material production. . . . Beyond it begins that development of human power which is its own end, the true realm of freedom. . . . The shortening of the working day is its fundamental prerequisite.

MARX, *Capital,* vol. 3

Like slave labour, like serf labour, hired labour is but a transitory and inferior form, destined to disappear before associated labour plying its toil with a willing hand, ready mind and joyous heart.

MARX, Inaugural Address of the First International (1864)

19

Socialism and Beyond

I. Freedom and Self-Determination

Why should socialism be more humane, and therefore more desirable, than other rival systems? The answer is: because it satisfies authentic human needs better than they do or could. In the hierarchy of needs, the highest as well as the purely and exclusively human one is the need for self-determination. Self-determination is identical with an authentic human existence. "This principle stresses the *right* of every man to universal development of his powers and capacities, to full satisfaction of his needs and wants. This right . . . is at the same time a human *obligation* as well, and always represents 'the determination of man,' what gives sense and value to his life."[1] It implies self-actualization, that is, a full development of inherent personal capacities. It also implies what might be termed the specific conditions for full self-actualization: consciousness of one's situation, critical evaluation of the possibilities, and a creative change of environment and oneself.[2] The conditions and the goal together make possible a conscious determination of one's position in the world. The essential precondition for this is freedom. In fact, it is so essential that the totality of freedom—as distinct from various partial freedoms, such as freedom of action and of will, formal and effective freedom, etc.—can meaningfully be described only as self-determination. In particular, the traditional distinction between negative and positive freedom—freedom *from* and freedom *for*— disappears, and the two freedoms coalesce into one single freedom of self-determination.

Freedom is a subject on which libraries have been written. For the present task, there is no need to write another treatise on it. What I propose to do is complete its integration into the conceptual framework of this study.

Julius Nyerere aptly defined a socialist system as an "organization of man's inequalities to serve their equality."[3] One may paraphrase this definition and speak of socialism as a system of restrictions—such as the banning of private and state capital, wage labor exploitation, etc.—designed to maximize freedom. If freedom and equality are but two aspects of the same just society, as I argued in chapter 7, then a society based on equality is *eo ipso* a free society.

A free society, as Marx and Engels pointed out, is one in which the freedom of every individual is the condition for the freedom of all. Individuals live in natural and social environments. In order to act freely, they must be free with respect to nature, to themselves, and to the society. In other words, freedom has three components: physical, psychological, and social.

The *physical* component implies freedom from want. Want, of course, can be absolute, as when physical survival is threatened, or relative, as when measured in relation to a given level of living as determined by the productive forces. Many societies have managed to eliminate absolute want. Some so-called primitive societies successfully overcame even relative want. An adequate supply of food, clothing, and shelter under conditions of egalitarianism satisfies all existing material needs at a sufficiently low level of technology. A society of hunters did not need television sets because these did not exist. At a more advanced stage of technological development, the productivity of labor increased beyond the subsistence level, the society was soon differentiated into classes, and the ruling class appropriated the surplus. In all subsequent history—which is the history of class societies—relative want has persisted. Just a small minority can enjoy all the benefits of the rising social productivity of labor. The majority often continue to live at a subsistence level. It is only when a very high level of technological development is reached that essential goods and services become accessible to every member of the society, and qualitative differences in the level of living among social groups are reduced to merely quantitative ones. At this level, socialism becomes meaningful. Some people still have spacious family houses and others only modest flats, but every family has healthy accommodations with all the essential amenities. Some people have big cars while others have small ones, but every car does the job of transportation and automobiles are accessible to every family. Similarly, the difference between an ordinary television set and a color set is largely quantitative, and so is the difference between universal secondary education and higher education if the latter is accessible to everyone regardless of family income. Once such a level of living is reached, freedom from want becomes a reality and the need for self-actualization becomes an urgently felt need.

The *psychological* component of freedom implies undistorted mental development and well-being. According to Christian Bay, from whom I borrow the idea and the term, psychological freedom means a certain harmony between basic motives and overt behavior.[4] It makes the individual capable of knowing and expressing his inner self. As Sigmund Freud discovered, the natural drives of human beings are repressed in class societies (by "civilization," as he would say). As a consequence, various psychopathological symptoms develop. And sick individuals make a sick society—which was an obvious extension of Freudian analysis to the societal level undertaken by Erich Fromm. Freud focused his attention on the suppression of sexual drives. It is not difficult to see the role such suppression plays in preserving family wealth—and, consequently, class position—in a bourgeois society, and in preserving political discipline—and thus ruling class legitimacy—in a politocratic society.[5] Unless the meaning of libido is extended, however, to cover not only the sexual drive but all aspects of life, there are many other repressive features of a class society. In a society with a universal market, independence, freedom, and power are based on private property. The latter implies pretty unscrupulous competition. The ensuing rat race generates an acute feeling of insecurity, tends to reduce all human qualities to a single dimension that can be measured and expressed in money terms, and ultimately produces neurosis on a mass scale. The universalization of the state produces the same effect under etatism. Here the accumulation of power and of material possessions depends on one's position in the politocratic hierarchy. Acquisitiveness is oriented toward office, not money; but the competition is equally brutal, and man is again reduced to a single measurable dimension—now in terms of authority. In both systems, an authoritarian family, authoritarian school, and authoritarian factory—as required in a class society—produce an authoritarian syndrome or neurosis or both. In short, individuals are destined to live in a social environment. For this, they must be socialized. Socialization in a class society is necessarily repressive. The abolition of classes will not automatically produce full harmony between inherent predispositions and required overt behavior but will eliminate at least some important psychological distortions caused by repressive socialization.

The *social* component of freedom has three dimensions, for power is a three-dimensional category. If a society is to be free, its members must be free from *physical* coercion, from *economic* coercion, and from *manipulative* coercion. In other words, they must participate freely in political decision making, they must be free in the production process and, finally, they must be protected from manipulative attempts designed to mold their values or their cognitive processes in the interest of particular social groups. There is hardly anything to be added to our earlier analysis on that score. A participative political system takes care of political and moral-intellectual freedoms. Self-management and distribution according to work provide a foundation for economic freedom.

When men are not free, they are alienated from their human potential. Their own creations evade their control and become threatening forces. This is what happens with the market in the economy and with the state in the polity. Political and work alienation tend to complement each other and to produce modern class societies. If the lack of freedom implies alienation, the process of disalienation is nothing but the process of the universal liberation of mankind. Man gains control over the conditions of his freedom and shapes his freedom according to his own, authentic, and not extraneous, criteria. This is the humanist ideal of freedom.[6]

II. Socialist Commodity Production

Many Marxist economists and philosophers declare that socialist commodity production is a *contradictio in adjecto*. It is *either* socialist *or* commodity production. It cannot be both, since the latter implies market relationships, which result in competition, periodic slumps, commodity fetishism, and various other phenomena of alienation incompatible with socialism. Socialism requires planning, which is a negation of market. Criticizing "market socialism" in Yugoslavia, Paul Sweezy argues that the market restricts socialist relations and transforms social ownership into a sort of collective ownership. Material incentives and market orientation necessarily generate a profiteering mentality. The evaluation of social usefulness by profit is characteristic of a capitalist system. Gadgetry and acquisitiveness replace socialist values.[7] Desirable moral incentives cannot be developed in a market setting. From this flow alienation and moral degradation. If true, these are serious accusations indeed. Thus, we must scrutinize them very carefully. The frequent observation that abolition of the market leads to etatism and an omnipotent state, which is even less preferable, is not a satisfactory answer. The problem is more complex than that.

First of all, it is good to be reminded that in a historical perspective the market proved to be an emancipating force. Robert Lane suggests that "the market has contributed to the relaxation of the bonds of convention and group fixation (sociological release); has nurtured the desire for mastery over one's environment; . . . has encouraged cognitive complexity and more adequate information processing, and, more dubiously and selectively, has facilitated the learning of coping and adaptive behaviour."[8] All this is not to be interpreted, of course, as a gain outweighing alienation and reification. History, after all, is not an accountant with double-entry bookkeeping. But it focuses attention on the evolutionary properties of the institution.

In a more technical sense, the market is an efficient planning device because it can use prices as allocational instruments. Joan Robinson has enumerated the four main advantages of a rational price system. First, if prices are set so as to equilibrate demand and supply, there is no scope for black market speculation and no need for governmental administrative interventions. "The supply-and-demand pricing system is thus a bulwark of freedom and public morality." Next, the market (properly regulated) allocates scarce goods to those who find them most desirable and, consequently, to those who are most likely to derive satisfaction from them. Third, "it appears fair and reasonable that each family should pay for what it chooses to take from the common pool at the valuation that the market has put upon it." Finally, prices indicate the relative scarcity of various commodities and thus the structure of investment that will lead to the best possible alternative uses of available resources.[9]

Next, the statement that commodity production automatically generates capitalism ought to be reversed. Commodity production existed under slavery, feudalism, and capitalism, as well as under etatism. It clearly did not determine all these socioeconomic systems; on the contrary, it itself was determined by more fundamental social relationships and was shaped by the respective social systems.[10] Thus, for instance, capitalism resulted from universalized private ownership, and etatism from equally universalized state ownership. Since there are so many types of commodity production, it should not be surprising if we find socialist commodity production as well. The elimination of private ownership does not necessarily produce socialism, although it may restrict the role of the market considerably. If state ownership is substituted for private ownership, then capitalism is replaced by etatism and commodity fetishism by office fetishism. In both cases, relations among people are reified, social inequality is preserved, class exploitation continues, and authentic human existence is made impossible. In socialism, social ownership makes social capital equally accessible to everyone, while the authoritarianism of a privately managed or state-managed firm is replaced by self-management. Socialist commodity production means a market system in which, for the first time, labor power has ceased to be a commodity.

The contention of incompatibility between planning and market has already been exposed as a fallacy. In chapter 12, the market was shown to be simply an instrument of planning. There is no need for social usefulness to be evaluated in terms of the profits of *individual* firms. The actual relationship is in fact reversed: profits—or, rather, the income motive—is used to influence the allocation of resources in accordance with the social plan.

The juxtaposition of material and "moral" incentives—with the latter being somehow more noble and therefore preferable—is simply a mistake. "Moral" incentive is really a misnomer; the proper term would be "nonpecuniary incentive." "Moral" implies a sort of conduct that is good in itself, not because it leads to something else, while the meaning of an incentive is exactly the opposite. Thus, the term itself is even a contradiction. There is no social or ethical difference between the two types of incentives. If a man is induced to work by the bestowal of decorations, plaques, titles of rank, public praise by leaders, and increased status and prestige—or is discouraged from wrongdoing by a Board of Shame on which he may be named, depicted, or lampooned—he is no better a man than one inspired by money gain and restrained by money loss. In both cases, the individuals are *induced* to behave in a certain way, their egoistic instincts are exploited. If material incentives stimulate private greed, moral incentives impose conformity which suits the power hierarchy. Some authors treat moral incentives as collective, and material incentives as individual, attributing a greater social value to the former because the latter stimulate private gain. But this is a mistake based on an illusion skillfully exploited by propagandists. Supposedly collective incentives represent a means for manipulation at the hands of superiors and help to preserve the social hierarchy. Moral incentives imply competition just as do material incentives. This similarity is stressed when the awards are won through "socialist emulation." Finally, moral incentives are reminiscent of feudal nonpecuniary status differences. At the time of the German Revolution, in the program of the Spartakusbund described by Rosa Luxemburg, point 6 required "doing away with all status differences, decorations and titles."[11]

The real difference is not between the various types of incentives but between incentives and autonomous decisions. In a world of acute scarcity, which socialism inherits, work is felt as a burden and disutility. Justice requires, as we saw, that *ceteris paribus* equal labor be exchanged for equal labor. Since comparisons cannot be carried out directly, an instrument of evaluation, a common equivalent, is necessary. This is money or honors or both. Which incentive will be selected is primarily a matter of efficiency, not of ethics (though undesirable side effects must also be taken into account). It is a matter of common experience, and well explained by Amitai Etzioni, that organizations with economic goals are more efficient when they use remuneration than when they employ coercion or normative power as the predominant means of control.[12] Cuba, China, and some other countries, by experimenting on a national scale, unwittingly proved this proposition. Moral incentives reduced economic efficiency and made necessary police and other coercive interventions in order to induce lazy or irresponsible people to work.[13] Thus, on the national scale moral incentives imply not only lower efficiency but also increased repression.

A market of a special type is thus fully consistent with socialism. But it is not devoid of all dangers. The market is an *instrument* of allocation of social resources. But no instrument is entirely neutral. Exchange, even when stripped of all its exploitative consequences, is still—as Marx noted—a bourgeois notion. Material incentives and competition reinforce acquisitive instincts, not human solidarity. If exclusive reliance on money relations were to become a permanent feature of the society, self-management might gradually degenerate into a sort of capitalist cooperative. If the results of work were permanently evaluated in terms of income, warns Mihailo Marković, and if the desire to earn as much money as possible were to become a permanent and basic interest of a worker, the product would be a type of personality basically no different from that produced by capitalist society.[14] The higher the level of living, the smaller is this danger. The more fully lower level needs are satisfied, the less important pecuniary incentives become, and the greater becomes the emphasis on things that "money cannot buy." But the danger exists, and it is certainly not a good policy to wait passively until the force of material incentives is fully exhausted. Nor is it good to deal with it so as to replace material incentives by "moral" incentives. What should be done is to begin replacing incentives by self-determination, competition by cooperation, exchange by solidarity, accumulation of things by personal development, having by being. Socialism will not develop automatically. Conscious social action is required. In particular, education for domestication, appropriate for a class society, must be replaced by education for freedom, appropriate for a classless society. A free man is not likely to waste his life accumulating gadgets, despairing about a few additional dinars, or begging for the favors of superiors.

III. Developmental Trends

We saw that freedom from want is a first precondition for the successful construction of a classless socialist society. Unsatisfied material needs represent a physical constraint for our societal design. This constraint can be removed by the sufficient development of the productive forces. Let us examine some empirical evidence.

The available statistical data show a continuous increase in production, achievement of full literacy, and adequate or more than adequate caloric content of food consumption in advanced countries; they indicate that many diseases have been eradicated, that the expectancy of life is longer and longer and, in general, that the level of living is high and constantly increasing. Many other empirical data could be quoted to illustrate the same trends. I wish, however, to draw attention to just three strategically important developments: productivity trends, the length of the working week, and the distribution of income.

It is a banal truth that the level of living depends on the productivity of labor. Labor productivity is constantly increasing. Modern econometric methods make it possible to measure the total labor productivity—of both current and embodied labor—technically denoted as factor productivity. If we select a sufficiently large country (say, the United States) and observe for a sufficiently long period of time (say, a century and a half) so that regularities become apparent, we shall discover the following trend in output per unit of factor input (annual factor productivity growth in the U.S. private economy, in percent):[15]

1800–1855	0.3
1855–1905	0.5

1905–1927	1.5
1927–1967	1.9

Technological progress has accelerated. The century of liberal capitalist development was based primarily on the expansion of employment and capital formation. The subsequent period of organized capitalism saw a fourfold acceleration of technological progress. There is no reason to believe that this is the limit. Thus science, pure and applied, is becoming the dominant productive force. Employment in commodity-producing sectors (manufacturing, mining, construction, agriculture, forestry and fishing), on the other hand, has shrunk from 84 percent in 1820 to about one-third at present in the United States. Since these are the sectors dominated by technology, the potential adverse influence of technology on labor relations is growing smaller.

The length of the working week is an indicator not only of the degree of humanization of work but also of how much lower-level needs have been satisfied. Since the beginning of the last century, the average number of working hours per week decreased in the United States as follows:[16]

1800	78 hours
1850	70 hours
1910	55 hours
1940	44 hours
1960	39 hours
1975	36 hours

In Britain, France, Germany, and elsewhere, the trends have been more or less the same. In the period before the First World War, the working week was shrinking at a rate of two hours per decade; after the war, the rate increased to three hours per decade. By the end of the century, the working week will be reduced to 30 hours or less in most developed countries.

Finally, even bourgeois and politocratic societies are becoming increasingly egalitarian. Income differentials for various occupations and between manual and mental labor are being reduced.[17] In the first half of the last century, real wages were stagnant or even decreasing.[18] This implied increasing income inequality. In the second half of the last century, the index of inequality stabilized. The First World War, the world economic crisis, and the Second World War reduced inequality in income distribution rather sharply.[19] Apart from the reduced income differentials, the diminishing share of agricultural labor and the diminishing share of unskilled manual labor contributed to an overall egalitarian trend. Cross-sectional data tell the same story: development tends to increase income inequality at the lowest level, but as growth continues income distribution becomes more egalitarian. Finally, as etatist systems show, income differences can be drastically reduced by merely replacing capitalist institutions.[20]

We now have to derive the consequences of the observed trends. Once the working week is reduced to 30 hours or less, almost one-half of the calendar week will represent leisure time. This is too much time to be spent on passive television viewing or football games. The unspent energy will have to be used in active pursuits outside the routine of work. Modern liberated man, supported by many mechanical slaves, will spontaneously engage in the same pursuits as ancient free man, supported by his human slaves: he will participate in deciding on political matters concerning his community, he will occupy himself with sports, he will enjoy arts and cultivate philosophy. The active use of leisure time means developing one's faculties in order to achieve a full enjoyment of life. Technological change, leisure, and long life will make life-long education both a possibility and a necessity. The once fateful antitheses between manual and mental labor and between town and countryside will tend to disappear. Egalitarian income distribution will contribute to the equalization of life chances. That, in turn, will facilitate meaningful communication among the members of the society. Advanced technology works in the same direction. Computerized polling makes an instant referendum possible and extends direct political participation to the national level. Data banks, connected by TV channels with every home, put the enormous stock of accumulated social knowledge and current information at the disposal of every individual. Control devices and two-way channels permit communication among viewers and between viewers and speakers. Multiple channels and neighborhood hookups (UHF, microwave, satellite relays) make it possible for representatives and administrators to talk to citizens in their districts.

Unlike his ancient predecessors, the socialist free man is not likely to engage in wars. Having been liberated from sexual, economic, and other obsessions, he is more likely to become nonaggressive, for the instinct for destruction will no longer be reinforced by repression. Besides, technological advances make major wars suicidal. Socialization will never be a smooth and neutral process, of course—Freud was certainly right in that—

but socialist society "will only impose such restrictions upon him as allow for the sublimation of his potentially disruptive instincts."[21]

IV. A Historical Perspective

What has been said above may now be put into historical perspective. For our purpose, it will be sufficient to distinguish four typical societies, representing three crucial stages in the historical development of mankind: the original classless society, the most developed class society as represented by bourgeois and politocratic societies, and the communist classless society. The findings of our inquiry make possible the schematic representation of the major features of the four societies given in Table 13.

Every schematic presentation is quite simplified, of course, and may therefore be misleading. The purpose of the present scheme is nothing more than to give a condensed summary of the results of our analysis. It is mostly self-explanatory and will need only a few additional comments.

Paleolithic hunters and gatherers and neolithic agriculturalists do not earn their living but satisfy their needs directly by their own work. If the climatic conditions are not unfavorable, these people are neither poor nor destitute. As Marshall Sahlins and other anthropologists have shown, they live in a society of abundance.[22] The abundance is, of course, relative to their needs and technology. They work three to four hours a day, or about half of the time of the modern worker. One day of labor of hunting and gathering may feed four to five persons, which is higher than the interwar productivity of Yugoslav agriculture. They are well nourished and about equally as tall as the average modern-day person; when settled, they live in comfortable and healthy dwellings[23] and engage in numerous artistic activities. Since simple tools and other objects can easily be replaced, they are not particularly valuable. On the other hand, nomads have to weigh the accumulation of objects against the inconvenience of transporting them on their backs. Not surprisingly, they are pretty indifferent toward private property. Plenty of leisure time makes work interesting. Some Australian natives have the same word for work and for play. Neolithic man has no use for the concept of gain. He is motivated to work by tradition and complex social motives. Trob-

TABLE 13

Historical Trends in Social Organization[a]

		History			Project
	Ingredients of social organization	Original classless society	Most developed class society		Communist classless society
			Bourgeois	Politocratic	
Economy	*Basis of economic system*	direct satisfaction of needs	market	state allocation of resources	social planning
	Chief resource	land	machinery		information
	Dominant sector of production	hunting and/or agriculture	industry		services
	Technology	labor intensive	capital intensive		knowledge intensive
Polity	*Basis of political system*	solidarity	authority		self-governing participation
	Interests of:	community	class		plurality of self-governing associations
	Articulation and aggregation of interests by:	customs	parties	party	plurality of organizations and direct communication
Culture	*Basis of ethics*	religious myths	utility		human solidarity
	Norms	ordained by mythical powers	legal		moral (self-regulation)
	Object of identification (social horizon)	clan	nation		mankind
	Social character	collectivist/tradition dominated	acquisitive/conformist		cooperative/autonomous
	Relation between individual and society	individual dominated by the collectivity	individualist competition	bureaucratic hierarchy	cooperation of autonomous persons

[a]Such a scheme was suggested to me by my colleague Eugen Pusić. He bears no responsibility, however, for this elaboration of his suggestion.

riand islanders produce more than they can consume; the surplus is left to rot. They do not try to minimize work. In fact, they spend a lot of time working for what may be called aesthetic reasons (maintaining clean and orderly gardens, building beautiful and strong fences, etc.).[24] Useful things, even if they are very scarce, are not considered particularly valuable. But an object that required a disproportionate investment of high-quality labor will be held in great esteem.[25] In the course of thousands of years, this original *subsistence economy of abundance* gradually changed until it reached the contemporary stage of *affluent scarcity,* based on either market or state allocation of resources. The next evolutionary epoch ought to produce a new society of abundance.

So much for the economic system. Economic systems are matched by political systems. The latter must accommodate dominant interests and provide institutions for their articulation and aggregation. Economy and polity are matched by culture, which includes the dominant ethics, the norms that regulate social life, the identification of individuals and their relations to the society. The word *matched* implies that there is no unicausal determination. The three spheres of social life are interdependent and are connected by complex feedback loops. The three spheres have one developmental trait in common, however—a gradual liberation of man, and his growth toward self-determination.

Primitive polities have chiefs, but chiefs have little or no *political* authority. They are admired and followed because of their personal qualities. "Leadership is here a higher form of kinship, hence a higher form of reciprocity and liberality."[26] The state organization does not exist, as I explained earlier (see chapter 10, section I, note 19). Communal interests prevail and they are articulated and aggregated by customs. "No one in a Nuer village starves unless all are starving."[27] Further development generates state, authority, classes, and parties. Community disintegrates, and many people starve while others enjoy affluence.

In primitive society, man does not yet exist as an individual. He is immersed in the collectivity, he is mortally threatened by unfriendly nature and dominated by taboos, myths, and traditions. Besides, he considers only the members of his own tribe as humans and calls them so. Outsiders are a different species.[28] His gradual liberation with respect to nature is accompanied by a psychological liberation from the grip of the collectivity; he is becoming an individual. At the same time, his social horizon widens. When this process of individuation is completed, when every member of society becomes formally equal and legally responsible for himself, the social organization assumes its contemporary forms. If these individuals are related to each other through mediation of the market, they make a bourgeois society; if the agent of mediation is a politico-bureaucratic hierarchy, the society is politocratic. The fundamental value orientations of liberated and alienated individuals are acquisitiveness and personal advancement. As a result they are conformists and represent a "lonely crowd." Further development leads to a reintegration of individuals into society in such a way as to preserve personal independence. Individuals now care about being, not about having. This occurs under conditions of increasing freedom in which personal freedom and societal freedom are mutually determined and reinforced.

Anthropological research has shown that the concepts of egoism and altruism do not apply to every society. If, as is often the case in primitive societies, the chief is expected to be generous, then everybody will be happy if the chief acquires valuable things, because they will soon be distributed. Ruth Benedict noted that societies characterized by nonaggression have societal orders in which the individual serving his own advantage also serves that of the group. Such societies do not display higher moral standards, in terms of our contemporary notions, but their behavior represents a functional response to a corresponding structure. The chief is generous because chiefdom is a form of kinship and the latter is a relation of reciprocity and mutual aid. He and any "rich" man gain tremendous personal satisfaction in being generous.[29] The ordinary man is generous because that helps him avoid the unpleasantness he may experience if the partner considers the things received to be less valuable than the things given away. Two groups exchange gifts instead of commodities in order to avoid the risks inherent in contacts with strangers. A solicitory gift is a token of friendship which is expected to provide safe conduct and reciprocity.[30] Malinowski found that the main characteristic of wealth of the islanders was generosity, while avarice was the most despised of all vices. In Kula a generous man establishes ties with a greater number of people than a niggard.[31] Generosity means power, and the recipient is put in a circumspect and responsive relation to the donor during the period the gift is unrequited.[32] Under such circumstances, the possessive individualism of a bourgeois utilitarian is unknown and dysfunctional. "One can set up social institutions," comments Abraham Maslow, "which will guarantee that individuals will be at each others' throats; or one can set up social institutions . . . so that one person's advantage would be another person's advantage rather than the other person's disadvantage."[33] Bourgeois and politocratic orders correspond to the former case, communism to the latter.

In communism, personal wealth is no longer measured in economic terms, for rich is the man "in whom *his own fulfillment exists* as an interior necessity, as a *need*."[34] The identification is no longer with any particular human group but with mankind. Social character changes. The genuinely liberated man acts as an autonomous person, able to transcend egoism and conformism and to determine his position in the world by following his own criteria. The latter are rooted in his changed social existence, which has become more humane.

Increasing material affluence will gradually reduce the incentive content of wage differentials. They will lose their social justification and will tend to disappear. The allocation of labor will proceed according to capabilities consistent with self-determination. Most of unpleasant labor will be replaced by machines. If any labor of that sort remains, it will be shared. The increased productive power of the society makes it possible for preferences for idleness to be respected. The bourgeois morality, expressed in commutative justice and based on exchange, will gradually give way to communist morality, characterized by distributive justice. The meritorious person gives way to a contributing person. Freedom, like wealth, will be evaluated in terms of being, not of getting.

In a world of scarcity, work is an activity focused on survival. From this flows the role of incentives. The latter are an appeal to selfishness. Competition in a struggle for survival tends to color the meaning of life. From this follows the psychology of accumulation. Survival need not be reduced to biological survival—it refers to the standard of living made possible by technological development—but the closer to the subsistence level one lives, the more brutal is the struggle for the means of survival. In a society of abundance, survival is taken for granted, and the meaning of life is sought elsewhere. Wherever it is found, it requires cooperative interaction with other persons. In order to fulfill oneself, one needs others. Selfishness now implies solidarity. In this sense, abundance makes possible a different world, and it is up to us to exploit the possibilities.

"The world that we must seek," wrote Bertrand Russell, "is a world in which the creative spirit is alive, in which life is an adventure full of joy and hope, based rather upon the impulse to construct than upon the desire to retain what we possess or to seize what is possessed by others."[35] In such a world, "no one is compelled to work more than four hours a day, every person possessed of scientific curiosity will be able to indulge in it, and every painter will be able to paint without starving. . . . The work exacted will be enough to make leisure delightful, but not enough to produce exhaustion. . . . Ordinary men and women, having the opportunity of a happy life, will become more kindly and less persecuting and less inclined to view others with suspicion."[36] In such a world, as Danilo Dolci pointed out, command will be replaced by coordination, power by responsibility, exploitation by valorization, and obedience by agreement; sin will be considered as insufficiency, and punishment will give way to cure.[37] In such a world, which Marx denoted as a higher phase of communist society, "the enslaving subordination of the individual to the division of labour . . . has vanished; . . . labour has become not only a means of life but life's prime want; . . . the productive forces have also increased with the all-round development of the individual, and all the springs of cooperative wealth flow more abundantly." As a consequence "the narrow horizon of bourgeois right can be crossed in its entirety and society can inscribe on its banner: From each according to his ability, to each according to his needs!"[38]

This world is not without conflicts or problems. But they will be of a different kind. Such a world is not an inevitability, and, in particular, not a necessary next step in human history. It is only a possibility. If human beings are essentially free and creative creatures, then a free society does not simply happen; it does not evolve as a result of some natural law that needs only to be discovered. A communist society is a project. It ought to be created. It must be fought for.

Will it be a happier society? This is one of those false questions that is unanswerable. Schopenhauer would argue that the only choice available is between dissatisfaction and boredom. But that is not a good description of human reality either. The tragedy—or the fortune—of mankind consists in the fact that the goals can never be attained nor the wants fulfilled. Human beings are destined to be dissatisfied, "unhappy." The fulfillment of some goals generates new dissatisfactions at a higher level. Every new and higher stage of development increases the possibilities but also the aspirations. The two will never coincide. The race is eternal. The predicament of mankind is self-creation. And that must be considered as good.

Otherwise, development would come to an end, which would be the worst of all possible fates—a boring, aimless, and futile life. The consciousness of our human imperfections ought to put us on guard against fanaticism and intolerance. And that is exactly the meaning of humanism. If there is such a thing as happiness, it consists in coping with problems and developing one's own capacities in the process. Happiness must be conquered individually, it is not given or guaranteed by social arrangements. Thus, the future society may not be happier than the present one, but it will certainly be more desirable and better adjusted to human needs. We can assert this with confidence, for it is unlikely that its members would wish to reestablish our present alienating conditions of life. Being more desirable and more humane, such a society is worth fighting for.

Notes

FOREWORD

[1] "Associationist socialism is, therefore, extra-scientific, because it does not concern itself primarily with (critical) analysis—as does Marxism—but with definite plans and the means of carrying them into effect" (J. A. Schumpeter, *History of Economic Analysis* [New York: Oxford University Press, 1955], p. 454). In fact, my disagreement with Schumpeter is even more profound than indicated in the text: not only do I intend to show that concern with "definite plans and means of carrying them into effect" is a legitimate scientific inquiry, but also that Marxism *is* associationist socialism.

[2]"On the Limited Relevance of Economics," in D. Bell and J. Kristol, eds., *Capitalism Today* (New York: Basic Books, 1971), pp. 91–92.

CHAPTER 1

[1] A century and a half earlier, similar ideas were propounded by Levellers and Diggers in the first successful bourgeois revolution, the English Revolution in the seventeenth century. Levellers fought for general suffrage, freedom of conscience, and equality before the law. Diggers or True Levellers tried to eliminate economic inequality, pointing out that political democracy could not exist without economic democracy. Diggers influenced the thinking of Robert Owen, the first associationist and a utopian predecessor of modern socialism.

[2] Similarly, though somewhat less precisely, the American Declaration of Independence (1776) states that "all men are created equal and are endowed by their Creator with certain inalienable rights such as Life, Liberty and the Pursuit of Happiness."

[3] See G. D. H. Cole, *Essays in Social Theory* (London: Macmillan, 1950), pp. 132–44.

[4] G. Lefebvre, *The Coming of the French Revolution* (1939), trans. by R. R. Palmer (New York: Vintage Books, 1962), p. 248.

[5] A century later this awareness was already very much present. In a proclamation in August 1914, the peasant leaders allied with Emiliano Zapata in the Mexican Revolution accused their bourgeois partners of the intention to introduce "freedom of the press for those who do not know how to write, the freedom to vote for those who do not know the candidates and the correct administration for those who will never make use of lawyers' services."

[6] H. J. Laski, *The British Cabinet: A Study of Its Personnel,* Fabian Tract no. 223 (London, 1928).

[7] R. T. Nightingale, *The Personnel of the British Foreign Office and Diplomatic Service, 1851–1929,* Fabian Tract no. 232 (London, 1930).

[8] K. Mannheim, *Freedom, Power and Democratic Planning* (New York: Oxford University Press, 1950), p. 99.

[9]

Ten Countries with the Longest History of Political Democracy

	Universal male suffrage	Secret ballot	Responsible government	Years of conventional democracy by 1979
Switzerland	1848	1872	1848	107
New Zealand	1879	1870	1856	100
Australia	1858	1859	1892	87
Canada	1898	1874	1867	81
Norway	1898	1884	1884	77*
United States	(1870)	1904	1789	75
France	1848	1913	1875	62*
Sweden	1908	1866	1917	62
Finland	1907	1907	1917	62
United Kingdom	1918	1872	1832	61

Source: C. Hewitt, "The Effect of Political Democracy and Social Democracy on Equality in Industrial Societies: A Cross-National Comparison," *American Sociological Review,* 1977, p. 457.

*Democracy suspended during 1940–44.

[10] In 1900 women were permitted to vote only in the settler nations: New Zealand (from 1893 on), South Australia (from 1895 on), and four states in the United States.

[11] N. Pašić, *Uporedni politički sistemi* (Belgrade: Institut za političke studije, 1976), p. 93.

[12] Lj. Tadić, *Tradicija i revolucija* (Belgrade: Srpska književna zadruga, 1972), p. 224. Harold Laski describes English judicial practice, in many respects the most advanced in the capitalist world, as follows: "There is one law for the rich and another for the poor whenever the preparation of a defence is an item of importance in the case. Nor is that all. In the personal relations of life, as in divorce, for instance, lack of means generally implies lack of access to the courts. . . . Another region of inequality is notable. If a poor person steals, conviction follows rapidly; if a rich person steals, she is usually bound over on the plea of nervous trouble. If a taxi-driver is proved to have been drunk in charge of a car, he pays the penalty; but it is notorious that magistrates do not like to convict the rich young man in a similar position, since he will usually appeal and often get his case reversed on appeal. . . . If directors of a company in high social position pay no attention to the affairs of the company, they are not held responsible when it is compulsorily liquidated; but if a petty official is confused in his accounts, charges of embezzlement are difficult to avoid." It is important to realize that these defects *cannot* be remedied by legislation. They are *socially* conditioned: "A magistrate who sees guilt

in a poor thief, but nervous disease in a rich one, will continue to make the distinction until differences of economic status are negligible; a judge who does not believe that distinguished directors of public companies ought to be responsible for a negligence they are paid to prevent, will only find them responsible when there is a genuine relation between income and service" (*A Grammar of Politics* [London: Allen and Unwin, 1928], p. 565).

[13] F. Sternberg, *Socijalizam i kapitalizam pred sudom svetske javnosti* (Belgrade: Jugoslavija, 1954), p. 31.

[14] F. Engels, *Die Lage der arbeitenden Klasse in England* (Leipzig, 1845).

[15] A. F. K. Organski, *The Stages of Political Development* (New York: Alfred A. Knopf, 1965), p. 7.

[16] This is not very different from medieval Russian judiciary practice, as exemplified by the famous case of the Estonian Jaan the Miller, who tried to sue his landowner in 1740. The College of Justice in St. Petersburg ruled that peasants did not have right to sue their masters.

[17] In our century, workbooks reappeared in Stalinist Russia.

[18] A. Gerschenkron, "Reflections on European Socialism," in *Essays in Socialism and Planning in Honour of Carl Landauer,* ed. by G. Grossman (Englewood Cliffs, N.J.: Prentice-Hall, 1970), p. 6.

[19] J. E. Meade, *Efficiency, Equality and the Ownership of Property* (London: Allen and Unwin, 1969), p. 27.

[20] It is instructive to recall that Darwin got the inspiration for his theory of natural selection among animals from the economic theory of Malthus, an economist of liberal capitalism.

[21]

The Proletarianization of the U.S. Labor Force (in percent)

	1780	1920	1969
Wage and salary employees (excluding managers and officials)	20.0	73.9	83.6
Salaried managers and officials	—	2.6	7.2
Entrepreneurs and self-employed	80.0	23.5	9.2

Source: R. C. Edwards, M. Reich, and T. E. Weisskopf, *The Capitalist System* (Englewood Cliffs, N.J.: Prentice-Hall, 1972), p. 175.

[22] This is seen easily when changes in the share of top *plants* are compared with changes in the share of top *firms.* Prais found that in Britain, between 1935 and 1963, the share of the one hundred top plants in manufacturing remained constant at 11 percent, while the share of the one hundred top firms increased from 24 percent to 38 percent (L. Hannah, *The Rise of the Corporate Economy* [London: Methuen, 1976], p. 183).

[23] The merger is not necessarily forced. It is often voluntary, as when a company needs capital for expansion and lacks access to the capital market, or when two companies improve their position on the market by merging. Large estate taxes also induce owners to sell out before death and leave their heirs cash and/or securities that are more readily marketable. Modern aggressive takeovers largely exploit the peculiarities of stock exchange operations and of the tax system. These peculiarities may be denoted as the price/earnings effect and the profit tax effect. In the former case, the aggressor is a corporation with an inflated (share) price/earnings (per share) ratio. Typically, the aggressor first secretly buys shares of the victim (which has a low P/E ratio) up to the percentage of total stock (10 percent in the United States) that need not be disclosed to the controlling government agency. Then the management of the target company is approached. If the deal is rejected, the aggressor makes a tender offer to the stockholders of the victim at a price sufficiently above the market price to induce sale. The purchase is financed out of the difference between the P/E ratios of the two corporations. In the second case, involving the profit tax effect, the aggressor offers more profitable debentures in exchange for the shares of the victim's stockholders. The gain is financed out of savings on the profit tax, for interest on debentures is deducted as cost. A sound, conservatively managed corporation is likely to have a slowly growing stock (to which the market will assign a low P/E ratio) and to shun debt. Thus, it will be doubly vulnerable to the attacks of reckless speculators. This explains the phenomenal growth of conglomerates during the last two decades. It is also obvious that this type of growth cannot be stabilizing, nor has it anything to do with productive efficiency.

[24]

Nonagricultural labor employed:

In enterprises with more than 200 employees in Germany	1882 11.9%	1905 20.3%	1925 23.5%	1961 45.1%
In enterprises with more than 500 employees in France	1896 9.3%	1906 11.7%	1926 19.3%	1958 29.8%
Employment in American manufacturing firms with more than 1,000 employees		1909 15.3%	1929 24.2%	1955 33.6%

Source: E. Mandel, *Marxist Economic Theory*, vol. 2 (New York: Monthly Review, 1968), pp. 395–97.

[25] A. Berle and G. C. Means, *The Modern Corporation and Private Property* (New York, 1939), pp. 33–35. In 1963 in Britain 180 firms employed one-third of the labor force in manufacturing and effected one-half of capital expenditures. In Germany industrial concentration is scarcely smaller. Here, in 1960 only 100 firms controlled two-fifths of industrial turnover, employed one-third of the labor force, and

accounted for 50 percent of manufacturing exports (M. Kidron, *Western Capitalism Since the War* [Harmondsworth: Penguin, 1970], p. 27).

[26] Kidron, *Western Capitalism,* p. 26.

[27] Hannah, *Rise of Corporate Economy*, pp. 13, 216.

[28] B. Horvat, "Klasifikacija područja svijeta prema Karakteristikama privredne razvijenosti," *Economic Analysis,* 1971, p. 282.

[29] J. Wakeford et al., eds., *Power in Britain* (London: Heinemann, 1973), p. 317.

[30] Using this technique, even before the war the Royal Dutch–Shell Company, to cite an example, succeeded in evading the payment of taxes to the Yugoslav government for some ten years. When the evasion was discovered, the company bribed the officials involved. See B. Horvat, *Industrija nafte u Jugoslaviji,* vol. 2: *Prerada Nafte* (Belgrade: Jugoslavenski institut za ekonomska istraživanja, 1966), pp. 117–20.

[31] R. J. Larner, "Ownership and Control of the 200 Largest Nonfinancial Corporations, 1929 and 1963," *American Economic Review,* 1966, p. 781.

[32] F. Pryor, *Property and Industrial Organization in Communist and Capitalist Nations* (Bloomington: Indiana University Press, 1973), p. 119.

[33] In the United States, almost two-thirds of the identifiable markets, accounting for about 60 percent of the value of manufacturing output, showed significant elements of oligopoly (C. Kaysen, "The Corporation," in *The Logic of Social Hierarchies,* ed. by E. Lanmann et al. [Chicago: Markham, 1971], p. 217). In smaller countries, this percentage will necessarily be higher.

[34] Mandel, *Marxist Economic Theory,* p. 426; also, E. Mandel, *Der Spätkapitalismus* (Frankfurt: Suhrkamp, 1972), pp. 476–78.

[35] The first to realize this was the English bourgeois radical, Mundella, who as early as the 1860s told a Royal Commission, "we [the employers] could have done nothing without the organization of the unions" (Z. Bauman, *Between Class and Elite* [Manchester: Manchester University Press, 1972], p. 122). Mundella was not applauded by his less imaginative and less intelligent colleagues. Several decades passed before his position was generally accepted by English employers, and two or three decades more before American employers caught up. Today his remark sounds almost like a truism.

[36] S. Lynd and G. Alperovitz, *Strategy and Program* (Boston: Beacon Press, 1973), p. 38.

[37] J. K. Galbraith observes that an "important service of the union to planning is to standardize wage costs between different industrial firms and to insure that changes in wages will occur at approximately

the same time. This greatly assists price control by the industry. And it also greatly facilitates the public regulation of prices and wages. . . . one of its [industrywide union's] tasks will be to insure that rates of pay will be more or less the same for the same kinds of work. This is done in the name of fairness and equity but it means too that no firm can reduce prices because of lower wage rates and none will be impelled to seek higher prices because its rates of pay are higher" (*The New Industrial State* [Boston: Houghton Mifflin, 1967], pp. 278–79).

[38] P. M. Sweezy, *Modern Capitalism and Other Essays* (New York: Monthly Review Press, 1972), p. 8.

[39] In the United States, this share increased from 7.4 percent in 1903 to 9.8 percent in 1929 (P. A. Baran and P. M. Sweezy, *Monopoly Capital* [New York: Monthly Review Press, 1966], p. 146). Another possible measure of the role of the state is the number of civil servants. The corresponding data for four characteristic years in Britain are: 1797—16,267; 1851—39,147; 1901—116,413; 1955—633,000 (Bauman, *Between Class and Elite,* p. 250).

[40] Galbraith, *New Industrial State,* p. 229.

[41] Paul Sweezy argues, however, that Japanese and German growth can be explained at least in part by the Korean and Vietnam wars and by the expanding American market (which decisively influences the world market) fed by military expenditures ("Capitalism, for Worse," in L. Silk, *Capitalism* [New York: Praeger, 1974], pp. 125–27).

[42] As Robert McKenzie describes the British scene: "Two great monolithic structures face each other and conduct furious arguments about the comparatively minor issues that separate them" (*British Political Parties* [London: Heinemann, 1955], p. 586). It is not difficult to agree with R. H. S. Crossman that, in his book, McKenzie "has shown conclusively that the two great parties have developed in accordance with the law of increasing oligarchy which operates in industry, in the trade unions and in Fleet Street" (*Socialism and the New Despotism,* Fabian Tract no. 258 [London, 1956], p. 21).

[43] The term was coined by J. K. Galbraith to denote the power pyramid in the modern corporation. The technostructure "embraces all who bring specialized knowledge, talent or experience to group decision-making" (*New Industrial State,* p. 71).

CHAPTER 2

[1] "It is a well-known, undeniable fact that without a free, unfettered press, without an unhindered association and assembly life, a government of the wide popular masses cannot be imagined at all." "Freedom only for the supporters of the government, only for the members

of the party . . . is not freedom. Freedom always means freedom for those who think differently" (R. Luxemburg, *Die Russische Revolution* [Hamburg: Oetinger, 1948], pp. 52, 53).

2 "We stand for the withering away of the state. And at the same time we stand for the strengthening of the dictatorship of the proletariat, the most powerful and the most potent of all state powers that have existed until now. The higher development of the state power in order to prepare the withering away of the state power—that is the Marxist formula. . . . this contradiction . . . reflects the dialectics of Marx" (J. Stalin, "Report to the XVI Congress of the Party," *Sochinenia,* vol. 12 [Moscow: Gospolitizdat, 1949], pp. 369–70).

3 J. Stalin, *Voprosy leninizma* (Moscow: Ogiz, 1945), p. 394. This sort of dialectics is not entirely a novelty. It was developed as early as the fourth century B.C. at the court of the Ch'in dynasty in China. The intellectual ancestor of Stalin was not Marx but Lord Shang, who said of the future classless society: "The way in which a sage administers a state is by unifying rewards, unifying punishments and unifying education. The effect of unifying rewards is that the army will have no equal; the effect of unifying punishments is that orders will be carried out; the effect of unifying education is that inferiors will obey superiors. Now if one understands rewards, there should be no expense; if one understands punishments there should be no death penalty; if one understands education there should be no changes, and so people would know the business of the people and there would be no divergent customs. The climax in the understanding of rewards is to bring about a condition of having no rewards; the climax in the understanding of punishments is to bring about a condition of having no punishments; the climax in the understanding of education is to bring about a condition of having no education" (*The Book of Lord Shang,* trans. by J. J. L. Duyvendak [London, 1928], p. 208). The Stalinist methods of government are foreshadowed by Shang in great detail. For Shang—as for Stalin—the chief goal is to maximize the power of the state. The ruler must hold in esteem peasants ("the working class") and soldiers, and scorn orators and wandering scholars ("the intelligentsia"). Peasants are indispensable for production and soldiers for state power, and that is all that matters. Punishment ought to be brutal even for minor offenses; the ruler must punish even before the offense is committed (the Moscow trials), and especially if his orders are not obeyed; otherwise, it is impossible to rule over people. In addition to achievements in production and war, spying on fellow citizens ought also to be rewarded by noble titles. A penetrating mind causes disorder, virtue ruins discipline, and kindness and humaneness are the mother of offense; these qualities are among the "eight parasites" that must be eradicated. Humanistic literature is ideologically undesirable and should be destroyed. Where the eight parasites exist, the people are strong and, consequently, authority is weak. In order for the state to be strong, the people must be made

weak. Then people will be content and will love the ruler. The recommendations of Shang were followed, and the state of Ch'in expanded. At about the same time as Lord Shang, another minister of another powerful ruler, Kautilya in India, wrote a similar book called *Arthashastra,* or the Book of State Organization. He describes an omnipotent state that regulates all public and private life and uses a hierarchically organized bureaucracy. Lord Shang and Kautilya lived in societies that Marx denoted as oriental despotism.

[4] For a succinct Marxist critique of etatism, see S. Stojanović, *Between Ideals and Reality* (New York: Oxford University Press, 1973; Yugoslav edition: Belgrade, 1969).

[5] A. Bebel, *Budushchee obshchesvto* (Moscow: Kolokol', 1905), p. 37.

[6] I put moral incentives in quotation marks because, as they have been applied in practice, they do not differ from material incentives. If shock workers, for instance, are given decorations, are widely heralded, and are offered political posts, that increases their prestige, their social power, and not infrequently, though indirectly, their material well-being also. The only real moral incentive, the one that transcends individual egoism and the bourgeois world in general, is a variety of Kantian categorical imperative: do good work for its own sake. (See also chapter 19, section II.)

[7] The former socialist, Benito Mussolini, made that very clear: "If the nineteenth was the century of the individual (Liberalism means individualism), it may be expected that this one may be the century of collectivism and therefore the century of the State." He continues: "For Fascism the State is an absolute before which individuals and groups are relative" ("The Doctrine of Fascism" [1932], quoted in A. Arblaster and S. Lukes, eds., *The Good Society* [New York: Harper and Row, 1971], pp. 315–16, 317). Stalin would not disagree, except that he would refer to the state as Soviet and not fascist. (See chapter 6, section IB.)

[8] K. Marx, *Economic and Philosophic Manuscripts of 1844*, trans. by T. B. Bottomore, in E. Fromm, *Marx's Concept of Man* (New York: Frederick Ungar, 1961), p. 125.

[9] Socialist realism was contemporaneous with state realism (the glorification of an assumed reality) in Fascist Italy and Nazi Germany. See Elio Vittorini, *Otvoren dnevnik* (Zagreb: Zora, 1971), pp. 45–46.

[10] In the spring of 1850, Marx and Engels allied themselves with the Blanquists for a few months. This alliance produced a joint declaration in which the phrase appears for the first time: "Le but de l'association est la déchéance de toutes les classes privilégiés, de soumettre ces classes a la dictature des prolétaires en maintenant la révolution en permanence jusqu'à la réalisation du communisme qui doit être la dernière forme de constitution de la famille humaine" (quoted in G.

Lichtheim, *The Origins of Socialism* [London: Weidenfeld and Nicolson, 1972], p. 289). At about the same time, in his political tract *The Class Struggles in France 1848–1850,* Marx mentions Blanqui in connection with revolutionary socialism and adds that this socialism is "the *class dictatorship* of the proletariat as the necessary transit point to the *abolition of class distinctions generally*. . . ." Blanqui and his followers stood for popular insurrection organized by a small, secret group of dedicated conspirators. The resulting dictatorship would dispossess the rich and establish social equality. Blanqui's teacher was Buonarrotti, the principal successor of Babeuf, who in turn was the leader of the Conspiracy of the Equals in 1796–97. Marx dropped secrecy and substituted class dictatorship for oligarchic dictatorship. The Bolsheviks replaced class by party dictatorship, which in practice degenerated into oligarchy (called collective leadership) or into one-man despotism. (See also chapter 10, section I.)

[11] In her evaluation of the Russian Revolution, written in 1918 in jail a few months before she was murdered, Rosa Luxemburg described this clearly and unambiguously: "The basic mistake of the Lenin-Trotsky theory is that they, like Kautsky, oppose dictatorship to democracy. '*Either* dictatorship *or* democracy'—so the question was formulated by both the Bolsheviks and Kautsky. The latter decided . . . in favor of bourgeois democracy. . . . On the contrary, Lenin-Trotsky opted for dictatorship against democracy and thereby for the dictatorship of a handful of persons, i.e., for dictatorship according to the bourgeois pattern. . . . It is the historical task of the proletariat, when it acquires power, to create socialist democracy in place of bourgeois democracy, not to eliminate every democracy" (*Die Russische Revolution*, pp. 59, 60).

[12] Quoted in H. Draper, "Marx and the Dictatorship of the Proletariat," *Cahiers de l'INSEA*, no. 129, September 1962, serie 5, no. 61, 5–74, quote from p. 14.

[13] Ibid.

[14] Quoted in M. Nomad, "The Anarchist Tradition," in M. M. Drashkovich, *Revolutionary Intellectuals, 1864–1943* (Stanford: Stanford University Press, 1966), pp. 57–94, quote from p. 64.

[15] Ibid., p. 68.

[16] "The Program of the Blanquist Fugitives from the Paris Commune" (1874), quoted in Draper, "Marx and the Dictatorship of the Proletariat," p. 63.

[17] K. Marx and F. Engels, *Correspondence 1846–1895* (New York: International Publishers, 1935), p. 486.

[18] Commission of the Central Committee of the CPSU(b), *History of the Communist Party of the Soviet Union (Bolsheviks)* (New York: International Publishers, 1939), pp. 356–57.

[19] The contempt for democracy expressed so often and so strongly by the ruling parties of the etatist societies comes dangerously close to a similar attitude ("impotent democracy") of fascist regimes. H. Lefebvre, a French Marxist, wrote before the war: "By a strange turning this image [ascetism, uniformity, hopeless mediocrity associated with 'socialism'] becomes more and more convenient to fascism, which orients all tendencies to primitivism, ascetism and naturalism; which officially calls 'socialism' the sacrificing of the individual to the collective, his levelling in a general misery and his uniformity. This ideology has nothing in common with Marxism which is a theory of richness, which rehabilitates the multiplicity of needs against all kinds of naturalism and primitivism" (*Le nationalisme contre les nations* [Paris, 1937], p. 38). The circle is closed.

[20] W. Brus, "The Polish October: Twenty Years After," in R. Miliband and J. Saville, eds., *The Socialist Register 1977* (London: Merlin Press, 1977), p. 183.

[21] This does not imply that capitalism is free from religious vestiges. It suffices to mention the numerous sects, widespread superstition, and all sorts of foolish beliefs existing in the most bourgeois of all countries—the United States. The most recent example is the collective suicide of several hundred members of a sect known as the People's Temple in 1978. Yet capitalism is not dominated by religion; rather, it is the other way around. The church is run like any other enterprise, preachers behave like salesmen, and holy books are advertised like any other commodity. Thus the Protestant Council of New York City advises its radio and TV speakers that, in a very real sense, they are "selling" religion. If marketing is poor, the listener will turn the dial and select another program (W. Whyte, Jr., *The Organization Man* [London: Jonathan Cape, 1957], p. 378). In 1900 the Reverend M. D. Babcock declared that "business is religion, and religion is business" (R. Bendix, *Work and Authority in Industry* [New York: Harper and Row, 1963], p. 257). If people go to church, they make it a shopping center. As described by S. Rowland: "The main mood of many a suburban church on Sunday is that of a fashionable shopping center. . . . On weekdays one shops for food, on Saturday one shops for recreation and on Sundays one shops for the Holy Ghost" (quoted in F. Pappenheim, *The Alienation of Modern Man* [New York: Monthly Review, 1959], p. 120).

[22] "As we survey man's history, we cannot . . . escape the following conclusion. The motive power of a value judgment is often greatly increased when it appears within the rationale of those who hold it, not under its proper logical flag as a value judgment but in the disguise of a statement of fact" (G. Gergmann, "Ideology," in M. Brodbeck, ed., *Readings in the Philosophy of the Social Sciences* [Toronto: Macmillan, 1969], p. 129).

[23] Letter to F. Bolte, November 23, 1871.

[24] In order to understand the Marxian influence psychologically, Russell suggests the following dictionary (*History of Western Philosophy* [London: Allen and Unwin, 1947], p. 383):

Yahweh = Dialectical Materialism
The Messiah = Marx
The Elect = The Proletariat
The Church = The Communist Party
The Second Coming = The Revolution
Hell = Punishment of Capitalists
The Millennium = The Communist Commonwealth

On the same page, Russell draws attention to the interesting historical paradox of Nazis' professing the ideas of the Jewish Old Testament.

[25] Note that *rational* is not antithetical to *idealist.* A man may be rational and highly motivated by ethical ideals (as Marx was, for instance), or religious and mean (as are characters in Dante's *Inferno*). The other two combinations are also possible, since the four dimensions of behavior are relatively independent. It is essential to distinguish very clearly between the structure of consciousness and the moral qualities of the actors.

[26] J. Nyerere, *Freedom and Socialism* (Dar es Salaam: Oxford University Press, 1974), p. 14.

[27] Even such an independent mind as Trotsky shared this view. When, in 1924, at the Thirteenth Congress of the Bolshevik Party, Trotsky was asked to renounce his views, he refused but admitted: "In the last instance the Party is always right because it is the only historic instrument which the working class possesses for the solution of its fundamental tasks. . . . I know that one ought not to be right against the Party. One can be right only with the Party and through the Party" (I. Deutscher, *The Prophet Unarmed* [London: Oxford University Press, 1959], p. 139). Contrast this with Engels' warning to party leader Bebel: "No party in any country can condemn me to silence if I decided to talk" (May 1–2, 1891).

[28] A few years later Slánský was posthumously rehabilitated as innocent.

[29] S. Stojanović, "Staljinistička partijnost i komunističko dostojanstvo," *Praxis,* 1973, pp. 679–96, quote from p. 686.

[30] André Gide reports the following story from his visit to the Soviet Union in 1936: "as we went through Gori, the little village where he [Stalin] was born, I thought it would be a kind and courteous attention to send him a personal message as an expression of gratitude for the warm welcome we had received. . . . I handed in a telegram which began: 'Passing through Gori on our wonderful trip I feel the impulse to send you——' But here the translator paused and said that he could not transmit such a message, that 'you,' when addressed to Stalin, was

not sufficient. It was not decent, he declared, and something must be added. He suggested 'You leader of the workers' or else 'You Lord of the people.' It seemed to me absurd and I said that Stalin must surely be above such flattery, but in vain. Nothing would budge him, and he would not transmit the telegram unless I agreed to the amendation" (A. Gide et al., *The God that Failed* [New York: Bantam Books, 1954], p. 193). The first of the two phrases in the text above is widely used in Korea. Thus, for instance, the entire front page of *The Pyongyang Times* on Saturday, August 25, 1975, consists of the following four articles: "The Respected and Beloved Leader Comrade Kim Il Sung Receives Delegation of Korean Youth in Japan"; "The Respected and Beloved Leader Kim Il Sung Sends Gifts to Iraqi President"; "Korean People under Great Leader's Wise Guidance Will Fight with Redoubled Efforts to Promote Country's Independent, Peaceful Reunification"; and "The Respected and Beloved Leader Kim Il Sung" (eight times) sends telegrams to different statesmen abroad. Similar phrases, though less extreme, are used in other etatist countries.

But *The Pyongyang Times* cannot match *Pravda,* which, on the occasion of Stalin's seventieth birthday, succeeded in filling its pages with greetings and eulogies for almost two years.

In comparison with the leadership cult in some etatist countries, the following description by M. Einaudi gives an impression of Italian fascism as somewhat restrained: "Psychologically, the unique position of the leader was carefully maintained by all the devices of communication and propaganda typical of totalitarian states. The identification of fascism with Mussolini was made compulsory in meetings of parlimentary assemblies, of the Fascist party, of economic bodies, of school children, of every form of group life" ("Fascism," *International Encyclopedia of the Social Sciences* [New York: Macmillan, 1968], vol. 5, pp. 334–41, quote from p. 336).

31 Petrus Abelardus, *Epistolae,* letter III.

32 E. Durkheim, *O podeli društvenog rada* [*De la division du travail social*]: (Belgrade: Prosveta, 1972), p. 214.

33 Ibid., p. 193.

34 Alexis de Tocqueville, an aristocratic conservative, noted in 1856 the religious qualities of the French Revolution: "In all the annals of recorded history we find no mention of any *political* revolution that took this form; its only parallel is to be found in certain *religious* revolutions. . . . Thus the French Revolution, though ostensibly political in origin, functioned on the lines, and assumed many of the aspects, of a religious revolution" (*The Ancien Regime and the French Revolution,* reproduced in A. Pizzorno, ed., *Political Sociology* [Harmondsworth: Penguin, 1971], pp. 23–24). Michael Walzer analyzed religious features of the English Revolution of 1640. Oliver Cromwell

told the Parliament in 1654 that he would not have acted as he did had not God opened a clear view. "It can only be suggested," continues Walzer, "that in the sixteenth and seventeenth centuries radical innovation in politics . . . was inconceivable without the moral support of religion . . . " (*The Revolution of the Saints,* ibid., pp. 324–25). More generally—and this is of particular interest with regard to our subject—revolutionaries of that time were committed "to the creation of the Holy Commonwealth in which the conscientious activity would be encouraged and even required. The saints saw themselves as divine *instruments* and theirs was the politics of wreckers, architects and builders—hard at work upon the political world. They refused to recognize any inherent or natural resistance to their labours. They treated every obstacle as *another example of the devil's resourcefulness* . . ." (ibid., p. 322, second emphasis added).

[35] Durkheim, *O podeli društvenog rada,* p. 160.

[36] Ibid., p. 201.

[37] Ibid., p. 381.

[38] Collective consciousness is defined as a set of beliefs and feelings common to the average members of a society (ibid., p. 119). A person has two types of consciousness: collective consciousness is common to the entire group and, consequently, it is not an individual himself but his society that lives in and acts through him. Individual consciousness represents only the person himself in what is personal and specific and makes him a separate being (ibid., pp. 159–60).

[39] Ibid., p. 202.

[40] Ibid., p. 185.

[41] Socrates was found guilty and executed because he "did not believe in gods in which the state believed."

[42] See L. R. Arias-Bustamante (*De la propriedad privada a la propriedad comunitaria* [Caracas: Monte Avila, 1971], pp. 41–43) for a collection of appropriate quotations.

[43] This linguistic incongruity has a simple psychological explanation. If members of the opposition (such as those who hold different opinions) are not different in kind but only in degree from the enemies (such as those who throw bombs), then it is logical to use a single combined phrase, "members of the enemy."

[44] *Quotations from Chairman Mao Tse-tung* (Peking: Foreign Languages Press, 1967), p. 277. Also: "careerists and conspirators like Khrushchev . . ." (ibid., p. 278).

[45] Political bosses are well aware of that. Hitler, for example, wrote in *Mein Kampf:* "It is necessary to suggest to the people that the most

varied enemies all belong to the same category; and to lump all adversaries together so that it will appear to the mass of our own partisans that the struggle is being waged against a single enemy. This fortifies their faith in their rights and increases their exasperation against those who would assail them" (quoted in J. Ellul, *The Technological Society* [New York: Vintage Books, 1964], p. 367). The organizational manual of the National Socialist German Workers' Party declared Jews, freemasons, Jesuits, and the political priesthood as the most dangerous enemies. Other enemies commonly denounced were anarchist and Catholic elements, Marxists, communists, plutocrats, cosmopolitans, Zionists, liberals, and pacifists. Some of these enemies appear on both Nazi and Stalinist lists.

[46] See Djuro Šušnjić, *Ribari ljudskih duša* (Belgrade: Mladost, 1976), p. 83.

[47] In the tradition of their people, Yugoslav partisans described historical developments, including changes in attitude, in numerous songs. One such Montenegran song says: "We do not believe in wonders any longer but in Marx and Engels and their illustrous books" (this information was passed on to me by Jozo Županov). Another song goes: "We don't believe in heaven but in Marx and Engels" (Dj. Šušnjić, "Religija i znanost," in Š. Bahtijarević, ed., *Religija i ateizam u samoupravnom socijalističkom društvu* [Zagreb: Centar za društvena istraživanja Sveučilišta, 1979], p. 87). Similar is the statement by Fidel Castro of Cuba: "We believed in Marxism, we believed that this was the most correct, most scientific, the only truthful theory, revolutionary theory . . . . I am a Marxist-Leninist and I shall be a Marxist-Leninist until the last day of my life" *(Selección de discursos* [Havana, 1963], p. 119). This statement may be colored by the emotional needs of an orator. Nevertheless, compare it to the statement of the famous Russian medieval presbyter Avakum (1621–82): "I shall keep as I received until my death. . . . I believe in what was written; what the saint teachers wrote is good for me" (A. I. Timofeev, *Teorija književnosti* [Belgrade: Prosveta, 1950], p. 398).

[48] "The theory of Marx, Engels, Lenin and Stalin is universally applicable." "It is revisionism to negate the basic principles of Marxism and to negate its universal truth" (*Quotations from Chairman Mao Tse-tung*, pp. 306 and 20). I have consistently been asked by the editors of journals and newspapers to delete from my articles such statements as "Marx made a mistake when . . ." or "Lenin was wrong because . . ." In the early etatist period of the then strong Soviet ideological influence, my party membership was jeopardized because I had once pointed out that the *translation* of Marx's *Capital* contained typographical and terminological errors.

[49] *Ribari ljudskih duša* (Belgrade: Mladost, 1976), p. 176.

[50] In order to avoid misunderstanding—almost inevitable when dealing with such an emotionally loaded subject—I should like to stress

again that no statement in this section must be interpreted in ethical terms. I am not arguing that the party is something bad—or good, for that matter. I am simply describing what happens and why. Moreover, at this stage of discussion, no implication is warranted about such problems as whether party congresses ought to determine party line and how, or to do something else. The message of the analysis is only the following: all social facts—ideas, institutions, activities—reflect a religious structure of consciousness and are similar to what happens in similarly religiously oriented societies. Behavioral patterns are not arbitrary but structurally determined.

[51] The Jewish Talmud informs us characteristically that Jesus was crucified because he had seduced and split Israel.

[52] In order to attack effectively an adversary in the international labor movement, Lenin wrote the book, *Proletarian Revolution and the Renegade Kautsky*. Half a century later, the Chinese Maoist leadership talk of the "renegade Tito clique" (*Is Yugoslavia a Socialist Country?* [Peking: Foreign Languages Press, 1963]) and of the "renegade clique of Brezhnev" (*Fundamentals of Political Economy* [1974] [White Plains, N.Y.: M. E. Sharpe, 1977], p. 207).

[53] Gide et al., *The God that Failed,* p. 102. Describing the fate of expelled Trotskyites in Poland, Isaac Deutscher writes: "the leadership succeeded in stifling all discussion and terrorizing Party members to such an extent that they began to shun us with the superstitious fear with which faithful members of the church used to shun excommunicated heretics" (*Marxism in Our Time* [Berkeley: Ramparts, 1971], p. 153).

[54] The phenomenon is, in fact, much more general and can be observed in many other countries. The liberation of a former colony involves sudden politicization of its citizens. The political culture is lacking. What happens is well described by Edward Shils: "Intense politicization is accompanied by the conviction that only those who share one's principles and positions are wholly legitimate members of the polity and those who do not share them are separated by a steep barrier. The governing party in many sovereign underdeveloped states, and those intellectuals who make it up or are associated with it, tend to believe that those who are in opposition are separated from them by fundamental and irreconcilable differences. They feel that they *are* the state and the nation, and that those who do not go along with them are not just political rivals but *total* enemies" ("The Intellectuals in the Political Development of the New States," in J. Finkle and R. Gable, eds., *Political Development and Social Change* [New York: John Wiley and Sons, 1966], pp. 338–64, quote from p. 355).

[55] Andrija Krešić drew my attention to this interpretation as a likely one.

[56] The term *ideology* is used in the Marxian sense of false consciousness

serving the interests of the ruling class. Of course, when it serves one's own interests, one's consciousness is correct.

[57] E. Fischer, "Marksizam kao naučna metoda," *Naše teme,* 1967, pp. 2077–83, quote from p. 2079.

[58] Even if we neglect the fundamental question about who establishes the progressiveness of a class and who evaluates its interests, the following consequence of the doctrine still remains valid. Since not *all* truth is class determined—mathematics and everyday statements of fact are not, for otherwise communication would be impossible—obvious lies are an indisputable proof that activity is running against proletarian interests. Lies can be justified on the basis of class interests only by replacing a theory with a tautology: whatever I do is in the class interests of the proletariat. The famous identification of the interests of General Motors with the interests of the American people belongs to the same class of statement and has the same class origin. On a practical level, the principle is stated somewhat differently, and in this form it received the following persuasive treatment by East German poet Wolf Biermann (*Mit Marx—und Engelszungen* [Berlin: Wagenbach, 1968]):

> Du sagst: Das Eingeständniss unserer Fehler
> nütze dem Feind.
> Gut. Aber wem nütze unsere Lüge?

[59] These are, for instance, the first and the third among ten criteria adopted at the University of Belgrade for judging fitness for a university appointment. See P. Kozić, "Idejno-politička i moralna podobnost univerziteskih nastavnika," *Univerzitet danas,* 1976, nos. 1–2, 81–88, espec. pp. 83–84. Similar criteria, of course, are used, tacitly or overtly (*Berufsverbot* being perhaps the best known example) in a number of more developed countries. But there they are at least felt as oppressive and are not self-imposed.

[60] Its formal publication was discontinued in 1966.

[61] Purged "antiparty elements" simply disappear from the history books and encyclopedias, even from paintings and photographs. It is important to realize that this is not at all simple dishonesty; at least, in many cases honesty is not in question. An example will clarify the matter. After the death of Mao, some photographs were falsified in the Chinese press (the Gang of Four disappeared). Neil Burton, living in Peking, gives the following illuminating explanation: "the appearance of leaders in or their removal from, photos is basically a matter of general approval, or strong disapproval, of those leaders and their political lines. You could reply that this was nonsense, that any photograph is only a reflection of a factual occurrence. I have good reason to believe that you would be met with disagreement, and perhaps with the additional information that had anybody tried to force the printers

to print unaltered photos of the leadership lined up at the funeral services for Chairman Mao . . . there would have been forceful obstruction by printers themselves . . . . Finally, if you . . . wondered aloud how history could have any meaning at all, your listeners would probably not understand your dilemma—or if they did, might reply that history is the business of archivists and historians, that the practice in question concerned not 'history' but current class struggle, and that no decent historian could aspire to illustrate a work with photographs of such despicable people as the Four in any case" ("In Defense of the New Regime," *Monthly Review*, 1978, no. 3, pp. 15–36, quote from pp. 27–28).

[62] At that time the forging of charters and deeds was customary. The forgers thought they were right because all they did was to provide a written basis for already existing claims. Their contemporaries did not find that illegal either. Only after the humanistic movement developed critical attitudes toward the Middle Ages was the authenticity of historical sources examined.

[63] Thus, for instance, Gentile praises anti-intellectualism, announces (in *The Foundation of Fascism*) that fascism is bound by no principles, and declares meaningless loyalty to any truth that lies outside or beyond the practical aims of Fascist politics. In the words of Herbert Marcuse: "Theory as such and all intellectual activity are made subservient to the changing requirements of politics" (*Reason and Revolution* [Boston: Beacon Press, 1960], p. 409).

[64] This similarity was also noted by B. Ward in *The Socialist Economy* (New York: Random House, 1967), ch. 5, and by L. A. Coser in "The Militant Collective: Jesuits and Leninists," *Social Research*, 1973, pp. 110–28.

[65] Mao Zedong, "New Phase," report at the Central Committee session in 1938, *Speeches and Articles* (Serbocroatian edition: Belgrade: Trideset dana, 1949, p. 84). In the strict logic of this definition, the Central Committee cannot possibly be wrong—and never has been.

[66] "Then said Jesus unto his disciples, if any man will come after me, *let him deny himself,* and take up his cross, and follow me" (Matthew 16:24, emphasis added). In the sixteenth century Saint Ignatius Loyola wrote that the mere executing of commands "does not deserve the name of obedience . . . unless it rises to the second degree which is to make the superior's will one's own in such a way that there is not merely the effectual execution of the command, but an interior conformity . . ." (*Letters of St. Ignatius Loyola,* selected and trans. by W. J. Young [Chicago: Loyola University Press, 1959], p. 289). If the word *superior* is replaced by the word *party,* the quotation also describes a twentieth-century view. Thus the Russian revolutionary Victor Serge points out: "Every Communist . . . feels himself to be the humblest servant of an infinite cause. The highest praise that can be bestowed

on him is to say that he has 'no private life,' that his life has fused totally with history. . . . It is the Party that does everything. Its orders are not to be discussed" (*The Year One of the Russian Revolution* [New York: Holt, Rinehart and Winston, 1972], p. 367).

[67] E. Fromm, *Bekstvo od slobode* (Belgrade: Nolit, 1964), pp. 206 and 243.

[68] Quoted in V. Kravchenko, *I Chose Freedom* (London: Robert Hale, 1947), p. 275.

[69] Quoted in F. Venturi, *Roots of Revolution* (London: Weidenfeld and Nicolson, 1960), pp. 365–66.

[70] Danko Grlić, from whom I take this quotation, adds, for the sake of comparison, the admission of Adolf Eichmann before the court in Jerusalem in 1961: "During my entire life I was accustomed to obey . . . I did fully and up to the end always only listened to my party" ("Marginalije uz Čehoslovačku i nove tendencije u socijalizmu," *Praxis*, 1969, pp. 316–24).

[71] B. Moore, Jr., *Political Power and Social Theory* (New York: Harper and Row, 1965), p. 69.

[72] J. Stalin, *Sochineniia*, vol. 7 (Moscow: Ogiz, 1947), p. 344.

[73] Moore, *Political Power and Social Theory*, p. 73.

[74] K. Mannheim, *Ideologie und Utopie* (Frankfurt-am-Main: Schulte-Bulmke, 1965), passim.

[75] By "charismatic," I mean possessing the transcendental quality ascribed to the bearer of charisma because it is believed that he (the leader) or it (the party, the teaching) is associated or possessed of some ultimate value or power.

[76] The Pope himself was occasionally a slaveowner. See J. Kulischer, *Opća ekonomska povijest* [Allgemeine Wirtschaftsgeschichte I] [Zagreb: Kultura, 1957], p. 91. In 1851 a book by Presbyterian minister George D. Armstrong, *The Christian Doctrine of Slavery* (New York: Charles Scribner, p. 134), appeared in which he wrote: "It may be that Christian slavery is God's solution of the problem [the relation of labor and capital] about which the wisest statesmen of Europe confess themselves at fault." A few years later, Rev. Fred. A. Ross, in his book *Slavery Ordained of God* (Philadelphia: Lippincott, 1857, p. 5), claimed: "slavery is ordained of God, and to continue for the good of the slave, the good of the master, the good of the whole American family, until another and better destiny may be unfolded." As late as 1900, the American Book and Bible House published a work in which the author argued that the Negro was not a descendent of Adam and Eve, but "simply a beast without a soul" (C. Carroll, *The Negro a Beast* [St. Louis], p. 339; quoted in E. F. Frazier, *Black Bourgeoisie* [London: Collier, 1970], pp. 115,121,122).

[77] "Aktueller und nichtaktueller Begriff des Marxismus," in W. Oelmüller, ed., *Weiterentwicklungen des Marxismus* (Darmstadt: Wissenschaftliche Buchengesellschaft, 1977), p. 15.

[78] L. Gottschalk et al., *The Foundations of the Modern World* (London: Allen and Unwin, 1969), book 2, ch. 9.

[79] There are two exceptions: East Germany and Czechoslovakia. The former is a special geopolitical case. The latter is one of the socially most mature countries in Europe. When, in 1968, Czechs and Slovaks tried to replace etatism with socialism, they were prevented by the military intervention of concerted etatist powers.

[80] At the Berlin conference in 1976, Santiago Carillo, the Spanish communist leader, remarked: "Sufferings due to the persecution of communists resulted in combining scientific socialism with a certain type of mystical sacrifice and predetermination. We became a sort of a new church with martyrs and prophets. For years Moscow . . . was our Rome. We talked about the Great Socialist October Revolution as of our Christmas. That was our youth. Today we have grown up. . . . We lose the character of a church more and more" (quoted in W. F. Haug and E. Wulff, "Prilog samorazumevanju naučnog socijalizma u sadašnjosti," *Sociajalizam u svetu*, 1977, *3*, 141–55, quote from p.145).

[81] That socioeconomic development need not be—and in fact *is not*—linear will be taken as obvious by Marxists. See K. Marx, *Pre-Capitalist Economic Formations* (New York: International Publishers, 1964).

[82] It will be of interest to quote a clear and reasoned statement by Peter Kropotkin in the article "Anarchism" in *Encyclopaedia Britannica* (1910): "The state organization, having always been . . . the instrument for establishing monopolies in favour of the ruling minorities, cannot be made to work for the destruction of these minorities. The Anarchists consider, therefore, that to hand over to the state all the main sources of economical life . . . would mean to create a new instrument of tyranny. State capitalism would only increase the powers of bureaucracy and capitalism. True progress lies in the direction of decentralization . . . and of free federation from the simple to the compound, *in lieu* of the present hierarchy from the centre to the periphery." Much earlier Bakunin envisaged "the most shameful lie: the red bureaucracy" unless the Russian state were destroyed, and then went on to make a straightforward prediction: "Take the most radical revolutionary and . . . give him dictatorial power . . . before a year is over he will be worse than the tsar himself" (A. Künzli, "Problem moći u anarhističkoj kritici marksizma," *Praxis*, 1970, pp. 117–25, quote from p. 120). In March 1920 Kropotkin wrote to Lenin: "Russia became a revolutionary republic in name only. . . .Today there is government not by the soviets but by party committees. . . . If the present situation lasts any longer, the word 'socialism' will be turned

into an abuse, as happened with 'equality' forty years after the rule of the Jacobins" (ibid., p. 121).

Criticizing the well-known book by Lenin, *State and Revolution*, Luis Fabri wrote in 1921 in *La crisis del anarquismo:* "If the state is also turned into an owner, then we shall have state capitalism and not socialism, and even less the abolition of the state or anarchy. . . . In an owner-state, all proletarians would become hired laborers of the state instead of hired laborers of private capitalists. The state would be an exploiter, which means that a mass of higher and lower rulers and an entire bureaucracy would constitute a new ruling and exploiting class" (V. Stanovčić and A. Stojanović, eds., *Birokratija i tehnokratija* [Belgrade: Sedma sila, 1966], p. 164, book 1).

[83] Well-known is the long polemic of Rosa Luxemburg with Lenin during 1904–18. As early as 1904, she wrote: "In actuality nothing surrenders so young a labor movement to power-thirsty intellectuals more easily and securely than the compression of that movement into the armor of bureaucratic centralism, which degrades the fighting workers to a compliant instrument of some 'committee' "(*Izabrani spisi* [Zagreb: Naprijed, 1974], p. 98). Plekhanov accused the Bolsheviks of aiming at a party dictatorship over the proletariat.

A decade before the October Revolution, the German economist and historian Werner Sombart wrote: "There is nothing sillier than socialism based on state ownership . . . because that would essentially be only bourgeois-capitalist production, and the social structure corresponding to that production would remain, only slightly modified: in these enterprises the same hierarchy would remain; similarly, the hierarchy of government . . . officials would not change. One hierarchy would be replaced by another. What for? On the contrary, it is necessary to aim for the removal of the hierarchic-bureaucratic system in the factory and the state. And this goal can be achieved only if autonomous labor organizations, trade unions, become bearers of production and if state organs are not allowed to interfere with their business affairs" (*Socijalizam i socijalni pokret*, translated from the eighth German edition [Belgrade: Djurdjević, 1922], pp. 120–21).

The great English philosopher and humanist Bertrand Russell foresaw the subsequent development very clearly in 1918: "State Socialists argue as if there would be no danger to liberty in a State not based upon capitalism. This seems to me an entire delusion. Given an official caste, however selected, there are bound to be a set of men whose whole instincts will drive them towards tyranny. Together with the natural love of power, they will have a rooted conviction (visible now in the higher ranks of the Civil Service) that they alone know enough to be able to judge what is for the good of the community. Like all men who administer a system, they will come to feel the system itself sacrosanct. The only changes they will derive will be changes in the direction of further regulations as how the people are to enjoy the good things kindly granted to them by their benevolent despots" (*Roads to Freedom* [London: Allen and Unwin, 1918], pp. 136–37).

[84] N. Bukharin, *Historical Materialism: A System of Sociology* (Ann Arbor: University of Michigan Press, 1969), pp. 310–11.

[85] E. Fromm makes a similar observation: "While Marx's theory was a critique of capitalism, many of his adherents were so deeply imbued with the spirit of capitalism that they interpreted Marx's thought in the economistic and materialistic categories that are prevalent in contemporary capitalism. Indeed, while the Soviet Communists, as well as the reformist Socialists, believed they were the enemies of capitalism, they conceived of communism—or socialism—in the spirit of capitalism. For them, socialism is not a society humanly different from capitalism, but rather, a form of capitalism in which the working class has achieved a higher status . . ." (*Marx's Concept of Man* [New York: Frederick Ungar, 1969], p. 6).

[86] It has also been called bureaucratic collectivism (Bruno Rizzi, *La bureaucratisation du monde* [Paris, 1939]). Three years later the same term was adopted by American communist Max Schachtman: "This new social order . . . is neither capitalist nor proletarian. To distinguish it from either one of these two and at the same time to underline its outstanding characteristics as tersely as possible, this new state was designated as *bureaucratic collectivism*" (*The Bureaucratic Revolution* [New York: Donald Press, 1962], p. 62). The term has now become popular in some communist circles in Italy. I do not adopt it because it is clumsy and because it suggests that there also exists nonbureaucratic collectivism, which is socialism. Yet, collectivism is the opposite of individualism, while socialism supersedes both.

[87] This universal faith can be traced far back into the nineteenth century. In 1859 Marx wrote: "Bourgeois productive relationships are the last antagonistic form of the social process of production. . . . With this social system, therefore, the pre-history of human society comes to a close" (quoted in Fromm, *Marx's Concept of Man*, p. 219).

[88] They even supported Stalin. In cinemas in worker districts, for example, people still applaud when Stalin appears on the screen (R. Medvedev, *Knjiga o socialističeskoj demokratii* [Paris: Grasset et Fasquelle, 1972], p. 55). Obviously, it was not only the workers. "Stalin was supported by the majority of the Soviet people," observed Roy Medvedev, "not only because he was clever enough to deceive but also because they were backward enough to be deceived"(*Let History Judge* [New York: Alfred A. Knopf, 1972], p. 428). To illustrate his point, Medvedev quoted the following passage from the nineteenth-century Arab thinker and social activist Abd al Rahmān al-Kawākibī: "The common people are the despot's sustenance and his power; he rules over them and with their help oppresses them. He holds them captive and they extol his might; he robs them and they bless him for sparing their lives. He degrades them and they praise his grandeur; he turns them against each other, and they take pride in his craftiness. . . . and if some of them are reproachful, rejecting despotism, the people will fight the rejectors as if they were tyrants" (ibid.).

[89] This view is common among Yugoslav social scientists and will also be found in my earlier work. See *An Essay on Yugoslav Society* (White Plains, N.Y.: International Arts and Sciences Press, 1969), ch. 2. One of the earlier Marxist writers, Anton Pannekoek, denotes the Soviet system as state capitalism and its state bureaucracy as a new ruling class (*Lenin as Philosopher,* 1938). Predrag Vranicki describes the process that brought about this state of affairs as a "bureaucratic-etatist counterrevolution" (*Marksizam i socijalizam* [Zagreb: Liber, 1979], p. 253).

[90] K. Marx, *Capital,* vol. 1 (New York: International Publishers, 1967), p. 217.

[91] David Horowitz summarizes the most glaring contradictions of Stalin's counterrevolution as follows: "While breaking the back of rural individualism, the Stalin régime fostered a furiously competitive *Stakhanovism* among the traditionally collectivist Russian working class. While encouraging learning and the acquisition of scientific knowledge on an unprecedented scale, it propagated grotesque intellectual doctrines [Zhdanov, Lysenko] and launched witch-hunting attacks on those sections of the intelligentsia that sought to assert any independence. While introducing large-scale social welfare services and glorifying human labour, it reintroduced, in the penal camps, the most hateful form of labour. While proclaiming its objective to be a 'classless' society, it created inequality and privilege on an extensive scale. While exorcizing religion in the name of Marxism and scientific rationality, it religicized Marxism and deified both the ruler and the state. Finally, while proclaiming its own continuity with 'Leninism,' it encouraged the resurgence of Russian nationalism, the rejection of which had been the very basis of the Leninist break with Social Democracy" (*Imperialism and Revolution* [London: Penguin, 1969], p. 150).

[92] See F. Pryor, *Property and Industrial Organization in Communist and Capitalist Nations* (Bloomington: Indiana University Press, 1973), p. 88.

[93] This is well illustrated by the available data for Czechoslovakia. If we compare data for 1939 (capitalism) with those for 1945 (expected socialism evolving toward etatism), we find that all important differences in earned incomes were radically reduced:

	1939	1945
Workers vs. employees	100/253	100/145
Auxiliary vs. skilled workers	100/169	100/142
Women vs. men	100/182	100/155
Agriculture vs. industry	100/290	100/155
Low-wage vs. high-wage industries	100/192	100/166

Source: J. Kosta, *Abriss der sozialökonomischen Entwicklung der Tschechoslowakei, 1945–1977* (Frankfurt am Main: Suhrkamp, 1978), p. 4.

[94] A. Sakharov, *Wie ich mir die Zukunft vorstelle* (Zurich: Diogenes, 1973).

[95] A. Inkeles, *Social Change in Soviet Russia* (Cambridge, Mass.: Harvard University Press, 1968), p. 58.

[96] A. Solzhenitsyn, *Archipelag GULAG* (Paris: YMCA, 1973).

[97] K. Štajner, *7000 dana u Sibiru* (Zagreb: Globus, 1971).

[98] GULAG = *glavnoe upravlenie lagerej,* or Main Administration of Camps.

[99] *Wie ich mir die Zukunft vorstelle,* p. 46.

[100] J. Deutscher, *Prognani prorok* (Zagreb: Liber, 1976).

[101] G. K. Schüller, "The Politburo," in H. Lasswell and D. Lerner, eds., *World Revolutionary Elites* (Cambridge, Mass.: MIT Press, 1965), pp. 97–115. In his report to the Eighteenth Party Congress, Stalin referred to Trotsky, Zinoviev, Kamenev, Iakir, Tukhachevsky, Bukharin, and others as "spies, murderers and wrongdoers" and told his audience that they were shot.

[102] N. Khrushchev, "Speech Before the 20th Congress, February 25, 1956," in C. Wright Mills, ed., *The Marxists* (New York: Dell, 1962), p. 370. The Soviet working class still has not been given the text of this speech.

[103] M. Matthews, *Privilege in the Soviet Union* (London: Allen and Unwin, 1978), p. 151.

[104] The four philosophers were Mitin (editor of the chief philosophical review), Konstantinov (director of the academy's Institute of Philosophy), Iudin, and Berezdnev. Mitin distinguished himself in 1930 for being probably the first to declare publicly that Stalin was the fourth classic. The passage quoted here was taken from a letter they wrote to the Central Committee after having been accused by another philosopher and old Bolshevik, P. I. Shabalkin; the latter was sent to a concentration camp in 1936, was rehabilitated in 1956, and wrote a letter to Khrushchev in 1961 (B. Lewytzkyj, *Die Linke Opposition in der Sowietunion* [Hamburg: Hoffman und Campe, 1974], p. 24).

[105] Quoted in *Politika,* March 18, 1979, p. 4. It should be added, however, that public protest forced the Ministry of Education to withdraw the textbook.

[106] Kolakowski, "The Eurocommunist Schism," *Dissent,* Winter 1978, pp. 33–37, quote from p. 33.

[107] See A. London, *L'aveu dans l'engrenage du proès de Prague* (Paris: Gallimard, 1968).

[108] Results obtained in a dissertation by D. Neubauer and reported by R. A. Dahl in "The Evaluation of Political Systems," in I. de Sola Pool, ed., *Contemporary Political Science* (New York: McGraw-Hill, 1967), p. 173.

CHAPTER 3

[1] B. Russell even declares that power is the fundamental concept in social science in the same sense that energy is the fundamental concept in physics; power, "like energy, must be regarded as continually passing from any one of its forms into any other, and it should be the business of social science to seek the laws of such transformations" (*Power* [London: Allen and Unwin, 1967], pp. 9–10). In attributing to power the central place, Russell was preceded by a compatriot, Thomas Hobbes, who in his *Leviathan* argued that the will for power was responsible for social differentiation and that wealth, knowledge, and honors are but the different kinds of power (Yugoslav edition: Belgrade: Kultura, 1961), p. 61.

[2] At the enterprise level, R. Lickert finds in the United States that the democratization of management increases the influence of all groups (*New Patterns of Management* [New York, 1961]). Veljko Rus finds that, in Yugoslavia, "power sharing increases the total amount of influence in all organizations which have developed division of labour, under the circumstances that social environment discourages strict hierarchical relations within organizations" ("De Facto Participation" [Berlin: International Institute of Management, 1978], p. 31 [mimeo]).

[3] A. Giddens, *The Class Structure of the Advanced Societies* (New York: Harper and Row, 1973), p. 130.

[4] Usually only three types of power are distinguished. F. L. Neumann speaks of three basic methods at the disposal of the power group: persuasion, material benefits, and violence ("Approaches to the Study of Political Power," *Political Science Quarterly*, 1950, pp. 161–80). J. R. Commons distinguishes physical, economic, and moral power (*Legal Foundations of Capitalism* [Madison: University of Wisconsin, 1957], pp. 47–64). A. Etzioni lists coercive power (e.g., military forces), utilitarian power (backed by economic sanctions), and persuasive power (e.g., that of the church). He lumps together the allocation of symbolic rewards and deprivations with the manipulation of mass media into a single category of persuasive or normative power (*The Active Society* [New York: Free Press, 1968], p. 357; *A Comparative Analysis of Complex Organizations* [New York: Free Press, 1961], p. 5).

[5] For this reason Marx thought that property relations determined class relations; society was dichotomized into antagonistically juxtaposed owners and nonowners. Max Weber reduced the formation of classes to exclusively economic interests connected with the existence of the market and then added power and status as two separate di-

mensions of social relations. Both authors designed their conceptual frameworks for the analysis of capitalist societies. Marx would find it somewhat difficult, and Weber simply impossible, to explain the class character of an etatist society. We shall see later that Marxists generally use a special construction of "collective bureaucratic ownership" for the purpose, while Weberians agree with Stalinists that etatism is classless.

[6] R. Dahrendorf, "On the Origin of Inequality among Men," in E. Laumann et al., eds., *The Logic of Hierarchies* (Chicago: Markham, 1970), p. 26.

[7] "It is clear, then, that some men are by nature free, and others slaves, and that for these latter slavery is both expedient and right" (Aristotle, *Politics,* 1255a). Saint Paul and Saint Peter held a similar view, as one can see in some of their letters to the early churches.

[8] Interviewing workers in one large American automobile plant in 1946–47, Ely Chinoy found the following: "I guess I'm just not smart enough, said one worker. It's my own fault, said another. . . . By thus focusing criticism upon the individual rather than upon its institutions, society protects itself against the reactions of those who fail" ("Opportunity and Aspirations of Automobile Workers," in N. J. Smelser, ed., *Readings on Economic Sociology* [Englewood Cliffs, N.J.: Prentice-Hall, 1965], pp. 38–46, quote from p. 44). If the worker does not blame himself, he just resigns in some sort of fatalistic pessimism, as the following often-heard working class expressions indicate: "What is to be will be"; "That's just the way things are"; "Give and bear it"; "You've got to take life as it comes"; "It's no good mourning"; etc. (R. Hoggart, *The Uses of Literacy* [London: Pelican, 1958], p. 92). Closely related to the lack of perception of a possible alternative is the lack of class consciousness as reflected in the voting behavior of the working class. In France in 1956, 30 percent of industrial workers and 44 percent of agricultural workers supported conservative and bourgeois parties. In Italy in 1953, this percentage varied between 19 percent for the lowest category to 48 percent for the best paid workers; and in Germany in 1953, between 49 percent for unskilled and 39 percent for skilled workers. In Britain about 45 percent of manual workers voted for nonlabor parties in 1964. In Switzerland this percentage was about 39; in Japan in 1960, 44. In Britain in 1945–66, more than one-third of workers voted Conservative while only one-tenth of the upper middle class voted Labour. In fact, more than one-half of all votes cast for Conservatives in 1959–1966 came from workers. Only in Sweden did less than 30 percent of all workers vote for bourgeois parties (in 1974). While between one-third and one-half of workers vote for bourgeois parties (in some countries, such as the United States, labor parties do not even exist), only between 10 and 20 percent of employers and the managerial middle class vote for workers' parties. See S. M. Lipset, *Political Man* (New York: Doubleday, 1963), pp.

235, 237, 253; J. Raynor, *The Middle Class* (London: Longmans, 1970), p. 104; R. Girad, "Milieux politique et classes sociales en Suisse," *Cahiers internationaux de sociologie,* 1965, pp. 29–54; J. LaPalombara, *Politics Within Nations* (Englewood Cliffs, N.J.: Prentice-Hall, 1974), p. 437; W. Korpi, *The Working Class in Welfare Capitalism* (London: Routledge and Kegan Paul, 1978), p. 274; S. E. Finer, *Comparative Government* (London: Penguin, 1970), pp. 143, 145. Recent research has indicated that a part, perhaps a large part, of class-inconsistent vote is due to upward and downward social mobility, which generates identification with the ruling class. Upwardly mobile workers, those who aspire to enter nonmanual strata, try to imitate the attitudes and adopt the values of these strata. Former white-collar employees who have been forced to take manual jobs consider this degradation as temporary and, as a proof to themselves and to others that this is so and that they really belong to the establishment, they stress even more strongly their right-wing preferences. Jean Blondel finds that union membership strongly improves class consistency. In Britain unionized manual workers are three times more likely to vote Labour than Conservative Party; nonunionized manual workers are about evenly divided (D. Thompson, *The Democratic Citizen* [Cambridge: Cambridge University Press, 1970], p. 130). Unions themselves, however, are also ideologically harnessed. Charles Lindborn describes how an American coal miners' union for decades did not press for enforcement of mine-safety legislation. "They simply feared for their jobs if the companies were to be forced to practice safety and bear the high costs of doing so. Their constrained minds could not seriously entertain an alternative—for safety procedures to be paid for by government funds, by subsidies to mining companies, or by subsidies to their own union" (*Politics and Markets* [New York: Basic Books, 1977], p. 210).

[9] In this respect the following passage by Karl Kautsky, characterized by Lenin as "profoundly true," provides a summary of the historical experience of European socialist movements: "The vehicle of science is not the proletariat, but the *bourgeois intelligentsia:* it was in the minds of individual members of this stratum that modern socialism originated, and it was they who communicated it to the more intellectually developed proletarians who, in their turn, introduced it into the proletarian class struggle where conditions allowed that to be done. Thus, socialist consciousness is something introduced into the proletarian class struggle from without and not something that arose within it spontaneously." The passage appeared in *Neue Zeit* (1901–02, XX, I, no. 3, 79) and was quoted in V. I. Lenin, "What Is to Be Done?" (1902), *Selected Works in Three Volumes* (Moscow: Progress, 1970), p. 150.

[10] C. J. Friedrich distinguishes three primary forms of coercion: physical (brute force applied in a military or police action), economic (withholding the means of securing livelihood), and psychic (by propaganda or by charismatic leadership). See *Man and His Government* (New York: McGraw-Hill, 1963), p. 168.

[11] "If we often fail to see the reality of economic coercion," explains A. P. Wertheimer, "because our conceptual distinctions tend to conceal it, there are still other reasons for this misconception. The rule makers and enforcers of the political system are far more visible or public than the agents of economic coercion. We know who is responsible for enforcing selective service laws, but who compels a family to starve? The diffuseness of economic rules: the lack of concentration of power in clearly defined offices and places, makes identification and understanding of economic coercion the more difficult. . . . Those who feel the squeeze of political coercion more severely than economic coercion are also more apt to be knowledgeable, articulate, able to determine the agents responsible for the coercion, and ready to make a reform of some kind." See "Political Coercion and Political Obligation," in J. R. Pennock and J. W. Chapman, eds., *Coercion,* Nomos XIV (Chicago: Aldine, 1972), pp. 230–31.

[12] "The Poor Law of 1834 finally abolished all grants in aid of wages, restricted outdoor charitable relief within the narrowest limits, and established the workhouse system as it was known in the nineteenth century. The laws no longer compelled anyone to work. Forced labour was henceforth a term of approbrium. For troublesome, violent and noisy systems of legal constraint had been substituted the peaceful, silent, unremitting pressure of hunger. The worker was a free man—left to his own judgment and discretion. He was free to starve with his family, to enter the workhouse (in which case he would be separated from his family) or to enter a factory. So long as care was taken to make life in the workhouse harder and more degrading than the life of a factory worker, the end was achieved. The labour revolution was complete. Labour power was a commodity sold by its owner and bought by the employer who wanted it under a freely negotiated contract. The labour market, which was a necessary part of the laissez-faire capitalist system, had been established" (E. H. Carr, *The New Society* [London: Macmillan, 1951], p. 43). (See also chapter 6, section IA.)

[13] That overly popular leaders may represent a threat to the society was already known to the ancient Greeks. They institutionalized a defense against this threat by inventing ostracism. Charisma is defined by A. Etzioni as "the ability of an actor to exercise diffuse and intense influence over the normative orientations of the actors" (*A Comparative Analysis of Complex Organizations* [New York: Free Press, 1961], p. 203).

[14] F. Parkin, *Class Inequality and Political Order* (New York: Praeger, 1971), p. 44.

[15] See W. Wesolowski, "The Notions of Strata and Class in Socialist Society," in A. Béteille, ed., *Social Inequality* (Harmondsworth: Penguin, 1969), p. 143.

[16] In feudal times, political power was dominant, and at the turn of the fourteenth century Ibn Khaldun could assert: "The possession

of power is the source of riches" (quoted in S. Ossowski, *Class Structure in the Class Consciousness* [London: Routledge and Kegan Paul, 1963], p. 24). In capitalism, economic power is dominant, and so English sociologist T. Bottomore can conclude: "A rich man may have difficulty in entering the kingdom of heaven, but he will find it relatively easy to get into the higher councils of a political party, or into some branch of government. He can also exert influence on political life in other ways: by controlling media of communication, by making acquaintances in higher circles of politics, by taking a prominent part in the activities of pressure groups and advisory bodies" (*Elites and Society* [London: Watts, 1964], p. 116).

[17] " . . . social status is determined by several factors," wrote Polish sociologist Stanislaw Ossowski, "and . . . within certain limits at least, these factors may compensate for one another. Lack of education or inferior birth can be offset by economic power: a *nouveau riche* must be richer than other people in the class to which he aspires. Inadequate income may to a certain degree be offset by high social status, or by the fact of having wealthy forebears." As Holbwacks wrote: "Le qualité de riche ne se perd pas avec la richesse" (in Ossowski, *Class Structure,* p. 47). "If . . . the discrepancy between an individual's economic position and the level of his education is too great in relation to approved norms in a particular milieu, then the individual deviates from the personality pattern accepted in a given social class; this affects both his social status and his psychological attitudes, whether he has a high income and a glaring lack of elementary education or holds two university degrees but earns barely enough to keep himself alive" (p. 53).

[18] Polish Marxist Adam Schaff expresses a widely shared view when he notes that "ex definitione a social class cannot exist in a society in which private ownership of means of production is abolished." But he immediately points out that the real problem is in the sphere of alienation (*Marksizm a jednostka ludzka* [Warsaw, 1965]; quoted from the Serbo-Croatian edition: *Marksizam i ljudska jedinka* [Belgrade: Nolit, 1967], p. 167).

[19] M. Pečujlić, "Teorijski okvir za proučavanje klasnih promjena u socijalizmu," *Sociologija,* 1966, pp. 5–26, quote from p. 8. Marx would have said: "It is always the direct relationship of the owners of the conditions of production to the direct producers . . . which reveals . . . the hidden basis of the entire social structure, and with it . . . the corresponding specific form of the state" (*Capital,* vol. 3 [New York: International Publishers, 1967], p. 791).

[20] R. Dahrendorf, for example, talks of the ruling groups (who, on the basis of their position, are able to set up binding norms), the service class (which helps the ruling groups in rule-forming tasks by applying the norms and also by advising and supporting the rulers), and subject groups (who are subject to the rule of rulers and their

servants). He adds intellectuals as a separate group outside the structure of rulers and ruled (*Konflikt und Freiheit* [Munich: Piper, 1972], pp. 111–12).

[21] "The functions of capitalist appear subdivided in a steadily growing number of salaried employees of the very highest and of the high and of lower rank. . . . These new aides are neither capitalists nor workers: they are not owners of capital, they do not create value by their work, but they do control values created by others." Thus social development "puts alongside the capitalist who owns and functions the other one who owns but does not function. . . . What is more: it also produces the noncapitalist who exercises capitalist functions, who therefore does not own but functions as a capitalist" (K. Renner, *Die Wirtschaft als Gesamtprocess und die Sozialisierung* [Berlin, 1924], pp. 119 and 375); quoted in R. Dahrendorf, *Class and Class Conflict in Industrial Society* [London: Routledge and Kegan Paul, 1967], pp. 94 and 84). "The capitalist makes use of paid assistants who replace him gradually in his functions" (K. Renner, *Wandlüngen der modernen Gesellschaft* [Vienna: Wiener Volksbuchhandlung, 1953], p. 211).

[22] In Britain unskilled manual workers reach peak income at the age of thirty (skilled workers, ten years later); income subsequently drops 15–20 percent (for skilled workers, 10–15 percent). In 1966 manual workers worked 44 hours, white-collar workers 38 hours per week (A. Giddens, *The Class Structure of Advanced Societies* [New York: Harper and Row, 1973], p. 180).

[23] Collin Clark found the following rates of unemployment for various groups in Britain in 1931 (quoted in W. G. Runciman, *Relative Deprivation and Social Justice* [London: Routledge and Kegan Paul, 1966], p. 81):

Unskilled manual workers	30.5%
Skilled and semiskilled manual workers	14.4
Clerks and typists	5.5
Higher office workers	5.1
Proprietors and managers	1.3

[24] Empirical research shows that nonsupervisory white collar employees are markedly more satisfied with their working conditions than blue collar employees (75 percent against 47 percent) and also like their jobs more (75 percent against 57 percent). See D. Katz and R. L. Kahn, "Some Recent Findings in Human Relations Research in Industry," in G. E. Swanson, T. M. Newcomb, and E. L. Hartley, eds., *Readings in Social Psychology* (New York: Holt, 1952), p. 655.

[25] In England and Germany, two-thirds of the new middle class vote for conservative, one-third for radical parties (R. Dahrendorf, *Class and Class Conflict in Industrial Society,* p. 53).

[26] See Z. Bauman, *Between Class and Elite* (Manchester: Manchester University Press, 1972), p. 256.

[27] R. Dahrendorf summarizes the findings of four such studies for the United States (R. Centers, 1949), United Kingdom (R. Hogart, 1957), West Germany (H. Popitz et al., 1957), and French Switzerland (A. Willener, 1957) in *Class and Class Conflict in Industrial Society,* pp. 281–88. A more recent British study by W. G. Runciman (*Relative Deprivation and Social Justice*) arrives at the same conclusions. So do J. Goldthorpe and his associates, who studied affluent workers (*The Affluent Worker,* vol. 2 [Cambridge: Cambridge University Press, 1970], p. 79).

[28] "The Nature of Class Conflict," in R. Bendix and S. M. Lipset, eds., *Class, Status and Power* (New York: Free Press, 1966), p. 85.

[29] In France, 41 percent of high-ranking military officers enter business; in 1974, 30 percent of private bankers came from the civil service (P. Birnbaum et al., *La classe dirigeante française* [Vendôme: Presses universitaires de France, 1978], pp. 65, 69).

[30] In 1950, in the United States, top executives were almost exclusively the sons of businessmen (57 percent), farmers (15 percent), and professionals (14 percent). In Britain, 30 percent of high-level civil servants in 1929–50 came from the families of property owners and professionals, who constituted 3 percent of the population. In France, 84 percent of *les grands corps de l'état* are recruited from upper and upper middle class families and less than 1 percent from the families of industrial workers and agricultural laborers (Bottomore, *Elites and Society,* pp. 74, 81–82). In the United States, 68 percent of very rich people come from upper class families (C. Wright Mills, *The Power Elite* [New York: Oxford University Press, 1956], p. 116). As for the families of wage earners, in America they produce only 3 percent of ambassadors, 5 percent of military and political leaders, 10 percent of high-level civil servants, less than 12 percent of business executives—and one-half of the work force (Suzanne Keller, *Beyond the Ruling Class* [New York: Random House, 1963], p. 312). In the Netherlands one or more directors and top managers are related to the founders in over two-thirds of public companies and in three-quarters of private firms. "Almost half of the boardroom elite," commented J. Pen, "are related to other top businessmen! Inbreeding in the group seems to be greater than that on remote islands" ("What About Managers," in K. Rothschild, ed., *Power in Economics* [Harmondsworth: Penguin, 1971], p. 210).

[31] In France just two schools, l'Ecole polytechnique and l'Ecole nationale d'administration, educate 24 percent of the ruling class (in 1974) (Birnbaum et al., *La classe dirigeante française,* p. 125). In Britain, so-called public (i.e., prestigious private) schools provide 76 percent of judges and Conservative MPs, 70 percent of ambassadors and lief-

tenants general and above, 67 percent of governors of the Bank of England, 66 percent of bishops, and 64 percent of chief executives in the hundred largest firms as against 3 percent for the rest of the population (H. Glennester and R. Pryke, "The Contribution of the Public Schools and Oxbridge," in J. Urry and J. Wakeford, eds., *Power in Britain* [London: Heinemann, 1973], p. 214). From public schools these people move to just two universities—Oxford and Cambridge. Around 1957, about 70 percent of ministers and senior civil servants had an Oxbridge education.

[32] Before the Second World War, the difference in height between university students and manual workers ranged from 2.5 centimeters in Italy to 7.7 centimeters in Germany (K. Svalastoga, *Social Differentiation* [New York: McKay, 1965], p. 86).

[33] In Chicago, for whites, the difference in life expectancy between the highest and the lowest economic class was ten years in 1920 and eight years in 1940 (ibid., p. 84).

[34] At midcentury, in Europe infant mortality was twice as high in the lowest economic class as in the highest (ibid.).

[35] In the Netherlands, in 1958–59 the upper 5 percent of the population produced 45 percent of male and 66 percent of female university students (ibid., p. 137). In the United States, 56 percent of upper middle class boys with an IQ in the lowest quintile expect to go to college, while only 29 percent of the ablest boys (IQ in the highest quintile) from the families of unskilled workers expect to do so. On the average, 80 percent of upper middle class boys, 19 percent of sons of skilled workers, and 12 percent of sons of unskilled workers expect to go to college (J. A. Kahl, *The American Class Structure* [New York: Rinehart, 1957], p. 282). In Western Europe, workers represent about one-half of the total population, but their sons and daughters comprise only 4 to 8 percent of the higher education student body. In France, the chances of access to university study vary from 1 percent for the sons of agricultural wage earners to 70 percent for the sons of businessmen and more than 80 percent for those of members of the liberal professions (R. Miliband, *The State in Capitalist Society* [New York: Basic Books, 1969], p. 41).

[36] The English upper class accent and vocabulary is only the most conspicuous example of a socially differentiated language, which can be found in other advanced countries as well.

[37] *Beyond the Ruling Class*, p. 305.

[38] G. W. Domhoff, *Who Rules America* (Englewood Cliffs, N.J.: Prentice-Hall, 1967), p. 9.

[39] At least two-thirds of the income of top corporation managers is derived from property holdings (C. W. Mills, *White Collar* [New York: Oxford University Press, 1953], p. 104).

[40] Paraphrased from "The Practice of Socialist Democracy in Jugoslavia," in C. Wright Mills, *The Marxists* (New York: Dell, 1962), p. 418.

[41] S. Ossowski, *Class Structure in the Social Consciousness* (London: Routledge and Kegan Paul, 1963), p. 116. Roy Medvedev indicates that for the highest positions the ratio, including various privileges, increases to 1:100 (*Let History Judge* [London: Spokesman Books, 1976], p. 540).

[42] After the Second World War, a systematic questioning of Soviet expatriates was undertaken at Harvard University. Some 40 percent of them left the Soviet Union voluntarily. While only 28 percent of the intelligentsia showed hostility toward the Soviet regime, the percentage was 45 for skilled workers and 58 for unskilled workers and peasants. Primary reasons for hostility were police terror and personal dissatisfaction with the jobs they had had (J. C. Davies, *Human Nature in Politics* [New York: John Wiley and Sons, 1963], p. 20). G. Lenski summarized the results of the research as follows: "the intelligentsia emerged as the most harmful class in Soviet society in the opinion of workers and peasants, while working class emerged as the most harmful in the opinion of the intelligentsia and white-collar employees" (*Power and Privilege* [New York: McGraw-Hill, 1966], p. 423). Alex Inkeles pointed out that, although there was a clear division into manual and nonmanual strata, the differences were not perceived as pronounced; he attributed this to low class consciousness. The really fundamental cleavage existed between party members and others. For these two categories, Soviet terminology has two special words: *partiinye* and *bespartiinye.* Concerning party personnel, there was "virtual unanimity in perceiving that group as having received more than its fair share, as having interests in conflict with those of other classes, and as being foremost in having done them harm" (*Social Change in Soviet Russia* [Cambridge, Mass.: Harvard University Press, 1968], p. 105).

[43] M. Haraszti, *A Worker in a Worker's State* (Harmondsworth: Penguin, 1977), p. 175. Haraszti's observation regarding social polarization into *them* and *us* was not crosschecked by the usual sociological research. Nevertheless, its validity was proved in the most authoritative way: he was promptly arrested and sentenced, and the publication of his manuscript was prevented.

[44] Cited in R. Dobson, "Social Status and Inequality of Access to Higher Education in the USSR," in J. Karabel and A. H. Halsey, eds., *Power and Ideology in Education* (New York: Oxford University Press, 1977), pp. 254–75, espec. p. 256.

[45] Cited in S. M. Lipset and R. B. Dobson, "Social Stratification and Sociology in the Soviet Union," *Survey,* 1973, no. 3, pp. 114–85, espec. p. 164. Data refer to Novosibirsk in 1963 and are taken from V. N.

Shubkin, "Molodezh' vstupaet v zhizn'," *Voprosy filosofii,* 1965. Other studies indicate ratios of educational chances between the first and third groups of 1:16 to 1:24 (Lipset and Dobson, "Social Stratification," p. 166). On the basis of extensive empirical research, Soviet sociologist O. I. Shkaratan concluded: "The educational level of the individual at the start of his work activity is to a large degree predetermined by the family, and this has a significant impact on the distribution of new members of the work force among the socio-occupational groups." See "Social Ties and Social Mobility," in M. Yanowitch and W. A. Fisher, eds., *Social Stratification and Mobility in the USSR* (White Plains, N.Y.: International Arts and Sciences Press, 1973), p. 317, originally published in Shkaratan, *Problemy sotsial'noi struktury rabochego klasa* (Moscow: Mysl', 1970).

[46] Dobson, "Social Status and Inequality."

[47] In the Soviet Union, this system is known as the Fourth Directorate of the Ministry of Health. Other bureaucracies enjoy similar privileges. In the United States, for instance, Walter Reed hospital in Washington, D.C., is reserved for the army and high government officials. Western managers have generous fringe benefits such as holiday houses, hunting cabins where business partners are received, private planes, expense accounts, and stock options.

[48] They appear to be from five to eight times higher than stipends at ordinary schools (*International Encyclopedia of the Social Sciences* [New York: Macmillan, 1968], vol. 2, p. 212).

[49] R. A. Medvedev, *Let History Judge,* p. 540.

[50] The corresponding group in a capitalist society are corporate executives, who "are treated with delicacy in the United States" (C. Lindblom, *Politics and Markets* [New York: Basic Books, 1977], p. 225).

[51] M. Matthews, *Privilege in the Soviet Union* (London: Allen and Unwin, 1978), p. 54.

[52] K. Svalastoga, citing a comparison of prestige ratings of various occupations in Denmark and Poland, noted that various skilled manual occupations carry much higher prestige in the latter country than in the former (*Social Differentiation,* p. 25). A. Sarapata compared prestige ratings in Poland and Germany, as well as in Poland before the war and in the 1960s, and found in both cases that skilled manual work has been upgraded and white collar work downgraded. A bookkeeper ranks above a skilled worker in Germany but below a skilled worker in Poland ("Stratification and Social Mobility," in J. Szczepanski, ed., *Empirical Sociology in Poland* [Warsaw: Polish Scientific Publisher, 1966], pp. 38, 43). The questioning of 2,146 Soviet displaced persons after the Second World War indicated that workers

ranked higher in the Soviet Union than in the United States, the United Kingdom, and New Zealand, but farmers were invariably rated lower (A. Inkeles and P. H. Rossi, "National Comparisons of Occupational Prestige," *American Journal of Sociology,* 1956, no. 4, pp. 324–39, espec. p. 334).

[53] M. Yanowitch, *Social and Economic Inequality in the Soviet Union* (London: Robertson, 1977), p. 30.

[54] The hostility between workers and members of the intelligentsia found among Soviet displaced persons was already mentioned. Polish sociologists found that the largest group of their respondents identified three classes: peasants, workers, and intelligentsia (D. Lane, *The End of Inequality* [Harmondsworth: Penguin, 1971], p. 103).

[55] In the USSR, the figure is 14.5 percent; in the USA, 7.8 percent. The data are not strictly comparable, however, and are somewhat biased in favor of the USSR (S. M. Miller, "Comparative Social Mobility," *Current Sociology,* 1960, pp. 1–89, espec. p. 37).

[56] In 1966, 16 out of 47 members of the Federal Council of Ministers were of working class origin. Of a total of 27 members of the various Politburos for the period 1917–51 and of 21 members of the party Presidiums during 1960–71, 8 and 9, respectively, were children of manual workers (Lane, *The End of Equality,* pp. 123, 126). Of all American presidents and cabinet members during the period 1789 to 1934, only 5 percent had fathers who were workers; 38 percent came from farmer families, while the majority—58 percent—were brought up in the homes of businessmen and professionals. In general, Soviet political leaders have come primarily from proletarian or peasant backgrounds, while American leaders have come from upper middle class and middle class backgrounds (Z. Brzezinsky and S. Huntington, *Political Power: USA/USSR* [New York: Viking, 1964], pp. 134, 135). In Sweden, 39 percent of government members during 1960–76 were of working class origin (W. Korpi, *The Working Class in Welfare Capitalism* [London: Routledge and Kegan Paul, 1978], p. 106).

[57] No direct comparison exists, but the conclusion can be derived indirectly. International comparative research has found that the power of the husband relative to his wife is greater the higher his social status. If an index is constructed to measure this power, it turns out that in Germany this index was 6.0 for entrepreneurs and 4.6 for skilled workers. In Yugoslavia, the relation between the husband's power and his status (measured by education) proved to be reversed. See Karl O. Hondrich, *Theorie der Herrschaft* [Frankfurt: Suhrkamp, 1973], pp. 165–67.

[58] Lane, *The End of Equality,* pp. 88, 89.

[59] M. Yanowitch, *Social and Economic Inequality,* p. 106.

[60] R. Aron, "Social Structure and the Ruling Class," *British Journal of Sociology,* 1950, *1* (16), 126–43, quotes from pp. 8, 9, 131, 132, 137.

[61] M. Pečujlić, "Teorijski okvir za proučavanje klasnih promjena u socijalizmu," *Sociologija,* 1966, pp. 5–26, espec. p. 14.

[62] Virtually the same is the reasoning of Isaac Deutscher: "The bureaucrats enjoy power and some measure of prosperity, yet they cannot bequeath their prosperity and wealth to their children. They cannot accumulate capital, invest it for the benefit of their descendants: they cannot perpetuate themselves or their kith and kin. . . . Until this day the Soviet bureaucracy has not managed to acquire that social, economic and psychological identity of its own which would allow us to describe it as a new class. . . . It has to acknowledge ever anew that it manages industry and finance on behalf of the nation, on behalf of the workers. Privileged as they are, the Soviet managers have to be on their guard. . . . They thrive on the apathy of the workers who so far have allowed them to run the state on their own behalf. But this is a precarious position, an incomparably less stable foundation than that sanctified by tradition, property and law" ("Roots of Bureaucracy," in R. Miliband and J. Saville, eds., *The Socialist Register 1969* [London: Merlin Press, 1969], pp. 25–26). The facts are described correctly but hardly interpreted appropriately. Capitalist directors also manage on someone's behalf—on behalf of shareowners. Descendants inherit the dominant values of the system—wealth in capitalism, and political position in etatism. The position of etatist managers is hardly more precarious than that of capitalist managers; it is sanctified by what I called theological socialism (chapter 2, section II).

[63] "The state apparatus represents a new ruling class. As a collective owner of the means of production, it employs labor power and exploits it. . . . In etatist society . . . the ruling class is a *collective* owner of the means of production, and hence a part of surplus value, which its members appropriate for personal consumption, is determined by their status in the state hierarchy" ("Etatistički mit socijalizma," *Praxis,* 1967, pp. 33–34). Similar is the position of Milovan Djilas, who considers the new class to be an ownership class (*The New Class* [London: Allen and Unwin, 1966], pp. 64–65). Even in 1921 the worker opposition expressed the view that the Soviet bureaucracy was becoming a new class that exploited and oppressed workers and peasants. The first to formulate the collective ownership explanation was Bruno Rizzi. In his book *La bureaucratisation du monde,* published in Paris in 1939 and immediately seized and destroyed, Rizzi argued that in Soviet society the exploiters do not appropriate surplus value directly—as do capitalists by cashing dividends of their enterprises—but indirectly, by means of the state, which appropriates the entire national surplus value and distributes it among the functionaries (pp. 31, 47, 48, 65, 103). The idea was independently rediscovered in

Eastern Germany by Rudolf Bahro, who wrote that party, state, and high business officials were antagonistically juxtaposed to direct producers and that the working masses were again confronted with concentrated state property (*Zur Kritik des real existierenden Sozialismus* [Cologne: Europäische Verlaganstalt, 1977], pp. 284–85). Since Bahro was promptly jailed, the government unwittingly proved that he was right.

[64] He points out, however, that under the conditions of modern capitalism it is more meaningful to consider the differential distribution of authority—not of ownership—as the basis of class formation (*Class and Class Conflict in Industrial Society* [Stanford, Calif.: Stanford University Press, 1959]).

[65] Gaetano Mosca saw this very clearly as early as 1896: "all political classes tend to become hereditary in fact if not in law. . . . Wealth and military valor are easily maintained in certain families by moral tradition and by heredity. Qualification for important office—the habit of, and to an extent the capacity for, dealing with affairs of consequence—is much more readily acquired when one has had a certain familiarity with them from childhood. Even when academic degrees, scientific training, special aptitudes as tested by examinations and competitions open the way to public office, there is no eliminating that special advantage in favour of certain individuals which the French call the advantage of *positions déjà prises*" (*The Ruling Class*, quoted in A. Pizzorno, ed., *Political Sociology* [Penguin, 1971], pp. 105–6). Kenneth Boulding conjectures: "One suspects that the class mobility in some socialist [read: etatist] countries may be even less than it is in the more fluid capitalist ones, simply because the inheritance of the family status, history and tradition may be much more significant in determining the life pattern of an individual than the inheritance of stocks and bonds and cash" ("The Dynamics of World Distribution," in M. Pfaff, *Grenzen der Umverteilung*, Vol. 1 [Berlin: Duncker and Humblot, 1978], pp. 17–32, quote from p. 24).

[66] An investigation of the career intentions of schoolchildren in Novosibirsk Oblast in 1962–63 showed that 71 percent of children of the intelligentsia intended to become specialists (i.e., intelligentsia) while none of the peasant children cherished the same hope (M. Matthews, *Class and Society in Soviet Russia* [New York: Walker, 1972], p. 263).

[67] S. C. Kolm, *Les élections sont elles la démocratie?* (Paris: CERF, 1977), p. 12.

[68] Stalin's daughter, Svetlana, provides a drastic illustration of the rule. She first fell in love with a Jewish movie man named Kapler. He was promptly arrested and sent to a prison camp. Stalin was enraged. "Apparently the fact that Kapler was a Jew was what bothered him most of all," noted his daughter. Then, as a student, Svetlana married a Jewish student. Her father agreed under the condition that he never meet him. It was only when Svetlana married for the second time—

to the son of Zhdanov, formerly second in command in the Soviet hierarchy—that her father was pleased. Svetlana reports that he "had always hoped the two families might one day be linked in marriage" (Svetlana Alliluyeva, *Letters to a Friend* [London: Hutchinson, 1967], pp. 193 and 203).

[69] A good analysis of how an elite party school operates can be found in the autobiographical book by Wolfgang Leonhard, *Child of the Revolution* (London: Collins, 1957). He describes the Comintern school which he himself attended.

[70] O. G. Brim and S. Wheeler, *Socialization after Childhood* (New York: John Wiley and Sons, 1966), p. 3.

[71] A. Nove, "Is There a Ruling Class in the USSR?" *Soviet Studies,* 1975, no. 4, pp. 615–38, quote from p. 635. Nove himself was prompted to assert: "The ruling stratum could perhaps be formally defined as all those persons holding appointments deemed to be significant enough to figure on the Central Committee's establishment nomenclatures of such appointments, i.e., who are on the *nomenklatura*" (ibid., p. 615).

[72] Quoted in R. Bahro, *Die Alternative* (Cologne: Europäische Verlagsanstalt, 1977), p. 207.

[73] "The political system of the communist countries seems to me to approach the pure type of a 'power elite,' that is, a group which, having come to power with the support or acquiescence of particular classes in the population, maintains itself in power chiefly by virtue of being an organized minority confronting the unorganized majority . . ." (T. B. Bottomore, *Elites and Society,* p. 37).

[74] This rigidity is well illustrated by a story Solzhenitsyn tells about himself. When he was arrested and escorted to Moscow in a group, he insisted that his luggage be carried by fellow prisoners of a lower rank. This was accepted by both the police and the prisoners—for he was an officer. At that time any possible reproach for this attitude, explains Solzhenitsyn, would have been incomprehensible to him, since clearly he was an officer! (*Archipelag GULAG,* p. 175).

[75] Charles Bettelheim and Paul Sweezy talk about a "state bourgeoisie," which seems confusing. See Paul Sweezy, "Toward a Program of Studies of the Transition to Socialism," *Monthly Review,* 1972, *9,* 1–13, especially p. 6: "It [state bourgeoisie] rules not through private ownership of the means of production, as in capitalist society, but through occupying the decision-making positions in the party, the state, and the economy; and it is a class and not simply a stratum because its sons and daughters have a much better chance of occupying the same positions of power than do the children of the rest of the population."

[76] Apart from the well-known activities of Agitprop and the strictly controlled mass media, persuasive power is exercised through political

activists (members of the party and of its youth organization). K. W. Deutsch estimates that the Soviet Union has three times as many political activists as advanced capitalist countries (9 percent as against 3 percent of the population). See his *Politics and Government* (Boston: Houghton Mifflin, 1970), pp. 48 and 50.

77 "All submissiveness is rooted in fear . . ." (Russell, *Power,* p. 14).

CHAPTER 4

1 P. Freire, *Pedagogy of the Oppressed* (Harmondsworth: Penguin, 1973), pp. 70, 96.

2 See G. Petrović, "Man and Freedom," in E. Fromm, ed., *Socialist Humanism* (New York: Doubleday, 1965), p. 273. *Praxis* is a somewhat elusive concept that has been given different meaning by different authors. Basically, its meaning is either descriptive or normative. In the former case praxis signifies specifically human activities, of which work is the most important, while others include artistic creation and contemplation. The normative meaning was elaborated most fully by M. Marković, who suggested the following definition: "Praxis is the human activity in which man creates the *optimal* possibilities of his being, an activity that is thus a *goal-in-itself* rather than a mere means to the achievement of some other goal" ("Dialectic Today," in M. Marković and G. Petrović, eds., *Praxis* [London: Reidel, 1979], pp. 3–43, quote from p. 27; see also his *From Affluence to Praxis* [Ann Arbor: University of Michigan Press, 1974], pp. 664–67).

3 E. Fromm, *Marx's Concept of Man* (New York: Frederick Ungar, 1964), p. 47.

4 M. Marković, *From Affluence to Praxis,* p. 75.

5 Ibid., p. 12.

6 G. Petrović, *Filosofija i marksizam* (Zagreb: Mladost, 1965), pp. 110–11, 195. In a later book, Petrović insists that alienation is an exclusively philosophical concept. He indicates an interesting possibility for overcoming the dichotomy between "normative" and "positive": "A man is not only what he is but also what he can be and ought to be. Yet, he is not a man of 'is' and 'ought to.' Before the decomposition into 'is' and 'ought to,' a man is already somebody in his essence, and concepts of alienation and disalienation are used for this realm of 'essence' (which precedes the rift between the realm of facts and that of values). These are only two among the concepts which are used for a philosophical analysis of man as a free creative being of praxis" (*Filozofija i revolucija* [Zagreb: Naprijed, 1973], p. 97).

7 See A. Schaff, *Marksizam i ljudska jedinka* (Belgrade: Nolit, 1967), pp. 98–102 (original Polish edition: *Marksism a jednostka ludzka,* Warsaw, 1965).

[8] R. Dahrendorf, *Essays in the Theory of Society* (London: Routledge and Kegan Paul, 1968), p. 13.

[9] In the study of American automobile workers cited earlier, Ely Chinoy observes that workers "seek to maintain the illusion that they themselves are still striving by constantly talking about their intention to leave the shop, even though . . . they admit when pressed that they would probably never do so" (Smelser, ed., *Readings on Economic Sociology,* p. 45).

[10] K. Marx, *Economic and Philosophic Manuscripts of 1844,* quoted in E. Fromm, *Marx's Concept of Man,* pp. 98–99. Robert Blauner claims that the concluding statement of the quotation was disproved by observation and research and that "the need for sheer activity, for social intercourse, and for some status identity in the larger society keeps even unskilled workers on the job after they are economically free to retire" (*Alienation and Freedom* [Chicago: University of Chicago Press, 1964], p. 31). It is true that social isolation is even worse than alienated labor; but that is beside the point. Physical compulsion means the need for close supervision in order to extract labor from the worker.

[11] M. Haraszti, *A Worker in a Worker's State* (Harmondsworth: Penguin, 1972), p. 53.

[12] See B. Ollman, *Alienation* (Cambridge: Cambridge University Press, 1971), p. 133.

[13] Marx, *Economic and Philosophic Manuscripts,* p. 95.

[14] Ibid.

[15] K. Marx, *The Holy Family,* quoted in J. Israel, *Alienation* (Boston: Allyn and Bacon, 1971).

[16] This condition implies that the simpleminded expectation that an abundance of goods will *necessarily* eliminate alienation is unjustified. Thus Soviet philosopher Oiserman argues: "In a society in which an abundance of material things is operatively available to all, the things will not be able to dominate men" ("Alienation and the Individual," in H. Aptheker, *Marxism and Alienation* [New York: Humanities Press, 1965], p. 149). If hierarchy remains, alienation will not disappear. The party and the state are also things, products of man's praxis, and they clearly can dominate men.

[17] G. Lukács, *Geschichte und Klassenbewusstsein* (Berlin: Malik, 1923). See particularly the chapter, "The Phenomenon of Reification."

[18] Israel, *Alienation,* pp. 59–60.

[19] M. Marković, "The Problem of Reification and Verstehen—Erklären Controversy," *Acta Sociologica,* 1972, *15,* 27–38, espec. p. 27.

[20] Quoted in Israel, *Alienation,* p. 44.

[21] K. Marx and F. Engels, *Njemačka ideologija* (Belgrade: Kultura, 1964), pp. 257–58.

[22] E. Fromm, *Revolucija nade* (Belgrade: Grafos, 1978), p. 92.

[23] K. Marx, *Das Kapital* (Hamburg, 1867), ch. 1, sec. D.

[24] (London: Routledge and Kegan Paul, 1960). The book by American economist Milton Friedman, *Capitalism and Freedom* (Chicago: University of Chicago Press, 1962) would serve equally well, as would any book on *bourgeois* freedom.

[25] Moreover, after these lines had already been written, Hayek was awarded the Nobel Prize.

[26] Hayek, *Constitution of Liberty*, p. 120.

[27] Ibid., p. 121.

[28] English liberal economist Lionel Robbins expresses the same idea in the following way: "The only sense which the economist can attach to the term exploitation of labour is as a description of what happens where a group of competing workers is confronted by a monopolistic buyer" (*The Economic Basis of Class Conflict and Other Essays in Political Economy* [London: Macmillan, 1939], p. 8). The reified mind, enchanted by the market, is unable to comprehend that the very *confrontation* of *workers* and *buyer* involves exploitation.

[29] Hayek, *Constitution of Liberty*, p. 123.

[30] Ibid., pp. 134–35.

[31] Ibid., p. 269.

[32] Ibid., p. 273

[33] Ibid., p. 299.

[34] Ibid., p. 140.

[35] F. A. von Hayek, *Law, Legislation and Liberty*, vol. 2 (London: Routledge and Kegan Paul, 1979), pp. 64–65, 83, and 96.

[36] Herbert Marcuse, *One Dimensional Man* (Boston: Beacon Press, 1964).

[37] W. Weisskopf, *Alienation and Economics* (New York: E. P. Dutton, 1971), p. 190.

[38] S. M. Lipset, "Social Class," in *International Encyclopedia of the Social Sciences* (New York: Macmillan, 1968), p. 304.

[39] K. Marx and F. Engels, *Der historische Materialismus Frühschriften* (Leipzig, 1932); translated by Karl Mannheim in *Freedom, Power and Democratic Planning* (New York: Oxford University Press, 1950), p. 238.

[40] B. Horvat, *Towards a Theory of Planned Economy* (Belgrade: Jugoslavenski institut za ekonomska istražavanja, 1964), p. 83.

[41] M. Marković, "The Problem of Alienation," p. 29.

[42] "Some years ago a shocking calculation was made that, in New York State at least, one person in twenty may be expected to spend some time in a mental hospital during his life . . ." (R. E. L. Faris, "Contemporary and Prospective Social Disorganization," in A. and E. Etzioni, eds., *Social Change* [New York: Basic Books, 1964], p. 414). Even when alienation does not generate neurosis, it is in one sense similar to it: a neurotic need not be conscious of his mental sickness; an alienated person is usually not aware of his dehumanized existence.

[43] Israel, *Alienation,* p. 32.

[44] From H. Aptheker, ed., *Marxism and Alienation* (New York: Humanities Press, 1965), p. 139.

[45] E. Fromm, "The Application of Humanist Psychoanalysis to Marx's Theory," in E. Fromm, ed., *Socialist Humanism* (New York: Doubleday, 1966), p. 236.

[46] Ibid., p. 231.

[47] Like the legendary Yugoslav Partisan and American cowboy who fire shots into the villain on the movie screen.

[48] M. Fritzhand, "Marx's Ideal of Man," in Fromm, *Socialist Humanism,* pp. 172–73.

[49] Ibid., p. 180.

[50] E. Fromm, *Let Man Prevail* (New York: Socialist Party, 1967), p. 14.

[51] D. Riesman, *The Lonely Crowd* (New Haven: Yale University Press, 1961).

[52] Two have already been mentioned in the footnotes. The other two are *The Sane Society* (New York: Rinehart, 1955) and *Escape from Freedom* (New York: Rinehart, 1941).

[53] It is hardly necessary to point out that the Marxism-Leninism of party compendia has nothing to do with Marxism and very little to do with Leninism.

[54] "Zimski filozofski susreti, Tara 1972," *Filozofija,* 1972, no. 1, recorded discussion, p. 73. For an analysis of the authoritarian personality in etatist society, which Svetozar Stojanović calls the oligarchic-etatist type of man, see his *Izmedju ideala i stvarnosti* (Belgrade: Prosveta, 1969), pp. 163–68.

[55] As has been demonstrated experimentally under laboratory conditions. In concluding his report, the experimenter poses a disturbing question: "If in this study an anonymous experimenter could suc-

cessfully command adults to subdue a fifty-year-old man, and force on him painful electric shocks against his protests, one can only wonder what government with its vastly greater authority and prestige, can command to its subjects" (S. Milgram, "Some Conditions of Obedience and Disobedience to Authority," in E. Laumann et al., eds., *The Logic of Social Hierarchies* [Chicago: Markham, 1971], pp. 465–66).

56 A friend of mine visited a historical museum in Moscow as a member of a Yugoslav delegation. He was shown around by the director of the museum. At one point he saw a rather well known painting of the first Soviet government, with Trotsky missing. "Is the entire government here?" my friend wondered. "Yes," came the answer. "Wasn't Trotsky a member?" "Yes, he was," replied the director. "And why isn't he here?" the guest inquired. With a benevolent smile, the director commented, "Tovarish B. vy opportunist" [Comrade B., you are an opportunist].

57 When in November 1956 Russian troops suppressed the Hungarian uprising, Prime Minister Imre Nagy and several members of his government took refuge in the Yugoslav embassy in Budapest. A treaty signed by the new Hungarian government guaranteed Nagy and his comrades safe conduct. They left the embassy and were promptly kidnapped by Soviet troops. Soon afterward Nagy was executed. The Yugoslav ambassador in Moscow lodged a protest to Khrushchev, pointing out that world public opinion was outraged. Khrushchev replied that he would have done the same, and then took the ambassador to task for referring to world opinion, since communists have different, class, criteria regarding such things (V. Mićunović, *Moskovske godine 1956/58* [Zagreb: Liber, 1977], pp. 463–64). Machiavelli would have agreed—but he would not have claimed that this was for the benefit of the working class.

58 "In factory, *we* is used in a way curiously at odds with its dictionary meaning. This little word, which brings to mind the idea of community and togetherness, acquires in the bosses' mouths shades of warning and a mark of distinction which separates them from the rest. . . . 'We have made it our aim . . . our objective is,' or '. . . we decided . . . we achieved . . . ' (Haraszti, *A Worker in a Worker's State,* p. 72).

59 P. Vranicki, "Socialism and the Problem of Alienation," in Fromm, *Socialist Humanism,* p. 303.

60 As in those Swiss towns where only the families falling into approximately the same tax class dance with one another (M. Weber, "Class, Status, Party," in Laumann et al., *Social Hierarchies,* p. 74).

61 H. Marcuse, *An Essay on Liberation* (Harmondsworth: Penguin, 1972), p. 14.

CHAPTER 5

[1] The quotation comes from the Introduction to Marx's *Class Conflicts in France* and was written in 1895. In this text Engels provided important information for the evaluation of his friend's and his own thinking. About their expectations concerning the 1848 Revolution he wrote: "History showed that neither we nor all those who thought similarly were right. It clearly showed that the state of economic development on the Continent was then far from ripe for the elimination of capitalist production; it showed this by the economic revolution that occurred after 1848 throughout the entire Continent . . . and all this on a capitalist foundation that, in 1848, was still capable of expansion." He went on to say that the conditions for fighting had changed fundamentally. "The rebellion of the old style, street fighting with barricades, which in 1848 was finally decisive everywhere, has grown quite obsolete." In his opinion, German workers transformed universal suffrage from a means of deceit into an instrument of liberation. And that led to a completely new way of fighting for the proletariat. "And so it happened that bourgeoisie and government came to fear the legal action of the workers' party much more than the illegal one, they fear election success more than success in a rebellion."

[2] It was only Serbian Social Democrats, Russian Socialists, and the Irish Trade Union Congress who defied bourgeois patriotism. So did the Socialist Party of America and the Italian Socialist Party (the United States and Italy were the two countries that entered the war at a later date).

[3] G. D. H. Cole, *A Short History of the British Working Class Movement 1789–1947* (London: Allen and Unwin, 1938), ch. 6, secs. 3, 4.

[4] A. Austin, *The Labor Story: A Popular History of American Labor (1786–1949)* (New York: Coward-McCann, 1969), ch. 4. For a good general study of Fourier, see O. Blagojević, *Charles Fourier* (Niš: Univerzitet u Nišu, 1971).

[5] S. Vidalenc, *Louis Blanc (1811–1882)* (Paris: Press Universitaire de France, 1948), p. 37.

[6] Ibid., pp. 38–39.

[7] G. D. H. Cole, *Socialist Thought* (London: Macmillan, 1953), vol. I: *The Forerunners 1789–1850*, pp. 177–78.

[8] Quoted in R. L. Pavićević, *Drźava kao federacija komuna* (Belgrade: Institut za meotunarodni radnički pokret, 1969), p. 96.

[9] Proudhon's syndrome—ignorance *cum* pretentiousness—can be found often in the history of socialist thought and so deserves an additional evaluation. Discussing Proudhon's economics, Joseph Schumpeter

remarked: "And we are interested in his economics only because it affords an excellent example of a type of reasoning that is distressingly frequent in a science without prestige: the type of reasoning that arrives, through complete inability to analyse, that is, to handle the tools of economic theory, at results that are no doubt absurd and fully recognized as such by the author. But the author, instead of inferring from this that there is something wrong with his methods, infers that there must be something wrong with the object of his research, so that his mistakes are, with the utmost confidence, promulgated as results. . . . He was, among other things, unable to produce a workable theory of market value. But he did not infer: 'I am a fool,' but: 'Value is mad' (*la valeur est folle*)" (*History of Economic Analysis* [New York: Oxford University Press, 1955], p. 457). In order to evaluate correctly Proudhon's complex personality, it is also good to know that he held some surprisingly reactionary views, such as anti-Semitism and sympathy toward the South on the question of American slavery; he thought that women were inferior beings and the inequalities among races inherent.

[10] Cole, *Socialist Thought,* vol. 1, p. 202.

[11] William Morris, *News from Nowhere or an Epoch of Rest, Being Some Chapters from a Utopian Romance* (London: Reeves and Turner, 1891). See also G. D. H. Cole, *Socialist Thought* (London: Macmillan, 1957), vol. II: *Marxism and Anarchism,* p. 420.

[12] G. D. H. Cole, *Socialist Thought* (London: Macmillan, 1967), vol. III: *The Second International,* pp. 565, 863.

[13] G. Lichtheim, *The Origins of Socialism* (London: Weidenfeld and Nicolson, 1969), pp. 53, 56, 122, 219.

[14] Marxist Social Democratic parties began to be created while Marx was still alive and soon were established in most European countries: in 1869 in Germany; in 1879 in Spain (by Pablo Iglesias) and Denmark; in 1882 in France (Partie ouvrière by Jules Guedes); in 1883–84 in Britain (Hyndman's Social Democratic Federation); in 1883 in Russia (Emancipation of Labor group by Plekhanov and Axelrod); in 1887 in Norway; in 1888 in Austria and Switzerland; in 1889 in Sweden and Holland (Social Democratic League); in 1892 in Italy, Poland, Finland, and Bulgaria; in 1903 in Serbia, etc. Thereafter, they began to be formed in non-European countries.

[15] For a more complete analysis, see B. Horvat, *An Essay on Yugoslav Society* (White Plains, N.Y.: International Arts and Sciences Press, 1969), ch. 9: "Marx and Engels on Socialist Economy."

[16] Cole, *Socialist Thought,* vol. II, pp. 202–4.

[17] Accordingly, syndicalism—or anarchosyndicalism—has become a derogatory word in the working class vocabulary. It is of some interest

to note that the opponents of workers' self-management invariably use this term in order to denote—and disparage—those who favor it even if the latter have no connection with syndicalism.

[18] Quoted in Cole, *Socialist Thought,* vol. III, p. 347.

[19] The document was prepared by the graduates of the Central Labor College, which was founded in 1909 as a breakaway from Ruskin College by dissident Marxist students and teachers. See K. Coates and T. Topham, eds., *Workers' Control* (London: Panther Modern Society, 1970), p. 5.

[20] G. D. H. Cole, *Guild Socialism Re-Stated* (London: L. Parsons, 1920), p. 13.

[21] Ibid., p. 46.

[22] Ibid., pp. 136–37.

[23] N. Carpenter, *Guild Socialism: An Historical and Critical Analysis* (New York: D. Appleton, 1922), p. 205.

[24] Evaluating this development a few years later, G. D. H. Cole concluded: "With coming of the slump, the demand for workers' control, though it remained a feature of the political and industrial programmes into which it had forced its way at an earlier stage, ceased to figure effectively in immediate trade union policy. The unions were fighting, not to make fresh gains, but to hold what they held, and it was of no use to preach to them policies which had no chance of success under the existing economic conditions. Guild Socialism passed under a cloud, not because the National Building Guild collapsed, but because it ceased to have any relevance to the immediate situation which the working classes were compelled to face." At that time Cole became very pessimistic about the practical implementability of guild socialist ideas: "It is good to be free, I argued, and therefore men ought to be free whether they wish it or not. So far I would still go; but I used to push the doctrine to logical conclusions which now seem to provide no solid basis for practical building of policy. Men must be forced to be free, I used to urge; and I added that they should be forced to use their freedom in the particular ways that appealed to me. The idea of work under an externally imposed discipline was repellent to me in my own crafts of writing and teaching; and I therefore assumed that it ought to be repellent to everybody, whatever the character of his job and whatever the cast of his own mind might be. I despaired of making most work interesting in itself, in the way in which my own work interests me; and I sought to find a substitute for this inherent interest in the adventitious interest of collectively controlling a naturally uninteresting job. I ignored the fact that most men's daily work is dull, and that, provided it is not positively irksome, they do not even want to find in it the overmastering interest which I find in my own job. They have other fish to fry; but of that

I did not take proper account. Self-government—the conscious and continuous exercise of the art of citizenship—seemed to me not merely good in itself—which it is—but the good—which it is not. Accordingly, I constructed, along with other politically-minded persons, a politically-minded person's Utopia of which, if it could ever exist, the ordinary man would certainly make hay by refusing to behave in the manner expected of him" (*The Next Ten Years in British Social and Economic Policy* [London: Macmillan, 1930], pp. 158–61; more easily accessible in Coates and Topham, *Workers' Control,* pp. 275–76).

[25] Useful information about contemporary revolutions is to be found in R. Bonchio, ed., *Storia delle rivoluzioni dell XX secolo,* 4 vols. (Rome: Editori riuniti, 1966).

[26] As a social phenomenon, the occupation of factories by workers is as old as the labor movement. In February 1819 English tobacco workers, after eleven weeks of strike, began to organize production by themselves. A century and a half later in 1964, during a general strike in Argentina 3 million workers occupied 4,000 enterprises and began to organize production (E. Mandel, ed., *Contrôle ouvrier, conseils ouvriers, autogestion* [Paris: Maspero, 1970], pp. 7–8). In a Colombian study it was found that *tomas de fábricas* were undertaken for three main reasons: because of the indebtedness of the enterprise, which stopped paying out wages; because of the danger that the enterprise would be closed down; and after prolonged strikes. The largest Colombian enterprise taken over employed 250 workers. The enterprises were operated by the workers themselves or by their unions (Centro Colombiano de Investigaciones Marxistas, *Las tomas de fábricas* [Bogotá, 1967], pp. 21, 60–61, and passim). In Chile enterprises taken over by the workers formed a national association called Empresas y Brigadas de Trabajadores; it had about one hundred members in 1972.

[27] It is of some interest to note the testimony of the well-known sociologist G. Gurwitch, who took part in the formation of factory committees in Petrograd and later emigrated to France. Gurwitch claims that the first soviets were organized by the Proudhonists among the social revolutionaries and by the left wing of the Social Democrats (S. Duvignaud, "Georges Gurwitch: A Sociological Theory of Self-Management," *Autogestion,* 1966, no. 1, pp. 5–6).

[28] In M. Brinton, *The Bolsheviks and Workers' Control* (Montreal: Black Rose, 1975), p. 21.

[29] Ibid. Characteristically enough, at the founding congress of the German Communist Party in January 1919, Rosa Luxemburg reversed the argument and proclaimed that trade unions would disappear, being replaced by soviets and factory committees (ibid., p. 30).

[30] Paul H. Avrich, "The Bolshevik Revolution and the Workers' Control in Russian Industry," *Slavic Review,* 1963, pp. 47–63, espec. p. 62.

[31] Quoted in R. V. Daniels, *The Conscience of Revolution* (New York: Clarion, 1969), pp. 85–86.

[32] A. Pankratova, "Comités d'usines en Russie à l'époque de la révolution (1917–1918)," written in 1923 in Russian and translated in *Autogestion,* 1967, no. 4, pp. 3–63.

[33] Quoted in Isaac Deutscher, *Soviet Trade Unions* (London: Oxford University Press, 1950), p. 29.

[34] Ibid., p. 34.

[35] P. Kropotkin, *Oeuvres* (Paris: Maspero, 1976), p. 338.

[36] There was a complete lack of communication between the two men. After a talk with Kropotkin, Lenin—according to the report of his secretary—commented: "How he has grown old. He lives in a country in which the revolution boils, the fighting is everywhere, and he finds nothing else to suggest but the cooperative movement. Here now you have the poverty of ideas of the anarchists . . ." (ibid., p. 411).

[37] *Terrorism and Communism* (Ann Arbor: University of Michigan Press, 1961), p. 162. This view was not prompted by the tactical requirements of the situation; it was Trotsky's considered opinion, which he never revised. Thus in 1931, already in exile, he wrote: "If such were the case [the state in the hands of the proletariat], we would have not workers' control of production but rather control of production by the workers' state as preparation for a regime of statified production founded upon nationalization. For us, the concept of workers' control exists within the scope of a capitalist regime. . . . Thus, a workers' control regime . . . can only be thought of as a provisional, transitional regime during the period of the shattering of the bourgeois state" ("A Letter to a Comrade" [Berlin, 1931], in *New International,* 1951, vol. 17, pp. 175–78 [New York: Greenwood Reprint, 1968]).

[38] Brinton, *Bolsheviks and Workers' Control,* pp. 69, 72, 73.

[39] J. Klikovac, "Učestvovanje radnika u upravljanju poduzećem" [The Participation of Workers in Managing the Enterprise], in J. Djordjević et al., eds., *Teorija i praksa samoupravljanja u Jugoslaviji* (Belgrade: Radnička štampa, 1972), pp. 209-26.

[40] *Socialist Thought* (London: Macmillan, 1958), vol. IV: *Communism and Social Democracy,* p. 150.

[41] Even a man like Kurt Eisner declared that the concept of socialization was very unclear to him. If it meant the takeover and man-

agement of enterprises by the workers, Eisner considered that to be "a dangerous utopia, a new form of capitalism and not socialism" (K. Eisner, *Sozialismus als Aktion* [Frankfurt: Suhrkamp, 1975], p. 127). For an extensive report on the socialization debate in Germany and Austria, see E. Weissel, *Die Ohnmacht des Sieges* (Vienna: Europaverlag, 1976).

42 Quoted in D. Bell, "Socialism," *International Encyclopedia of the Social Sciences*, vol. 14 (New York: Macmillan, 1968), pp. 506–34, quote from p. 509.

43 Otto Rühle, *Baupläne für eine neue Gesellschaft* (Hamburg: Rowohlt, 1971), p. 128.

44 *Capitalism, Socialism and Democracy* (New York: Harper, 1950), p. 310. In this respect Karl Kautsky fully agreed with his bitter adversary, Lenin. He admitted that German conditions were more favorable than Russian, but insisted that the proletariat was not yet mature enough for self-management (*Die proletarische Revolution und ihr Programm* [Stuttgart: Dietz, 1922], p. 159).

45 Rühle, *Baupläne für eine neue Gesellschaft*, pp. 123-25. Eisner shared this opinion. In the program of his Bavarian government, published on November 15, he declared: "We say quite frankly that it looks to us impossible to transfer industry into social ownership at the time when the productive forces of the country are almost exhausted. It is impossible to socialize when there is hardly anything that can be socialized" (quoted in V. Pantić, *Radnička veća u Nemačkoj* [Belgrade: Institut za međunarodni radnički pokret, 1972], p. 147). But Hilferding ("Die Einigung des Proletariats," February 1919) was in favor of the rapid nationalization of mines and the establishment of some sort of industrial democracy. In enterprises, workers' councils were to be elected as controlling bodies for the management and as auxiliary organs to carry out socialization. The delegates of workers' councils were to meet annually at a congress and elect a central council. See W. Gottschalch, ed., *Parlamentarismus und Rätedemokratie* (Berlin: Wagenbach, 1968), pp. 90–93. See also D. Schneider and R. Kuda, *Mitbestimmung* (Munich: Deutsher Taschenbuch Verlag, 1969), pp. 91, 96, 150.

46 Quoted in E. Kassalow, *Trade Unions and Industrial Relations* (New York: Random House, 1969), p. 45. A telling contrast is provided by another contemporaneous Social Democratic government, that of Sweden. In a Riksdag debate in 1932, Ernest Wigforss, the leading Marxist theoretician within the Social Democratic Party, explained to his bourgeois colleagues an economic phenomenon to be known later as the demand and employment multiplier. Expanding state expenditures became the main issue in the election campaign during the same year. Social Democrats formed a minority government. Wigforss became the minister of finance and pursued the policy Hilferding rejected. For the next two generations, Swedes elected Social Dem-

ocratic governments, and the population is now enjoying the highest standard of living in the world.

[47] Like their German colleagues, Austrian Social Democrats refused to assume responsibility for the regulation of the capitalist economy in crisis. They emerged from the election of 1930 as the largest party, but did not enter the government in order to avoid becoming discredited. Three years later, the parliamentary democracy collapsed and civil war followed.

[48] There was a revolution in Hungary, an abortive uprising in Vienna, a civil war in Finland, communist governments in the three Baltic countries, massive seizure of factories and land in Italy, and rapidly expanding communist vote and sympathies in Yugoslavia. In Sweden "there was intense flaring up of the demand for a democratization of the constitution; the masses moved immediately for this and other reforms. . . . But many believed that now the final bell had tolled for the existence of bourgeois power. . . . The Ministers of War and Naval Affairs found that 'the atmosphere was very much one of revolution.' Cautionary measures had been taken in several respects. Especially untrustworthy troop units had been demobilized. . . . The bolts had been taken from all arms in the supply depots and left with trustworthy officers" (Z. Höglund, *Hjalmar Brantig och hans livsgärning,* vol. 2 [Stockholm, 1928], quoted in B. Abrahamsson and A. Broström, *The Rights of Labour* [London: Sage Publications, 1980], p. 103). Even victorious Britain did not feel safe. There outbreaks of mutiny and refusal to obey orders occurred in both the army and the navy. But the docility of the unions and the Labour Party helped. While in Britain "the authorities actively considered the possibility of an insurrection, the most militant elements in the British proletariat proved unable to give their struggle anything more than a trade union character" (Walter Kendall, *The Revolutionary Movement in Britain 1900–21* [London: Weidenfeld and Nicolson, 1971], p. 168; see also pp. 188, 190, 194). See also J. Westergaard and H. Resler, *Class in a Capitalist Society* (London: Heinemann, 1975), p. 383.

[49] Karl Korsch, *Arbeitsrecht für die Betriebsräte* (Berlin, 1922).

[50] The first internal commission (*commissione interna*) was established in 1906 in the "Italia" automobile factory in Turin on the basis of a collective agreement between the management and the metalworkers' union. Its task was to resolve the conflicts emerging from collective agreements. During the First World War, the Italian government recommended internal commissions as instruments of cooperation, and they were set up in a number of enterprises. See B. Pribičević, ed., *Industrijska demokratija* (Belgrade: Institut za izučavanje radničkog pokreta, 1967), p. 186.

[51] G. Maione, "Expérience d'autogestion en Italie (1919–1956)," *Autogestion,* 1969, nos. 9–10, pp. 89–120, espec. p. 95.

[52] See Ian Clegg, *Workers' Management in Algeria* (New York: Monthly Review, 1971).

[53] J. Osers, "First Attempts Towards the Introduction of a Self-Management System in Czechoslovakia," *Economic Analysis and Workers' Management,* 1977, pp. 181–94.

[54] M. Bárta, "Les conseils ouvriers en tant que movement social, " *Autogestion,* 1969, nos. 9–10, pp. 3–36, quote from p. 30.

[55] In China, soviets had been organized sporadically since 1927. But they differed radically from the Russian revolutionary soviets. Their nature was well described by Mao Zedong: "In certain places councils of deputies were convened, but they are considered only as provisional organs whose main function is to elect executive committees; after the elections all power is concentrated in the hands of committees and there is no more talk about the councils of deputies. One cannot say that no council of workers', peasants' and soldiers' deputies, worth its name, is in existence; one can find them, but very few. This is explained by an insufficiency of propaganda and of educational work concerning this political system" (quoted in E. Mandel, ed., *Contrôle ouvrier,* p. 296). In December 1927, an uprising established the Canton Commune. In her historical monograph on the Chinese Revolution, E. Calloti Pischel commented: "the participation of the people in the democratic elections of the red government was quite limited, and according to certain sources it was purely imaginary" (*Storia delle rivoluzioni del XX secolo*, vol. IV: *La rivoluzione cinese*).

[56] The oldest works council still in existence in Britain is that of the Bourneville Works of the cocoa and chocolate manufacturing firm, Cadbury Brothers, Ltd. Works committees were established at the beginning of the century in this firm. The aim of the management was defined as the *rapprochement* of the employer and workers (*A Works Council in Being. An Account of the Scheme in Operation at Bourneville Works* [Publication Department, Bourneville Works, 1921]).

[57] For the sake of completeness, an interesting German attempt ought to be mentioned. The Industrial Commission of the revolutionary National Assembly, which met in Frankfurt in 1848, put forward a resolution asking that factory committees, consisting of employers' and workers' representatives, issue work rules subject to approval by district factory councils elected by the factory committees of a district. The resolution was not enacted because the revolution collapsed shortly afterward (C. W. Guillebaud, *The Works Council* [Cambridge: Cambridge University Press, 1921], p. 1).

[58] J. B. Seymour, *The Whitley Councils Scheme* (London: P. S. King, 1932), p. 9.

[59] *Joint Consultation over Thirty Years* (London: Allen and Unwin, 1950), p. 16.

[60] Characteristic of the mood of workers was the following published statement of Clyde workers: "We hold the view that the trade union officials are the servants, not the masters, of the rank and file, and that they require some pressure at times to move them in the path the rank and file desire them to tread" (H. Wolfe, *Labor Supply and Regulation* [Oxford: Clarendon Press, 1923], p. 151). D. Kirkwood, one of the leading members of the Clyde workers' committee, told the visiting prime minister Lloyd George at a meeting in December 1915 that they had organized the strike "in defiance of you, in defiance of the Government . . . and in defiance of the Trade Union officials" (B. Pribičević, "Demand for Workers' Control in the Railway, Mining and Engineering Industries 1910–1922," doctoral dissertation, Nuffield College, Oxford, 1957, p. 568; a shortened version was published as *The Shop-Stewards' Movement and Workers' Control, 1910–1922* [Oxford: Blackwell, 1959]). Comparable to the British shop stewards' movement was the German works councils movement after 1918. And similar to the statements of Clyde strikers was the following published statement of the striking metalworkers in Düsseldorf in 1924: "In a great number of towns the Trade Unions have adhered to the general strike proclaimed by the Works Councils. Where this has not yet taken place, the workers must force them to join the movement. The leaders of the unions who refuse must be ejected from their offices" (Guillebaud, *The Works Council*, p. 70).

[61] Seymour, *Whitley Councils Scheme*, p. 191.

[62] Disillusioned by the failure to establish workers' self-management, shop stewards passed through an interesting transformation and from ardent supporters turned into fierce opponents. In the Foreword to Pribičević's book *The Shop-Stewards' Movement and Workers' Control, 1910–1922*, G. D. H. Cole gives the following evaluation of the two movements, which were leading advocates of workers' control during and just after the First World War: "The Guild Socialists' weakness was that they never faced the fundamental problem of power and of large-scale organization and planning, whereas the weakness of those who led the shop stewards' movement was that, though during the war they were occupied largely with day-to-day workshop problems, no sooner was the fighting over than they became exclusively preoccupied with the central problem of class power and forgot all about control at the works and workshop level and indeed even denied that such control had anything to recommend it thus forfeiting the human basis of their appeal. They thus became centralist and totalitarian democrats, and lost sight of the essential purpose of the movement for workers' control in its relation to ordinary men and women."

[63] C. A. Myers, *Industrial Relations in Sweden* (Cambridge, Mass.: Technology Press, 1951), p. 55.

[64] Ibid., pp. 56–58.

[65] Quoted in K. C. Alexander, *Participative Management* (New Delhi: Shri Ram Centre, 1972). Two other studies dealing with the Indian experience and issued by the same publisher are: N. R. Sheth, *The Joint Management Council* (1972), and Ž. Tanić, *Workers' Participation in Management: Ideal and Reality in India* (1969).

[66] E. Mandel, "Contrôle ouvrier," *La gauche* (Brussels), 1970, p. 50.

[67] That co-determination is an unstable arrangement should be obvious. But joint consultation also implies an inherent contradiction that generates forces of change. W. E. S. McCarthy described well this contradiction: "the notion of joint consultation involves a paradox. . . . It presumes that there are some areas of management activity . . . which are fit and proper subjects of joint determination by collective bargaining; on the other hand there are other areas . . . which must remain the *exclusive* prerogative of management, although they may be discussed with workers' representatives. Yet it is also assumed that the main advantage of holding such discussions is that in matters of this kind the interests of the two sides converge rather than conflict. . . . Thus we come to the paradox . . . we reach a position in which it is suggested that agreements are only possible when the two sides are basically opposed; when they are really united, there cannot be any question of an agreement" (*The Role of Shop Stewards in British Industrial Relations*, Research Paper 1, Royal Commission on Trade Unions and Employers' Associations [London: Her Majesty's Stationery Office, 1966], pp. 35–36).

[68] International Labor Office, *Labor-Management Co-operation in United States War Production*, Studies and Reports no. 6 (Montreal, 1948), pp. 197 and 257.

[69] *Joint Consultation,* p. 100.

[70] "In many instances the idea took shape in the minds of individual employers or managers faced with rapidly expanding personnel, and was originally intended as no more than a substitute, of sorts, for that direct personal contact which is so easily lost when the pay-roll lengthens and the ratio of skilled and semi-skilled workers increases." Such was the testimony of G. S. Walpole, also an employer (*Management and Men* [London: Jonathan Cape, 1945], p. 39).

[71] The research team of the National Institute of Industrial Psychology records: "A number of younger executives told us that their favorable attitude to joint consultation had been acquired through experience in the services during the war" (*Joint Consultation in British Industry* [London: Staples Press, 1952], p. 69).

[72] Ibid., p. 59. This situation is also well reflected in the contemporary management literature. K. Robertson describes participative management as "the discipline whereby an organization learns how to tap something of the latent potential of its members. It involves entirely

new skills of behaviour. . . . It is . . . the gradual, stressful, risk-taking process of experience by which management matures from its outmoded role of directing, controlling and governing to its new role of enabling, encouraging, assisting and reinforcing achievement of others" ("Managing People and Jobs," *Personnel Management*, September 1969, p. 24).

[73] M. Weber, *The Theory of Social and Economic Organization* (London: W. Hodge, 1947), p. 300.

[74] On joint consultation, see W. H. Scott, *Industrial Leadership and Joint Consultation* (Liverpool: University Press of Liverpool, 1952); E. Jaques, *The Changing Culture of a Factory* (New York: Dryden Press, 1952); International Labor Organization and National Institute of Industrial Psychology studies already quoted. On workers' management, see P. Kovač and Dj. Miljević, *Samoupravljanje proizvodjača u privredi* (Belgrade: Savremena administracija, 1958); J. Vanek, *The Economics of Workers' Management: A Yugoslav Case Study* (London: Allen and Unwin, 1972).

[75] *Management and Men*, p. 166.

[76] *Joint Consultation*, p. 119.

[77] International Labor Office, *Workers' Management in Yugoslavia* (Geneva, 1962), p. 203.

[78] J. Espinosa and A. Zimbalist, *Economic Democracy* (New York: Academic Press, 1978), p. 141.

[79] T. E. M. McKitterick and R. D. V. Roberts, *Workers and Management*, Fabian Research Series no. 160 (London, 1953), pp. 9 and 20.

[80] National Institute of Industrial Psychology, *Joint Consultation*, pp. 64, 65.

[81] Describing conditions in the United States, the ILO study cited above stated: "A considerable number of prewar plans for joint committees in factories had been developed primarily by management in order to interest workers in the successful operation of factories and in many instances had been aimed at undercutting the development of unionism" (*Labor-Management Co-operation*, p. 185).

[82] The resulting deep psychological conflict of workers is well described by E. Jaques: "it seemed as though the only time the members of the Council could hold their heads high was if there was a management-worker fight on; if there was no fight, they felt guilty as if they were not doing what was expected of them." " . . . the desirability of employment with the firm has led workers to look to the management rather than to the trade unions for security of employment, and has aroused in the workers' leaders an acute conflict over loyalties divided between the firm and the trade unions" (*Culture of a Factory*, pp. 122, 179).

[83] Historical illustrations are not difficult to come by. Take the German works councils of the Weimar period, of which Guillebaud (*The Works Council*, pp. 212–13) says: "To the German masses the workers' councils stood for the democratization of the industrial system and the attainment, in the economic sphere, of the same rights of self-government and self-determination as they thought they had achieved by the Revolution of 1918 in the political sphere. . . . when it came to the practical working out of the basic and, to the individual workers, the most important part of the structure—the Works Councils, they found that the bulk of the political leaders of labor were in league with the employers to prevent any too wide extension of powers to these Councils." Unions were apprehensive of losing leadership (ibid., p. 41), and hence were anxious to ensure that works councils did not become really effective; they and their political allies, the majority socialists, "were backed up to the utmost by the employers, who were at least as much concerned to fetter the Works Councils and to confine them within the organization of the Unions. Of the latter the employers were not afraid . . . " (ibid., p. 11).

[84] An empirical illustration is offered by two authoritative pronouncements of British unions and party views. In the parliamentary debate on joint consultation in 1950, Mr. Gunter declared: "There has been an amazing revival of the old syndicalist idea of direct workers' control in certain sections of labor. In my opinion it is impossible to envisage any great development in the sphere of joint consultation if we imagine that this old, wooly idea of workers' control can operate. In the last resort management must be allowed to manage and to make decisions, and must accept the responsibility. What we seek is that their decisions and policy shall be translated to the workers so that they may understand their objectives, and thereby help to ensure that co-operation which can result in much better and higher production. I cannot leave the trade union side without expressing my belief that the majority of trade unionists do not desire to see the establishment of workers' control, as it is sometime called" (in National Institute of Industrial Psychology, *Joint Consultation*, p. 82). His remarks were evaluated by the National Institute of Industrial Psychology as a "very well expressed Trade union view" (ibid., p. 82). In the Labour Party's 1957 policy document on nationalized industries, the chapter on workers' participation asks the question: "Direct Representation?"—and answers it negatively: "The syndicalist view of industry run by workers, either through their trade unions or through elected boards was objected to by the Labour Movement many years ago" (*Public Enterprise: Labour's View of the Nationalized Industries* [London, 1957], p. 39). Note the reference to "syndicalism" in both these quotations. The situation on the other side of the ocean was described by James Matles, secretary of the United Electrical, Radio and Machine Workers of America, in an interview in 1965: "The key problem facing the rank and file workers in the shop and trade union movement today is the destruction of the shop steward system. The shop steward has been destroyed,

undermined or neutralized through the combined efforts of employers and top union leadership" (Coates and Topham, *Workers' Control*, p. 408).

[85] See H. A. Clegg: "To-day industrial discipline is a different matter in all industries from the pre-war period of heavy unemployment. This is often said to be one of the greatest difficulties of British industry to-day. At the same time, full employment has done more to make industry more democratic and to raise the status of the worker than any legislation or any machinery for joint consultation could do" (*Industrial Democracy and Nationalization* [Oxford: Blackwell, 1950], p. 78). This is a very lucid statement, but the concluding antithesis is spurious; the causation is different from the one implied: the democratization of industrial organization produced joint consultation, not the other way around. Once generally applied, joint consultation becomes a social institution and cannot be abolished without social upheaval. But neither can it be petrified in its present form, with the attention of workers channeled toward welfare matters while management reserves the right to make the crucial managerial decisions. Very soon workers will begin to insist that this "toilet democracy" be replaced by "proper democracy." C. A. Myers unintentionally described something of the kind happening in Sweden when he noted: "unless the committees begin to tackle real problems . . . the 'stagnation' may turn into disgust and revulsion. 'Toilet democracy' as one person described the current concern for better washrooms, lighting, etc., may suffice for a time, but it is hardly the 'industrial democracy' that the labor movement said it was seeking" (*Industrial Relations in Sweden*, p. 71).

[86] *Joint Consultation*, p. 29.

[87] Glacier Metal Company is an interesting English example. Its works council constitution says: "The functions of the Council shall be: . . . to carry the responsibility of deciding the principles and policies which shall govern the Management of the Factory in the light of the opinions of producers and managers, in the light of the interest of consumers, shareholders and the nation at large, and in the light of total Company Policy" (Jaques, *Culture of a Factory*, p. 153). In seeking to achieve this aim—management surrendering arbitrary executive power and the workers developing responsible and effective collective decision making instead—both management and workers had to overcome enormous difficulties caused by their learned attitudes and the totally uncongenial institutional framework within which they were to work. Other interesting examples are Scott Bader Commonwealth in Britain (F. H. Blum, *Work and Community* [London: Routledge and Kegan Paul, 1968]); Dynavac Pty, Ltd., in Australia (L. Cupper, "Worker Participation in the Dynavac Organization," *Journal of Industrial Relations*, June 1976, pp. 124–41); and the American insurance firm International Group Plans (D. Zwerdling, "At IGP, It's Not Business as Usual," *Working Papers for a New Society*, 1977, no. 1, pp. 68–81).

[88] See C. H. Bishop, *All Things Common* (New York: Harper and Brothers, 1950). Boimondeau was sold in 1971, after three decades of existence. Its life history is rather instructive and representative of other similar cases. Such a community is an alien island in a sea of a different culture. The founders are usually immune to this hostile environment, because they believe in their cause and are imbued with a feeling of mission. Newcomers, however, are socialized to capitalist society. They tend to work for wages, do not feel responsibility for the community, and retire to their privacy after work. When business is depressed, wages are low and newcomers leave. When business is booming, there is a tendency to transform the community into a capitalist firm. In order to survive longer, it helped if the community was sealed off from the disruptive influence of the outside world by strong religious beliefs. Thus, compared to various Owenite, Fourierist, and other experiments, religious communities lasted longer. The most conspicuous and, in a way, unique example is the Hutterite Brethren in America. Hutterites are descendants of an Anabaptist sect organized in Moravia in the sixteenth century, and the continuity of the sect's existence has been fully preserved. In his historical study *Vorläufer des neuren Sozialismus* ([Stuttgart: Dietz, 1923], vol. II, chs. 1–5), Kautsky evaluated the Hutterite community in Moravia as "of greatest significance for the history of socialism" for "it represents the most mature product of heretical communism." Hutterites settled in America in 1874. Their settlements are communist organizations with common ownership of goods and distribution according to needs. The important decisions are made by the council or by the male congregation. In 1964 there were 154 Hutterite colonies in Canada and the United States with a combined population of 14,700 (See V. Peters, *All Things Common* [New York: Harper and Row, 1971]).

[89] The project was started by Don José María Arizmendi, who settled in Mondragón in 1941 and who prided himself on never having made decisions for others. As a former participant in the Spanish Civil War on the Republican side, he could not engage in political or trade union activities, and so tried to achieve social reforms through cooperation. He began by reviving two church associations, which led to the foundation of a polytechnical school. The first cooperative, with forty members, was established in 1956. By the end of 1976, the year of Don José's death, the system included sixty-five firms with 14,665 members. It continued to expand, adding four firms with 1,500 members in the next two years. The Mondragón system has the following characteristics: (a) the ratio between top and bottom pay levels has been reduced from 15:1 to 3:1; (b) the management board is elected annually and selects persons for the key managerial posts; (c) new members pay an initial contribution in installments; (d) the surplus earned is largely reinvested and the members' personal accounts credited accordingly; (e) this "embodied labor" is the source of annual interest payments to the workers; (f) past labor can be fully recovered, i.e., the principal taken out, at the time of retirement; (g) a credit

union serves as an investment bank. Mondragón thus eliminated two sources of failure of other producer cooperatives: the lack of capital and the dilution of shares by employment expansion, which would induce the founders to treat newcomers as hired labor (A. G. Johnson and W. F. Whyte, "The Mondragón System of Worker Production Cooperatives," *Industrial and Labour Relations Review*, 1977, pp. 18–30).

[90] J. Cable and F. Fitzroy studied a sample of forty-two German enterprises classified into high-participation and low-participation firms. The former outperformed the latter by 5 percent in terms of output per man, 177 percent in output per unit of capital, and 33 percent in profitability (rate of return on capital) ("Cooperation and Productivity: Some Evidence from West German Experience," p. 19, mimeographed).

CHAPTER 6

[1] J. S. Mill, *Principles of Political Economy,* book IV (New York: Kelley, Reprints of Economic Classics, 1961), p. 753. It is of some interest to note how surprisingly similar this aristocratic theory appears to the theory of the leading role of an elitist vanguard party in the early stages of etatism. The relation between rich and poor is replaced by that between leaders and masses. Leaders must not command but explain and persuade—an affectionate tutelage. The masses must not think for themselves or try to determine their destiny; they are expected to follow. The lot of the masses is regulated for them, not by them. The party has an absolute political monopoly.

[2] *Dissertation on the Poor Laws by a Wellwisher of Mankind,* quoted in K. Polanyi, *The Great Transformation* (Boston: Beacon Press, 1971), pp. 113–14. In *Capital* (ch. 23, sec. 4) Marx exposed Townsend as a "delicate priestly sychophant" because he not only discovered the disciplining power of hunger but also rationalized it as a divine principle: "It seems to be a law of nature that the poor should be to a certain degree improvident, so that there may always be some to fulfil the most servile, the most sordid, the most ignoble offices in the community. The stock of human happiness is thereby much increased, whilst the more delicate . . . are left at liberty without interruption to pursue those callings which are suited to their various dispositions." In his own way, Townsend, as we shall see in a moment, accurately predicts "that Poor Law (i.e. helping the poor) tends to destroy the harmony and beauty, the sympathy and order, of that system which God and nature have established in the world."

[3] Quoted in Bendix, *Work and Authority in Industry* (New York: Harper and Son, 1959), p. 75.

[4] Polanyi, *The Great Transformation,* p. 79.

[5] *Principles of Political Economy,* book IV, p. 756.

[6] *Paternalistic Capitalism* (Toronto: Copp Clark, 1972), p. 6.

[7] *Work and Authority,* p. 294.

[8] A. Tannenbaum and his associates observed: "Workers in the American plants . . . do not *feel* as alienated as workers elsewhere but in fact they *are* powerless with respect to basic policy issues. Because of 'human relations' a discrepancy exists between the subjective and objective experience of alienation. . . . The approach no doubt works in mitigating some of the psychological effects of hierarchy, but it does so without making any basic changes in hierarchy" (*Hierarchy in Organizations* [San Francisco: Jossey-Bass, 1974], p. 220).

[9] R. M. Steers and L. W. Porter, *Motivation and Work Behavior* (New York: McGraw-Hill, 1975), p. 20.

[10] J. Barbash, "Humanizing Work—A New Ideology," *The AFL-CIO American Federationist,* July 1977, pp. 8–15, espec. p. 14.

[11] *Paternalistic Capitalism,* p. 108.

[12] V. I. Lenin, "Immediate Tasks of the Soviet Government" (April 1918), and "Left-Wing Childishness and Petty-Bourgeois Mentality" (May 1918).

[13] *Ekonomia polityczna socjalismu* (Warsaw: Państ wowe wydawnictwo ekonomiczne, 1963), pp. 56, 58.

[14] In the anthology edited by V. G. Afanas'ev, *Nauchnoe upravlenie obshchestvom* (Moscow: Mysl', 1967), p. 61. The book was prepared by the Department of Scientific Communism of the Academy of Social Sciences together with the Central Committee of the Communist Party of the Soviet Union, and as such may be considered as the most authoritative source.

[15] Ibid., p. 69.

[16] "Social Structure and the Functions of Management," in M. Yanowitch and W. A. Fisher, eds., *Social Stratification and Mobility in the USSR* (White Plains, N.Y.: International Arts and Sciences Press, 1973), p. 50; originally published in N. M. Rutkevich, ed., *Izmenenie sotsial'noi struktury sotsialistisheskogo obshchestva* (Sverdlovsk, 1965).

[17] In Afanas'ev, *Nauchnoe upravlenie obshchestvom,* p. 88. It is somehow forgotten that Lenin himself, in his often-quoted book *The State and Revolution,* stressed in 1917 that "*every* state is *non*-free and *non*-popular," and declared that Marx's statement that all previous revolutions had perfected the state, while in reality the state has to be crushed, is "the basic text in Marxist teaching about the state" (*Sochineniia,* 4th ed., vol. 25 [Moscow: Gospolitizdat], pp. 370, 378).

[18] In Afanas'ev, *Nauchnoe upravlenie obshchestvom,* p. 97. Benito Mussolini's ideas about the state read as if they had directly inspired the paragraph quoted: "It is the state which educates citizens, makes them

conscious of their mission, calls them to unity; harmonizes their interests in justice; hands on the achievements of thought in the sciences, the arts, in law, in human solidarity" (in A. Arblaster and S. Lukes, eds., *The Good Society* [New York: Harper and Row, 1971], p. 317).

[19] Feliforov, in Afanas'ev, *Nauchnoe upravlenie obshchestvom,* p. 96. For a more precise definition of democratic centralism, see that by Mao Zedong given in chapter 2, section II.

[20] M. Formanek, "Preimućstva socijalističkog političkog sistema i čehoslovačko iskustvo," *Socijalizam u svetu,* 1977, no. 7, pp. 33–53, espec. p. 45. (The article was a paper presented to the international roundtable at Cavtat, and so the phrasing had to be careful.)

[21] Feliforov, in Afanas'ev, *Nauchnoe upravlenie obshchestvom,* p. 88.

[22] Formanek, "*Socijalističkog političkog sistema,*" p. 52.

[23] C. A. Yampol'skaia, *Obshchestvennye organizacii i razvitie socialisticheskoy gosudarstvennosti* (Moscow: Iuridicheskaia literatura, 1965), p. 32.

[24] Sadykov, in Afanas'ev, *Nauchnoe upravlenie obshchestvom,* p. 79.

[25] *Marx-Engels Werke,* vol. 25 (Berlin: Dietz, 1964), p. 614.

[26] M. Matthews, *Class and Society in Soviet Russia* (London: Penguin, 1972), p. 218. In Leningrad only 3.7 percent of unskilled workers are party members.

[27] K. W. Deutsch, *Politics and Government* (Boston: Houghton Mifflin, 1970).

[28] M. Hirszowicz, "Is There a Ruling Class in the USSR?—A Comment," *Soviet Studies,* 1976, no. 2, pp. 262–73, espec. p. 267.

[29] Quoted in M. Yanowitch, *Social and Economic Inequality in the Soviet Union* (London: Robertson, 1977), p. 137. One is reminded of the ignoble Führer principle.

[30] This is found by A. Whitehorn, who compared Yugoslav and Canadian enterprises ("Workers' Self-Management—Socialist Myth or Prognostication," *Revija za sociologiju,* 1976, no. 2–3, pp. 17–30).

[31] See A. Tannenbaum et al., *Hierarchy in Organizations,* pp. 73, 77, 86, 100, 108, 143, 213. This is a comparative research project undertaken by an international team in Yugoslavia and Israel (worker management, twenty industrial plants), and Austria, Italy, and the United States (traditional capitalist organization, thirty plants). We still lack comparable empirical data for etatist enterprises.

[32] For a good critical review of the Mayo studies, see Paul Blumberg, *Industrial Democracy: The Sociology of Participation* (New York: Schocken Books, 1969), pp. 14–46.

[33] D. Bell, "Work, Alienation and Social Control," *Dissent*, Spring 1974, pp. 207–12, quote from p. 210. An official task force reports: "the productivity of workers is low—as measured by absenteeism, wildcat strikes, sabotage, poor-quality products, and a reluctance by workers to commit themselves to their work tasks. Moreover, a growing body of research indicates that, as work problems increase, there may be a consequent decline in physical and mental health, family stability, community participation and cohesiveness while there is an increase in drug and alcohol addiction, aggression and delinquency" (J. O'Toole et al., *Work in America* [Cambridge, Mass.: MIT Press, 1973], p. XVI).

[34] Interview with Leonard Woodcock (president of the United Automobile, Aerospace and Agricultural Implement Workers of America), "There's Still a Car in Your Future," *Challenge*, May–June 1974, pp. 29–36, quote from p. 30.

[35] "The Post-Industrial Organization," *Bureaucrat*, 1974, pp. 285–300, quote from p. 291.

[36] In Britain three-quarters of all strikes are of this kind and are related in particular to offending working arrangements, rules, and discipline. See C. Pateman, *Participation and Democratic Theory* (Cambridge: Cambridge University Press, 1970), p. 56.

[37] "Information and Efficiency: Another Viewpoint," *Journal of Law and Economics*, 1969, p. 7.

[38] In the early 1960s, Lockheed Missiles and Space Co. had two levels of supervisors, four levels of managers, and one directoral level—seven levels altogether. If direct line assistants are included as a level, the number increases to eleven. The firm had a span of management at the upper level of 1:5–10 (one manager to five to ten subordinates) and at the middle level of 1:15–18 (H. Koontz, "Making Theory Operational," in J. H. Donnelly, J. L. Gibson, and L. M. Ivanchevich, *Fundamentals of Management* [Dallas: Business Publications, 1971], pp. 77–91, p. 84).

[39] *Principles of Political Economy*, book IV.

[40] "Sur le contenu du socialisme," *Socialisme ou barbarie*, 1957, no. 22; translated as *Workers' Councils and the Economics of a Self-Managed Society* (London: Solidarity, 1972), p. 59.

[41] J. E. S. Ross, quoted in R. Dahrendorf, *Konflikt und Freiheit* (Munich: Piper, 1972), p. 131.

[42] J. L. Gray and P. Meshinsky, "Ability and Opportunity in English Education," in L. Hogben, ed., *Political Arithmetic* (London: Allen and Unwin, 1938), p. 416. In 1967, in the United States, 20 percent of the children of families with incomes of less than $3,000 went to

college; this percentage rose to 76 percent for families with incomes in excess of $15,000 (S. Bowles, "Protivrečnosti u visokom skolstvu," *Marksizam u svetu*, 1975, no. 1, pp. 53–90, espec. p. 60).

[43] "Recent concern about talent utilization has uncovered a surprisingly high proportion of intellectually promising people who . . . fail to achieve advanced education" (K. Svalastoga, *Social Differentiation* [New York: McKay, 1965], p. 143).

[44] While hardly any substandard poor children reach the university, a substantial number of substandard privileged children do. If pupils are classified into fee-paying and others, then in England in 1933–34 a substandard child in the fee-paying group had an opportunity of receiving a higher education between 58 and 162 times greater than that of a similar child in the other group (Gray and Meshinsky, "Ability and Opportunity," p. 372).

[45] W. L. Warner and J. C. Abegglen, *Occupational Mobility in American Business and Industry 1928–1952* (Minneapolis: University of Minnesota Press, 1955), p. 38.

[46] Ibid., p. 41.

[47] Ben Lewis has described well the peculiar position of the top management of a capitalist corporation: "The market for corporation top executives is indeed a peculiar affair. Through its control of the proxy machinery, top management determines the selection of the board which selects top management; top management sits across from itself at the bargaining table, hiring itself and setting the terms of its own employment. Top management is a vitally important factor of production, but operating in the context of the corporation its precise functional character has never been thoroughly examined or buttoned down. It can be hired on a fixed-dollar contract, and in this sense is a labour service; it can 'invest' itself for a possible return of profit . . . and in this sense its provision partakes of entrepreneurship. . . . And when one contemplates competing top management pursuing competing top managements and luring them away from other competing top managements in a kind of incestuous, fenced in, closed circle, using a teeming witches' brew of wages, bonuses, options and the rest as bait, the totality presents a bizarre scene in contrast with which the hiring and paying of top executives by nationalized industries is almost pastoral" ("British Nationalization and American Private Enterprise: Some Parallels and Contrasts," *American Economic Review, Papers and Proceedings*, 1965, no. 2, pp. 50–64, quote from p. 63).

[48] J. D. Phillips calculated that in the United States, in the early 1960s, waste in distribution, corporate advertising, and surplus employee compensations in finance, insurance, real estate, and legal services reached almost one-tenth of the gross national product (P. A. Baran and P. M. Sweezy, *Monopoly Capital* [New York: Monthly Review,

1966], p. 389). In the late 1960s, advertising and other sales promotion expenditures alone amounted to $60 billion, which is about the same as the nation's expenditures on education and health (C. Lindblom, *Politics and Markets* [New York: Basic Books, 1977], p. 214).

[49] S. E. Finer, *Comparative Government* (London: Penguin, 1970), p. 389.

[50] A Soviet law of 1940 treated tardiness and truancy as criminal offenses punishable by up to six months' corrective labor and a wage cut of up to 25 percent. The law was in force until 1956. This law is reminiscent of the British Master and Servant Act, in effect until 1875, under which workers who struck in breach of contract could be prosecuted under criminal charges and imprisoned. The only important difference appears to be that Britain did not pretend to be ruled by workers, and so the terminology used was consistent with the facts.

[51] *Czechoslovakia: The Bureaucratic Economy* (White Plains, N.Y.: International Arts and Sciences Press, 1972), p. 20. Yugoslav political leaders voiced similar complaints during the country's etatist development. Josip Broz Tito declared: "In 1949 . . . 18 percent of all workers and employees failed to participate regularly in the work. Of these, 9.5 percent were absent from work with no justification." Edvard Kardelj commented in 1948: "In some enterprises complete theories existed about the need to set the plan as low as possible. . . . Not infrequently . . . the controlling agency finds that machines are utilized at only the 50 or 60 percent level. . . . The controlling agency found that a major share of cases of rejects and poor product quality . . . were made possible in large degree by the insufficient readiness of the management . . . to overcome difficulties" (quoted in D. Bilandžić, *Historija SFR Jugoslavije* [Zagreb: Školska knjiga, 1979], pp. 124–25).

[52] As an illustration, Kornai cited the case of a Budapest factory which, in a period of seven weeks, was subject to sixteen inspections by seven control authorities. That did not include inspections carried out on behalf of district and city party committees (*Overcentralization in Economic Administration* [London: Oxford University Press, 1959], pp. 110–11).

[53] Ibid., p. 112.

[54] A. A. Matejko, *Social Change and Stratification in Eastern Europe* (New York: Praeger, 1974), p. 136.

[55] Kornai, *Overcentralization*, p. 208.

[56] "The economic problem of society is . . . a problem of how to secure the best use of resources known to any of the members of society for ends whose relative importance only these individuals know. Or, to put it briefly, it is a problem of the utilization of knowledge not given

to anyone in its totality" ("The Use of Knowledge in Society," *American Economic Review,* 1945, pp. 519–30, quote from p. 519). "If . . . the economic problem of society is mainly one of rapid adaptations to changes in the particular circumstances of time and place, it would seem to follow that the ultimate decisions must be left to the people who are familiar with these circumstances, who know directly of the relevant changes of the resources immediately available to meet them" (ibid., p. 524). Hayek framed his argument so as to prove the superiority of the free market over central planning. In the context of this book, it may be of some historical interest to note the following claim made by Hayek in 1945: "nobody has yet succeeded in designing an alternative system in which certain features of the existing one can be preserved which are dear even to those who most violently assail it—such as particularly the extent to which the individual can choose his pursuits and consequently freely use his own knowledge and skills" (ibid., p. 528). I shall not leave this challenge unanswered.

57 Inventories can be twice as large as in the average capitalist firm. See B. Horvat, *Business Cycles in Yugoslavia* (White Plains, N.Y.: International Arts and Sciences Press, 1971), p. 92.

58 But not as egalitarian as it could be while fostering economic efficiency. A bureaucratic hierarchy, in order to function, requires substantial income differences. Such income differences represent the maintenance cost of the system.

59 The Soviet estimate quoted by M. Ellman in *Planning Problems in the USSR* (London: Cambridge University Press, 1973), p. 32. Ellman compares the role of *tolkachi* in the etatist sellers' market to the role of salesmen in the capitalist economy with a buyers' market.

60 T. Bauer, "Investment Cycles in Planned Economies," *Acta Oeconomica*, 1978, 243–60, quote from p. 246.

61 " . . . the buyer of the screw factory bribes the stock-keeper of the steelworks: he should telephone immediately on arrival of the much-awaited steel. . . . Or he pays something to the sales department man: if there are several claimants, he should be given the product and not someone else. Bribery is made sometimes in money, sometimes in the form of some 'present.' . . . There are . . . numerous indirect forms of recompensing favours, which are impossible or almost impossible to prosecute by law. . . . Every 'buyer' is a 'seller' somewhere. Everybody who has received a favour somewhere is able to return it somewhere else. And, if the claim of mutual favours is well built up, it may considerably influence selection processes. This chain of mutual services is much more important than the common direct corruption which is easy to detect and therefore too risky" (J. Kornai, "Economics of Shortage," prepublication manuscript [Budapest, 1979], pp. 122–23). See also H. Smith, *Les russes* (Paris: Belfond, 1976), p. 104.

[62] M. Crozier, "De la bureaucratie comme système d'organisation," *Archives européens de sociologie,* 1961, pp. 18–52, espec. p. 42. It may be noted that the state of permanent crisis and the ideology of the ubiquitous enemy (chapter 2, section II) reinforce each other.

[63] M. Crozier listed the following characteristics of the Soviet bureaucratic (dis)equilibrium: "authoritarian relations, great subordination on the part of inferiors, at the same time a lot of passive resistance on the part of powerful informal groups and a *circulus vitiosus* of bureaucratic controls superimposed upon each other, whose oppressive weight necessarily generates passive resistance which exactly strengthens suspicion and the need for control" (ibid., p. 41 n.).

[64] "The implementation of the economic reforms of the sixties, and the various forms of 'loosening' the branch management hierarchy were accompanied by the emergence of tensions in several countries. As it emerges from the present survey, leading party and state organs reacted in such situations usually by strengthening the administrative elements of control and hierarchical subordination, even if there was no demonstrable connection between the extent of decentralization and disequilibrium troubles" (T. Bauer and L. Szamuely, "The Structure of Industrial Administration in the European CMEA Countries: Change and Continuity," *Acta Oeconomica,* 1978, pp. 371–93, quote from p. 386).

[65] See B. Horvat, "The Relation Between Rate of Growth and Level of Development," *Journal of Development Studies,* 1974, pp. 382–94; "Welfare of the Common Man in Various Countries," *World Development,* 1974, no. 7, pp. 29–39.

[66] The conclusion cannot be verified statistically because only two countries (East Germany and Czechoslovakia) fall into this group, and no etatist country has yet reached the most advanced stage of development. On the other hand, East Germany and West Germany share the same national and cultural environment, and the latter has developed faster: before the war per capita GNP was about equal in the two countries; in 1976, West German GNP was 17 percent higher and product per employed person showed an even larger spread (K. C. Thalheim, *Die wirtschaftliche Entwicklung der beiden Staaten in Deutschland* [Berlin: Landeszentrale für polit. Bildungsarbeit, 1978], pp. 40, 137). On the other hand, since 1960, both countries have achieved roughly equivalent rates of growth in GNP and industry (P. Gregory and G. Leptin, "Similar Societies Under Differing Economic Systems," *Soviet Studies,* 1977, no. 4, pp. 519–42). The Berlin Wall and the exodus of several million people from the East may be taken as deciding the issue.

[67] This can be illustrated by the data on Soviet economic growth. I add comparable data for Japan and Italy, two capitalist countries of approximately the same level of economic development. Output per

unit of input is measured by the residual estimated from the following production function:

$$\Delta Y + \alpha\Delta L + \beta\Delta K + \delta\Delta A + \Delta R, \alpha + \beta + \delta = 1$$

where Y = real national income; L = labor input adjusted for quality; K = capital input; A = land input; R = output per unit of input; Δ = rate of increase; and α, β, δ = shares of L, K, and A.

Annual Rates of Growth

	Output	Capital	Labor	Combined factor productivity
USSR: 1950–62	6.1	8.8	2.4	1.7
1962–70	5.4	8.4	1.8	1.7
Japan: 1955–68	10.1	10.5	1.9	5.5
Italy: 1950–62	6.0	3.5	1.3	4.3

Source: S. M. Cohn, "The Soviet Path to Economic Growth: A Comparative Analysis," *Review of Income and Wealth*, 1976, pp. 49–60, Tables 1, 2, 3, and 7.

The Soviet rate of growth of output is no higher than the rates of growth of the other two countries, and the growth in productivity is substantially lower. Besides, with the reduction in employment growth, the expansion of Soviet production tends to be reduced. Employment includes educational changes as well. The exact specification and quantification of the factors causing a reduction in the Soviet rate of growth is a difficult technical problem that cannot be discussed here. See P. Desai, "The Production Function and Technical Change in Postwar Soviet Industry: A Reexamination," *American Economic Review*, 1976, pp. 372–81; S. Gomulka, "Slowdown in Soviet Industrial Growth 1947–1975 Reconsidered," *European Economic Review*, 1977, pp. 37–50. The rapid and continuous deceleration of Soviet growth is most clearly visible if we look at the rate of industrial growth in consecutive postrecovery five-year plan periods (percent per annum):

1950–55	13.1	1960–65	8.6	1970–75	7.4
1955–60	10.4	1965–70	8.5	1975–80	6.3 (plan)[a]

Source: Comecon bulletins.
[a]The achieved rate of growth for the first three years, 1975–78, is 5.1 percent.

Over the last twenty-five years, the rate of industrial growth declined by 61 percent.

[68] In fact, we need not remain that agnostic and can extract more information from our data. If it can be assumed that a pioneering country developing under not especially favorable conditions will perform below the standards of efficiency that can reasonably be expected from an established economic system, then the Yugoslav results are likely to be located left of the mean of the still nonexistent distribution.

Thus, if this mean is replaced by Yugoslav data, we surely make a conservative estimate. All that remains is to test the statistical significance of the difference between the two means, assuming that the variances of the two distributions are approximately the same.

[69] See B. Horvat, "Nationalism and Nationality," *International Journal of Politics*, 1972, no. 1, pp. 19–46.

[70] For details, see B. Horvat, *The Yugoslav Economic System* (White Plains, N.Y.: International Arts and Sciences Press, 1976).

[71]

Rates of Growth

	1952–64	1964–78
Gross national product	8.6	5.6
Industrial output	12.7	7.1
Agricultural output	4.5[a]	1.7
Industrial producer prices	1.2	10.9
Real wages	5.4	4.1

Sources: *Statistički godišnjak Jugoslavije*, 1971 and 1978.
[a] 1953–64.

A comparable productivity analysis for the post-1964 period is available for manufacturing and mining:

Rates of Growth

	1955–64	1964–74
Output	11.9	7.3
Labor (working hours)	6.0	1.3
Capital	13.7	8.1
Combined factor productivity	4.4	3.7

Source: A. Puljić, "Efekti neopredmećenog i opredmećenog tehnološkog napretka na stopu rasta industrijske proizvodnje," doctoral dissertation, University of Zagreb, 1979, pp. 195 and 204.

[72] For a summary of the literature, see Blumberg, *Industrial Democracy*, pp. 123–34. Blumberg concludes: "There is hardly a study in the entire literature which fails to demonstrate that satisfaction in work is enhanced or that other generally acknowledged beneficial consequences accrue from a genuine increase in workers' decision-making power. Such consistency of findings, I submit, is rare in social research" (ibid., p. 123). S. Melman compared the efficiency of traditional managerial firms with that of self-governing firms belonging to kibbutzim in the same industries in Israel and found that the productivity of labor and capital, as well as profitability, were higher, while administrative costs were lower, in the self-managing firms ("Industrial Efficiency under Managerial vs. Cooperative Decision-Making," *Review of Radical Political Economy*, 1970, no. 1, pp. 9–34).

In terms of yields per acre, productivity per worker, technical and innovative efficiency, advanced training, and marketing, kibbutzim are more efficient than other sectors of Israeli agriculture in almost all areas of agricultural production (see J. R. Blasi, *The Communal Future* [Norwood, Pa.: Norwood Editions, 1978], p. 109). For other references see J. Espinosa and A. Zimbalist, *Economic Democracy* (New York: Academic Press, 1978), pp. 160–61.

73 Ishak Adizes reported that supervision costs were eliminated in two worker-managed plants (*Industrial Democracy* [New York: Free Press, 1971], p. 192). Espinosa and Zimbalist found in Chile that participation improved work discipline, reduced absenteeism and frequency of strikes, and affected innovative behavior favorably (*Economic Democracy,* pp. 141, 184). Paul Bernstein reported on a producer cooperative that was sold by its aging worker-owners to a large conglomerate. As a consequence, eight more foremen were needed though there were 100 fewer workers ("Workplace Democratization," doctoral dissertation, Stanford University, 1975, p. 29). E. S. Greenberg reported that co-ops employ one or two supervisors per shift, while the standard firms surveyed use six to seven per shift ("Producer Cooperatives and Democratic Theory: The Case of the Plywood Firms" [Palo Alto: Center for Economic Studies, July 1978]).

74 Income distribution will be discussed further in chapter 9.

CHAPTER 7

1 See M. Kangrga, *Razmišljanja o etici* (Zagreb: Praxis, 1970), pp. 22–23.

2 Thus, with few exceptions, social scientists advocate the status quo in their respective environments. In order to preserve "value neutrality," they take the dominant value system as given. As a result, radical social changes *will not* be contemplated. The ensuing analysis leads to findings that conform to what has been observed. This is interpreted in favor of the establishment. Therefore, radical social changes *ought not* be undertaken.

3 "The Value-Oriented Bias of Social Inquiry," in M. Brodbeck, ed., *Readings in the Philosophy of the Social Sciences* (Toronto: Macmillan, 1969), pp. 101–2.

4 "The process of social investigation inescapably embroils the investigator in his subject in a way that is different from that of the natural scientist. For the latter, the discovery of an anomaly may constitute a blow to his intellectual 'security,' perhaps even to his psychological 'integrity.' *But it does not threaten his moral position as a member of a social order*" (R. L. Heilbroner, "Economics as a 'Value-Free' Science," *Social Research*, 1973, pp. 129–43, quote from p. 139).

5 In the Introduction to G. Myrdal, *Value in Social Theory*, edited by P. Streeten (London: Routledge and Kegan Paul, 1958), p. xvii. The program is defined as a "complex of desired ends, means and pro-

cedures, and effects other than ends which may be inevitable outcomes, all of which is conditioned by valuations" (ibid., p. xiv).

6 Strictly speaking, even factual statements cannot be proved but only disproved.

7 Here *persuasion* implies a rational cognitive process free of any emotional manipulation. The scope of the scientific discussion of value judgments was well described by Max Weber in a lecture delivered in 1913 ("Der Sinn der 'Wertfreiheit' der soziologischen und ökonomischen Wissenschaften"): (1) the elaboration and examination of the consistency of the ultimate value axioms; (2) the deduction of implications for other value judgments; (3) the analysis of factual consequences regarding both the means and the undesirable by-products; and (4) the uncovering of conflicting value judgments. (See A. Brecht, *Political Theory* [Princeton: Princeton University Press, 1959], pp. 227–28.)

8 This may be considered as an important advantage of the second approach. By refraining from insistence on one single best arrangement of the world, it preserves individual freedom.

9 K. Marx and F. Engels, *German Ideology* (1846), quotation from *Sochinenia,* vol. 3 (Moscow: Gospolitizdat, 1955), p. 409.

10 This famous formula only appears simple and unambiguous. Consider two situations that generate the same total volume of happiness. In one, happiness is distributed equally throughout the community; in the other, the distribution is extremely unequal. Which situation is to be preferred? If total utility is slightly higher in the second situation, a utilitarian will opt for it. Thus utilitarianism may be very antiegalitarian. To illustrate exactly that point, Amartya Sen constructed the following example: A cripple derives less utility from additional income than the average individual. Since total utility is maximized when marginal utility of income is rendered equal throughout the community, the cripple will get less and the healthy man more. The unfortunate handicapped man is punished twice: first by nature and then by utilitarians (*On Economic Inequality* [Oxford: Clarendon Press, 1973], pp. 16–18).

11 *A Theory of Justice* (London: Oxford University Press, 1973), p. 26.

12 M. Životić, *Čovek i vrednost* (Belgrade: Prosveta, 1969), pp. 76–77.

13 *The Ethical Foundations of Marxism* (London: Routledge and Kegan Paul, 1972), pp. 163–64.

14 "Thou shalt love thy neighbor as thyself" (Mark 12:31). "Act in such a way that you always treat humanity, whether in your own person or in the person of any other, never simply as a means, but always at the same time as an end" (I. Kant, *Groundwork of the Metaphysic of Morals,* trans. by H. J. Paton, originally titled *The Moral Law* [London:

Hutchison, 1956], p. 96). "The critique of religion ends with the teaching that man is the highest being for man, consequently, with the categorical imperative that all relations in which man is a humiliated, oppressed, abandoned, despised being be destroyed" (K. Marx, *Werke*, vol. 1 [Berlin: Dietz, 1957], p. 385).

[15] *Theory of Justice*, p. 426.

[16] "Reply to Alexander and Musgrave," *Quarterly Journal of Economics*, 1974, pp. 633–55, espec. pp. 634–39.

[17] *Theory of Justice*, p. 143.

[18] Ibid., p. 252.

[19] R. A. Wolff, *Understanding Rawls* (Princeton: Princeton University Press, 1977), p. 185.

[20] Rawls, *Theory of Justice*, p. 12.

[21] Ibid., pp. 60, 302.

[22] Ibid., p. 542.

[23] I used essentially the same principle, but operationalized within the self-governing framework, to derive the optimum distribution of income in my dissertation (1958), published later as *Towards a Theory of Planned Economy* (Belgrade: Jugoslavenski institut za ekonomska istraživanja, 1964), pp. 122–26. In the present book, it is further elaborated in chapter 9.

[24] *Theory of Justice*, p. 100.

[25] Ibid., p. 180.

[26] Ibid., p. 179.

[27] Ibid., p. 21.

[28] J. Charvet, "The Idea of Equality as a Substantive Principle," in A. de Crespigny and A. Wertheimer, eds., *Contemporary Political Theory* (New York: Atherton Press, 1970), p. 159.

[29] *Theory of Justice*, p. 503.

[30] James Sterba puts forward the following principle: "The results of voluntary agreement and private appropriation are morally justified provided each person is guaranteed the liberty necessary for satisfying both those basic needs he shares with other persons and those he has which can be satisfied by only slightly restricting the liberty of others" ("Neo-Libertarianism," *American Philosophical Quarterly*, 1978, pp. 115–21, quote from p. 121).

[31] *Anarchy, State and Utopia* (New York: Basic Books, 1974), p. 211.

[32] *Theory of Justice*, pp. 274, 258.

[33] A few illustrations from Rawls's own country may suffice. In 1960, in the United States the nominal tax rate for an income of $200,000 per year was 91 percent; the actual tax paid on incomes of $5 million or more was only 24.6 percent. In 1958, nominal inheritance tax on estates of $20 million or more was 69 percent; the inheritance tax actually paid was 15.7 percent (G. E. Lenski, *Power and Privilege* [New York: McGraw-Hill, 1966], p. 343). Gabriel Kolko (*Wealth and Power in America* [New York: Praeger, 1962], p. 34) found that the poorest people contributed in taxes more than enough to pay for the total amount they receive from welfare expenditures. It appears that the rich do not pay taxes and the poor do not reap benefits.

[34] *Theory of Justice,* p. 258.

[35] For this reason, Jan Pen is right in remarking that "the difference principle may cover almost any amount of income differential and ill-gotten gain. . . . *A Theory of Justice,* which looks at first sight like an egalitarian book, may in the hands of a clever conservative become a plea for inequality" ("A Theory of Justice," *Challenge,* March–April 1974, pp. 59–62).

[36] *Understanding Rawls,* p. 195.

[37] *Theory of Justice,* p. 3.

[38] *Yearbook of the United Nations 1948–1949* (New York, 1950), p. 535.

[39] Karl Kautsky gave a very different answer. He argued that an ethical ideal of the rising classes results from needs, aspirations, and will concerning something contrary to what exists. It is an opposite of the ruling morality and, as such, purely negative. In all class societies, the ruling morality protects unfreedom, inequality, and exploitation. Therefore, the ethical ideal of all rising classes has been a negation of the ruling class morality: freedom, equality, and fraternity. But this concordance of the ethical ideals of different historical periods is only very superficial, and it hides differences in social goals (*Ethik und die materialistische Geschichtsauffassung* [1906] [Stuttgart: Dietz, 1922], p. 136). That inequality and equality are opposites is obvious. But why the former should be an original phenomenon and the latter merely a negative response, Kautsky left unexplained. The best minds of the human race have advocated the three "negative ideals," and so did the ruling classes—but only for their members. Thus, it seems more reasonable to assume that the three "negative ideals" are in fact original and that, when they are thwarted, people rebel (if they can). Of course, clearly the ruling class reinterprets the ethical ideals in such a way as to justify its social position.

[40] E. Fromm undertook a detailed analysis of human destructiveness in his book *Anatomy of Human Destructiveness* (New York: Holt, Rinehart, and Winston, 1973). Fromm examined the question of whether destructiveness is inherent in human nature. He came to the

conclusion that there are two different types of aggression, one benign and the other malign. The former is a biologically adaptive response when vital interests are in jeopardy. It is phylogenetically programmed and is common to animals and humans; it is reactive and defensive. The latter is pure destructiveness, not a defense against danger; it is not programmed, and it is biologically harmful and socially disruptive. Malign aggression is a product of the social conditions of human existence and, as such, changes with these conditions.

[41] *Ethik,* p. 137.

[42] Justice conceived as equal liberty is more or less generally accepted. But solidarity, as the third component, is occasionally absent. This absence creates insuperable problems, and so solidarity is subsequently added under some other name and in some special relationship. Characteristic in this respect is the analysis of R. W. Baldwin, who defines justice as equal liberty and then concludes that justice alone is not enough and that the second great rule of morality is altruism or beneficence (*Social Justice* [Oxford: Pergamon, 1966], p. 112).

[43] *A Grammar of Politics* (London: Allen and Unwin, 1928), p. 275.

[44] Ibid., p. 153.

[45] Ibid., p. 142.

[46] Ibid., pp. 146–48.

[47] But this is not at all obvious—as the following quotation illustrates: "unfortunately, general equality (as distinct from political) is almost impossible to define" (R. A. Dahl and C. E. Lindblom, *Politics, Economics and Welfare* (New York: Harper and Bros., 1953), p. 46.

[48] *Naturrecht und menschliche Würde* (Frankfurt am Main: Suhrkamp, 1961), p. 187.

[49] In this context, it is of some interest to contrast bourgeois and socialist morality as described by B. Gallie. Bourgeois (in his terminology, liberal) morality implies commutative justice (equal exchange), the meritorious individual (deservingness as a basis of distribution), and the moral necessity of free choice and contract. It might be added that it also implies a specific individualism characterized by the absence of social responsibility. Socialist morality implies distributive justice (exchange modified by needs), the contributing individual, and the freedom to be, not to get ("Liberal Morality and Socialist Morality," in P. Laslett, *Philosophy, Politics and Society* [Oxford: Blackwell, 1956], pp. 116–33, espec. p. 128).

[50] They are fundamental social roles because they cannot be abandoned unless a person leaves the society. Other roles—being a father, being a member of a club, etc.—can be so abandoned. The first to

apply a similar approach was the Slovenian economist Franc Černe in a practically unknown work (a reflection of the fate of a scholar in a small nation) representing his doctoral dissertation on planning and the market in socialism. In Černe's view, socialism is characterized by the following three elements: (1) equal rights of members of the community as producers; this implies social ownership; (2) equal rights in terms of income distribution; the implied consequence is distribution according to work; (3) equal rights in political life; as citizens, members of the community enjoy socialist democracy ("Planiranje in tržni mehanizam v ekonomski teoriji socijalizma," Ljubljana, 1960, p. 281).

[51] This is a misnomer, for all planning is at least partly or in the final analysis central.

CHAPTER 8

[1] The change has already begun under the old system, of course. As Miroslav Pečujlić observed, private property has passed through a process of depersonalization. Roman and classical bourgeois laws hardly dealt with legal persons as legal subjects. They were developed for physical persons. Besides, formerly undivided right disintegrated into two components: one generating benefits (*nudum ius*) and the other providing an authorization for management (*Klase i savremeno društvo* [Belgrade: Savremena administracija, 1967], p. 39).

[2] "Social Ownership—Collective and Individual," in B. Horvat, M. Markovic, and R. Supek, eds., *Self-Governing Socialism: A Reader,* vol. 2 (White Plains, N.Y.: International Arts and Sciences Press, 1975), pp. 151–63 (originally published in *Gledišta,* 1968, pp. 531–44).

[3] For an analysis in terms of a particular empirical setting, see B. Horvat, "The Postwar Evolution of Yugoslav Agricultural Organization: Interaction of Ideology, Practice and Results," *Eastern European Economics,* 1973–74, *12* (2), 1–106.

[4] If the individual producer employs no outside workers, the analysis in the text applies strictly. If he employs several such workers (a small number, usually up to five, which is strictly limited by law), a transitional category comes into being, with additional complications. The uninterrupted development of a one-man business into a small-scale family enterprise, and then into a worker-managed firm poses further problems. For a detailed analysis, see B. Horvat, *An Essay on Yugoslav Society* (White Plains, N.Y.: International Arts and Sciences Press, 1969), ch. 4.

[5] It is important to notice that work teams or, as they are sometimes called, autonomous work groups have strictly limited functions. Veljko Rus and Mitja Kamušič, on the basis of research conducted at a Slovene factory, suggest that they "should be limited to those functions only which could not be performed by any other body in the work

organization. We have in mind self-organization and self-control of group work, which represent a condition for the abolition of hierarchical organization and control on the part of lower and middle management. . . . Autonomous work groups should not decide about hiring and firing, and also not about promotion and education of their members. In this way, autonomous work groups will be unifunctional and partial, and not multifunctional and total" ("Autonomous Work Groups Within a System of Self-Management," Conference on Workers' Participation on the Shop Floor, Dubrovnik, February 1976, p. 36 [mimeographed]).

[6] V. Rus, "Novi model samoupravljanja i njegova relevantna društvena okolina," in J. Obradović, V. Rus, and J. Županov, eds., *Proizvodne organizacije i samoupravljanje* (Zagreb: Sveučilište, 1975), p. 46.

[7] I borrow the name from the statute of the Scott Bader Commonwealth but assign to the organ a different function. See F. H. Blum, *Work and Community* (London: Routledge and Kegan Paul, 1968), p. 156.

[8] "One of the major problems in the United States is that a great many decisions are made solely to overcome the unintended consequences of earlier decisions. . . . Most of the time, the unintended consequences affect individuals and groups who were not consulted before decisions were made. There can be no better way of discovering as many such problems as possible than to include in decision processes those individuals most likely to be affected by them. Although this would slow down the process, it would produce more effective decisions which, because hidden consequences had been discovered in advance, would become cost-effective through *cost avoidance*" (F. C. Thayer, *An End to Hierarchy! An End to Competition!* [New York: Watts, 1973], p. 39).

[9] "The Post-Industrial Organization," *The Bureaucrat*, 1974, pp. 285–300, quote from p. 290.

[10] "An adaptive, temporary system of diverse specialists solving problems, coordinated organically via articulating points, will gradually replace the theory of bureaucracy" (W. Bennis, "A Funny Thing Happened on the Way to the Future," in H. Leavitt et al., eds., *Organizations of the Future* [New York: Praeger, 1974], pp. 3–28, quote from p. 8).

[11] See chapter 5, section VI.

[12] M. Rosner, B. Kavčič, A. S. Tannenbaum, M. Vianello, and G. Weiser, "Worker Participation and Influence in Industrial Plants of Five Countries," in *Participation and Self-Management*, Proceedings of the Dubrovnik Conference, vol. 4 (Zagreb: Institute for Social Research, 1973), pp. 91–102, quote from p. 100.

[13] R. Townsend, *Up the Organization* (New York: Alfred A. Knopf, 1970), p. 49.

[14] *Wealth of Nations,* ed. by E. Cannan (New York: Random House, 1937), p. 700.

[15] "Uloga kolegijalnih izvršnih organa u procesu samoupravnog odlučivanja," *Ekonomski pregled,* 1971, pp. 511–31, espec. p. 520.

[16] Yugoslav legislation after 1973 was based largely on this misconception.

[17] On another occasion, I evaluated a council decision as meaningless. I was told that the council cannot take meaningless decisions—the council represents the will of the community—and that in any case the director cannot evaluate the council's decisions. On a third occasion, the council refused to accept a contract between the work organization and one of its members. It was considered self-evident that an individual member has certain obligations toward the work organization, but that the converse is not true. The council cannot be bound by contract stipulations in its dealings with individual workers. The individual and the collectivity cannot have equal rights; the former must be subordinated.

[18] The empirical research referred to here is cited in Veljko Rus, "Klike u radnim organizacijama," *Gledišta,* 1966, pp. 1079–98.

[19] Describing the Yugoslav scene in 1974, Jozo Županov wrote: "The idea that Economic Units should be autonomous self-sufficient units capable of earning and distributing their own income . . . prevailed over a sociological proposal . . . of fusing formal and informal organization on the lowest possible level into basic building blocks of the organization. . . . In most firms management was successful in preserving a *de facto* centralized organization" ("The Self-Management Work Organization—The Ideal and Reality in the Light of an Organizational Theory" [mimeographed]).

[20] V. Rus et al., "Participative Decision-Making under Conditions of Uncertainty," paper presented at the Second International Conference on Participation, Workers' Control and Self-Management, Paris, 1977 (mimeographed).

[21] One possible contribution to the development of such culture is to study malpractices and expose them publicly. A manual of self-management ought to contain not only constructive rules but also a systematic discussion of all possible misuses.

[22] J. Županov (*Samoupravljanje i društvena moć* [Zagreb: Naše teme, 1969], pp. 54–56) and V. Rus ("Novi model samoupravljanje i njegova relevantna društvena okolina," in J. Obradović, V. Rus, and J. Županov, eds., *Proizvodne organizacije i samoupravljanje* [Zagreb: Sveučilište u Zagrebu, 1975], p. 50) noticed this tendency and documented it by empirical research.

CHAPTER 9

[1] Made in opposition to an earlier Louis Blanc formula of distribution according to needs, which Proudhon considered unrealistic. In fact, the first to use the phrase was Saint-Simon's disciple Bazard, who wrote in *Exposition* (1830) that the society without exploitation is the one "in which all individuals will be classed according to their capacities and remunerated according to their work."

[2] In this section I am adopting the same general approach as in my book *Towards a Theory of Planned Economy* (Belgrade: Jugoslavenski institut za ekonomska istraživanja, 1964), ch. 6.

[3] See various theoretical writings and practical proposals by Professor Jaroslav Vanek. I also held a similar view in my first book on the theory of a self-governing economy.

[4] See B. Horvat, "Raspodjela prema radu medu kolektivima," *Naša stvarnost,* 1962, no. 1, pp. 52–66.

[5] For a general treatment of such cases, see B. Horvat, "Utvrđivanje rente u proizvodnji nafte," *Ekonomist,* 1979, pp. 203–9.

[6] Market valuations fuse the two aspects into one single productivity aspect. It is the product that is sold and bought. If wage costs increase, product price will increase, demand will decrease and, in the absence of perverse slopes of demand and supply curves, a new equilibrium will be struck at a higher marginal productivity of labor.

[7] The income gap between an unskilled worker and the general manager in a firm employing 5,000 workers is about 1:5 at a $1,000 per capita level of development. In a comparable capitalist firm, it is at least five times as great.

[8] Barry Bluestone reports that in the American economy the wages of qualified workers differ as much as 110 percent. He also finds "that the American labour market is considerably inefficient in terms of matching what we have called endogenous productions (potential output of an individual given his endogenous productivity characteristics) to marginal products or wages. Much of the labour force appears to be paid at rates not consonant with their measured human capital" ("The Determinants of Personal Earnings in the U.S.," p. 54 [mimeographed]).

[9] See chapter 12, section IV.

[10] Whenever a capitalist system cannot achieve a target or solve a problem, neoclassical theory claims that it is inherently impossible.

[11] It may also depend on genetic or environmental accidents, and therefore the labor income of the disabled and mentally retarded people must be complemented by a social subsidy that may also be conceived as a global social insurance payment.

[12] Thus, for example, the protective services of the police represent an intermediate, not a final good. Total social product does not consist of GNP *plus* police services. The output of a shoe factory consists of a certain number of pairs of shoes, *not* of the latter *plus*, for example, the services of nightwatchmen. Preserving law and order is a *precondition* for the system to be able to produce final goods and services, not an addition to final output. See B. Horvat, "The Conceptual Background of Social Product," *Income and Wealth,* series IX (London: Bowes and Bowes, 1961), pp. 339–52; and "An Integrated System of Social Accounts for an Economy of the Yugoslav Type," *Review of Income and Wealth,* 1968, pp. 19–36.

[13] We observe a similar phenomenon in individual consumption. In the strict logic of the marginal utility calculus, and under the assumption of divisibility, satiation could occur only for all wants simultaneously, or for none of them. Even at modest incomes, however, the consumption of various goods (sugar, salt, water, etc.) is brought to the satiation level.

CHAPTER 10

[1] Foreword to *Zur Kritik der politischen Ökonomie,* 1859.

[2] T. Parsons and N. Smelser, *Economy and Society* (New York: Free Press, 1956), pp. 16–19; T. Parsons, *Structure and Process in Modern Societies* (Glencoe, Ill.: Free Press, 1964), pp. 45–47; T. Parsons, "On the Concept of Political Power," in R. Bell, D. Edwards, and R. H. Wagner, eds., *Political Power* (New York: Free Press, 1969), pp. 251–84, espec. p. 280. For an interesting modification of this conceptual scheme, see R. Holt, "A Proposed Structural-Functional Framework," in J. C. Charlesworth, ed., *Contemporary Political Analysis* (New York: Free Press, 1967), pp. 86–107.

[3] "Toward a Pure Theory of Threat Systems," in Bell, Edwards, and Wagner, *Political Power,* pp. 285–92, espec. p. 285.

[4] D. Bell, *The Coming of Post-Industrial Society* (New York: Basic Books, 1973), pp. 10–12; *The Cultural Contradictions of Capitalism* (London: Heinemann, 1976), pp. 10–14.

[5] *Cultural Contradictions,* p. 10.

[6] This is the position taken by, among others, Robert Dahl. See his paper "Fundamental Rights in a Democratic Order," presented at the Moscow Congress of the International Political Science Association in 1979.

[7] As Robert Lane pointed out to me in a letter, such a nonnormative definition of legitimacy would legitimize the Nazis. This is true; but it is also the virtue of the definition. There is no point in hiding the fact that Nazis *were* popular in their country. Besides, I wish to avoid intermingling value considerations in my analytical framework. I pre-

fer to introduce the latter into the discussion in an orderly way and, if possible, at a single point. I believe that in this way the analysis gains in rigor and the communication is less likely to be misunderstood. Clearly, people may disagree for two very different reasons: (a) because the analysis seems somehow deficient; and (b) because the values held are different. It is therefore advisable to keep the two issues separate. The same considerations were involved in choosing the definition of revolution later on (chapter 14, section II).

[8] With minor modifications, I borrow these two definitions from Hans Kelsen, *General Theory of the Law and State* (Serbo-Croatian translation: *Opšta teorija prava i države* [Belgrade: Arhiv za pravne i društvene nauke, 1951], pp. 17 and 188).

[9] See B. Horvat, *An Essay on Yugoslav Society* (White Plains, N.Y.: International Arts and Sciences Press, 1969), ch. 2, "The Transition Period and the Dictatorship of the Proletariat."

[10] J. Lapenna, *State and Law: Soviet and Yugoslav Theory* (New Haven: Yale University Press, 1964), p. 16.

[11] K. Marx, *Civil War in France*, 1971; F. Engels, Introduction to the text by Marx, 1891.

[12] V. I. Lenin, *Gosudar'stvo i revoliuciia,* 1917, ch. 5, sec. 2 and ch. 1, sec. 4.

[13] V. I. Lenin, "On the History of the Question about Dictatorship," *Sochineniia*, 1920, vol. 31, p. 326.

[14] V. I. Lenin, *Proletarskaia revoliutsiia i renegat Kautsky* (1918) (Moscow: Ogiz-Gospolitizdat, 1947), p. 14.

[15] Also polemicizing against Kautsky, Trotsky wrote in 1920: "No social organization except the army has ever considered itself justified in subordinating citizens to itself in such a measure, and controlling them by its will on all sides to such a degree, as the State of the proletarian dictatorship considers itself justified in doing, and does" (*The Defense of Terrorism* [London: Allen and Unwin, 1921], p. 130). "The State, before disappearing, assumes the form of the dictatorship of the proletariat, i.e. the most ruthless form of State, which embraces the life of the citizens authoritatively in every direction" (ibid., p. 157). In fact, this is more than just political dictatorship; it is full-fledged totalitarianism. Kautsky, whose book Lenin and Trotsky attacked, maintained correctly that the mature Marx, in using the phrase *dictatorship of the proletariat*, "only intended to describe a political *condition*, and not a *form of government*" (*The Dictatorship of the Proletariat* [1918] [Ann Arbor: University of Michigan Press, 1971], p. 140).

[16] S. A. Golunski and M. S. Strogovich declared: "even to the Marxist genius of Engels the concrete form of the proletarian state was still

that of a parliamentary republic" ("The Theory of State and Law," in *Soviet Legal Philosophy*, vol. 5 [Cambridge, Mass.: Harvard University Press, 1951], p. 354).

[17] G. Zinoviev, "Pressing Questions of the International Labour Movement," *Communist International*, June–July 1920, pp. 2109–56, quote from p. 2131.

[18] J. V. Stalin, "O treh osnovnyh lozungah partii po Krest'ianskomu voprosu" (1927), in *Voprosy leninizma* (Moscow: Ogiz, 1945), p. 163.

[19] In so-called primitive societies, in which class stratification is absent, the state does not exist either. These have been described in *Tribes without Rules* (Y. Middleton and D. Tait, eds. [London: Routledge and Kegan Paul, 1964]). Stateless societies have political action, but not specialized political institutions and, even less, professional politicians; territorial boundaries are not definitive, there is no exclusive sovereignty, and central monopoly of legitimate force does not exist. Aidan Southall ("Stateless Society," in *International Encyclopedia of the Social Sciences* [New York: Macmillan/Free Press, 1968], vol. 15, pp. 157–67) enumerates five characteristics of stateless societies: (1) they are multipolities, which means that there is no single, all-embracing organization covering the entire society; the boundaries of language do not coincide with those of warfare, or of intermarriage, clanship, or ritual observance; (2) global social integration is achieved by rituals; during festival periods conflicts and disputes are abandoned and general truce established; (3) societal segments keep a dynamic equilibrium by handling tensions and conflicts through complementary opposition; the same applies to (4) cleavages and transcendant interconnections in nonunilineal kinship systems; (5) since there are several nonhierarchically placed polities within a single society, legitimacy is distributive, and legitimate political action belongs to multiple points and levels. Leaders are not political professionals. Chiefs have no political authority or sanctions; their preeminence depends on their bravery and generosity and, in general, on doing better than others in activities important for group life. Leadership by consent is the only basis for legitimacy. "In stateless societies every man grows up with a practical and intuitive sense of his responsibility to maintain constantly throughout his life that part of the fabric of society in which at any time he is involved. . . . But if every man is thus for himself, he is so only within a very tight framework of reciprocal obligation that he cannot avoid absorbing. The lack of specialized roles and the multiplex quality of social networks mean that neither economic nor political ends can be exclusively formed by anyone to the detriment of society, because these ends are intertwined with each other and further channeled by ritual and controlled by the beliefs which ritual expresses" (ibid., p. 167).

[20] Isaak Deutscher illustrates the point: "I think it was Trotsky who used a very plain but very telling metaphor: the policeman can use

his baton either for regulating traffic or for dispersing a demonstration of strikers or unemployed. In this one sentence is summed up the classical distinction between administration of things and administration of men" (Roots of Bureaucracy," in R. Miliband and J. Saville, eds., *The Socialist Register 1969* [London: Merlin, 1964], p. 20).

[21] L. Duguit, *Les transformations du droit public* (Paris, 1913).

[22] See E. Pusić, *Problemi upravljanja* (Zagreb: Naprijed, 1971).

[23] The first to formulate the doctrine was Charles Dallison (*The Royalists Defense*, 1648). For a comprehensive history of the doctrine, see M. J. C. Vile, *Constitutionalism and the Separation of Powers* (Oxford: Clarendon Press, 1967).

[24] For Locke, legislative power was of central importance and was to be divided between king, lords, and commons. Executive and federative powers were to be left in the hands of the king. Montesquieu transformed the executive into the judicial power, and the federative into the executive power. Locke *divided one* power; Montesquieu *separated three* powers. The British insistence on legislative power survived in the British parliamentary government, but the power was undivided. The idea of the separation of different powers gave rise to the American presidential system. As usual, the intellectual origin of the idea of division or separation of powers can be traced back to Plato and Aristotle. See K. Čavoški, "Problemi slobode u demokratiji," *Filozofske studije* (Belgrade: Filozofsko društvo Srbije, 1973), pp. 3–70.

[25] Charles Louis de Secondat, Baron Montesquieu, *De l'esprit de loix* (1748), book XI, ch. 6, translation from H. Laski, *A Grammar of Politics* (London: Allen and Unwin, 1928), p. 297.

[26] The reader may note that I use the term "self-management" in relation to business affairs and the term "self-government" when I refer to political affairs. Consequently, I speak of "workers' self-management" and of "citizens' or political self-government." I also use self-government as a generic term when I denote socialism as a "self-governing society."

[27] Sun Yat-sen, "Die Fünf-Amter-Verfassung" (1921), in K. A. Wittfogel, *Sun Yat Sen* (Vienna: AGIS, n.d.), pp. 239–50, quote from p. 248. According to Sun, the ancient Chinese government system consisted of three independent authorities: the control authority, the examination authority, and the emperor's authority. The latter performed three functions: judicial, administrative, and legislative. The control authority inflicted all punishments and could even suggest the punishment of the emperor (ibid., pp. 246–47).

[28] The open competitive examination for entrance into the civil service was introduced in Great Britain in 1854.

[29] Laski, *Grammar of Politics,* pp. 398–99.

[30] E. Pusić, *Problemi upravljanja,* p. 107.

[31] A similar idea was formulated by English socialists and reformers Sidney and Beatrice Webb: "What we shall call the Political Democracy, dealing with national defence, international relations and the administration of justice, needs to be set apart from what we propose to call the Social Democracy, to which is entrusted the national administration of the industries and services by and through which the community lives." That would involve establishing two assemblies: political parliament, which would function along traditional lines, and social parliament, which would sit for a fixed term of years with dissolution possible only under special circumstances (*A Constitution for the Socialist Commonwealth of Great Britain* [London: Longmans, Green, 1920], pp. 111 ff.). The Webbs also take as a basis of their analysis the threefold classification of man as producer, man as consumer, and man as citizen (ibid., pp. xvii and passim). The same idea reappeared in the turbulent times of the German Revolution. Two majority socialists, Max Cohen and Julius Kaliski, trying to combine parliamentarism with the council system, proposed at the Second Councils Congress in Berlin in 1919 that a separate Chamber of Labor (*Kammer der Arbeit*) be added to the People's Chamber (*Volkskammer*). All employed in enterprises were to elect production councils. These councils were to be integrated vertically up to the central production council; all councils were to send their delegates to chambers of labor at the corresponding levels (W. Gottschalch, *Parlamentarismus und Rätedemokratie* [Berlin: Wagenbach, 1968], pp. 26, 83–84). The idea was tried out for the first time in Yugoslavia soon after the introduction of workers' management.

[32] The two aspects of social power—distribution and amount—are often confused. It is vitally important, however, to keep this distinction clear. An analogy with wealth may help. A society may be poor or wealthy, and in both cases wealth may be equally or unequally distributed. What we would like to achieve is a wealthy *and* egalitarian society. Similarly, the political system ought to be designed in such a way as to maximize power potentials for solving social problems while equalizing the distribution of power in the sense that no group of citizens can impose its will on the disagreeing majority.

[33] C. J. Friedrich, *Constitutional Government and Democracy* (New York: Blaisdell, 1964), p. 113.

[34] Before World War II, courts with constitutional responsibilities were extremely rare. They existed primarily in federally organized polities, such as the United States, Canada, and Australia. After the war constitutional courts were established in the Federal Republic of Germany, Italy, India, Yugoslavia, and elsewhere.

[35] V. Rajović, *Sudovi udruženog rada* (Belgrade: Službeni list, 1975).

[36] *Grammar of Politics*, p. 546.

[37] How justice is administered to ordinary citizens in contemporary capitalist democracies may be illustrated by a description of the practices in New York City, which certainly are not the worst to be found. J. Newfield spent a month observing a municipal courtroom and found the following: "Routinely, lives are ruined and families broken by 30-second decisions. Some judges quit work at 2:00 P.M. to play golf, while some 8,000 men and women presumed innocent under the Constitution wait months for trial in the city's overcrowded detention jails. Other judges have tantrums on the bench and call defendants 'animals' and 'scum.' Cops pay court attendants . . . $5 to call their cases first. Legal Aid lawyers defend 50 poor clients a day with not a second for preparation. The bail system lets bondsmen buy freedom for the rich and well-connected. Clerks sell advance word on court assignments and decisions. Civil cases almost always get decided in favor of the landlord or businessman or city agency" (quoted in M. Parenti, *Democracy for the Few* [New York: St. Martin's Press, 1974], p. 120). The British administration of justice—considered one of the best in the world—is described by J. Westergaard and H. Resler as follows: "Most . . . are bewildered by the court proceedings; they complain that the atmosphere prevents a fair hearing, and that court officials are unhelpful. So, too, in penal cases, where the great majority of the defendants are manual working class; and where the safeguards intended to protect prisoners are often denied to them. Those held first at police stations are usually, if they ask, refused access to a solicitor at the time. Magistrates rarely grant bail against police objections, although the case on subsequent trial often proves not to result in a jail sentence; and most of those refused bail are not told of their right to appeal on the point. Legal representation is uncommon in the courts, even when defendants plead not guilty; and at least a large majority of those sentenced to prison by magistrates have had no lawyer to put their case. Advice about, and help in making, an appeal are often inadequate. So, whether the proceedings are civil or penal, working-class people in court are victims of procedures they do not understand and for which they receive little help that is formally prescribed; often sheer indifference or direct hostility" (*Class in a Capitalist Society* [London: Heinemann, 1975], pp. 189–90).

[38] *Grammar of Politics*, p. 567.

[39] In the Soviet Union (with its *prokuratura*) and some other etatist countries, this control is rather extensive. The public prosecutor supervises the administration of justice and is also responsible for a general supervision over the legality of administrative acts. The latter implies review of subordinate legislation and monitoring of the implementation of laws. Any citizen may raise a complaint about an abuse of his rights to the procuracy, which is expected to investigate the matter and take the appropriate steps with the authorities.

[40] The term *ombudsman* comes from *om* = about and *bud* = messenger, and referred to the collection of a fine from the offender in Viking times. Later the term came to mean any kind of agent.

[41] The constitution stipulated that the *justitieombudsman*, "in capacity of the representative of parliament, shall supervise the observance of laws and statutes, as applied by the courts and by public officials, and institute proceedings before competent courts against those who, in execution of their official duties have, through partiality, favouritism, or other causes, committed any unlawful act or neglected to perform their official duties" (quoted in A. Bexelius, "The Origin, Nature and Functions of the Civil and Military Ombudsmen in Sweden," in *The Ombudsman or Citizen's Defender: A Modern Institution, Annals of the American Academy of Political and Social Science*, May 1968, *377*, 10–19, quote from p. 11).

[42] Bexelius, "Civil and Military Ombudsmen," p. 15.

[43] S. Thune, "The Norwegian Ombudsman for Civil and Military Affairs," *The Ombudsman or Citizen's Defender*, pp. 41–54, espec. p. 51.

[44] H. J. Abraham, "The Danish Ombudsman," in *The Ombudsman or Citizen's Defender*, pp. 55–61, espec. p. 58.

[45] Since 1976, a similar body has functioned at the international level. It is called the Human Rights Committee and is elected by secret ballot from a list of persons nominated by the states party to the International Covenant on Civil and Political Rights. The committee receives and considers communications from individuals who claim to be victims of a violation by a participating state of any of the rights set forth in the covenant and who have exhausted all available domestic remedies. The committee brings any communication submitted to it to the attention of the signatory state, which is obliged to submit a written explanation clarifying the matter and the remedy taken.

[46] J. Coleman, *Power and Structure of Society* (New York: W. W. Norton, 1974), p. 76.

[47] The type of leader appropriate for socialism is that described by the ancient Chinese sage Laozi: "A leader is best when men barely know he is there, not so good when men obey and acclaim him, worse when they despise him" (quoted in C. J. Friedrich, *Man and His Government* [New York: McGraw-Hill, 1963], p. 159). What I have in mind, and what Laozi probably meant as well, is the leader as a chief, a Führer, the supreme head of a hierarchy issuing commands. Leaders as creative coordinators inspiring people for collective action are welcome in any society, of course. This clarification is prompted by a critical remark by Robert Lane.

[48] To stress institutional differences, parliament, government, and ministries are denoted in the figure as the Assembly, the Executive

Council, and secretariats. Once these differences are grasped, the two sets of terms may be used interchangeably.

[49] T. Parsons, *Structure and Process,* pp. 250–79.

[50] E. Pusić, *Lokalna zajednica* (Zagreb: Narodne novine, 1963), p. 69.

[51] At the turn of the century, communal administration in Croatia comprised 30 groups of activities classified into 7 branches. Half a century later, there were 250 groups and 12 branches (general administration, economy, finance, city planning and construction, education, culture, health, social policy, labor relations, communal services, police, and defense) (Pusić, *Lokalna zajednica,* p. 101).

[52] Ibid., p. 116.

[53] If the number of states is too great, the Presidium can be formed on a rotational basis, with one state dropping out and another coming in each year.

CHAPTER 11

[1] C. J. Friedrich, *Man and His Government* (New York: McGraw-Hill, 1963), p. 549.

[2] M. Duverger, *Janus—les deux faces de l'Occident* (Paris: Fayard, 1972), pp. 16, 48.

[3] Duverger, *Les deux faces.*

[4] The undemocratic practices of communist parties in power have nothing to do with Marx, or Marxism, or the original traditions of the socialist movement. But the seeds of future evils were already visible in early social democratic parties. The critique of Robert Michels will be quoted later. Here I cite a few extracts from letters by Friedrich Engels. When left-wing opponents were expelled from the Danish Socialist Party, Engels wrote to Trier (December 18, 1889): "The workers' movement is based on the sharpest criticism of existing society; criticism is its vital element; how then can it itself avoid criticism, try to forbid controversies? Is it possible for us to demand from others freedom of speech for ourselves only in order to eliminate it afresh in our own ranks?" When the leadership reacted to the opposition of Jungen, Engels wrote to Sorge (August 9, 1890): "The Party is so big that absolute freedom of debate inside it is a necessity. . . . The greatest party in the land cannot exist without all shades of opinion in it making themselves fully felt." This, of course, is diametrically opposite to the Stalinist insistence on "monolithic unity." In connection with Marx's *Critique of the Gotha Programme,* which the party leadership suppressed as too critical, Engels wrote to Kautsky (February 11, 1891): "It is also necessary that people cease to treat party functionaires—their servants—with silk gloves and before them, as infallible bureaucrats, stand submissively instead of critically." See also M. Johnstone, "Marx and Engels and the Concept of Party," *Socialist Register* (London: Merlin, 1967), pp. 121–46.

[5] I have taken this classification from Polish political scientist Jerzy Wiatr and modified it in two ways: I added the classifying characteristic, "Number of candidates" and left out his category "Hegemonic party system" (formally several parties, but no legal opposition, as in Poland) because it is not meaningfully different from a one-party system (J. Wiatr, "The Hegemonic Party System in Poland," in E. Allard and S. Rokkan, eds., *Mass Politics* [New York: Free Press, 1970], pp. 312–21, espec. p. 318; originally published in J. Wiatr and J. Tarkowsky, *Studies of the Polish Political System* [Warsaw: Ossolineum, 1967], pp. 108–23).

[6] "A campaign for a Congressional seat can easily cost $15,000–25,000 and a Senatorial campaign can cost half a million dollars or more" (R. A. Dahl and C. E. Lindblom, *Politics, Economics and Welfare* (New York: Harper and Brothers, 1953), p. 315. In 1966–68, a campaign for the House of Representatives in Connecticut cost $53,000. Nelson Rockefeller's 1966 campaign for the governorship of New York State cost $5 million. The presidential campaign of Richard Nixon in 1972 spent $37.6 million in gifts and $1.6 million in loans (C. Anderson, *Statecraft* [New York: John Wiley and Sons, 1977], pp. 157–58). Evaluating this aspect of contemporary elections, Joseph LaPalombara has noted: "The cost of competing for public office in the United States has reached truly astronomical proportions. . . . For every presidentially aspiring haberdasher like Harry S. Truman, there are several multimillionaires like John F. Kennedy or Averell Harriman. For less wealthy but well-heeled aspirants like Richard Nixon, enormously wealthy backers stand ready to turn dollars into votes—sometimes by means that are flagrantly in violation of law" (*Politics Within Nations* [Englewood Cliffs, N.J.: Prentice Hall, 1974], pp. 486–87).

[7] In the United Kingdom, the stature and personal magnetism of individual parliamentary candidates affects the outcome by only some ±500 votes per constituency (H. R. Winter and T. J. Bellows, *People and Politics* [New York: John Wiley and Sons, 1977], p. 160).

[8] "Two or three candidates who eventually fight for people's vote," declared Bertrand de Jouvenel, "are in any case chosen by an 'inner leadership group.' " He added characteristically: "That can hardly be otherwise. It is completely impossible to leave the choice to the people without restricting it" (*Reine Theorie der Politik* [Berlin: Luchterhand, 1967], p. 149).

[9] Duverger, *Les deux faces*, p. 65.

[10] *Political Parties: A Sociological Study of the Oligarchical Tendencies of Modern Democracy* (Glencoe, Ill.: Free Press, 1949; originally published in 1911 under the title *Zur Soziologie des Parteiwesens in der modernen Demokratie*).

[11] Ibid., p. 16.

[12] *Revolution and Counterrevolution* (New York: Basic Books, 1968), pp. 413, 415. In almost exactly the same terms, Frank Deppe and his colleagues described the trade union and Social Democratic Party (SPD) apparatus in West Germany as manifesting: (a) a centralization of decision-making authority; (b) a tendency of functionaries to become bourgeois; (c) a concentration of the union and party press; (d) manipulation of congresses, which become staged shows; and (e) a concentration of financial power (*Kritik der Mitbestimmung* [Frankfurt am Main: Suhrkamp, 1969]).

[13] *Political Parties*, p. 16.

[14] G. M. Carter and J. H. Herz, *Government and Politics in the Twentieth Century* (London: Thames and Hudson, 1965), p. 108.

[15] R. Rose, *The Problem of Party Government* (Harmondsworth: Pelican, 1976), p. 1.

[16] Ithiel de Sola Pool, "The Public and the Polity," in I. de Sola Pool, ed., *Contemporary Political Science* (New York: McGraw-Hill, 1967), pp. 22–52, quote from p. 35.

[17] V. Dennis et al., "Political Socialization to Democratic Orientations in Four Western Systems," *Comparative Political Studies*, 1968, pp. 71–101, espec. pp. 78, 86. Later research has indicated that children tend to change with the society and seem to be less respectful now.

[18] "Public and Polity," p. 39.

[19] G. A. Almond and G. B. Powell, *Comparative Politics* (Boston: Little, Brown, 1966), p. 117.

[20] *Politics Within Nations*, pp. 154–61.

[21] "Political Parties: Some Sceptical Reflections," in R. C. Macridis and B. E. Brown, eds., *Comparative Politics* (Homewood, Ill.: Dorsey Press, 1972), pp. 233–51, quote from p. 239.

[22] Ibid., pp. 249–50.

[23] Ibid., p. 243.

[24] Quoted in ibid., p. 246.

[25] "The Hegemonic Party System in Poland," in Allard and Rokkan, *Mass Politics*, pp. 317–21, quote from p. 315. Najdan Pašić distinguishes three functions of the Soviet Communist Party as a constituent part of the state apparatus: (1) the party selects functionaries for the state administration; (2) it directly controls the activities of all state organs; (3) all important decisions of state organs are preceded by relevant decisions of the respective party bodies (*Uporedni politički sistemi* [Belgrade: Institut za političke studije FPN, 1976], p. 199).

[26] Two practical examples may be illuminating before we proceed to a more complete analysis. Close to two-thirds of American communities with more than 5,000 inhabitants hold nonpartisan elections. But in such cases candidates depend more on business contributions than when party money is available (T. N. Clark, "Community Structure and Decision Making," in T. N. Clark, ed., *Community Structure and Decision Making* [San Francisco: Chandler, 1968], pp. 91–128, espec. p. 108). In Switzerland, the federal government is elected on a nonpartisan basis (though not the parliament).

[27] An example of nonpartisan information is the *Washington Star-News,* a newspaper, and the League of Women Voters, an organization working to promote political responsibility, which together publish election guides with information about candidates and the offices to which they aspire. In the 1974 election the candidates for the House of Representatives were asked to answer the following three questions: "1. What special qualifications, education or experience do you have which would contribute to your effectiveness as delegate . . . ? 2. Now that the District of Columbia has an elected mayor and city council, how do you see (a) the role of the District of Columbia delegate to Congress, and (b) the role of the congressional District committees? 3. What actions in Congress will you initiate or support to deal with the most crucial needs in the District of Columbia?" ("Electoral Guide," *Washington Star-News,* October 24, 1974, p. 2). Concerning financing, Germany was probably the first country to provide systematically for public financing of competing political parties. In Norway the state pays the expenses of nominating conventions if they follow prescribed procedures. In Tanzania only one party exists, but there may be many candidates for every political office and the campaigning of the two who are most successful in the primaries is financed publicly.

[28] Representatives are not political *leaders* but public *servants.* Voters should select them, declared Marx in his address on the Civil War in France in 1871, in the same way that any other employer selects his workers, supervisors, and accountants.

[29] This system of referenda and initiative (*Volksbegehren*) works in Switzerland, where citizens decide on ten to eighteen political issues annually. Participation runs between 50 and 60 percent (E. Gruner and B. Junker, *Bürger, Staat und Politik in der Schweiz* [Basel: Lehrmittelverlag, 1968], pp. 114, 116). Carl Friedrich evaluates Swiss experience as follows: "The recurrent refusal of the general electorate to sanction constitutional and legislative measures designed to benefit particular interest groups suggests that referendum is an integrating mechanism" (*Trends of Federalism in Theory and Practice* [London: Pall Mall, 1968], p. 152).

[30] "Even in the first years of application [of *Volksbegehren*] it became apparent that the population as a whole tends to be more conservative than the elite in Parliament" (Gruner and Junker, *Bürger, Staat und*

Politik, p. 119). In one evaluation of ten countries (Switzerland was not included in the sample), Sweden appeared to have the most democratic political system (R. A. Dahl, "The Evaluation of Political Systems," in de Sola Pool, *Contemporary Political Science,* pp. 166–81, espec. p. 173). An inquiry into Swedish political life in 1974 revealed that supporters of each parliamentary party, left and right included, were more conservative than their respective leaderships. Citizens of Yugoslav communes are more conservative than officials of the local government apparatus (E. Pusić). It has been suggested that elites engage in change in order to increase their power, that active political participation will alter attitudes, and the final outcome may prove to be the reverse of present conditions (Vesna Pusić).

[31] See C. B. Macpherson, "The Maximization of Democracy," in P. Laslett and W. G. Runciman, eds., *Philosophy, Politics and Society* (Oxford: Blackwell, 1967), pp. 83–103, espec. p. 84.

[32] E. H. Carr, *The New Society* (London: Macmillan, 1951), pp. 62–63.

[33] Consider two well-known passages from *The Social Contract:* "In order that the social compact may not be an empty formula, it tacitly includes the undertaking, which alone can give force to the rest, that whoever refuses to obey the general will shall be compelled to do so by the whole body. This means nothing less than that he will be *forced to be free;* for this is the condition which, by giving each citizen to his country, secures him against all personal dependence" (book I, ch. 7; emphasis added). ". . . the citizen is no longer the judge of the dangers to which the law desires him to expose himself; and when the prince says to him: 'It is expedient for the State that you should die,' he ought to die, because it is only on that condition that he has been living in security up to present, and because his life is no longer a mere bounty of nature, but a gift made conditionally by the State" (book II, ch. 5). Read "general will" as "the historical interest of the working class" (as against the "will of all," which is "bourgeois liberalism") and you get statements such as etatist ideologues make all the time. But Rousseau clearly was also—perhaps predominantly—a source of genuinely democratic theorizing.

[34] H. Lasswell and A. Kaplan, *Power and Society* (New Haven: Yale University Press, 1950), p. 218.

[35] P. Bachrach, *The Theory of Democratic Elitism: A Critique* (Boston: Little, Brown, 1967), p. ix.

[36] *Rulers* define goals, formulate and execute rules, adjudicate, and contend for political support. The *ruled* are subject to rules, demand adjudications, and wish to influence legislators (H. V. Wiseman, *Political Systems* [London: Routledge and Kegan Paul, 1966], p. 131). One of the basic functions of the parties is to perpetuate this division,

since parties select leaders and provide links between the ruled and the rulers (see Friedrich, *Man and His Government*, p. 518). The same obviously applies with even greater force to etatist vanguard parties.

[37] This has already been noted by Talcott Parsons, though he drew different conclusions from this correspondence. See "An Overview," in T. Parsons, ed., *American Sociology* (New York: Basic Books, 1968), pp. 319–35, espec. p. 331.

[38] Ibid.

[39] "Once one representative has a party, his opponents must. So great are the political advantages of a party that in a representative democracy a politician without party is a politician without power" (R. A. Dahl, *After the Revolution?* [New Haven: Yale University Press, 1970], p. 74).

[40] J. A. Schumpeter, *Capitalism, Socialism, Democracy* (New York: Harper and Bros., 1950), p. 283.

[41] Considering the idea of a classless society, R. Dahrendorf remarked that "it is possible to conceive of a society whose structure contains positions equipped with different authority rights but which does not enable any group of persons to occupy these positions regularly and exclusively. . . . where there is no group which is capable of monopolizing positions of authority, it is virtually impossible for coherent conflict groups to emerge, and the society or association in question is therefore classless" (*Class and Class Conflict in Industrial Society* [London: Routledge and Kegan Paul, 1967], p. 219).

[42] Characteristically, it comes from economist Joseph Schumpeter (*Capitalism, Socialism, Democracy*, pp. 242, 269). He also observed that in democratic voting "the social function is fulfilled, as it were, incidentally—in the same sense as production is incidental to the making of profits" (ibid., p. 282).

[43] C. Pateman, "A Contribution to the Political Theory of Organizational Democracy," paper delivered at the 1974 Annual Meeting of the American Political Science Association.

[44] In postulating politics without parties I am, of course, swimming against the current of contemporary political theory. Apart from anarchists (who have been discredited) and a few Marxist humanists (who are considered benevolent utopians), hardly anyone has even registered such a "strange" idea. Let me therefore record at least one voice of support. It comes from Mihailo Marković, who, not unexpectedly, has been exposed to the same cultural environment and revolutionary experiences as myself. Marković has suggested that parties "might be gradually replaced by a pluralism of flexible *ad hoc* political organizations which would represent various interest groups, which would offer incomparably more opportunity for the direct par-

ticipation of each citizen, and which would offer a much wider range of programs and candidates. The distinguishing characteristics of these political organizations would be the absence of permanent party machines and party bureaucracies. They would no longer be instruments of the privileged elites which keep concentrated economic and political power in their own hands. Instead, they would become forms of genuine political democracy both direct and indirect" (*From Affluence to Praxis* [Ann Arbor: University of Michigan Press, 1974], pp. 166–67). The elimination of political parties need not represent a great difficulty or a complete break with tradition. There are already many signs of the decay of the party system (extraparliamentary opposition) and the delegitimation of political parties (decline in support for the parties as established by various surveys, the weakening of party loyalties, etc.). See J. Christiansen et al., "Political Parties and Capitalist Development," *Kapitalistate*, 1977, no. 6, pp. 7–38, espec. pp. 31–32.

[45] Dahl, *After the Revolution?*, p. 64.

[46] Both declarations were preceded and influenced by the postrevolutionary English Bill of Rights of 1689. Yet the latter bill was not intended to define general human rights; its purpose was to limit the power of the king by strengthening the power of Parliament and the courts.

[47] Forty-eight states voted in favor; six (etatist countries, South Africa, and Saudi Arabia) abstained. Let me add that even dictators like Salazar and Stalin had to recognize the same fundamental rights by including them, at least formally, into the Portuguese and Soviet constitutions, respectively.

[48] While the declaration was morally binding, the covenant is legally so. It was adopted with 106 votes in favor and none against. It entered into force on March 1976, when the number of ratifying countries reached thirty-five.

[49] This was well reflected in the first Russian postrevolutionary constitution of 1918, known as Lenin's Constitution. This constitution placed at the disposal of workers and peasants technical and material means for the publication of newspapers and books and also facilities for public gatherings. Yet, negative freedoms were not guaranteed, nor even mentioned. As a result, freedoms of expression and of assembly remained empty declarations.

[50] These rights, together with the right to fair wages, social security, and freedom from hunger, are protected by the 1066 International Covenant on Economic, Social and Cultural Rights. The recognition of these rights is an important contemporary achievement fully absent

at the time of the bourgeois revolutions. One might, perhaps, say that eighteenth-century bourgeois revolutions produced civil and political rights, while twentieth century anticapitalist revolutions produced economic and social rights.

[51] Article 8 of the Covenant on Civil and Political Rights explicitly forbids slavery and servitude but not hired labor. In other words, it condemns slaveowning and feudal orders but not capitalism or etatism. In this sense, the covenant is a representative document of its epoch.

[52] Writing about Britain—one of the oldest and most developed democracies in the bourgeois world—Frank Ward, a Labour Party officer, asked: "The right of the electorate to information free from inaccuracies and distortions will have to be established as a basic democratic right. The whole community must be able to influence the content of the media and challenge its value judgements instead of leaving it, as at present, in the hands of a narrow clique of newspaper proprietors operating through carefully selected editors and journalists who voluntarily conform to their standards, or in the hands of the tightly-knit establishment of the BBC and ITV" (*In Defence of Democratic Socialism* [London: Rye, 1978], p. 126).

[53] Two separate problems must be clearly distinguished: the *distribution* of control and the *total amount* of control exercised. "An organization may exert little control over its members and be seen by them as quite benign, even though control which is exercised is in the hands of a few leaders. Another organization may be extremely coercive of the individual member, even though its decisions are reached by and enforced by majority processes" (A. Tannenbaum and R. L. Kahn, *Participation in Union Locals* [Chicago: Row, Peterson, 1958], p. 237). Similarly Isaiah Berlin noted: "a man may leave a vigorous and genuinely 'participatory' democratic state in which the social or political pressures are too suffocating for him, for a climate where there may be less civil participation, but more privacy, a less dynamic and all embracing communal life, less gregariousness but also less surveillance" (*Four Essays on Liberty* [London: Oxford University Press, 1969], p. lvii).

CHAPTER 12

[1] L. Robbins, *An Essay on the Nature and Significance of Economic Science* (London: Macmillan, 1932), p. 113. Robbins' paradox is transformed into the "basic inconsistency in socialism" in the six editions of a book by William Loucks, who argues "that a socialist economy, with its necessary choice of comprehensive goals and its arbitrary pricing to those ends, cannot exist *without substantially interfering with either freedom of consumers' choice or the freedom of occupational choice or both.* If com-

prehensive goals are chosen, individual action must conform to them; whereas, if individual actions are left free, the comprehensive results will be determined thereby" (*Comparative Economic Systems* [New York: Harper and Row, 1961], p. 257). Loucks apparently is still unaware of the century-long experience indicating that "if individual actions are left free, the comprehensive results" will consist of business cycles, unemployment, monopoly distortions, and similar other unintended effects that replace free choice by the vagaries of the market. The commonsense conclusion that genuine consumer and producer freedom requires appropriate control of the market to make expectations and realizations coincide, somehow escapes a bourgeois mind. Commodity fetishism again.

[2] K. V. Ortrovitianov et al., *Politicheskaia ekonomiia* (Moscow: Gospolitizdat, 1955), chs. 29, 30.

[3] M. Dobb, *On Economic Theory and Socialism* (London: Routledge and Kegan Paul, 1955), p. 79.

[4] See B. Horvat, "The Rule of Accumulation in a Planned Economy," *Kyklos,* 1968, pp. 239–68.

[5] R. A. Nisbet, "Cooperation," in *International Encyclopedia of the Social Sciences* (New York: Macmillan, 1968), vol. 3, pp. 388–90, quote from pp. 388–89.

[6] A. Smith, *The Wealth of Nations* (New York: Modern Library, 1937), p. 423.

[7] B. Ward, "The Firm in Illyria: Market Syndicalism," *American Economic Review,* 1958, pp. 566–89.

[8] Since the critique is ideologically based, for the most part it is not scientifically interesting. All its essential points, developed at book length, can be found in H. Lepage, *Autogestion et capitalism* (Paris: Masson, 1978). For my critical evaluation of the book, see B. Horvat, "Autogestion: efficacité et théorie néo-classique," *Revue économique,* 1979, pp. 361–69.

[9] See Y. Simon and H. Tézenas du Montcel, *Economie des ressources humaines dans l'entreprise* (Paris: Masson, 1978).

[10] This was achieved admirably by Jaroslav Vanek in *The General Theory of Labor Managed Market Economies* (Ithaca, N.Y.: Cornell University Press, 1970).

[11] B. Horvat, "Prilog teoriji jugoslavenskog preduzeća," *Ekonomska analiza,* 1967, pp. 7–28.

[12] The two hypotheses about the behavior of the worker-managed firm—per capita income maximization and surplus maximization—were tested by a student of mine, Janez Prašnikar, in his master's dissertation, "Testiranje hipoteze o obnašanju samoupravnega podjetja," Zagreb University, 1979. Prašnikar examined forty Slovene firms. His findings corroborate the surplus maximization hypothesis.

[13] The other parameters used were: capital-output ratio $k = 3$, and average investment maturation period $m = 3$ years (B. Horvat, "Problemi u vezi s izborom stope investiranja," *Ekonomski pregled,* 1961, pp. 40–46).

[14] The argument is basically reproduced from my article, "The Optimum Rate of Investment Reconsidered," *Economic Journal,* 1965, pp. 572–76.

[15] For a formal model incorporating these features, see B. Horvat, "A Model of Maximal Economic Growth," *Kyklos,* 1972, pp. 215–28.

[16] If the maturation period is $m = 3$ years, the last three years of investment will have no effect on output. With the capital-output ratio $k = 4$, it will take four years for investment to be recuperated by increased production. If the share of consumption in output is $c = 0.6$, it will take $4{:}0.6 = 7$ years for investment to be recuperated by increased consumption. Thus, in order for output maximization not to conflict with consumption maximization, the life span of a generation must be longer than $T = 25 + 3 + 7 = 35$ years.

CHAPTER 13

[1] Marx made the same discovery three-quarters of a century earlier, but Keynes did not pay much attention to what he called "the underworld of Karl Marx." The ideological stupidity of an otherwise enlightened environment was well described by Joan Robinson, a leading Cambridge economist: "There was Great Britain with never less than a million workers unemployed, and there was I with my supervisor teaching me that it is logically impossible to have unemployment, because of Say's Law. Now comes Keynes and proves that Say's Law is nonsense (so did Marx, of course, but my supervisors never drew my attention to Marx's views on the subject)" (*On Re-reading Marx* [Cambridge: Students' Bookshop, 1953], pp. 19–20).

[2] In capitalist countries this type of inflation is the result of a struggle between unions and employers. When unions were weak—at the time of Marx and Keynes—it was unknown. In a self-management economy, it is generated by differential productivity growth in various industries unmatched by appropriate policy measures (see B. Horvat, *Ekonomska politika stabilizacije* [Zagreb: Naprijed, 1976]).

[3] See B. Horvat, "Kompenzacije kao instrument ujednačavanja uvjeta privređivanja," *Ekonomski pregled*, 1977, pp. 629–36.

[4] Individuals are not barred politically from establishing such foundations as well. Because of the egalitarian distribution of income, however, the possibility for this to happen is not great.

[5] Aristotle on the polis in *Politics* III, 130.

[6] The following example may provide an idea of the orders of magnitude involved. In Yugoslavia, where fiscal decentralization is relatively well developed—in fact, more thorough than anywhere else—communal budgets amount to 50 percent of all budgets not including defense. Communes account for the highest percentage of expenditures on public utilities (84 percent against 16 percent for the states) and on education (78 percent as against 22 percent for the states); in both cases federal expenditures are nil. See B. Horvat, "Yugoslav Economic Policy in the Post-War Period," *American Economic Review*, June 1971, supplement, p. 157.

CHAPTER 14

[1] There is a terminological difficulty here which may cause confusion. One speaks of bourgeois (not capitalist) revolutions and, in the reverse fashion, of socialist (mostly not proletarian) revolutions. In the first case it is the class, in the second the system, that characterizes the revolution. The reason for this is that the revolutionary bourgeoisie were not aware that they were building capitalism (the term did not even exist), while socialist revolutionaries often are not proletarians. A further complication arises from the fact that, as a rule, (violent) socialist revolutions result in etatism, not socialism. To avoid ambiguity and confusion, I use a negatively defined term and speak of anticapitalist revolution.

[2] *The New Economics,* trans. by B. Pierce (Oxford: Clarendon Press, 1966), p. 79. Since this is a point of great theoretical and practical significance, let me cite some other formulations of it. Three years before Preobrazhensky wrote his book, the well-known Marxist philosopher, György Lukács, an active participant in the Hungarian Revolution of 1918, wrote: "Surely, also, a proletarian revolution would be unthinkable if its economic presumptions and preconditions were not already produced in the lap of capitalist society by the development of capitalist production. There is an enormous difference between the two types of development, however, in that, *as a mode of economy, capitalism already developed within feudalism, destroying it.* At the same time, it would be a fantastic utopia to imagine that anything in the direction of socialism can originate within capitalism except, on the one hand, *objective economic presumptions of its possibilities*—which,

however, can be *transformed* into real elements of a socialist mode of production only after capitalism's destruction . . . —and, on the other hand, the development of the proletariat as a class" (*Geschichte und Klassenbewusstein* [Berlin: Malik, 1923]; Serbo-Croatian translation [Zagreb: Naprijed, 1970], pp. 337–78). The best-known formulation of the same thesis was given by Stalin in 1926 (see his *Voprosy leninizma* [Moscow: Ogiz, 1945], pp. 111). The most recent version of the doctrine has been aptly formulated by Ernest Mandel: "Marxists reject all theories according to which a gradual transformation of the capitalist mode of production, or a gradual conquest of power within the framework of bourgeois-democratic state institutions, would be possible. For them, according to their basic theory of classes, models of production and state power are *structures* which cannot change their basic features. . . . Such a change presupposes their overthrow, the substitution of one class rule for another . . . of one predominant set of relations and production for another. This is only possible under conditions of *revolutionary crisis,* which cannot be artificially 'produced,' but which arises unavoidably at certain moments out of the inner contradictions of bourgeois society" ("Late Capitalism, State Power and the Transition to Socialism in Western Europe," symposium paper, Uppsala, June 1977, p. 11 [mimeographed]). Examples are May 1968 in France and March–November 1975 in Portugal.

[3] J. Stalin, *Ob osnovah leninizma* (1924) (Moscow: Gospolitizdat, 1945), p. 50. Stalin took over this theory from Lenin, Trotsky, and Bukharin.

[4] P. M. Sweezy and C. Bettelheim, *On the Transition to Socialism* (New York: Monthy Review, 1971) p. 113.

[5] Declared J. Stalin: "when the *entire* leadership *completely* passed into the hands of one party, which does not share and cannot share the ruling of the state with another party. This we call the dictatorship of the proletariat" (*Voprosy leninizma* [Moscow: Ogiz, 1945], pp. 163).

[6] E. Mandel, "Zehn Thesen zur sozialökonomischen Gesetzmässigkeit der Übergangsgesellschaft zwischen Kapitalismus und Sozialismus," in P. Hennicke, ed., *Probleme des Sozialismus und der Übergangsgesellschaften Suhrkamp* (Frankfurt am Main, 1973), pp. 15–37, espec. pp. 16–22. Mandel clearly was inspired by James Burnham; the latter drew a very different conclusion, however. In his *Managerial Revolution* (New York: John Day, 1941), Burnham argued that, just as the oppressed peasantry did not succeed the feudal lords but both were displaced by the bourgeoisie, so the proletariat would not succeed capitalists but both would be replaced by managers as the new ruling class.

[7] A Gallup report indicated that, in 1973–77, only 14 percent of the American population lacked confidence in the "free enterprise" system. Robert Lane reported interviews with working and lower middle class men who "expressed almost no resentment of the very rich, but

considerable resentment of the poor living on welfare" (R. Lane, "The Legitimacy Bias," in B. Denitch, ed., *Legitimation of Regimes* [London: Sage, 1979], pp. 55–80, espec. pp. 64 and 70–71).

[8] In Russia almost one-half of the workers queried answered Yes to the question, "Do you consider yourself to be one of the proprietors of socialist production?"; 22.5 percent replied No and 22.1 percent did not know. David Lane describes the Soviet worker as an "incorporated worker" who "has certain forms of solidarity with the factory. He accepts the authority structure on the basis of its performance capacity. He participates actively in improving production, and he is closer to the administration both socially and politically than the worker in a capitalist society" (D. Lane, "Soviet Industrial Workers," in Denitch, *Legitimation of Regimes,* pp. 177–94, espec. pp. 184 and 190).

[9] Young Marx is responsible to some extent for the spurious predictability of "historical necessity." In *The Holy Family* (1845), he and Engels wrote: "It is not a matter of what this or that proletarian or even the proletariat as a whole *pictures* at present as its goal. It is a matter of *what the proletariat is in actuality* and what, in accordance with this *being*, it will historically be compelled to do" (quoted in R. Tucker, *The Marx-Engels Reader* [New York: W. W. Norton, 1972], p. 105). True enough. But we are still left with the task of finding out what the proletariat will do. And in this respect history has mostly ignored the recommendations of well-meaning reformers and revolutionaries. I shall take up the same question and the same quotation in section IIA.

[10] Mancur Olson notes that "unless there is coercion or some other special device to make individuals act in their common interest, *rational, self-interested individuals will not act to achieve their common or group interests.*" He then cites the case where over 90 percent of workers "will not attend meetings or participate in union affairs; yet over 90 percent will vote to force themselves to belong to the union and make considerable dues payments to it." He concludes that "the workers were not inconsistent: their actions and attitudes were a model of rationality when they wished that everyone would attend meetings and failed to attend themselves. For if a strong union is in the members' interests, they will presumably be better off if the attendance is high, but . . . an individual worker has no economic incentive to attend a meeting" (*The Logic of Collective Action* [Cambridge, Mass.: Harvard University Press, 1974], pp. 2, 86).

[11] Sweezy and Bettelheim, *Transition to Socialism.*

[12] This view was common among the leaders of the Second International. In 1901, in a speech concerning the project of the program of the Austrian Social Democratic Party, Karl Kautsky insisted that modern socialism was created by individual members of the bourgeois

intelligentsia; that, therefore, a socialist consciousness must be introduced into the proletarian class struggle from outside; and that this struggle does not generate it spontaneously. In Russia, Lenin was preceded by Petr Tkachev, who argued that the masses needed an intellectual elite that would organize and inspire them to fight against the misery that surrounded them. (See F. Venturi, *Roots of Revolution* [London: Weidenfeld and Nicolson, 1960], p. 402.) Tkachev's organizational ideas were applied by the clandestine populist association Zemlia i Volia [Land and Liberty] and were later developed by Lenin into organizational principles of the Bolshevik Party.

[13] S. Mallet, *Nova radnička klasa* (Belgrade: Komunist, 1970).

[14] A third, value element is often added. M. Marković defines revolution as "any qualitative transformation that contributes to the liberation of man" ("Dialectic Today," in M. Marković and G. Petrović, eds., *Praxis* [London: Reidel, 1979], pp. 3–43, espec. p. 21). Revolution is supposed to be something good, progressive. For this reason, today gangs of political criminals, such as Pinochet in Chile or Papadopulos in Greece, call their activities "revolutions." For analytical purposes, it seems desirable that the concept of revolution be stripped of value connotations and used in a technical sense. It is much easier to agree on whether a historical event represented a structural change than on whether it was progressive. Determination of the progressiveness or regressiveness of a revolution is a matter of a very difficult, separate analysis—in fact, of a full-fledged social theory.

[15] The banker Laborde and the wealthy merchant Boscary provided funds to equip insurgents with arms and compensate them for lost wages (C. G. Lefebvre, *The Coming of the French Revolution* [New York: Vintage Books, 1962], p. 86).

[16] It is of some interest to note that Lyon, the most industrially developed city in France, became one of the centers of counterrevolution.

[17] N. Birnbaum, *The Crisis of Industrial Society* (London: Oxford University Press, 1969), p. 28. The first spinning mill equipped with a steam engine was put into operation in England in 1785.

[18] C. Brinton, *The Anatomy of Revolution* (New York: Vintage Books, 1960), p. 101.

[19] See E. H. Norman, *Japan's Emergence as a Modern State* (New York: Institute of Pacific Relations, 1940).

[20] The Cambridge historian John Dunn gave the following description of events: "When the peasant armies of Zapata challenged the Constitutionalist government in 1914–15, the organized working class was either neutral or favoured the government against what seemed to them reactionary hordes. . . . There could be nothing in common between peasants organized for and by themselves and a proletariat

most of which was at least as anti-foreign or anti-clerical as it was anti-capitalist. The Mexican working class in the face of revolution decided in the great majority to accept being bought off for the largest amount they could get and for the most part they have stuck to their choice ever since" (*Modern Revolutions* [Cambridge: Cambridge University Press, 1974], p. 69).

[21] A. de Tocqueville, writing around the middle of the last century, seems to have been the first to notice this: "Thus it was precisely in those parts of France where there had been most improvement that popular discontent ran highest. . . . Patiently endured so long as it seemed beyond redress, a grievance comes to appear intolerable once the possibility of removing it crosses men's minds. . . . At the height of its power feudalism did not inspire so much hatred as it did on the eve of its eclipse" (*The Old Regime and the French Revolution* [Garden City, N.Y.: Doubleday, 1955], pp. 176–77).

[22] It is often disputed whether the American War of Independence also had the character of a social revolution. There was no feudalism in America, it is argued; capitalism existed before the Revolution as well as after, and so there could be no revolution. Though the European type of feudalism did not exist in America (it did not develop in all parts of Europe either), the society was definitely prebourgeois. There was a "union of kinship, solidarity and land," as the social environment was described aptly by Robert Nisbet ("The Social Impact of the American Revolution," *Dialogue,* 1975, no. 1, pp. 30–39, quote from p. 34). Primogeniture and entail, together with very large estates, established great landowners as an indigenous aristocracy. In addition to independent small farmers, below the landowning class were the relatively numerous tenant farmers, indentured servants, and Negro slaves. A high degree of localism, a fusion of economic and political power, and an absence of government centralization were further characteristics of the prerevolutionary environment. Finally, the church was legally established. All these aspects of social life were radically changed. Many great landowners took the Loyalist side. They were expelled and their estates confiscated, which made possible a redistribution of large areas of land. Primogeniture and entail were abolished in almost all states within a decade. Freedom of conscience, written into the first constitutional amendment, secured the disestablishment of religion. Slaves were freed in the northern states. Noble titles and ranks were abolished. The parafeudal society of rank and status was replaced fairly rapidly by a society of bourgeois equality.

[23] Q. Hoare and G. N. Smith, eds., *Selections from the Prison Notebooks of Antonio Gramsci* (London: Lawrence and Wishart, 1971), p. 6, see also pp. 4–8.

[24] L. P. Edwards, *The Natural History of Revolution* (Chicago: University of Chicago Press, 1927), p. 41; Brinton, *Anatomy of Revolution*, pp. 41–45, 267.

25 See F. Venturi, *Roots of Revolution* (London: Weidenfeld and Nicolson, 1960).

26 F. Engels, "On Authority," in K. Marx and F. Engels, *Selected Works,* vol. 1 (Moscow, 1958), p. 638.

27 Quoted in H. J. Laski, *The Socialist Tradition in the French Revolution* (London: Fabian Society/Allen and Unwin, 1930), p. 23.

28 I. Deutscher, *Razoružani prorok* (Zagreb: Liber, 1978), p. 18. T. Draper quotes a figure of 11,000 members for May 1917 (*The Roots of American Communism* [New York: Viking Press, 1959], p. 101).

29 I. Deutscher, "Maoism: Its Origin and Outlook," in R. Blackburn, ed., *Revolution and Class Struggle* (Sussex: Harvester, 1978), pp. 191–223, espec. p. 193.

30 *Democracy in America* (1840) (New York: Vintage Books, 1957), p. 318.

31 This analogy belongs to Marx (*Misère de la philosophie,* 1846). It is appealing but also misleading. There is a fundamental asymmetry in the positions of the two classes. The bourgeoisie were *not* an exploited class and remain the *ruling* class in the new *class* society. The proletariat were an *exploited* class and *cannot* become the ruling class in a *classless* society.

32 This is the mature formulation of the original idea expressed in 1843 as a sociophilosophical postulate. The 25-year-old radical democrat and patriot Karl Marx asked: "Where is there a *real* possibility of emancipation in Germany?" He continued emphatically: "*This is our reply.* A class must be formed which has *radical chains,* a class in civil society which is not a class of civil society, a class which is a dissolution of all classes, a sphere of society which has a universal character because its sufferings are universal, and which does not claim a *particular redress* because the wrong which is done to it is not a *particular wrong* but *wrong in general.* There must be formed a sphere of society which claims no traditional status, a sphere which is not opposed to particular consequences but is totally opposed to the assumptions of the German political system, a sphere, finally . . . which is . . . a *total loss* of humanity and which can only redeem itself by a *total redemption of humanity.* This dissolution of society, as a particular class, is the *proletariat.*" In this way the old Judeo-Christian vision of a redeemer was revived and secularized. Marx, however, was too much of a scholar to remain at that level; most of his epigones were not, and the consequences have already been indicated. Another passage is both revealing and full of implications: "Just as philosophy finds its *material weapons* in the proletariat, so the proletariat finds its *intellectual* weapons in philosophy. And once the lightning of thought has penetrated deeply into this virgin soil of the people, the Germans will emancipate themselves and become *men*" ("Critique of Hegel's Phi-

losophy of Right," in *The Marx-Engels Reader*, ed. by R. Tucker [New York: W. W. Norton, 1972], pp. 22–23). In our own century, the muse of history transformed philosophers into party leaders and replaced Germans with various other peoples. Two years after the latter passage was written, the idea of the "historical interests of the proletariat"—so much abused today—was introduced. Because of the reasons cited above, "the proletariat itself can and must liberate itself. But it cannot liberate itself without destroying its own living conditions. It cannot do so without destroying *all* the inhuman living conditions of contemporary society which are concentrated in its own situation. . . . It is a matter of *what the proletariat is* in actuality and what, in accordance with this *being*, it will historically be compelled to do. Its goal and its historical action are prefigured in . . . its own life-situations. . . . There is no need to harp on the fact that a large part of the English and French proletariat is already *conscious* of its historical task and is continually working to bring this consciousness to full clarity" (Marx and Engels, *The Holy Family*, quoted in ibid., pp. 105–6). Was it not true of the slaves and the serfs as well, one might ask, that they "could not liberate themselves without destroying their own living conditions"? And what were they "historically compelled to do"?

[33] See, for instance, Mao Zedong, *Chinese Revolution and the Communist Party of China,* December 1939 (*Kineska revolucija.* [Belgrade: Vuk Karadžić, 1968], p. 47).

[34] Friedrich Engels attributed the opportunistic attitudes of English workers to colonial exploitation and world market domination, in which they participated along with the bourgeoisie, and to the fact that, among other concessions, the ruling class undertook to fulfill the requests of the Chartist program ("English Elections," 1874; see also the letter to Karl Kautsky, September 12, 1882).

[35] P. Sweezy, *Modern Capitalism and Other Essays* (New York: Monthly Review, 1972), p. 160. Howard Wachtel shares this opinion and describes the American scene as follows: "radical economists have identified several dimensions along which labour is stratified. . . . Summarizing briefly their argument, labour is stratified by industry and occupation (U.S. Steel had between 45,000 and 50,000 separate job titles), by race . . . , by sex and by ethnic groups. The educational system reinforces work stratification by means of the hierarchical differentiation in the school system. . . . The net effect of all this is to divide labour along status lines, thereby mitigating its class solidarity, while at the same time legitimizing the inequalities inherent in the functioning of capitalism" (Class Consciousness and Stratification in the Labour Market," in R. C. Edwards, et al., eds., *Labor Market Segmentation* [Lexington, Mass.: D. C. Heath, 1979], p. 106).

[36] From 1928 to 1933, the share of workers' parties (socialists and communists) in the total vote decreased by 8 percent; that of the

conservative party, by 40 percent; and that of middle-class parties, by 79 percent (S. M. Lipset, *Political Man* [New York: Doubleday, 1963], p. 139). A caveat must be added, however. Though manual workers (and even more so, peasants) were substantially underrepresented in the Nazi Party in 1933, it is nevertheless true that they comprised 31.5 percent of all members; industrial and agricultural workers represented 42.5 percent of the members of the Italian Fascist Party in 1921 (R. Bendix, "Social Stratification and Political Power," *American Political Science Review*, 1952, pp. 357–75). Industrial workers represented 51 percent of the Hungarian (Arrow Cross) Fascist Party in 1937, while they comprised only 23 percent of the population (I. Deak, quoted in H. Kahn and A. Wiener, *The Year 2000* [London: Macmillan, 1967], p. 269). These percentages correspond to the share of workers in the communist parties.

37 Marx saw this very clearly. In the last paragraph of his lectures "Wage, Price and Profit," delivered at the two meetings of the General Council of the International in 1865, he suggested the following conclusion: "Trade unions work well as centres of resistance against the encroachments of capital. . . . They fail generally from limiting themselves to a guerilla war against the effects of the existing system, instead of simultaneously trying to change it, instead of using their organized force as a lever for the final emancipation of the working class, that is to say, the ultimate abolition of the wage system."

38 In 1820, one-half of all factory workers were children of 9 and 10 years working thirteen hours per day. Five-sixths of all persons imprisoned in 1830 in the northern and middle Atlantic states were debtors.

39 Even today social mobility seems to be higher in the United States than in other capitalist countries. G. Lenski provides the following data for upward and downward mobility across the manual-nonmanual line:

United States	34%	Denmark	30%	West Germany	25%
Sweden	32	Norway	30	Japan	25
Britain	31	France	29	Italy	20

Source: G. Lenski, *Power and Privilege* (New York: McGraw-Hill, 1966), p. 411.

40 R. Lane, "The Legitimacy Bias," in Denitch, *Legitimation of Regimes*, p. 63.

41 Quoted in I. Bernstein, *The Lean Years* (Baltimore: Penguin, 1966), p. 381.

42 Ibid.

43 Quoted in M. Dobb, *Studies in the Development of Capitalism* (New York: International Publishers, 1963), pp. 354–57.

44 Quoted in ibid.

[45] Ibid.

[46] S. M. Lipset, *Political Man,* p. 401. S. Cohen observes: "Labour leaders are not a breed apart from other men. They live in a society where people are stratified and accorded status on the basis of the symbols that mark life within the society. The typical labour leader is not a deviant in the free enterprise society. Since he accepts free enterprise in principle, he has no quarrel with the basic forces that motivate men in such a society. On the contrary, he is motivated by these very forces. He wants to be successful. In his case that means that he wants power, prestige, the respect of the people he relates to and a salary that is large enough to give him status as well as comfort" (*Labour in the United States* [Columbus, Ohio: Merrill, 1970], p. 193).

[47] "It is our guess," write S. M. Lipset and R. Bendix, "that the creed of the 'individual enterpriser' has become by and large a working class preoccupation. Though it may have animated both working class and middle class in the past, it is no longer a middle-class ideal today. Instead, people in the middle class aspire to become professionals and, as a second choice, upper-white-collar workers" (*Class, Status and Power* [Glencoe, Ill.: Free Press, 1953], p. 462).

[48] The 1963 convention of the AFL-CIO adopted a resolution urging all affiliates to remove "the last vestiges of racial discrimination" (Cohen, *Labour in the United States*, p. 163).

[49] It should be pointed out, however, that on the whole workers (and the lower middle class) displayed a more positive attitude toward ending the Vietnam war than the upper middle class, which was in favor of tough options (see R. F. Hamilton, *Class and Politics in the United States* [New York: John Wiley and Sons, 1972], p. 453).

[50] In 1946, Ernest Bevin, Labour government foreign minister and former trade union secretary, declared in Parliament: "I am not prepared to sacrifice the British Empire, because I know that if the British Empire fell . . . it would mean the standard of life of our constituents would fall considerably" (R. Blackburn, ed., *Revolution and Class Struggle* [Sussex: Harvester, 1978], p. 356).

Arghiri Emmanuel described the economic interests at stake in the following terms: "When . . . the relative importance of the national exploitation from which a working class suffers through belonging to the proletariat diminishes continually as compared with that from which it benefits through belonging to a privileged nation, a moment comes when the aim of increasing the national income in absolute terms prevails over that of improving the relative share of one part of the nation over the other. From that point onward the principle of national solidarity ceases to be challenged in principle, however radical and violent the struggle over the sharing of the cake may be. Thereafter a *de facto* united front of the workers and capitalists of the well-to-do countries, directed against the poor nations, coexists with an international trade-union struggle over the sharing of the loot.

. . . To an increasing extent the attitude of the working class in the advanced capitalist countries as a whole in relation to the Third World is becoming like that of the British working class toward the rest of the world all through the nineteenth century: struggles for wage-and-hour demands . . . inside the country; a united national front against the outside world, with the working class sometimes taking up vanguard positions" (*Unequal Exchange* [New York: Monthly Review, 1972], pp. 180, 182). This generalization, however, must not be interpreted as implying an absolute necessity or inevitability. As usual, there is a great scope for social action. Swiss workers voted against extending aid to less developed countries; in Sweden survey research indicates that workers favor such extension.

[51] In South Africa white workers, led by union and communist leaders, engaged in an armed rebellion against the government in order to prevent the employment of Africans in the mines under conditions similar to theirs. This 1921 uprising marked the beginning of the apartheid regime. It also produced the most bizarre slogan in all of labor history: "Workers of the world unite and fight for a white South Africa." Today no progressive white working class organization exists in South Africa (R. Davies, "The White Working-Class in South Africa," *New Left Review,* 1973, no. 82, pp. 40–59). In Algeria the European proletariat "mobilized in defense of French Algeria and supplied the OAS killers. For them it was a question of life and death. *Their* privileges was [*sic*] their quality as Europeans and whites. . . . They earned in a few days what an Algerian earned in a month" (Emmanuel, *Unequal Exchange*, p. 184). White workers in Bissau behaved in the same way. British dockers barred colored labor from the docks.

[52] Lipset, *Political Man,* p. 108.

[53] H. Arendt, *Elemente und Ursprünge totaler Herrschaft* (Frankfurt am Main: Europaïsche Verlaganstalt, 1962), pp. 460–61.

[54] Staffer provided the following profile of attitudes toward civil liberties for communists (the sample comprised males, excluding retirees):

Percent tolerant of those with opinion

	Professionals and semiprofessionals	Proprietors, managers, and officials	Manual workers	Farmers and farm laborers
Communists should be allowed to speak	53	41	27	20
Communist books should be in the library	62	44	25	18
Communists ought to be jailed	68	58	36	28

Source: In Hamilton, *Class and Politics*, p. 436.

Attitudes toward atheists were similar. Even proprietors, managers, and officials appear to be substantially more tolerant than workers. By far the most tolerant are professionals; the least tolerant are farmers. Hamilton points out that worker authoritarianism regarding communists indicates acceptance of the leads provided by government and private "opinion leaders," while intolerance toward atheism is explained to some degree by the cultural conservatism of the small towns and rural environments from which many workers come (*Class and Politics*, p. 448).

[55] The following are some pertinent survey research results. Workers (unskilled and semiskilled workers more than skilled) prefer one-party systems to multiparty systems more than any other occupational group, though farmers come close. The same is true for the less educated as against the more educated. Only farmers and farm workers are less tolerant than workers with respect to civil liberties issues. Political tolerance increases with education (Lipset, *Political Man*, pp. 93, 95, 101). A. Kornhauser found that industrial workers tend to oppose racial equality—nearly 60 percent of Detroit factory workers held segregationist views—and show great admiration for strict authority. He suggested that the same occupational and social disadvantages that tend to produce low personal morale and other features of poor mental health also lead to certain antidemocratic feelings (*Mental Health of the Industrial Worker* [New York: John Wiley and Sons, 1965], pp. 212, 233, 234, 261, 267). Emphasis on the intrinsic qualities of a job (how much opportunity the job provides for exercising one's abilities, how interesting the work is, how much opportunity it offers to help people) increases with socioeconomic status, while emphasis on extrinsic qualities (hours of work, fringe benefits, how tiring the work is, job security, absence of too much pressure) decreases (M. L. Kohn, *Class and Conformity* [Homewood, Ill.: Dorsey Press, 1972], p. 78). The lower the socioeconomic position of an individual, the more rigidly conservative his view of man and of social institutions and the less his tolerance of noncomformity—which are characteristics of authoritarian attitudes (ibid., p. 80). German fathers of the lowest of the four strata rank the trait of "obedience" as the most valuable; American lower class fathers rank it in second place (after "honesty") (K. O. Hondrich, *Theorie der Herrschaft* [Frankfurt am Main: Suhrkamp, 1973], p. 175; see also W. H. Sewell, "Social Class and Personal Adjustment," *International Encyclopedia of the Social Sciences* [New York: Macmillan, 1968], vol. 10, pp. 222–25). Though the two working class parties in Germany resisted naziism more than bourgeois parties, the difference was not dramatic. Erich Fromm, himself a German and also a contemporary observer, explains the reasons: "The onslaught of Naziism did not meet with political opponents, the majority of whom were ready to fight for their ideas. Many of the adherents of the leftist parties, although they believed in their party programs as long as their parties had authority, were

ready to resign when the hour of crisis arrived. . . . A great number of them were of a personality type that has many of the traits of . . . the authoritarian character. They had a deep-seated respect and longing for established authority. The emphasis of socialism on individual independence versus authority, on solidarity versus individualistic seclusion, was not what these workers really wanted on the basis of their personality structure" (*Escape from Freedom* [New York: Rinehart, 1941], p. 281). Murray Bookchin, an American anarchist, observes: "From the family, through the school and religious institutions, the mass media, to the factory and finally trade union and 'revolutionary' party, capitalist society conspires to foster obedience, hierarchy, the work ethic and authoritarian discipline in the working class. . . . The factory and the class organizations that spring from it play the most compelling role in promoting well-regulated, almost unconscious docility in mature workers—a docility that manifests itself not so much in characterless passivity as in a pragmatic commitment to hierarchical organizations and authoritarian leaders" ("Introductory Essay," in S. Dolgoff, ed., *The Anarchist Collectives* [New York: Free Life, 1974], p. xxxiv).

56 Generally, workers' parties seem to be less authoritarian than bourgeois parties. An examination of teachers in Belgium, England, France, West Germany, the Netherlands, Norway, and Sweden showed that teachers who preferred conservative, Christian, and Liberal parties scored higher on authoritarianism than those who preferred Social Democratic, Labor, and Communist parties (S. Rokkan, *Citizens, Elections, Parties* [Oslo: Universitetsforlaget, 1970], p. 337).

57 J. Županov, *Samoupravljanje i društvena moć* (Zagreb: Naše teme, 1969), p. 56.

58 V. Rus, "Novi model samoupravljanja i njegova relevantna društvena okolina," in J. Obradovič, V. Rus, and J. Županov, eds., *Proizvodne organizacije i samoupravljanje* (Zagreb: Filozofski fakultet, 1975), p. 50.

59 Ž. Marković, "Samoupravljanje i klasna svest komunista," *Gledišta,* 1975, pp. 609–20, espec. pp. 618–19.

60 Ideological dimensions were defined as follows:

Self-government as against centralism, bureaucratism, and state managerialism
Openness toward the world or internationalism as against isolationism
Modernism as against traditionalism.
Acceptance of social ownership as against insistence on private ownership
Humanism, i.e., the acceptance of man as a supreme value, as against treating him as a means

Collectivism as against individualism, i.e., importance attributed to collective as against individual interests
Materialist orientation (hedonism, utilitarian attitudes, consumerism) as against nonmaterial orientation (idealism, spiritual values, asceticism)

Persons were grouped into three categories according to whether they tended toward one or the other polar view or showed mixed attitudes.

Proportion of Persons in the Social Group Expressing a Preference for the Given Value (in percent)

	Self-government	Openness toward world	Modernism	Social property	Humanism	Collectivism	Materialist orientation
Humanist intelligentsia	86	81	77	75	65	62	48
Technical intelligentsia	76	73	71	77	60	58	55
Industrial skilled workers	72	47	39	75	42	52	63
Unskilled urban workers	55	38	27	65	45	47	67
Peasants	34	27	8	37	44	25	66

Source: D. Pantić, "Ideološke orijentacije i ideološki sistemi društvenih slojeva," in *Društveni slojevi i njihova svijest* (Belgrade: Institut društvenih nauka, 1975), charts 1–8 (mimeographed).

Note that for materialist orientation, the ranking is reversed, which is what one would expect. The data should be interpreted with caution, for in Yugoslavia the self-government orientation is an official ideology and better-educated strata are more likely to give "correct" answers, thus exaggerating the differences. The first conclusion drawn by the author in interpreting the results of his study is rather characteristic: "The members of higher social strata . . . are more than others makers of the self-governing ideological system and as an avant-garde most completely see the historical interests of the working class reflected in that system" (Pantić, "Ideološke orijentacije," p. 179). Why should they see the interests of the working class and not their own?

61 M. Janićijević, "Predstave o društvu i socijalne identifikacije društvenih slojeva," in *Društveni slojevi*, p. 118.

62 N. Rot and N. Havelka, *Nacionalna vezanost i vrednosti kod srednjoškolske omladine* (Belgrade: Institut društvenih nauka, 1973), p. 247.

[63]

	Religious believers (in percent)
Peasants	97.0
Laborers and operatives	66.0
Skilled workers	45.5
White collar workers	40.2
Intellectuals	25.0

Source: S. Vrcan, "Radništvo, religija, crkva," *Revija za sociologiju*, 1977, p. 12.

[64] The following statement by Karl Kautsky, chief theoretician of the Second International, indicates how pseudorationalist reasoning was substituted for empirical analysis: "Being the lowest of all classes, [the proletariat] is also the most democratic of all classes" (*Die Soziale Revolution* [Berlin: Vorwärts, 1904], p. 5).

[65] Studying the attitudes of British affluent workers, John Goldthorpe and his associates found absence of a solidarity orientation (*The Affluent Worker in the Class Structure* [Cambridge: Cambridge University Press, 1971], p. 157). S. M. Miller and F. Riesman cited antielitism, outspokenness, and orientations toward cooperation and informality as prodemocratic attitudes of American workers, as against antidemocratic middle class conventionalism, competitiveness, status concern, fear of authority, overintellectualism, and snobbery. On the other hand, they identified an authoritarian potential of workers consisting of the desire for strong leadership and definite structure, anti-intellectualism, and a punitive ("tough") attitude toward the violation of law ("Working-Class Authoritarianism: A Critique of Lipset," *British Journal of Sociology*, 1961, pp. 263–76, espec. p. 272).

[66] The basic difference between the old and the new middle class consists in the fact that the former owns property while the latter generally does not, but is hired to do a job. Consequently, while the former has a bourgeois existence, the latter has at most a bourgeois life-style. Since they belong to the genus of hired labor—like workers—middle class groups that do not hold managerial and other commanding jobs are potential candidates for proletarianization.

[67] In the United States, industrial workers represented the following percentages of the labor force: 1900, 36 percent; 1950, 41 percent; 1970, 35 percent. For male workers only (females were increasingly taking clerical and sales jobs), the percentages are as follows: 1900, 38 percent; 1950, 48 percent; 1970, 47 percent. If service workers are included in the category of blue collar workers, we get the following percentages: 1900, 45 percent; 1950, 52 percent; 1970, 47 percent (*Historical Statistics of the United States*, 1970, p. 225). The share of manual labor attained a maximum in 1950. In West Germany, the share of workers in the active population reached a peak around 1955 and, in three characteristic years, was as follows: 1925, 47 percent;

1955, 52 percent; 1968, 47 percent (K. Meschkat and O. Negt, eds., *Gesellschaftsstrukturen* [Frankfurt am Main: Suhrkamp, 1973], p. 33).

[68] Shifts in the sectoral employment structure in the last century and a half can be illustrated by the data available for Britain and the United States.

Composition of the Labor Force (in percent)

	Great Britain			United States		
	1811	1951	1963	1820	1950	1964
Agriculture, forestry, fishing	34	5	4	72	13	7
Manufacturing, mining, construction	39	49	47	12	37	34
Services	27	46	49	16	50	59

Source: R. Richta et al., *Civilizacija na raskršću* (Belgrade: Komunist, 1972), p. 315.

Relative industrial employment reached a maximum around 1950.

[69] In their 1921 Görlitz Program, German majority Social Democrats proclaimed: "Die Sozialdemokratische Partei Deutschland ist die Partei des arbeitenden Volkes in Stadt und Land" [the Social Democratic Party of Germany is the party of the working people in city and country].

[70] Here I respond to a critique raised by my colleague Jozo Županov.

[71] The periodization used is based essentially on the studies of G. D. H. Cole (*Studies in Class Structure* [London: Routledge and Kegan Paul, 1955], pp. 37–40) and Z. Bauman (*Between Class and Elite* [Manchester: Manchester University Press, 1972]).

[72] E. P. Thompson, *The Making of the English Working Class* (London: Gollancz, 1964), p. 193.

[73] Frank Ward provides a very impressive illustration: "in relation to the knowledge of the time, the ability levels of the skilled carpenter or stone mason of 1800 would rank on a par with today's computer manager or middle executive. Intelligence and mental agility would equate; only the tools have changed as technology has altered" (*In Defence of Democratic Socialism* [London: Rye, 1978], p. 76). The *Book of English Trades* lists apothecary, attorney, and optician alongside carpenter, currier, tailor, and potter (see Thompson, *English Working Class*, p. 237).

[74] Bauman, *Between Class and Elite*, p. 41. Around the middle of the century, H. Mayhew observed that artisans were "almost to a man red-hot politicians. They are sufficiently educated and thoughtful to have a sense of their importance in the state." On the other hand, "the unskilled labourers are a different class of people. As yet they are as unpolitical as footmen, and instead of entertaining violent democratic opinions, they appear to have no political opinions whatever;

or, if they do . . . they rather lean towards the maintenance of 'things as they are,' than towards the ascendancy of the working people" (quoted in Thompson, *English Working Class*, p. 240).

[75] E. J. Hobsbawm, *Labouring Men* (London: Weidenfeld and Nicolson, 1968), p. 297.

[76] Quoted in W. Lazonick, "The Subjection of Labour to Capital," *Review of Radical Political Economics*, 1978, pp. 1–31, quote from p. 22.

[77] In a letter to Adolph Sorge (December 7, 1889), Engels described these workers as a "worker aristocracy" and added that what was most disgusting was that they were impregnated by bourgeois "respectability." Hobsbawm, a contemporary writer, noted: "The artisan creed with regard to the labourers is that the latter are an inferior class and that they should be made to know and kept in their place." Hobsbawm quoted the secretary of the Boilermakers' Union, who, appalled at the idea of a laborer being allowed to do craftsmen's work, asserted that "it would not be desirable for a man of one class to go to another class." Hobsbawm also noted that most members of the present-day Amalgamated Engineering Union would not have been admitted to its predecessor (*Labouring Men*, pp. 275, 325).

[78] This was the only socialist interlude in all of American political history. Eugene Debs, a union organizer and presidential candidate of the Social Democratic Party formed in 1898, polled 96,000 votes. The socialist vote quadrupled in the 1904 election, and in 1912 Debs collected 897,011 votes, representing 5.9 percent of the total cast. Soon afterward political socialism had already begun to go downhill.

[79] Consequently, "most full-time officers rate themselves among the holders of middle class posts" (H. A. Clegg, A. J. Killick, and R. Adams, *Trade Union Officers* [Oxford: Blackwell, 1961], pp. 85, 90).

[80] More than one-half of former British trade union officials become civil servants or officials in state corporations; one-tenth of them take managerial jobs in private industry; and only one-tenth return to the shop floor (M. Kidron, *Western Capitalism Since the War* [Harmondsworth: Penguin, 1970], p. 125).

[81] In 1971 clerks earned slightly less than all male manual workers on average (J. Westergaard and H. Resler, *Class in a Capitalist Society* [London: Heinemann, 1975], p. 76). At about the same time in Soviet industry the wages of clerical and office personnel amounted to 81 percent of workers' wages (M. Yanowitch, *Social and Economic Inequality in the Soviet Union* [London: Robertson, 1977], p. 30).

[82] The following data compiled by Lennart Forsebäck regarding the percentage of employees belonging to unions are suggestive:

	Blue collar	White collar	Together
France			25
United States			30
West Germany			35
Japan			35
Italy			45
Britain	50	35	
Norway	80	50	
Denmark	85	55	
Sweden	95	75	

Source: L. Forsebäck, *Industrial Relations and Employment in Sweden* (Stockholm: Swedish Institute, 1976), pp. 30–31.

Forsebäck points out that, in Sweden, "it is indicative of the times that the concept of wage earner has practically come to replace the previous categorization blue-collar/white-collar in public documents and in everyday use of language" (*Industrial Relations*, pp. 30–31).

[83] *The Affluent Worker in the Class Structure* (Cambridge: Cambridge University Press, 1971), p. 27. In an earlier paper, also concerned with the British scene, J. Goldthorpe and D. Lockwood explained the reasons for this convergence: "On the side of the working class, twenty years of near full employment, the gradual erosion of the traditional, work-based community, the progressive bureaucratization of trade unionism and the institutionalization of industrial conflict have all operated in the same direction to reduce the solidary nature of communal attachments and collective action. At the same time, there has been greater scope and encouragement for a more individualistic outlook so far as expenditure, use of leisure time and general levels of aspiration are concerned. Within the white-collar group, on the other hand, a trend in the opposite direction has been going on. Under conditions of rising prices, increasingly large-scale units of bureaucratic administration and reduced chances of upward 'career' mobility, lower level white collar workers, at any rate, have now become manifestly less attached to an unqualified belief in the virtues of 'individualism' and more prone to collective, trade union action of a deliberately apolitical and instrumental type" ("Affluence and the British Class Structure," *Sociological Review*, 1963, no. 2, p. 152). In the United States, empirical research, based on hierarchical clustering methods, has failed to find evidence supporting embourgeoisement and manual-nonmanual division theories, while they do provide support for a hypothesis of proletarianization of white collar work. The majority of clerical workers and even technicians are more similar to manual workers than to those in middle class occupations. Thus the manual-plus-clerical versus nonmanual split appears to be the basic division in the American occupational structure (R. Vanneman, "The

Occupational Composition of American Classes," *American Journal of Sociology*, 1977, pp. 783–807).

[84] One author commented: "I believe that we are moving toward a period when manual work in industry will be just as objectively reactionary a factor as was the work in backward agriculture at the time of Marx" (E. Pusić, "Razlikovanje u pojmu klase i činioci društvenog procesa," *Naše teme*, 1965, p. 985).

[85] Radovan Richta and his associates give the following data on the typical skill requirements of production at various levels of technology:

Proportions of Total Labor Force (in percent)

	Unskilled	Semiskilled	Skilled	Secondary professional school	University
Traditional industrial system					
a. Universal machinery	15	20	60	4	4
b. Conveyor belt	—	57	33	8	2
Automation					
c. Partial	—	38–43	45–55	13–30	4–12
d. Complete	—	—	40–50	40–60	20–40

Source: R. Richta, *Civilizacija na raskršću* (Belgrade: Komunist, 1972), p. 125.

Technologies (a), (b), and (c) correspond to phases 2, 3, and 4 in the text. The assembly line eliminates unskilled workers. In the USA and the USSR, for instance, unskilled workers practically disappeared from manufacturing. Complete automation eliminates semiskilled workers as well.

[86] Extrapolating such trends, V. A. Thompson suggests that bureaucratic organization will be transformed into an innovational organization that "will be much more professional than most existing ones. Work will be much less determined by production-oriented planners on the Smith's pins model and more determined by the extended periods of pre-entry training. The desk classes will decline in number and importance relative to professional, scientific and technical workers. There will be a great increase in interorganizational mobility and a corresponding decline in organizational chauvinism. The concept of organizations as organic entities with some claim to survive will tend to be replaced by the concept of organizations as opportunities for professional growth. In the innovative organization, professional orientations and loyalties will be stronger relative to organizational or bureaucratic ones. Esteem striving will tend to replace status striving. There will be less control by superiors and more by self and peers. Power and influence will be much more broadly dispersed" ("Bureaucracy and Innovation," *Administrative Science Quarterly*, June 1965, *10*, 1–20, espec. p. 12).

[87] The proportions are 25 percent in the Soviet Union and Canada, and more than 40 percent in the United States, on the average; in American urban areas, the share with higher education is already 60 percent.

[88] According to the estimates of Guy Routh, in the last half century (between 1913–14 and 1960), the standard of living of various British occupational groups increased by the following percentages: professionals, 20 percent; clerks, 52 percent; skilled workers, 78 percent; unskilled workers, 88 percent (in J. Raynor, *The Middle Class* [London: Longmans, 1970], p. 59). In France, from 1911–13 to the end of 1956, the real salaries of state counselors decreased by 47 percent, while the real wages of Parisian skilled workers increased by 20 percent and those of agricultural laborers by 71 percent (J. Fourastié, *Civilizacija sutrašnjice* [Zagreb: Naprijed, 1968], p. 152). In 1961 about 50 percent of German small merchants did not earn an income larger than that of industrial workers (S. Keller and R. Vahrenkamp, "Iluzije kasnog kapitalizma," *Marksizam u svijetu,* 1975, no. 1, p. 25). In the civil service, from 1875 to 1955 extreme income differentials decreased from 7.1:1 to 5.4:1 in the United States (for undersecretary of the treasury vs. messenger), from 14.6 to 5.1 in France (for directeur général des finances vs. huissier) and from 32 to 15.9 in the United Kingdom (for permanent head vs. sorter) (T. Scitovsky, "International Comparison of the Trend of Professional Earnings," *American Economic Review,* 1966, pp. 25–42, espec. p. 27).

[89] Workers themselves are not sure. W. G. Runciman found in a 1962 survey in Britain that 22 percent of persons in manual occupations declared themselves as middle class and an additional 7 percent as lower middle class. Nineteen percent of those in nonmanual occupations, on the other hand, considered themselves as workers (*Relative Deprivation and Social Justice* [London: Routledge and Kegan Paul, 1966], p. 158). Also in Britain, Kahan and his associates found that 8 percent of unskilled and 17 percent of skilled workers consider themselves middle class, while 21 percent of persons in higher managerial and professional occupations (usually considered upper middle class) and 37 percent of those in lower managerial and administrative occupations (middle class) identified themselves with the working class (see Raynor, *The Middle Class,* p. 10). A 1968 French survey showed that 29 percent of employed women married to clerks were workers or service personnel, while 39 percent of the wives of workers were clerks or even members of middle cadres (M. G. Michal, "L'emploi féminine en 1968," *Collection de l'INSEE,* November 1973, série D, no. 109, Table 12). In Sweden in 1975, less than 50 percent of workers identified themselves with the working class, and the share is falling. Besides, even on the lesser paid rungs of the working class, around 85 to 90 percent consider a transfer of national income to solve environmental and social problems of equal or greater importance than

a pay rise (U. Himmelstrand, "Socialism and Social Liberalism in the Context of Swedish Societal Change," *Community Development,* 1977, no. 37–38, pp. 37–66, espec. p. 51).

[90] For instance, in 1964, 90 percent of American married workers outside the South owned cars as compared with 89 percent for the lower middle class and 97 percent for upper middle class families. Twenty-nine percent of working class families owned two or more cars; the corresponding percentages for the other two classes were 26 and 46, respectively (R. F. Hamilton, *Class and Politics in the United States* [New York: John Wiley and Sons, 1972], p. 385).

[91] "Affluence," p. 157.

[92] Karl Marx would have agreed. Consider the following, somewhat clumsily phrased, paragraph from the draft (not incorporated into the published text) of book 1, chapter 6, of *Capital:* "with the development of a *real subsuming of labor under capital* . . . the *real performer* in the overall labor process is not the individual worker, but increasingly a *socially combined labor power,* and the various labor powers, which are in competition with one another and constitute the entire productive machine, participate in very different ways in the direct process of creating commodities . . . one works with hands, another more with his head, one as a manager, an engineer, a technician, or even a helper. Thus the *functions of labor power* will increasingly be included in the direct concept of productive labor, while the bearers of these functions will be increasingly related to the category of *productive workers,* directly exploited by capital and *subordinated* to its process of consumption and production. If we consider the *total worker,* of whom the shop consists, then his *combined activity* is materialized directly in the *total product* . . . while it is quite irrelevant whether the function of an individual worker, who is only one of the links of this total worker, is further away or closer to direct manual work" (K. Marx and F. Engels, *Sochineniia,* 2nd ed., vol. 49 [Moscow: Politizdat, 1974], p. 95).

[93] Kahan and his associates found that in Britain the largest cleavage in subjective class identification occurs not between manual and nonmanual groups but between skilled or supervisory nonmanual and lower nonmanual (Raynor, *Middle Class,* pp. 9–10). This finding is consistent with the foregoing analysis, which indicated that lower level nonmanual employees would be placed closer to workers than to other nonmanual employees. Prestige scores for skilled manual occupations (such as carpenter) may be higher than for lower middle class job titles (such as clerk in a store) (see L. Reissman, *Class in American Society* [Glencoe, Ill.: Free Press, 1959], p. 156). If the social gaps between groups of occupations are measured by the percentage of workers stating that they would choose similar work again, then American society looks as follows:

University professors	93%
Firm lawyers, school superintendents	85
Journalists	82
White collar workers (nonprofessional)	43
Skilled printers	52
Skilled autoworkers and steelworkers	41
Unskilled steelworkers	21
Unskilled autoworkers	16

Source: R. L. Kahn, "The Work Module," in J. O'Toole, ed., *Work and the Quality of Life* (Cambridge, Mass.: MIT, 1974), p. 204.

[94] Even this has been denied. Daniel Bell observes that the effort of professional and kindred categories of American labor to reassert their status through membership in high-prestige associations, stiffer requirements for professional certification, and changes in school curricula represents an attempt at differentiation and not amalgamation with other social groups (*The Coming of Post-Industrial Society* [New York: Basic Books, 1973], pp. 153–54). True enough. And so were the efforts of displaced craftsmen two centuries earlier to preserve their guilds and societies, and of skilled workers in the second half of the nineteenth century to preserve their new model unions in the face of masses of unskilled workers whom they did not recognize as their social equals. Yet the final result was the formation of a relatively homogeneous social group called the proletariat or, more neutrally, blue collar labor.

[95] M. Dobb, *Studies in the Development of Capitalism* (New York: International Publishers, 1963), pp. 265–66.

[96] As in Thomson-Houston, the leading French electronics firm, where engineers refused to join the corporate organization of managerial personnel and instead joined the workers' union (see Serge Mallet, *La nouvelle classe ouvrière* [Paris: Seuil, 1963]). In May 1968 technicians, and even managers, participated in the factory strikes and occupations in the electronics, chemical, and petrochemical industries and in Electricité de France. It was not the traditional economic demands but self-management that excited them most. Students and workers virtually brought the French economy and the state to a standstill in May 1968.

[97] This frame of mind is well expressed in a letter to the editor written by a Harvard University student in 1968: "We are concerned by a system that we had no part in creating and, more important, we will not have an opportunity, however token, to change it before it works its will on us. At graduation we are immediately faced with an obligation that we have inherited, and we must judge" (*Dialogue,* 1969, no. 2, p. 19).

[98] A. Gorz, *Strategy for Labour* (Boston: Beacon Press, 1968), p. 106.

[99] B. Denitch, "Is There a New Working Class?" *Dissent*, July-August 1970, pp. 351–55, quote from p. 353.

[100] E. Mandel, "Radnici i permanentna revolucija," *Marksizam u svetu*, 1974, no. 11, pp. 28–46, espec. p. 36.

CHAPTER 15

[1] A. Maslow, *Motivation and Personality* (New York: Harper and Row, 1970); and *Toward a Psychology of Being* (New York: Van Nostrand, 1968). The theory was first presented in "A Theory of Human Motivation," *Psychological Review*, 1943, pp. 370–96.

[2] Maslow, *Motivation and Personality*, p. 46.

[3] Maslow, *Psychology of Being*, p. 30.

[4] See J. C. Davies, *Human Nature in Politics* (New York: John Wiley and Sons, 1963).

[5] B. Horvat, *Towards a Theory of Planned Economy* (Belgrade: Jugoslavenski institut za ekonomska istraživanja, 1964), ch. 11.

[6] *Motivation and Personality*, p. 98.

[7] Ibid.

[8] Ibid.

[9] Ibid.

[10] Ibid., pp. 273–74.

[11] See *Escape from Freedom* (New York: Farrar, Straus and Giroux, 1941); *The Sane Society* (New York: Holt, Rinehart and Winston, 1955).

[12] C. P. Alderfer, "An Empirical Test of Human Needs," *Organizational Behavior and Human Performance*, 1969, pp. 143–75; M. A. Wahba and L. G. Bridwell, "Maslow Reconsidered: A Review of Research on the Need Hierarchy Theory," *Academy of Management Proceedings*, 1974, pp. 514–20. The results of empirical tests are rather ambiguous. It has been pointed out that needs are intrinsically interdependent, and that therefore the research technique used (factor analysis) was methodologically wrong. Instead of orthogonal rotation, which forces independent factors, oblique rotation, which allows for interdependence among the underlying constructs, ought to be used. V. F. Mitchell and Pravin Moudgill used an oblimin technique and obtained a loading pattern displaying close correspondence with Maslow's classification ("Measurement of Maslow's Need Hierarchy," *Organizational Behavior and Human Performance*, 1976, pp. 334–49).

[13] C. P. Alderfer, *Existence, Relatedness and Growth* (New York: Free Press, 1972).

[14] Ibid., pp. 9–12.

[15] Ibid., pp. 148–49.

[16] "The U.S. Internal Security Act of 1950 established six standby concentration camps . . . to be activated at the president's discretion in case of an internal security emergency and gave broad powers to hearings officers to incarcerate citizens without trial" (C. Lindblom, *Politics and Markets* [New York: Basic Books, 1977], p. 264).

[17] M. Dobb, *Studies in the Development of Capitalism* (New York: International Publishers, 1963), pp. 234–35. Stalinist collectivization was not essentially different.

[18] *An Essay on Liberation* (Penguin, 1972), p. 25. Another representative writer is Norman Birnbaum: "As for the proletariat, it is neither in its culture nor in its politics a harbinger of the future or a revolutionary force. Today's avant-garde in industrial societies will be found amongst the young, particularly students (that is to say, those without immediate responsibilities or bondages to the existing order), and amongst intellectuals, those with a certain freedom from routine and a certain proclivity to employ their critical faculties" (*The Crisis of Industrial Society* [London: Oxford University Press, 1969], p. 94).

[19] *Essay on Liberation*, p. 57.

[20] Ibid., pp. 71–73.

[21] A. Smith, *The Wealth of Nations* (1776) (New York: Modern Library, 1937), book 3, ch. 4, pp. 387 and 391.

[22] On the reasons for classifying countries into these three groups instead of the more common two (developing and developed), see my article, "The Relation Between Rate of Growth and Level of Development," *Journal of Development Studies*, 1974, pp. 382–94. The three groups can be defined in terms of (logarithms of) per capita GDP. Since the value of money changes, however, it is more convenient to specify them in terms of percentage share of agricultural population in the total active population. The two measures are highly correlated (r^2 = 0.81). The undeveloped group includes countries with more than 60 percent agricultural population; the industrializing group occupies the interval between 60 and 25 percent; while in developed countries, the share of agricultural population is below 25 percent. These percentages should be interpreted as only very rough benchmarks. It may be added that, in the developed countries, the population is fully literate.

CHAPTER 16

[1] K. Marx, "The Chartists," *New York Daily Tribune*, August 25, 1852

[2] Letter to Turati, February 6, 1892.

[3] N. Q. Herric, "Who's Unhappy at Work and Why," *Manpower*, Jan-

uary 1972, pp. 3–7. A Canadian study conducted a few years later produced similar findings. It turned out that the single most important consideration in the minds of Canadians was interesting work, and "that intrinsic aspects of work such as having sufficient information and authority outweighed the importance of extrinsic features such as salary or comfortable surroundings" (M. Burstein et al., *Canadian Work Values: Findings of a Work Ethic Survey and a Job Satisfaction Survey* [Ottawa: Information Canada, 1975], pp. 29–30). In another American study, based on a sample survey of 3,101 men, it was found that lack of control over the work process (closeness of supervision, routinization, and substantive complexity) has an appreciable direct affect on feelings of powerlessness, self-estrangement, and normlessness. The author points out that "insofar as workers are closely supervised, are caught up in a repetitive flow of similar tasks and do work of little substantive complexity, their work does not permit self-direction" (M. L. Kohn, "Occupational Structure and Alienation," *American Journal of Sociology*, 1976, pp. 111–30, espec. p. 112). Work discontent is not peculiar to capitalist countries; it can be found equally in an etatist environment, though it is not so well researched. V. A. Iadov and A. A. Kissel' found that only 20 percent of young Leningrad workers employed in low-skilled jobs were satisfied with their work ("Work Satisfaction," *Sociologicheskie issledovania*, 1974, no. 1, pp. 85). Insofar as labor turnover is an indication of work dissatisfaction and conflict, the following data are of some interest: about 5 percent of the work force changed their jobs each year between 1967 and 1972 in Germany, and about 4.8 percent in 1970 in the USA; the comparable figure for the USSR was 21 percent in 1970 (W. Teckenberg, "Labour Turnover and Job Satisfaction," *Soviet Studies*, 1978, no. 2, pp. 193–211, espec. p. 194).

[4] Report by H. Johnson and N. Kotz in the *Washington Post*, April 10, 1972.

[5] Walter Reuther, president of the United Automobile Workers union, in a television interview a few weeks before his death (quoted in R. Edwards, M. Reich, and T. Weisskop, *The Capitalist System* [Englewood Cliffs, N.J.: 1972], p. 259).

[6] G. L. Staines, "Is Worker Dissatisfaction Rising?" *Challenge*, May-June 1979, pp. 38–45.

[7] D. Yankelovich, "Changing Attitudes Toward Work," *Dialogue*, 1974, no. 4, pp. 3–13, quote from p. 12.

[8] See H. Wachtel: "Class Consciousness and Stratification in the Labor Process," in R. Edwards et al., *Labor Market Segmentation* (Lexington, Mass.: D. C. Heath, 1977), pp. 95–122, quote from p. 112.

[9] The story of the Saab-Scania plant in Trollhättan is instructive in this respect. The assembly line work organization created a high absentee rate (23.1 percent in 1974) and an extremely high turnover of

personnel (75–80 percent). Something had to be done, and the initiative for change came not from the labor union but from middle management. In 1975 autonomous groups replaced individual workers working according to the dictate of the assembly line. The expenses for the change were paid off in less than three years. Both job satisfaction and profits increased (Berit Härd, "A Better Quality of Working Life Should Be Accessible to All," *IFDA Dossier 12*, October 1979, pp. 19–26).

[10] W. Korpi, *The Working Class in Welfare Capitalism* (London: Routledge and Kegan Paul, 1978), p. 325.

[11] R. Aronson and J. C. Cowley, "The New Left in the United States," in R. Wiliband and I. Saville, eds., *Socialist Register* (London: Merlin, 1967), p. 84.

[12] Evidence to the Sankey Commission on the Nationalization of the Mines, 1919.

[13] S. M. Lipset, *Political Man* (New York: Doubleday, 1963), p. 64.

[14] October 7, 1965; again on November 6, 1968 (quoted in F. Deppe et al., *Kritika saodlučivanja* [Belgrade: Komunist, 1974], p. 153).

[15] Something of the kind seems to have happened in Sweden after 1965. From that time on, reports Edmund Dahlström, there was increased "criticism towards social structure and policy in Sweden. Most established institutions got their part. The critical theme concerned very much industrial relations and exploitation of the rank and file. Employers, unions and bureaucrats were made responsible for the unsatisfactory conditions. Several novels occurred showing the damaging effect of working conditions, piece-work, hard-working rules, inhumane supervisions etc. Journalists, film producers and theatrical groups tried to elucidate the exploitive relations. Through mass media they spread to a large proportion of the people. Even popular culture in its different manifestations transmitted some of the ideas. It is hard to deny the effect of these ideas" ("Efficiency, Satisfaction and Democracy in Work," paper prepared for the Dubrovnik conference on self-management, January 1977, p. 18). In 1975 Meidner's report (to be discussed later) appeared. A year later the Trade Union Congress gave strong support to requests for self-management. In the same year, the Social Democrats were defeated after having held power for almost half a century. That can be taken as a sign of too little, rather than too much, genuine socialism.

[16] "Cognition, Consciousness and Depression," paper presented at the Eleventh World Congress of the International Political Science Association, Moscow, 1979, p. 39.

[17] "Why Is France Blocked?" in H. Leavitt et al., eds., *Organizations of the Future* (New York: Praeger, 1974), pp. 42–56, quote from p. 50.

[18] See B. Denitch, "Legitimacy and the Social Order," in *Legitimation of Regimes* (London: Sage, 1979), pp. 5–22; J. Habermas, "Conservatism and Capitalist Crisis," *New Left Review*, 1979, no. 115, pp. 73–86.

[19] "Work is the objectification of human powers: while shaping the confined object, man projects unto it his own consciousness, thoughts, desires, needs and imagination. Through it, he realizes the potential capacities of his being. At the same time, production enables the worker to satisfy needs, his own and those of others. Work, therefore, *could be* an activity through which the individual expresses all of the fundamental characteristics of his human nature, and through which he produces and confirms himself as a man" (M. Marković, *From Affluence to Praxis* [Ann Arbor: University of Michigan Press, 1974], p. 121).

[20] *The Cultural Contradictions of Capitalism* (London: Heinemann, 1976), p. 84.

[21] Ibid., pp. 71–72.

[22] Quoted in M. Marković, "Nova ljevics i kulturna revolucija," *Praxis*, 1970, pp. 927–44, quote from p. 943.

[23] Worker discontent with the traditional role of unions already leaves union leaders bewildered. Jerry Wurf, president of the Federation of State, County, and Municipal Employees (AFL-CIO) complains: "The greatest labor leader avocation these days is to gripe about the lack of their members' appreciation for all that they are doing for them." A U.S. government task force concluded: "There is considerable evidence that (1) alienated workers are less loyal to their unions than are non-alienated workers and (2) workers in jobs with little intrinsic satisfaction are least favorably inclined toward unions regardless of their age" (J. O'Toole et al., *Work in America* [Cambridge, Mass.: MIT Press, 1973], p. 113).

[24] "We are no longer divided," writes Italian socialist Lelio Basso, "into supporters of revolution and the supporters of gradual conquest of power; instead we are divided into those willing to be integrated into capitalist society and those who believe that the present society, conditions, and chances are ripe for a socialist reconstruction of the society" ("Prospects of European Left," in M. Pečujlić et al., eds., *Marksizam* [Belgrade: Službeni list, 1976], p. 919).

[25] In the United States management prerogatives were accepted in practice but not defined until after the Second World War, when President Truman called a conference of high-ranking business and labor representatives to discuss problems and settle differences in the common interest. The resulting management report insisted on the right to manage as defined by exclusive managerial control over six areas: (1) the determination of output, and the location of new and

closing of old units; (2) the determination of layout, equipment, and production techniques; (3) the determination of financial policies and customer relations; (4) the determination of management organization and promotion of executives; (5) the determination of job content, size of work force, and selection of employees; and (6) the determination of safety, health, and property protection measures. In a reflection of changed power relations, unions refused to commit themselves, arguing that it was not wise to build a fence around the rights and responsibilities of the parties. No agreement was reached (S. Cohen, *Labor in the United States* [Columbus, Ohio: Merrill, 1970], p. 222).

[26] J. S. Mill, *Principles of Political Economy* (1848), ed. by W. J. Ashley (New York: Kelley, 1961), p. 764.

[27] The following table provides some information about the point made:

Number of Working Days per 1,000 Employees Lost due to Industrial Actions (average for 1964–73)

Sweden	43
West Germany	43
Japan	217
France	277
Britain	633
United States	1247

Source: L. Forsebäck, *Industrial Relations and Employment in Sweden* (Stockholm: Swedish Institute, 1976), p. 67.

Of the countries listed, various forms of co-determination exist only in West Germany and Sweden. It may be of some interest to note that until the mid-thirties Sweden had one of the highest rates of strikes among all the developed countries. Strikes also lasted long. In 1932 the Social Democratic government assumed power. A few years later the strike rate had declined substantially, and soon Sweden came to rank lowest in the frequency of industrial disputes (W. Korpi, *The Working Class in Welfare Capitalism* [London: Routledge and Kegan Paul, 1978], pp. 95–96).

[28] Additional evidence is provided by various surveys. A study conducted by Deutsches Gewerkschaftsbund in 1968–69 showed that unionized workers considered the extension of co-determination second in importance (after employment security) and nonunionized workers put it in third place (D. Jenkins, *Job Power, Blue and White Collar Democracy* [London: Heinemann, 1974], p. 121). A few years later, a Hart poll in the United States revealed that 66 percent of persons questioned favored employee ownership and control of large corporations, while 56 percent said they would "probably support" or "definitely support" a presidential candidate who favored employee

ownership and control of U.S. companies (G. Alperovitz and J. Faux, "An Economic Program for the Coming Decade," *Democratic Review,* November 1975, pp. 1–2). In a French opinion poll in 1974, nearly one-third of those surveyed said that the single most important reform they wanted was industrial democracy (J. Rifkin, *Own Your Own Job* [New York: Bantam, 1977]).

[29] The more sophisticated version of the argument is the widely accepted theory of the American economist Frank Knight, who argued that an entrepreneur bears uninsurable risks called uncertainty.

[30] As was argued by the Swedish trade union economist Rudolf Meidner, in the debate on the wage earner funds (*Ekonomisk debatt,* 1976, no. 1, p. 78).

[31] In the United Kingdom, 1 percent of the population owns 42 percent of the total personal wealth, represents 60 percent of all taxpayers who own shares of stock, and owns 81 percent of all company stocks (J. Westergaard and H. Resler, *Class in a Capitalist Society* [London: Heinemann, 1975], p. 116). In the United States, in 1953, 1.6 percent of the total adult population, who at that time had $60,000 or more each in total assets, owned 82 percent of all corporate stock, virtually all state and local government bonds, and from 10 to 33 percent of every other type of personal property; 1 percent of the adult population received 40 percent of the total property income; 2.3 percent of households owned about 80 percent of the national productive capital (S. J. Lampman, *The Share of Top Wealth-Holders in National Wealth: 1922–1956* [Princeton: National Bureau of Economic Research, Princeton University Press, 1962], pp. 23, 195, 108). In Sweden, 1 percent of taxpayers owns three-quarters of equity capital and 5 percent of taxpayers owns one-half of personal wealth (R. Meidner et al., *Löntagarfonder* [Stockholm: Tiden, 1975], pp. 38, 43).

[32] Rudolf Meidner and his colleagues wrote a book showing how this method could be applied most advantageously in the Swedish economy, and then prepared a report for the 1976 Trade Union Congress. The congress accepted it (see *Löntagarfonder* [Stockholm: Tiden, 1975]; *Kollektiv Kapitalbildning genom löntagarfonder* [Stockholm: Prisma, 1976]).

[33] The Danish Federation of Trade Unions presented a plan whereby employers would be obliged to contribute to an "employees' investment and dividend fund" in amounts increasing gradually from an initial 0.5 percent to 5 percent of the total wage bill. Two-thirds of the contributions to the fund may be claimed back by the employer for investment in the firm. It has been estimated that the fund's share in corporate stock would amount to 14 percent after ten years and to 26 percent after twenty years. A bill to implement the first stage of the plan was defeated in parliament.

[34] H. C. Cars, "Meidners Modell—Kritik och alternativ," *Frihetlig socialistisk tidskrift,* 1975, no. 6, pp. 15–21. In an attempt to show that

Marx's labor theory of value was wrong, Paul Samuelson unwittingly provided a "proof" for the two-factor theory: "If labor grows at an exponential rate $1 + g$ and goods are priced at their synchronized labor costs: then the bourgeois pricing formula $A_0(g) = a_0(1 + g) \times [I - a(1 + g)]^{-1}$ must be charged by rational planners" ("Understanding the Marxian Notion of Exploitation," *Journal of Economic Literature,* 1971, pp. 399–431, quote from p. 429). Here a_0 stands for unit labor inputs, a is unit capital inputs, and g is the rate of profit, the same for both inputs.

[35] Spanish engineer J. Luis Montero de Burgos distinguishes capital and labor (remunerated by interest and wages) from risk-bearing capital and risk-bearing labor (sharing in profits). The firm is defined as an association of persons supplying active (workers) or passive (capitalists) labor (*Una nueva empresa para una nueva sociedad* [Madrid: Fragua, 1977], pp. 53, 54, 56).

[36] British unions are demanding co-determination over the investment of the $40 billion in pension funds in that country. In the United States, private and public pension funds own between 20 and 25 percent of the equity listed on the New York Stock Exchange, hold nearly 40 percent of corporate bonds and, as a source of investment capital, are four times larger than all individual savings. It is true that most pension funds are controlled by management or investment counselors, but this need not remain so (J. Rifkin and R. Barber, *The North Will Rise Again* [Boston: Beacon Press, 1978]).

[37] The general formula for this sort of calculation is

$$\frac{F_t}{S_t} = 1 - \left[\frac{(1 + \pi(1 - \lambda - u)}{(1 + \pi(1 - u)}\right]^t$$

where F = fund, S = stock, π = gross rate of profit, λ = the share of contributions in gross profit, u = dividends + taxes, t = year. (See Meidner, *Löntagarfonder,* p. 129.)

[38]

	Without fund contribution tax 40%, interest 5%	With fund contribution Tax 40%, interest 5%	Tax 40%, interest 10%	Tax 50%, interest 5%
Profit before tax	100	100	100	100
Contribution to the fund (20%)	—	−20	−20	−20
Tax	−40	−32	−32	−40
Profit after contribution and tax	60	48	48	40
Dividends	60	48	48	40
Value of stock (dividends ÷ interest rate)	1200	960	480	800
Contributions ÷ value of stock	—	2.15%	4.2%	2.5%

[39] Thus, the Federation of Swedish Industries and the Swedish Confederation of Employers' Organizations reacted promptly to Meidner's report. In their own report published in 1976, employers argued that wage earners' funds would cause a breakdown of the capital market, profits would no longer be the criterion for investment, and a planned economy would gradually emerge. Besides, they declared, the accumulation of shares in the labor funds amounts to a form of expropriation probably incompatible with fundamental principles of justice.

[40] M. Weber, *Economy and Society* (Totowa, N.J.: Bedminster Press, 1968), p. 1395.

[41] L. E. Karlsson, "Experiences in Employee Participation in Sweden: 1969–1974," *Economic Analysis and Workers' Management*, 1975, pp. 296–330, quote from p. 316. A few examples—two from a capitalist and one from an etatist environment—are illuminating. David Jenkins quoted Polaroid's training director Ray Ferris, who explained why an apparently efficient corporation program was terminated: "It was too successful. What were we going to do with the supervisors—the managers. We didn't need them any more. . . . The employees' newly revealed ability to carry more responsibility was too great a threat to the established way of doing things and to the established power pattern" (*Job Power: Blue and White Collar Democracy* [Garden City, N.Y.: Doubleday, 1973], pp. 314–15). A highly publicized job enrichment experiment in a dog food factory in Kansas was brought to an end because, though successful economically, "it became a power struggle" and "was too threatening to too many people," reported Stephen Marglin. Marglin also surveyed other American and British experiments in participation which increased productivity substantially but were discontinued because established power and social relationships tended to be disrupted ("Catching Flies with Honey," paper presented at the Dubrovnik Conference on the Economics of Workers' Management, September 11–13, 1978). An experiment in management democratization in a state grain farm at Akchi in Kazakhstan in 1968–70 serves as an etatist counterpart to the above examples. In terms of labor productivity, production costs, and profits per worker, the Akchi experiment proved extremely successful. Yet it was discontinued. The application of the principle that "all should manage in turn" could not win favors from professional managers and party functionaries. "The implicit threat which the experiment posed to the power and privileges of such groups was undoubtedly the source of its undoing" (M. Yanowitch, "Pressures for More 'Participatory' Forms of Economic Organization in the Soviet Union," *Economic Analysis and Workers' Management*, 1978, pp. 403–18, quote from p. 416).

[42] See D. C. Jones, "The Economics and Industrial Relations of Producer Cooperatives in the United States 1791–1939," *Economic Analysis and Workers' Management*, 1977, pp. 295–317; "Workers' Management in Britain," *Economic Analysis and Workers' Management*, 1975, pp.

331–38; "Producer Cooperatives in the U.S.," paper contributed to the Walton Symposium on Labour-Management, Glasgow, 1979.

[43] This statement is based on the evidence provided by the performance of kibbutzim, the Basque cooperatives in Mondragón, American plywood co-ops, and French producer co-ops. Since the first two have already been discussed, I add only information on the remaining two. The sixteen worker-owned plywood firms in the American Pacific Northwest show greater physical productivity, higher product quality, and greater economy in the use of materials. The value productivity is 30 to 50 percent higher than in conventional capitalist mills. "Members of cooperatives not only work harder and more carefully, but perform supervisory, executive, maintenance and plant improvement functions, as well as becoming able and being willing to do a variety of production jobs as needed (Katrina V. Berman, "Worker-Management in U.S. Plywood Manufacturing Cooperatives," paper contributed to the Walton Symposium on Labour-Management, Glasgow, June 1969). Eric Batstone studied a sample of sixty co-ops (mainly in construction and printing) in the Paris region. He found that supervisory personnel were reduced to one-half in printing (in building, the number was about the same as in the capitalist sector); the ratio of value added to net value of capital equipment was 46 percent higher in printing co-ops and 28 percent higher in building co-ops; and the co-ops survived for longer periods than the typical capitalist enterprise ("Some Aspects of the Economic Performance of French Producer-Cooperatives," paper contributed to the Walton Symposium on Labour-Management, Glasgow, June 1969).

[44] In 1978, the U.S. Congress passed a bill creating a cooperative bank and encouraging worker and community groups to buy capitalist enterprises. In an opinion poll conducted in 1975, two out of three Americans said that they would prefer to work for a worker-owned and -controlled company if they were given the choice (B. Stokes, *Worker Participation—Productivity and the Quality of Work Life*, Worldwatch Paper 25 [Washington, D.C., 1978], p. 42). In Britain, the Industrial Common Ownership Act was passed in 1976 and later a Cooperative Development Agency was established. In other countries new laws concerning producer cooperatives either have been passed or are under active consideration.

[45] Two recent European examples, both of which occurred in 1974, are the Triumph motorcycle plant in Meriden, England, with 1750 workers, and the Lip watch factory in France, employing 1300 workers. Japanese competition compelled the Triumph management to close up shop. Workers occupied the plant, obtained a government loan, and preserved at least 700 jobs. The production of motorcycles per worker increased from fourteen to twenty-two. Lip was sold to Swiss interests, and the factory was then closed. The workers struck and later continued to produce and sell watches. The government sent in the police, but the population lent support by buying Lip

watches. In Chile, the case was rather bizarre. Here the junta attempted to sell off state-owned enterprises. In the prevailing chaos, not many businessmen were willing to assume political and economic risks; thus, the workers often were the only interested buyers. In some fifty firms more than 5000 workers assumed management and ownership responsibilities in order to preserve their jobs.

CHAPTER 17

[1] N. Bukharin, *Economics of the Transformation Period* (New York: Humanities Press, 1971), p. 158.

[2] H. Braverman, *The Future of Russia* (New York: Grosset and Dunlap, 1966), p. 110.

[3] I. Deutscher, *Nedovršena revolucija* (Belgrade: Centar za društvena istraživanja pri Predsjedništvu SKJ, 1971), p. 27.

[4] I. Deutscher, *The Prophet Unarmed* (London: Oxford University Press, 1959), ch. 1.

[5] This explanation was suggested to me by Zaga Golubović.

[6] In this respect Marx was very precise: "If the proletariat . . . by means of revolution . . . makes itself the ruling class and, as such, sweeps away by force the old conditions of production, then it will, along with these conditions, have swept away the conditions for the existence of . . . classes generally, and will thereby have abolished its own supremacy as a class" (*Communist Manifesto*). Our authors know the quotation, of course, but prefer to ignore it—together with many others, and for obvious reasons.

[7] S. A. Styepanian, ed., *Rabochiy klass SSSR i yego vedushchaia rol' v stroitel' stve kommunizma* (Moscow: Nauka, 1975), p. 310.

[8] P. Demichev, "Razvitoy socializm—stupen' na puti k kommunizmu," *Problemy mira i socializma,* 1973, no. 1, pp. 9–15.

[9] A. K. Belyh, *Upravlenie i samoupravlenie* (Leningrad: Nauka, 1972).

[10] G. M. Manov et al., *Demokratiia razvitogo socialisticheskogo obshchestva* (Moscow: Nauka, 1975), pp. 90, 98, 105–6, 110, 118, 219, 146.

[11] B. Topornin, "The Dynamic Political System of Developed Socialism," in *Political Systems: Development Trends* (Moscow: Social Sciences Today, 1979), p. 12.

[12] Analyzing Soviet ideological development, Sava Živanov notes that the Eighteenth Party Congress in 1939 proclaimed that the Soviet Union had entered the period "of completing the building of the classless socialist society and of gradual transition from socialism to communism." The Twenty-first and Twenty-second congresses shifted the transition to the 1980s. The new program of 1961, adopted at the Twenty-second Congress, announced that "a communist society

will in the main be built in the USSR" in twenty years, i.e., by 1980. In the 1970s, in the discussions connected with the preparation of the new constitution, new authoritative statements indicated that after socialism had been established, there would be a long period of development of socialism and no transition to communism ("Novi ustav i osnovni pravci razvitka političkog sistema SSSR," *Socijalizam u svetu*, 1979, no. 12, pp. 193–209, p. 197).

13 During the Hungarian uprising, the Soviet troops stationed in Hungary or Romania had to be replaced with fresh, brainwashed contingents from the less developed areas of the Soviet Union. In the Report of the Special Committee on the Problem of Hungary to the Eleventh General Assembly of the United Nations, it was stated: "At times the Hungarians met with sympathy from Soviet troops. . . . Some Russian officers and soldiers appear to have fought and died on the Hungarian side" (A/3592, 1957, pp. 24–25). Jiři Pelikan described the behavior of Russian soldiers occupying Czechoslovakia as follows: "The ordinary Soviet soldier was very confused and demoralized. Everywhere our people were asking them why they were invading a brother socialist country and the Russian soldiers did not know what to answer. There were a number of suicides of Soviet soldiers at this time" (R. Blackburn, ed., *Revolution and Class Struggle* [Sussex: Harvester, 1978], p. 257).

14 According to M. N. Rutkevich, in M. Pečujlić et al., eds., *Marksizam*, vol. 3 (Belgrade: Službeni list, 1976), p. 204.

15 Soviet dissidents realize this and build their hopes on the conflict between the "scientific intelligentsia" and the "administrative class." According to the underground paper *Seiatel'* (1971, no. 1), the former is the only class in history which, by definition, consists of free thinking people for whom intellectual and informational freedom represents a precondition for their socially useful productive activity. The latter bases its absolute power and privileges on the suppression of intellectual freedom, the propagandist brainwashing of the population, and the withholding of information.

16 So does the increasingly open opposition to imperialist adventures and political arrests. The occupation of Czechoslovakia, the trials of dissidents, and the internments into psychiatric hospitals are followed by (limited) demonstrations and (more numerous) protesting letters to state and party authorities.

17 They have already begun their work of revolutionizing the consciousness of the society. According to the well-informed Soviet dissident communist Roy Medvedev, all dissident and radical groups inside and outside the party are composed of intellectuals (see *Kniga o sotsialisticheskoi demokratii* [Paris: Grasset and Fasquelle, 1972]). But the workers are not entirely absent either. In the group of eight demonstrating on August 25, 1968, at Red Square against the occupation of Czechoslovakia, two were workers. In the same year, 738

people sent letters protesting the trial of Galansky and Ginzburg. Two-thirds of the protestors were scholars and artists, 6 percent were workers, and the rest were professionals and students (A. Amal'rik, *Prosushchestvuet li Sovietskiy Soyuz do 1884 goda* [Amsterdam: Fond imeni Gercena, 1969], p. 12). Dissidents (*inakomysliashchie*) are a specific extrasystemic opposition in an etatist environment.

[18] L. Kolakowski, *Main Currents of Marxism*, vol. 3 (Oxford: Clarendon, 1978), pp. 90–91.

[19] The term was apparently coined by Frane Barbieri, a Yugoslav journalist reporting from Rome. Santiago Carrillo, its chief spokesman, explains that Eurocommunism means "the need to move toward socialism democratically, which implies party pluralism, parliament and representative institutions, and popular sovereignty exercised regularly through universal suffrage; . . . trade unions independent both from the state and from the parties, freedom of opposition, human rights, religious freedom, freedom of cultural, scientific, and artistic creation, and the development of the most extensive popular participation at all levels and in all sectors of social activity" (*'Eurocommunisme' et état* [Paris: Flammarion, 1977], p. 165).

[20] In June 1976, a wave of strikes swept Polish cities because of a sudden increase in food prices. The authorities reacted with various measures of repression. In September, a group of Polish intellectuals created the Committee for the Defense of Workers (KOR) with the aim of rendering legal, medical, and material help to the persecuted workers. This was the first independent organization created in postwar Poland that represented at the same time a left-wing opposition. The committee demanded full public inquiry into police brutality. A year later, the KOR was transformed into the Committee for Social Self-Defense, which had the following objectives: (1) to struggle against any form of repression on political, religious, or racial grounds and to give support to persons so persecuted; (2) to struggle against all violations of law and to help the victims of such violations; (3) to fight for the institutional respect of civil liberties and rights; and (4) to support and defend every social initiative intended to apply the rights of man and citizens (Z. Erard and G. M. Zygier, *La Pologne: une société en dissidence* [Paris: Maspero, 1978], p. 41).

[21] Socialist opposition in etatist countries seems to be reaching a similar conclusion. Roy Medvedev attributes special significance to words of truth and quotes approvingly an anonymous dissident who declared: "Unlike the revolutionary transformations in the past, the coming revolutionary transformation of our country may possibly be crucially affected by *words*. An idea overcoming the masses can now become a 'material force' in an almost direct sense. . . . The attack on the Winter Palace, as a method of revolutionary activity, continued and reproduced the attack on the Bastille. The attack on our bureaucratic fortresses will be of a *radically* different nature: they will begin to

crumble under the blows of thought itself" (*Kniga o sotsialisticheskoi demokratii,* pp. 377–78). The Polish historian and activist in the democratic opposition, Adam Michnik, scorns revolutionary programs and conspiratorial practices as serving only to enable the police to engineer mass hysteria and to make possible police provocation. Pressing for reforms, for the extension of human rights, is "the only path to be followed by the dissidents in Eastern Europe" ("Nowy evolucjonizm," *Aneks*, 1977, nos. 13–14, pp. 33–48, quote from p. 42). The Soviet group Seiatel' rejects conspiratorial activities outright.

22 See W. Brus, *The Economics and Politics of Socialism* (London: Routledge and Kegan Paul, 1973), pp. 105–11.

23 Tamara Deutscher, "Voices of Dissent," in R. Miliband and J. Saville, eds., *The Socialist Register 1978* (London: Merlin, 1978), pp. 21–43, espec. p. 41. One of the patients was said to be "suffering from nervous exhaustion brought on by her quests for justice." Deutscher comments: "What an indictment of a system in which 'quest for justice' leads into a psychiatric ward."

24 In the more developed etatist countries, workers do this spontaneously all the time. They did so after Budapest and Poznań in 1956, after Prague in 1968, after Gdańsk and Szczecin in 1970–71. Dissident groups almost invariably request self-management.

25 Quoted in M. Yanowitch, *Social and Economic Inequality in the Soviet Union* (London: Robertson, 1977), p. 146.

26 For a good survey of the literature, see M. Yanowitch, "Pressures for More 'Participatory' Forms of Economic Organization in the Soviet Union," *Economic Analysis and Workers' Management,* 1978, pp. 403–18.

27 Quoted in ibid., p. 408–9.

28 Studying the attitudes of former Soviet citizens, A. Inkeles finds: "The Russians do not seem to expect initiative, directedness and organizedness from an average individual. They therefore expected that the authority will of necessity give detailed orders, demand obedience, keep checking up on performance and use persuasion and coercion intensely to insure steady performance" (*Social Change in Soviet Russia* [Cambridge, Mass.: Harvard University Press, 1968], p. 117). These findings are corroborated by an observation by the Soviet dissident Andrei Amal'rik: "the ideas of self-government, of equality under law for all and of personal freedom—and the responsibility that goes with these—are almost completely incomprehensible to the Russian people. . . . The very word 'freedom' is understood by most people as a synonym of the word 'disorder.' . . . As for respecting the rights of the individual as such, such an idea simply evokes bewilderment. One can feel respect for force, authority, even, ultimately, intelligence or education, but that human personality of itself should represent any kind of value—this is a preposterous idea in the popular

mind" (quoted in G. R. Urban, ed., *Eurocommunism* [London: M. T. Smith, 1978], p. 237). It is as if not much has changed since the times of Ivan Turgenev, who remarked: "The attitudes of slavery are too deeply planted into our heart; we shall not soon part with them. We need a master in everything and everywhere" (*Dim* [Smoke] [Zagreb: Matica Hrvatska, 1963], p. 28). The ordinary citizen expects a hierarchical ordering and guidance in everything. A group is taken through an art gallery; the guide explains the characteristics of various paintings; the more vocal members of the group protest, "You did not tell us which of them is *the most beautiful!*" The Russian members of a family visit their relatives in Belgrade; the visitors express their dislike for the local press: "Your newspapers are confusing, they do not tell you what *is correct!*" Let me add that here, as elsewhere, anecdotes are no substitute for scholarly research. Etatism being what it is, however, anecdotes are often the only available source of information.

[29] A bourgeois order combines political democracy and economic autocracy. A politocratic order may do the reverse and combine economic democracy and political autocracy. The ruling class maintains monopoly in the sphere where its base of power lies.

[30] "Economic Organization in the Soviet Union," p. 415.

[31] Ibid., p. 18.

[32] And the conscience of a number of Russian citizens was stirred up. One of the protestors at Red Square in Moscow in 1968, Natalia Gorbanevskaia, later told the court: "My comrades and myself are happy that we participated in this demonstration. At least for a moment have we broken through the stream of unhindered lies and timid silence. We have shown that not all citizens of our country agree with that act of violence carried out in the name of the Soviet people." The wave of protests culminated in an act of despair, committed by mathematics student Ilia Rips, who carried a poster proclaiming, "I protest against the Occupation of Czechoslovakia," to Freedom Square in Riga and burned himself (see W. Leonhard, "Prager Frühling and Eurokommunismus," in U. Gärtner and J. Kosta, eds., *Wirtschaft und Gesellschaft* [Berlin: Duncker and Humblot, 1979], pp. 389–418, espec. p. 411).

CHAPTER 18

[1] M. Duverger, *Janus—Les deux faces de l'Occident* (Paris: Fayard, 1972), p. xiii.

[2] Quoted in *What Now*, the 1975 Dag Hammarskjöld Report, presented in *Development Dialogue*, 1975, nos. 1–2, p. 59.

[3] In 1967 forty-three out of sixty African parties opted for socialism in their programs (J. Hadži-Vasileva, *Afrika i socijalizam* [Belgrade:

IMRP, 1973], p. 33). In many cases, however, socialism stood merely as a proxy for nationalism and economic growth.

[4] J. Nyerere, *Freedom and Socialism* (Dar es Salaam: Oxford University Press, 1974), pp. 24–25.

[5] *What Is to Be Done,* 1902, chs. 2, 4.

[6] For sixty-six countries, the correlation between the proportion of children in primary schools and the frequency of revolution was 0.84 (S. P. Huntington, *Political Order in Changing Societies* [New Haven: Yale University Press, 1968], p. 47).

[7] In the more passionate language of Frantz Fanon, the ideologue of the Algerian revolution, "in the colonial countries the peasants alone are revolutionary, for they have nothing to lose and everything to gain. The starving peasant, outside the class system, is the first among the exploited to discover that only violence pays. For him, there is no compromise, no possible coming to terms; colonization and decolonization are simply a question of relative strength" (*The Wretched of the Earth* [New York: Grove Press, 1968], p. 61).

[8] In the 1950s and 1960s, some thirty-seven Asian, African, and Latin American countries had larger proportions of unionized labor force than the United States (Huntington, *Political Order,* p. 284).

[9] Ibid., pp. 279–280. See also Joan Nelson in B. Ward et al., eds., *The Widening Gap* (New York: Columbia University Press, 1971), pp. 141–43.

[10] Mao Zedong, *Chinese Revolution and the Communist Party of China,* December 1939.

[11] B. Russell, *Power* (London: Unwin, 1967), p. 18.

[12] Huntington, *Political Order,* pp. 7–8.

[13] This rule need not apply to other continents: witness Chile. Here, perhaps, as in the case of Italy and Germany, another rule is applicable: unsuccessful socialist revolutions generate fascist regimes.

[14]

Number of Successful Coups in Modernizing Countries, 1945 or Date of Independence through 1966

		Countries with coups	
Type of political system	Number of countries	Number	Percent
One party	26	6	25
Dominant party	18	6	33
Two parties	16	7	44
Multiparty	20	17	85

Source: Huntington, *Political Order*, pp. 408, 423.

No coups succeeded in communist countries.

[15] *Wretched of the Earth,* pp. 181–82.

[16] *Freedom and Socialism,* p. 36.

[17] After the Revolution, in 1945, the agricultural population represented 75 percent of the total population in Yugoslavia. By 1971, this percentage had been reduced to 36.4 (B. Horvat, *The Yugoslav Economic System* [White Plains, N.Y.: International Arts and Sciences Press, 1976], p. 77). Bulgaria achieved a similar rate of population transfer.

[18] R. Bićanić, "Kapitalni koeficijent, tehnički napredak i teorija praga ekonomskog razvoja," *Ekonomski pregled,* 1961, pp. 251–300.

[19] B. Horvat, "The Relation Between Rate of Growth and Level of Development," *Journal of Development Studies,* 1974, pp. 382–94.

[20] See B. Horvat, "Real Fixed Capital Costs Under Steady Growth," *European Economic Review,* 1973, pp. 85–103, espec. p. 102.

[21] See A. Puljić, "Utjecaj neopredmećenog tehnološkog napretka na stopu rasta," doctoral dissertation, University of Zagreb, pp. 339–41; L. Johansen, "A Method for Separating the Effects of Capital Accumulation and Shifts in Production Functions upon Growth in Labour Productivity," *Economic Journal,* 1961, pp. 775–82.

[22] Japan achieved a rate of 9 percent.

[23] I base this assumption primarily on my analysis of Yugoslav economic and social processes (see B. Horvat, *An Essay on Yugoslav Society* [White Plains, N.Y.: International Arts and Sciences Press, 1969]; *Yugoslav Economic System).* This level of development makes possible full literacy, universal ten-year education, egalitarian income distribution, and political democracy. It may be remarked that Western European countries have left the 1939 level of development far behind and have not built socialism. The answer is that they were trying to preserve capitalism, not construct socialism. They were not using shortcuts but detours.

[24] *Ribari ljudskih duša* (Belgrade: Mladost, 1976), pp. 24–26.

[25] In Yugoslavia the land maximum is set at 10 hectares. In 1967, personal consumption per member of peasant household for various categories of land holders was as follows (where consumption of lowest category = 100):

up to 2 ha.	100
2-3 ha.	100
3-5 ha.	94
5-8 ha.	97
more than 8 ha.	100

Source: B. Horvat, "Jugoslovenska agrarna teorija i politika u posleratnom razdoblju," *Pregled,* 1976, p. 757.

Larger households have larger estates and fewer family members working outside the estate.

[26] This was the position taken by the ruling Tanzanian party in its 1967 Arusha Declaration.

[27] E. Fromm, *Zen budizam i psihoanaliza* (Belgrade: Nolit, 1964), p. 229.

[28] E. Fromm, *Bekstvo od slobode* (Belgrade: Nolit, 1964), p. 259.

[29] What Marx thought of the minority position in the party is shown by his attitude toward the German Social Democratic Party Congress in Gotha in 1875. He wrote a critique of the proposed program. The party leadership suppressed it. In the letter of criticism he sent to Bracke on May 5, 1875, he stated that he and Engels would disagree with the congress and added, "it is my duty not to recognize even by diplomatic silence, a programme that is in my conviction completely unacceptable and demoralizing to the party." Today the Gotha Programme is remembered primarily because of Marx's *Critique!*

[30] Letter to Herson Trier, December 1889.

[31] V. F. Asmus, *Logika* (Moscow: Ogiz, 1947), p. 373.

[32] *Borba,* October 9, 1966, p. 4.

CHAPTER 19

[1] Marek Fritzhand, *Etička misao mladoga Marksa* (Belgrade: Nolit, 1966), p. 76.

[2] "Ability to act self-consciously, critically and creatively in principle separates human beings from all other living organisms and the rest of nature" (M. Marković, "On Human Freedom and Self-Determination" [Washington, D.C.: Woodrow Wilson International Center for Scholars, 1976], p. 8 [mimeographed]).

[3] *Freedom and Socialism* (Dar es Salaam: Oxford University Press, 1974), p. 4.

[4] *The Structure of Freedom* (New York: Atheneum, 1965), pp. 84, 371.

[5] E. Tiryakian finds public acceptance of sexual promiscuity as one of the indicators heralding the outbreak of a revolution. This is so because "social organization involves, among other things, the subordination of sexual and other forms of hedonistic gratification . . . to socially constructive, goal-oriented 'instrumental' activities. A sudden significant increase in hedonistic behaviour matched with a legitimation and/or a public acceptance of this implies . . . loss of the normative cohesion of the society in question" ("A Model of Societal Change and Its Lead Indicators," in S. Z. Klausner, ed., *The Study of Total Societies* [New York: Doubleday, 1967], p. 93).

[6] R. Supek, *Participacija, radnička kontrola i samoupravljanje* (Zagreb: Naprijed, 1974).

[7] P. Sweezy, "The Transition from Socialism to Capitalism," *Monthly Review,* 1964, pp. 569–90.

[8] "Autonomy, Felicity, Futility: the Effects of the Market Economy on Political Personality," *Journal of Politics,* 1978, pp. 1–24, quote from p. 14.

[9] J. Robinson, *Exercises in Economic Analysis* (London: Macmillan, 1961), pp. 203–5.

[10] Edward Kardelj remarked pertinently that the market does not determine the character of production relations but, on the contrary, the production under the respective class relations determines the character of the market (*Pravci razvoja političkog sistema socijalističkog samoupravljanja* [Belgrade: Komunist, 1977], p. 73).

[11] W. Gottschalch, *Parlamentarismus und Rätedemokratie* (Berlin: Wagenbach, 1968).

[12] "Production is a rational activity, which requires systematic division of labour, power and communication as well as a high level of coordination. It therefore requires also a highly systematic and precise control of performance. This can be attained only when sanctions and rewards can be readily measured and allocated in close relation to performance. Remunerative sanctions and rewards are the only ones that can be so applied, because money differentials are far more precisely measurable than force, prestige or any other power differentials" (A. Etzioni, *A Comparative Analysis of Complex Organizations* [New York: Free Press, 1961], p. 80).

[13] In 1971, the Cuban government passed a law aimed at 400,000 loiterers and providing penalties ranging from six months to two years of forced labor in rehabilitation centers for those convicted of malingering or habitual absenteeism from work or school. The Soviet Union has applied similar coercive measures in the past.

[14] M. Marković, "Socijalizam i samoupravljanje," in *Smisao i perspektive socijalizma* (Zagreb: Praxis, 1965), pp. 54–71, espec. p. 70. Something of the kind seems to have happened to a certain extent in Yugoslavia. In order to enhance worker management autonomy, weaken the hierarchy, avoid nationalistic disputes, and prevent the meddling of the state, *dohodovni princip* (the income principle) was extolled as the supreme principle of organization. Each collective was to be the master of "its" income, and all contributions of individuals were measured in money. The resulting chase of money in economic units, offices, universities, and research institutes had deeply alienating effects. Needless to say, the same task could have been accomplished—and much better, at that—by a more sophisticated design that would have eliminated most of the alienating consequences.

[15] M. Abramovitz and P. A. David, "Reinterpreting Economic Growth," *American Economic Review,* May 1973, p. 430.

[16] A. Dragičević, *Potrebni rad i višak rada* (Zagreb: Kultura, 1957), p. 355. R. Richta et al., *Civilizacija na raskršću* (Belgrade: Komunist, 1972), p. 333. *Economic Report of the President* (Washington, D.C., 1976), p. 204.

[17] In the countries for which data are available, in 1968 the annual earnings of persons with a university education were higher than those of persons with a primary education by the following factors:

Eight less developed countries	6.4
Six industrializing countries	3.4
Six developed countries	2.4

Source: M. Ratković, *Cost-Benefit analiza investiranja* (Belgrade: Institut ekonomskih nauka, 1976), p. 87.

Workers' management, of course, accelerates the process. In Yugoslavia, in the same year the comparable factor was 2.1; a comparison with the prewar (1938) capitalist arrangements gives the following picture:

	1938	1957
Wages of unskilled workers	100	100
Wages of skilled workers	330	149
Wages of all workers	100	100
Salaries of government employees	166	135
Salaries of business employees	200	

Source: B. Horvat, *Towards a Theory of Planned Economy* (Belgrade: Jugoslavenski Institut za ekonomska istraživanja, 1964), p. 125.

[18]

Real Wages in France

	1750–60	1801–10	1820–40	1861–70	1911–13
Skilled workers in Paris	100	140	120	190	240
Miners	-	-	60	85	135
Agricultural laborers	45	54	45	55	85

Source: J. Fourastié, *Civilizacija sutrašnjice* (Zagreb: Naprijed, 1966), p. 152.
Note: Wages of skilled workers in Paris in 1750–60 = 100.

For Britain, see E. J. Hobsbawm, *Labouring Men* (London: Weidenfeld and Nicolson, 1964), pp. 64–119.

[19] A. M. Carter's inequality index of the distribution of personal income after taxes in England illustrates that process: 1880, 41; 1913, 38; 1928, 30; 1937, 23; 1948/49, 16 (*The Redistribution of Income in*

Postwar Britain [New Haven: Yale University Press, 1955], p. 75). The inequality index represents the percentage income which would have to be transferred from high to low income groups in order to achieve an equal *per capita* distribution; thus 0 percent expresses absolute equality and (almost) 100 percent, absolute inequality.

20

Income Distribution at Various Levels of Development

	Mean per capita product (U.S.)	Average Gini ratio	Share of top 5% (in %)
Capitalist countries			
Seven countries	53	0.37	32
Thirteen countries	118	0.47	30
Fourteen countries	197	0.48	34
Ten countries	408	0.46	27
Six countries	715	0.43	22
Twelve countries	1950	0.41	20
Etatist countries			
Five countries	795	0.27	14

Source: J. Cromwell, "The Size Distribution of Income: An International Comparison," *Review of Income and Wealth*, 1977, p. 296.

The inverted U shape of the inequality curve and the egalitarian influence of etatism were confirmed by a student of mine, Miroslav Glas, in his dissertation "Razdelitev dohodka v procesu ekonomskega razvoja" (Ljubljana, 1978). Glas fitted the curve $N = A \exp B (\ln y/\bar{y})^2 \exp CS$ to data of 28 countries. N is an inequality measure, y is per capita GNP, $\bar{y}$ is per capita GNP for which N is in maximum, S is a social system variable, while A, B, and C are parameters. The coefficient of determination turned out to be $R^2 = 0.77$ for the top 5 percent and $R^2 = 0.88$ for the Gini ratio. C had a negative sign, indicating that etatism lowers inequality (ibid., Table 5-7).

21 A. Stern, *The Science of Freedom* (London: Longmans, 1969), p. 125. The author speaks of the "stage of solidarity" and does not mention socialism.

22 M. Sahlins, "La première société d'abondance," *Les temps modernes*, 1968, no. 268, pp. 641–80.

23 Marvin Harris mentions that "the skeletal remains of the hunters themselves bear witness to the fact that they were usually well-nourished." He quotes L. Angel's data regarding the height of males: 30,000 B.C., 177 cm; 10,000 B.C., 165 cm; 1960 American males, 175 cm. As for "housing standards," Harris says: "In Czechoslovakia winter dwellings with round floor plans twenty feet in diameter were already in use more than 20,000 years ago. With rich furs for rugs and beds, as well as plenty of dried animal dung or fat-laden bones for the hearth, such dwellings can provide a quality of shelter superior

in many respects to contemporary inner-city apartments" (*Cannibals and Kings. The Origins of Cultures* [New York: Random House, 1977], pp. 10, 14).

[24] B. Malinowski, *Argonauts of the Western Pacific* (London: Routledge and Kegan Paul, 1972); Yugoslav edition: *Argonauti zapadnog Pacifika* (Belgrade: Beogradski irdavačko-grafički zavod, 1972), pp. 52–54, espec. p. 140.

[25] Ibid., pp. 154–55.

[26] M. Sahlins, *Stone Age Economics* (London: Tavistock, 1974), p. 132.

[27] Quoted in ibid., p. 213.

[28] Ruth Benedict, *Patterns of Culture,* Serbo-Croatian translation by B. Marković (Belgrade: Prosveta, 1976), p. 35. The foreigner is even an enemy (Malinowski, *Argonauti,* p. 305).

[29] Abraham Maslow describes the behavior of a "rich" Northern Blackfoot Indian at the Sun Dance ceremony: "At one point in the ceremony . . . he . . . told of his achievements. 'You all know that I have done so and so, you all know that I have done this and that, and you all know how smart I am, how good a stock man I am, how good a farmer, and how I have therefore accumulated great wealth.' And then, with a lordly gesture, a gesture of great pride but without being humiliating, he gave this pile of wealth to the widows, to the orphaned children, and to the blind and diseased. At the end of the Sun Dance ceremony he was stripped of all his possessions, owning nothing but the clothes he stood in. He had, in this synergic way (I won't say either selfishly or unselfishly because clearly the polarity had been transcended) given away everything he had, but in that process had demonstrated what a wonderful man he was, how capable, how intelligent, how strong, how hard-working, how generous and therefore how wealthy" (*The Further Reaches of Human Nature* [Harmondsworth: Penguin, 1971], pp. 211–12).

[30] Sahlins, *Stone Age Economics,* pp. 133, 303.

[31] Malinowski, *Argonauti,* p. 87.

[32] Sahlins, *Stone Age Economics,* p. 133.

[33] Maslow, *Human Nature,* p. 221. That this is literally true was demonstrated by Margaret Mead in her classic study of three neighboring tribes in New Guinea (*Sex and Temperament in Three Primitive Societies* [1935] [New York: New American Library of World Literature, 1962]). In one tribe work was conceived as friendly cooperation, warfare was infrequent and superficial, and the leadership was necessary only during ceremonies and great feasts. The problem of social life was to force the few more capable individuals to undertake, against their will, the responsibility for organizing exciting ceremonies. At a

distance of about 160 kilometers lived a tribe of cannibals whose social organization was based on the idea of natural hostility among persons of the same sex. Men and women were equally reckless and aggressive, and no rule was honored. The third was a tribe of artists in which the conventional roles of men and women were interchanged. Here women dominated while men were less responsible and emotionally dependent. Colin Turnbull described similar contrasts between socially minded and cooperative Mbuti hunters of the rain forest in northeastern Zaïre and individualistic and asocial Ik farmers in the mountains of neighboring northern Uganda ("Human Nature and Primal Man," *Social Research,* 1973, pp. 511–530). Further research may perhaps show that all these differences are due partly or largely to reproductive pressure, intensification, and environmental depletion (cf. M. Harris, *Cannibals and Kings;* and *Cultural Materialism* [New York: Random House, 1979]). However, such a finding, if true, would be largely irrelevant for our present situation. The potential mastery over nature rendered possible by advanced modern technology and scientific research is so great that we cannot only destroy our environment and ecological balance, but also re-create them and improve them. In other words, material-environmental constraints are much less potent at the present level of technological advance than at that of nomads and primitive farmers. Consequently, the determinism is less stringent and the range of choice much greater.

[34] K. Marx and F. Engels, *Rani radovi* (Zagreb: Kultura, 1953), p. 197.

[35] B. Russell, *Socialism, Anarchism and Syndicalism* (London: Allen and Unwin, 1918), p. 210.

[36] B. Russell, "In Praise of Idleness" (1932), quoted in E. Fromm, ed., *Socialist Humanism* (New York: Doubleday, 1966), pp. 258–59.

[37] D. Dolci, "Reflections on Planning and Group," quoted in Fromm, *Socialist Humanism,* p. 422.

[38] K. Marx, "Critique of the Gotha Program," in R. C. Tucker, *The Marx-Engels Reader* (New York: Norton, 1972), p. 388.

Index of Names

Index of Subjects